Encyclopedia of
Rural America
The Land and People

Encyclopedia of
Rural America

The Land and People

Volume 2
M-Z

Gary A. Goreham
Editor

ABC-CLIO

Santa Barbara, California
Denver, Colorado
Oxford, England

Library of Congress Cataloging-in-Publication Data

Encyclopedia of rural America : the land and people / Gary A. Goreham,
    general editor.
        p. cm.
    Includes bibliographical references (p.   ) and index.
    ISBN 0-87436-842-1 (alk. paper)
    1. Country life—United States—Encyclopedias. 2. United States—
Rural conditions—Encyclopedias. 3. United States—Geography—
Encyclopedias. I. Goreham, Gary.
E169.12.E5   1997
973'.09173'4—dc21   97-23320
                                                       CIP

04 03 02 01 00 99 98 97   10 9 8 7 6 5 4 3 2 1

ABC-CLIO, Inc.
130 Cremona Drive, P.O. Box 1911
Santa Barbara, California 93116-1911

This book is printed on acid-free paper ⊗ .
Manufactured in the United States of America

General Editor

Gary A. Goreham
North Dakota State University

Advisory Board

Don E. Albrecht
Texas A&M University

Michael D. Boehlje
Purdue University

Emmett P. Fiske
Washington State University

Cornelia Butler Flora
Iowa State University

Lorraine E. Garkovich
University of Kentucky

William D. Heffernan
University of Missouri, Columbia

Patrick C. Jobes
Montana State University

Martin Kenney
University of California, Davis

Phyllis Gray-Ray
North Carolina Central University

Sonya Salamon
University of Illinois

CONTENTS

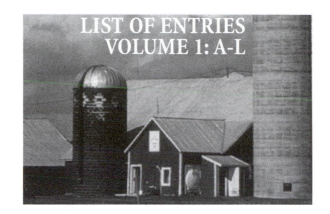

LIST OF ENTRIES
VOLUME 1: A-L

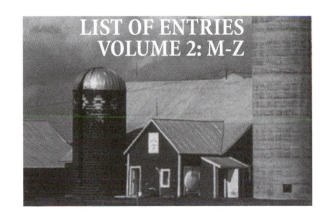

LIST OF ENTRIES
VOLUME 2: M-Z

Encyclopedia of
Rural America
The Land and People

Manufacturing Industry

Enterprises involving the large-scale conversion of materials into salable products, typically by use of machinery. This entry discusses the importance of manufacturing to rural economies and the number of manufacturing jobs that were added in many rural counties during the 1980s. It points out that most rural manufacturing jobs are in low-wage industries and that wages and labor productivity are lower in rural manufacturing. Finally, two problematic issues are examined: fewer rural manufacturing jobs than urban ones are in export industries, and rural industries pollute more than urban industries.

Importance in Rural Economies

Manufacturing industries have been significant sources of jobs and income in many rural (or nonmetropolitan) communities for decades. With the long-run decline of employment in farming and other resource-based industries, manufacturing will continue to be a key component of rural economies for the foreseeable future. In 1993, there were 4.2 million jobs in rural manufacturing industries, slightly more than in the peak reached in 1979. An important difference, however, is that manufacturing made up 19.3 percent of all rural jobs in 1979, but only 16.7 percent 1993. In 1969, there were 3.5 million rural manufacturing jobs, or 20.1 percent of all rural jobs. Manufacturing is even more important as a source of income, accounting for 23 percent of total rural earnings in 1993. Although the economywide shift in employment from goods-producing industries to service-related industries reduced manufacturing's share of jobs by over one-sixth since 1970 manufacturing's share of rural earnings declined by just 6 percent from the 1969 level of nearly 25 percent.

Not all rural areas are equally dependent on manufacturing for jobs and income. In 1993, the rural counties most dependent on manufacturing were less urbanized counties (nonmetropolitan counties with total urban populations of between 2,500 and 19,999). Manufacturing accounted for 18 percent of all jobs and 24 percent of all earnings in these counties in 1993. Urbanized nonmetropolitan counties (nonmetropolitan counties with total urban populations of between 20,000 and 50,000) were highly dependent on manufacturing; 16 percent of jobs and 22 percent of earnings in these counties were from manufacturing industries. In completely rural counties (counties with total urban populations of less than 2,500), manufacturing is a less important but still significant source of jobs and income, accounting for 14 percent of jobs and 18 percent of earnings.

Looking only at averages does not provide a complete picture of the importance of manufacturing because there is wide variation among counties, with manufacturing's importance varying according to the degree of urbanization. In 1993, almost one-third of all urbanized nonmetropolitan counties were highly dependent on manufacturing for jobs in the sense that manufacturing accounted for 20 percent or more of total jobs, whereas one-half were highly dependent on manufacturing for income. About the same proportion of less urbanized counties were highly dependent for jobs but a slightly lower proportion, just under one-half, were highly dependent for income. For rural counties, only 18 percent were highly dependent for jobs and 30 percent for income.

The nation's rural manufacturing jobs are regionally concentrated, as three regions account for over three-quarters of all rural manufacturing jobs. The Southeast has the largest share, with over 43 percent of the nation's rural manufacturing jobs. In addition, over one-half of all rural jobs in the furniture and chemicals industries and over three-quarters of all rural jobs in the tobacco, textiles, and apparel industries are in the Southeast. The next largest region is the Great Lakes, with 21 percent of the nation's rural manufacturing jobs, followed by the Plains, with 13 percent. None of the other five regions (New England, Mideast, Rocky Mountain, Southwest, Far West) have more than 7 percent of rural manufacturing jobs.

These regions also differ markedly in terms of manufacturing's importance as a source of jobs and income within each regions economy. Manufacturing is the most important in the Great Lakes. Just over 20 percent of all rural jobs and 31 percent of all rural earnings in the Great Lakes region were in manufacturing industries in 1993. Manufacturing accounted for 22 percent of rural jobs in the Southeast and 28 percent of rural earnings. The fact that manufacturing accounts for a higher proportion of jobs in the Southeast than in the Great Lakes, but a lower proportion of income, reflects the fact that much more of the Great Lakes' manufacturing jobs are in relatively high-wage durables manufacturing industries, whereas the Southeast is dominated by low-wage nondurables manufacturers. For example, the four largest industries in the Great Lakes region are industrial machinery, electrical machinery, primary metals, and transportation equipment, together accounting for 43 percent of rural manufacturing jobs in the region. In contrast, the top four industries in the Southeast, accounting for 50 percent of the region's manufacturing jobs, are apparel, textiles, lumber, and food processing. Manufacturing is the least important in the Southwest, Rocky Mountain, and Far West regions. In each of these three regions, manufacturing accounts for between 8 and 10 percent of jobs and between 11 and 14 percent of earnings.

Jobs Added during the 1980s

Manufacturing job growth has been an important determinant of the overall economic performance of rural economies. Between 1969 and 1979, the number of manufacturing jobs in nonmetropolitan counties increased by 18 percent (631,000 jobs). This job growth abruptly ended with the back-to-back recessions of 1980 and 1981–1982, when rural areas lost 509,000 (12 percent) manufacturing jobs. Although these losses were much less severe than the 1.7 million manufacturing jobs lost in urban areas, the losses were nevertheless quite serious for many rural communities. During this period, 458 nonmetropolitan counties lost 25 percent or more of their

manufacturing jobs and 95 of these lost more than 50 percent. The number of manufacturing jobs in rural areas rose fairly steadily between 1982 and 1989, the longest business cycle recovery in the postwar period. Job losses of the preceding recessions were more than made up during this seven-year recovery as 525,000 rural manufacturing jobs were added, more than twice the number of manufacturing jobs added in urban areas and more than rural areas had lost during the recessions of the first three years of the 1980s. The number of jobs fell slightly as a result of the 1990 recession, but job gains during the subsequent recovery pushed the number of rural manufacturing jobs to an all-time high of 4.2 million.

Manufacturing job growth since 1982 has been relatively widespread. Almost two-thirds of all nonmetropolitan counties added manufacturing jobs during this period. The 776,000 manufacturing jobs added in these counties represent a 34 percent increase over 1982. In contrast, the nonmetropolitan counties that did not add manufacturing jobs between 1982 and 1993 lost a total of 226,000 jobs, a 17 percent decline from 1982. Not surprisingly, the economies of counties that added manufacturing jobs were stronger than the economies of counties that did not add manufacturing jobs. For instance, the population of counties that added manufacturing jobs grew twice as fast during both the 1970s and 1980s than did rural counties with no manufacturing job growth. The total number of jobs also grew twice as fast in these counties with manufacturing job growth than in rural counties that did not add manufacturing jobs. Earnings likewise grew substantially faster in counties experiencing manufacturing job growth. However, the substantial job and earnings growth did not translate into significant wage gains. Earnings per job grew at approximately the same rate in both groups of counties so that in 1993 earnings per job in the counties with manufacturing job growth were still approximately 10 percent below average earnings per job in the rural counties with no manufacturing job growth.

Although a large number of rural counties experienced added manufacturing jobs, this growth was by no means uniform. During the 1970s, all three types of rural counties experienced substantial manufacturing job growth: urbanized counties added 139,000 jobs, less urbanized counties added 425,000 jobs, and completely rural counties added 67,000 jobs. Between 1979 and 1982, urbanized counties lost 187,000 jobs (15 percent), less urbanized counties lost 292,000 jobs (14 percent), and completely rural counties lost 40,000 jobs (10 percent).

Rural Manufacturing, 1992

	Total U.S. Jobs in Industry (%)	All Rural Manufacturing Jobs (%)	Pay (%)	Productivity (%)
Lumber and wood products	55.6	9.5	97.3	109.3
Textile mill products	46.3	7.4	95.4	103.8
Leather and leather products	38.5	1.0	75.0	88.5
Apparel and other textile products	35.8	9.2	80.4	80.9
Food and kindred products	30.1	11.8	76.4	64.0
Furniture and fixtures	30.0	3.7	86.6	91.4
Paper and allied products	28.6	4.7	112.6	122.4
Stone, clay, and glass products	26.6	3.2	91.1	98.8
Rubber and miscellaneous plastics products	24.8	5.8	93.8	102.6
Primary metal industries	20.0	3.4	90.1	91.4
Industrial machinery and equipment	19.5	8.9	79.4	84.5
Fabricated metal products	18.2	6.5	86.0	99.0
Misc. manufacturing industries	17.9	1.7	85.8	101.9
Electronic and other electric equipment	17.4	6.5	73.4	82.3
Chemicals and allied products	14.7	3.2	88.6	89.5
Petroleum and coal products	14.2	0.4	84.0	83.6
Transportation equipment	13.9	5.9	68.5	82.0
Tobacco products	13.1	0.1	65.2	43.7
Printing and publishing	13.0	5.1	69.1	70.3
Instruments and related products	7.9	1.9	71.5	90.4
Total	100.0	22.6	75.4	76.8

Source: Bureau of the Census. *Annual Survey of Manufacturers.* Washington, DC: Bureau of the Census, 1994.

Most of the manufacturing jobs added during the 1980s were in less urbanized or completely rural nonmetropolitan counties. Completely rural counties experienced the fastest rate of job growth, with the number of manufacturing jobs increasing by 27 percent between 1969 and 1979 and by 29 percent between 1982 and 1993. Manufacturing jobs in less urbanized nonmetropolitan counties grew more slowly but accounted for a much larger number of new jobs. Since 1982, less urbanized nonmetropolitan counties have added 388,000 manufacturing jobs. This is just 9 percent fewer jobs than were added during the so-called rural renaissance of the 1970s and 33 percent more than the number of jobs lost between 1979 and 1982. Urbanized nonmetropolitan counties added only 81,000 jobs between 1982 and 1993. In contrast to the other two group of counties, urbanized counties have not recovered fully the jobs lost during the recessions of 1980 and 1981–1982.

Jobs in Low-Wage Industries

The industry with the highest proportion of all U.S. jobs in rural areas (based on 1992 data) is lumber and wood processing, with 56 percent of all U.S. jobs in rural counties (see table). This is followed by textiles, leather, apparel, food processing, and furniture industries, each with 30 percent or more of total jobs located in nonmetropolitan

counties. The least rural industry is instruments, with less than 8 percent of U.S. jobs, followed by printing, tobacco, transportation equipment, petroleum, and chemicals, each with less than 15 percent of total U.S. jobs.

The four largest employers (food and kindred products, lumber and wood products, apparel, and industrial machinery) employ 39 percent of all rural manufacturing workers. With the exception of industrial machinery, these industries pay significantly less than the U.S. average manufacturing wage. However, just as was the case in urban areas, low-wage industries experienced the largest job losses. Between 1977 and 1993, manufacturing job growth in rural areas occurred mostly in printing, food processing, transportation equipment, rubber, and paper. Together, these industries added 293,000 jobs. The five industries with the largest losses included some of the most rural and the lowest-paid industries. Apparel, textiles, lumber, leather, and primary metals lost a total of 267,000 jobs.

Wages and Labor Productivity

Wages in most manufacturing industries are substantially lower in rural than in urban areas. While wages in six rural manufacturing industries (textiles, paper and allied products, lumber and wood products, rubber and plastic products, stone and clay products, and primary metals) were at least 90 percent of the corresponding urban wages in 1992, six industries (tobacco, printing and publishing, leather, electronic equipment, transportation equipment, and instruments) paid 75 percent or less of the corresponding urban wage. Overall, wages paid by manufacturers in rural areas were 75 percent of urban wages.

Labor productivity (measured by value added per worker) in rural industries is, in general, below that of urban industries. Furthermore, despite significant rural productivity growth during the 1980s, a substantial productivity gap remains. At the end of the 1970s, value added per worker in rural manufacturing was 22 percent less than value added per worker in urban manufacturing. By 1992, this gap had widened slightly to 30 percent. Rural labor productivity was lower in almost all types of manufacturing, being higher than urban in only five industries (textiles, lumber and wood products, paper and allied products, rubber and chemicals, and miscellaneous products). Some of this gap is the result of the fact that urban areas experienced much larger job losses in low-productivity industries, such as textiles and apparel, than did rural areas.

Fewer Rural Jobs in Export Industries

Firms that produce for the export market tend to be more successful than firms that do not export in a number of important ways. They have higher growth rates of both output and jobs, they pay higher wages, and they tend to survive longer. As the global economy expands, it will become increasingly important for rural firms to participate in export market. Data from the *Annual Survey of Manufactures,* which is conducted by the U.S. Bureau of the Census, indicate that rural industries do not export as much as urban. Over 37 percent of all urban manufacturing jobs are in industries that export at least 15 percent of their total output, compared to only 27 percent of rural manufacturing jobs, a difference of over one-third. If pulp mills and logging are excluded, the gap increases to over 45 percent. These differences imply that rural manufacturing industries are less likely than urban industries to benefit from increased exports.

Rural Industries' Pollution

Rural areas are considered attractive for many manufacturing industries because of the perception that rural communities are more willing to accept noxious and polluting industries than are urban communities. If this is true, many rural communities may face the difficult

choice between more jobs or a clean environment, as new industries will provide much-needed jobs but at the same time degrade the environment and even pose health risks to residents. Data from the Environmental Protection Agency indicate that rural industries are indeed more polluting than their urban counterparts. In 1992, rural areas accounted for 29 percent of all releases of toxic chemicals from manufacturing establishments, significantly more than their share of either manufacturing jobs or manufacturing output.

The form of release is important for determining the potential risk that the release of a specific chemical poses. Of the three major forms of chemical releases (into air, water, or on land), air and water releases constitute the more important potential health risks because chemicals released into either the air or water are much more likely to come into contact with large numbers of people. Overall, 33 percent of all air releases and over 50 percent of all land releases were in rural areas in 1992, but only 23 percent of all water releases were in rural areas.

—G. Andrew Bernat, Jr.

See also
Community; Development, Community and Economic; Employment; Entrepreneurship; Environmental Protection; Labor Force; Labor Unions; Policy, Rural Development; Regional Planning; Underemployment; Work.

References
Barkley, David, ed. Economic Adaptation: Alternatives for Nonmetropolitan Areas. Boulder, CO: Westview Press, 1993.

Bernat, G. Andrew, Jr. "Manufacturing Restructuring and Rural Economies: Job Growth but Lagging Wages." *Rural Development Perspectives* 9, no. 3 (June 1994): 2–8.

Bernat, G. Andrew, Jr., and D. McGranahan. "Rural Manufacturing Links to Rural Development." Agriculture Information Bulletin No. 664–52. Washington, DC: U.S. Department of Agriculture, July 1993.Bureau of the Census. *Annual Survey of Manufacturers.* Washington, DC: Bureau of the Census (various years).

Testa, William A. "Trends and Prospects for Rural Manufacturing." Working Paper WP-1992-12. Chicago: Federal Reserve Bank of Chicago, 1992.

Marijuana

Also known as hemp, a broadleaf plant that produces a stick resin that, when smoked or eaten, has an intoxicating effect on the user. Marijuana was originally brought to the United States for industrial purposes, but today is used primarily for recreation and medicine. Marijuana may be one of the largest cash crops in America. Both the geography and the culture of rural areas make them well suited for marijuana cultivation, and it is likely that marijuana cultivation will be an issue in rural areas for some time. Contained in this entry is a description of early industrial and medical uses of marijuana and of the crop's cultivation methods. The marijuana industry is described, as are marijuana growers and the comparative advantage of rural over urban cultivation.

Early Uses

Marijuana has been a feature of the rural landscape since the first settlers came to America. It is now primarily a recreational drug, but its earliest uses in the United States were industrial and medicinal. There is only one species of marijuana, but there are several varieties, which differ in their size, density of growth, coloration, and intoxicating properties. Marijuana plants are dioecious—that is, each plant matures as either a male or female, although on rare occasions plants may switch sex during growth or grow with characteristics of both sexes. It is a hearty plant that is grown in every state and grows best in the same climate and soil conditions that are ideal for growing corn.

As an industrial product, the stalk of the plant is a source of strong fiber, long used for the manufacture of fine linen, paper, canvas, and rope. The first paper and cloth probably were made from hemp fibers. Until the late 1800s, most of the paper in the world was made from hemp fiber, including the paper used to print the Gutenberg Bible and the first two drafts of the Declaration of Independence. Until the 1900s, hemp was used for nearly all sails, riggings, cargo nets, and other ropes and cloths used on ships. Compared with cotton, the hemp fiber is stronger, softer, warmer, and more water absorbent. Oil from the hemp plant resembles linseed oil and was used in paints. Much of the wild marijuana that grows throughout the Midwest was planted for industrial purposes, including military applications during World War II when the Japanese capture of the Philippines cut off an important source of sisal rope for the U.S. military. The sterilized seeds of marijuana plants are still used in some bird feed, and it is claimed that marijuana would be more cost effective than wood in the production of paper. There are periodic calls for the legalization of marijuana for industrial purposes, but the development of synthetic fibers undercut some of the economic pressure for legalization.

Marijuana contains over 400 chemicals, including THC (tetrahydrocannabinol), the primary psychoactive chemical in marijuana. THC provides both the "high"

A marijuana plant.

experienced by recreational smokers and the benefits claimed by those who use it for medical purposes. During the 1800s and early 1900s, marijuana was used in medicines to treat a wide variety of illnesses. Although illegal in all states but California, where it can be used for medical purposes, it nevertheless is used today to treat glaucoma and prevent the nausea that often accompanies chemotherapy for cancer patients. Conclusive scientific tests have not been conducted, but it appears that marijuana generally is effective for these purposes and may work better than synthetic substitutes.

Marijuana has been used as a recreational drug by fringe groups for some time. It was not until the 1960s that it became widely used among the general population. At that time, nearly all marijuana was imported, primarily from Mexico. Even though demand for marijuana was high, there were periodic shortages. American marijuana smokers quickly learned that by planting the seeds that came with their imported marijuana, they could produce their own marijuana at relatively low cost. From this it was a short step to crossbreeding and experimenting to raise the THC level of plants and to increase their yield.

Ways the Plant Is Grown

There are three different ways in which marijuana can be found growing in America today. First is wild marijuana, or "ditchweed." Usually of low potency, ditchweed originally was bred for its fiber rather than its psychoactive properties. Most frequently found in the Midwest, the amount of wild marijuana is substantial. In 1992, of the 272 million marijuana plants the Drug Enforcement Administration reports were eradicated in the United States, over 264 million (97 percent) were ditchweed. Furthermore, five midwestern states accounted for more than 90 percent of the eradicated ditchweed. Demand for ditchweed is low among marijuana smokers because of its low potency and harsh taste. Even so, ditchweed can yield the harvester anywhere from $100 to $200 per pound.

A second way that marijuana is grown is through cultivation of the plants and harvesting of them at maturity, producing what is known as commercial-grade marijuana. Growers generally will select varieties of marijuana that are more potent and thus can command a higher selling price. The packaged leaves and flowering tops will sell for between $700 and $1,500 per pound, depending on quality and current market conditions.

Finally, some growers produce a particular type of marijuana known as sinsemilla, a Spanish term for "without seeds." To cultivate sinsemilla, plants grow until their sex can be determined. At this point, all male plants are removed. Female plants continue to grow and produce flowering bud tops. Ordinarily these flowering tops are fertilized by pollen from male plants, pollen that sticks to the resin produced by these tops. This resin is loaded with THC, the psychoactive agent that gives marijuana its high. In the absence of male plants, however, pollination does not occur, and the female plants continue to produce more resin to catch any passing pollen. Harvesters of sinsemilla are interested primarily in these flowering bud tops and often discard the leaves and the rest of the plant. And because the leaves typically are not harvested, the sinsemilla grower has no interest in growing tall bushy plants. Rather, the plant is pruned to produce the greatest number of flowering buds. A sinsemilla grower will not obtain as much product weight from a single plant as would an ordinary commercial grower. The cultivation of sinsemilla also is much more labor intensive. However, sinsemilla is far more valuable than commercial marijuana, yielding the seller between $2,000 and $5,000 per pound.

The Industry

Because the cultivation of marijuana is an illegal activity, there are no precise measures of the size of the marijuana industry in the United States, its economic impact, or of the number of people involved. Even conservative estimates, however, place the gross sales of domestic marijuana at over $60 billion each year, surpassing such legal cash crops as corn, wheat, or soy beans. Estimates of the number of people involved vary wildly, from 90,000 to 250,000 commercial growers, and from 1 to 2 million people who grow smaller amounts for personal use. Virtually every state reports marijuana cultivation, although the highest producing states are in the Midwest.

Who Grows the Plant?

Who are domestic marijuana growers? In particular, who are the people who grow larger amounts and consequently have the greatest impact on the domestic marijuana market? As with any activity, simplistic descriptions are inadequate. Many types of people are involved in marijuana growing, but there are general trends. The typical commercial grower is over age 30, White, male, and living in a rural area. They often are employed in legitimate jobs, particularly as independent business operators or farmers.

In general, there are three types of commercial marijuana growers, with the types varying both in their motivations for growing and in the sizes of their operations. The most typical type of grower has a relatively small operation and is motivated by both a fascination with growing and a desire to provide himself or herself with low-cost and high-quality marijuana. This type, also known as a communal grower, may find marijuana growing profitable but is not involved primarily for the money. The fascination with growing often leads to complex growing operations in which the grower constantly is experimenting with new technology and with plant breeding. Like the amateur gardener or the amateur wine maker, the rewards for these growers come primarily from the process of cultivation and their ability to impress their marijuana-using friends with their high-quality product.

A second category of grower, the pragmatist, is smaller in number, but the operations of pragmatists are somewhat larger than those of the communal grower.

Pragmatists grow out of economic necessity, and the size of their operations often are dictated by the depth of their economic problems. Some may have dabbled previously in marijuana cultivation for their own consumption, but their activities now are driven by the need to meet economic problems. Sometimes these are farmers who face foreclosure. In other cases, they are people who have lost their legal jobs or for whom financial emergencies have arisen, such as unanticipated medical expenses. Some of these growers believe that what they are doing is wrong but feel that they have few options to resolve their current economic problems. Unlike communal growers, pragmatists often derive little inner satisfaction from what they are doing. To the contrary, they are often anxious and full of guilt, looking forward to the day when they can get out of marijuana cultivation.

A third type of grower, the hustler, is the least frequent type of grower but is also the type with the largest operations. These individuals are motivated by the idea of grand success and pride themselves on the size and efficiency of their operations. The profits made by hustlers can be considerable. Money from growing is important for hustlers, but primarily as a symbol of their business acumen and entrepreneurial skills. Hustlers often feel no particular commitment to marijuana cultivation as a social or political statement and easily can drift from growing into other get-rich-quick schemes and questionable business activities. Hustlers are as different from communal growers as corporate farms are from small family-owned farming operations.

Marijuana growers may be exposed to other types of drugs, use them, and even expand their business to include trafficking in other drugs. For example, there is evidence that some large-scale marijuana growers in Kentucky may be moving into the transshipment of cocaine. This is probably not typical, however. More common is the commercial marijuana grower who does not become involved in the sale or distribution of other drugs. There also are a number of growers who use no other drugs and even some who never use marijuana.

Unlike the conspicuous consumption and extravagant lifestyles that the media portrays for large-scale dealers in cocaine and heroin, the marijuana grower is best served by maintaining a low profile. Marijuana cultivation ties the grower to a particular geographic area and exposes him or her to the risk of arrest or the theft of the crop for a period of about four months, or year-round in the case of indoor growers. Consequently, it is in the grower's best interest to maintain a low profile in the community and avoid behavior that might arouse suspicion. An approach that downplays flashiness and extravagance also is consistent with the culture of many rural areas. Violence associated with marijuana growing is not common except in those areas where the local culture already is associated with violence. Violence, like conspicuous consumption, draws unwanted attention to the grower and the area.

The Rural Setting of Cultivation

Although the rise of indoor growing makes it possible to cultivate marijuana in urban and suburban areas, rural areas have several distinct advantages. First is the issue of geography. Outdoor growing often involves plants that are quite large, but in rural areas they can blend more easily with other vegetation. In addition, some varieties emit a strong odor while growing, something less likely to be detected in sparsely populated rural areas. Rural areas, particularly those in the Midwest, often have rich soil in abundance. Most national news organizations and most researchers who study the drug problem are located in urban areas. To these groups rural marijuana cultivation is largely invisible. Lacking public attention, legislators have few pressures to stress rural marijuana cultivation in their public speeches or lawmaking.

A second advantage of rural areas for marijuana growing is the rural culture. For example, hunting and fishing provide excellent opportunities for growers to locate remote growing sites and to justify frequent trips to those sites without arousing suspicion. In addition, basic knowledge of horticulture is obtained easily in rural areas where gardening is a common hobby and in those rural areas where farming is still a common occupation. Rural marijuana growers benefit from the antigovernment attitudes of many rural areas. There are rural areas where the government, particularly the federal government, is disliked more than the growers. Eastern Kentucky provides a striking example of this mind-set. A final aspect of rural culture is the tendency in many rural areas to keep problems within to avoid damaging the reputation of the community. Such an attitude serves to hide the scope of the problem from public view. Thus, domestic marijuana cultivation is a large industry that is heavily concentrated in rural areas. The ease with which growing can be learned and the money that can be made by growing marijuana make it likely that it will persist for some time. Both geography and rural culture make it likely that rural areas will continue to be the primary setting for marijuana cultivation.

—*Ralph A. Weisheit*

See also
Addiction; Crime; Culture; Policing; Poverty; Values of Residents.
References
Bonnie, Richard J., and C. H. Whitebread II. *The Marihuana Conviction: A History of Marihuana Prohibition in the United States*. Charlottesville: University Press of Virginia, 1974.

Grinspoon, Lester, and James B. Bakalar. *Marihuana: The Forbidden Medicine*. New Haven, CT: Yale University Press, 1993.

Herer, Jack. *The Emperor Wears No Clothes*. Van Nuys, CA: HEMP, 1990.

Himmelstein, Jerome L. The Strange Career of Marihuana: Politics and Ideology of Drug Control in America. Westport, CT: Greenwood Press, 1983.

Kleiman, Mark A. *Marijuana: Costs of Abuse, Costs of Control.* Westport, CT: Greenwood Press, 1989.

Weisheit, Ralph. A. *Domestic Marijuana: A Neglected Industry.* Westport, CT: Greenwood Press, 1992.

Weisheit, Ralph A., David N. Falcone, and L. Edward Wells. *Crime and Policing in Rural and Small-Town America*. Prospect Heights, IL: Waveland Press, 1996.

Marketing

All the business activities involved in the flow of products and services from farms and ranches to the final consumers. Marketing enables farm products to be converted into food products. This conversion requires a coordinated system, regulated by the government, to provide healthy and nutritious food to consumers. Marketing begins when products leave the farm or ranch and move to the first handler. It starts with the milk truck from the local cooperative on the New England dairy farm, the tobacco auction in North Carolina, the soybean processor in central Illinois, the grain elevator in Kansas, the feeder cattle auction in Colorado, and the vegetable processing cooperative in California. In addition, the marketing system must deliver these products and services when consumers want them, at a place they can acquire them, in a form they desire, and at an acceptable price. Thus, marketing is said to add different kinds of value to the farmers' raw products: "time value" involves the storage function, "place value" relates to transportation services, and "form value" relates to processing. This entry examines the importance of agricultural marketing to the American economy and describes marketing channels and the coordination of the production marketing system. The role of agricultural cooperatives in the marketing system is discussed. Various market regulations are listed.

Significance

In the mid-1990s, the economic value of all farm sales approached $200 billion, whereas the amount spent by consumers for domestically produced foods and beverages exceeded $700 billion. The farmer's share of the food consumption dollar was 24 percent, with a 76 percent share for marketing. Current trends are toward more marketing services including more processing, greater convenience, more variety, more colorful packaging, larger and more convenient retail outlets, and sharp increases in spending for food eaten away from home. A primary driving force of the desire for more marketing services has been the declining costs of food in relation to disposable income. As an example, Americans currently spend only about 11 percent of their disposable income on food. These trends are expected to continue in the future.

The components of the marketing bill as estimated by the U.S. Department of Agriculture (USDA) in the mid-1990s showed that labor costs dominated the food marketing bill, making up 47 percent of the total marketing costs. Large amounts of labor are required to process, transport, and retail food in stores and restaurants. Also important to the food marketing bill are packaging, 11 percent; transportation, 5 percent; fuel and electricity, 5 percent; and other items, including advertising, depreciation, interest, rent, and repairs, 28 percent. Corporate profits represent about 4 percent of the total marketing bill.

The farmer's share of the each dollar spent at retail varies from product to product. On eggs, as an example, the farmer receives about 58 percent of each retail dollar spent on eggs. The farmer's share of the retail dollar for other food products is as follows: chicken, 54 percent; beef, 52 percent; milk, 42 percent; dried beans, 36 percent; pork, 35 percent; peas and corn, 21 percent; bread, 7 percent; corn flakes, 5 percent; and corn syrup, 4 percent. When more marketing services are required, the farmer's share is lower.

Channels

The marketing channel involves the steps that farm products go through on their way to final consumers, with successive market services, often by a number of different owners, being added. Farmers often deliver their products to a local market. This local market may be a dealer who accumulates volume, sorts, weighs, and grades the product before it is shipped to the processing facility. Grains and soybeans often are sold in this manner. Another common local market is the auction market. Auctions are centralized locations where many sellers can bring their goods to be shown to buyers and where buyers and sellers have access to information about the volume and quality of products in the market that day. Auctions are important markets for tobacco, feeder livestock, and cull cattle and hogs.

Some agricultural products, such as poultry, eggs, vegetables, fruit, and cotton, are delivered directly from the farm to the processing plant. These products need immediate processing because of perishability or need to be stored. From the processor, products move to another processor or distributor, who further refines the product or begins to move it toward final distribution. This group often is called wholesalers. Finally, the product is distributed to retail outlets, where another set of merchants prepare, display, and sell to the consumer.

The trend in recent years has been to reduce the number of parties involved in the marketing channel and eliminate unneeded functions. Many "middlemen" have been eliminated and marketing costs often have been cut by a streamlining of the channel. Today, it is much more likely that farmers will deliver their raw materials directly to a large food processor who takes the product all the way to the final consumption location.

Coordination of the System

The food system must deliver wholesome food products and services to millions of customers around the globe several times per day. This involves the enormous task of production coordination, processing, transportation, and retail delivery. In addition, consumers demand that this coordination be efficient so that products are affordable. Producers must make decisions of what raw food materials to produce and when to supply them, processors must have raw materials to process, and retailers need a constant supply of what is sometimes a perishable product with a short shelf life.

Coordination can be divided into three general types: price and profit incentives, contracts, and vertical integration. The majority of agricultural marketing is coordinated by price and profit incentives. Producers make decisions to raise certain crops or animals based on expected prices and profits. High prices and profits give producers incentives to expand. Alternatively, when prices and profits are low, producers have incentives to decrease production. Agricultural product prices in the United States form a complex system that includes not only current or spot prices but also forward cash prices for delivery at later time periods. In addition, futures markets have developed that are paper obligations either to make or take delivery at a future period of time. Futures markets are legally binding commitments, but one of their advantages is that they can be offset easily.

Those who buy a futures contract make a commitment to take delivery at a set price, whereas those who sell futures make a commitment to make delivery at a set price. If the futures position is offset before delivery, the holder simply pays or receives the difference in the price change from the initial commitment. A further refinement of the futures market is the agricultural options market. Options provide the buyer with the right, but not the obligation, to take a position in the futures market.

Futures and options are traded for many of the major agricultural commodities, including corn, wheat, soybeans, cotton, live cattle, feeder cattle, live hogs, and milk. These markets enable the price system to more accurately, effectively, and efficiently transmit price signals to producers and consumers. There are at least four ways they achieve this. First, these markets provide a central area to collect orders, which represent vast amounts of information. The trading pits where futures and options prices are established receive orders from buyers and sellers around the world. Each market participant brings information about the worldwide marketplace, and the evaluation of this information results in buy or sell orders. Second, this information is analyzed and prices are determined. Through the process of bringing buyers and sellers together, the price level at which one party is willing to buy and another to sell is found. This processes of "finding" the market price is called "price discovery." Third, futures and option prices help guide both producers and consumers in their decision making. For example, since futures prices are quoted for about one and one-half years into the future, producers can use these prices to help determine which crop will be most profitable for them to plant next year. And fourth, these markets provide a place for businesses to transfer their price risk to others who want to take more price risk for the chance of profiting from price change. A farmer who feels that the price of his or her growing wheat crop is favorable can use futures to establish the price several months before harvest. In doing so, the farmer establishes the price to be received, and thus someone else who purchased the wheat accepts the financial risk of price changes. Options prices can be used by the farmer to establish a minimum price for the growing wheat crop in case prices drop, yet be able to take advantage of better prices if they rise.

Contracts are a second way that markets are coordinated between producers and consumers. It is common in the vegetable industry, as an example, for the vegetable processor to contract with producers to raise vegetables in set volumes that meet specific grades and standards established by the processor. Other agricultural products that have important amounts of contract production include seed production, broilers, turkeys, eggs, and hogs.

Vertical integration is a final way that coordination occurs between production and consumption. In vertical integration, one firm controls production processing and distribution to consumers. In the early 1990s, the U.S. Department of Agriculture estimated the percent of production in various foods that were produced in highly integrated operations. The USDA found that 100 percent of broilers (chicken) were vertically integrated; processed vegetables, 98 percent; market eggs, 95 percent; turkeys, 85 percent; fresh vegetables, 65 percent; hogs, 12 percent; and feed grains, 2 percent.

The Role of Cooperatives

Farmer cooperatives are a common way to market products. Marketing cooperatives are businesses owned by the farmers themselves. Individual farmers generally do not have the financial means to own their own marketing or processing facilities. However, by combining their investments with other farmers, they are able to form a cooperative large enough to service the needs of many farmers. Marketing cooperatives are different from other corporations because they are owned by those farmers (patrons) who use the services of the cooperative. The cooperative has a profit motive, but profits are paid back to those who use the cooperative in the form of patronage dividends.

Marketing cooperatives are sometimes formed to provide just the initial handling of the farm products. This often is true for grains and soybeans where the local grain elevator is a farmer cooperative. In many cases, however, the marketing cooperative has been extended to be both the local buying point and a processing facility. This allows the farmer-owners to add more value to their products, to extend their services more closely to the consumer, to seek more outlets for the products they produce, and, they hope, to generate a profit on further processing. Examples of farmers owning cooperatives that do further processing include milk marketing cooperatives, meat processing plants, sugar beet refining facilities, and fruit processing and marketing cooperatives.

Regulation

Farmers generally are small and have little individual power in the marketplace. In contrast, many marketing and processing firms are large and have a greater ability to exert influence on markets by potentially manipulating prices or volumes purchased. This apparent inequality in relative market power requires that markets be regulated by state and federal governments for fairness to all participants to provide common grades and standards for trade and to maintain food safety and sanitation.

Some of the key regulations include the Sherman Anti-Trust Act (1890), which was the initial legislation to ban monopoly practices. This was followed by the Clayton Act (1914) and the Federal Trade Commission Act (1914), which helped to define fair trade more clearly. The Packers and Stockyards Act (1921) regulated livestock movement through marketing channels and determined the way farmers and ranchers had to be paid for livestock. The Capper-Volstead Act (1922) established the legal framework for farmer cooperatives to be established, but also helped to define and regulate the way they could operate. The U.S. Grain Standards Act of 1976 established standards for grain weighing and handling. The Meat Inspection Act (1906) and the Federal Meat Inspection Act (1967) standardized meat inspection at either the federal or state level. Commodity futures and options markets are regulated by the Commodity Futures Trading Commission, established in 1974.

The United States believes in a free marketplace. But over time, Americans also have learned that total freedom can result in unfair practices that result in monopoly profits, poor efficiency, and unsafe products. Markets left to themselves are generally not self-regulating, and thus governmental guidelines are necessary. These regulations help to protect market participants and consumers and help to provide a set of fair trade standards for all.

—Chris Hurt

See also

Agricultural and Resource Economics; Agricultural Law; Agricultural Prices; Agro/Food System; Futures Markets; Grain Elevators; Markets; Trade, International; Trade, Interregional; Value-Added Agriculture.

References

Agricultural Outlook (Washington, DC: U.S. Department of Agriculture, Economic Research Service), various issues.

Chicago Board of Trade. Education and Marketing Services Department. "Introduction to Agricultural Hedging." Chicago: Chicago Board of Trade, 1988.

Chicago Mercantile Exchange. *A Self-Study Guide to Hedging with Livestock Futures.* Chicago: Chicago Mercantile Exchange, 1986.

Kohls, Richard L., and Joseph N. Uhl. *Marketing of Agricultural Products.* 7th ed. New York: Macmillan, 1990.

Manchester, Alden. *Rearranging the Economic Landscape.* AER-660. Washington, DC: U.S. Department of Agriculture, Economic Research Service, 1992.

McCoy, John H., and M. E. Sarhan. *Livestock and Meat Marketing.* 3d ed. New York: Van Nostrand Reinhold, 1988.

National Food Review (Washington, DC: U.S. Department of Agriculture, Economic Research Service), various issues.

Purcell, Wayne D. *Agricultural Marketing: Systems, Coordination, Cash, and Futures Prices.* Reston, VA: Reston, 1979.

Tomek, William G., and Kenneth L. Robinson. *Agricultural Product Prices.* 3d ed. Ithaca, NY: Cornell University Press, 1990.

Markets

The range of economic sectors and/or the aggregation of the supply and demand for goods and services existing in a specified geographical area. "Rural markets" is used in this entry to refer to the range of economic sectors and/or the supply and demand for goods and services existing in areas meeting the census definition of rural—populations less than 2,500. Rural markets are examined from the standpoint of their economic health and various conditions that either facilitate or impede economic vibrancy. They are indicative of the general economic structure of such areas, the status of labor markets, and approaches employed to improve the economic health of rural areas.

Definitions

The term *market* represents several related ideas. It refers to a region in which goods can be bought and sold. It also represents the extent to which there are a demand and a supply of a particular good or service. The existence of markets is predicated on the notion that there is an agreement between buyer and seller or producer and consumer on the price at which goods and services will be exchanged. Thus, one may focus narrowly on rural labor markets, retail markets, and geographic or regional markets.

The term *rural regions* refers to the population base or density across a geographical area. From a pejorative standpoint, the term paints an expansive picture of an area and a people that lag economically and culturally behind mainstream America. Scholars usually define several distinct rural regions: central Appalachia, Black Belt South, Mississippi Delta, Missouri Ozarks, lower Rio Grande valley, cutover region of the Upper Midwest, northern New England, timber region of the Pacific Northwest, and rural California. The economies in these regions are typified by poor infrastructure, low tax bases, poverty, low per capita income, and low education levels.

Economic Structure

Many rural regions typically do not have diversified economies. The size of rural markets is influenced by several factors. First, markets of any type are influenced by economies of scale. Regions with significant economies of scale (high demand for goods and services) are able to offset the cost associated with transporting goods and services across low-density areas. Regions with industries that have large economies of scale have large market areas. Economies of scale usually are associated with high fixed costs. Operating with large volume serves to offset high fixed costs. A second factor that affects market size is demand density. Demand density is the quantity demanded per unit of land area (the quantity demanded per person times the population density). The larger the demand density or population density is, the greater is the number of producers who can operate in a given market area. Finally, transportation costs may affect market size. High transportation costs represent an impediment to producers and influence an industry's decision to locate in a particular location or region.

The impact that economies of scale, demand density, and transportation costs have on rural markets is intuitive. Specific features of rural areas include low economies of scale, low demand density, and high transportation costs associated with shipping both raw materials and finished products. Thus, economic diversity is less common in rural areas. Many rural areas are one-industry towns; their economic survival hinges on the presence and prosperity of one or two sizable operations (such as manufacturing plants or military bases). The collapse of the single industry in a location translates into the collapse of the region's economic base.

The national economy experienced a major structural change in the 1970s and 1980s and into the 1990s. The global reach of the economy signaled a shift from goods-producing to service-producing industries in advanced industrial nations. This has had the effect of altering regional economies. Local markets have been forced to restructure and conform to the type and level of demand from outside markets.

The success of a region or local economy, whether rural or urban, is based on its ability to bring money into the community by exporting goods that are produced within the region. If most rural areas fortuitously depend on marginal manufacturing operations to sustain their economies, the collapse of such operations spells doom for those areas. Some economist argue that a service-based national economy will result in greater inequality as the skilled blue-collar jobs that offer occupational and social mobility evaporate and as the occupational structure becomes skewed, with low-skilled, low-wage jobs at one end and highly paid professional service jobs at the other end. For rural or regional economies, and hence regional or rural markets, the restructuring of the nation's economy further incapacitates traditionally stagnant manufacturing markets. The ability of rural areas to generate basic or export income is severely stifled, and it often is difficult for these areas to diversify or enter into other markets.

Labor

Labor markets are a set of relations between buyers and sellers of labor, with employers representing buyers of labor and regions representing sellers of labor. In terms of viability, labor markets narrowly construed refers to the readiness of a region's civilian workforce to occupy a variety of jobs. If a company considers relocating to a particular area, what are the chances that the location has a pool of qualified individuals ready to perform the whole range of activities needed to start and sustain the company's activities? Key questions become, What is the average education level of the area's civilian labor force? What is the average skill level of the area's civilian labor force? To what extent does the labor market in a rural area increase or decrease its chances for economic growth?

The restructuring of the economy in the 1970s and 1980s resulted in increased demand for a highly educated national workforce. This created problems for economies that historically have been typified by production industries: agriculture, mining, timber, and routine manufacturing. There has been a growing imbalance between the skills of the workforce and the higher skills desired by employers, which creates a special problem for rural areas, where average education levels are relatively low. Those who study components of rural America often refer to this two-faceted problem as the education and rural crisis. There is a linkage between the two problems in that the rural crisis stemmed directly from the low education levels of the rural workforce. Consequently, the growth and skill levels of rural jobs are limited by the education levels of rural workers. The shift in the economic structure that occurred in the 1980s hurt rural areas because employers no longer looked for reliable, low-skilled, low-paid workers. Rural labor markets have less appeal to employers searching for high-skilled labor.

Economic structure and rural labor markets have a poignant impact on rural markets. Each determines the nature of the goods and services to be produced and sold. A region's viability hinges on its ability to bring money into the community by exporting goods and services.

Poorly leveraged economies and low-skilled labor markets do not serve as catalysts for economic activity.

Economic Development

Markets, when thought of as regional areas in which economic activity is either vibrant or stagnant, often seek to alleviate their sundry maladies. Conditions such as poor infrastructure, low tax bases, poverty, low per capita income, and low education levels represent impediments to economic growth and opportunity. Economic development activities have at least three major goals: job creation, fiscal improvement, and physical improvement. Within these three goals are a range of activities geared to achieve each. Historically, the focus of economic development activities was rooted in business recruitment to increase the growth of manufacturing sectors. Many of the activities centered on developing tools aimed at improving the business climate and the infrastructure, with the intended outcome of attracting manufacturing concerns to a specific region. With the shift from a manufacturing economy to a service economy, many regions were forced to modify their approach to economic or fiscal improvement. In addition to continuing efforts at business recruitment and infrastructure development, regions sought ways to develop labor markets. These provided prospective service sector industries with incentive either to base their operations in the area or to include them in their expanded service area.

References to rural markets need not be followed by expressions of doom. Rather, technology has the potential to evaporate the remoteness of rural communities. Rural economic development strategies must take advantage of technological developments to create propitious conditions leading to economic growth.

—Franklyn L. Tate

See also

Development, Community and Economic; Employment; Labor Force; Manufacturing Industry; Policy, Rural Development; Quality of Life; Regional Planning; Technology; Trade Areas; Underemployment.

References

Ayres, Janet, F. Larry Leistritz, and Kenneth E. Stone. *Revitalizing the Retail Trade Sector in Rural Communities: Lessons from Three Midwestern States.* Ames, IA: North Central Regional Center for Rural Development, 1989.

Blair, John P. *Urban and Regional Economics.* Homewood, IL: Irwin, 1991.

Christensen, James, R. C. Maurer, and Nancy L. Strang. *Rural Data, People, and Policy: Information Systems for the Twenty-First Century.* Boulder, CO: Westview Press, 1994.

Flora, Cornelia B., and Jan A. Christenson. *Rural Policies for the 1990s.* Boulder, CO: Westview Press, 1991.

Johnson, Thomas, Brady J. Deaton, and Eduardo Segarra. *Local Infrastructure Investment in Rural America*. Boulder, CO: Westview Press, 1988.

Lyson, Thomas A., and William W. Falk. *Forgotten Places: Uneven Development in Rural America*. Lawrence: University of Kansas Press, 1993.

Tickamyer, Ann R., and Cynthia Duncan. "Poverty and Opportunity Structure in Rural America." *Annual Review of Sociology* 16 (1990): 67–86.

U.S. Department of Agriculture. *Education and Rural Economic Development: Strategies for the 1990's*. Washington, DC: U.S. Department of Agriculture, Economic Research Service and Agriculture and Rural Economy Division, September 1991.

———. *Labor Market Areas for the United States*. Washington, DC: U.S. Department of Agriculture, Economic Research Service, 1987.

Marriage

A social institution under which two people formalize their decision to live as partners who are committed to each other. This entry considers the simple myths and complex realities of rural marriages. Focusing on farm and ranch couples, the entry reviews issues of couple relationship to the enterprise; couple involvement with older and younger generations in the agricultural enterprise; issues of gender, division of labor, and communication; and issues related to marital difficulty, divorce, and death of the spouse.

Myths and Realities

Farm and ranch marriages may be America's mythic traditional marriages. However, the reality is that the couples who farm or ranch are enormously diverse and must struggle with daunting challenges that are far from the mythic traditional ideal. The American notion of a traditional marriage is part of American cultural mythology. To a large extent, the mythic traditional marriage is rural. However, rural couples are enormously diverse, representing hundreds of different cultures and an enormous range in level of affluence, quality of relationship, reasons for living in rural America, understandings of what marriage should be, understandings of their own marriage, role division, relationship to the economy and the community, obedience to the law, commitment to living in rural America, and identity as "rural." Many couples in rural America are not married or not heterosexual. Some rural marriages are quite divergent from what most people consider a traditional marriage: for example, couples who do not live together, who do not have a sexually exclusive relationship, who live in isolation from their local community, whose relationship involves a great deal of intimidation and beating by the man, whose lives are dominated by the use of alcohol, who live in communes, or whose income derives from illegal activities.

Farm and Ranch Couples

Perhaps the marriage that most often comes to mind when people think of rural marriage is that of a farm or ranch couple. There are fewer than 1 million such marriages in America, and the number is steadily decreasing. Which couples farm or ranch and which do not reflect many factors, including the history of economic exploitation in America. For example, Blacks in a southern community may value the owning of farmland as much as Whites do, but Blacks will be far less likely to own such land (Gröger 1987).

Farm and ranch marriages have in common their connection to the agricultural enterprise. The stereotype of such couples is that the man owns and operates the enterprise, the woman works in the house, and the couple is identified with farming as a way of life. The reality may be quite different. The couple may see farming as simply a job and a way to produce income or perhaps as worth doing because it is what one of the partners wants to do. Barlett (1993) found many farm wives in a Georgia study who were not identified with farming and in some cases did not want the family to continue farming.

Some farms are operated by women, and on many farms operated by a married couple, the woman's work is primary (Rosenfeld 1985; Rosenfeld and Tigges 1988). On many other farms, the woman's work is as essential to the enterprise as the man's. This is so even on farms where the woman does not work in the enterprise much, if at all, but produces off-farm income that is necessary for the family to continue in farming.

Although many farms could not be operated without the work of both adult partners, it is common for family members and others to downplay the contribution of a woman. This can be understood as partly a matter of societal and family values that credit whatever the man does as the real work of the farm. That women may not be credited for their contribution to the enterprise is an important matter in terms of self-esteem and fairness. Women whose husbands acknowledge their farmwork are less stressed (Keating 1987) and presumably more satisfied with farmwork and marriage. Moreover, acknowledgment of a woman's contribution to the agricultural enterprise is extremely important when it comes to legal rights in probate and divorce situations.

This idealized image of a young couple represents the romantic myth that surrounds rural marriage—a myth belied by the realities of rural life.

Attention to the ethnicity of a farm couple can be extremely helpful in understanding the two people's relationship to each other, to other family members, and to the agricultural enterprise (Salamon 1992). Among the important examples in Salamon's work are substantial ethnic group differences in how central the farm is to the couple's way of life and how much the crucial solidarity in working the farm is husband-wife (versus father-son or brother-brother).

Intergenerational Relationships

Many farm couples work in an intergenerational operation, perhaps at first working with the husband's parents and later working with one or more of the couple's own adult offspring. To understand such farm couples, one must attend to those multigenerational relationships. The crucial alliance, the relationship that most involves one in day-to-day activity, frequently is intergenerational. Sometimes the intergenerational relationship seems to create marital difficulties. For example, a wife may be treated as an outsider and be blamed for most family tensions by her parents-in-law and husband.

The stereotypical farm couple can work amicably, but farm couples, like other couples, struggle with their differences, the imperfection of communication, and inadequate resources of money, time, and personal energy. In farm couples, the enterprise can become an important ingredient in power struggles. For example, a husband may assert that something must be done because it is necessary to the farm. He thus makes the needs of the farm and his expertise in assessing those needs part of the couple power struggle. If she brings in an off-farm income, she may assert that she should have control over that income and claim a right to review certain farm expenditures. If the couple works in conjunction with either person's parents, those parents or beliefs and assertions about those parents can be part of couple power battles. For example, he may rely on his parents as allies or say that because he cannot go against their wishes, the couple must accept or do something he claims is what his parents want. She may try to recruit his mother as an ally, but she also may need to ally with her husband in trying to deal with his parents. So power struggles in farm couples are related to aspects of the farm enterprise and dynamics in the larger family. Similarly, as Barlett (1993) showed, aspects of the farm enterprise are related to what goes on in the couple: for example, the standard of living one or both wants to achieve. And dynamics in the larger family are related to what goes on in any specific couple in the family.

Gender, Division of Labor, and Communication

There is a rich literature on the division of labor in farm couples, often focusing on how much the woman does on the farm and how much the man does in the home. That literature typically deals with concrete chores but also with division of labor in broader terms. For example, many farm women are crucial in managing relationships within the farm family in ways that promote effective farmwork by children and others and in building and maintaining ties to the community that can pay off economically for the farm enterprise (Kohl 1976).

Many farm couples work in proximity to their residence. This may facilitate the work of the enterprise, but it may mean that they never get away from work (Rosenblatt and Anderson 1981). Living in close proximity to work may make it easier for family members to know what one another does, to be available to help one another, and to be in a position to communicate richly. However, knowing what one's spouse does and being in a position to communicate richly may create difficulty if they lead to resented criticism or to difficult and painful differences of opinion. Farm couples often work with physical separation and with a strict separation of work responsibilities. Each partner may have a personal sphere of work, including the work of managing the family and maintaining the household. The physical separation and the division of labor may limit how much each member will know of what the other does, how much they will criticize, and how much they will talk about important aspects of their daily life. For example, her bringing up an issue of farm safety may be unlikely if both see the farm operation as his responsibility. She may feel that she has a right to bring up such matters when safety issues are relevant to her work area: for example, if the care of children is primarily her responsibility and the safety of a child is at issue.

When partners do not communicate well, they may not deal effectively with a crisis: for example, when the farm operation is in economic difficulty. Farming is in many ways a very stressful way of life. Because farming is one of the most dangerous occupations in America, farm couples must deal with work-related hazards, illnesses, and injuries. Farming also is hazardous economically, with farm income at the mercy of weather, insect pests, plant and animal diseases, variations in supply and demand, changes in interest rates and land values, changes in federal law, control of pricing by agribusinesses, and international events that radically increase the cost of fuel and fertilizer. It is small wonder, then, that farm marriages may be rocked by economic crises (Conger, Ge, and Lorenz 1994; Rosenblatt 1990).

Troubles

Farm couples are no different in needing social services, such as marriage counseling, that can support their relationship, yet rural America has a relatively low density of such services. One reason for the low density of services is that it is harder to provide services when the number of people in the catchment area is relatively small. Another factor is that there is relatively little anonymity in a rural community. Consequently, couples in rural America who are concerned about reputation may not want to risk being seen entering a counseling office. This is particularly so when relatively few people in one's community have received a service such as counseling or are willing to acknowledge receiving such services; then it is difficult for others to learn about the service and to understand how it could be beneficial. It would be an error to point to the lower divorce rate in rural America (Shelton 1987) and say that marital-support services are not needed in rural areas. Many rural couples for whom divorce would be a route to greater happiness, safety, sanity, and well-being for one or both partners do not divorce. That farm couples divorce less often than urban couples may say more about reputation issues in rural America and the lack of economic and social alternatives than about the relative wholesomeness of farm marriages.

Farm marriages often end with the death of a spouse. In farm couples, a spouse's death can be extremely challenging if the spouse was actively involved in the farm operation. The surviving partner may have to deal not only with the death but also with the immediate demands of the farm enterprise (Rosenblatt and Karis 1993). Early bereavement is a bad time to have to make major decisions, but the grieving spouse may have to do so if the enterprise cannot be operated without the spouse who has died. A decision to sell the farm may have devastating consequences for relationships with other family members (the surviving partner may be selling the opportunity to farm) and for the bereaved person (the surviving partner may be selling a home and way of life as well as an economic enterprise she or he no longer can manage).

—*Paul C. Rosenblatt*

See also
Culture; Domestic Violence; Ethnicity; Family; Intergenerational Land Transfer; Mental Health; Rural Women; Values of Residents.

References
Barlett, Peggy F. *American Dreams, Rural Realities: Family Farms in Crisis.* Chapel Hill: University of North Carolina Press, 1993.
Conger, Rand D., Xiao-Jia Ge, and Frederick O. Lorenz. "Economic Stress and Marital Relations." Pp. 187–203 in *Families in Troubled Times: Adapting to Change in Rural America.* Edited by R. D. Conger and G. H. Elder Jr. New York: Aldine de Gruyter, 1994.
Gröger, Lisa B. "The Meaning of Land in a Southern Rural Community: Differences between Blacks and Whites." Pp. 189–207 in *Farm Work and Fieldwork: American Agriculture in Anthropological Perspective.* Edited by M. Chibnik. Ithaca, NY: Cornell University Press, 1987.
Keating, Norah C. "Reducing Stress of Farm Men and Women." *Family Relations* 36 (1987): 358–363.
Kohl, Seena. B. *Working Together: Women and Family in Southwestern Saskatchewan.* Toronto: Holt, Rinehart and Winston, 1976.
Rosenblatt, Paul C. *Farming Is in Our Blood: Farm Families in Economic Crisis.* Ames: Iowa State University Press, 1990.
Rosenblatt Paul C., and R. M. Anderson. "Interaction in Farm Families: Tension and Stress." Pp. 147–166 in *The Family in Rural Society.* Edited by R. T. Coward and W. M. Smith Jr. Boulder, CO: Westview Press, 1981.
Rosenblatt, Paul C., and Thomas A. Karis. "Economics and Family Bereavement Following a Fatal Farm Accident." *Journal of Rural Community Psychology* 12, no. 2 (1993): 37–51.
Rosenfeld, Rachel Ann. *Farm Women: Work, Farm, and Family in the United States.* Chapel Hill: University of North Carolina Press, 1985.
Rosenfeld, R. A., and Leann M. Tigges. "Marital Status and Independent Farming: The Importance of Family Labor Flexibility to Farm Outcomes." Pp. 171–192 in *Woman and Farming: Changing Roles, Changing Structures.* Edited by W. G. Haney and J. B. Knowles. Boulder, CO: Westview Press, 1988.
Salamon, Sonya. *Prairie Patrimony: Family Farming and Community in the Midwest.* Chapel Hill: University of North Carolina Press, 1992.
Shelton, Beth Ann. "Variations in Divorce Rates by Community Size: A Test of the Social Integration Explanation." *Journal of Marriage and the Family* 49, no. 4 (1987): 827–832.

Mechanization

The use of tools and machines to enhance and replace human labor. This entry describes the labor problems faced by agricultural producers. It examines the emergence of mechanization as a solution to many of these labor problems. The consequences of the mechanization of agriculture were extensive, and some of these consequences are described.

Essential Elements in Production
There are several elements in the production of food and fiber that are absolutely essential. This list of essential elements includes, but is not limited to, soil, water, sunshine, and the force or energy necessary to accomplish agricultural tasks (Schlebecker 1975). This force or energy, or simply labor, is needed to prepare the soil, plant the seeds, remove the weeds, harvest the crop, and numerous other tasks. Throughout human history, and even during most of the era of European settlement in North America, humans have been the major source of agricultural labor (Cochrane 1979; Vassey 1992). But mechanization of agriculture has changed the sources and organization of farm labor. This mechanization process consists of the development and use of machines that allow human labor to be more efficiently used and to be largely replaced by machines. The mechanization of agriculture is perhaps the most prominent cause of change in the development of American agriculture and in the transformation of rural America.

The Unique Labor Problems of Agriculture
There are several factors that make the labor problems of agriculture unique and troublesome, especially when compared to the problems of industrial labor (Mooney 1983; Friedland 1984). Most prominent is that the production of many agricultural commodities is seasonal. Throughout the year, there are periods of extensive labor, such as during planting and the harvest, which are followed by periods where the labor requirements are minimal as biological processes unfold (Mann and Dickinson 1978). Employing an agricultural labor force large enough to meet peak requirements would mean that during most of the year this labor force would be used very inefficiently. But if attempts to obtain a sufficient labor force during critical periods fail, the result could be utter ruination. In contrast to agriculture, an industrial labor force can be used consistently and efficiently throughout the year.

Attempts to deal with these labor issues in agriculture have taken a variety of directions throughout human history. During the colonial years, and after the initial establishment of the United States, the family farm was the primary means by which farm labor was organized in this country. Family farms were typically medium-sized

Mechanization has greatly increased the efficiency and productivity of farms. This seeding machine saves the farmer days of back-breaking work.

operations where the vast majority of the labor inputs was from the farmer and other family members. Family labor was relatively effective in dealing with the unique labor issues of agriculture because family members could be used extensively on the farm when needed and then idled with minimal costs when not needed (Buttel, Larson, and Gillespie 1990). Of course, the family farm did not exist everywhere, and there were other approaches used for dealing with farm labor problems. The plantations of the early South with slave labor and the large fruit and vegetable farms of California with extensive hired labor forces were examples of efforts to meet the labor needs of agriculture outside of the family farm enterprise. Slave labor was used prominently in cotton production, which required a variety of low-skill tasks to be performed throughout the year and thus allowed the labor force to be used efficiently. California producers were dependent on having migrants or other populations available that were desperate enough to take the low wages and temporary employment that agriculture offered.

During the years when agriculture depended on human labor, the major factor limiting the sizes and production capabilities of American farms was the labor capacity of family members. To early American farmers, there was generally plenty of land available, but having the labor resources to operate this land was a more difficult concern (Berardi and Geisler 1984; Dorner 1983). As a result, the typical American family farm existed at about the subsistence level. Most farmers were able to produce enough to meet the needs of the family but generally had little surplus for the marketplace. Thus, it was necessary for most of the American population to be involved in farming. The first U.S. census, in 1790, found that 96 percent of the population was rural and that most of these rural residents were living on farms (Albrecht and Murdock 1990).

Historical Emergence

From early on in the development of American agriculture, emphasis was placed on developing machines as a more consistent solution to farm labor problems. In

American agriculture, machines had several major advantages over human labor. First, once a machine was purchased, it could be stored during periods of disuse for little additional cost and made quickly available when needed. Second, machines could eliminate much of the back-breaking work once associated with farming.

During the nineteenth century, several major technological breakthroughs occurred. Among the more important were the iron moldboard plow, grain drill, mechanical grain reaper, grain-threshing machine, and cotton gin. New technologies substantially increased the labor capacity of family farms, allowing them to operate a larger acreage to produce more per acre and thus to have a surplus that could be sold in the marketplace. Surplus made it possible for some of the population to be released from agriculture and to pursue endeavors not directly related to food production. At the same time, the expansion of industry attracted workers to urban areas. By 1880, the nonfarm population exceeded the farm population for the first time, and by 1920 the urban population had surpassed the rural population (Albrecht and Murdock 1990).

Despite these nineteenth-century developments, the United States of the early twentieth century was still largely an agricultural nation. In 1940, farmers remained the largest occupational group in the country. At that time, there were over 6 million farms in the United States, the farm population exceeded 30 million people, and about 25 percent of the total U.S. population lived on farms. But after 1940 the mechanization of agriculture proceeded rapidly; the impacts of this process have been more dramatic than anyone could have imagined. The mechanization of agriculture changed the very nature of farm work and totally transformed the face of rural America.

Perhaps the mechanization process of the twentieth century is best exemplified by the all-purpose tractor that first appeared in the 1920s. The tractor could pull a plow as horses had before the tractor was invented, but the tractor could pull a bigger plow, pull it faster, and pull it longer. Consequently, farmers could complete their plowing in a much shorter time than before. In addition, the tractor used fossil fuels as its energy source rather than eating part of the crop, as horses did. With a tractor and other machines, farmers could either operate a much larger farm or complete the farmwork in less time, which made it possible to be involved in other endeavors, such as off-farm employment.

It is estimated that about 30 billion hours of human labor went into in the production of food and fiber in the United States in 1930 (Bertrand 1978). The use of more and continually improved farm technologies resulted in a steady decline in the amount of human labor required. By 1984, only 3.7 billion hours of human labor were needed in agriculture. In 1940, the average farmer produced enough food and fiber to supply 10.7 persons. By 1970, the average farmer was producing enough for 47.9 persons, and by 1984 this number had increased to 77. Using modern machines in the 1980s, a farmer could accomplish in 1 hour what had taken 14 hours in 1920 (Poincelot 1986).

Farm Structure Consequences

With the labor needs in agriculture reduced so dramatically, the most evident consequences between 1940 and 1970 were an increase in the size of the average farm and a reduction in the farm population. Technology made it possible for farmers to operate a much larger farm, and the economies of scale associated with the purchase of new machines made such farm expansion almost compulsory. Mechanization resulted in the smaller and less competitive farms becoming less economically viable, and as a result many of them went out of business. The reduction in farm numbers was rapid. By 1950, the number of farms was down to 5.4 million. These numbers were further reduced to 3.7 million in 1959 and to 2.7 million in 1969. Between 1940 and 1970, the size of the average American farm increased from 175 acres to 390 acres. Reduction in the farm population was even more dramatic, as farm population declines were compounded by the increasingly smaller size of the farm family. By 1950, the farm population had been reduced to 23 million. It was further reduced to 15.6 million in 1960 and to 9.7 million in 1970 (Albrecht and Murdock 1990).

Despite continuing technological developments, major changes in the direction of farm structural change occurred after 1970. Specifically, the trend toward fewer and larger farms slowed dramatically. Since 1970, the number of farms and the farm populations have continued to decline, and farm sizes have continued to increase, but the rates of these changes have been much smaller. In 1992, there were 1.9 million farms, the size of the average farm was 440 acres, and the farm population was down to 3.9 million.

The most apparent result of mechanization in recent years is the emergence of the large, highly capitalized farm. In 1992, only 2.4 percent of U.S. farms had farm sales of $500,000 or more; yet these farms had 45.9 percent of the total farm sales. The movement toward large-scale farms has not been consistent for all commodities as technological developments have been much more amenable for some commodities than others. For some commodities, new technologies allowed production to occur in an assembly-line fashion and allowed an efficient and steady use of labor. For example, most poultry production now consists of the production, processing, and distribution conducted by a single, large firm. The independent small poultry producer largely has been eliminated. An increasingly larger proportion of the nation's dairy production occurs in specialized dairy farms with 500 or more cows. These farms purchase most or all of their feed and rely heavily on hired labor. Similarly, very large hog and beef feeding operations have emerged in recent years that in many ways resemble a factory more than they do a farm. For each of these farm enterprises, the emergence of such large capitalized farms is possible because seasonality is not an issue and production occurs steadily throughout the year. Furthermore, production can be confined to a small area that can be highly capitalized, and there is no need for large landholdings. The effects of mechanization have been somewhat less extensive on the more land-intensive, seasonal crops. There are some commodities where machines have not been invented yet to perform many of the tasks and human labor remains paramount.

Community Consequences

The mechanization of agriculture has consequences far beyond farmers and farm families. With labor needs reduced so extensively in agriculture, many areas with high concentrations of the workforce employed in agriculture experienced heavy out-migration and large population declines between 1940 and 1970. Even during the nonmetropolitan population turnaround of the 1970s, counties most dependent on agricultural employment continued to lose population. Population declines dramatically influenced rural communities as many nonfarm businesses were forced to close. Urban communities were affected as millions of former rural and farm residents moved to the city, often without the skills to compete in the urban labor force.

Technological developments will continue to have dramatic consequences for American agriculture. For example, the emergence of biotechnology could greatly impact farm structure and rural communities. It is critical that researchers and policymakers keep abreast of these changes and that we improve our ability to understand and predict the consequences of future technological developments.

—*Don E. Albrecht*

See also
Agricultural Engineering; Agriculture, Structure of; Community; Employment; History, Agricultural; Technology; Work.
References
Albrecht, Don E., and Steven H. Murdock. *The Sociology of U.S. Agriculture: An Ecological Perspective.* Ames: Iowa State University Press, 1990.
Berardi, Gigi M., and Charles C. Geisler. *The Social Consequences and Challenges of New Agricultural Technologies.* Boulder, CO: Westview Press, 1984.
Bertrand, Alvin L. "Rural Social Organizational Implications of Technology and Industry." Pp. 75–88 in *Rural U.S.A.: Persistence and Change.* Edited by Thomas R. Ford. Ames: Iowa State University Press, 1978.
Buttel, Frederick H., Olaf F. Larson, and Gilbert W. Gillespie Jr. *The Sociology of Agriculture.* Westport, CT: Greenwood Press, 1990.
Cochrane, Willard W. *The Development of American Agriculture: A Historical Analysis.* Minneapolis: University of Minnesota Press, 1979.
Dorner, P. "Technology and U.S. Agriculture." Pp. 73–86 in *Technology and Social Change in Rural Areas: A Festschrift for Eugene A. Wilkening.* Edited by Gene F. Summers. Boulder, CO: Westview Press, 1983.
Friedland, William H. "Commodity System Analysis: An Approach to the Sociology of Agriculture." Pp. 221–236 in *Research in Rural Sociology and Development.* Vol. 1: *Focus on Agriculture.* Edited by Harry K. Schwartzweller. Greenwich, CT: JAI Press, 1984.
Mann, Susan A., and James M. Dickinson. "Obstacles to the Development of a Capitalist Agriculture." *Journal of Peasant Studies* 5 (1978): 466–481.
Mooney, Patrick H. "Toward a Class Analysis of Midwestern Agriculture." *Rural Sociology* 48 (1983): 563–584.
Poincelot, Raymond P. *Toward a More Sustainable Agriculture.* Westport, CT: AVI, 1986.
Schlebecker, John T. *Whereby We Thrive: A History of American Farming, 1607–1972.* Ames: Iowa State University Press, 1975.
Vassey, Daniel E. *An Ecological History of Agriculture, 10000 B.C.–A.D. 10000.* Ames: Iowa State University Press, 1992.

Media

The means or channels of communication, especially technological ones, and mass media aimed at a widespread audience, typically providing information, news, entertainment, and persuasive messages. More commonly, the media refer to television, radio, newspapers, magazines, and, increasingly, interactive computer channels. Rural areas tend to be less well served by mass media, largely for economic reasons. Social influences of media vary by the context in which individuals use them, and the impact of newer communication technologies on rural life remains unclear. Extension programs continue a vital role for farmers, with private, commercial sources gaining strength. The rural mass media systems and their effects on the public are described in this entry. Emerging communication technologies and the use of media by farmers are examined.

Weekly newspapers are an important source of local information; Thomas Burford, editor of the Farmers Independent *in Bagley, Minnesota, displays his paper.*

Rural Systems

Mass media serve rural communities less well than urban ones primarily because of smaller, more dispersed rural populations. Communication systems generally reflect the societies and communities they serve, and media are used in widely ranging ways by their audiences, with diverse consequences. However, little study has been done of differences between rural and urban media impacts. Recent advances in media technologies may benefit some rural areas but present more problematic influences in others. Farmers form a distinct media audience with narrower and more pragmatically defined channel and message preferences. Extension programs enhanced agricultural communication over the decades.

Mass media are distributed unequally across America. Its rural communities, regardless of region or type, tend to be media poorer in terms of access. Simple economics is a major reason; mass media thrive on mass audiences, preferably those they can reach with lower distribution costs. Commercial advertising–driven media are most prone to this. Newspapers serve as a classic example. Large urban dailies provide dozens of pages of news, features, and advertisements in several editions, driven by subscriber lists of over 100,000 and a concentrated, competitive retail advertising base. Rural communities are more likely to be served by a combination of small-town weekly and smaller-city daily papers, typically providing considerably less depth and breadth in coverage. Whereas major urban dailies still reach many rural areas, increasing distribution costs drive up subscription prices. Current trends suggest many of these papers are pulling back to their core advertising market areas for greater profit.

Broadcast media also tend to underserve the rural landscape because they are economically limited by the number of households within their maximum signal areas. Small-town and open-country residents are apt to have far fewer radio and television stations to choose, and these usually lack the diversity of formats and attendant quality of stations in more populous, competitive markets. Cablecasting overcame some of these disadvantages in small cities and towns, but at a price to users. Satellite dishes are a boon to country dwellers, but at a cost prohibitively high to many. Statewide public radio and television networks level the field, with many providing higher-quality informational and cultural programming to even the most remote populations. Nonetheless, the dynamism and diversity of contemporary broadcasting are muted in most rural areas. For both rural broadcast outlets and newspapers, employee salary levels tend to be lower than in larger market areas, probably drawing less experienced and/or less proficient staffs. Rural markets are regarded by some as training grounds for journalists working their way up to more urban venues, which can result in relatively high rates of turnover and less familiarity with local issues.

Magazines are the most geographically unrestricted medium, provided a person can subscribe by mail and pay the attendant cost. However, rural areas are unlikely to have the advantage of large newsstands or bookstores relatively close at hand, limiting the value of browsing and single-issue purchases. Availability of books and audio and video recordings similarly is constrained by rural areas having smaller, more widely separated distribution outlets, including libraries. The reduced selection of channels across all major media has consequences in rural audiences having less mix of competing voices from which to choose in news and public affairs coverage. Knowledge of statewide and national issues may suffer among rural publics for their not receiving topical news from a variety of broadcast and print sources, with differing information formats and editorial policies. As a result, there may be an increasing knowledge gap on current affairs between rural and metropolitan audiences.

Effects on the Public

Social observers going back to Robert Park in the 1920s related community size and attendant aspects of community structure to variations in mass media institutions and in turn to the quantity and quality of their content. Those factors likewise affect how audiences access and use media and what the impact of media is likely to be. Theories of media effects have evolved during the century from ones attributing to media substantial ability to influence individuals and society, to more limited-effects models in which media have little, if any, power, to current ones depicting more interactive transactions between audiences and media. Media gratifies needs such as surveillance, information, social interaction, inclusion, escape, and arousal. Media effects can be seen, in part, as consequences of the search for such gratifications.

Publics vary in their dependence on media according to a number of psychosocial, demographic, and cultural factors. Other approaches to media effects on individuals and society focus on prosocial and antisocial socialization of children and adults, on construction and transmission of media-based depictions of social reality, on the ability of media to set issue agendas for audiences, and on a range of media influences on the development, adaptation, and inhibition of public opinion. Unfortunately, little work has been done recently on to differential uses of media by rural versus metropolitan dwellers and the effects of such use in terms of information gain, attitudinal or behavioral changes, or cultural consequences. The preponderance of media distribution outside of rural areas may contribute to this neglect.

Emerging Communication Technologies

Mass media technologies can be viewed as having a generally positive impact on rural communities in that they reduce social isolation; increase access to information for personal, family, and business decision making; increase access to news, public affairs, and general cultural content; and contribute to a broader economic base by providing advertising, employment, and technological diffusion. Nearly all forms of emergent communication

technologies, from the telegraph to the telephone and radio, have had singularly beneficial impacts on rural lifestyles and economies. Less clear is the extent to which those same technologies have advanced urban society even more, widening an informational and cultural gap between urban and rural. The documented disadvantages in rural communities of such requisites as health care and transportation heighten the advantages that increased information services could perform for them. As with the diffusion of any innovative technologies, the anticipation of the rate of adoption and full range of consequences remains speculative.

It also remains unclear whether the technological, largely computer-driven, distribution changes in media now under way will improve the lot of rural audiences. Most information highway scenarios offer the availability of multiple arrays of information and entertainment through telephone, cable, and satellite hookups, dispelling traditional boundaries between print and electronic communication. Although the telecommunications infrastructure in many, if not most, rural communities may now be less than adequate, the promise holds for relatively cheap distribution of and access to the same electronic information sources available to residents of larger, wealthier urban areas. One possibility is that of improved access primarily to the more educated, upscale populace, increasing the gap between them and the have-nots. Microcomputer and videotex use, for example, has been found to increase more among large-scale farmers who already have more informational resources and skills at hand. Migration of information industry workers to more desirable countryside locations, both near and away from urban zones, may add to economic and lifestyle divisions.

Often overlooked in more promising information society scenarios is the fact that the initial cost of computer equipment, although sharply declining, is still problematical for many, as are the basic processing skills required. Whereas rural residents may be as likely as nonrural ones to have telecommunication technologies in their homes, there is considerable variation across types of rural communities (for example, agricultural versus light industry–based versus bedroom). The impact of new information technologies on rural America may be highly split across the increasing diversity of rural locales, unlike the case of more traditional mass media in which rural communities in general were less endowed. Metropolitan encroachment into rural areas seemingly would bring urban media channels into greater play in those areas, but little study has been done on how these sources displace or interact with existing rural media (for example, weekly newspapers and small-town radio stations) or on the role of media as older communities undergo relatively rapid growth and related changes.

Farm Use

Farmers and other agricultural producers form a subculture tied to, yet distinct from, other rural populaces. They attend to the typical rural media for general information and entertainment but also depend on a network of specialized channels providing them with often critical information for making short- and long-term economic and production decisions. Local newspapers, radio, and television outlets cater to the farm audience with news on agriculturally salient issues, market reports, weather, and often informative advertising on farm-related products. Whereas farmers clearly rely on these channels for recent, updated information, they are more apt to name farm magazines and newspapers as their most popular and credible source. These subscription publications provide more detailed stories on agricultural practices, finances, and government policy. They range from more general national publications (such as *Farm Journal)* to regional or activity-specific ones (such as *Hoard's Dairyman, Western Livestock Reporter, and Iowa Farmer Today*). More specialized newsletters aimed at particular kinds of producers have grown in recent years, as have a range of telecommunication and computer services that disseminate immediate and in-depth information on an increasing variety of subjects. Cost clearly becomes a factor, with the more sophisticated channels serving larger, more profitable enterprises.

Social research on media use among farmers often is couched in terms of adoption and diffusion of innovations models, and media typically are credited with making farmers more aware of and familiar with new farm technologies and practices, whereas interpersonal communication appears more important later in the process when decisions to adopt are being made. It does appear likely that media have accelerated the rate of diffusion of innovative farm practices and technologies. The current, more globally oriented farm economy appears driven in part by worldwide media systems that efficiently link producers to one another.

It is difficult to assess rural media, especially farm media, without noting the role of university extension programs. Developed largely in the early 1900s to extend the latest agricultural research from the campus to the producers, extension from the beginning capitalized on mass media to improve its reach. Innovations included the now-familiar printed bulletins informing farmers in common language of how to apply the newest production techniques, to early public radio programming aimed at farm and home audiences, to instructional films, and now to videotapes, telephone, and video teleconferencing. Much of the research-based content of agricultural magazines, local newspapers, and rural commercial radio and television stations still depends heavily on input from state and local extension offices. Surveys of farmers name extension media as quite close to magazines in frequency of use and typically higher in credibility. Extension also continued early efforts at home economics instruction with programs aimed at nutrition, family, and consumer education, primarily in rural areas. Current trends, however, suggest an increasing privatization of agricultural information, with producers turning more and more to commercial information sources and paid consultants. Agribusiness companies aggressively promote their products by providing substantial information of value to farmers. The validity and credibility of such nonpublic information may come under greater scrutiny in the future.

Promoting Change

As with mass media systems in general, rural media largely reflect the infrastructures and cultures they serve, including their strengths and weaknesses. The extent to which media are capable of promoting, reinforcing, or inhibiting social change is still an open question, as is what kinds of situations advance one possibility or another. More emphasis on these questions in rural societies may be particularly important given the challenges they face.

—Garrett J. O'Keefe and Julie A. Rursch

See also
Computers; Consumer-Goods Advertising; Consumerism; Cooperative State Research, Education, and Extension Service; Land-Grant Institutions, 1862; Land-Grant Institutions, 1890; Public Libraries; Technology; Technology Transfer; Telecommunications; Trade Areas; Trade, Interregional.

References
Abbott, Eric A., and J. Paul Yarborough. "Inequalities in the Information Age: Farmers' Differential Adoption and Use of Four Information Technologies." *Agriculture and Human Values* 9 (1992): 67–79.
Fett, John. *Sources and Use of Agricultural Information: A Literature Review.* Madison: University of Wisconsin, Department of Agricultural Journalism, 1993.
LaRose, Robert, and Jennifer Mettler. "Who Uses Information Technologies in Rural America?" *Journal of Communication* 39 (1989): 48–60.

McQuail, Dennis. *Mass Communication Theory: An Introduction.* 3d ed. London: Sage, 1994.

Park, Robert E. "The Natural History of the Newspaper." Pp. 8–23 in *Mass Communication.* Edited by W. Schramm. 2d ed. Urbana: University of Illinois Press, 1975.

Rogers, Everett M. *The Diffusion of Innovations.* 4th ed. New York: Free Press, 1995.

Tichenor, Philip J., George A. Donohue, and Clarice N. Olien. *Community Conflict and the Press.* Beverly Hills, CA: Sage, 1980.

———. "Community Structure, Media, and Knowledge." *Sociology of Rural Life* 12 (1992): 1–2, 7.

Yarborough, Paul. Information Technology and Rural Economic Development: Evidence from Historical and Contemporary Research. Washington, DC: U.S. Congress, Office of Technology Assessment, 1990.

Mental Health

A state in which the individual is able to function psychologically in a way that he or she is effective in most spheres of life and is reasonably free of pain or discomfort. This entry summarized recent data on the prevalence of alcohol, drug abuse, and mental health (ADM) problems in rural areas. It has been commonplace to assert that rural America suffered from what Ginsberg (1997) aptly termed an *auditory* gap—a difficulty in being heard. The intervening two decades however, witnessed a remarkable reduction in this gap, particularly in the area of mental health. This has been the result of vigorous advocacy and legislative initiatives. This entry describes the history of rural mental disorders research and compares urban and rural populations with respect to mental disorders. It examines the impact of the farm crisis of the early 1980s on mental health and compares it with the mental health impacts of energy booms and life in isolated frontier areas. The entry concludes with a discussion of alcohol and drug abuse in rural areas.

Psychiatric Epidemiology

Research in psychiatric epidemiology can be characterized in terms of three generations of instruments. The first employed case records; the second, field instruments that measured generic psychiatric distress; and the third, field instruments that related to standard diagnostic categories of disorder. In regard to the epidemiology of ADM problems in rural America, two separate but related questions need to be raised. First, are rates for disorder reliably higher in rural or in urban areas? Second, how much mental disorder exists in rural areas? The first question has ideological and philosophical, as well as scientific, aspects. For several millennia, cities have been viewed with suspicion as morally unhealthy environments, as counterpoised to the healthfulness of rural venues. More recently, advocates of rural health and mental health services have stressed the greater number of mental health problems in rural areas. First- and second-generation studies produced inconsistent findings, and a definitive answer to the question was not possible because of a lack of comparable research.

Since the 1970s, changes in psychiatric nomenclature enabled investigators to develop field instruments directly tied to diagnostic categories. Several recent, large, third-generation studies attempted to answer the question of rural/urban differences in psychopathology. The first, the Epidemiologic Catchment Area (ECA) program, was a major multisite study of five catchment areas (three urban, one mixed urban/rural, and one predominantly rural) that queried over 18,000 respondents using a standardized psychiatric instrument. The evidence suggests that there are no rural/urban differences in the lifetime prevalence of aggregate mental disorder. However, in terms of specific disorders, with the exception of alcohol abuse/dependence and cognitive deficit, which are higher in rural areas, the rates for most disorders are higher in the urban setting. Clusters of depressive symptoms show some rural predominance. The research results highlight the importance of differentiating specific disorders in any study of the relation between psychiatric morbidity and rural/urban residence. The ECA investigators stressed that a simple rural/urban dichotomy is insufficient to explain differences in prevalence. One must examine characteristics of the rural environment that predispose persons to disorder, as well as the presence of persons at high risk for disorder (Robins, Locke, and Regier 1991).

The Colorado Social Health Survey (CSHS) examined rural/urban differences in mental disorder (defined as "need for mental health/substance abuse services"). Using two definitions of rural, the researchers arrived at different conclusions. Under the first, the need for services in the two areas was approximately equal. In terms of the second, the need for services was significantly *higher* in urban areas (Ciarlo and Tweed 1992).

The most recent data addressing rural/urban differences in psychopathology come from a national probability sample of the United States, the National Comorbidity Study (NCS). Using a standardized instrument similar to that employed by the ECA investigators, NCS researchers queried approximately 8,000 respondents. Unlike the ECA and, congruent with the CSHS, they found no significant difference in the rates for either overall or specific disorders by urbanicity. The only significant difference was higher rates for comorbidity (multiple disorders) in the urban area (Kessler et al. 1994).

Special note must be made of the relationship between rurality and suicide. The notion that there is a link between type of social organization and rates of suicide has been known at least since the work of Durkheim at the beginning of this century. Historically, changes have been noted in urban/rural differences in suicide. Early in the century, rates were higher in urban areas. By midcentury, there was essential parity. In recent years, there tended to be a rural predominance. A clear explanation of the change in the pattern is not evident, but it has been suggested that it might be related to migration patterns, the spreading of urban values, and methods of recording vital statistics (Wilkinson and Israel 1984). The instability of the rural economy made it susceptible to cycles of boom and bust. These cycles created stressors, which, in turn, had significant impact on the mental health of its residents.

The Farm Crisis. The farm crisis of the 1980s focused national attention on the plight of this important segment of the population. Several research studies and anecdotal and services use evidence underscored the magnitude of the mental health aspects of the crisis. Mental health centers experienced sharp increases in services utilization. A study of the response of community mental health centers in 12 midwestern Grain Belt states to the farm crisis found that there was significant increase in client dysfunction and that almost one-half of the caseload were clients with problems directly related to the agricultural crisis (Mermelstein and Sundet 1986). The majority of presenting problems seen in the clinics were depression, withdrawal and denial, crisis behaviors, substance abuse, spouse abuse, and psychosomatic responses. Disturbingly, traditional sources of referral to mental health services did not operate. Public health nurses, clergy, and agricultural extension specialists, traditionally central to rural life, were ranked low as sources of help for personal problems.

A large number of cross-sectional surveys in farm states and provinces in the United States and Canada underscored the elevated levels of distress and psychopathology. A study conducted in Nebraska provided important longitudinal data. The investigators found that households in farm communities went from having the lowest rates of psychological disorder in 1981 (a period of farm prosperity) to the highest in 1986 (during the farm crisis). Of particular note was the rate of reported depressive symptomology, almost doubling from 11 to 21 per-

cent. With the easing of the farm crisis, the percent of farm respondents reporting high levels of symptoms dropped to 12, close to the precrisis rate (Wagenfeld et al. 1994).

The Energy Boom. The economic downturn of the farm crisis produced social disorganization and substantial distress. Likewise, the energy crisis of the 1970s, by rapidly transforming a number of small, isolated rural communities into boomtowns, engendered widespread social disorganization that affected both newcomers and longtime residents. Several reports and studies documented elevated levels of stress and psychopathology (cf. Davenport and Davenport 1979).

Frontier Areas. Recently attention has been paid to the mental health problems of the most isolated of rural areas: frontier counties. Many of these areas are experiencing population changes—both rapid increases and gradual depopulation. The former includes the problems of boomtowns. In the latter, this erosion in some cases threatens community viability. Anecdotal data document the mental health consequences, but no systematic empirical data exist. Duncan (1993) wrote a compelling journalistic account of life in frontier areas. Popper and Popper (1987) articulated a very controversial history and prospects of frontier areas.

Epidemiology of Alcohol and Other Drugs of Abuse

Some data on the prevalence of alcohol and other drugs of abuse (AODA) problems already have been discussed in connection with the third-generation psychiatric surveys. In addition, numerous special-purpose studies have been conducted on adolescent and adult rural populations to gauge levels of use and abuse. In general, these studies suffer from serious conceptual and methodological flaws and are of limited value (see Wagenfeld et al. 1994) for a summary of the research findings).

The energy crisis boomtowns provided some data on AODA problems. Significant increases were reported in substance abuse–related problems (for example, driving while under the influence, public intoxication, domestic violence) associated with the uncontrolled growth. In addition, there was a change in the environment where drinking occurred (bars rather than homes), a change in the purpose and function of alcohol use, and an alteration in the consequences of excessive drinking.

National survey data on the prevalence of AODA in both adolescent and adult populations in metropolitan and nonmetropolitan areas indicate that there are virtually no differences in lifetime prevalence of alcohol and marijuana use beween urban and rural areas. The use of illegal drugs is less common in the nonmetropolitan areas, with the exception of stimulants. Compared to earlier surveys, the metropolitan/nonmetropolitan differences are narrowing. In terms of abusive behavior (daily use of alcohol or marijuana within the past month), students in nonmetropolitan areas are slightly more likely to have consumed alcohol on a daily basis than their more urbanized counterparts.

In sum, the best available data suggest that levels of ADM disorders in rural areas are either equivalent to, or lower than, in urban areas. There is little support for the argument of higher rates of psychopathology in rural areas. The reasons for this are not entirely clear but may relate to characteristics of the rural environment, perceptions of problems, and help-seeking patterns. At the same time, rural areas traditionally have been underserved by treatment facilities. The rural economy is more prone to cycles of boom and bust, and these engender stress-related consequences. The net result is a high degree of suffering.

—*Morton O. Wagenfeld*

See also
Addiction; Domestic Violence; Health Care; Mental Health of Older Adults; Policy, Health Care; Policy, Socioeconomic.
References
Ciarlo, J. A., and D. L. Tweed. "Exploring Rural Colorado's Need for Mental Health Services: Some Preliminary Findings." *Outlook* 2, no. 3 (1992): 29–31.

Davenport, J. H., and J. A. Davenport III. *The Boomtown and Human Services.* Laramie: University of Wyoming Press, 1979.

Duncan, Dayton. *Miles from Nowhere.* New York: Penguin Books, 1993.

Ginsberg, L. "Social Work in Rural Areas," Pp. 3–17 in *Social Work in Rural Areas: Preparation and Practice.* Edited by Ronald K. Green and Stephen A. Webster. Knoxville: Tennessee School of Social Work, 1977.

Kessler, R. C., K. A. McGonagle, S. Zhao, C. B. Nelson, M. Hughes, S. Eshleman, H-U. Wittchen, and K. S. Kendler. "Lifetime and 12-Month Prevalence of DSM-III-R Psychiatric Disorders among Persons Aged 15–54 in the United States: Results from the National Comorbidity Study." *Archives of General Psychiatry* 51 no. 1 (January 1994): 8–19.

Mermelstein, J., and P. Sundet. "Rural Community Mental Health Centers" Response to the Farm Crisis." *Human Resources in the Rural Environment* 10 (1986): 21–26.

Popper, Deborah Epstein, and Frank J. Popper. "The Great Plains: From Dust to Dust." *Planning* 53, no. 12 (1987): 12–18.

Robins, Lee, Ben Z. Locke, and Darrel A. Regier. "An Overview of Psychiatric Disorders in America." Pp. 328–366 in *Psychiatric Disorders in America.* Edited by Lee N. Robins and Darrel A. Regier. New York: Free Press, 1991.

Wagenfeld, Morton O., J. D. Murray, D. Mohatt, and J. C. DeBruyn. *Mental Health and Rural America: 1980–1993.* Washington, DC: U.S. Government Printing Office, 1994.

Wilkinson, Kenneth P., and J. D. Israel. "Suicide and Rurality in Urban Society." *Suicide and Life-Threatening Behavior* 14 (1984): 187–199.

Mental Health of Older Adults

Mental disorders (e.g., dementia and depression) observed among individuals over age 65. These disorders usually are chronic and may be associated with one or more of the following influences: social, psychological, physiological, and neurological. This entry has as its focus the mental health of rural older adults (people aged 65 and over) in general and older adults with dementia (OAD) and their family caregivers (FCs) in particular. The entry examines the barriers that rural OAD and their FCs face in seeking health and community-based services in rural America. The entry first examines trends in the numbers and proportions of older adults across rural America and discusses age and dementia composition among this group. The entry then reports on the deleterious effects on FCs of caring for an OAD and describes the barriers influencing health and community support services. The entry closes with some suggestions to rural planners and policymakers for modifying the present delivery system in rural America.

Numbers

Research on the mental health of older adults living in rural areas (counties outside of a metropolitan statistical area) of the United States receives little attention. Data from the 1990 census show that 8.2 million older adults resided in rural areas (26 percent of the total older adult population). Of this population, 10 percent (847,000) were aged 85 and over (oldest-old), a group increasing and expected to grow well into the future relative to those living in metropolitan areas (Clifford and Lilley 1993). With a substantial proportion of the rural older adult population in general, and the rural oldest-old in particular, the number with dementia (impairment of memory and deterioration of intellectual thinking) will increase, having tangible implications for societal institutions such as health care institutions and families. Ramifications will include the provision of effective and equitable health services at modest costs for rural OAD and their FCs.

Dementia Composition

Dementia is a prevalent psychiatric disorder among older adults. It is considered one of "the most costly both in terms of patient care costs and quality of life issues" (Rathbone-McCuan 1993, 149) and an unidentified mental health problem in rural communities. Therefore, reduction of the overall economic burden and improvement of quality of life for rural OAD and their FCs are important since most of the expenses of caring for OAD are sustained by their FCs rather than third-party payers (Hooyman and Kiyak 1996, 258).

Dementia prevalence rates are difficult to obtain among rural older adults, primarily because diagnostic and evaluation services are excessively limited (Buckwalter, Smith, and Caston 1994). The national prevalence rate of dementia clearly increases with age. It affects approximately 10 percent between the ages of 65 and 75 and 25 to 30 percent over age 85. The prevalence of Alzheimer's disease, the most common form of dementia, is twice as great in women as in men (Schneider 1995). Approximately one-half of OAD live in the community and are cared for by a spouse or child (Hooyman and Kiyak 1996). With no cure for dementia, a goal for treatment is to slow the cognitive and intellectual deterioration and to prevent institutionalization for as long as possible (Schneider 1995). Certain types of health and community-based services provided at the early stages of the chronic condition of dementia help maintain the independent health and functioning of OAD and slow the decline of cognitive impairment in OAD (Krout 1994).

Effects of Dementia on Family Caregivers

Dementia affects not only a particular older adult but also the spouse or other family members who may be providing the care. The stress of caring for an OAD typically leads to deterioration of the FCs' physical and psychological health (Hooyman and Kiyak 1996, 262; Schmall and Webb 1994). An important consideration is to provide social, emotional, and support services at a reasonable cost for FCs to OAD because these services are expensive and may involve lost workdays (Buckwalter et al. 1994; Hooyman and Kiyak 1996, 258–262). Services such as respite and adult care programs are fitting because they provide planned temporary or periodic relief to FCs. Specifically, respite and adult day care services provide FCs "with much-needed breaks in caregiving, giving them time to pursue personal interests and activities and to take care of other business, thus enabling them to continue providing care" (Schmall and Webb 1994, 157). Respite and adult day care services also help OAD remain active and retain learned skills and keep them in the community longer (Nelson 1994). However, rural OAD and their FCs, compared with their urban counterparts, are less likely to use respite and adult day care (Buckwalter et al. 1994; Rathbone-McCuan 1993).

It is too premature to conclude that rural residence directly influences the use of services. Without more systematic information on the distribution of dementia and factors influencing service use, both states and local communities in rural America will remain in a difficult position vis-à-vis to planning for the care of OAD. Such information could contribute to case identification and planning for the use of services in rural areas (Rathbone-McCuan 1993).

Barriers to Services

Even with a lack of research, five primary characteristics are considered barriers to care for rural older adults: the availability, accessibility, affordability, and acceptability of services and the lack of coordination among the mental health and aging service systems in rural areas (Krout 1994; Nelson 1994). Availability refers to adequacy of supply of services to meet the rural OAD's needs. In rural areas, compared with urban areas, mental health services (geropsychiatric inpatient and outpatients services) and mental health professionals (psychiatrists, psychologists, and social workers) trained to treat dementia are less available (Buckwalter et al. 1994). Additionally, compared with urban areas, rural areas are less likely to have community-based services, especially respite care, adult day care centers, and homemaker and meal preparation services (Krout 1994). This occurs because community service agencies usually lack the population base in rural areas necessary profitably to employ skilled workers or the budget to travel long distances into remote rural areas.

Accessibility, or distance to care or services, is a major barrier to service use for OAD living in rural areas. Services tend to be less accessible for them because of geographical distances and lack of public transportation. Increasing the distance or time to get rural older adults to services or services to them significantly hinders utilization (Krout 1994). Rural OAD also have less access to mental health professionals trained in geropsychology or geropsychiatry and must rely on primary-care physicians, who are usually not equipped to accurately diagnose and treat dementia (Buckwalter et al. 1994).

Affordability relates to whether individuals have enough family income and insurance coverage for health and community-based services. Services are less affordable for rural older adults because of high and persistent insurance coverage rates among them (Buckwalter et al. 1994; Schmall and Webb 1994). The percentage of underinsured and uninsured rural older adults is large and growing; and Medicaid eligibility and reimbursement often are restricted in rural states. The lack of Medicare and Medicaid coverage for mental health and other types of community-based services is seen as a barrier to professional geriatric expertise in rural areas (DeCroix-Bane, Rathbone-McCuan, and Galliher 1994). Rural FCs to OAD are unwilling to use or delay using community-based services because of the costs of services or anticipated future health care costs (hospital and nursing home care) (Schmall and Webb 1994).

Acceptability refers to the social labeling (or stigma) associated with seeking care. Based on service refusal data from a mental health outreach program, Buckwalter and her associates (1994) found that 13.1 percent of the older adults refused services because of stigma. Dementia, by its intellectual incompetence, produces a changed status or identity, which can result in social unacceptability or inferiority (Cotrell and Schulz 1993). Rural FCs to OAD could perceive that neighbors and friends will know about their relative's dementia and presence of problematic behaviors associated with the disease and "become the topic of town gossip and the brunt of bad jokes, and will be avoided, shunned, or ostracized" (Buckwalter et al. 1994, 217). To counteract the notion that services are less acceptable for rural OAD and their FCs, the content and presentation of services must correspond with the particular attitudes and values found among OAD and their FCs and must dispel the myths associated with dementia (Krout 1994).

In many rural areas, there is little or no cooperation and coordination across components of the mental health and aging systems (for example, community mental health and Area Agencies on Aging, respectively). Research suggests that if state-level initiatives were created to maintain cooperative planning and funding between aging and mental health systems, then the provision of services in rural areas would be available, accessible, and acceptable (DeCroix-Bane, Rathbone-McCuan and Galliher 1994). To understand better the cooperation (or lack of) among these systems, DeCroix-Bane et al. (1994) conducted a national survey of need and availability of mental health services. Data were collected from the executive directors of 615 Area Agencies on Aging (response rate 70 percent). The study found that Alzheimer's disease support groups were less likely to be found in rural areas, even though respondents reported that older adults with Alzheimer's disease were the second neediest population (out of a possible ten populations).

Proposals for the Future

The proportion of rural OAD and their FCs will continue to grow. Rural OAD and their FCs face barriers to utilization of necessary services. Services are less available, accessible, affordable, and acceptable, and the mental health and aging service systems lack coordination and cooperation. To provide equitable services for rural OAD and their FCs, rural planners must address these barriers. However, at the present time insufficient information exists on the planning, development, and effectiveness of community-based services for rural OAD and their FCs. Rural OAD will continue to be viewed by the service providers as high-risk clients who are set unanchored among health and community support service agencies (Rathbone-McCuan 1993). Some future federal initiatives may encourage states to develop comprehensive respite and adult day care support programs for FCs, with reducing caregiver stress and enhancing caregiver well-being as primary purposes (Schmall and Webb 1994). However, with changes in the policy and service delivery initiatives, a family-oriented approach is needed because rural individuals tend to use family and friends rather than professional services. In this approach, families must made better aware of the availability of services. Thus, rural planners should find a compassionate individual within the service system and have information readily obtainable on service availability and eligibility (Schmall and Webb 1994). Future research should develop alternative programmatic approaches to providing community-based services to rural OAD and their FCs that would aid practitioners and advise policymakers (Krout 1994). Alternative programmatic approaches should be devised to meet the diverse characteristics, values, and beliefs among OAD and their FCs living in heterogeneous areas of rural America (Krout 1994).

—Neale R. Chumbler

See also
Elders; Health Care; Mental Health; Nursing Homes; Policy, Health Care; Policy, Socioeconomic; Senior Centers.

References
Buckwalter, Kathleen, C. Marianne Smith, and Catherine Caston. "Mental and Social Health of the Rural Elderly." Pp. 203–232 in *Health Services for Rural Elders*. Edited by R. T. Coward, C. N. Bull, G. Kukulka, and J. M. Galliher. New York: Springer, 1994.
Clifford, William B., and Stephen C. Lilley. "Rural Elderly: Their Demographic Characteristics." Pp. 3–16 in *Aging in Rural America*. Edited by C. N. Bull. Newbury Park, CA: Sage, 1993.
Cotrell, Victoria, and Richard Schulz. "The Perspective with Alzheimer's Disease: A Neglected Dimension of Dementia Research." *Gerontologist* 33 (1993): 205–211.
DeCroix-Bane, Share, Eloise Rathbone-McCuan, and James M. Galliher. "Mental Health Services for the Elderly in Rural America." Pp. 243–266 in *Providing Community-Based Services to the Rural Elderly*. Edited by J. A. Krout. Newbury Park, CA: Sage, 1994.

Hooyman, Nancy, and H. Asuman. Kiyak. *Social Gerontology: A Multidisciplinary Perspective*. 4th ed. Boston: Allyn and Bacon, 1996.

Krout, John A. "An Overview of Older Rural Populations and Community-Based Services." Pp. 3–18 in *Providing Community-Based Services to the Rural Elderly*. Edited by J. A. Krout. Newbury Park, CA: Sage, 1994.

Nelson, Gary M. "In-Home Services for Rural Elders." Pp. 65–83 in *Health Services for Rural Elders*. Edited by Raymond T. Coward, C. Neil Bull, Gary Kukulka, and James M. Galliher. New York: Springer, 1994.

Rathbone-McCuan, Eloise. "Rural Geriatric Mental Health Care: A Continuing Service Dilemma." Pp. 146–160 in *Aging in Rural America*. Edited by C. N. Bull. Newbury Park, CA: Sage, 1993.

Schmall, Vicki L., and Linda C. Webb. "Respite and Adult Day Care for Rural Elders." Pp. 156–178 in *Providing Community-Based Services to the Rural Elderly*. Edited by J. A. Krout. Newbury Park, CA: Sage, 1994.

Schneider, Lon. "Efficacy of Clinical Treatment for Mental Disorders among Older Persons." Pp. 19–71 in *Emergent Issues in Mental Health and Aging*. Edited by M. Gatz. Washington, DC: American Psychological Association, 1995.

Migrant Farmworkers

Individuals who are employed in agriculture either seasonally or temporarily and are absent overnight from the permanent residence (Public Law 97-470, 1983). This entry reviews recent literature on migrant farm labor, with illustrating examples from southern New Mexico, where migrant families enter from south Texas and migrant single males enter from Mexico.

Seasonal Cycles

Texas is home base for the largest number of migrant farmworkers in the United States. Residents of the lower Rio Grande valley typically are employed in Texas from December until June in vegetable and citrus production and then fan out into the northern states and to both coasts to harvest a wide variety of crops. Another major population of migrants work the winter fruits and vegetables in Florida and then move up the eastern seaboard and into the states around the Great Lakes during the summer. They are an ethnic mixture from several Caribbean and Central American countries. Mexico supplies yet another major stream of migrants, who move north up the West Coast and into the Midwest during the harvest season. Many Mexican migrants were legalized under the special agricultural worker (SAW) provision of the Immigration Reform and Control Act of 1986 (Public Law 99-603), but substantial undocumented immigration continues as well.

"Day haul operation" is defined in the Migrant and Seasonal Agricultural Act of 1983 as "the assembly of workers at a pick-up point waiting to be hired and employed, transportation of such workers to agricultural employment, and the return of such workers to a drop-off point on the same day" (Public Law 97-470, Sec. 3). Day haul and migrant workers may appear to be exclusive categories, but along the U.S.-Mexico border they overlap substantially.

Literature

In an extensive review of migration literature, Massey (1987) found that the most powerful predictors of whether a household head migrates was land and business ownership. He found that once begun, migration networks tend to develop and mature, making U.S. employment less risky and problematic for those with relatives or neighbors in the United States. Tienda (1989) picked up the latter theme in her essay on the social effects of migration from Mexico to the United States and predicted that the Immigration Reform and Control Act of 1986 would be ineffective in stemming illegal migration. She argued that migration from Mexico to the United States is so much a part of so many Mexicans' expectations and family strategies—in short, so institutionalized—that it is probably impossible to control. Linder (1992) made a similar argument for labor laws in general, suggesting that market forces overwhelm the government's legislative efforts to ameliorate workers' problems.

Stoddard (1976) argued that American policy on Mexican immigration has vacillated ever since the national boundary was established. Governed by U.S. labor needs, a cyclical pattern of facile entry followed by involuntary deportation is documented. This vacillation undermines government attempts to regulate immigration. Stoddard (1986) described informal networks that span the border and operate to institutionalize, if not legalize, immigrant workers. Workers obtain U.S. documents, such as a driver's license, social security card, and/or union membership, which provide the facade of a legitimate appearance. They bide their time until an opportunity to obtain legal papers occurs.

Whereas the literature on migratory labor elsewhere is substantial and accessible, most studies on Texas farmworkers have been done by state agencies and exist only in difficult to obtain in-house reports or manuscripts. One exception, Briody (1986), employed a sociohistorical approach and work histories of a sample of south Texas migrants. She found that households tended to enter the migrant stream either as newly formed units or later in the cycle when the children's labor could be used. Job

During peak periods migrant workers like these Mexican laborers near Salinas, California, pick strawberries 10 to 12 hours a day, 7 days a week.

insecurity at home of the primary income earner also influenced him or her to enter the migrant stream.

Fuller (1991), at the end of a long career studying farm labor in California, offered a valuable perspective on migrant labor. He asserted that migratory workers do not exist because the farm economy needs them; they exist because society has a large backlog of unsolved social and economic problems. More particularly, Mexico, Central America, and the Caribbean have a backlog of unsolved social and economic problems that pushes workers into the migrant stream and into the United States. Fuller argued that people do not become poor from working in agriculture; they become agricultural workers because they already are poor. Migrant work provides opportunities for those not accepted elsewhere to obtain temporary farm employment until more acceptable work is available.

It is worth noting that the native-born Black Americans who did the farmwork in Florida in 1960 no longer dominate the agricultural workforce. They have been replaced with successive waves of immigrants. While in Florida the successive waves are often of different nationalities, further west, Mexican-born immigrants predominate in the fields. This indicates there is at least intergenerational mobility out of migratory farmwork (Frontline 1990).

Empirical Observations

The agriculture of southern New Mexico illustrates migrant farmworkers' current situation. Two crops generate the bulk of the demand for seasonal migrant labor in southern New Mexico: chiles and onions. The region is well known for its chile, but onion production draws little attention even among local residents. Onion harvest begins in late May or early June and slows down in August when green chile harvest begins. Chile harvest continues until November or December. In spite of the dovetailing of the two seasons, there has been a substantial differentiation of labor forces between the two crops. Into the early 1980s, onions were harvested by migrants from south Texas. These migrants come primarily as families and return to Texas at the end of onion harvest. They typically have a connection to a labor contractor and know they will have work before they leave home. The labor contractor may even provide assistance in finding housing and advance some expenses. In return, the contractor has a loyal worker who will not jump to another crew when working conditions and earning potential appear better. Daily movement of workers among harvest crews is one of the most frequent complaints of farm labor contractors. With the doubling of onion production between 1984 and 1992, local and day haul workers entered the onion fields in large numbers. As these workers gained onion experience, they became competitive with the south Texas migrants.

Migrants from south Texas encounter some hostility from local residents who ask why these people are coming to take jobs away from locals. Local offices allegedly refuse food stamps to migrants at least partially on the grounds that resources to meet even local residents' need are inadequate. When migrants first arrive in the area, they can, and many do, receive a box of groceries from private charities to last until the first paycheck. Labor contractors sometimes advance rent and/or grocery money to them. When absolutely necessary, migrants obtain local medical services, occasionally with assistance from a labor contractor or farmer, more frequently on their own. Aside from the aforementioned services, migrants generally do not expect or apply for other social services.

During the chile harvest season, hundreds of workers cross the Santa Fe bridge from Cuidad Juárez to El Paso starting about 3:00 A.M. to board buses for the long ride (2.5 to 3 hours) to harvest fields as far away as Deming and Hatch, New Mexico. The buses return to El Paso around 7:00 P.M. At first glance these workers appear to be day haul workers. However, many, if not a majority, of these workers are required to be absent overnight from their permanent place of residence and therefore also fit the migrant farmworker definition. Some sleep on the street because the round-trip journey to and from their lodging in a Juárez *colonia* (suburb) could take as much as three or four hours out of an already short night. Many

come for the season from permanent residences in the interior of Mexico.

The most precise farm labor wage rate data available were collected by the New Mexico Agricultural Statistics Service (1991). They conducted three annual surveys from 1989 to 1991 to determine the prevailing wages and practices in the New Mexico chile industry. Almost all chile harvest work is paid on a piece-rate basis, which varies by type of chile and field conditions. Chile workers averaged between $5.70/hour and $7.10/hour depending on the type of chile. Wage rates ranged from $1.93 to $16.80/hour, reflecting the wide range of working conditions and worker abilities. No worker theoretically should earn less than the minimum wage of $5.15/hour, and workers who cannot generally are not employed very long.

However, average hourly wage data provide an incomplete picture of farmworker earnings; the picture has to be filled out by information on how many hours are worked. One of the most common farmworker complaints is about the uncertainty of how much work will be available. Farmworkers may even ride two or three hours to a field only to find there is no work that day. They do not get paid for their travel time. Day haul workers may leave the El Paso pickup point at 4:00 A.M., work only six or seven hours, wait an hour or two to get paid, and arrive back in El Paso at 7:00 P.M. The schedule can be exhausting, and it is easy to understand why farmworkers may not want to work every day.

Annual household income data are much less precise for the simple reason that over an entire year various members of the household work at various jobs for various employers for varying amounts of time. They probably receive W-2 forms for part of the income and no W-2 for other parts. Migrant families in New Mexico from south Texas reported annual household incomes in the range of $5,000 to $13,000. Family size ranging from two to seven workers accounts for much of the variation in earnings. A principal reason that migrant families incur the expense and inconvenience of migration is the opportunity for summer employment for all able-bodied family members. In very few cases were the annual incomes of farmworker households above the official poverty income, defined as $13,812 for a family of four, including two children less than 18 years of age (U.S. Bureau of the Census 1991). Migrants in New Mexico, traveling alone, reported individual incomes in the range of $3,000 to $7,200. These workers typically worked six to eight months in two or three commodities and spent several months with their families in Mexico. The younger males tend to be single and the older ones married. Men leave this migrant stream as they situate wives and children either in border communities or in the United States. A serious problem for those legalizing under SAW status has been the difficulty of legalizing family members; consequently many members remain undocumented.

Both the Migrant and Seasonal Agricultural Act and the Immigration Reform and Control Act contained provisions making it illegal to hire undocumented workers. However, such workers continue to find employment. Surveys of farmworkers in fields in Doña Ana and Luna Counties in New Mexico indicate there are relatively few undocumented aliens working close to the border. Meanwhile, across the country employer sanctions have been ineffective at preventing, and have not significantly curtailed, the employment of unauthorized workers in agriculture. Both the Migrant and Seasonal Agricultural Act and the Immigration Reform and Control Act are federal laws, and their enforcement is largely left up to federal officials. In New Mexico, local and state police detain only undocumented individuals who have been stopped for some other violation and who subsequently are found not to have proper residence or visitor documents. In those cases, the U.S. Border Patrol will be notified. There is a high concentration of Border Patrol agents along the border with Mexico; farmers know their workers, and records are likely to be checked. That, together with a plentiful supply of documented workers, leads to a relatively high rate of compliance. Without effective deterrence and with a reduced labor supply, the rate of compliance declines.

Future Prospects

The current generation of migrant workers is not made up of sons and daughters of a previous generation of migrant farmworkers; this is predominantly a foreign-born generation. This demographic indicates that there is at least intergenerational movement out of migratory farmwork. A continual oversupply of labor defeats attempts to ameliorate working and living conditions, even as migrants leave the stream from one generation to the next. Along the U.S.-Mexico border, a very large labor supply was legalized by the SAW provisions of the Immigration Reform and Control Act. Away from the border, beyond the effective reach of the Border Patrol, undocumented workers continue to swell the ranks of the workforce. The scramble to obtain work leaves many workers willing to accept substandard wage rates and conditions. Even when hourly wage rates exceed minimum stan-

dards, an adequate annual income is not guaranteed. Ultimately, improvement of migrant labor conditions requires tighter control on immigration, and that will be difficult until there is improvement in the social and economic conditions in the sending areas.

—*Clyde Eastman*

See also
Agricultural Law; Employment; Ethnicity; Latinos; Poverty.
References
Briody, Elizabeth K. *Household Labor Patterns among Mexican Americans in South Texas.* New York: AMS Press, 1986.
Eastman, Clyde. "Impacts of the Immigration Reform and Control Act of 1986 on New Mexico Agriculture." *Journal of Border-Land Studies* 6, no. 2 (1991): 105–130.
Frontline. *New Harvest, Old Shame.* Public Broadcasting Service, 1990. Video.
Fuller, Varden. *Hired Hands in California's Farm Fields.* Giannini Foundation Special Report. Davis: University of California, Davis, June 1991.
Linder, Marc. *Migrant Workers and Minimum Wages.* Boulder, CO: Westview Press, 1992.
Massey, Douglas S. "Understanding Mexican Migration to the United States." *American Journal of Sociology* 92, no. 6 (May 1987): 1372–1403.
New Mexico Agricultural Statistics Service. Unpublished chile harvest wage data. 1991.
Stoddard, Ellwyn R. "A Conceptual Analysis of the 'Alien Invasion': Institutionalized Support of Illegal Mexican Aliens in the U.S." *International Migration Review* 10, no. 2 (Summer 1976): 157–189.
———. "Identifying Legal Mexican Workers in the U.S. Borderlands: Perceptions and Deceptions in the Legal Analysis of Border Migration." *Southwest Journal of Business and Economics* 3, no. 4 (Summer 1986): 11–26.
Tienda, Marta. "Looking to the 1990s: Mexican Immigration in Sociological Perspective." Pp. 109–147 in *Mexican Migration to the United States.* Edited by Wayne A. Cornelius and Jorge A. Bustamante. San Diego: Center for U.S.-Mexican Studies, University of California, San Diego, 1989.
U.S. Bureau of the Census. *Poverty in the United States: Current Population Report: Consumer Income.* P-60, no. 181. Washington, DC: Bureau of the Census, 1991.
U.S. Public Law 97-470. Migrant Worker Protection Act. 97th Cong., 2d Sess., January 14, 1983.
U.S. Public Law 99-603. Immigration Reform and Control Act of 1986. 99th Cong., 2d Sess., November 6, 1986.

Migration

Migration: a relatively permanent residential movement from one legally designated area to another, which includes changes of residence across county, state, and regional boundaries and between urban and rural places. In rural America, migration has been a formative and dynamic process. It continues to pass through phases affecting the use of land and resources and the composition and size of communities. Migration has been regarded as the demographic process that has had the most defining influence on American character. Theoretical orientations explaining migration are diverse and have changed with the substantive nature of migration. Current studies of migration generally emphasize the relative importance of economic and quality-of-life motivations.

Introduction

Migration has been and continues to be the most dynamic demographic process shaping the geographic and social structures of rural areas. Migrants weigh both economic and quality-of-life factors. Communities experience contributions and conflicts as residents leave and newcomers arrive. Migration flows are complex, varying according to age, gender, education, and numerous other demographic variables. Such information is increasingly important for planning and development in rural areas.

Immigrants bring both contributions and problems to host communities. They are conveyors of innovation and development, but they also disproportionately create difficulties for local institutions. Confrontations frequently take on an "old-timer" versus "newcomer" polarity. Benefits and problems associated with migration are intensified as the magnitude increases, as in boomtowns. Rural areas continue to grapple with achieving a prosperous and stable balance when facing changes in population, whether through in-out or flow-through migration. (In-migration is the number of people moving permanently into a geographic area; out-migration is the number of people moving permanently out of an area. Adding in- and out-migration together results in net-migration, which may be a net-out-migration or a net-in-migration from an area. Flow-through migration [or mobility] is the number of people who temporarily reside in an area on their way to another area.)

William Petersen (1958) distinguishes primitive, free, impelled/forced, and mass migration. Historically, in rural America, each of these types of migration has been a social force. Prior to the Colombian Exchange—the colonial expansion into the New World—primitive migration typically followed cyclical seasonal routes within a territory by indigenous people. Free migration became a dominant force, imposed by fiat on the indigenous population. The initial colonization by European settlers was eventually followed by as many as 15 million Africans forced into slavery, primarily on southern plantations. Mass migration, the largest in world history, eventually ensued, settling the entire area between the

Appalachians and the Pacific Ocean in about 60 years, between 1830 and 1890. Forced migration occurred as Indians were sequestered onto reservations. The attraction to Europeans had been to the vast tracts of lands, with their rich legacies of natural resources. The adaptation made by settlers to the vast frontier have been used, following the nineteenth-century historian Frederick Jackson Turner, to describe the American personality and American communities: independent, self-reliant, and practical. Classification of the rural villages established during this period was among the earliest contributions of rural sociology. C. J. Galpin (1918) classified rural communities on the basis of their economic origins and their spatial patterns.

Economic and Quality-of-Life Explanations

The popular theories of migration are skewed toward economic explanations, which are particularly viable from the perspectives of most migrants and most researchers. Although the ability to survive economically in any location is fundamental, the assumption that people make moves based on economic optimization is not always borne out by the experience of migrants.

There have always been settlers seeking change in quality of life, albeit with economic security. Pennsylvania and Rhode Island were havens for religious freedom. The religious minorities of the Anabaptists, Moravians, Hutterites, Amish, and Mennonites exemplify the search for particular qualities in settings free of urban congestion and based on idealized intentions that persisted through the communal period of the mid-1800s. Oneida and New Harmony were the most famous of the many utopian rural communes established in the United States in the nineteenth century. In the 1960s and 1970s, a spate of religious rural communes, such as Rajneeshpuram and the Church Universal and Triumphant, and hippie communes followed this tradition. In the 1980s and 1990s, the thrust of quality-of-life migration has been from urban people moving to safer, cleaner, less crowded environments. In part, this is an extension of White flight beyond suburbia. However, the most rapidly expanding communities have been in rural scenic and natural recreation areas, in mountain, lake, and coastal areas. This migration is especially popular among the elderly.

Realistically, there is an amalgamation of motives for migration based on weighing the advantages of rural lifestyle against the lost economic opportunities of urban life. Human ecological theories look to improvements in communication and technological access as primary factors attracting migrants into rural areas. Partially skirting the social-psychological motivational controversy distinguishing economic from quality-of life-theories, human ecology theory looks beyond individual migrants to focus on structural changes that made rural areas more accessible, comfortable, and feasible for making a living. Wardwell (1980) provided a general summary of developments in transportation and communication systems. Dillman and Beck (1988) emphasized the pivotal importance of the improvements brought to rural areas through the information age.

Differential Migration

Data concerning rural and urban migration are extremely detailed and complex, making reporting cumbersome. Tables can occupy several pages. Imagine comparing the numbers and rates of migration between rural-to-urban and urban-to-rural at 10-year intervals between 1970 and 1990. That table alone would require four pages and yet would lack dozens of important variables such as race, gender, education, occupation, income, place of birth, and years in residence. Careful attention to these details is crucial to understand population dynamics. Such data, drawn from the U.S. Census Bureau's *Current Population Surveys*, have been interpreted by Fuguitt, Brown, and Beale (1989). In one table, for example, they demonstrate that rural/urban movement is very much a two-way process with many residents moving from each type of location to the other. The magnitude of population change is somewhat invisible because the effects of these counterstreams of migrants largely cancel each other out. Moreover, there are distinctive and influential differences between different age groups. Between 1970 and 1975, the net increase of nonmetropolitan areas was 1,595,000, but for 20–29 year olds there was a net decrease of 335,000. Five years later, the nonmetropolitan net had declined to –642,000. By 1983, the net total was –351,000 and for 20–29 year olds it was –265,000. In most years since then a net loss has occurred in nonmetropolitan areas in spite of millions of people each year moving into rural areas.

Rural areas are and have been regarded as less mobile than cities. They are less mobile, but only for those who stay. Historically, rural areas have supplied the populations for cities. Most young people in the United States have left their rural hometowns. Frontier farm towns were hubs of new people, often establishing the ethnic origins of towns. Successive waves of nationalities migrated to the United States, a pattern that persists as Hispanic and Asian migrants continue to enter the country.

During the rapid western migration, rural populations frequently grew beyond the capacities of local resources to sustain them. Some resources, particularly minerals, forests, and marginal agricultural lands, were immediately exploited and then abandoned when they played out or became unprofitable. More persistently, rural populations moved away as labor was displaced by technology. One well-equipped farmer, logger, or miner in 1995 can do the work of 20 or more laborers one century earlier. Technological advancement and declining resources led to proportional rural population loss from out-migration in southern and central states, which precipitated in-migration in northern and western cities. This dominant flow continued from the first census in 1890 until 1960, except for a brief period during the early 1930s. Since the 1950s there has been a heavy migration flow to rural areas adjacent to southern and western cities. The turn-around migration (the shift from rural-to-urban net-migration to urban-to-rural net-migration) first noted by Calvin Beale (1975) generated many hopes of a rural renaissance, but the growth was short-lived, lasting from the late 1960s through the 1970s.

Migration as a Source of Social Problems

Migration in rural America is a persistent force that brings both problems and prosperity. There is an absence of viable, recognizable organizations of the rural disenfranchised. "The tyranny of the majority" forgets there is rural crime and rural poverty, which are strongly associated with migration. Out of sight, and a minority, they are out of mind. Boomtowns experience unique problems. The eagerness for growth and profit, on the part of both outside corporations and local residents, tends to make them neglect the consequences of development and, eventually, the bust following the boom. Boomtowns experience great stress, particularly during the temporary construction phase, when immigration is high. Abandonment, bankruptcy, and desolation typifying the bust phase are common among western mining towns. Similar phases occur in agriculture- and timber-based rural economies, although the magnitude of variation and the speed and intensity of changes are especially evident in the boom and bust of mining. Informal social systems and structural and economic capacities to handle problems are particularly vulnerable.

The most obvious and immediate needs in areas about to experience or already experiencing rapid growth are infrastructural services: sewer, water, and road systems and fire, police, health, and educational services.

However, caution must be exercised to prevent overconstruction and development of delivery systems and service structures, since their costs are too high for communities to bear if growth does not become self-sustaining. Focusing on such systems may draw attention away from informal social systems such as neighboring, family, and friendships, which are fundamental, crucial aspects of rural life.

Residential Conflicts:
Newcomers versus Old-Timers

Conflicts between newcomers and old-timers are especially evident due to rural migration. Differences in lifestyles, commitment, and social and demographic characteristics are common, particularly when migration is heavy and the origins of newcomers are remote. Consequently, clashes over identity and proprietary rights are common. Such differences are more common in rapidly growing scenic recreational areas than in more traditional extractive areas, although boomtowns are an exception. Spin-around migration exacerbates such conflict. Spin-around migration involves people who move into an area, often one high in natural amenities, for quality-of-life reasons. However, their residency is short-lived (usually less than ten years), despite initial intentions of permanent residence, because of limited economic opportunities. Community has been regarded as the unifying construct in rural life. The rapid spin-around migration in scenic recreational areas elicits the issue of what the implications of such migration are for modern postindustrial society. It leads to questions of the meaning of that rural cornerstone—community. Rural communities historically were composed of a small population of relatively immobile residents who earned their living from the area and shared common values. Each of these defining qualities of traditional community is questionable in modern tourist recreation-based locales. Janet Fitchen (1991) identified a less common, but nevertheless persistent, type of rural migration that both reflects the broader problems of society and manifests those problems in small towns—migration of urban poor people to rural areas because of lower costs and a hope for safer, more secure, healthier lives.

Recent Applications
of Information about Migration

Migration in rural America is a dynamic phenomenon that has stimulated new solutions to perennial problems. Rural sociologists practicing in social impact assessment and in community development and planning developed models and methods to optimize development while minimizing social disruption. Political rhetoric and commendable intentions for community planning emphasize the importance of development and planning for generating opportunities to retain young residents. Residents, especially young people, from rural areas dependent on natural resource conversion will undoubtedly continue to move away in the foreseeable future. The hopes for rapid development in many communities are unrealistic. However, a process of gradual in-filling will increasingly occur as old residents stay and new residents move into areas of relatively sparse population.

— *Patrick C. Jobes*

See also

Community; Development, Community and Economic; Infrastructure; Policy, Rural Development; Quality of Life; Regional Planning; Settlement Patterns; Urbanization.

References

Beale, Calvin. *The Revival of Population Growth in Nonmetropolitan America.* ERS-605. Washington, DC: U.S. Department of Agriculture, E.S.C.S., 1975.

Beaulieu, Lionel, and David Mulkey, eds. *Investing in People.* Boulder, CO: Westview Press, 1994.

Brown, David L., and John M. Wardwell, eds. *New Directions in Urban-Rural Migration.* New York: Academic Press, 1981.

Dillman, Don A., and Don M. Beck. "Information Technologies and Rural Development in the 1990s." *Journal of State Government* 61, no. 1 (1988): 29–38.

Fitchen, Janet M. *Endangered Spaces, Enduring Places.* Boulder, CO: Westview Press, 1991.

Fuguitt, Glen, David L. Brown, and Calvin L. Beale. *Rural and Small Town America.* New York: Russell Sage Foundation, 1989.

Galpin, Charles J. *Rural Life.* New York: Century, 1918.

Jobes, Patrick C., William F. Stinner, and John M. Wardwell. *Community, Society and Migration.* Lanham, MD: University Press of America, 1992.

Petersen, William A. "A General Typology of Migration." *American Sociological Review* 23, no. 2 (1958): 256–266.

Wardwell, John M. "Toward a Theory of Urban-Rural Migration in the Developed World." Pp. 71–114 in *New Directions in Urban-Rural Migration: The Population Turnaround in Rural America.* Edited by David L. Brown and John M. Wardwell. New York: Academic Press, 1980.

Military Personnel and Industry

Government and civilian activity devoted to the defense of the United States. Military spending is disproportionately concentrated in certain states and in urban areas. Projected cuts in military spending on procurement and research and development are expected to have little impact on rural America. Additional closures of bases would affect some rural communities that may find economic recovery more difficult than urban areas affected by such closures. Military spending is described in this entry. The effect of military procurement, research and development expenditures, base closures, and payments to military retirees on rural economies are examined.

Spending

Military spending includes spending on research and development, military hardware, civilian and military personnel, and retired military personnel. Its influence on economic activity in rural America varies substantially by location and type. Defense spending on research and development and on military hardware is centered in urban areas. Wages and salaries paid to civilian employees and to military personnel and payments to retired military and to reserve and National Guard units have a stronger influence on rural economies. Cuts in military spending may hurt selected rural communities, especially those experiencing base closures. Rural America can expect net gains in economic activity if spending reductions are applied to federal budget deficit reduction.

Defense spending for fiscal year 1995 was $266 billion (in 1995 dollars), a decrease of less than 1 percent in constant dollars from 1994 (U.S. Bureau of the Census 1996). Recent concerns centered on the effect of declining military spending. The defense spending share of gross domestic product is projected to decline from 6.5 percent in 1986 to 3.6 percent in 1997 (Hamrick 1992/1993).

Effect of Procurement and Research and Development Cuts

Expenditures on procurement and research and development accounted for over 53 percent of all Department of Defense spending in 1993 (U.S. Department of Defense 1994). The overall effects of procurement expenditures on rural areas is limited, however. Three-fourths of procurement expenditures are concentrated in communications equipment, aircraft and parts, ordnance, business services, shipbuilding and repair, and new construction (Whitehead 1991). These defense industries usually are located in urban areas. For example, only 6 percent of employment in communications equipment was in nonmetropolitan locations in 1990 (Hamrick 1992/1993). In 1988, over 30 percent of defense procurement and research and development spending was concentrated in seven major urban centers (Atkinson 1993). A few rural communities close to defense industry plants may be adversely affected by changes in the level and composition of military spending. But only 3.6 percent of all U.S. counties with a population of under 50,000 have per capita defense contract awards exceeding the national per capita average (Atkinson 1993).

Research on subcontracting and the indirect effects of military spending reinforces the notion that procurement and research spending mainly affects urban centers. Defense contractors often subcontract substantial amounts of work to other firms. But subcontracting increases the concentration of defense spending in major cities (Atkinson 1993). Likewise, the indirect effects of procurement spending generally are felt in urban industries. Defense contractors and subcontractors often form a web of firms in urban locations where agglomeration economies (costs savings due to close proximity of connected firms) exist.

OhUallachain (1987) estimated location quotients (a measure of the contribution of a given industry to an economy) for military procurement spending at the state level in 1983. He found a strong and positive relationship between the relative importance of defense procurement spending and changes in employment from 1978 to 1984. Increased defense spending may help explain the stronger economic growth observed in urban, as opposed to rural, economies in the 1980s.

Researchers indicated the regional winners and losers in the distribution of defense procurement expenditures. Based on location quotients and per capita estimates, defense procurement spending has been concentrated in the New England states; the states surrounding Washington, D.C.; California; Washington; and in other states such as Kansas and Mississippi (Atkinson 1993; Crump 1989; Whitehead 1991). Department of Defense personnel expenditures follow a different pattern, with southeastern states and most states west of a line running from North Dakota to Texas receiving a disproportionally large share (Atkinson 1993). The same percentage of workers in urban areas and rural areas (2 percent) work at bases and other military facilities (Hamrick 1992/1993).

Impact of Base Closures

Several rural communities depend on local military bases to generate economic activity, and some communities have been affected by base closures. The impacts on communities of closures range from significant decreases in economic activity to beneficial effects. The latter occur when base infrastructure is devoted successfully to alternative uses that engender economic activity.

Rowley and Sternberg (1993) compared the economic impact of base closings in 33 metropolitan communities and 50 nonmetropolitan communities from 1961 to 1990. The ability of rural communities to recover from base closures varied. Ten out of the 50 rural counties examined in their study did not regain all the civilian jobs that had been lost, whereas 12 additional counties did not recover all of the civilian jobs plus transferred military jobs. Although the remaining counties ultimately filled the gap in reduced employment, rural areas generally felt a greater impact from base closure than urban areas. Civilian job losses were a higher percentage of total employment in nonmetropolitan, as opposed to metropolitan, communities experiencing base closings. Employment, income, and population growth rates were slower in rural communities that experienced the loss of a base than in urban counties where bases had closed. Rural counties experiencing base closures had slower growth in income, employment, and population than the average across all rural counties.

Determinants of the ability of rural communities to recover from base closures included success of base redevelopment efforts, which partly hinged on speed of base acquisition by local groups and the existence of a airstrip. Smaller communities had more difficulty organizing development efforts in response to a base closure. Remote rural communities tended to experience more problems in recovering from a closure (Rowley and Sternberg 1993).

Military Retirees

Little attention has been given to the impact on rural communities of payments to retired military. States with larger than average shares of retired military include Virginia, with per capita military retiree payments of $320; Florida, with per capita payments at $197; and Nevada, with per capita payments of $219 (U.S. Bureau of the Census 1994). Unless the distribution and spending patterns of retired military differ from those of retired individuals in general, the literature on the impacts of retirement on rural communities should address this issue.

On balance, cuts in military spending should help more than hurt rural areas, although certain rural communities certainly will be negatively affected. Cuts in defense devoted to federal budget deficit reduction should lower interest rates and engender economic activity that will more than compensate for any losses in economic activity in rural America as a whole.

—*David W. Hughes*

See also
Development, Community and Economic; Employment; Income.
References
Atkinson, Robert D. "Defense Spending Cuts and Regional Economic Impact: An Overview." *Economic Geography* 69 (1993): 107–122.
Crump, Jeffrey R. "The Spatial Distribution of Military Spending in the United States." *Growth and Change* 20 (1989): 50–62.
Hamrick, Karen S. "Defense Cuts Pose Difficult Adjustment for Some Rural Communities." *Rural Conditions and Trends* 3 (Winter 1992/1993): 6–7.
OhUallachain, Breandan. "Regional and Technological Implications of the Recent Buildup in American Defense Spending." *Annals of the Association of American Geographers* 77 (1987): 208–223.
Rowley, D. Thomas, and Peter L. Sternberg. *A Comparison of Military Base Closures Metro and Nonmetro Counties, 1961–90.* Staff Report No. AGES 9307. Washington, DC: U.S. Department of Agriculture, Agriculture and Rural Economy Division, Economic Research Service, April 1993.
U.S. Bureau of the Census. *Federal Expenditures by State for Fiscal Year 1993.* Washington, DC: U.S. Department of Commerce, March 1994.
———. *Statistical Abstract of the United States: 1996.* 116th ed. Washington, DC: U.S. Government Printing Office, 1996.
U.S. Department of Defense. *Atlas/Data Abstract for the United States and Selected Areas: Fiscal Year 1993.* Washington, DC: Washington Headquarters Services, Directorate for Information, 1994.
Whitehead, David D. "The Impact of Private-Sector Defense Cuts on Regions of the United States." *Economic Review* 76 (March 1991): 30–41.

Miners

People who engage in the process, occupation, or business of working in mines or getting ore, coal, precious metals, fuels, and other substances out of the earth. This entry includes discussion of miners' role in society, health and safety issues, training, political action, and life in mine towns.

Role in Society

Just as American farmers fed an industrializing nation, so American miners provided the materials to construct it. They produced the fuel, metals, and stone products necessary to generate and store electricity, drive vehicles, power factories, and construct and roads and buildings. Miners extracted fuels, minerals, and metals from the earth. The public generally associates mining with underground extraction in which miners either drill or blast a shaft vertically into the earth or horizontally into a mountainside to recover ore. Whereas this kind of mining continues to be important in the industry, open pit or strip mining has become increasingly prevalent throughout this century. Strip miners recover ore by using large earth-moving equipment to remove tons of soil and rock. Both mining processes include a wide range of complicated extraction and processing tasks, many of which pose considerable physical risk to mine workers. Both also displace earth, alter the landscape, and have negative effects on both the surface and groundwater, factors that influence the environment and living conditions of mining communities. Both types of mining increasingly require complicated technology and therefore demand relatively large amounts of capital expenditure.

Health and Safety Issues

Mining, particularly underground mining, is a dangerous occupation. In 1993, for instance, 200 miners died and 20,000 suffered disabling injuries. Miners died at a rate of 33 per 100,000 workers, a figure that compares closely to the 1993 agricultural death rate of 35 per 100,000 workers. Mining and agriculture are significantly more dangerous than the third most dangerous industry, construction, which boasted a 22 per 100,000 worker death rate in 1993 (U.S. Bureau of the Census 1995).

Some mine workers and mine owners argue that theirs is an inherently dangerous enterprise: increased capital expenditure, enhanced training programs, tougher safety and health regulations, and stricter governmental enforcement of these regulations, they claim, could never fully eliminate the danger of mining. Miners can be crushed in equipment accidents or by falling rock and earth, either in landslides (surface) or roof falls (underground). They may be blown up by explosives or, in the case of underground mining, by methane gas ignited by an electrical spark. Electrically powered mining machines running in damp, underground work areas may burn or electrocute their operators or those working nearby. Sharp drills and cutting devises cause injury and amputations. Mining dislodges and circulates dust and fibers through the air, placing miners at an increased risk for respiratory illnesses such as emphysema, bronchitis, silicosis, and pneumoconiosis.

During much of this industry's history, mine health and safety training and regulation remained in the hands of individual coal operators, who were governed by a variety of state and local codes concerning occupational safety. In 1910, the federal government created the Bureau of Mines to coordinate governmental oversight and regulation of the national mining industries. In 1941, Congress passed the Mine Inspection Act, which mandated federal inspection of mine operations and authorized inspectors to make nonbinding recommendations to mine owners. Subsequent legislative action introduced binding safety regulations, funded federal mine inspectors, created the Mine Safety and Health Administration, and established a fund for workers' compensation for black lung (pneumoconiosis). Consequently, from 1941 to the present, national mine death and accident rates consistently have declined and provisions for the care of disabled miners and their families have expanded. Nevertheless, the U.S. safety records never has compared favorably to those of European mining districts. Large mine disasters, such as the 1968 Farmington, West Virginia, disaster, which claimed 78 lives, and the 1984 explosion and fire in Orangeville, Utah, which killed 27, continue to occur (Wallace 1987).

Training

The topic of miners' training is connected to the issue of safety inasmuch as mining is a complicated and technical operation that demands considerable skill and knowledge from the workers. In the nineteenth and early twentieth centuries, miners dislodged minerals, stone, and ore with hand-powered auger drills and explosives; loaded the materials with a shovel; and used animals to haul them to the processing or transport area. Whether workers were independent prospectors or entrepreneurs, subcontractors with a large company, or employees working under the supervision of a mine foreman, they usually learned their trade from more experienced miners, either as formal or informal apprentices.

Mining historically required physically strenuous labor from workers rather than formal education. Miner training, like safety inspection, was under the supervision of the mine owners and employees themselves during this period. Mine work was mechanized by the 1950s. Miners no longer worked side by side in teams doing similar tasks; they became increasingly specialized and isolated. Many miners sit alone to operate bulldozers, augers, continuous mining machines, and, more recently, long-wall mining machines, which dislodge and unearth rock, ore, and earth. These materials are then transported by electric or diesel-powered buggies or conveyor belts to processing sites.

Much of the training of America's miners continues to be done by the mine companies themselves. Since the mid-1960s, many vocational schools and colleges in mining areas have offered mine training and engineering programs. In 1977, the Federal Mine Safety and Health Amendments Act required mine operators to implement health and safety training programs, including at least 40 hours of paid job and safety training for underground miners and 8 hours for surface miners, with refresher courses scheduled every 12 months. Mining still does not require substantial formal education of its workers.

Labor Unions and Political Action

Political action, labor strikes, and lobbying by miners and miners' unions played a central role in enhancing the health, safety, and training of the nation's miners. Since the early days of commercial mining in the Northeast, miners have joined together to protect and support one another through social clubs, beneficial societies, and, eventually, labor unions. Many of the early miners from Wales and Germany brought with them a strong labor union tradition and working-class identity.

However, throughout the twentieth century the mining industry expanded to the South and the West. At the same time, it integrated former agricultural workers from the United States and other countries into its workforce. With the influx of Appalachian and midwestern farmers, African American tenant farmers, Native American agriculturalists and craftsmen, and immigrants from Europe and Central America, the miners' labor union movement lost much of its strength and coherency. There have been a variety of local, regional, and national miners' unions covering a broad range of ideological positions from anarchism to communism and liberal reformism. These include the Molly Maguires, the National Miners Union (of the American Communist Party), the Progressive Miners Union, the Mine and Mill Workers Union, and the United Mine Workers of America (UMWA), to name a few.

Of these, the United Mine Workers of America achieved the most success during this century. Under the leadership of John L. Lewis, this union beat its rivals and consolidated its power during the Great Depression, when the federal government for the first time protected the right of American workers to unionize. Lewis emerged as a national political figure during the 1930s and was even considered as a possible running mate for Franklin D. Roosevelt. The 1940s and 1950s could be considered a high point for the UMWA as it was central in achieving increased federal mine safety and health regulation and enforcement. The UMWA achieved relatively favorable wage rates for its members and established a medical care system and health and pension plans that had a substantial impact on miners' families in central Appalachia. However, the UMWA and other miners' unions have not been able to protect the jobs of America's miners. These jobs have been eliminated through mechanization programs and the overseas movement of mining operations by the multinational corporations, which increasingly control the industry. Since the 1950s, employment in mining generally has declined even as production has increased. Autocratic leadership styles, corruption, nepotism, and internal conflict weakened the UMWA throughout the 1960s and 1970s, and the antiunionism of the Reagan-Bush administrations eroded the power of the UMWA and other miners' unions throughout the 1980s.

Although mineral industry workers may be an ethnically, racially, and regionally diverse group, the mining industry historically has been a male-dominated endeavor. Although mine companies have employed women as secretaries, clerks, and bookkeepers, they have been slow to incorporate women into mineral production jobs. During the 1970s, women made some inroads into this field, only to be harassed and discriminated against by both their bosses and their co-workers. Women continue to make up only a small percentage of mine workers in this country.

Towns

Mining, like farming, is usually a rural pursuit. There are two reasons for this. First, mining occurs where the ore is located regardless of how remote that location may be from urban centers. Second, mining disrupts the physical environment, sometimes enough to destroy the landscape and buildings surrounding it and to pose a nuisance to its neighbors. For miners and their families, this means that they must either endure a long commute to the workplace or live in mining towns.

Mining towns range from small, urban centers providing a variety of services, amenities, and comfortable houses to rapidly constructed enclaves of trailers, shacks, and other temporary shelter. Before 1950, it was common for mining companies to construct entire villages, including houses, stores, churches, schools, medical facilities, and entertainment facilities, for their workers. Some of these towns were considered models of urban planning and construction. This arrangement offered drawbacks to both the owners and workers, however. Owners found it increasingly difficult and expensive to maintain the infrastructure of their company-owned towns, and workers found their employers' control over their lives to be oppressive. Mine owners could, after all, evict them from their homes, control their utilities, monitor communications and leisure activities, administer health care, educate children, and even control local government and law enforcement.

Towns located near mine sites typically must contend with many hardships. Houses, buildings, and streets are often dirty and difficult to keep clean. Piles of mine waste and puddles of polluted water accumulate in and around mine towns. It often is difficult for residents to obtain clean water, as strip mine runoff pollutes streams and underground mining destroys water tables. Landslides are common around strip mines, and underground mining can cause subsidence (the land over the mine can collapse, leaving a crater where a store or home once stood). The transportation of mine materials can clog small city streets, rural routes, and railways, making travel difficult. And depending upon the history, landownership patterns, and other resources in the area, mining can so dominate a town's economy that diversified, alternative economic development can be blocked. Because the mining industry typically is vulnerable to boom-bust cycles, mine towns that do not attract or develop alternative nonextractive industries often suffer from high poverty rates and eventually may be abandoned when mine companies close their operations.

Cyclical fluctuations in this industry, combined with the extractive nature of mining itself, make American miners a relatively mobile occupational group. Miners often move from place to place to pursue work. According to the 1992 U.S. census on mineral industries, miners were employed in each of the 50 states. States with the most miners included West Virginia (33,000), Kentucky (30,600), Colorado (17,300), Virginia (15,900), Wyoming (15,800), New Mexico (14,500), and Arizona (13,800). The oil and gas drillers of Texas (149,900), Louisiana (47,800), California (33,700), and Alaska (10,400) also accounted for many mineral industry employees. Although mining persists in eastern Appalachian states, these figures reflect the movement of mining to the West and Southwest and the increasing importance of oil and natural gas extraction throughout the twentieth century.

Diversity

Mineral industry workers may be an ethnically, racially, and regionally diverse group, but the mining industry has been a male-dominated endeavor. Although mine companies have employed women as secretaries, clerks, and bookkeepers, they have been slow to incorporate women into mineral production jobs. During the 1970s, women made some inroads into this field, only to be harassed and discriminated against by both their bosses and their co-workers. Women continue to make up only a small percentage of mine workers in this country.

—*Shaunna L. Scott*

See also
Culture; Environmental Regulations; Injuries; Labor Force; Labor Unions; Land Stewardship; Mining Industry; Mountains; Natural Resource Economics; Petroleum Industry; Work.

References
Corbin, David. *Life, Work, and Rebellion in the Coal Fields: The Southern West Virginia Miners, 1880–1922.* Urbana: University of Illinois Press, 1981.

Francaviglia, Richard V. *Hard Places: Reading the Landscape of America's Historic Mining Districts.* Iowa City: University of Iowa Press, 1991.

Gaventa, John. *Power and Powerlessness: Quiescence and Rebellion in an Appalachian Valley.* Urbana: University of Illinois Press, 1980.

Kingsolver, Barbara. *Holding the Line: Women in the Great Arizona Mine Strike of 1983.* Ithaca, NY: ILR Press, 1989.

Lewis, Ronald L. *Black Coal Miners in America: Race, Class, and Community Conflict.* Lexington: University Press of Kentucky, 1987.

Michrina, Barry P. *Pennsylvania Mining Families: The Search for Dignity in the Coalfields.* Lexington: University Press of Kentucky, 1993.

Rosenblum, Jonathon D. *Copper Crucible: How the Arizona Miners' Strike of 1983 Recast Labor-Management Relations in America.* Ithaca, NY: ILR Press, 1995.

Scott, Shaunna L. *Two Sides to Everything: The Cultural Construction of Class Consciousness in Harlan County, Kentucky.* Albany: State University of New York Press, 1995.

U.S. Bureau of the Census. *Statistical Abstract of the United States.* Washington, DC: U.S. Department of Commerce, Economics and Statistics Administration, Bureau of the Census, 1995.

———. *U.S. Census: Census of Mineral Industries.* Washington, DC: U.S. Department of Commerce, Economics and Statistics Administration, Bureau of the Census, various years.

Wallace, Michael. "Dying for Coal: The Struggle for Health and Safety Conditions in American Coal Mining, 1930–82." *Social Forces* 66 (1987): 336–364.

Mining Industry

The science, technique, and business of mineral discovery and exploitation. Mining has been part of American history since the first settlements. During this period of time, it had an impact on many aspects of American development, including labor relations, settlement patterns, and the environment. This entry describes the history of the mining industry and its impact on rural communities. The needs of the mining industry, the industry's environmental impact, and the struggle between management and labor are examined.

History

Mining and rural North America have been together since 1598, with the permanent Spanish settlement in New Mexico, and 1607, with the English establishment of Jamestown, Virginia. It may not quite make sense to speak of rural and mining America as synonymous. The

Coal mining has been the dominant industry in many rural areas; it presents many environmental problems as well as hazards to the miners themselves.

mining frontier was an urban frontier that sometimes existed in a rural environment, but by the very nature of mining, it collided with and changed all that it touched. Those areas that returned to a rural setting after mining left were never the same again. The industry left a permanent mark upon the land.

Mining inspired the early settlement of North America. The Spanish hoped to find another Inca or Aztec golden kingdom as their mining frontier drove northward up the Rio Grande. They failed to find one either in future New Mexico or Arizona, but they changed forever the history of that region. The English aspired to emulate the Spanish but found no success at all along the eastern coast, despite repeated hopes and efforts. For over a century in both areas, mining failed to live up to early expectations. Slowly the English expanded westward, and the Spanish eventually settled in California and Texas. Finally, in the nineteenth century coal, copper, lead, and, eventu-

ally, iron mining started in the Midwest, but what investors really wanted was the quicker road to fortune: gold or silver mines.

The discovery of gold in the 1820s in the Auraria, Georgia, region and in neighboring North Carolina touched off the initial successful North American gold excitement. The real rush came with the discovery of gold on the south fork of the American River in 1848. Ironically, this California discovery happened just weeks before Mexico ceded the territory to the United States. What the Spanish and Mexicans sought for years at long last had been discovered.

For the next 60 years, mining directed the settlement of much of the West—California, Nevada, Colorado, Idaho, Montana, Alaska, and parts of Utah, New Mexico, and Arizona. Gold and silver mining seized headlines, while copper, coal, lead, zinc, and, ultimately, molybdenum and tungsten became profitable once uses for them were found. Areas that may never have been settled opened and then were later abandoned within a season or two. Nevertheless, the ultimate result was regional permanent settlement.

During these same decades, miners and investors developed the great Pennsylvania coalfields, the Michigan copper mines, the Minnesota iron deposits, and Midwestern lead districts. Various other smaller discoveries followed, including borax, diatomite, and mercury in California; oil shale in several western states; sulfur in Louisiana, Mississippi, and Texas; and feldspar, stone, gravel, and marble in a host of states, to name just a few products from this North American treasure box. The United States emerged as a major world mining nation.

Little slowdown occurred in the twentieth century. Uranium, lithium, potassium, bauxite, and renewed interest in older districts kept mining moving throughout the country. New mining equipment, techniques, and processes allowed reworking of nineteenth-century mines and development of mineral deposits that could not have been mined economically even 50 years earlier. Strip mining and open pit mines dotted the landscape from the East to the West Coast, huge trucks and stream shovels replaced the old labor-intensive industry, and regions that never thought they would see mining activity found themselves involved in a rush to open low-grade deposits.

Impact

All this activity created a tremendous impact on rural America, from population growth to long-range environmental repercussions. The regions where the miners and their companies worked would never be the same again, nor would the people who had lived and worked there before the miners arrived. The most obvious impact for visitor and resident alike was the striking fact that the advance of mining implied an urban advance. Miners did not have the time, or the inclination, to provide needed services, although they had money, at least in theory, to pay for them. As a result, people came to provide those services "to mine the miners." Mining camps (smaller in population, business district, and with fewer support mines), mining towns (larger, wealthier, and with richer mines), and company towns (owned and operated by one corporation) dotted the American landscape. Where urban settlement may not have taken root otherwise, in high mountain valley and on desert floor, it did and thrived as long as the mines operated. Whether the community lasted several seasons or became permanent, it changed the surrounding rural environment.

These communities created development faster than had had been witnessed in rural America and provided nearby markets for their agriculture neighbors unlike anything they had experienced earlier. Mining communities served as cultural transmitters, bringing newspapers, theaters, "fads," schools, churches, sports, and urban society with a rapidity and extent not witnessed in the more slowly developing world around them. They also came to dominate politically their neighbors. A mining community could jump from a few hundred to several thousand people in a season; some of the largest would reach five figures in a year or two. They simply overwhelmed old-time political alliances and issues. This could unsettle completely the local political scene and create tensions over such issues as the site of the county seat and the creation of a new county, with the corresponding economic loss to older counties. A rural-urban split developed that lasted far beyond its origins.

Mining could upset completely local mores and even landownership. Residents of rural Appalachia (West Virginia and Kentucky) sold their mineral rights in the nineteenth century and then found out what this meant when the strip miners arrived in the twentieth century. The result was the devastation of the land and people; they have not recovered since. State borders did not shield rural America. The Ducktown, Tennessee, copper mines and smelters spilled water pollution and smoke into neighboring rural Georgia. This led to a series of court cases. Finally, the U.S. Supreme Court in 1915 issued an injunction to prevent the spreading of sulfurous fumes over the Georgia border.

The money to be made in a variety of ways attracted business and investors, who changed the pace and direction of progress. For example, these communities made a major impact on local water, land, and air, what nineteenth-century people would have described as environmental repercussions. The towns and their mines created regional publicity, both good and bad, to a degree unmatched by other contemporary developments; the legend of the mining West and East was born. They created tourism as people came to "see the elephant," as the old mining saying went, and sample a lifestyle generally unknown in older, more established communities.

Often these communities did not survive the closing of their mines, a fact that did not lessen their impact. Mining helped to create transportation networks, develop regional business centers (such as Denver and San Francisco), and achieve a more balanced economy (industry and agriculture stimulated by mining). During their lifetime, mines and miners pumped money into the local economy that remained even after they had disappeared. In some areas, they left behind ghost towns that became tourist attractions and roads that opened rural America to visitors and those who came to look and wonder about what transpired here.

Needs

Mining needed three elements to survive—economically feasible mineral deposits, excellent transportation systems, and financial investment. The mines and their communities encouraged the development of that nineteenth-century wonder, the railroad. Few mining districts reached their full potential until the coming of this cheap, fast, and year-round mode of transportation. Railroads affected the entire surrounding rural regions by lowering the cost of living, providing ready access and egress, promoting local resources and attractions, and encouraging population growth and economic development.

Investors came, lured by the expectation of getting rich without working. They developed a variety of businesses besides mining—lumbering, irrigation projects, electric power, tourists resorts, feeder railroads, agriculture, industry, and almost anything that crossed the mind of Americans of the nineteenth and twentieth centuries. These businesses created jobs, wide-ranging development, and more opportunity for rural Americans. Although all of these effects might have occurred without mining, mining provided the promotion and investment that quickened the pace, sometimes by several generations.

Environmental Impact

Mining furnished blessings and made problems for rural America. One conspicuous impact was concisely defined by a Breckenridge, Colorado, dredge operator whose operations threatened that town and its beautiful setting: "Industry is always to be preferred to scenic beauty" (Smith 1993, xi). A look at the environmental heritage of mining in Breckenridge or Minnesota's Mesabi range or the tristate (Oklahoma, Kansas, Missouri) lead mining district makes clear that this philosophy too often guided development.

With rare exceptions, the scramble to develop natural resources resulted in a "profit first" philosophy. Profit guided all. The earth was opened and exploited; streams were polluted with minerals, trash, and sewage; trees were cut down, roads and railroads sliced through forests, over deserts, and around mountains; towns generated urban pollution; and mining dumps and tailing piles

marked the miners' passage. The impression of English poet James Thomson (1963, 245–246), who visited Central City, Colorado, illustrated mining's consequences everywhere: "Prospect holes, primitive loghuts, millsheds, of which many are idle, fragments of machinery that proved useless from the first, heaps of stone and poor ores, and all sorts of rubbish. No one has ever cleaned up anything here. . . . The hills surrounding us have been flayed of their grass, and scalped of their timber; and they are scarred and gashed."

Who was to blame? Certainly, the transitory mining companies and miners exhibited little concern for the future beyond profit from the ore deposits. The federal government encouraged this development and virtually gave away the nation's natural resources in the name of progress and growth. The state governments and local boosters took great pride in this progress without regard to what might occur in future years. Absentee stockholders wanted dividends, not profits spent on reclamation or more environmentally concerned mining practices. The public demanded low-priced coal and cheap minerals to improve its lifestyle. Each of these groups must accept responsibility for the results.

The world rushed into rural America with the coming of mining. The rush occurred not simply because of a population explosion, economic transformation, political turmoil, or environmental problems. Rather, rural Americans had been isolated from some epidemics and medical problems plaguing the cities. Now urbanization brought to rural settings sanitation problems, polluted water, crowded conditions, and hastily built housing fostering illness and disease. The establishment in some mining districts of nearby hot springs as health resorts alleviated these problems somewhat, as did the building of hospitals in many mining towns. Doctors more commonly opened offices in mining communities than in other types of rural areas.

Owners versus Miners

The struggle between management and labor, with the corresponding development of unions, captured more headlines than medical worries. Rural America had not seen anything like the breadth and depth of this conflict. Miners worked at a dangerous, difficult job for low pay, whereas management and the stockholder reaped most of the profits. Conflict proved even worse in the company towns, where the company nearly controlled the workers' and their families' lives from birth to death.

Starting in the late nineteenth century, the United

Mine Workers in the eastern, then western, coalfields and the Western Federation of Miners in the western hard rock mining districts fought management across the country; Pennsylvania, Illinois, Oklahoma, South Dakota, Idaho, and Arizona furnished some of the battlegrounds. Violence, death, civil rights violations, destruction of property, and hatred followed in the conflict's wake. The struggle continued for well over a century as unions relentlessly tried to organize workers.

Although no generalization can be made about the reaction of rural Americans and their communities to this struggle, like much of the rest of the country in the nineteenth and early twentieth centuries, they seemed appalled and displayed widespread disapproval of violent, "un-American" activities. The basic conservatism of rural America failed to comprehend the problems of emerging modern America and the new industrial system.

The press and public blamed a generous share of the guilt for this labor conflict on foreign agitators. The mining communities contained a much more diverse ethnic population than did their rural neighbors. The company towns (copper, coal, and iron) in particular embraced ethnic populations that contrasted sharply with their predominantly northern European neighbors. The demographic disparity between the mining towns and their rural neighbors led to misunderstanding and sometimes fear on the part of rural residents about what was happening to America then and in the future.

Mining also brought more federal government involvement in rural America's life, particularly in the twentieth century. The presence of the federal government became more obvious, especially with the appearance of federal agencies regulating issues such as mine safety, health, labor, and environmental questions. Sometimes this intervention proved quite sweeping. For example, during the uranium rush, which occurred during the cold war era, government agencies built roads, operated smelters, purchased ore, and regulated the industry beyond anything experienced earlier. The impacts on rural Utah, Arizona, New Mexico, Colorado, and Wyoming were startling, not the least of which was the environmental mess, some of it nuclear, left behind when the boom ended in the 1960s. Similarly, after the oil shale excitement in Colorado in the 1970s and 1980s was exhausted, rural towns and counties plunged into severe depressions. When rural America puts its faith on the assumption that finite extractive industries will provide a permanent economic pillar, disappointment seems sure to arrive eventually.

Finally, the trend in mining over the past century has been from the individual to corporate control. Labor difficulties reflected this tendency. However, its impact on rural America reached even further. Corporations could dominate a county, or sometimes even a state, as the Anaconda Mining Company did in Montana, by controlling newspapers and politicians. The influence of these companies spread far beyond their mines and towns.

Present-Day Influence

Today mining does not play the significant role it once did in rural America. Nevertheless, the industry helped to open rural America and left behind a transportation, urban, industrial, economic, and tourism heritage. Primarily in the gold and silver districts of the West, ghost towns and seasoned mining camps have emerged as tourists' favorites and old mining roads and railroad routes have opened the high country to hikers and jeepers. The core industry may be gone, but its influence lives. In areas such as northern Nevada, mining is booming again, and in older districts, such as the Pennsylvania coalfields and the Homestake mine in Lead, South Dakota, mining continues to operate.

As an extractive industry with finite ore bodies, mining depleted part of the natural resources of rural America. It left behind an environmental mess that stretches from the coalfields, to the uranium mines and mills, to the open pit copper mines and the hard rock districts. Only recently has the government undertaken major cleanup efforts in some of these areas. Rural America will be affected for generations to come; Appalachia is only one of many examples of what mining's environmental legacy means to the land and people.

Where miners prospected and mined, mining invariably transformed rural America. It quickened the pace of settlement and growth; brought promotion, investment, environment problems, urbanization, and population; and then typically left. The profits from the industry often went elsewhere, and the industry left behind an environment changed forever.

—*Duane A. Smith*

See also
Environmental Regulations; Labor Force; Labor Unions; Land Stewardship; Miners; Mountains; Natural Resource Economics; Urbanization.
References
Caudill, Harry M. *My Land Is Dying*. 2d edition. New York: Dutton, 1973.
Francaviglia, Richard V. *Hard Places: Reading the Landscape of*

America's Historic Mining Districts. Iowa City: University of Iowa Press, 1991.

Gordon, Robert B., and Patrick M. Malone. *The Texture of Industry: An Archaeological View of the Industrialization of North America.* New York: Oxford University Press, 1994.

Gordon, Suzanne. *Black Mesa: The Angel of Death.* New York: John Day, 1973.

Gulliford, Andrew. *Boomtown Blues: Colorado Oil Shale, 1885–1985.* Niwot: University Press of Colorado, 1989.

Smith, Duane A. *Rocky Mountain Mining Camps: The Urban Frontier.* Reprint, Niwot: University Press of Colorado, 1992.

———. *Mining America: The Industry and the Environment, 1800–1980.* Reprint, Niwot: University Press of Colorado, 1993.

Ridler, Anne, ed. *Poems and Some Letters of James Thomson.* London: Centaur Press, 1963.

Tanzer, Michael. *The Race for Resources: Continuing Struggles over Minerals and Fuels.* New York: Monthly Review Press, 1980.

Toole, K. Ross. *The Rape of the Great Plains.* New York: Atlantic Monthly, 1976.

Mountains

Landforms rising at least 1,000 feet above local base elevations. The mountain geography of the United States is marked by tremendous spatial variation in physical and cultural landscapes. However, the key unifying traits of rural mountain areas are vertical zonation of vegetation, isolation, cultural variety, resorts and recreation, natural hazards, conflicts over land use, and economies strongly linked to natural resources. This entry describes five mountainous regions of the United States: the Appalachian Highlands, Rocky Mountains, Western Basin and Range, Sierra Nevada and Cascade Mountains, and the Alaskan mountains.

Appalachians

The Appalachian Highlands of the eastern United States consist of scores of ranges, ridges, and plateaus separated by narrow valleys. The Appalachians are ancient folded and thrust-faulted terrain. Paleozoic and Mesozoic sedimentary rocks, such as shale, limestone, sandstone, and conglomerate, are found. Igneous intrusions of granite and gabbro cut across these units. Intense folding metamorphosed many rocks to slate, phyllite, schist, and gneiss. Erosion by water rounded the mountains relative to the much younger ranges of the West. During the Pleistocene era, continental glaciers descended south as far as New Jersey. The ranges north of the continental ice sheets, such as the Adirondacks, were smoothed and beveled by glacial action. The soils of these areas are shallow and poor in fertility compared to those to the south that continued to develop throughout the Ice Age.

In 1890, C. H. Merriam conducted the first scientific studies of the vertical zonation of climate and vegetation in mountains. His "life-zone" concept (strata on a mountainside where different vegetation and plant life are found as a result of climate and growing conditions) came from field research in the San Francisco peaks north of Flagstaff, Arizona. However, vertical zones are easily seen in the humid Appalachians as well. In New England, montane zone forests contain maple, birch, and oak. Higher in the mountains are the spruce-fir forests of the subalpine zone. Summits such as Mountain Washington (6,288 feet) in New Hampshire and Mount Katahdin (5,267 feet) in Maine are above treeline. In the southern Appalachians, the Great Smokies contain peaks such as Clingmans Dome (6,643 feet), where dwarf Fraser firs grow but no true alpine ecosystems exist. Lower-elevation deciduous forests are characterized by ash, basswood, beech, maple, hickory, and poplar. The Great Smoky Mountains National Park has the most diverse deciduous forests in the world, with over 160 species of trees.

The Appalachian Mountains collect immense amounts of precipitation that move toward the sea in hundreds of rivers. The Connecticut, Hudson, Susquehanna, Potomac, Ames, Santee, Savannah, and other rivers deliver waterpower to a long chain of industrial "fall-line" cities with large rural hinterlands that provide raw materials (such as Providence, New York, Philadelphia, Baltimore, Richmond, Raleigh, and Macon). The Tennessee Valley Authority built scores of dams in the southern Appalachians. Rural valleys along the Chattanooga, Tennessee, Hiawassee, and other rivers have been inundated by reservoirs and local residents relocated.

The Appalachian Mountains contain many cultures. Rural New England has a mix of people of English and French-Canadian heritage. The landscape now is used mostly for dairy farming, timber harvest, ski resort development, and rural residential homesites. The southern Appalachians were settled mostly by poor immigrants from Scotland and Ireland. Bluegrass and country music evolved when isolated rural farmers adapted the music of their homelands to fiddles, banjos, mandolins, and flat-topped guitars. Until recently, this remoteness allowed a unique mountain culture, with its own accent, music, crafts, food, and fundamentalist Christian religious sects, to persist in the "hollers" (a narrow valley separated from adjacent valleys by a high ridge) of the South. Improved road systems now are crossing many former mountain barriers, and these rural enclaves are breaking down. Backpackers are becoming numerous along the 2,147-mile

Mountain areas contain many of the country's national parks, as in this image of the Grand Teton range located in northwestern Wyoming.

Appalachian Trail, from Springer Mountain, Georgia, to Mount Katahdin, Maine.

Rockies

The Rocky Mountain cordillera consists of dozens of ranges extending from New Mexico to the Canadian border. The southern Rockies contain the Sangre de Cristo and Jemez Mountains of New Mexico, the high country of Colorado, and the Laramie range of Wyoming. The central Rockies consist of the Wasatch and Uinta Mountains of Utah and the Wind River, Wyoming, Big Horn, and Teton ranges of Wyoming. The northern Rockies include all the ranges of Idaho and Montana. The Rockies were upthrust during the tertiary geologic period, starting about 70 million years ago. Tremendous volcanic activity accompanied the faulting of Precambrian and younger rocks. Yellow-stone National Park is a huge caldera (volcanic crater). Basalt poured out across areas ranging from Taos, New Mexico, to the Snake River Plain of Idaho. Most of the region's dramatic peaks grace the tops of fault block mountain ranges. The Grand Teton (13,771 feet) in Wyoming and Pike's Peak (14,110 feet) in Colorado are well-known examples. During the Pleistocene era, mountain glaciers carved the rounded Rockies into their present rugged topography of cirques (glacial basins), aretes (ridgelines), cols (passes), and horns (peaks). Ice sheets carved U-shaped valleys and deposited unsorted moraines where glaciers stagnated. Meltwater streams reworked glacial till (morainal material) into outwash plains that filled many mountain valleys with sand and gravel.

The Rocky Mountains are noted for dramatic vegetation changes with elevation. Abundant alpine areas exist. Much of the Rockies are mantled in coniferous forests dominated by ponderosa pine, Douglas fir, lodgepole pine, and various species of spruce and fir. Aspen groves are widespread. Valley bottoms are generally semi-arid or arid and support grasslands or desert shrublands.

Ranching and farming are the dominant land uses at low elevations. Cattle and sheep are grazed in the mountains during the summer on land leased from the federal government. Rural ranchers, miners, and loggers face opposition to the long-standing western tradition of wide-open resource use on mountain lands managed by the U.S. Forest Service and Bureau of Land Management. Conservationists challenge federal subsidies for grazing, water and mineral development, and timber harvest. Residents of small towns across the Rockies organized various "Sagebrush Rebellions" over the years in opposition to higher use fees and less consumptive forms of management. However, recreational use of public lands contributes increasing revenues to rural economies. The Continental Divide Trail traverses the length of the Rockies.

During the 1990s, the Rocky Mountain West experienced a massive influx of people fleeing the crime and economic recession of America's cities. More than 25 percent of the population growth in the Rocky Mountain states between 1990 and 1995 came from California immigrants alone. In Utah, the effects are most acutely felt in what was traditionally a Mormon cultural landscape based on farming and sheep raising. In Colorado, most rural areas are dependent on incomes from the state's two dozen ski areas. In northern New Mexico, wealthy immigrants raised the cost of living to the point where working-class Hispanos and other residents no longer can afford to buy homes. The land was originally occupied by indigenous Native American tribes. Land grants were established for the Indians and the Hispano poulations during the Spanish and Mexican settlement of the region. The United States acquired the region through the Treaty of Guadalupe Hidalgo in 1848, and most of these lands fell into the hands of Anglo ranchers and the federal government. The Hispanos' land grants set up by the Spanish and Mexicans were maintained by the United States.

In Montana, extensive land subdivision and housing development threaten to eliminate ranching in landscapes such as the Greater Yellowstone Ecosystem. Rural land conservation groups known as land trusts protect open space through tools such as direct purchases and conservation easements (donation of development rights). However, in this same area ranchers opposed the 1995 reintroduction of the endangered gray wolf in Yellowstone National Park.

Basin and Range

The Basin and Range physiographic province consists of more than 200 mountain ranges extending in a southeast-trending arc from southern Oregon to southern New Mexico. These fault block mountain ranges are oriented north-south. Broad, deep basins run between them. Local relief averages about 5,000 feet. However, the maximum vertical rise extends from the bottom of Death Valley (282 below sea level) to the 9,000-foot summits of the Panamint range. The mountains contain vegetation somewhat similar to the Rockies, yet endemic (geographically unique) species are numerous. Valley bottom vegetation encompasses North America's four great deserts: the Great Basin, Mojave, Sonoran, and Chihuahuan.

The Basin and Range region contains some of America's most remote settlements. "Rural" in Nevada can mean a 100-mile drive to the nearest movie theater. U.S. Route 50 runs east-west across Nevada and is called the "Loneliest Highway in America." Over 88 percent of Nevada is public land. Huge military bases are widespread in the Basin and Range, with rural towns deriving substantial economic benefit. Most public lands are used for livestock grazing. A unique cowboy culture evolved in Nevada based on transhumance (horse-mounted cowboys moving cattle up and down the mountains with the seasons). The influence of Spanish ranching practices is obvious. Nevada cowboys are called "buckaroos," wear "chaps," and use "lariats and "riatas" (ropes)—all words derived from Spanish. Buckaroo is from the Spanish vaquero. Elko and Winnemucca host "cowboy poetry" gatherings where buckaroos read their verse.

The rural Basin and Range region has several massive open-pit mines employing thousands of people. Copper mines exist in Utah (Bingham Canyon), Nevada (Ely), Arizona (Globe, Miami, Clifton, and Morenci), and New Mexico (Silver City). Gold mines near the boomtowns of Carlin and Elko, Nevada, are some of the largest in the world. In the past, mineral development in the Basin and Range consisted of small-shaft gold and silver mines. Mining is a boom-bust industry, and the region is dotted with ghost towns and barely surviving rural communities. Goldfield, Nevada, once had a population of 30,000; today perhaps 50 people reside there. Tombstone, Arizona, became a tourist attraction based on the lore of its violent frontier past.

Sierra Nevada and Cascades

The Sierra Nevada and Cascade ranges are defined by their proximity to metropolitan centers. Urbanites in California, Oregon, and Washington travel to the rural towns and high-country environments of these mountains during weekends and summer vacations. California's granitic Sierra Nevada, Yosemite, Kings Canyon, and Sequoia National Parks have become so crowded that reservations through Ticketron are required months ahead. Ski resorts, from Heavenly Valley in southern California to Mount Baker in northern Washington, are destination-area attractions. The local economies of many Sierra and Cascade communities are highly dependent on tourism and recreation. The Pacific Crest Trail traverses these ranges from Mexico to Canada.

The Cascades are capped by a chain of composite volcanoes with a significant risk of eruption. In 1980, Mount Saint Helens (Washington) exploded, killing 57 people and causing over $1 billion in damage. Rural residents of the Cascades have worked as sawyers and in sawmills for generations. The result has been deforestation of old-growth forests—those previously undisturbed by human beings. Less than 5 percent of the original forests remain. A heated conflict exists between the forest products industry and conservationists over the practice of clear-cutting (harvesting all the trees in a stand). The presence of the endangered Northern Spotted Owl resulted in hundreds of thousands of acres being put off-limits to logging. Rural loggers consequently were put out of work. Conservationists argue that this is inevitable if the owl and old-growth forests are to survive. The economy of the region is being redirected into tourism and high-technology industries, such as the manufacturing of silicon computer chips.

Alaska

Perhaps nowhere in America is the conflict between resource extraction and conservation more intense than in Alaska. This "last frontier" is the scene of decades of court battles over fishing rights, timber harvest, oil and gas development, and management of wildlife. The Trans-Alaska pipeline from the North Slope (north of the Brooks range) and Valdez was completed in the 1970s. Rural life changed dramatically as a result of a huge in-migration of workers during the construction boom. Once the pipeline was finished, many rural Alaskans found themselves looking for work. The Exxon Valdez oil spill of 1989 seriously reduced the amount of fish caught in Prince William Sound. Rural towns still suffer economically. In 1996, a major conflict concerned opening the Arctic National Wildlife Refuge to oil and gas development. Native Alaskans living in rural villages are afforded

special hunting and fishing rights in refuges and other portions of the state. However, debates rage over who sets seasons and quotas for the harvesting of key migratory species such as caribou. Across America, rural life in the mountains is changing. Land use issues are likely to remain pivotal for gaining an understanding of the geography of these regions.

—*John B. Wright*

See also
Cowboys; Culture; Desert Landscapes; Environmental Protection; Forestry Industry; Mining Industry; Parks; Regional Diversity.
References
Arno, Stephen F., and Ramona P. Hammerly. *Timberline: Mountain and Arctic Forest Frontiers.* Seattle: Mountaineers, 1984.
DeBuys, William. *Enchantment and Exploitation: The Life and Hard Times of a New Mexico Mountain Range.* Albuquerque: University of New Mexico Press, 1985.
Hunt, Charles B. *Physiography of the United States.* San Francisco: Freeman, 1967.
Peirce, Neal R. *The Mountain States of America.* New York: Norton, 1972.
Price, Larry W. *Mountains and Man: A Study of Process and Environment.* Berkeley and Los Angeles: University of California Press, 1981.
Wright, John B. *Rocky Mountain Divide: Selling and Saving the West.* Austin: University of Texas Press, 1993.
Wyckoff, William, and Larry M. Dilsaver. *The Mountainous West: Explorations in Historical Geography.* Lincoln: University of Nebraska Press, 1995.

Municipal Solid Waste Management

The way with which residual materials generated by production and consumption activities are collectively dealt. An effective municipal solid waste management (MSWM) system comprises several coordinated components: collection, processing, marketing, disposal, transportation, and financing. The first four components are sequential in relation to one another, whereas transportation serves to link the components and financing generally is dealt with for the system as a whole. This entry outlines the most important options or questions relating to each component in the current rural setting.

As noted in each of the previous sections, the transportation component of municipal solid waste management systems in rural areas is a critical one from the standpoint of maintaining a cost-effective system. With rural communities moving to provide more comprehensive collection services for solid waste and recyclables, efficiency in moving materials to a disposal or processing facility depends upon employing appropriate container and truck technologies. These technologies may not be

The challenges posed to municipalities everywhere by solid waste management are heightened in rural areas, where limited financial resources conflict with increasingly stringent federal regulations governing waste disposal.

the same as what a densely populated urban community would typically employ. In addition, the trend toward fewer regional disposal facilities means that transportation costs may increase as a proportion of overall systems costs. Rural communities may find that contracting with private haulers will be more economical than maintaining their own containers and trucks, particularly if they are not used on a full-time basis. While container and truck technologies have been changing rapidly through the 1990s, Bumpus (1993) provides a fairly recent and very useful primer on basic options and their relative costs.

Current Rural Setting

Three key realities have created significant challenges for rural communities in the 1990s regarding MSWM. One pertains to new federal regulations regarding landfill design and operation and state-level requirements for planning, collection, and recycling. The second relates to the concerns of rural citizens, who demand opportunities to engage in recycling and other activities viewed as part of the solution to the solid waste crisis. They want more influence over local disposal facility siting decisions and activities such as solid waste importation from other counties or states. The third reality is the existence of substantial economies of scale regarding some components of solid waste management systems, particularly the processing and marketing of recyclable materials and solid waste disposal. These realities force many rural communities to consider a bewildering array of options and to deal with substantially higher costs. The overall challenge facing leaders in rural communities is to identify a solid

waste management system that satisfies the constraints of federal and state regulations and the demands of local citizens within local fiscal constraints.

Collection

Solid Waste. Although attention increasingly focuses on collection of recyclables in rural areas, collection of solid waste in general remains a problem. Some rural areas have no publicly provided solid waste collection system outside of municipalities, although private haulers may offer service to rural residents. Many rural areas have either a green box or a convenience center system. A green box system involves placement of dumpsters (typically 6- or 8-cubic yard size) at numerous locations throughout a county on public road rights-of-way. A convenience center system involves establishment of a limited number of drop-off sites on major roads where dumpsters are concentrated or compactor containers are used. The sites have a gravel or paved surface and are fenced to limit access to certain hours when an attendant is present.

A rather dramatic shift from green box systems and toward convenience center systems was driven by economic factors and problems of green box systems related to littering, scavenging, and vandalism. Interest in collection of recyclables from rural areas brought to light the compatibility of convenience center systems with drop-off recycling approaches. Some analysts argue that a house-to-house system with relatively small compactor trucks operated by one person can be relatively cost effective and assure that a high percentage of solid waste is collected from rural areas and disposed of properly.

Recyclables. During the 1980s, several small-scale buy-back recycling centers were established in rural areas. To drive participation, these centers relied on the relatively strong economic incentives to collect aluminum cans. Many residents bought glass, newspaper, and, in some cases, scrap metal, corrugated board, and plastic. These centers had small-scale equipment to compact materials for shipment to markets. Because these centers paid for most, if not all, materials and many processed an extremely small tonnage of materials, they often faced relatively high net costs per ton of material diverted from disposal.

More prevalent in rural areas today are drop-off systems in which either dedicated sites are established or separation of recyclables is encouraged at convenience centers. The performance of drop-off systems is affected by the convenience of the location and hours of operation, the extent of educational efforts and publicity, the socio-economic characteristics of residents, and the range of materials accepted. Convenience centers have controlled access and an attendant present, so quality control should not be the problem it sometimes is with unattended drop-off sites. Container and transportation technologies greatly affect the overall costs of a system. Some systems rely on private contractors to provide specialized rental containers and transportation of materials to a buyer. Others employ homemade containers, existing trucks, and county employees to collect and transport materials. Because transportation of recyclables from drop-off sites to a centralized processing facility generally is done before materials are compacted, this activity can be relatively expensive compared to transporting compacted solid waste.

Processing

Solid Waste. Once solid waste has been collected, the question of processing arises. Solid waste may go directly to a landfill without any processing. However, there are several processing activities that can divert materials from the landfill or reduce their volume. The composting of organic matter to produce a resource for sale or to be given away is receiving much attention. Numerous composting options exist, from yard waste only to mixed solid waste composting in which most or all of the organic fraction is used. The co-composting of solid waste with municipal sewage sludge has been demonstrated to be a viable option. However, given the likelihood of small amounts of yard wastes as a percentage of solid waste in rural areas, the pressure for and potential of pay-off from composting activities appears limited.

Debate continues over how incineration should be viewed within integrated solid waste management systems. However, it does represent a processing activity that greatly reduces the amount of residual material to be landfilled. Conventional wisdom dismisses incineration as a viable economic option for rural areas because of the lack of economies of scale and the absence of markets for the energy produced.

Recyclables. Two related questions pertain to processing recyclables once they are collected in rural areas. First, to what extent, or in what way, should materials be processed before marketing? Second, should processing be done on a small scale at the point of collection, on a small scale at a central place in a rural county, or on a larger scale at a regional processing center in a larger urban area?

Although some small, rural processing centers have invested in specialized equipment (such as plastic shredders), if such centers are to do any processing at all, a versatile baler may be sufficient in most situations. The key objective should be to reduce volume in order to decrease transportation costs to buyers rather than preparing materials to specification for remanufacturing. However, even simple baling can be expensive on a per ton basis if volumes are low.

The second question pertains to the trade-off between the lower processing costs and higher transportation costs of regional processing strategies. There are marketing advantages on a regional basis, although this could be achieved through a cooperative marketing arrangement without regional processing. A recent analysis of an eight-county region in eastern Tennessee suggests that cost savings from processing on a regional basis would more than offset the higher transportation costs, even under assumptions regarding levels of participation, processing costs, and transportation costs that would tend to favor processing on an individual county basis (Park, Holt, and Roberts 1991). The sum of regional processing costs plus transportation costs (from central points in each county to a processing center near the center of the region) was 17 to 34 percent lower than total processing costs for eight individual-county operations. The same trade-off can be looked at from the standpoint of an individual county trying to decide whether to tie in with an existing regional processor. This same analysis shows for a given volume of material how far away from a regional processor a rural community must be to economically justify its own processing center or, for a given distance from the regional processor, how high material volume must be to justify economically the community's own processing center. The presence of substantial economies of scale in the processing of recyclables warrants serious evaluation of regional strategies for rural areas.

Marketing

From the standpoint of marketing recyclables, the goal is to achieve a satisfactory combination of price and buyer stability. However, typical characteristics of recycling centers in rural areas work against the achievement of this goal. Low volumes and an isolated location may put such centers at a disadvantage in negotiating a contract with buyers who want full truckloads on a regular basis. Small operations normally rely on buyers to provide transportation or make arrangements with an independent trucking firm. In addition, obtaining information from alternative buyers or new market outlets is a time-consuming activity in which there are economies of scale. Thus, marketing cost per ton may be higher for smaller centers than for larger ones.

Another factor in the marketing of recyclables is the importance of clean materials to buyers. Whole loads or bales may be rejected for certain types of contamination. The likelihood of using drop-off systems for collections of materials in rural areas puts a premium on oversight and monitoring of the quality of recyclable materials being collected and processed.

There are several possible strategies for dealing with the marketing problems facing small processing operations in rural areas. These strategies range from establishing a state or regional clearinghouse to provide information on market outlets, buyers, and prices, to developing a cooperative marketing arrangement among rural communities to accumulate full loads, improve negotiating positions, and provide increased stability (Schoenrich 1994).

Disposal

Landfilling will continue to be the primary method for solid waste disposal in rural areas. However, the new Subtitle D requirements of the Federal Resource Conservation and Recovery Act of 1976 already set in motion a rapid transition to fewer, larger, regional landfills and probably a greater proportion of private landfills. Required levels of capital investment and professional management may render landfilling a nonviable alternative for most rural counties. The economies of scale clearly favor larger landfills, as cost per ton falls rather dramatically from that of a facility scaled to serve a single rural county with, say, between 10,000 and 20,000 population to that of a facility scaled to serve an urban area or region with 100,000 population or more.

Although the number of new sites needed in the future may decline, gaining acceptance for any particular new site will remain problematic. Rural areas still will be viewed by public and private entities that wish to construct landfills as attractive locations for regional landfill sites, but these areas may resist strongly. If a new site is to serve a number of counties, efforts should be made to ensure that the host community or jurisdiction (1) has the opportunity to participate in planning, decision making, and monitoring; (2) gains commitments for mitigation of known or potential negative impacts; (3) is guaranteed compensation for any actual damages; and (4) receives rewards for willingly hosting the site.

Financing

Rural areas, by choice or by mandate, face the prospect of higher costs associated with upgrading solid waste collection systems, providing recycling options, and meeting new landfill standards. Historically, the financing of solid waste management in rural areas relied on revenues generated by local property or sales taxes. Landfill tipping fees have been nonexistent or below the true cost of disposal; user fees for curbside collection in municipalities or at convenience centers in unincorporated areas have been the exception rather than the rule. However, increasing numbers of small municipalities and rural counties are implementing successfully volume-based user fees, even within drop-off collection systems (Park 1995). Such strategies to finance the increasing costs of solid waste management systems have the advantage of (1) paying for the system from other than general tax revenues, (2) making the costs of the system more explicit, and (3) tying charges directly to waste volume or services. The achievement of these objectives would enhance the economic efficiency of a system and its equity by providing incentives for waste reduction and recycling.

Challenges

Rural communities face a tremendous challenge as they move into a new era for municipal solid waste management, one fraught with increased regulation, citizen demands, and economic pressures. Most rural communities are ill equipped to meet this challenge. The most serious constraint to meeting this challenge may be limited financial resources. However, some observers emphasize the lack of sufficient leadership and expertise in many rural communities to plan, implement, monitor, evaluate, and revise strategies for improved MSWM. Privatization may seem the simplest thing to do, but it may or may not be less expensive or best for the community.

Another constraint on rural communities' ability to meet the MSWM challenge stems from the difficulty of forging and sustaining effective arrangements for regional or multicommunity cooperation. As previously noted, cost-effective MSWM will require regional cooperation of some sort for many rural communities or counties with small populations. This is no simple task, even if rural communities are willing to work together, which is not always the case. States implemented a variety of strategies to encourage or facilitate cooperation; however, the results have been somewhat mixed. Regionalization is occurring, especially for landfills, although often in an ad hoc or de facto manner rather than as the result of a conscious effort to develop an integrated MSWM plan (Environmental Protection Agency 1994).

Public agencies in most states provide technical assistance for MSWM. However, the resources are meager in relation to the challenge facing rural communities and coordination among agencies is limited. There have been several major efforts to identify or develop written materials designed to aid rural communities in making MSWM decisions. First, a task force sponsored by the Southern Rural Development Center (1995) developed an annotated bibliography of guidebooks, computer models, research reports, articles describing case studies, and other items. Second, the Coastal Georgia Regional Development Center (1994) developed a comprehensive two-volume guidebook for rural solid waste management. One volume is a "regional planning user guide"; the other, a "sample regional plan." Third, the Solid Waste Association of North America (1994) developed a series of four relatively short guidebooks that focus on public-sector decision making, capacity assurance, regionalization, and financing. These resources should be helpful to rural community leaders in considering and making the changes that are needed in their MSWM systems.

—*William M. Park*

See also

Environmental Regulations; Impact Assessment; Infrastructure; Policy, Environmental; Public Services.

References

Bumpus, Lewis D. *Solid Waste: Transportation and Other Costs.* Knoxville: County Technical Services, University of Tennessee, 1993.

Coastal Georgia Regional Development Center. *Rural Solid Waste Management: Regional Planning User Guide.* Brunswick: Coastal Georgia Regional Development Center, 1994.

———. *Rural Solid Waste Management: Sample Regional Plan.* Brunswick, GA, 1994.

Doeksen, Gerald A., et al. *A Guidebook for Rural Solid Waste Management Services.* Mississippi State: Southern Rural Development Center, 1993.

Environmental Protection Agency. "Joining Forces on Solid Waste Management: Regionalization Is Working in Rural and Small Communities." EPA 530-K-93–001. Washington, DC: Environmental Protection Agency, 1994.

MaCC Group. *Waste Reduction Strategies for Rural Communities.* Washington, DC: American Plastics Council, with the Tennessee Valley Authority, 1994.

Malia, James E., and Janice Morrisey. *Rural Communities and Subtitle D: Problems and Solutions.* Knoxville: Tennessee Valley Authority, 1994.

Park, William M. "Using Volume-Based User Fees in Rural Areas: How Do They Work?" *Resource Recycling* 14, no. 1 (January 1995): 30–37.

Park, William M., Jeffery Holt, and Roland Roberts. "Regional Coordination for Processing of Recyclables from Rural Areas: A Case Study of the First Tennessee Development District."

SW-5–91. Knoxville: University of Tennessee, Waste Management Research and Education Institute, 1991.

Schoenrich, Lola. *Case Studies of Seven Rural Programs Cooperatively Marketing Recyclables.* St. Paul: Minnesota Project, 1994.

Solid Waste Association of North America. *Rural Solid Waste Management Series.* Silver Spring, MD: Solid Waste Association of North America, 1994.

Southern Rural Development Center. *Decision Aids for Municipal Solid Waste Management in Rural Areas: An Annotated Bibliography.* Mississippi State: Southern Rural Development Center, 1995.

Music

The various folk music traditions and commercial derivatives with which Americans identify. Although musical heritages vary regionally, and even from community to community, depending on the cultural identity of the original inhabitants, modern mobility and the media have helped to create a homogeneous musical culture among modern rural Americans. Knowledge, availability, and commercial consumption of national trends in recorded music since the 1920s, particularly among young people, have caused the original folk and ethnic styles of immigrant settlers to be acknowledged and experienced historically rather than as current, everyday music. Ethnic musical genres have undergone numerous changes in style and instrumentation as a result of extensive twentieth-century commercialization and the inevitable processes of acculturation. This entry covers major musical genres that add to the identities of rural American cultures and that have their roots in the original folk and ethnic styles unique to particular regions and peoples.

Hillbilly and Country Western Traditions

Appalachian. Southeastern mountain music was developed before the twentieth century by descendants of the region's Scotch-Irish and German settlers. Pre-twentieth-century instrumentation included the three- or four-string dulcimer from Germany, the fiddle from Ireland, and the banjo, which was introduced into Appalachian music during the mid-nineteenth century. As the style became more widely known through commercial recordings in the 1920s, the mandolin and guitar were added. The singing style is known for its vocally tense and forced high-pitched sound, with slides often occurring between melody notes and on the last notes of phrases. Traditional and original melodies and texts are based on the storytelling styles of English ballads and to some extent on the popular American ballads typical of nineteenth-century minstrel shows and parlor song literature. The fundamentalist revivalism of the early nineteenth century accounted for a strong religious component, which resulted in hymns and spirituals often sung in three- and four-part harmony. Modernization, travel, and mass communication altered the once-isolated lives of Appalachian residents. However, the musical traditions live on through a few elderly musicians, commercial and archival recordings, and young musicians wishing to recapture this musical heritage for performance in old-time fiddling contests and folk music festivals.

Bluegrass. Bluegrass music has the sound and texts with which many rural Americans identify, especially those with roots in the southeastern and south-central states. It is not a true folk music but rather a commercial, highly polished adaptation of mountain musical styles developed in the mid-l940s by skilled professional musicians led by mandolinist Bill Monroe. Monroe's Blue Grass Boys, named for his Kentucky roots, became the style's namesake through requests for his distinctive "blue grass" tunes by radio fans of the Grand Ole Opry heard over WSM in Nashville. Access to bluegrass music by rural Americans is through recordings, radio, and live performances at annual bluegrass festivals, the first of which was held in Roanoke, Virginia, in 1965.

Typical bluegrass music structure includes solo verses, harmonized vocal choruses, and instrumental breaks in which individual band members get featured solos. The vocal style is usually high pitched and straight toned. Standard instrumentation consists of five acoustic-stringed instruments: mandolin, banjo, fiddle, guitar, and string bass. The texts typically relate stories about famous people and events, affairs of the heart, and sentimental feelings of home and family. Bluegrass repertoire includes vocal gospel trios and quartets sung a cappella in the tightly harmonized, high-pitched style typical of mountain singing. Today's bluegrass recordings and festivals also feature bands with a more progressive approach (for example, the New Grass Revival) that tends to appeal to younger audiences; this approach fuses rock styles and techniques with bluegrass instrumentation and vocal style.

Country Western. Country Western music enjoys a wider appeal in rural America than any other commercial music idiom, especially in the Midwest, Southwest, and Far West. Known as hillbilly music before World War II, it was first popularized commercially on "barn dance" radio shows of the late 1920s and 1930s (such as WLS in Chicago and WSM in Nashville) and on the broadcasts of the Grand Ole Opry over WSM beginning in the late 1920s. During the 1930s, hillbilly music began to expand stylistically and instrumentally in order to become more commercially appealing to a wider audience.

The adaptability of country music to its expanding audiences and the ability of its producers to incorporate styles of other popular music idioms have been hallmarks of the genre's continued commercial success. Country music's evolution and adaptations since the 1920s have included Swiss yodeling (late 1920s); the Hawaiian steel guitar (1930s); cowboy songs and the western garb of the movies (1930s); big band jazz styles and instrumentation—western swing (1940s); the infusion of blues elements—Texas honky-tonk (1940s); the founding of sheet music publishers and record companies devoted to recording and marketing country music (1940s); country crooning (early 1950s); female soloists with female points of view (early 1950s); the fusion of early rock-and-roll styles and instrumentation—rockabilly (mid-1950s); and the nonconformist, country "outlaw" appeal to young audiences (1970s).

Traditional style elements that continue today include a somewhat strait, vibratoless vocal sound; a lonesome or plaintive vocal delivery; a tendency for the voice to break for heightened emotional impact; vocal slides between pitches; a southern accent with dialectic pronunciations; and stereotypical cowboy costuming. Especially appealing to rural Americans are the simple melodies and harmonies and the sentimental texts that deal with values and human conditions with which rural Americans can identify readily—personal, real-life issues such as loneliness, male-female relationships, family values, morality and patriotism, religious faith, and the desire to return home after traveling long distances or moving away from one's rural roots. The trend in contemporary country music, often called the people's music, is less regional and more generalized in order to appeal to a wide cross-section of Americans, both rural and urban.

European Immigrant Traditions

European immigrants brought a varied body of national and ethnic traditions in music that played a major role in their lives and influenced the nature and evolution of American popular music culture. In the late nineteenth century, many immigrants settled throughout the rural Midwest, where they often created new communities with single ethnic identities. Until World War I, these communities maintained relatively isolated musical identities reflecting those of their original homelands, which included community band music, dance music, and ethnic song literature.

In the late 1920s, hundreds of rural musicians toured regional communities as professional ethnic bands. These early professionals recognized the need to internationalize their repertoire with a more generalized Old World sound and with the inclusion of some mainstream popular music in order to satisfy the tastes of various ethnic identities throughout a larger touring territory. These crossover territory bands often included members representing more than one ethnic identity, and their instrumentation expanded to include the relatively new piano accordion and the standard dance band instruments, such as trap set percussion, clarinet, saxophone, trumpet, trombone, and tuba. This music was especially appealing to many second-generation Europeans who failed to share their parents' desire to maintain close cultural ties to the old country.

Throughout the 1930s and 1940s, rural ethnic populations danced to these bands in community ballrooms and listened to them on radios, phonograph records, and juke boxes. By the 1940s, international music had become a standard part of the mainstream popular music culture in both rural and urban areas, with touring polka bands such as those led by Lawrence Welk (German-Russian from North Dakota), Frankie Yankovic (Slovenian from Indiana), and "Whoopie John" Wilfarht (German from Minnesota). Their musical style is still preferred by many older rural midwesterners. The desire of younger musicians to learn original ethnic styles from older musicians has grown since the mid-1970s, and old-time ethnic music is performed and danced to at the many ethnic festivals and celebrations held annually throughout the Midwest.

Louisiana Cajun Traditions

One of the most unusual rural musical styles to develop in the United States comes from the "French triangle" occupying the swamp and bayou region of Louisiana. Cajun (altered form of Acadian) is the common designation for the French-derived White folk music of southern Louisiana developed by French-descended refugees from Acadia, now Nova Scotia. Contemporary Cajun music retains many of its original style traits and in recent years has seen a marked growth in commercial popularity throughout the United States.

The fiddle is the instrument associated most with Cajun dance music and provides lively music for the popular all-night dance party called a *fais do-do.* The accordion was added to the Cajun band during the 1920s and,

with the acoustic guitar and triangle (*tit fer*), became an integral part of the Cajun instrumental sound. The songs are typically lighthearted and sung in the French patois of the region with a straight-toned, nasal quality and with interjections of various types of shouts. Waltzes and lively two-steps are the most popular dance styles.

Regional African Americans have translated Cajun music into what is called zydeco (Cajun slang for the French "les haricots," or green snap beans), a blend of Cajun style and rhythm and blues. Zydeco bands use the accordion and typically include drums, electric guitar, piano, and rub-board, similar to the jug-band washboard. Cajun music performed in its original style is seeing a gradual revival both in commercial recordings and among rural performers attempting to reconnect with bayou folk music traditions.

Southern African American Traditions

Music characteristic of contemporary African Americans living in the rural South is tied closely to the nineteenth-century folk styles (spirituals, field songs, and work songs) of their ancestors. African slaves brought a rich musical heritage, and through acculturation with the Anglo-Saxon styles with which they came in contact, a new African American folk music heritage emerged.

Sacred Traditions. Nearly 200 years of acculturation between the African-based musical expressions of slaves and the hymn singing of Anglo Americans created a sacred musical folk culture among Blacks in the antebellum South, with stylistic traits and practices that can be heard in some rural churches. Dating back to the camp meetings of the great revivals in the early nineteenth century, musical expression has been an integral part of the emotions felt and expressed in African American services. As sermons build in emotion, preachers often begin intoning their messages, with spontaneous responses coming from the congregation (call-response singing is elemental to both African musical practice and African American folk music). Whereas the old lining-out method of hymn singing is now dated (the preacher sings a line, and the congregation sings it back), the tendency for members of the congregation to sing hymn melodies in an improvised, embellished manner (basing) continues in many rural churches. At times services may include a spontaneous church house moan by the women of the congregation, an improvised segment of blueslike humming following a highly charged outpouring of emotional singing, preaching, and kinetic energy (shout). Many rural churches include modern, highly stylized gospel performances by soloists backed up by the choir, by congregational hand clapping, and by instruments.

Secular Traditions. As with sacred music, secular music styles indigenous to rural African Americans in the South date back to nineteenth-century folk idioms such as work songs, fiddle playing, and the hollers of fieldworkers. Rural musical developments after the turn of the century included ragtime instrumental styles played by guitarists, pianists, string bands, and jug bands and folk blues styles sung around campfires, on street corners, and in railroad yards. Blues singing is a solitary, particularly African American form of lament rooted stylistically in nineteenth-century field hollers and socially in problems related to discrimination, unemployment, and loneliness. The songs of rural blues legends such as Robert Johnson, Leadbelly (Huddie Ledbetter), and Blind Lemon Jefferson are sung by modern blues singers as a tribute to the heritage of the style, even though many of the social ills from which these songs arose no longer exist to such an extreme.

Many of today's blues singers perform in country roadhouses and small-town juke joints throughout the rural South. Their styles range from the zydeco music of Louisiana Creoles to contemporary, pop-oriented soul blues accompanied by a small instrumental combo (electric guitar, keyboard, and drum set). The African American blues heritage is celebrated at annual blues festivals such as the King Busquit Blues Festival held in Helena, Arkansas. Festivals that are particularly popular with rural populations are those that feature regional performers, such as the Sunflower River Festival in Clarksdale, Mississippi.

Southwest Hispanic Traditions

Sacred Traditions. Hispanic American music of the rural Southwest has folk roots that date to the sixteenth century. The earliest sacred Hispanic music appeared in what is now New Mexico. The valleys of the upper Rio Grande and the Pecos River were relatively isolated, and contemporary musical expressions of the region are rooted in centuries-old traditions. A famous example is the musical accompaniment to Los Hermanos Penitentes (the Penitent Brothers), the religious rituals begun by early Catholic laypeople. The *alabado,* an unmetered sacred song type performed in unison (similar to Gregorian plainsong), is characteristic of the Penitentes. Another body of religious folk songs performed in California, New Mexico, and Texas is sung in conjunction with two Christmas liturgical dramas or mystery plays:

Los Pastores (The Shepherds) and *Las Posadas* (The Lodgings).

Secular Traditions. The secular music of rural Hispanic Americans is more widespread and varied than surviving sacred forms. A secular category popular with many rural Hispanics is a mariachi-type of dance music ensemble called *conjunto de la música norteña* (ensemble of northern music). The traditional instrumentation consists of the button accordion and guitar. Recent additions include a saxophone (played in thirds with the accordion melody), drum set, and electric bass. The metrical styles tend to be indicative of polkas or waltzes. The appearances of the button accordion and polka styles reflect the probable influence of early German settlers in the region.

The two most significant secular song types are the *corrido* and the *canción.* The *corrido* is similar in structure and function to a folk ballad. Originating in mid-nineteenth-century Mexico, it is a strophic song type used to tell stories of significant people and events in the lives of Hispanic Americans. *Corridos* are written and performed mostly in the lower Rio Grande region, but recordings of the songs are popular with Hispanic Americans throughout the Southwest. Recent songs deal with such subjects as César Chávez (of the farm labor movement) and the assassinations of the Kennedys and Martin Luther King, Jr. The *canción* is more lyrical and sentimental and less socially relevant. One of the best-known song titles from this genre is "Cielito Lindo."

Native American Traditions

The musical practices of Native Americans were unique to each of the some 1,000 tribes that inhabited what is now the continental United States before the arrival of European settlers. Although some general musical traits and practices still reflect certain regional or tribal traits, contemporary Native American music is more homogeneous in style. Like other rural Americans, Native Americans listen to popular radio stations and buy recordings that reflect the national trends in commercial music. However, many Native Americans increasingly wish to recapture and celebrate musical values, practices, and styles basic to their past traditions. The celebrations that best exemplify Native American musical practices are intertribal powwows sponsored by clubs, Indian associations, and schools.

Powwows are well-organized, public events in which singing and dancing play important roles. Some feature invitational competitions in music and dance, such as that held near Hartford, Connecticut. The performers are generally paid professionals, often with national reputations. Typical performing groups of musicians or dancers represent many tribal identities and perform traditional songs, new songs, and songs written or popularized by other performing groups. Although the original functions of ritualistic singing and dancing have been replaced largely by public performance settings, the spiritual gift and inspiration to write a new song are still believed to be inherent to song composition.

Regional traits evident in contemporary musical performance include tendencies to sing in low or high vocal ranges (southwestern or northern tribal traditions, respectively) and the use of higher degrees of melodic and rhythmic complexity (Pueblo Indian tribes of New Mexico). As in the past, dance is associated closely with the singing. Professional dancers showcase traditional dance styles, with interested powwow participants joining in during large-group dance segments. New songs are written either in the native language of the composer or in English. Songs in English are more popular among younger generations because most younger Native Americans have little or no working knowledge of their traditional languages. Older songs and new songs in Native American languages are favored by elders. These songs often have no specific text and use only groupings of vowel-like sounds or Native American language syllables, a trait typical of pre-twentieth-century music. Some professional performers incorporate into their repertoire humorous renditions of well-known American popular songs sung with traditional Indian vocal inflections (for example, "Happy Birthday" and "Achy Breaky Heart"). The most commonly used instruments are flutes and percussion types (drums of various sizes and assorted rattles).

Public School Traditions

The earliest form of organized music education in rural America began during the early nineteenth century in New England with Protestant church–sponsored singing classes that taught musical notation and the proper manner in which to sing hymns. During the 1830s, Lowell Mason developed the first vocal music curriculum for use in public schools. Because of a lack of music specialists in rural areas, plus a need for relatively few faculty, small rural schools offered little or no organized music education until the 1920s. Through the 1950s, most country and small-township schools treated musical experiences as extracurricular activities taught or led by part-time teachers, teachers with other specialties, or circuit teachers who taught in different schools during the week. Since

the 1950s, dwindling rural populations and economic resources have caused most rural schools to consolidate into multitownship districts. As a result, offerings in music education and group performance opportunities have expanded.

Modern rural school districts, like their urban counterparts, generally offer chorus and band, and since the 1930s interested students have been able to participate in district- and state-level solo and ensemble music contests. Both levels of contests tend to hire certified education specialists in music and adhere to the curricular and pedagogical standards set by the Music Educators National Conference, although these practices were not typical in rural school districts until the 1960s. Many rural schools can hire only one full-time music teacher for all grade levels of chorus and band. Because of the heavy workload and inability of teachers to focus on either choral or instrumental music, rural schools tend to experience a greater frequency in music teacher turnover. Rural schools have not had any tradition in string education or orchestral performance opportunities. This is due to a lack of strong traditions in art music string playing among rural Americans, a lack of available string teachers and conductors in rural regions, and a lack of the financial resources and student numbers necessary to support string education and performance.

The percentage of rural students who participate in music (often over 50 percent) is usually higher than in urban schools, as is the case for other extracurricular activities. This is due in large part to the smaller, more cohesive student populations and to long-established extracurricular traditions among the community at large. Smaller student populations allow greater familiarity between students and teachers, thereby enhancing recruitment by the music faculty. Since the 1920s, band programs have been the strongest component of rural music education, probably because of small-town community band traditions, the European ethnic band music traditions established by early settlers, and the functional nature and visibility of band programs to the school and community (for example, holiday parades, pep bands, and graduation marches).

—*Robert W. Groves*

See also
African Americans; American Indians; Arts; Cultural Diversity; Culture; Educational Curriculum; Ethnicity; Latinos; Recreational Activities; Religion.
References
Chase, Gilbert. *America's Music*. 3d ed. Urbana: University of Illinois Press, 1989.

Greene, Victor. *A Passion for Polka: Old-Time Ethnic Music in America*. Berkeley and Los Angeles: University of California Press, 1992.

Hitchcock, H. Wiley. *Music in the United States: A Historical Introduction*. 3d ed. Englewood Cliffs, NJ: Prentice-Hall, 1987.

Hitchcock, H. Wiley, and Stanley Sadie, eds. *New Grove Dictionary of Music in the United States*. 4 vols. New York: Macmillan, 1984.

Kingman, Daniel. *American Music: A Panorama*. 2d ed. New York: Schirmer Books, 1990.

Malone, Bill. *Country Music, USA*. Rev. ed. Austin: University of Texas Press, 1985.

Nettl, Bruno. *Folk and Traditional Music of the Western Continents*. 3d ed. Englewood Cliffs, NJ: Prentice-Hall, 1990.

Recorded Anthology of American Music. New York: New World Records, 1977–present. Recordings and historical notes.

Southern, Eileen. *The Music of Black Americans: A History*. 3d ed. New York: W.W. Norton, 1983.

Native Americans

See American Indians

Natural Resource Economics

The quantity, quality, conservation, and use of natural resources in rural America. Natural resources have played a pivotal role in the long and checkered evolution of the rural economies of the United States. This entry is a brief survey and synthesis of the economics of natural resource use in rural America and its evolving future directions. The first part of the entry provides a glimpse of major natural resource concerns from a historical perspective and sets the stage for the discussion that follows. The second part presents a survey of use of specific natural resources in rural America. The third part discusses the philosophical change that is transforming the pace and pattern of natural resource use. The final part sets forth future directions for natural resource policy in rural America.

Historical Setting

Natural resource problems have been a source of serious concern among economists and noneconomists for nearly two centuries in the United States and abroad. These concerns, for analytical purposes, can be grouped into three main categories: quantity (resource scarcity), quality, and conservation. A sketch of some representative thinking on these issues is presented as a backdrop for the following discussion.

Early concern about the adequacy of natural resources to support human life if resource use and population growth continued undiminished at the then-pre-vailing rate was expressed by British classical economists Thomas Malthus in the late eighteenth century and David Ricardo in the early nineteenth century. According to Malthus, population tended to increase far more rapidly (in "geometric progression") than agricultural production and the supply of food, leading inevitably to economic disarray. The relatively fixed quantity of land was considered largely responsible for this situation. Malthus discounted technological improvement and factor substitution as possible means to correct the situation.

Ricardo theorized that soil quality differences largely accounted for differences in land rent. He held the view that the most productive land was cultivated first, followed by land of progressively decreasing quality, resulting in an increasing scarcity of high-quality land and eventual resource exhaustion. Ricardo extended his analysis to natural resources in general, although empirical evidence was lacking in other areas, for instance, mining. Nevertheless, this was an important insight into the pattern of natural resource utilization, as subsequent experience has shown.

John Stuart Mill struck a more positive note about the future of natural resources in the mid-nineteenth century. Mill differed from Malthus and Ricardo in an important respect; he argued that the margin of productivity was limitless, as it could be extended both extensively and intensively. Mill, however, was deeply concerned about possible deterioration in the quality of natural resources due to overcrowding caused by rapid population growth—a first glimmer of what twentieth-century economists call "congestion externalities" (deleterious external effects of overcrowding).

The most perceptive recent analysis of natural resource scarcity in the United States was published by

The environmental movement has heightened awareness of noneconomic considerations in natural resource management. Preservation of the environment for recreational uses is a factor that needs to be balanced against the financial concerns of natural resources industries such as logging and mining.

Barnett and Morse (1963). Unlike their predecessors, they arrived at a rather optimistic conclusion: Resource scarcity has been averted by technological progress, making substitution of lower-grade resources possible due to corresponding increases in their effective supplies.

Natural resource conservation has long been a source of concern in the United States. Marsh, as far back as 1865, expressed concern about human activities and their impact on ecological balance. Later, Pinchot (1910, 123), often considered the founder of the American conservation movement, wrote extensively about the need to conserve "wood, water, coal, iron, and agricultural products," which he considered indispensable for human survival.

Ciriacy-Wantrup (1952) in his seminal book *Resource Conservation* explored the economic and policy dimensions of resource conservation from a largely institutional perspective. He identified the following key economic forces as shaping the decisions of resource users: prices, property rights, tenancy, credit, taxation, and market form. He effectively articulated the need to establish a "safe minimum standard" of conservation to prevent resource depletion and exhaustion. More recent conservation studies extended the analysis through economic modeling and econometric and other quantitative studies.

Natural Resource Use in Rural America

Natural resource use in rural America has been rooted primarily in the philosophy of production agriculture embodied in profit maximization through output expansion. The notion of sustainable agriculture and resource use has not been an integral or important part of the commonly held agricultural creed. The discussion that follows focuses on problems of quantity, quality, and conservation in the context of specific natural resources: water, land, forest, and energy.

Water. Water consumption in rural America increased substantially over the second half of the twentieth century as a result of the dramatic increase in irrigated agriculture, especially in the West. In 1982, for instance, the 17 western states accounted for a little over 80 percent of the total irrigated agriculture in the United States (approximately 49 million acres in farms). Expansion of crop production to arid and semi-arid regions through extensive water storage and transfer systems, as in California, significantly added to the demand for limited water resources over the years. Quality of both ground- and surface waters deteriorated due to salinization and contamination from pesticides, nitrates, and selenium. Rachel Carson's *Silent Spring* (1962), a chilling account of the consequences of organic pesticide use in agriculture, drew national attention and created a new awareness of its hidden dangers. The comparative abundance and cheapness of water in many areas of rural America in the past accounted for the slow adoption of water conservation technologies such as drip irrigation. The market for and pricing of water were seldom considered seriously in the planning and allocation of water. However, today, quantity, quality, and conservation are issues of paramount importance in the effective planning, management, and allocation of the dwindling surface- and groundwater supplies in rural America.

Land. Soil erosion continues to be a major source of concern. The productivity of land in rural America has been severely affected as a result of unabated soil loss. Over the years, several techniques have been developed to keep soil in place such as reduction or elimination of tillage, reduction of runoff through irrigation management, and covering soil with plants and mulch. However, the problem of soil erosion is far from contained.

Soil quality is another important issue in land management. It is a key element in the sustainability of agricultural production. Over the years, soil quality suffered irretrievable losses in many areas of rural America due to monoculture and other crop management systems that use large quantities of inputs to maintain output.

Soil conservation assumed a new prominence in the context of land management in rural America because of pervasive soil erosion and soil quality losses. Soil conservation is intended to help soils retain their productive capacity by preventing depletion and limiting average soil losses from erosion ideally to a maximum of 4 tons per acre per year. (For a comprehensive discussion of land economics issues, see van Kooten, 1993.)

Forests. Forestry or forest resources figure prominently among America's natural resources. Forestry provides an early example of the application of science to natural resources management in the United States. Major issues center on the multiple uses of the public forest lands and on timber harvesting practices. The former include uses such as wilderness, mining, recreation, and timber. The latter deal with a panoply of problems, among them optimum rotation and clear-cutting. Rapid deforestation resulting from unchecked cutting of trees for lumber has been and continues to be a source of serious conflict. The impact of greenhouse gases (chlorofluorocarbons) on the forests is an area of looming concern.

Energy. Energy use in U.S. agriculture periodically

has been subject to intense scrutiny, especially in the wake of the Organization of Petroleum Exporting Countries (OPEC) oil embargo of 1973 and the natural gas shortages in the winter of 1976–1977, because of the highly energy-intensive nature of agriculture. Gasoline, diesel oil, fuel oil, liquid propane (LP) gas, and natural gas traditionally have accounted for a significant part of energy use in agriculture. In addition to direct use in agricultural and livestock production, large quantities of petroleum products go into the production of chemicals and fertilizers used in agriculture.

This traditional pattern of energy use is now changing. Recent studies suggest a reduction in the energy intensity of western U.S. agricultural production. Gopalakrishnan (1994) points out that energy used to produce a dollar's worth of agricultural output registered an almost 9 percent decrease between 1974 and 1978. Measures to substitute nonenergy (e.g., physical labor or biotechnology) for energy (e.g., petroleum oil or electricity) and the adoption of various energy conservation measures such as tillage and weed control, fertilizer management, better irrigation practices, optimal tractor performance, and efficient feed handling, processing, and distribution practices contributed to substantial energy savings. The conclusion is that U.S. agriculture has become less energy-intensive in the wake of sharp escalations in energy prices.

Although U.S. agriculture over the past several decades has become increasingly capital-intensive, the potential for capital-energy substitution still exists in the U.S. farming sector. In addition, it might be possible to substitute land or labor for energy in the agricultural sector; for example, more labor-intensive farming techniques could be used in place of energy-intensive ones.

Sustainability: The Guiding Principle

Recent years, roughly the last two decades of the twentieth century, witnessed a major change in the philosophy underlying natural resource use in America. This philosophical change is embodied in what has come to be widely known as sustainable resource use. The focus is on keeping the natural resource bounty of a country intact by regulating its rate of use on a sustained basis so that its depletion or exhaustion is averted. The key to such regulation is to ensure that the rate of resource replenishment matches or exceeds the rate of depletion of the natural resource. This marks a distinct departure from the production-oriented approach to resource use, which was in vogue for many years in America.

Sustainable agriculture is gaining widespread acceptance within mainstream agriculture. The environmental costs associated with many of the earlier agricultural practices are addressed by sustainable agriculture, with its focus on the avoidance of air, water, and land pollution. Sustainable agriculture views natural resources from a functional approach as living, vital, dynamic entities integrally intertwined with the environment, as opposed to independent, free-floating resource commodities. Sustainable resource use thus encapsulates a new vision of natural resources as logical extensions of the environment, a view analogous to Zimmermann's (1951) earlier vision of the tripartite interaction of humans, nature, and culture.

Natural Resources in Rural America:
Future Directions

Major changes that should occur in the formulation of a natural resource policy for rural America reflecting the tenor of the times are briefly touched on under four broad categories: economic, institutional, technological, and ethical-environmental. Economic changes would encompass the more vigorous use of market and price to allocate increasingly scarce resources among competing demands in an economically sustainable fashion. A case in point is water. Water markets and water pricing will take on new importance, especially in the water-short western states, as is evident from the recent experience of California (Carter, Vaux, and Scheuring 1994), Arizona, and Colorado, among others. Fuller use of input substitution in response to relative price changes, as in the case of energy use in agriculture discussed earlier, is another likely economic change. Regulation of the rate of resource use through the rigorous enforcement of quotas, standards, zoning, and taxes represents another economic change.

Institutional changes connote broad and sweeping changes in natural resources policy stemming from or instigated by shifts or variations in the sociocultural milieu. (See Rutherford 1994 for a discussion of the role of institutions in economics.) Modifications in current natural resource laws are also an integral part of such change. Resource conservation, sustainable resource use, and resource quality will assume a new importance in shaping rural America's natural resource policy. Pollution-abatement policies will be more widely accepted and adopted. Water, land, and forestry resources will be directly affected by the broad sweep of these changes.

Technological changes will address resource scarcities of the Ricardian variety in an attempt to extend the margin of resource use to ever-farther limits. Changes in technology, for instance, could make an increasing array of renewable energy sources, such as biomass, solar, wind, and waves, cost-effective and well within the reach of large segments of population. Water-conserving irrigation technologies and other resource-conserving and sustaining techniques will become far more common in the rural America of the twenty-first century.

Perhaps the most important group of changes affecting the quantity, quality, and sustainability of resource use in rural America will be the result of altered environmental and ethical perceptions. The view of natural resources as impersonal resource commodities, and thus as economic production inputs, is being steadily replaced by a notion of resources as an integral part of the larger environment. There is growing recognition today that resources must be used with great care as to their possible environmental impacts. The notion of a safe minimum standard and the utilitarian ethos of intergenerational equity (relative equality among people from generation to generation) are the core elements of this evolving philosophy. In brief, this marks a distinct shift in the underlying resource use philosophy from the economics of the marketplace to the moral standing of the marketplace.

—Chennat Gopalakrishnan

See also

Agricultural and Resource Economics; Agriculture, Alternative; Conservation, Energy; Conservation, Soil; Conservation, Water; Environmental Protection; Ethics; Forests; Future of Rural America; Land Stewardship; Policy, Environmental; Soil; Water Use.

References

Barnett, Harold J., and Chandler Morse. *Scarcity and Growth: The Economics of Natural Resource Availability*. Baltimore: Johns Hopkins University Press, 1963.

Carter, Harold O., Henry J. Vaux, Jr., and Ann F. Scheuring, eds. *Sharing Scarcity: Gainers and Losers in Water Marketing*. Davis: University of California Agricultural Issues Center, 1994.

Carson, Rachel. *Silent Spring*. Boston: Houghton Mifflin, 1962.

Ciriacy-Wantrup, S. C. *Resource Conservation*. Berkeley: University of California, Division of Agricultural Sciences (originally published in 1952), 1963.

Gopalakrishnan, Chennat. *The Economics of Energy in Agriculture*. Aldershot, UK: Avebury, 1994.

Marsh, George P. *Man and Nature: Or Physical Geography as Modified by Human Action*. New York: Charles Scribner, 1865.

Pinchot, Gifford. *The Fight for Conservation*. New York: Doubleday, Page and Co., 1910. Reprint: Seattle, WA: University of Washington Press, 1967, 1973.

Rutherford, Malcolm. *Institutions in Economics*. Cambridge, UK: Cambridge University Press, 1994.

van Kooten, Cornelis G. *Land Resource Economics and Sustainable Development*. Vancouver, Canada: UBC Press, 1993.

Zimmermann, Erich W. *World Resources and Industries*. New York: Harper and Brothers, 1951.

Nurses and Allied Health Professionals

Nonphysician health care providers. This entry addresses the shortage of nurses and allied health professionals in rural areas and means by which such professionals are being recruited to fill the gap; the practices of rural nursing and allied health; and legislative initiatives that support rural health care practices.

The Rural Shortage

A shortage of nurses and allied health professionals exists in rural America. Numerous factors have been cited as to why rural areas may be less attractive practice sites. Governmental agencies, educational institutions, and professional health organizations are pursuing strategies to increase the recruitment and retention of nurses and allied health professionals in rural areas.

There has been concern for a number of years regarding the provision of health care to populations in rural areas. A rural shortage of nurses and allied health professionals is a major factor related to the lack of optimal health care service provision. Other factors that contribute include a rural-urban maldistribution of physicians and, in some instances, a lack of rural health care facilities. According to an American Hospital Association survey, 36 percent of hospital closings in the 1980s were in rural areas (Burke et al. 1994). Certain types of health problems are more prevalent in rural settings and this different health problem profile may influence the practice decisions of health care professionals. Rural areas generally have higher rates of chronic disease and more problems related to maternal and child health. Agricultural work presents a higher risk for health problems and injury than work in other sectors.

Studies that focus on reasons why rural areas fail to recruit and retain adequate numbers of nurses and allied health professionals identify various contributory factors. These include a perception of limited recreational and family educational opportunities; a lack of ready access to state-of-the-art health information and professional continuing education opportunities; heavier patient/client demands; limited ability to consult with colleagues or professional specialists; higher numbers of patients with less ability to pay for health care; and difficulties encountered with reimbursement from insurance companies and government agencies (Travers and Ellis 1993; Willis 1993; Price 1993; Muus, Stratton, and Ahmed 1993; Straub and Wright 1993). In some instances, salaries in rural areas may be less competitive than those in urban

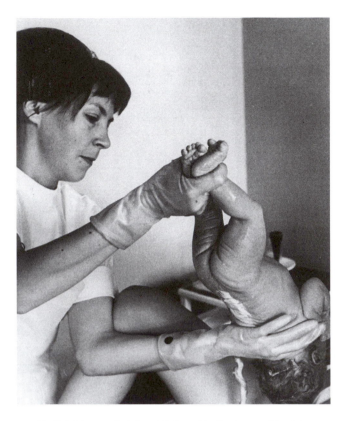

A midwife holds a newly delivered baby. Midwifery is one of the oldest paraprofessional occupations but is only now gaining acceptance in the modern medical community.

areas (Bigbee 1993). Lack of employment opportunities for spouses in rural areas may also play a role.

Statistics concerning the precise nature of the nursing and allied health professional shortage in rural America are limited (Office of Technology Assessment 1990). According to government statistics, 17 percent of the country's registered nurses (RNs) in 1988 worked in rural areas. Of those, the majority were based in the more populated rural counties. Only 8.7 percent were employed in counties of less than 50,000 residents, and most were employed in counties of greater than 25,000 residents. When compared to urban RNs, rural RNs were "more likely to work full-time, more likely to work in nursing home or public health settings, less likely to work in hospitals, and less likely to have a baccalaureate degree" (Office of Technology Assessment 1990, 265–266). Counties with small populations were more likely to have nurses prepared at the minimum of a baccalaureate degree level. The conclusion can be drawn that more remote areas perhaps required higher levels of nursing expertise.

Statistics on numbers of allied health professionals in rural areas are even more scarce than those for nurs-

ing. To some extent, this reflects a lack of consistency in use of the term "allied health professional" as well as the large number of health professions included under the umbrella of allied health. However, available evidence and anecdotal reports indicate rural shortages among a wide range of allied health professionals.

Recruitment to Rural Areas

Efforts are currently under way to recruit and retain more nurses and allied health professionals in rural practice. In part, these efforts have been driven by a lack of rural physicians. Nurse practitioners (NPs) and physician assistants (PAs) received particular attention in attempts to increase health care delivery services to rural areas. This focus resulted from recognition that these health care practitioners can provide basic health care services to areas that lack direct physician coverage. In the arena of primary care, NPs and PAs can accomplish 75 to 90 percent of physician duties (Osterweis and Garfinkel 1993).

The NP is generally an RN with a graduate degree. Some NPs, however, obtain their education through certificate programs. According to a 1990 survey, NPs who obtained their credentials through a certificate program were more likely to work in rural settings. The movement away from granting the NP credential through certification and solely through graduate programs has been defined as a potential obstacle for the production of rural NPs. The PA generally holds a minimum of a baccalaureate degree. There are PA programs, however, that are certificate, associate degree, or master's degree programs. The practice of PAs is legally linked with physician practice, while NPs are trained to work in an independent practice.

The professions of NP and PA both emerged in the 1960s in response to concerns about shortages of physicians. Both kinds of practitioners are now in high demand in urban and rural areas alike.

Nurse practitioners located in rural areas are more frequently specialists in family health employed in primary care clinics. They also are more likely to have admitting privileges for hospitals and nursing homes. An analysis of 1991 surveys of migrant and community health centers found that NPs and certified nurse midwives (CNMs) were more likely to serve as physician substitutes in rural settings than were PAs (Shi et al. 1993). The majority of NPs are based in counties with higher population bases. In 1988, 85 to 91 percent of NPs practiced in counties with greater than 50,000 population (Fowkes 1993).

In 1990, only 12.9 percent of PAs practiced in rural areas (Travers and Ellis 1993). Rural PAs differ from their urban counterparts in that they are more frequently primary care specialists. The majority of rural PAs (83 percent) are located in states that give PAs the authority to write prescriptions (Willis 1993). Cawley (1993) noted a trend for fewer PAs to practice in rural areas and cited as factors contributing to this decline increased numbers of females in the profession, retirement of rural PAs, and increased demand for PAs in specialty practices and in the hospital setting.

Community and migrant health centers are major organizations employing both NPs and PAs in rural settings. Such clinics on average employ 2.2 full-time equivalent NPs or PAs per site (Fowkes 1993).

Certified nurse midwives (CNMs) and certified registered nurse anesthetists (CRNAs) are also important health professionals in the rural setting. Appropriately trained CNMs manage uncomplicated pregnancies. CRNAs provide anesthesia services and may be the sole providers of such services in rural areas. There is concern that CNMs and CRNAs practice in less than optimal numbers in rural settings. Of the 42 CNMs certified in Arizona, only 10 were found to practice in rural areas (Gordon and Erickson 1993). These investigators found that Arizona CNMs practicing in rural areas were less likely than their urban counterparts to be prepared at the master's degree level and had fewer years of practical experience.

The 1990s phenomenon of downsizing allayed the nursing shortage in many urban areas. Some urban professionals who saw their jobs disappear decided to relocate to rural areas to practice. Any shift toward rural areas as the result of urban downsizing may be influenced by future patterns of rural hospital closure and by the presence in rural communities of clinics, offices, home health services, and long-term care facilities. One scenario foresees the change from acute care beds to long-term care beds in rural hospitals coupled with the development of rural emergency care clinics serving as feeders to urban hospitals (Rubenstein 1989).

The managed care movement will influence patterns of rural health care practice. Rural practitioners will need to be in alliances that allow them to benefit financially. The tendency of managed care to use more technician-level allied health practitioners may be felt in rural areas. Managed care should promote increased use of NPs and PAs. This may benefit rural areas because of increased pressure for adequate NP and PA remuneration under the rubric of cost-effectiveness.

Rural Health Care Practice

Rural practice has advantages. For example, nurses and allied health professionals working in rural areas tend to have greater and more diverse responsibilities and freedoms in the work environment. The rural environment also provides opportunities for greater recognition and appreciation from members of the community. In some instances, rural health care facilities offer higher base salaries and salary bonuses in an attempt to attract nonphysician health care providers. Organizations of allied health professionals in some states are active in rural recruitment and retention.

Telemedicine and other uses of computer technology, such as telecourses and teleconferencing, make health information and access to specialists a reality for the rural nurse or allied health care worker. These technologies may overcome the perceived rural practice barriers of lack of information and professional interaction. Other innovations that should help enhance the ability of rural health practitioners to communicate are the increasing availability of medical and health care resource software, the Internet, CD-ROMS, and fax machines.

Educational programs allowing students to train in rural areas are beneficial in expanding the numbers of students who choose to enter rural practice upon graduation. In 1991, the Committee on Allied Health Education and Accreditation (CAHEA) of the American Medical Association (AMA) collected and analyzed data concerning rural training. The survey found that training for the following allied health occupations was offered in 150 or more rural locations: radiographic technician, respiratory therapy technician, medical record technician, occupational therapy, physician assistant, and medical assistant. Rural allied health training was more likely to occur in more populated rural areas and in professions with a primary care focus as opposed to professions that are more specialized and equipment intensive (Gupta and Konrad 1992). A 1992 survey of all programs accredited to train PAs found that 58 percent of programs offered practice experience in rural counties and two accredited PA programs were based in rural counties (Hooker, Gupta, and Konrad 1994). Scholarships for those willing to serve in medically underserved rural areas after graduation is another strategy being used to recruit allied health professionals into rural locations.

Some programs target high-school students in rural areas in an attempt to develop interest in and provide academic preparation for health care careers. These programs operate under the premise that individuals who come from a rural environment are more likely to return to that environment to practice. Walker (1991) emphasized that local training in health care will enable rural residents to help meet their own health care workforce needs.

A new health educational model relevant to preparing individuals to work in rural health is the cross-training or multiskilling approach, which educates allied health professionals and nurses in multiple areas outside of their traditional scope of practice. The Agency for Health Care Policy and Research of the U.S. Public Health Service has outlined models for rural health care using a single class of allied health worker trained to accomplish tasks in radiology, laboratory science, and emergency medicine. This agency also believes it feasible to cross-train nurses to provide therapy services and to fulfill other nonnursing functions (Agency for Health Care Policy and Research 1991).

Legislative Initiatives Supporting Rural Health-Care Practice

State legislative initiatives and federally funded programs actively promote rural nursing and allied health practices. For example, Nebraska and Kentucky have funded programs to increase the number of rural students entering health programs (Straub and Wright 1993). Texas is using cooperative programming and distance learning to link health-science centers with rural academic universities and is funding rural health outreach programs to provide continuing education to nurses in rural areas. In addition to education on technical topics, the rural outreach program provides stress reduction and burnout prevention programming (Okimi, Reed, and Bernhardt 1992). Federally funded area health education centers (AHECs) plays a major role in supporting rural health practice by providing preprofessional and continuing education programs.

In addition to legislative initiatives dealing with education, recent legal measures allowing for more independent practice and greater reimbursement potential likewise support rural health care practice by nonphysician providers. States that allow nurses and allied health professionals, particularly NPs and PAs, to expand the scope of their practice are more conducive to rural practice and primary care. Areas covered under scope-of-practice legislation include type of required physician supervision, types of procedures that can be performed, and medication authority.

Other legislative initiatives being considered, such as those that would permit Medicare to allow more flexible on-site time commitments for rural health facility personnel, might also enhance the provision of rural nursing and allied health care. For example, a law that would allow rural hospitals to deviate from the requirement that an RN be present 24 hours per day is currently under debate by health care professionals in rural communities. Government health care reimbursement policies also have been revised to include coverage for more services offered by NPs and PAs. Services of NPs and PAs in designated rural health professional shortage areas are now eligible for Medicare reimbursement. PAs and NPs in rural areas are eligible in many states to receive Medicaid reimbursement. The Rural Health Care Services Act passed in 1977 was modified to aid in recruitment and retention of nonphysician health care providers by modifying provisions related to reimbursement. However, problems with both governmental and nongovernmental health insurance coverage still exist with regard to these and other allied health care practitioners.

Nonphysician health care professionals (nurses and practitioners in allied health) are critical to the provision of appropriate health care services in rural America. Attempts will continue to recruit and retain these individuals in rural settings.

—*Judy E. Perkin*

See also
Health and Disease Epidemiology; Health Care; Injuries; Policy, Health Care.

References
Agency for Health Care Policy and Research. *Delivering Essential Health Care Services in Rural Areas: An Analysis of Alternative Models.* AHCPR Pub. No. 91-0017 (May). Washington, DC: U.S. Department of Health and Human Services, Agency for Health Care Policy and Research, 1991.

Bigbee, Jeri L. "The Uniqueness of Rural Nursing." *Nursing Clinics of North America* 28 (1993): 131–144.

Burke, George C., III, Grant T. Savage, Kelly C. Baird, Veronda L. Durden, and Robert A. Pascasio. "Stakeholder Impact on Two Rural Hospital Closures." *Texas Journal of Rural Health* 8 (1994): 5–13.

Cawley, James. "Physician Assistants in the Health Care Workforce." Pp. 21–39 in *The Roles of Physician Assistants and Nurse Practitioners in Primary Care.* Edited by D. Kay Clawson and Marian Osterweis. Washington, DC: Association of Academic Health Centers, 1993.

Fowkes, Virginia. "Meeting the Needs of the Underserved: The Roles of Physician Assistants and Nurse Practitioners." Pp. 69–84 in *The Roles of Physician Assistants and Nurse Practitioners in Primary Care.* Edited by D. Kay Clawson and Marian Osterweis. Washington, DC: Association of Academic Health Centers, 1993.

Gordon, Ilene, and Julie R. Erickson. "Comparison of Rural and Urban Certified Nurse-Midwives in Arizona." *Journal of Nurse Midwifery* 38 (1993): 28–34.

Gupta, Gloria C., and Thomas R. Konrad "Allied Health Education in Rural Health Professional Shortage Areas of the United States." *Journal of the American Medical Association* 268 (1992): 1127–1130.

Hooker, Roderick S., Gloria C. Gupta, and Thomas R. Konrad. "Rural Health Training Sites for Physician Assistants." *Journal of the American Academy of Physician Assistants* 7 (1994): 353.

Murphy, John. "Taking the Less-Traveled Road." *Advance for Physical Therapists* 6 (1995): 8–9.

Muus, Kyle J., Terry D. Stratton, and Kazi A. Ahmed. "Medical Information Needs of Rural Health Professionals." *Texas Journal of Rural Health* 1st Quarter (1993): 10–15.

Office of Technology Assessment. *Health Care in Rural America.* OTA-H-434 (September). Washington, DC: U.S. Congress, Office of Technology Assessment, 1990.

Okimi, Patricia H., John C. Reed, and Jacqueline E. Bernhardt. "Continuing Education for Rural Nurses: A State Funded Program." *Texas Journal of Rural Health* 2nd Quarter (1992): 7–12.

Osterweis, Marian, and Stephen Garfinkel. "The Roles of Physician Assistants and Nurse Practitioners in Primary Care: An Overview of the Issues." Pp. 1–9 in *The Roles of Physician Assistants and Nurse Practitioners in Primary Care.* Edited by D. Kay Clawson and Marian Osterweis. Washington, DC: Association of Academic Health Centers, 1993.

Price, Diane. "PAs in Rural Practice." *Journal of the American Academy of Physician Assistants* 6 (1993): 423–427.

Rubenstein, David A. "The Rural Hospital in the Year 2001." *Texas Journal of Rural Health* 2nd Quarter (1989): 29–34.

Shi, Leiyu, Michael E. Samuels, Thomas R. Konrad, Thomas C. Ricketts, Carleen H. Stoskopf, and Donna L. Richter. "The Determinants of Utilization of Nonphysician Providers in Rural Community and Migrant Health Centers." *Journal of Rural Health* 9 (1993): 27–39.

Straub, La Vonne A., and W. Russell Wright. "Preparing Rural Students for Health Careers." *Texas Journal of Rural Health* 1st Quarter (1993): 16–27.

Travers, Karen L., and Robert B. Ellis. "Why PAs Leave Rural Practice: A Study of PAs in Maine." *Journal of the American Academy of Physician Assistants* 6 (1993): 412–417.

Walker, Mary. "Non-Physician Health Professionals and Rural Health Care." *Texas Journal of Rural Health* 2nd Quarter (1991): 8–12.

Willis, Judith B. "Barriers to PA Practice in Primary Care and Rural Medically Underserved Areas" *Journal of the American Academy of Physician Assistants* 6 (1993): 418–422.

Wright, Kathleen A. "Management of Agricultural Injuries and Illness." *Nursing Clinics of North America* 28 (1993): 253–266.

Nursing Homes

Licensed health care facilities that provide long-term services to chronically impaired people of all ages. Rural nursing homes are an important source of long-term care in rural areas. Access to nursing homes, unlike that to many other care-providing institutions, may be better in rural than in urban areas. However, it is unclear whether the quality of care afforded to rural nursing home residents is better or poorer than that given to urban nursing home residents. The conversion of small rural hospitals to skilled nursing facilities has improved access to skilled nursing care in rural areas. Findings regarding the quality of care in rural facilities suggest that they may provide adequate palliative care but are less adequate at providing aggressive rehabilitative services. There is clear although limited evidence that nursing homes in rural areas may be highly integrated into their local communities. In order for rural nursing homes to be successful in the future, they must ensure high-quality care, maintain community integration, and serve as catalysts for related home and community services.

An Important Source of Care

Long-term care services provided by nursing homes include assistance with activities of daily living, such as help with eating, dressing, toileting, bathing, and movement. Such assistance may be needed by people of any age, but older people are more likely than others to require it. There is some evidence that rural older Americans have higher levels of chronic impairment than do other elders, which could lead to a greater need for long-term care services, including nursing home care. However, rural elders appear less likely than urban elders to view nursing homes as an appropriate arrangement for meeting their long-term care needs (McAuley and Blieszner 1986).

Access

Although access to many kinds of health and long-term care services is generally more limited in rural areas, this is not true of nursing home care. Nonmetropolitan areas of the United States tend to have substantially more nursing home beds relative to their populations than do urban areas (62 certified beds per 1,000 rural elders, versus 45 per 1,000 elders in metropolitan settings), even though the latter tend to have larger facilities (Shaughnessy 1994). However, it appears that rural areas have a much higher variation in nursing home beds per 1,000 older people than urban areas.

Characteristics of Residents

There is evidence that residents of rural nursing homes are younger and somewhat less functionally impaired than urban nursing home residents. Greene (1984) hypothesized that this difference may be the result of limited community services in rural areas, leading to the premature institutionalization of rural elders. However, findings based upon national data have been incongruent, with some showing better functioning among rural nurs-

A retirement center and nursing home in Albert City, Iowa.

ing home patients and others showing no significant difference between rural and urban patients (Dor et al. 1990; McConnel and Zetman 1993).

Development of Swing Beds

One of the most interesting developments in rural institutional long-term care has been the growth of swing beds in small rural hospitals. Rural hospital swing beds provide packages of skilled nursing services that fall between the acute care offered by hospitals and the traditional long-term care services provided in nursing homes. Swing-bed care has been called "short-term long-term care" or "sub-acute care." Relatively few rural nursing homes can provide this type of skilled care, so hospital swing beds appear to offer a very useful service in rural areas. The development of rural hospital swing beds was supported by the Omnibus Budget Reconciliation Act of 1980 as a way to improve the financial viability and financial resources of rural nursing homes and to extend access to cost-effective nursing home care in rural areas.

Currently, about half of all eligible rural hospitals (those with fewer than 50 beds) offer swing beds. Evaluations of the swing-bed program found that swing-bed patients are hospitalized less frequently and are more likely to experience improvements in their activities of daily living than residents of rural nursing homes. Swing-bed patients see physicians ten times more frequently than nursing home patients, and they received more lab tests and other services, suggesting a more aggressive therapeutic regimen. Swing-bed care is less expensive than skilled nursing home care but offers similar or better overall quality. The rural hospital swing-bed program appears to have improved the quality of long-term care in

rural areas and increased access to long-term care services without increasing costs. The overall success of rural hospital swing beds has led some to call for similar programs in urban areas.

Quality of Care

The sparse evidence regarding quality of care indicates that rural nursing homes may provide adequate chronic, palliative care, but they may do less well than urban facilities or rural hospital swing beds at providing high-quality, aggressive rehabilitation services (Shaughnessy, Schlenker, and Kramer 1990). There is some anecdotal evidence (Shaughnessy 1994) that staff in rural nursing homes are more mindful of their patients' functional and support needs than is typical in urban facilities. The difference may be due to lower staff turnover in rural facilities or to the smaller size of rural communities and facilities, which promotes continuing social interaction between nursing-home staff and administration with family members and friends of patients both within and outside the facility. However, there may be some quality-of-care problems in rural facilities, such as poor training and the overprovision of assistance with activities of daily living, which could limit rehabilitation or even hasten functional decline in some nursing home residents.

Community Ties and Permeability

In an in-depth, multimethod study of one 90-bed rural nursing home in Kentucky, Rowles (1996) identified a high level of economic, social, psychological, and historical integration between the nursing home and the rural community, leading to a sense of community ownership and support for the facility. Rowles also discovered a high level of permeability, or consistent exchange, of people and communication between the nursing home and the community. This high degree of permeability made it possible for many patients in the facility to continue to feel that they were residents of the rural community. According to Rowles, the level of integration and permeability that existed in this rural nursing home is far more feasible in rural than urban areas. However, the trend toward medicalization of long-term care may limit the integration of rural nursing homes with their communities.

Ensuring Success

The nursing home is likely to be a continuing component of long-term care in rural areas because institutional care is the best alternative for a select portion of chronically impaired individuals. Several related issues must be addressed in order to assure that rural nursing homes operate successfully and support the long-term care needs of impaired rural residents. These issues include: (1) how to assure the quality of rural nursing home care; (2) how to ensure that rural nursing homes and their residents maintain, to the fullest extent possible, their ties with the community; and (3) how to enhance the role of rural nursing homes as catalysts for improved community-based and home-care services, which are frequently limited in rural areas. Because of their flexibility, the specialized administrative and long-term care expertise of their staff, and the extraordinary level of visibility they experience within their communities, rural nursing homes may have strong potential to adapt themselves to meet the future long-term care needs of rural residents (Rowles 1994).

—William J. McAuley

See also
Elders; Health Care; Policy, Health Care; Senior Centers.
References
Dor, A., L. K. Dubay, M. Genevieve, and M. Perozek. "The Characteristics of Nursing Home Residents: An Urban-Rural Comparison." Working Paper No. 3971-01. Washington, DC: Urban Institute, 1990.
Greene, V. L. "Premature Institutionalization among the Rural Elderly in Arizona." *Public Health Reports* 99 (1984): 58–63.
McAuley, William J., and Rosemary Blieszner. "A Rural-Urban Comparison of Preferences Expressed by Elders for Long-term Care Arrangements." *Southern Rural Sociology* 4 (1986): 55–66.
McConnel, C. E., and M. R. Zetzman. "Urban/Rural Differences in Health Services Utilization by Elderly Persons in the United States." *Journal of Rural Health* 9 (1993): 270–280.
Rowles, Graham D., James A. Concotelli, and Dallas M. High. "Community Integration of a Rural Nursing Home." *Journal of Applied Gerontology* 15, no. 2 (June 1996): 188–201.
Shaughnessy, Peter W. "Changing Institutional Long-term Care to Improve Rural Health Care." Pp. 144–181 in *Health Services for Rural Elders*. Edited by Raymond T. Coward, C. Neil Bull, Gary Kukulka, and James M. Galliher. New York: Springer, 1994.
Shaughnessy, Peter W., Robert E. Schlenker, and Andrew M. Kramer. "Quality of Long-term Care in Nursing Homes and Swing-bed Hospitals." *Health Services Research* 25 (1990): 65–96.

Nutrition

The interaction between food and living things, encompassing physiological and biochemical processes and influenced by psychological, social, economic, environmental, and technological factors. Most rural Americans have an adequate intake of essential nutrients, but they do need help to improve their diets to comply with recommendations to decrease the intake of fat, saturated fat, and sodium. Delivery of nutrition education and other preventive and emergency food programs for the rural poor may be more difficult than in urban settings due to the logistical realities of rural living.

Recommendations for Rural Americans

Most Americans understand that diet plays an important role in causation and prevention of chronic diseases. Consensus now exists, based upon a number of national reports issued in the 1990s, about the urgent need for all Americans to decrease their intake of fat, saturated fat, cholesterol, and sodium, and to avoid putting on excess weight. Additionally, in order to ensure adequate intake of the recommended dietary allowances for essential nutrients, all Americans are urged to eat a variety of foods and especially to increase their consumption of fruits, vegetables, cereals, and grains, which are rich sources of vitamins, minerals, and fiber but are low in or devoid of fat. According to a nutritional guide put out by the U.S. Department of Agriculture (USDA), Americans should consume at least 5 servings of fruits or vegetables every day and 6 to 11 servings of bread, grain, pasta, or rice. The U.S. Department of Health and Human Services' Healthy People 2000 Nutrition Objectives also address the need to increase calcium intake, especially by youth between the ages of 12 and 24, and pregnant and lactating women, due to the essential role of calcium in formation and maintenance of bones and teeth and as a factor modifying the risk for developing osteoporosis later in life.

These recommendations apply to rural and urban dwellers alike, since the diets of the two groups are quite similar. The major sources of information about the diets of Americans are the National Health and Nutrition Examination Survey (NHANES) and the Continuing Survey of Food Intakes of Individuals (CSFII). Data collection and analysis for NHANES III, the most comprehensive nutrition monitoring survey to date, and CSFII are currently under way. Both surveys show that many Americans fail to consume a diet that includes foods from all the major food groups. NHANES II data show that 24 percent of Americans reported having eaten no dairy products, and 46 percent and 18 percent no fruits and vegetables, respectively, on the day of interview (Kant 1991). Only 29 percent of respondents had eaten the recommended number of servings of fruit and 29 percent, of grain; 51 percent had eaten the recommended number of servings of dairy products; 61 percent, of vegetables; and 71 percent, of meat. Data from CSFII corroborated the study by Kant et al. (1991), showing that even greater numbers of Americans reported no intake of at least one food group. Based on data analysis using the USDA's 1989 to 1991 CSFII and new methodologies for quantifying fruit and vegetable intake developed at the National Cancer Institute, the average intake by the general population is approximately four servings of fruits and vegetables per day, one fewer than the minimum recommended. The high cost of fruits and dairy products may partly account for the significant number of individuals failing to consume these foods, yet this is unlikely since persons in the highest income quartile showed disappointingly little improvement in food group consumption compared to lower-income respondents (Kant 1991).

Although dietary intake does not appear to differ significantly between rural and urban Americans, there is some evidence that blood cholesterol levels may be higher among individuals living in rural settings than in urban dwellers. While the reasons are unclear, traditional rural lifestyle may include diets that are somewhat higher in saturated fat.

Obesity is reportedly increasing rather than decreasing in the United States. This disturbing situation emphasizes the need to address physical activity and nutrition and lifestyle in educating children and youth as they establish patterns that will last their lives long.

Nutrition and Rural Elderly

Since one-quarter of individuals over the age of 65 reside in rural areas, several researchers have studied the diet of rural elders. As these analyses tend to target specific rural populations, they may not be informative about the diets of rural elderly in other locations. Lee et al. (1991; 1993), in a study of rural elderly in 11 southern states, found that 53 percent of respondents consumed two-thirds or less of the recommended daily calories, and 55 percent, less than two-thirds the recommended amount of calcium. Intake of vitamin A, folate, vitamin C, thiamin, and iron was similarly low, with 38, 34, 31, 25, and 23 percent of the elderly subjects, respectively, eating less than two-thirds of the recommended levels.

In a subsequent report, these researchers reported that four out of ten elderly individuals (43.5 percent) in this southern sample reported following a recommended special dietary regimen or were following self-prescribed food practices. The most frequently encountered of these special diets was a sodium-restricted regime, followed by low-fat/low-cholesterol, diabetic, low-calorie, high-fiber, and low-fiber diets. The elderly respondents on these diets were indeed attempting to follow them, which is

demonstrated by the significant differences in mean intake of targeted nutrients between those individuals trying to limit them as compared to elders who were not following the special diet. However, the compliance rates for these special diets were still quite low.

Nutrition and Rural Children

Data from 1,392 children between the ages of one and ten obtained from a USDA 1987–1988 nationwide food consumption survey showed that urbanization had a significant effect on children's eating patterns. Children residing in nonmetropolitan areas (N=426) had markedly higher intakes of calories, total fat, saturated fat, cholesterol, and sodium than central city or suburban children in the Healthy People 2000 Nutrition Objectives—amounts far exceeding current USDA nutritional recommendations. Rural children's intakes of each category follow, with the recommended levels in parentheses: 37.8 percent of calories as fat (30 percent), 14 percent of calories as saturated fat (10 percent), and 2,537 milligrams of sodium (2,000 mg). These higher intakes by rural children are of concern, since they could lead to increased risk of chronic diseases including heart disease, cancer, and stroke. Studies of both children and elderly point to the need for nutritional education in rural areas.

Nutrition Programs for Rural Residents

A variety of nutrition programs that provide food or nutrition information are available to rural residents, primarily targeting children. The USDA is responsible for the National School Lunch and Breakfast Programs, the Child and Adult Care Food Program (which serves child and adult day care sites), the Special Supplemental Nutrition Program for Women, Infants, and Children (WIC), and Nutrition Education and Training Program (targeting educational settings and educators). Nutrition programs for older adults such as Home-Delivered Meals and Congregate Meals are provided through authorization of the Older Americans Act.

Nutritional education and health promotion information and services may be less available to rural people than to urban ones, due to the shortages of health agencies and professionals and the resultant need to travel long distances to obtain services, a problem that can be particularly difficult in bad weather. The Cooperative State Research, Education, and Extension Services, community education programs, local hospitals and clinics, government food programs such as WIC, and some television and radio programming and printed materials are all sources of credible nutrition and health information. Government requirements for nutritional contents labeling on food products are also useful to rural consumers who are interested in and aware of how to read these labels.

Rural residents obtain nutritional information less often from physicians and dietitians than do urban residents, and they more often rely on cookbooks for dietary information. Focus group interviews with rural residents have indicated that physicians need to clearly prescribe special diets and emphasize that these diets make a difference in disease outcomes (Crockett et al. 1990). Repetition may be needed for retention of information and for building skills in food purchasing and preparation. Due to special transportation problems and long distances to health care facilities, audio tapes or written materials sent to the home may be most effective in delivering nutritional education. Mailing nutritional education materials is an effective delivery method for rural residents; but alone, this method may not be effective in stimulating behavioral changes (Crockett et al. 1992).

Food Cost and Availability

People living in rural areas rely on smaller and fewer grocery stores, experience limited food purchasing power, and have limited access to fresh foods high in vitamins A and C and iron. Morris, Neuhauser, and Campbell (1992) studied food item availability in 33 persistently poor rural counties in 22 states by pricing 77 nutritious, low-cost foods in 51 supermarkets and 82 small or medium-sized stores. In 1989, the USDA valued the weekly cost of the Thrifty Food Plan foods at $75. When the foods on the USDA's Thrifty Food Plan were priced in rural grocery stores, the cost was $102, or 36 percent more than the maximum food-stamp allotment (Morris et al. 1992). They found 3.8 supermarkets per county in rural America, compared to 29 in urban settings, meaning that rural residents had to travel farther to reach a store. The average cost of the 77 foods in rural supermarkets was 8 percent higher than in larger grocery stores. The researchers also verified that fresh foods were very limited in the small to medium-sized stores. However, other studies have shown similar discrepancies in some urban locations as well. These factors may influence nutritional adequacy and the ability of residents to follow recommended dietary guidelines.

Food Insecurity

Food insecurity is the mental and physical condition that comes from not eating enough food due to insufficient economic, family, or community resources. It is more problematic for Americans living in rural areas because of higher poverty rates. In 1992, almost 17 percent of rural Americans had incomes below the official poverty line, compared to less than 13 percent of urban Americans.

In Texas, Friedman (1991) showed that the emergency food packages supplied in both urban and rural settings were sufficient to provide a well-balanced diet for three days. Urban boxes supplied more legumes, fortified breakfast cereals, and enriched rice, and therefore supplied significantly more niacin, riboflavin, vitamin C, iron, and fiber. Rural boxes contained more bacon and canned soups and had significantly more sodium. However, Stevens, Grivetti, and McDonald (1992) found no differences between urban and rural residents in the nutrient content of home-delivered meals. Adequacy of emergency food boxes may be irrelevant if rural families do not seek the boxes in times of hunger. Some evidence indicates that rural values of self-reliance may deter families from seeking help when it is needed. Alleviating the problem of food insecurity is more difficult in rural areas than urban ones, due to the isolation and relative lack of emergency food services.

A very important nutritional issue for rural Americans is compliance with dietary recommendations that reduce the risk of developing chronic diseases. Also, poverty and problems of access to nutritional information, programs, and services must be overcome to ensure optimal nutrition for all rural Americans.

—*Susan J. Crockett and Joyce M. Merkel*

See also
Food Safety; Policy, Food.
References
Crockett, Susan J., Karen E. Heller, Joyce M. Merkel, and Jane M. Peterson. "Assessing Beliefs of Older Rural Americans about Nutrition Education: Use of the Focus Group Approach." *Journal of the American Dietetic Association* 90, no. 4 (April 1990): 563–567.
Crockett, Susan J., Karen E. Heller, Lois H. Skauge, and Joyce M. Merkel. "Mailed-home Nutrition Education for Rural Seniors: A Pilot Study." *Journal of Nutrition Education* 24, no. 6 (November–December 1992): 312–315.
Friedman, B. J. "Urban and Rural Food Agencies Provide Adequate Nutrition to the Hungry." *Journal of the American Dietetic Association* 91, no. 12 (December 1991): 1589–1590.
Kant, Ashima K., Gladys Block, Arthur Schatzkin, Regina G. Ziegler, and Marion Nestle. "Dietary Diversity in the US Population, NHANES II, 1976–1980." *Journal of the American Dietetic Association* 91, no. 12 (December 1991): 1526–1531.
Lee, C. J., J. Tsui, E. Glover, L. Glover, M. Kumelachew, A. P. Warren, G. Perry, S. Godwin, S. K. Hunt, M. McCray, and F. E. Stigger. "Evaluation of Nutrient Intakes of Rural Elders in Eleven Southern States Based on Sociodemographic and Life Style Indicators." *Nutrition Research* 11 (1991): 1383–1396.

Lee, Chung Ja, Ann P. Warren, Sandria Godwin, Jean C. Tsui, Geraldine Perry, Sharon K. Hunt, Rafida Idris, Retia Scott Walker, Hattie F. Evans, Flavelia E. Stigger, and Sylvia S. Leftwich. "Impact of Special Diets on the Nutrient Intakes of Southern Rural Elderly." *Journal of the American Dietetic Association* 93, no. 2 (February 1993): 186–188.

Morris, Patricia McGrath, Linda Neuhauser, and Cathy Campbell. "Food Security in Rural America: A Study of the Availability and Costs of Food." *Journal of Nutrition Education* 24, no. 1 (January–February 1992): 52S–58S.

Sizer, Frances Sienkiewicz, and Eleanor Noss Whitney. *Hamilton and Whitney's Nutrition: Concepts and Controversies.* 6th ed. St. Paul, MN: West Publishing, 1994.

Stevens, Debbi A., Louis E. Grivetti, and Roger B. McDonald. "Nutrient Intake of Urban and Rural Elderly Receiving Home-delivered Meals." *Journal of the American Dietetic Association* 92, no. 6 (June 1992): 714–718.

U.S. Department of Agriculture, Human Nutrition Information Service. *Making Healthy Food Choices.* Home and Garden Bulletin No. 250. Washington, DC: Government Printing Office, 1993.

Organic Farming

The process of producing wholesome crops and livestock without synthetic fertilizer or pest controls, through the creation of healthy soil and complex biological systems. Organic farming was the first type of farming practiced, and it has a history stretching back many centuries. In the last 200 years, synthetic fertilizers and pest controls were developed, and the methods of organic farming were gradually phased out. Fifty years ago, J. I. Rodale reintroduced organic farming to the United States, with the intent of maintaining healthy soil, food, and people. Today, many in the farming industry have returned to organic methods in response to a world deeply concerned about the health of people and their environment.

Industrialized Farming

The industrialization of American farming began in colonial times. Farming was the basis of the colonial economy, and most territorial expansion and settlement were done by farmers. Some settlers formed friendships with Native Americans, who showed them how to grow native crops like corn, squash, beans, and herbs. By the late eighteenth century, wealthy landowners, such as George Washington and Thomas Jefferson, saw farming as a way to show that the newly formed United States was a successful nation. This political motive, along with the need to feed a growing population, led to the development of industrialized farming, or the creation of farms modeled after factories.

Further technical developments continued this pattern. In Germany, chemist Justus von Liebig discovered that adding mineral nutrients to the soil helped plants to grow more abundantly. This was the beginning of synthetic fertilizer use, and with the introduction of the first chemical pesticides shortly thereafter, many traditional agricultural practices were abandoned. In 1859, the first steam-powered tractor went on display, further reinforcing the move away from traditional practices. Even then, there was concern for the new methods. President Lincoln questioned the direction farming was taking and warned that in the future, large industrial farms may not be sustainable.

J. I. Rodale Introduces Organic Farming

After World War I, industrial farming methods were expanded and intensified through the introduction of single crop plantings and synthetic fertilizer. By the beginning of World War II, industrialized farming was standard. In 1941, J. I. Rodale bought a run-down farm in Pennsylvania and decided to grow food for his family in the healthiest way possible. Rodale was concerned that many members of his family had died at an early age, almost all from heart attacks. He read the works of Sir Albert Howard, who had done scientific research in India. Howard had recognized the value of returning good nutrients to the soil by using compost and knew that poor soil could affect the health of the lands, and consequently, the human body. Rodale came to believe that the relationship of soil to healthy plants was the missing link to healthy people. Rodale was also inspired by F. H. King's *Farmers of Forty Centuries* and Lord Walter Northbourne's *Look to the Land*, where the term "organic farming" first appeared. Rodale started to publish his *Organic Gardening and Farming* magazine in 1942, and wrote *Pay Dirt* in 1945 and *Organic Front* in 1948.

Using the word "organiculture," Rodale began to spread his ideas. Initially, organic farming was not accepted by farmers, the government, or the academic

Farmers harvest soybeans on an organic farm. Organic farming has undergone tremendous growth in the last decades of the twentieth century in response to the demand for healthier products.

community. By the 1950s and 1960s, however, a growing band of gardeners, farmers, and traditionalist communities such as the Amish had adopted organic methods. In 1962, Rachel Carson's consciousness-raising *Silent Spring* alerted people to the effects of agricultural chemicals on the environment and human health. The week before Rodale died, in 1971, the *New York Times* carried a cover feature story about him. His ideas and the organic movement were beginning to gain recognition.

Establishing Scientific Credibility

J. I. Rodale's son, Robert, realized the need for greater scientific credibility in organic farming. This realization led him to seek a strong research program, and thus he founded the Rodale Research Center in 1971, on a 305-acre farm in Maxatawny, Pennsylvania. The farm, like most in the area, had been chemically treated for many years, and the research program was to study the introduction of organic methods. To do this, a partnership was formed with a neighbor who agreed to farm according to

the methods set out by the center. The neighbor was initially skeptical; however, within a few years, he saw yields of corn on the farm equal or exceed those of neighboring farms, his costs were lower, and the methods were safer because of the reduced use of chemicals. He then changed his own farm to an organic one. This success story and the growing popularity of organic farming led to the need to provide specialized information to the burgeoning number of organic farmers. The need was met in 1979 with the publication of the *New Farm* magazine, which grew out of *Organic Gardening*.

In 1980, a U.S. Department of Agriculture (USDA) team under the Carter administration gave the first official governmental recognition to organic gardening's merit. The team's report stated that the soil is a living system and must be fed so that the activity of beneficial organisms in the soil will not be restricted. Team members discovered organic farms of all sizes were productive, efficient, and well-managed, and that their practices controlled soil erosion, minimized water pollution, and conserved energy. The report praised organic farmers for their unique, innovative methods of soil management for pest control. It concluded that much could be learned from these farmers and that research and educational programs should be developed to better serve their needs.

The Conversion Project was started in 1981 at the Rodale Research Center to develop scientifically reliable statistics showing that organic farming can be as productive and profitable as conventional farming, and the effort continues today. Also in 1981, Robert Rodale coined the term "regenerative agriculture." This concept meant that soil could be regenerated when farmers broke the bonds of solidified thinking and became fluid in their ability to adapt, and so through chaos found a new, regenerated way of being. Just as a forest regenerates after a forest fire, so farmers must keep regenerating the soil, which must continually be reborn and revitalized.

U.S. Government Supports Sustainable Agriculture

In 1985, Congress authorized the Low Input Sustainable Agriculture program, or LISA. Funds were provided for projects to answer questions of farmers and researchers searching for ways to reduce off-farm inputs. Appropriations climbed from nearly $4 million in 1988 to more than $115 million in 1996. Several events occurred in 1990 relating to organic farming. First, a National Academy of Sciences report on alternative agriculture concluded that alternative farming systems are practical and provide economical ways to maintain yields, conserve soil, maintain water quality, and lower farm operating costs. Second, part of the Farm Bill called for federal organic certification standards. The USDA appointed a standards board, whose recommendations were implemented in 1996. Third, the nonprofit Rodale Institute was officially formed. The institute expanded beyond research to include educational outreach. Programs in Senegal, Guatemala, Russia, and China helped farmers to regain what they lost through the years when they attempted to industrialize.

Today's Organic Farmers

The Organic Farming Research Foundation can document about 5,000 certified organic farmers as of 1997. Through contacts at the farm, retail, and commercial levels, the foundation has gathered data indicating that an additional 8,000 farmers produce crops or livestock in organic management systems. The USDA reported that 1.13 million acres were used in organic agriculture in 1994, with nearly half that amount devoted to pasture and rangeland. Other sectors included 380,000 acres for human food crops, 174,500 for livestock feed crops, and 17,495 for cotton. Sales of organic produce have climbed steadily by more than 10 percent since 1988. The *Natural Foods Merchandiser*, an industry periodical, updates a careful statistical analysis annually that showed gains of more than 22 percent each year between 1990 and 1996. U.S. gross sales of all organic products hit $3.5 billion in 1996 and should reach $6 billion before 2000.

Many farmers who market their crops and livestock conventionally use some regenerative practices to cut input costs, increase biodiversity, clean land and water, protect the health of their families, and earn the respect of their communities as careful stewards of natural resources. Fred Kirschenman, a North Dakota organic farmer, observes that today's farmers are more concerned with safer ways to farm. They believe that healthy soil is the foundation for healthy crops that can resist disease, out-compete weeds, and provide healthy food for healthy people. They take special care to encourage good physical properties of the soil with abundant populations of microbes, earthworms, and other soil life. This helps to protect the environment and prevent erosion.

Organic farmers use complex crop rotations that alternate row crops with close-growing crops such as small grains or forages. They rotate crops like corn and other grains, which remove nitrogen from the soil, with legumes, which add free nitrogen from the air to the soil. Between cash crops, organic farmers often grow cover crops and "green manure" crops to improve the soil; these plants are not harvested but instead are plowed under to feed the soil. Such diverse rotations help to control weeds, insects, diseases, and other pests.

Livestock are an integral part of an organic farm because animals consume forages grown in complex rotations and help to recycle the nutrients to the fields through the manure they produce. The manure is managed carefully, often composted before it is applied to the fields so that the nutrients are not washed into groundwater or surface water, causing pollution. Composted soil has more stable nutrients, holds water better, encourages abundant root growth, and protects crops from soil disease. Leaves collected from municipalities are another source of organic matter that is turned into compost to improve the soil.

Organic farmers often sell their produce directly to the consumer to eliminate the middle person. The challenge for the future is to grow the produce as closely as possible to consumers. Consumers are willing to pay a higher price for organic produce because of the high quality, better taste, and freedom from pesticides. The concern for a healthier lifestyle is gaining momentum.

Today there is a network of farmers helping each other to recapture the best that was lost through the years before the introduction of chemical fertilizers. They are refining traditional practices by what is being learned today from studies of the soil and natural surroundings. They are learning how to close the circle that moves to the rhythm of life as it describes the harmonious whole.

—*Ardath Rodale*

See also

Agrichemical Use; Agriculture, Alternative; Biodiversity; Conservation, Soil; Cropping Systems; Farm Management; Groundwater; Land Stewardship; Pest Management.

References

Howard, Sir Albert. *An Agricultural Testament.* London: Oxford University Press, 1940. Reprint, Emmaus, PA: Rodale Press, 1979.

King, F. H. *Farmers of 40 Centuries: Or Permanent Agriculture in China, Korea, and Japan.* London: Cape, 1928. Reprint, Emmaus, PA: Rodale Press, 1979.

Kirschenman, Frederick. *Switching to a Sustainable System: Strategies for Converting from Conventional/Chemical to Sustainable/Organic Farm Systems.* Windsor, ND: Northern Plains Sustainable Agriculture Society, 1988. Reprint, Emmaus, PA: Rodale Press, Holding Library, 1996.

Lampkin, Nicolas. *Organic Farming.* Ipswich, UK: Farming Press Books, 1980.

National Research Council. *Alternative Agriculture.* Washington, DC: National Academy Press, 1980.

Northbourne, Walter Ernst Christopher James, Baron. *Look to the Land.* London: J. M. Dent and Sons, 1940.

Rodale, J. I. *Pay Dirt.* Emmaus, PA: Rodale Press, 1945.

———. *The Organic Front.* Emmaus, PA: Rodale Press, 1948.

Rodale, Robert D. *Land Reborn: The Triumph of Agriculture.* In press.

U.S. Department of Agriculture, National Agriculture Library. *Periodicals Pertaining to Alternative Farming Systems.* Beltsville, MD: Alternative Farming Systems Information Center, 1993.

———. *Sustainable Agriculture in Print: Current Books.* Beltsville, MD: Alternative Farming Systems Information Center, 1993.

Parks

Areas of open space available for public use and enjoyment. Parks come in all shapes and sizes and can be found in the smallest villages or the largest cities. Parks and open space are integral parts of a community and provide opportunities to enjoy the rural outdoors and our natural resources.

Community and Rural Parks

Throughout America's history, parks and recreation lands have played an important role in the cultural and social growth of its citizens. In the earliest settlements in the eastern part of the country, there were lands set aside as commons for general public use. The community parks of today evolved from the commons or village square of the past, as the concept spread westward.

The village square often was located in the center of a small rural community and was the focal point of social activities. The village bandstand was used not only for band concerts, but was also the platform from which great political and philosophical speeches and debates emanated. Special events, such as ice cream socials, community picnics, family reunions, and various contests were held and continue to be held in the village park or square. The business district often grew up around the commons or square, and the communities continued to grow in ever expanding circles around the square. Many larger cities can trace their origins to such a starting point.

Another derivation of this concept was the courthouse square in the county seats of rural America. Many classic architectural masterpieces are preserved throughout the country in the courthouse squares, which in many cases also functioned as community parks. Many old courthouses ceased to be functional and have been converted into historical museums. With this change in usage, the structures and parklike settings take on a different cultural character, but they are still there for public enjoyment.

The community school also was a focal point in rural areas. If enough land is associated with the school to provide facilities such as playgrounds, ball fields, and tennis courts, and if there is a gymnasium, the school functions as the community park and recreation center for the rural school district. Small rural communities and the surrounding agricultural area tend to provide parks and recreation facilities on a less formal basis (in other words, there are generally no special park districts or village park departments). Instead, these communities tend to rely on ad hoc committees and more volunteer participation to provide these amenities and activities.

With the demise of rural school systems through consolidation of districts and other mechanisms for efficiency, the older schools and associated land became surplus to educational needs. However, from the viewpoint of the community and rural areas, the structures and grounds are important elements to sustain a quality of life in these rural settings. Sometimes the buildings or parts of the buildings can be retained for community use, while in other instances the structures are razed and the land retained as a village or township park. Thus, these facilities, paid for by local taxes, continue to benefit the people who initially paid for them, or their descendants. It is important for the viability of rural areas and communities to have parks close to residents' homes, in the neighborhood or the township.

In the hierarchy of U.S. parks and park systems, most lands committed to parks and designated as open

Picnickers on the shore of Lake Louise in Mt. Rainier National Park, Washington.

space are found in rural or remote areas. This entry initially focused on the commons or village square because these areas were the basis for the park system concept. They were the precursors of our city, county, regional, state, and national park systems. With the exception of the city and urban park systems, all the other systems are located primarily in rural areas. The parks are found in rural areas because they are the primary locations for natural resources and provide the necessary land base.

National Parks

The United States has not been very progressive in land-use policies, but it did originate two land policies of world-wide significance—the creation of a national park system policy and the Tennessee Valley Authority policy. Our national park system policy has attracted the attention of natural resource leaders throughout the world and

has been copied or adapted in various ways by many foreign countries (Ise 1961).

The creation of our national park system came about as a result of the rapid expansion of the western frontier after the Civil War. Far-sighted leaders advocated conservation practices to ensure the protection of suitable lands and waters for future public enjoyment. There might have been little motivation to conserve at that time, when the store of these natural resources appeared inexhaustible; however, these leaders exerted a strong influence on national policy (Wirth 1980).

Congress acted as early as 1832 to reserve acreage in the Hot Springs, Arkansas, area for public use, and designated the first national park at Yellowstone in 1872. Not only was Yellowstone National Park the first of its kind in the United States, it also established a precedent for national parks throughout the world. In addition, Yellowstone was chosen for inclusion in the first group of World Heritage Areas, so designated in 1972, 100 years after its founding.

Until the early 1960s, almost all of the parks operated by the National Park Service were in rural areas, readily accessible to rural people, the reasons for establishing the national parks and related areas in the system were not compatible with the recreational needs of rural citizens. The primary intent of the national parks was to preserve areas of outstanding scenic beauty and cultural value and to make them accessible to urban and rural, domestic and foreign visitors alike.

State Parks

The success of the national park concept led to the establishment of state and county park systems throughout the country. There were a scattering of individual state parks in the 1860s, when California set aside Yosemite as a state park and later transferred it to the U.S. government as a national park. Other state parks established before 1900 include the Adirondack State Park in New York; Interstate Park, jointly established by Wisconsin and Minnesota; and Mackinac Island State Park, Michigan. All of these early parks were located in very remote rural areas, in some cases almost wilderness, so they were not much more accessible to rural populations than to urban ones.

The state park movement had its greatest boost as a result of the 1908 White House Conference on Conservation, called by President Theodore Roosevelt, who was well known for his interest in conservation of natural resources. This conference led to the creation of formal state park agencies in about one-third of the states over the next 15 years. This growth has continued slowly until today, when every state in this country has its own park system. The state parks are unique natural, cultural, or historic resources, and are predominantly located in rural settings where these unique sites are found. Therefore, the surrounding rural population has the easiest access to these sites. In some areas, the surrounding rural communities benefit substantially from the influx of visitors and the money that visitors are willing to spend in and near the parks.

County and Metropolitan Park Systems

The first county park systems to be established included Essex County, New Jersey, in 1895; Milwaukee County, Wisconsin, in 1897; and Nassau County, New York, in 1898. Today there are hundreds of county-level systems around the country with titles such as county park

department, county park and recreation commission, county forest preserve district, county conservation district, or county forestry and park department. Whatever their titles, all serve the citizens of and visitors to a particular county by helping meet their park, recreation, and open space needs (Weir 1928).

Like national parks, most of the county park and open space lands are in rural settings and therefore are readily accessible to rural residents in a county. Rural residents often relate more directly to county park systems. Since these residents are not a part of an incorporated area, they do not find it convenient to use facilities or participate in programs offered by metropolitan park systems. In some areas, if families are not taxpayers in a particular jurisdiction, they are precluded from participation in recreational activities or must pay a registration premium for participation.

The county park and open space areas in many metropolitan areas that were once in rural settings are now "green oases in the urban desert." These areas can still be used by the rural population, but they are not as accessible or inviting as they once were. Many choice county areas with outstanding natural resource attributes have been severely and adversely affected by an increased use load resulting from a burgeoning and encroaching population around them.

The rapidly expanding metropolitan areas led to the establishment of multicounty or metropolitan park systems around a few major population centers. This concept provides a broader tax base than is possible from a single county and allows the purchase of choice natural resource lands out in the more rural counties, where such land is still available. Examples of this type of system are: the Huron-Clinton Metro Park System, a six-county system around Detroit, Michigan; the Maryland–National Capital Park and Planning Commission, on the north and west sides of Washington, D.C.; the Oakland Bay Regional Park District, on the east side of San Francisco Bay; and the Hennepin Regional Park System, in the Minneapolis, Minnesota, area. This type of system should be more prevalent in the major metropolitan areas to serve both rural and urban populations.

Forests and Special Use Areas

Other natural resource–rich public lands, such as county, state, national, and industrial forestlands, cover over 300 million acres, most of which is open for a wide variety of recreational uses. Many of the outstanding scenic and recreational areas of these forests rival the parks operated by companion park agencies. Rural communities surrounded by public lands depend on sustainable use of these areas to maintain their economies. Recreational uses bring in visitors from urban areas and are an important source of revenue for rural counties. One of the benefits of this public/private-sector partnership is managing the natural resource base to maintain the economic and intrinsic values derived from these resources.

The relatively recent focus on buying up abandoned railroad rights-of-way and converting them to trails of various types provides one of the best examples of the greenway concept, a way of connecting rural areas to the urban environment. Linear patterns such as drainways, stream corridors, power line easements, and canals present opportunities to create greenways that cut across rural-urban imaginary boundaries. Trail systems developed in conjunction with greenways also can connect urban areas through the pastoral rural scene so that recreationists in both areas have mutual enjoyment.

Although financial return is not the basic intent of most trail systems, there can be an economic benefit to people living near a trail. They have the opportunity to provide services to trail users, such as bike, snowmobile, or horse rentals; camping; bed and breakfast; or food or other types of supplies. Some rural communities and individuals capitalized on such opportunities and benefited substantially. For example, a 1992 study by the National Park Service and Pennsylvania State University, *The Impacts of Rail-Trails,* examined three trails, the Heritage Trail in Iowa, the St. Marks Trail in Florida, and the Lafayette Trail in Louisiana. The study found that "use of the sample trails generated significant levels of economic activity.... The amount of 'new money' brought into the local trail county was $630,000, $400,000, and $294,000 annually for the respective trails (page ii)."

All citizens benefit to some degree from the country's diverse park systems. All major cities and most smaller communities and villages have parks, if not extensive park systems, available to residents. Rural residents can benefit from the various parks and park systems to an equal or greater degree than urban residents because usually they are in closer proximity to the resource-based areas operated by township, county, state, and national agencies. There is no shortage of parks and open space in rural areas in general, although there may be certain locations

in this country where parks and open space may still be at a premium. Continued planning to obtain and develop rural park and recreation areas is still badly needed in many areas because land-use planning has been tagged with an unfair connotation and felt to be undemocratic. If the parks and recreation needs of rural citizens are to be met in the future, there must be better land-use planning today.

—*Robert D. Espeseth*

See also
Camps; Development, Community and Economic; Environmental Protection; Land Stewardship; Regional Planning; Wilderness; Wildlife.
References
Ise, John. *Our National Park Policy: A Critical History.* Baltimore, MD: Johns Hopkins University Press, 1961.
Lapping, Mark B., Thomas L. Daniels, and John W. Keller. *Rural Planning and Development in the United States.* New York: Guilford Press, 1989.
Miller, S. *The Economic Benefits of Open Space.* Portland: Maine Coast Heritage, 1992.
National Park Service. *Economic Impacts of Protecting Rivers, Trails and Greenway Corridors.* Washington, DC: Government Printing Office, 1990.
National Park Service and Pennsylvania State University. *The Impacts of Rail-Trails: A Study of Users and Nearby Property Owners from Three Trails.* Washington, DC: Government Printing Office, 1992.
Weir, H. L. *Parks: A Manual of Municipal and County Parks.* New York: A. Barnes and Co., 1928.
Wirth, Conrad. *Parks, Politics and People.* Norman: University of Oklahoma Press, 1980.

Pasture

A grazing management unit separated from other units by fencing and devoted to forage production for harvest by grazing animals (Barnes 1995). This entry addresses the differences in the two main types of pasture found in America, management inputs required for each, and grazing management systems used in pastures.

Types of Pastures

Pastures are broadly divided into two categories, rangelands and pastureland. Rangelands are lands on which the native vegetation is predominantly grasses, grasslike plants, forbs, and shrubs suitable for grazing. Rangelands are the primary land type found in the world and comprise 70 percent of the land surface area of the earth (Holechek, Pieper, and Herbel 1995). Most rangelands in the United States are located west of the Mississippi River and account for 62 percent of the total land area.

Pastures consist largely of land that is unsuitable for crop cultivation, so it is used for the production of red meat and dairy products through the grazing of cattle.

Most rangelands are unsuitable for cultivation due to their semi-arid nature, excessive topographical relief, and lack of soil fertility. Because rangelands are unsuited to cultivation, their primary use is to convert solar energy captured by native plant species into red meat, milk, and fiber via the grazing ruminant.

Immediately west of the Mississippi River, there is adequate precipitation to support the rangeland ecotype classified as tallgrass prairie. The predominant forage species are little bluestem, big bluestem, Indian grass, and switchgrass. Available moisture declines from east to west, and the tallgrass prairie gives way to the short-grass prairie of the western Great Plains. The predominant forage species of this ecosystem are buffalo grass and blue grama, whereas in the intermontane region, wheat grasses and fescues are prevalent. In the arid country typical of west Texas, New Mexico, Arizona, and Nevada, or in the intermontane desert country of Utah, various shrubs such as mesquite, sagebrush, and junipers predominate. Many of the shrubs are classified as weed species with little value for livestock grazing because of unpalatable compounds or defensive mechanisms such as spines. These same shrubs, however, play an important role as wildlife food and cover.

Grazing systems commonly used on rangelands include continuous or season-long, deferred rotation, seasonal-suitability, best-pasture, rest-rotation, high intensity/low frequency, and short-duration (Holechek et al. 1995). Range grasses must be allowed rest between grazing events. Rest allows plants to mature and build an adequate supply of carbohydrates in root systems for subsequent growth. When plants do not receive adequate rest from grazing events, desirable species decline in number and are replaced sequentially by species of reduced palatability and eventually by weed species with little or no nutritive value for grazing animals.

Prescribed burning and proper grazing management are used to encourage persistence and productivity of desirable forage species. Although there are other interrelated factors, absence of fire combined with overgrazing degrades many rangelands to brush communities with little or no grazing value. Fire is a natural part of the rangeland ecosystem and is a useful management tool to control brush encroachment and release grass species from competition.

When grazing management alone will no longer improve rangeland condition, herbicides are often used to reduce the number of weed species and encourage production of desirable forage species. Proper grazing management and prescribed burning are then used as management tools to extend the treatment life of the herbicide application.

Pasturelands are distinguished from rangelands by the periodic use of agronomic inputs to maintain introduced forage species. These species typically have the potential to increase dry matter production, tolerate close or continuous grazing, and respond to fertilization. Examples of popular introduced species are Bermuda grass and tall fescue.

Precipitation

The most limiting factor to forage production is moisture. With the exception of the coastal areas of Washington, Oregon, and northern California, the greatest annual precipitation in the continental United States occurs east of the Mississippi River. Long-term annual mean precipitation levels in the eastern states approach 16 cm, and areas along the Gulf Coast and Atlantic seaboard routinely receive in excess of 20 cm per year (Martin, Leonard, and Stamp 1976). Not surprisingly, most pastureland is found in areas where precipitation is adequate to support high levels of forage production. These areas include the southeastern states from east Texas to the Atlantic seaboard, the Midwest along both sides of the Ohio River, and the Northeast.

Soil Fertility

High levels of precipitation in the eastern United States have resulted in the formation of acid soils of reduced fertility, due to leaching of basic cations from the upper soil horizons. Thus, where most of the pastureland is located, lack of soil fertility and not of moisture is the common limiting factor to forage production. Unlike precipitation, however, this factor is under direct control by the manager.

The first step in amending the soil is to perform a soil analysis in order to determine the levels of nitrogen, phosphorus, and potassium in the soil, and the soil pH (soil acidity). Under certain circumstances, analyses for other nutrients may be required. Written recommendations for the level of each fertilizer nutrient required,

based on the yield goal for specific forage crops, are furnished to the producer by the laboratory conducting the analysis.

Nitrogen is an important element required for optimal plant growth and is positively correlated with nutritive value. Unfortunately, soil nitrogen is usually very low and generally ranges from 0.03 to 0.4 percent in the top 30 cm of cultivated soils (Tisdale, Nelson, and Beaton 1985). Industrially supplied sources of nitrogen (for example, ammonium nitrate, ammonium sulfate, and urea) are commonly used as fertilizer in agriculture.

An alternative method of supplying nitrogen to the soil is through the use of legumes. Legumes are plants that have a symbiotic relationship with host-specific *Rhizobia* bacteria. In the symbiotic relationship, the legume serves as a host plant for the bacteria, while the bacteria fixes atmospheric nitrogen into a form readily used by the plant. Forage legumes have the ability to provide the equivalent of 50 to 200 pounds of actual nitrogen per acre to other non–nitrogen fixing plants under good growing conditions, thus reducing the need for nitrogen fertilizer.

Other nutrients such as phosphorus, potassium, sulfur, and boron are applied as required, based upon the soil test recommendations. Only a soil analysis will provide this critical information.

Acid soils generally do not have direct negative effects on plant growth; however, indirect effects can hamper plant production. Soil nutrients, particularly phosphorus, are most available at near-neutral pH levels. Many producers, therefore, apply crushed limestone (lime) to increase soil pH and to enhance nutrient availability for optimal forage production.

Pasture Use

Forages produced in pastures are used in one of four methods: conserved forage (either hay or silage), green chop, or direct harvest by grazing animals. Regardless of how forage is used, two aspects of forage production remain under direct control of the manager: the fertility program (previously discussed) and the stage of maturity of the forage at harvest.

Forage maturity and nutritive value are inversely correlated; that is, as the forage increases in maturity, the nutritive value declines. Thus, immature plants are highest in both nutritive value and digestibility. Obviously, dry matter production increases with stage of maturity and a balance between nutritive value and production must be achieved. Harvest schemes for hay, silage, or green chop should be timed to obtain an optimal quantity of forage of high nutritive value. Grazing systems likewise should attempt to maintain forage in a relatively immature stage to enhance animal performance.

Hay for livestock is second only to corn as the most important U.S. agronomic crop. Hay is produced on 25 million hectares and is valued at over $11 billion to U.S. agriculture (Albrecht and Hall 1995). Species used as hay include alfalfa, timothy, orchard grass, wheat, oat, rye, annual ryegrass, wheat grass, Bermuda grass, Bahia grass, sorghum and sudan-type grasses, clovers, and native species.

Silage is another form of conserved forage, but unlike hay, it is stored in airtight containers (silos or individual large round bales) at higher moisture levels, generally 65 to 70 percent. The forage undergoes a reduction in pH due to anaerobic bacteria and stabilizes at a pH level between 3.6 to 4.2. Under this acid condition, forage nutritive value remains constant indefinitely. The most common forage utilized as silage is corn, but forage sorghums, alfalfa, cereal grains, and even Bermuda grass have been conserved as silage.

Green chop is a system in which forage is harvested mechanically and brought to the livestock for consumption. The use of green chop increases forage harvest efficiency and reduces forage waste. However, equipment costs are high and individual animal performance is typically reduced compared with other grazing systems.

Grazing Management

The manipulation of the grazing animal by the manager with a defined goal or objective in mind is known as grazing management. Proper grazing management should match forage nutritive value and availability with the nutrient requirements of grazing livestock. In many cases, the only management change required for improved efficiency is to develop a controlled breeding season that matches seasonal forage availability with nutrient requirements of gestating or lactating females or growing animals.

There is no single grazing system that can meet the requirements of all producers. Certain parcels of land lend themselves better to certain types of grazing systems. Management philosophies and experience levels of producers will likewise dictate how livestock will be manipulated. However, generalized grazing systems have been developed that facilitate livestock movement and enable producers to have improved control over the forage budgeting process, and these systems are discussed below. A critical point to remember is that grazing systems generally have less impact on animal performance than do soil fertility or stocking rate.

Continuous Stocking

Continuous stocking is popular because it requires the least input from the livestock producer, and at moderate stocking levels, it generally results in the highest individual animal performance when compared with rotational stocking systems. Improved individual animal performance associated with continuous stocking is due to increased diet selectivity by the animal. In contrast, grazing systems that involve livestock movement between pastures often force animals to consume forage that they might not otherwise select, reducing performance.

The major disadvantage of continuous stocking relates to the variable growth rate of forages. For example, during early spring, warm-season grasses experience rapid growth that necessitates a relatively heavy stocking rate for proper harvest efficiency. Later, during periods of reduced precipitation levels associated with summer, forage growth rates decline, requiring a reduction in stocking. If a variable stocking rate that matches varying forage levels is not used, pastures will either be overstocked or understocked. Overstocking combined with poor soil fertility can result in weed invasion, a reduced carrying capacity of the pasture, and decreased profitability of the enterprise.

Conversely, understocking results in patch (or spot) grazing. Patch grazing occurs when animals repeatedly graze the same area because the immature regrowth is more palatable and of higher nutritive value. Ungrazed areas increase in maturity, decline in nutritive value, and become increasingly less palatable. The wasted forage reduces the potential profit from the livestock operation.

To optimize forage use under continuous stocking, a variable stocking rate should be used and may be accomplished by adjusting either livestock numbers or pasture size. The use of inexpensive electric fencing allows producers to rapidly adjust pasture size and maintain the proper stocking rate relative to the forage growth rate. Simply opening or closing gates of a multi-paddock operation will accomplish the same result. Excess forage from the portion of the pasture not grazed during the rapid-growth phase should be cut as hay. Cutting excess forage for hay or silage is one of the most effective methods of implementing the variable stocking rate pasture-management scenario.

Another variation of continuous stocking involves the installation of a creep gate. In a creep-grazing system, younger animals have free access to separate pastures planted to forages of higher nutritive value, but the size of the creep gate prevents entry into the pasture by mature animals. Forage species typically used in creep-grazing systems include small grains, ryegrass, and clovers for fall and winter grazing. Sorghum, sudan-type grasses, pearl millet, annual lespedezas, and cowpeas are used in summer programs.

Rotational Stocking

Rotational stocking requires that a single pasture be subdivided into two or more smaller units not necessarily equal in size. Livestock are moved from one paddock to the other at alternating intervals. The concentration of livestock results in a temporarily overstocked condition and allows for a high forage harvest efficiency.

The optimum time to move livestock from one paddock to another is critical in rotational stocking and requires considerable management expertise. Tenure in a paddock may vary from 1 to 10 days per paddock, depending on climatic conditions and forage growth rates. Rotational stocking systems where livestock are moved on a calendar basis will not achieve optimum animal performance or forage use. Varying forage levels may require producers to skip one or more paddocks in the grazing rotation and to harvest skipped units for hay during periods of excess forage production.

Rotational stocking allows for better control of livestock than other methods of pasture management. Potential health problems may be observed at an earlier stage since the producer spends more time with the livestock. Rotational stocking early in the spring may help to control early weed species.

The primary disadvantage of rotational stocking is reduced individual animal performance because of reduced diet selectivity. Another disadvantage relates to the expense of additional fence construction, although this may be offset by the use of low-cost electric fencing. Additional water development also may be necessary, and the costs of labor involved in routinely moving livestock also must be taken into consideration.

Some forage species may warrant the use of rotational stocking. For example, weeping lovegrass, if not rotationally stocked, is patch grazed by livestock and quickly becomes excessively mature and unpalatable. Reseeding annual clovers should be rotationally stocked to promote seed production and stand persistence. The use of rotational stocking may also help to maintain the nutritive value of warm-season perennial grasses, thus improving animal performance somewhat. Rotationally

stocking cool-season forages may not be as important to the grazing animal, but rest between grazing events may allow for increased dry matter production.

A modification of rotational stocking known as forward creep grazing may enhance growing animal performance. The livestock herd is split into two groups; "first and last" or "leader and follower" grazers. The first grazers (leaders) are usually younger animals with a higher nutritive requirement compared with mature animals. The leaders graze a paddock first and obtain forage of the highest nutritive value. When approximately one-third of the forage has been consumed, the first grazers are rotated to a new paddock. The last grazers (followers) are then rotated into the paddock just vacated by the first grazers. The last grazers are generally mature animals with lower nutritive requirements.

Strip grazing is yet another technique of rotational stocking, which uses two portable fences (typically electric) to allot a small area of pasture for grazing. As with other rotational stocking systems, the temporarily overstocked condition results in a high harvest efficiency, although animal performance is typically reduced. Strip grazing allows forage to be consumed with a minimum amount of trampling of the remaining forage.

One final grazing system to be considered is limit grazing. With limit grazing, separate pastures are generally planted to annual species of high nutritive value. Livestock are allowed to graze the pastures on a limited basis, either a few hours per day or a few days per week. This system typically is used during the winter, when forage growth is limited. Allowing livestock to have adequate quantities of good hay or dormant standing forage and limited access to pastures planted to cereal grains or ryegrass enables spring-calving brood cows to maintain their body condition at a reduced cost. Calves born in the fall experience improved weight gains compared to calves wintered on hay only. Weight gains are achieved at less cost than for cattle wintered on concentrates.

The key to proper grazing management is to think through the process with respect to expectations and the inputs required for each system. The manager should seek an optimal balance between harvest efficiency, resource conservation, individual animal performance, and most important, the economic returns from the total enterprise. Using either a continuous or rotational stocking system can result in a profitable livestock operation, depending on the managerial expertise.

Good management is an essential element of a sound pasture program. Close attention to soil fertility, forage maturity at harvest, and grazing management will enhance the probability for maximum economic return, and thus the sustainability, of the forage production system.

—*Larry A. Redmon*

See also
Agronomy; Biodiversity; Dairy Farming; Livestock Production; Ranching; Regional Diversity; Soil.

References
Albrecht, Kenneth A., and Marvin H. Hall. "Hay and Silage Management." Pp. 155–162 in *Forages. Volume I: An Introduction to Grassland Agriculture.* 5th ed. Edited by Robert F. Barnes, Darrell A. Miller, and C. Jerry Nelson. Ames: Iowa State University Press, 1995.

Barnes, Robert F., Darrell A. Miller, and C. Jerry Nelson, eds. *Forages. Volume I: An Introduction to Grassland Agriculture.* 5th ed. Ames: Iowa State University, 1995.

Heitschmidt, Rodney K., and Jerry W. Stuth, eds. *Grazing Management: An Ecological Perspective.* Portland: Timber Press, 1991.

Hodgson, John. *Grazing Management Science into Practice.* New York: John Wiley and Sons, 1990.

Holechek, Jerry L., Rex D. Pieper, and Carlton H. Herbel. *Range Management: Principles and Practices.* 2d ed. Englewood Cliffs, NJ: Prentice-Hall, 1995.

Martin, John H., Warren H. Leonard, and David L. Stamp. *Principles of Field Crop Production.* 3d ed. New York: Macmillan Publishing Co., 1976.

Tisdale, Samuel L., Werner L. Nelson, and James D. Beaton. *Soil Fertility and Fertilizers.* 4th ed. New York: Macmillan Publishing Co., 1985.

U.S. Department of Agriculture. *Agricultural Statistics.* Washington, DC: U.S. Government Printing Office, 1993.

Pest Management

An ecological approach to insect control. Although dictionaries define pests as "any destructive insect," the term pest has no ecological validity. Any organism that competes with humans for available resources of food and fiber is both destructive and pestiferous. Thus, weeds, fungi, microorganisms, rodents, and birds can also be categorized as pests. Insects and related arthropods, however, comprise more than three-quarters of all animal species and are by far the most numerous of pest species. The concept of pest management was first developed as an ecological approach to insect control. This will be the frame of reference in this entry, although the principles emphasized could be applied equally well to other pest organisms.

Integrated Pest Management

Pest management is philosophically similar to the more familiar concepts of forest, game, and fisheries management, being an effort to optimize pest control tactics in an ecological and environmentally sound manner. Integrated pest management (IPM) has been variously defined as: (a) a system where all available techniques are evaluated and consolidated into a unified program to regulate pest populations so that economic damage is avoided and environmental disturbances are minimized, and (b) intelligent selection and integration of pest control actions that ensure favorable economic, ecological, and sociological consequences.

IPM has three primary goals: The first is to determine how the life system of the pest needs to be modified to reduce its numbers to tolerable levels, that is, below the economic threshold; the second is to apply biological knowledge and current technology to achieve the desired modification, or applied ecology; and the third is to devise pest control procedures compatible with economic and environmental quality constraints, or economic and social acceptance (Metcalf and Luckmann 1994). Thus, IPM procedures rely on protection and conservation of natural enemies: parasites, predators, and diseases that regulate the biological balance of pest populations. IPM rejects the regular or preventive use of broad spectrum insecticides and the general philosophy of species eradication, which is unworkable.

The establishment of IPM programs is based on identifying the pests to be managed in the agroecosystem, defining the economic injury level as the pest population density that causes enough injury to justify the cost of treatment, and establishing the economic threshold as the level of pest damage where control measures should be applied to prevent an increasing pest population from attaining the economic injury level.

Although the IPM philosophy is equally applicable to vast agricultural operations or to the home garden, and although the insect pests that are economically important may be the same for each crops, the methods of pest control that are optimal in the home garden are often impractical for the commercial grower. The cosmetic requirements for home production of fresh fruits and vegetables are markedly different from those of the canning industry. In general, labor-intensive procedures such as hand worming and picking of pests, which are highly useful in small-scale production, are completely impractical for production of row crops or in commercial fruit orchards.

Components of IPM Programs

IPM is a system to minimize pest damage through a combination of compatible tactics that make life difficult for

This mechanical sprayer dusts vines with fungicide at the Buena Vista Winery in Sonoma, California. In addition to pest control, the sprayer also fertilizes and waters the grapevines.

the pest and that are economically, environmentally, and socially acceptable. Although it is the pest that is to be managed, pest management is people-oriented. As long as the pest manager accepts the ecologically oriented philosophy of IPM, many old practices of pest control are acceptable components of pest management systems. Doing nothing is also a valid IPM alternative, as time often will restore ecological balance between the pest and its environment.

There are several widely used insect control components that almost invariably form the framework for successful IPM programs. These should be considered in the order presented to develop a successful program.

Ecosystem Planning. The most appropriate way to avoid major insect pest control problems is through careful choice of the crops to be planted and of the genetic varieties to be produced. To grow highly susceptible plant

species having major insect enemies, one must be prepared for the annual battle with pests and for the necessity of frequent use of insecticides. Examples include home growing of cabbage, cauliflower, broccoli, and eggplant; growing apples and peaches; and landscaping with white birch, honey locust, and sycamore. The tactic of cultivar choice is an especially important one for arborists, landscapers, or house gardeners who are ill prepared philosophically or strategically for unsightly or unpalatable pest damage. Often the most appropriate answer is to plant only species of garden plants, shrubs, and trees that are of high tolerance.

Plant species can be systematically rated for susceptibility to insect pest damage according to the following five categories: (1) they are practically immune; (2) they have few and minor problems; (3) they have a single important pest; (4) they have a devastating enemy;

and (5) they have several important pests (see table). In general, it is prudent for the home gardener to consider cultivating plants at the top of the line. These ratings apply to insect and mite problems encountered in the Midwest. Other factors, such as aesthetics, taste, food quality, and susceptibility to climate and plant diseases, must also guide the choice. A large number of vegetables belonging to categories (1) and (2) can be grown without problems from insect pests and diseases. Troubles can be expected with the higher categories (Metcalf and Luckman 1994).

Resistant Varieties. For most commercially grown crops, specific varietal cultivars differ considerably in their degree of susceptibility to attack by insect pests and plant diseases. This tactic of host plant resistance is a basic component of IPM, and the commercial planting of resistant varieties is of major importance to suppress insect pests such as those of corn (corn earworm and European corn borer), sorghum (chinch bug), barley (greenbug), wheat (Hessian fly and wheat-stem sawfly), alfalfa (spotted alfalfa aphid), and cotton (lygus bugs). There is a continuing struggle between plant breeders developing such resistant varieties and insect pests evolving resistant biotypes to overcome the varietal resistances. New techniques of transgenic biology are already producing new varietal cultivars incorporating major host resistant factors, and these may become important in IPM programs. However, the struggle between plants and pests will always represent a series of genetic accommodations leading to both new and superior cultivars and more vigorous insect pests.

Biological Control. The greatest single factor in keeping plant-feeding insects from overwhelming the rest of the world is that they are fed upon by other insects (Metcalf and Metcalf 1993). Such entomophagous insects are considered in two groups: predators that catch and devour smaller or more helpless creatures, and parasites (sometimes called parasitoids) that live in or on the bodies of host animals.

The science of biological control is little more than 100 years old, dating from the successful importation in 1888 of the Australian ladybird beetle, *Rodolia cardinalis,* to control the cottony cushion scale, *Iceya purchasi,* which was destroying California citrus groves. Recent estimates indicate that at least 70 species of important insect pests of the United States are partially or completely controlled by establishment and manipulation of parasites and predators.

Several categories of biological control are important to agriculture: First on the list is classical biological control, which involves the importation and establishment of foreign, natural enemies to control exotic pests that were controlled by these predators in the area of their original endemicity. Second, augmentation of natural enemies involves efforts to increase populations of parasites and predators by periodically releasing them into the environment. Third, conservation of natural enemies involves efforts to preserve and maintain existing populations of natural enemies by altering pesticide use patterns or changing crop management practices. Biological control is totally compatible with the use of resistant crop varieties; and the two tactics, which are relatively inexpensive and have high benefit-risk ratios, together serve as the foundation of modern IPM.

Chemical Control. The use of insecticides has been the major tactic for insect pest control for well over 100

Susceptibility of Selected Plants to Insect Pest Damage

Plant Type	Insect Pest Damage Categories				
	(1) Practically immune	(2) Few, minor problems	(3) Single important pest	(4) A devastating enemy	(5) Several important pests
Vegetable	beet, chard, Chinese cabbage, lettuce, radish, pea	mustard, spinach, sweet potato	asparagus, corn (early), onion, tomato	bean, broccoli, cauliflower, cucumber, eggplant, squash	cabbage, corn (late), melon, potato
Fruit	strawberry	blackberry, cherry, raspberry	apricot, currant, grape, plum	nectarine, pear, quince	apple, peach
Shade tree	sweet gum, tree of heaven	burr oak; ginkgo; Norway maple; Oriental plane; scarlet, red, and white oak; sugar maple, tulip tree	American plane, blue ash, Chinese elm, hickory, mountain ash, spruce, white pine	box elder, buckeye, catalpa, European linden, hackberry, honey locust, horse chestnut, Scotch pine, walnut, willow	American and European elm, black ash, black locust, cottonwood, green ash, Lombardy poplar, Scotch elm, silver maple, white birch

Source: Metcalf et al. (1994).

years. Insecticides are the only tool for IPM that is reliable for emergency action, when pest populations approach or exceed the economic threshold. According to a publication of the National Academy of Sciences (1969, 456–457): "Chemical pesticides will continue to be one of the most dependable weapons of the entomologist for the foreseeable future.... There are many pest problems for which the use of chemicals provide the only acceptable solution. Contrary to the thinking of some people, the use of pesticides is not an ecological sin. Their use is indispensable to modern society." However, much insecticide use has been ecologically unsound; and misuse, overuse, and injudicious use have been major factors in the growth of interest in IPM. The IPM concept seeks to maximize the advantages of pesticide use and to minimize its disadvantages.

As a general principle in IPM, insecticides should be used only as a last resort, when other carefully planned control measures have failed and emergency intervention is necessary. This use should be integrated thoroughly into the IPM program; in other words, an effort should be made to identify and utilize the insecticide least likely to seriously damage beneficial insects, to pose unacceptable health hazards to the user and the consumer of treated produce, and to adversely affect environmental quality. Another important factor to be considered is the effect of the insecticide application in the presence of insect pest populations that are genetically resistant to one or more of the major classes of insecticides (that is, organochlorines, organophosphates, carbamates, and pyrethroids).

Ready to use (RTU) insecticide products that are formulated in both pressurized and pump dispensers provide a very appropriate way to deal with thousands of relatively minor insect pest problems. The components and concentrations of active ingredients in these RTU formulations are precisely formulated to provide insecticidal efficiency against specific groups of pests of home and garden, greenhouses, warehouses, markets, restaurants, animal quarters, and institutions. Thus, the IPM practitioner must be particularly knowledgeable about insecticide management, which is a recognized component of integrated pest management (see Metcalf and Luckmann 1994).

Insecticides composed of microbial toxins (for example, *Bacillus thuringiensis,* or Bt) and viruses that are specifically and nearly exclusively toxic to small groups of insect pests are rapidly growing additions to the armamentarium of the pest management specialist. Their use is compatible with all other IPM tactics.

Practical Pest Management

To practice IPM on any scale, whether as a home gardener, family farmer, commercial grower, or IPM specialist in agribusiness, it is necessary to proceed through a series of common steps. These differ only in the way the required information is obtained and in the complexity and sophistication of the specific procedures employed.

Potential Pest Problems. Every crop has a specific set of potential pests; infestations by any of these pests results in characteristic crop damage and predictably in crop loss. The information needed to address these problems is obtainable from reference books in local libraries or bookstores, through county extension agents and in experimental station bulletins and circulars, or by consulting a professional entomologist or IPM specialist. The advantages in becoming an IPM expert are that one will be aware of what to look for in anticipating the initial indications of pest problems and will have a good grasp of appropriate methods for dealing with it.

Scouting. Individual gardeners should check their plants for damaged leaves and fruits, as well as for insect eggs, larvae, and adults, as they work in the garden or admire the plants. When dealing with larger plots or fields, subsampling of discrete areas on a quantitative basis (for example, counting so many insects per leaf, fruit, plant, or foot of row) will be necessary to relate pest populations to their economic thresholds. Other quantitative sampling methods, such as the sweep net or sticky traps baited by volatile lures, are most useful in orchards and row crops. In large commercial operations, employment of professional scouts is an important part of IPM.

Management Decisions. The economic injury level (EIL) for each specific crop is the key to implementing IPM decisions. The EIL is defined as the pest population level at which damage is tolerable and above which economic loss occurs. The action threshold for pest control interventions is the economic threshold (ET)—that is, the pest density at which control measures should be applied to prevent an increasing pest population from reaching the EIL.

For practical use there are four categories of economic threshold. First, *nonthresholds* are where the pest population is always greater than the EIL, as is typical in vegetable and fruit crops where a premium is paid for cosmetic appearance, or where applied control is used as a form of crop production insurance. Second, *nominal* thresholds are those in which the exact relationships between pest injury and crop damage are undetermined, so that EIL values can only be approximated on the basis of experiment station and producer experience. This is the present situation with the majority of small vegetable and fruit crops. Third, *simple* thresholds are where ET values are calculated from EIL values, based on long-term study of generalized insect injury and crop response. These values represent the best current practices for commercial insect control on important crops. Fourth, *comprehensive* thresholds are where ET values are computed from EILs that are developed for major crops after extensive research into pest injury, crop phenology, and economics.

Many factors and attitudes affect individual growers' decisions about the levels of damage or crop loss that they are willing to accept. The garden hobbyist is unwilling to accept the slightest trace of insect injury to prized blossoms or fruits. On the other hand, the organic farmer often accepts damage that would make produce unmarketable in normal channels. The pest losses incurred can be partially offset by the organic premium that some consumers will pay to avoid residues of chemical insecticides on edible produce.

Treatment Decisions. Control interventions are needed only when the scouting data indicate that the population of the pest exceeds the ET. At this point, the grower must optimize the type of treatment on the basis of personal experience, extension service recommendations, prevailing market prices, and available resources. Each individual manager must make a decision based on personal philosophy, economics, and environmental impacts. From these factors, appropriate interventions will be selected from an array of pest management tools. Rescue treatments with chemical or microbial insecticides provide the only certain remedy when the economic threshold is breached, and thus are employed mostly as the last resort.

These are the decisions and control actions that comprise integrated pest management. Although the process may seem complex, an immense amount of relevant information is available from state and federal experiment stations and extension services (see Flint and Van den Bosch 1981; Davidson and Lyon 1987; Pedigo 1996; Olkowski, Door, and Olkowski 1991; Metcalf and Metcalf 1993). Practicing IPM specialists are available to provide the expert knowledge required and to assume the responsibilities for applied control.

Tools of Pest Management. The specific ways in which pests can be abated, controlled, and managed are outlined below, but limitations of space preclude detailed discussion. Readers might wish to consult the references cited for additional information.

First, *cultural methods* include agronomic practices such as the use of resistant crop varieties, crop rotations, crop refuse destruction, soil tillage, variations in timing of planting and harvest, and pruning and thinning. Second, *mechanical methods* involve hand destruction, exclusion by screens or barriers, and trapping and collecting. Third, *physical methods* make use of heat, cold, and radiant energy. Fourth, *biological methods* include protection and encouragement of natural enemies, introduction and artificial increase of specific parasites and predators, and propagation and dissemination of insect diseases. Fifth, *chemical methods* make use of attractants, repellents, and insecticides. Sixth, *genetic methods* involve propagation and release of sterile or genetically incompatible pests and genetically engineered crop plants. Finally, *regulatory methods* involve plant and animal quarantines, eradication, and suppression programs.

Combining these tools in ways that are applicable to one's pest control problem, commensurate with the scope of one's operation, feasible with the means at one's disposal, and in accord with one's philosophy is what pest management is all about.

—*Robert L. Metcalf and Lesley Deem-Dickson*

See also
Agrichemical Use; Agriculture, Alternative; Biodiversity; Cropping Systems.

References
Davidson, Ralph H., and William F. Lyon. *Insect Pests of Farm, Garden, and Orchard.* 8th ed. New York: Wiley, 1987.
Flint, Mary Louise, and Robert Van den Bosch. *Introduction to Integrated Pest Management.* New York: Plenum Press, 1981.
Metcalf, Robert L., and William H. Luckman. *Introduction to Insect Pest Management.* 3d ed. New York: Wiley, 1994.
Metcalf, Robert L., and Robert A. Metcalf. *Destructive and Useful Insects: Their Habits and Control.* 5th ed. New York: McGraw-Hill, 1993.
National Academy of Sciences. *Princioles of Plant and Animal Pest Control, Volume 3: Insect-Pest Management and Control.* Publication 1695. Washington, DC: National Academy of Sciences, 1969.
Olkowski, William, Sheila Daar, and Helga Olkowski. *Commonsense Pest Control.* Newton, CT: Tauton, 1991.
Pedigo, Larry P. *Entomology and Pest Management.* 2d ed. New York: Macmillan, 1996.

Petroleum Industry

The economic system that produces, refines, markets and transports petroleum products. This entry provides a brief overview of the petroleum industry and reviews available data on oil activity in the United States. The economic impact of the industry on local rural areas, including boom-bust cycles that strained some oil-dependent regions, is reviewed. Finally, environmental considerations related to the oil industry are discussed.

Overview

The petroleum industry played a central role in the development and evolution of many rural areas in America. Resource extraction is usually located in rural areas, thus extraction often provides jobs and income for the local economies of these areas. The structure of the petroleum industry includes four components: production, refining, marketing, and transportation. Production involves the location and extraction of oil and natural gas from underground reservoirs. Refining involves the manufacturing of finished products (for example, gasoline and jet fuel) from the crude oil. Marketing includes the distribution of finished products to consumers, including both wholesale and retail efforts. Finally, transportation includes the pipelines, tankers, barges, and trucks that move crude oil to refineries and on to markets. Production activities have been tied most closely to rural areas, but the other components of the industry also impact many rural areas. (See Measday and Martin 1986 for an overview of the evolution of the petroleum industry, including a history of the world market and key corporate and governmental players.)

Plank (1994) has described trends in the petroleum industry in recent years. The industry downsized and restructured, creating job losses of 450,000 over a seven-year period. The industry's future is challenged because of shrinking domestic supplies and because other countries have captured much of the U.S. market. Plank notes that U.S. natural gas exploration may be 40 years behind oil. However, a number of positive factors currently are influencing the domestic oil industry, including advances in technology (such as drilling), strong industry survivors, and more effective firms operating at lower costs. U.S. industrial policy will play a key role in future developments in the industry. Võ (1994) examined the global oil industry and U.S. relations with the international community. Future relations will be complex and unpredictable, given the political complications of past years. Rural areas dependent upon the oil industry will be affected directly inasmuch as the petroleum industry is affected.

Data on Oil Activity in the United States

Oil production is concentrated geographically in specific states and regions throughout the country. Data published in 1994 by the Independent Petroleum Association of America (IPAA) present a useful picture of petroleum oil activities. The top ten ranking states for crude oil production at that time were Texas, Alaska, Louisiana, California, Oklahoma, Wyoming, New Mexico, Kansas, and North Dakota—all located in the Southwest and the West. Other states also are impacted by crude oil production, and data for each state are included. Natural gas production is somewhat similar, with the following ten states being ranked highest: Texas, Louisiana, Oklahoma, New Mexico, Wyoming, Kansas, Alaska, Colorado, California, and Alabama. The IPAA publication provides historical data (production, imports, supply, demand, reserves, and price) in addition to the state rankings. Each state's petroleum industry is profiled, showing the number of wells drilled and the levels of production, and a list of petroleum associations and state agency contacts is provided.

Economic Impact on Local Rural Areas

Oil extraction has played a key role in the economy of many regions. Oil extraction is one of the natural resource–based activities that helped to shape rural America. Castle, Shriver, and Weber (1988) have reviewed the performance of natural resource industries (forestry, energy, mining, and fishing) and the resulting impacts on rural America. The key factor identified is instability, as these areas currently are adjusting to decline, lower incomes, and higher unemployment. As natural resource–based industries downsize, the impacts are relatively greater in nonmetropolitan areas, where a greater number of individuals are employed in natural resources.

Regional impact patterns exist both for oil extraction and natural resource activities. Most areas specializing in energy extraction are the coal- and natural gas–producing areas of the Rocky Mountains, the oil-producing areas of Texas, Oklahoma, and the Gulf Coast, and the coal fields of Southern Illinois, Kentucky, and the Appalachian Mountains. The more remote the location of these resources, the greater the impact of resource extraction, because these remote economies tend to be highly dependent on extractive activities, having few economic alternatives. According to Castle et al. (1988), major influences that affect resource-dependent economies are international events (such as Middle Eastern politics and the price of oil), environmental policies (the Clean Air Act and resulting impacts on production), and industry structure (deregulation of the natural gas industry and large oil firms). These macro issues and trends ultimately impact the local economies where oil extraction and other natural resource–based activity occur.

An oil well in California. Such small wells are a common sight in many rural oil-producing areas, where they can exploit limited reserves of oil.

Energy development had significant impacts on regions in the western United States. Murdock and Leistritz (1979) reviewed the impacts of activity with oil, natural gas, oil shale, coal, and uranium. Many of these resources are indirectly related to oil; oil shale and coal are alternatives to petroleum, and mining of these products results from high oil prices. Murdock and Leistritz presented an overview of energy technology and energy needs, a thorough literature review, and the effects of energy development on agriculture and local business. They discussed policies to provide impact information and deal with appropriate growth management options. They identified housing and community facility needs as results of economic development and resource extraction in many western regions.

Oil extraction activities also have indirect impacts. Platt and Platt (1989) noted that service industries often are linked to the oil and natural gas production industries. Whereas production is sensitive to general economic condition, the service industries are most sensitive to growth or decline in oil production, which demon-strates the linkages other sectors of the economy have to oil extraction.

Natural resource extraction often causes gains and losses not evenly distributed to all groups. Oil and natural gas extraction often occurs in remote areas with an indigenous population. McNabb (1990) noted how the off-shore oil and gas activities in Alaska impacted the native Eskimo population. The Eskimo population depends on fishing harvests that are negatively affected by oil exploration. The alternatives for the native population are few, and lower living standards result. McNabb has pointed out that although Alaska is a major exporter of oil, the Eskimo population has benefited little from those exports.

Boom-and-Bust Cycles

Each oil price cycle or industry restructuring represents a boom or a bust for communities dependent upon petroleum for their economic well-being. Rising prices bring growth and increased economic activity. Often this growth is faster than local infrastructure can support.

Frequently, there have been shortages of housing, retail services, and other goods, as economic booms occur in communities and regions with petroleum resources during times of rising oil prices. Investments in public and private infrastructures are made to respond to the rapid rise in demand. Eventually, oil prices decline and excess capacity exists in the community. Morse (1986) reviews the history of the oil market and the resulting boom-bust cycles. He notes this cycle impacts the industry itself, the end users of oil, and the global economy. Detomasi and Gartrell (1984) published 11 papers surveying research into specific problems faced by resource communities. Issues related to community services, housing, impact on income distribution, and impact on indigenous people are reviewed. Models and methods of analysis to better understand and predict impacts are reviewed and evaluated.

Leistritz and Murdock (1981) examined alternative methods to model the economic, demographic, public service, and fiscal impacts of major resource development projects. They included projects other than oil and gas in their analysis, but the approach and methodology are similar. They reviewed each component of impact analysis (economic, demographic, public services, fiscal, social) and discussed how to interface these components through computerized models. Since each component is related and linked, this is a critical concept. For example, new jobs in the economic sector often bring in new people and create new demands for public services such as schools and health care. Tax revenues often are not collected in the appropriate jurisdiction or during the right time period to pay for needed services. These types of impacts often occur during the boom or rapid growth periods of resource extraction communities.

Brabant (1983) explored the ways in which communities respond to needs for basic services. The impact of resource extraction varies across time, space, and type of impact. There is a strong need for development planning and community organization. Community leaders need to anticipate the changes that will occur as the community experiences the boom-bust cycle.

Specific examples of the local impact of petroleum industry boom-bust cycles are presented by Harrop (1990), who wrote about the Anadarko Basin in Oklahoma. Prior to 1980, oil was $15 per barrel; it rose to $35 per barrel in 1980–1981, but fell back to $15 by 1986. During the late 1970s and early 1980s, population almost doubled for some cities and counties in western Oklahoma. Following the bust in the late 1980s, there were tremendous levels of excess capacity in commercial and industrial properties. The boom of 1980 made the front page of the *Wall Street Journal,* where shortages of housing and strained infrastructure were noted (Padilla 1982). The real-estate market was reported to be thriving, although one local leader interviewed noted that any potential crash would not be pleasant.

Environment and Oil

Conflicts among production, economic growth, and environmental protection have become important factors in the U.S. petroleum industry (Gilbert 1993). Oil is used primarily as a transportation fuel, and Americans continue to rely on the automobile, showing little interest in using mass transit. Nonetheless, due to widespread concern with air pollution, emissions, and rising gasoline fees or emissions taxes, there is strong incentive to identify alternatives to oil. If shifts in demand occur, rural areas dependent on oil extraction will be affected. However, Gilbert noted that most environmental effects occur during transportation of crude oil to refineries. The Exxon *Valdez* spill of crude oil was a notable example of this, with a huge environmental impact on the communities of south-central Alaska. In 1989, the super-tanker *Valdez* was involved in an oil spill off Alaska's Prince William Sound. The effects on wildlife were devastating (Cohen 1993), and the long-term damage to the local resource base was great. Concern with environmental accidents, and laws like the Clean Air Act of 1990, will encourage increased reliance on alternative fuels (Kezar 1994–1995). However, alternative fuel options, such as natural gas, could cost more. Environmental concerns must be balanced with economic efficiency to determine the most effective choices.

Despite its many potential uses as a fuel and in the production of fertilizer, natural gas has been an under-utilized energy source and chemical feedstock, according to Hall, Hay, and Vergara (1990), who have profiled the historical development of the natural gas industry. The base or supply of natural gas is abundant in the United States; but serious obstacles to using this resource remain, including a lack of knowledge about gas valuation and pricing. Finley (1993) similarly assessed the U.S. natural gas resource base, concluding that it was an abundant, moderately priced resource. Natural gas eventually may serve as an alternative to coal and oil, if a viable producing industry and efficient delivery system are developed. Natural gas already plays an important role in many rural areas; for example, it serves as a power source for irrigation systems operating in the Great Plains. Large areas in this region have converted from dryland farming to irrigated farming, thus increasing their output and income levels. Barkley (1988) noted that deregulation of the natural gas industry had a mixed impact on rural areas; although the average price of natural gas went down, pricing generally became more volatile. This instability creates changes in farming patterns, which in the long term will depress the economies of towns in the Plains region.

Oil and the petroleum industry played a central role in many rural locales' economies. The nature of the industry led to boom-bust cycles in rural areas where oil is produced. Predicting the magnitude of these economic effects and identifying appropriate planning responses is a critical component of rural development efforts. The future impact of oil will depend on worldwide consumption, market trends, and environmental considerations.

—*Mike D. Woods*

See also

Conservation, Energy; Development, Community and Economic; Employment; Environmental Protection; Impact Assessment; Income; Mining Industry; Natural Resource Economics.

References

Barkley, Paul W. "The Effects of Deregulation on Rural Communities." *American Journal of Agricultural Economics* (December 1988): 1091–1096.

Brabant, Sarah. "From Boom to Bust: Community Response to Basic Human Needs." *Journal of Applied Sociology* 10 (1993): 23–47.

Castle, Emery N., Ann L. Shriver, and Bruce A. Weber. "Performance of Natural Resource Industries." Pp. 103–133 in *Rural Economic Development in the 1980's: Prospects for the Future.* D. Brown and K. Deavers. Washington, DC: U.S. Department of Agriculture, 1988.·

Cohen, Maurie J. "Economic Impact of an Environmental Accident: A Time-Series Analysis of the Exxon Valdez Oil Spill in South Central Alaska." *Sociology Spectrum* 13 (1993): 35–63.

Detomasi, Don D., and John W. Gartrell, eds. *Resource Communities: A Decade of Disruption.* Boulder, CO: Westview Press, 1984.

Finley, Robert J. "A Positive Assessment of the U.S. Natural Gas Resource Base." Pp. 1–7 in *The Role of Natural Gas in Environmental Policy.* Austin: University of Texas, Bureau of Business Research, 1993.

Gilbert, Richard J., ed. *The Environment of Oil.* Norwell, MA: Kluwer Academic Publishers, 1993.

Hall, Carl W., Nelson E. Hay, and Walter Vergara. *Natural Gas: Its Role and Potential in Economic Development.* Boulder, CO: Westview Press, 1990.

Harrop, Paul S. "The Life and Death of an Oil Field Boom Town: An Appraisal Profile of Elk City, Oklahoma." *The Real Estate Appraiser and Analyst* (Spring 1990): 4–10.

Independent Petroleum Association of America. "The Oil and Natural Gas Producing Industry in Your State." *Petroleum Independent* 64, no. 5 (September/October 1994).

Kezar, Michelle L. "New Law, New Fuels." *Cross Sections* 11, no. 4 (Winter 1994–1995): 1–5.

Leistritz, F. Larry, and Steven H. Murdock. *The Socioeconomic Impact of Resource Development: Methods for Assessment.* Boulder, CO: Westview Press, 1981.

McNabb, Steven. "Impacts of Federal Policy Decisions on Alaska Natives." *Journal of Ethnic Studies* 18, no. 1 (1990): 111–126.

Measday, Walter S., and Stephen Martin. "The Petroleum Industry." Pp. 38–73 in *The Structure of American Industry.* Edited by Walter Adams. New York: Macmillan, 1986.

Morse, Edward. "After the Fall: The Politics of Oil." *Foreign Affairs* (Spring 1986): 792–811.

Murdock, Steve H., and F. Larry Leistritz. *Energy Development in the Western United States: Impact on Rural Areas.* New York: Praeger Publishers, 1979.

Padilla, Maria. "Oklahoma's Oil and Gas Boom Brings Cash, People, Problems." *The Wall Street Journal* (March 16, 1982): 1.

Plank, Raymond. "The Future of Oil and Gas in North America." *Vital Speeches of the Day* (February 1994): 272–275.

Platt, Harlan, and Marjorie Platt. "Failure in the Oil Patch: An Examination of the Production and Oil Field Services Industries." *Energy Journal* 10, no. 3 (July 1989): 35–49.

Võ, Hân Xuân. *Oil, the Persian Gulf States, and the United States.* Westport, CT: Praeger, 1994.

Planning

See Regional Planning

Plantations

Large areas of land on which a single crop is usually grown. The word plantation arose during the European colonization of the tropics and subtropics of the New World. Plantations were self-sustaining communities where political and economic institutions were monopolized by the authority of the planter. This self-sufficient lifestyle was also characteristic of the Old South, where the plantation was the center of commerce. The Old South can be regarded as the part of America where the plantation has been the main history-making entity. This system incorporated its ideals of existence into the family, church, school, and state. Today, the term plantation is also used in forestry disciplines to mean fields of trees planted for future lumber, pulp, and paper production. This entry reviews the history of plantations, including discussions of mansions, slavery, and indentured servitude. In addition, various misconceptions of plantations and plantation life and the role of plantations today are discussed.

Brief History

Plantations came into existence in North America in the 1600s. Spain and Portugal already had established large plantations in Central and South America that were used

Belle Grove Plantation in Middleton, Virginia.

as models by the English. Many historians consider the tobacco trade the foundation of the southern planter. Tobacco farms were widespread throughout the southeastern states. Virginia was most successful in farming tobacco, whereas the Carolina area became a large producer of rice, and in Georgia planters farmed indigo. In time, cotton would become the primary crop in the South.

Plantations were developed in other parts of the world as well as in the United States. Those that most closely resembled the U.S. plantation model were found in Barbados, Jamaica, and Bermuda. Slave labor was used in these areas as well, with sugar being the staple crop.

The true planters in the United States were plantation owners. A person had to own at least 20 slaves to be considered a true planter, and very few of the planters owned plantations this large. As the beginning of the Civil War approached, only one in 500 planters owned a large plantation with more than 100 slaves (Stone 1993).

Mansions

By the 1720s, the plantation regions experienced enormous increases in wealth with the growth of the agricul-

tural economy, brought on by the formation of cotton and sugar-cane plantations. With this wealth came the determination of each plantation owner to construct the most immaculate mansion possible. Plantation houses, with their long, sloped roofs and hand-carved columns, faced a waterway whenever possible. The waterway frequently was the Mississippi River.

The labor-intensive plantations in the United States abruptly declined following the abolition of slavery, causing most existing plantations to be broken into small farms and operated by individual owners or tenant farmers. A few continued to operate as usual, using wage-laborers and sharecroppers instead of slaves. Many grand plantation homes were destroyed or deteriorated during the years of the Civil War. Some mansions were restored during the Reconstruction; others have been restored in recent years.

Misconceptions

One of the greatest misconceptions, especially when referring to the Old South, is that there was a large number of plantations. In fact, during the days before the Civil

War the typical southerner rarely visited a plantation, much less owned one. Only a small group of people enjoyed the lifestyle of the plantation owner.

Another widely held misconception about plantation life pertains to the prevalence of slave-holding. The master/slave model was not descriptive of as many plantations as most people believe. The slave population peaked prior to the American Revolution. This held true for absolute numbers as well as in proportion to the total population of the colonies. Even during these years, the master/slave model is descriptive of only a part of the plantation families. Less than half the planting families in Chesapeake (the oldest of the staple colonies) owned slaves on the eve of the Revolution (Land 1969). Although the Civil War brought a legal end to slave-holding, the relationship between power and slave-holding had already eroded to some extent by 1860.

Indentured Servitude

Behind the facade of the eloquent mansions and beneath the superstructure were the indentured servants and the slaves. Indentured servants were the main source of labor on plantations during the seventeenth century. Poor Europeans who wanted to go to the colonies received passage if they agreed to become servants for a specified number of years to pay their transportation debt. Criminals also were sent to the colonies, and in most cases, they were forced to be servants. Some Europeans were kidnapped and taken to the colonies as servants. Indentured servants were often, though not always, treated harshly, and usually were not granted freedom until after their contracted time was completed.

Slavery

For slaves, however, life on the plantation was a constant struggle both spiritually and physically. Slavery was introduced to plantations in Virginia in 1619. Blacks taken prisoner in Africa by slave traders were brought to America in chains and sold as labor to the owners of large estates and plantations, where they lived under racist oppression. The enslavement of Black Africans by White Americans is often referred to as one of history's greatest crimes.

Slaves were forced to create a livable world for themselves and their children while enduring the harshest of living conditions. Travelers to the South created a popular image of the living quarters of slaves as a one-room log cabin, commonly housing more than six slaves. Although there was some stability in the life of some slave families,

most families experienced disorganization and instability. Slave families who experienced a relatively cohesive life were generally those who worked on large plantations.

Plantation owners, especially those owning larger plantations, paid special attention to the physical condition of their slaves. Many looked upon their slaves as they did their cattle, breeding them thoughtfully and selectively. Plantation owners allowed their physically superior male slaves to move freely among their female slaves, thus providing larger and healthier children for future field hands.

On the more aristocratic plantations, masters instilled a pride of caste among their house servants, drawing a sharp social distinction between the slaves of the Big House and those of the quarters. (The Big House referred to the living quarters of the planter on a plantation. Although many were extravagant, most were fairly modest in size and decor; nonetheless, historical records show that the idea of the Big House reaffirmed the image of the master planter as a very powerful and wealthy figure.) For example, a cook in the Big House could not let her child play with the children of the field slaves. This expression of contempt for field slaves was an attempt by the house servants to raise their own image in society. Although the attempt was at the expense of other slaves, it narrowed the distance between Whites and Blacks (Genovese 1976).

Plantations in the Modern World

Plantations still exist today as a result of new and continuing economic interests. Some plantation sites produce agricultural and other goods, and others supply historical landmarks for tourists. Historic plantations can be visited, and although their romantic charm is easily embraced, present day labor-controlling systems perpetuate the Old South's paternalistic mentality.

Control over labor switched from slavery to sharecropping and the crop-lien system after the Civil War. Later, another economic mechanism, the Black Codes, was used to control labor. This mechanism created a dual system in the South, pitting Blacks and Whites against each other. The tension between races stemmed from Blacks being forced to work for low wages because of their skin color. Poor Whites were denied jobs because planters felt justified to pay Black workers less than White workers. This post–Civil War racial divide continues to fuel tension in race relations.

As cotton prices began to fall in the 1970s, other crops, such as catfish, began to replace cotton. In places such as Sunflower and Humphrey Counties, Mississippi, catfish surpassed cotton as the leading crop. Although catfish farming brought $350 million to the Mississippi Delta in 1990, almost all of the profit went to approximately 400 White landowners and supervisors, epitomizing how catfish farming strengthened the plantation mentality in the Delta (Schweid 1991).

Tourists are drawn from around the world to the plantations and mansions of rural America. Many states have restored mansions and plantations, which are now open to the public. The Waverly Plantation is a favorite in Columbus, Mississippi; Franklin, Tennessee, is home to the Carnton House; the Astabula Plantation is in Pendleton, South Carolina; and the John Dickinson Mansion is in Dover, Delaware. The South has many plantations, mansions, and other historic sights that give visitors a glimpse of what used to be.

Plantations used for touring continuously rise and fall in popularity. Overall, however, the plantation tourism industry is growing. In Greenwood, Mississippi, there are seven plantations open to visitors. Tour groups on average include between 50 and 60 people. Each group spends approximately $200 on tours alone. At the Cedar Wycke Plantation in Monroe County, Mississippi, tours are given by appointment only. They cost $5 per person, and the plantation receives between 400 and 500 visitors annually. In Natchez, Mississippi, even the antebellum vacation homes are big business. Homes in this area receive up to 200,000 tourists annually. Plantations outside of Mississippi also are following this growing trend.

Plantations played an important part in shaping rural America. Although many overlook their historical importance, one must only refer to the colonial era to witness the impact of plantations on the young nation. Mansions and southern belles are depicted in the romance of the plantation era, but slavery and its defenders will always be remembered for making the plantation an unjust system.

—*Terri L. Earnest and John J. Green*

See also
African Americans; Agriculture, Structure of; Architecture; Culture; Forestry Industry; History, Rural; Inequality; Landownership; Social Class.

References
Genovese, Eugene D. *Roll Jordan Roll: The World the Slaves Made.* 2d ed. New York: Vintage Books, 1976.
Land, Aubrey, ed. *Bases of the Plantation Society.* Columbia: University of South Carolina Press, 1969.
Schweid, Richard. "Down on the Farm." *Southern Exposure* Fall (1991): 15–21.
Stone, Lynn. *Plantations.* Vero Beach, FL: Rourke Publishing, 1993.

Policing
The component of the law-enforcement community that serves to protect citizens and to preserve the peace. The purpose of this entry is to review five important aspects of police department functioning in rural areas (that is, in towns of 2,500 or fewer inhabitants, and in the sparsely populated counties): (1) the scope of their responsibilities, (2) police-community relations, (3) sources of job-related stress among rural police, (4) budgetary constraints and challenges, and (5) educational and training issues. Unlike other existing research reviews, this discussion highlights the conditions and challenges unique to rural policing.

Introduction
Sociological and criminological research has focused heavily on policing in urban areas, largely neglecting important law-enforcement issues in the rural context. This is in spite of the fact that America has many large and important rural regions, which account for more than 80 percent of the land and which house 51 million people (21 percent of the national population). Furthermore, emerging research in rural policing has documented that of the 15,383 law enforcement agencies studied across the country, 7,461 (48.5 percent) have fewer than 10 sworn officers on their staff with an additional 6,245 (40.6 percent) of the reporting departments characterized by a range of 10 through 49 licensed police officers (Weisheit, Wells, and Falcone 1996). When researchers have studied rural police departments and their personnel, there has been a marked tendency to generate comparative rural-urban profiles, which in effect reinforces the salience of urban organizations, their staffs, and their problems.

Scope of Police Responsibilities
Numerous law-enforcement agencies have authority responsibilities in rural regions. Citizens of rural America are served and protected by small-town police and sheriff's departments, state police and highway patrol units, state conservation units, and federal agencies like the U.S. Forest Service. The county sheriff's department continues as the primary means of service and law enforcement protection in rural areas. Of the approximate 3,000 counties in the United States, most law enforcement units that serve the public at this level are independent county agencies, and the senior administrator is the elected county sheriff. This reflects the design of our colonial founders who structured the primary means of law enforcement at the local level and wanted it overseen by a locally elected official.

County sheriff's departments have a wide scope of responsibilities. These involve law enforcement, processing criminal and civil court orders, county jail administration, courtroom safety, property seizure, and the collection of fees and taxes. Many rural county sheriff's departments employ only a handful of deputies, several of whom work part-time, none of whom are specialists, and as a result, expertise in any single aspect of policing in virtually nonexistent. Congruent with this profile of wide responsibilities performed by a small labor force of generalists is the conclusion that per capita costs of rural law enforcement agencies tend to be lower than larger urban-based agencies where the staff are more highly specialized and salaried.

Citizen expectations of rural law enforcement personnel are higher than in the urban domain. This is handled by rural agencies in their heavy reliance on both interagency cooperation and interpersonal dynamics rather than a show of numerical and specialized technical force. Thus, the community policing concept has such a long-standing acceptance and reliance in rural America compared to urban areas, where it is a much more recently adopted police strategy of public service (Weisheit, Wells and Falcone 1994).

Community Relations

Whereas Wilson's (1968) threefold typology of legalistic, service, and watchman police styles is recognized as a beginning point to understand rural policing and its relationship with communities, Klonski and Mendelsohn (1970) long ago noted that the communal system of justice aptly describes and explains the cultural context in which rural police function. In this cultural milieu, rural law enforcement personnel rely heavily on informal rules of conduct as a foundation to conduct their work. As a result, local community standards, as compared to the content of legislatively established official standards of behavior, tend to influence decisions as to who will and will not be subject to the official actions of police and the related criminal justice bureaucracy. This sociocultural standard generates a partnership between the citizens and police in many rural areas, i.e., the conceptual core of community policing. Sociologists, criminologists, and police administrators have come to realize that this partnership produces a flow of information from the public to the police that contributes significantly to the ability of police to serve and protect the public more effectively. This is especially noticeable when compared to the conditions of alienated police-community relations found in urban America.

The rural ethos appears to connect to the higher rate of crimes that are cleared by arrest in rural as compared to urban jurisdictions. Weisheit, Wells, and Falcone (1996) point out that for all index crimes in 1992 the proportion cleared by arrest for rural counties is 23.0 percent, whereas in cities of 250,000 or more inhabitants the rate is 18.8 percent. More specifically the rate of clearance for violent crimes in rural areas is 60.7 percent and in urban areas it is 38.5 percent. For property crimes the rural rate of clearance is 18.4 percent whereas the level of arrest clearance for this crime category in urban cities is 14.3 percent. This may reflect, in part, the concept that rural police are more a part of their community than urban police who appear to be more apart from their constituents.

Job-Related Stress

The wide, open geographical terrain, extensive scope of functional responsibilities, and the importance of police-community relations combine to generate distinct conditions that foster stress among rural police. Sandy and Devine (1978) describe four factors that are unique to rural policing. The first of these is that of personal security. Rural patrol officers are keenly aware that security through backup may be an hour or more wait. Second, social factors contribute to the level of stress among rural officers. In a sheriff's department, for example, the patrol deputies are usually residents of the county that employs them. Whereas this benefits them insofar as they know their constituents on a personal basis, this condition produces a lack of anonymity and the resulting loss of personal privacy. More recently Bartol (1996) underscores that this "fishbowl factor" intensifies existing levels of stress caused by other job related factors. A third factor contributing to stress is the working conditions found in rural policing. Budgetary constraints, limited opportunity for vertical promotion, and lateral movement to another agency, such as an urban department that places a premium on specialization, contribute to the stressful nature of rural police work. Finally, inactivity leads to inadequate sensory stimuli, which constrains on officer's self-esteem. Unfortunately, administrators of rural departments recognize little if any need to confront stress, preferring instead to prioritize direct services to the public.

Budgetary Constraints and Challenges

Rural law enforcement agencies budget for service to the public more than protection of the public through rigid, official enforcement of criminal laws. As suggested earlier, this generates a composite economic evaluative profile that is cost effective in the use of taxpayer resources.

On the other hand, many rural regions are constrained increasingly by population declines and a shrinking tax base. This challenges the rural county sheriff's ability to adequately finance the full range of services that remain a priority for the public. The trends in economic restructuring and persistent poverty in rural America do not appear to bode well for rural law enforcement. Possible changes in federal economic policies that have supported rural regions will apparently intensify this difficulty. As nothing is inevitable, creative policy makers in rural regions have the opportunity to respond to these local and national changes through imaginative management strategies such as the consolidation of public services. Adjustments in economic and policing policy priorities must be designed to satisfy the needs and wishes of the local constituency. As much heterogeneity within rural America now exists, considerable variance in changes is quite likely.

Education and Training

The education and training needs of rural law enforcement personnel have been a low priority among administrators who work with town managers or chairs of county commissions. In this rural context the education and training of personnel is not needed nor is it viewed as a wise use of the budget. Thus, recruiting well-educated, highly trained law enforcement personnel in rural regions has been noticeably difficult. Releasing rural officers to attend educational programs and training workshops involves registration, lodging, and meal cost that are often viewed as prohibitive.

Technological developments, however, appear to be a means to adapt to this economic challenge. Interactive video networks allow educational programs to be brought to the agency, thereby avoiding the necessity to release staff to attend an educational conference. Similar innovations are available for training purposes, such as through the Law Enforcement Television Network (LETN). As a result, video recorded training sessions are readily available, economically priced and updated on a regular basis. This permits agency administrators to purchase a range of training programs and, as a result, build an impressive video training library. Field staff, on the other hand, are able to access these LETN training programs at a convenient point in their personal and professional schedules. Technological innovations appear to hold many benefits for the education and training of rural officers.

Whereas education and training for rural police have been low priorities at the local rural level, state laws increasingly mandate minimum standards on both of these items. Innovative technologies and creative law enforcement administration can assist small departments as these units respond to changes in state requirements regarding educational and training standards. Police leaders of rural law enforcement departments are now required and able to note these changes.

Conclusion

Rural law enforcement agencies are responsible for more than 80 percent of our territory and more than 20 percent of our citizens. Therefore, attention to this segment of U.S. law enforcement is warranted. While many conditions, constraints, and challenges exist, much more rural specific research is needed; it deserves a higher priority than has been the traditional work of sociologists and criminologists. This chapter has focused on the sociocultural milieu in which rural policing operates. While it may seem that the rural context is small and more easily managed than the research challenges of the urban context; researchers need keen alertness to the subtle complexities required by such endeavors in our rural areas. Theoretical models and methodological designs used successfully for research in the urban areas are of questionable and uneven value for research on rural policing. Attention to the complexities of rural research is essential if our inventory of knowledge about policing is to be useful for political and agency leaders. This is particularly true as rural policing enters the culturally complex and politically volatile changes that will challenge it in the twenty-first century.

—Thomas D. McDonald

See also
Crime; Domestic Violence; Gambling; Marijuana.

References
Bartol, Curt R. "Police Psychology: Then, Now and Beyond." *Criminal Justice and Behavior* 23 (1996): 70–89.
Klonski, James R., and Robert I. Mendelsohn. *The Politics of Local Justice.* Boston: Little, Brown, 1970.
McDonald, Thomas D., Robert A. Wood, and Melissa A. Pflug. *Rural Criminal Justice.* Salem, WI: Sheffield Publishing Co., 1996.
Rachlin, Harvey. "Small Town Training." *Law and Order* 40 (1992): 38–40.
Sandy, Joan Phillips, and Donald A. Devine. "Four Stress Factors Unique to Rural Patrol." *Police Chief* 45 (1978): 42–44.
Sims, Victor H. "The Structural Components of Rural Law Enforcement: Roles and Organizations." Pp. 41–54 in *Rural*

Criminal Justice. Edited by T. D. McDonald, R. A. Wood, and M. A. Pflug. Salem, WI: Sheffield Publishing Co., 1996.

Weisheit, Ralph A., David N. Falcone, and L. Edward Wells. *Crime and Policing in Rural and Small-Town America.* Prospect Heights, IL: Waveland, 1996.

Weisheit, Ralph A., and L. Edward Wells. "Rural Crime and Justice: Implications for Theory and Research." *Crime and Delinquency* 42, no. 3 (1996): 379–397.

Weisheit, Ralph A., L. Edward Wells, and David N. Falcone. *Crime and Policing in Rural and Small Town America: An Overview of the Issues.* Washington, DC: National Institute of Justice, 1994a, Draft.

———. "Community Policing in Small-Town and Rural America." *Crime and Delinquency* 40 (1994b): 549–567.

Wilson, James Q. *Varieties of Police Behavior: The Management of Law and Order in Eight Communities.* Cambridge, MA: Harvard University Press, 1968.

Policy, Agricultural

The range of actions taken by government and other public bodies to influence the people, economy, and course of events in agriculture, and through these to have an impact on rural America. At the founding of the country, agriculture was synonymous with rural life. The course of agricultural policy in rural America has been one of increasing disassociation, especially in the twentieth century. Today, agricultural policy is no longer rural policy, and sectors other than agriculture exert a primary influence on rural people. This entry examines three major epochs of agricultural policy, with special emphasis on the period since 1933.

First Epoch: Land and Settlement Policy

There have been three epochs in agricultural policy: The first, from the American revolution until the beginning of the twentieth century, witnessed the opening of the land and the peopling of the landscape. Agricultural policy was land policy and settlement policy. From 1900 until 1933, during the second epoch, government took the role of supporting infrastructure and resource conservation. Starting in 1933, the third epoch began, with direct government involvement in agriculture and in major economic decisions made on the farm. These changes mirrored the national trends toward government's increasing role in the life of its citizens.

Opening the land and peopling the landscape took over a century to accomplish. There are almost 2 billion acres in the lower 48 states, and roughly 400 million are cropland base. Another 200 million acres of lower-quality land could be brought into production. By 1956, the federal government had distributed the public domain as shown in the accompanying table.

Land in the Original Public Domain as of 1956

Recipients	Millions of Acres
Sales and grants largely to private individuals	455.5
National forests, parks, wildlife, military reservations	187.8
Unreserved and unappropriated public domain	170.6
Homestead and related grants	147.0
Railroads	131.0
States to support transportation and other infrastructure	125.0
States to support education	99.0
Military land bounties	73.5
Indian tribal and trust lands	52.8
Grand total (original public domain)	1,442.2

Source: Cochrane 1993, 175.

In the early days of the American republic, there was pressure to use land distribution to earn revenues and pay off the new nation's debt. Thomas Jefferson's view prevailed, however, and land was sold or granted on more favorable terms to create a nation of small yeoman farmers, central to Jefferson's notion of agriculturally based democracy. In this phase of settlement, the fertile land seemed endless. As people moved westward it was cultivated extensively—in terms of cultivating more land to produce more as well of moving on to better lands at the frontier when old lands had lost their fertility.

Second Epoch: Indirect Role of Government

The transition to the twentieth century and a different role for the federal government is best illustrated by the recommendations of the Country Life Commission shortly after 1900. The commission, appointed by Theodore Roosevelt, looked into the conditions of rural life and made recommendations about what government might do to improve it. The commission was led by Liberty Hyde Bailey and included Gifford Pinchot among its members. It held hearings around the country and surveyed the rural populace, receiving over 100,000 responses to a national questionnaire.

The conclusions of the commission were that the federal government should improve the environment for farmers and the infrastructure for rural life. Among its recommendations were to create savings banks, institute a rural free postal delivery, conduct extensive applied research and extension education at the land-grant colleges, and improve health education and transportation in rural areas. Over the next several decades, almost all of the recommendations were put into action. The focus was both rural and agricultural—the two were still synonymous. None of the recommendations involved government actively in the decisions of individual farmers or rural people; but the message of a positive role for government in rural affairs was clear, if indirect.

The Agricultural Depression and the Agricultural Adjustment Act

The role of government changed completely in 1933 (Rasmussen 1985). The early 1900s had been the golden age of agriculture. The notion of parity for agriculture was based on the experience of 1910 through 1914, when farmers had low costs for inputs and good prices for farm products. Agriculture boomed during World War I and the immediately succeeding years. But in the early 1920s, foreign agricultural markets collapsed and agriculture entered a depression that was ended only by World War II. Between the wars, farm incomes and land values plummeted. A farm selling in northern Indiana in 1919 at the end of the boom did not regain its nominal dollar purchase price until after World War II. Farms were lost, and there was severe economic distress in rural areas long before the stock market crash of 1929. When Franklin Roosevelt took office in 1933, incomes in rural areas on average were only 40 percent of incomes in urban areas, and unemployment in urban areas was around 30 percent.

The Roosevelt administration's mandate was to tackle this problem, and the Agricultural Adjustment Act of 1933 was passed. The task was to get cash into rural areas, and the tactic was to raise farm prices. Production was restricted on basic commodities important to farmers' incomes, in order to push prices higher. Prices were also supported through nonrecourse loans on crops, which brought the federal government into the commodity storage business if farmers turned over their crop rather than pay back a federal loan. Direct payments were made to farmers in some cases; marketing orders were set up to manage the supplies of specialty crops and dairy products; and new credit institutions were set up that were more suited to agricultural lending needs. The U.S. government purchased worn-out or nonproductive farms, and under the 1937 and 1938 Agricultural Adjustment Acts, paid farmers to adopt conserving practices, make physical improvements to their lands, or hold fragile land out of production. These provisions also helped to restrict supply and raise prices. These basic components of agricultural policy were still in effect through the early 1990s in rural America.

Most remarkable was the Roosevelt administration's willingness to try many new measures, jettison those that did not work, and move on to new measures that might work. Did these policies achieve their goals? In 1940,

George Tolley, the U.S. Department of Agriculture's (USDA's) chief economist under Secretary of Agriculture Henry A. Wallace, wrote that the policies of the New Deal had three objectives. One objective was to improve the viability of commercial agriculture; second, to enhance the life of the subsistence farmer, the rural poor, or the migrant laborer; and third, to protect the land and enhance conservation and the more productive use of resources. Tolley commented that the first task of underpinning commercial agriculture had been accomplished, but the tasks of helping those less fortunate and enhancing conservation and resource stewardship had not (USDA 1940).

Today, USDA income statistics show that farm family incomes are on a par with non–farm family incomes. Thus, the severe disparity between farm and nonfarm average income is no longer evident. Most farm families achieve this equality with additional off-farm income, just as nonfarm families also have more than one wage earner. However, the equality of income and living conditions for commercial farmers sought by the New Deal for the most part has been achieved.

Which Policy Matters?

To what extent does agricultural policy affect rural areas? Chester Davis, an early Agricultural Adjustment Act administrator, understood that agricultural policy was not necessarily the main influence on either the farmer or the rural populace. What really affected agriculture and rural areas was "expressed in a complexity of laws and attitudes which, in the importance of their influence on agriculture, shade off from direct measures like the Agricultural Adjustment Act through the almost infinite fields of taxation, tariffs, international trade, and labor, money, credit , and banking policy" (USDA 1940, 325). Then, as today, Davis saw that much of what moves rural America does not come from agricultural policy.

Agriculture and rural America have been affected greatly by monetary and credit policy. The Farm Credit Banks, Resettlement Administration, Farm Security Administration, and finally the Farmers Home Administration increased the availability of credit to the sector at critical times. The easy credit policy of the late 1970s, followed by the restrictive monetary policy of the Federal Reserve and the collapse in exports in the early 1980s, were factors in the farm financial crisis that proved disastrous for farms and rural areas. Massive agricultural price-support expenditures were made in the latter half of the 1980s to counter the hardships of the bust in the agricultural economic cycle.

Tax policy influenced the returns to agriculture and the size of farms. Cash accounting, special depreciation rules, and special inheritance provisions tended to increase the size of firms (USDA 1981). Other public policies coupled with economic forces also are capable of unleashing drastic economic change within agriculture. "We have credit policies that cheapen the cost of credit for large borrowers. We have tax policies that encourage vertical integration, agglomeration, and farm size enlargement" (Raup 1978, 305). One of the problems that many see is a synergism of agricultural and nonagricultural policies that depopulates rural America and decreases the economic linkages between the farm and its local community. There are trade-offs between the resiliency of the moderate-sized family farm and the greater efficiency of larger, more integrated units. And there are trade-offs between the positive economic and social role of many family farms in a rural community and the cost savings and improved efficiency of larger farms in obtaining inputs and capital from outside the rural area.

Technology and Productivity

The 1930s ushered in an era of increasing productivity and intensification in agriculture and direct government involvement in farming. The closing of the frontier was one factor in this change. Productivity was relatively stagnant from 1900 to the 1930s, as was the size of the farm population. From 1940 to 1990, farm population went from about 30 million to 4 million, while input productivity more than doubled. According to Mayer, "Postwar farm policies continued to support farm income, making more capital available for the purchase of new farm machines and, thereby, more labor available for other parts of the economy" (1993, 82). World War II, the flow of public technology available from the land-grant institutions, and the building of the interstate highway system led to farm consolidations, out-migration of labor from agriculture, and increasing proportions of farm inputs coming from large, centralized, off-farm suppliers. An engine of growth dominated and drove the structural changes in the agricultural sector.

Self-Perpetuating Programs

Why was there little change in American agricultural policy? When the federal government became actively involved in agriculture in the 1930s, the farming landscape was more homogeneous. It was believed that programs based on subsidizing farm products would be fair because the public perceived a large mass of small to mid-sized farms having similar output, productivity, and needs for support. However, "through a process of uneven consolidation, U.S. farm structure became increasingly skewed, and a wealthy minority of large-sized farmers eventually came to produce the majority of all supported farm products, thus capturing the majority of all support benefits" (Paarlberg 1989, 1161–1162). In essence, policies were initiated and continued whereby large operations obtained more program benefits and smaller firms remained more vulnerable to failure. The very characteristic of family farms—that they fail with relatively low cost to society as a whole—allowed a transition to occur with rapid farm consolidation almost unnoticed by many because the social costs were borne quietly, primarily by farm families.

Especially today, after farm consolidation and the changed relationship between farms and their communities, agricultural policy is not rural policy. There is increasingly a disconnection between agriculture and rural areas. Agricultural production enterprises are a shrinking part of rural economic activity. But for better or for worse, agriculture, forestry, and other rural-based industries have been major factors shaping the institutions and norms of rural areas (Castle 1993). It is in this sense that agriculture remains most important to rural areas today, not because of its economic activity or the impact of agricultural programs. Conditions in rural areas are different from the 1930s, yet the same norms, institutions, and policy devices persist.

The stresses of the 1980s accentuated the problems of agriculture and rural areas. Both suffered more from macroeconomic policy, deregulation, changes in international markets, and increased international competitiveness than many other sectors or regions. The question becomes one of how rural areas adapt to the changing circumstances around them, including the budget-driven changes in agricultural policy that eventually will further diminish the transfer of income to rural areas that exist today. To what extent will diminished agricultural programs increase the risk level for the farming community and add instability to the rural community? If much of the relative decline of rural economies since the 1930s has been due to successful adoption of labor-saving technology in agriculture and other rural pursuits, where will rural America wind up in a future that promises more of the same?

In the past, a rural area with a strong agricultural base could be an economic entity unto itself. This is no longer the case. Industrialization has "peripheralized the role of rural areas. . . . Most rural areas now constitute specialized components of larger regional economies, supplying a particular industry and/or factor of production" (Cooper 1993, 38). Agriculture is one of many in such a context. The old notion was that a rural place or region was related to an accompanying immobility of capital and labor, but this is no longer the case. Agriculture is no longer a core. Agricultural policy held a static view of place for agriculture. If the infusion of cash from agricultural programs in the late 1980s solved the farm crisis, it did not solve the rural crisis. Most rural employment is in other sectors, such as forest products, mining, manufacturing, and producer services. It is here that agricultural policy has not been able to address the sluggishness in rural economies that has persisted since the recession of the early 1980s. What we have seen recently is "a long term decline in the relative importance of resource industries as employers, the pressures of technology and foreign competition on employment in low-wage rural manufacturing industries, the endemic liabilities of small population concentrations and distance from major urban centers, and chronic weaknesses in the rural labor force due to lower education and poorer skills" (Reid 1989, 358). This trend cannot be turned around by agricultural policy alone.

Where is agricultural policy likely to go, and what effect is it likely to have on rural America? Over the next decade large income transfers to agriculture on the basis of one's specific crop or scale of production might well cease. If a successful argument is made that agriculture is more subject to and especially damaged by income volatility, then some sort of income insurance or other risk-reducing program might emerge. However, international competition, market specialization, technology and the imperative of its early adoption, tax measures, and credit policy are likely to continue to encourage consolidation and vertical integration of agriculture irrespective of the 1996 farm bill. A shift from the historic participation-based payments program to something like income risk insurance or needs-based transfers will not halt the drift of agriculture toward a position less important and less central to rural America. The basic political tenant of agricultural programs has been more toward income redistribution than productivity and capacity enhancement. Agricultural programs used by large producers and landowners have been skewed to favor income transfers to these effective interest groups. Little has been done to ease the adjustment of those leaving agriculture. To impact rural America, one needs not just good agricultural policies, but good policies that affect other components of the rural economy, encouraging productivity, enhancing economic capacity, and easing the transition of people from one economic sector to another.

—*Otto C. Doering III*

See also

Agricultural and Resource Economics; Agricultural Prices; Agricultural Programs; Agriculture, Structure of; Farms.

References

Castle, Emery N. "Rural Diversity: An American Asset." *Annals of the American Academy of Political and Social Sciences*, 529 (September 1993): 12–21.

Cochrane, Willard D. *The Development of American Agriculture: A Historical Analysis*. 2d ed. Minneapolis: University of Minnesota Press, 1993.

Cooper, Ronald S. "The New Economic Regionalism: A Rural Policy Framework." *Annals of the American Academy of Political and Social Sciences* 529 (September 1993): 34–47.

Mayer, Leo V. "Agricultural Change and Rural America." *Annals of the American Academy of Political and Social Sciences* 529 (September 1993): 80–91.

Paarlberg, Robert. "The Political Economy of American Agricultural Policy: Three Approaches." *American Journal of Agricultural Economics* 71, no. 5 (December 1989): 1157–1164.

Rasmussen, Wayne D. "Historical Overview of U.S. Agricultural Policies and Programs." *Agricultural-Food Policy Review: Commodity Program Perspectives*. Agricultural Economic Report No. 50 (July). Washington, DC: U.S. Department of Agriculture, Economic Research Service, 1985.

Raup, Philip M. "Some Questions of Value and Scale in American Agriculture." *American Journal of Agricultural Economics* 60, no. 2. (May 1978): 303–308.

Reid, J. Norman. "Agricultural Policy and Rural Development." *Emerging Issues*, Agricultural Economic Report No. 620. Washington, DC: U.S. Department of Agriculture, Economic Research Service, 1989.

U.S. Country Life Commission. *Report of the Commission on Country Life*. Chapel Hill: University of North Carolina Press, 1944.

U.S. Department of Agriculture. *Farmers in a Changing World: 1940 Yearbook of Agriculture*. Washington, DC: U.S. Department of Agriculture, 1940.

———. *A Time to Choose: Summary Report on the Structure of Agriculture*. Washington, DC: U.S. Department of Agriculture, 1981.

Policy, Economic

The set of laws, programs, and administrative rules that guide, encourage, or constrain economic activity. Reid and Long (1988) define policy as a "guiding and consistent course of action" and emphasize the importance of policy decisions in turn being guided by a consistent set of policy objectives. They refer to the set of programs selected to advance the chosen policy objectives as a "policy strategy," which is roughly equivalent to the way the term "policy" is used in this entry. Federal, state, and local governments, through taxing, spending, and regulatory actions, create economic policy. National policy designed to support the economies of urban areas (where three-quarters of Americans live) might work incidentally to the disadvantage of rural areas, which are sparsely populated, isolated, and often dependent on a narrow economic base. This has led some to suggest the creation of an explicit national- or state-level rural policy. The first section of this entry suggests three reasons why governments have economic policies. This is followed by a discussion of the rural context for economic policy—the distinctive characteristics of rural areas and the forces leading to rural change. The next two sections describe the economic policies of the federal government and of state and local governments and their impacts on rural areas. The final section is a discussion of the idea of comprehensive national policy to address the needs of rural areas.

Why Economic Policy?

National governments enact monetary, fiscal, and trade policies to establish the legal and monetary frameworks necessary for an economy to function smoothly. These frameworks provide security in trade and a basic social and physical infrastructure (for example, schools, water, and sewer systems). A certain level of taxation is necessary to support these activities.

Governments also often enact policies to correct market inefficiencies and undesirable social, economic, or environmental effects of private decisions. Within a basic market framework, firms and individuals often make decisions that are either economically inefficient or have undesirable side effects. For example, because of imperfect information, urban banks may deny a loan to a credit-worthy rural business in favor of a loan to a risky urban venture. Or a farmer's decision to apply pesticide may harm the habitat of an endangered species. The decisions of manufacturing firms to locate overseas may increase poverty and worsen the distribution of income in this country. Subsidized loan programs, pollution taxes, and welfare and job training programs are examples of economic policies that address these concerns.

Finally, in addition to providing a framework and correcting the negative impacts of market decisions, governments attempt through policy to enhance the overall level of economic activity and the health of certain sectors and regions as well as to achieve specific social goals.

The Rural Context for Economic Policy

Rural America is becoming increasingly similar to urban America in population and economic characteristics, values, and the availability of services and amenities. There are at least four characteristics, however, that distinguish rural areas, and that cause rural areas to be affected differently from urban areas by economic policy and global economic and social forces. First, rural areas tend to have a narrower economic base than urban areas, specializing in the natural resource industries of agriculture, forestry and wood products, energy extraction, and mining. Almost half of the rural counties in the United States depend on one of these industries for 20 percent or more of their labor and proprietor income; 30 percent of these counties depend on agriculture (farming, food processing, and agricultural services); and 14 percent depend on the other three natural resource industries.

Second, rural areas are isolated. They are, for the most part, distant from economic and political centers and thus they do not have ready access to the economic and political discussions that shape policy decisions.

Third, rural areas are sparsely populated. Nonmetropolitan counties average 19 people per square mile, whereas metropolitan counties have 332 people per square mile. Low population densities keep rural areas from attaining the economies of size and concentration that are possible in urban areas.

Fourth, rural people are more involved in local self-governance than are urban people. Although they have only 24 percent of the population, rural areas have 75 percent of the local government units. This places more demands on rural people to fulfill leadership roles, often in volunteer positions, and gives them more experience in self-governance (Weber et al. 1989).

There are at least four sets of forces that are changing the economies of rural and urban areas and are providing new constraints and opportunities for rural areas. First, technological change leads to new production processes and dramatic reduction in the costs of transportation and communication. While these changes reduced the need for firms to be close to markets or firm headquarters, they also tended to reinforce urban concentrations, because technological change tends to proceed faster in areas with denser concentrations of similar businesses.

Second, corporate organizational structures are moving toward flexible, multisource international production and away from vertically integrated structures in which a single firm is involved in all aspects of production, marketing, and distribution. Firms are coming to rely more on "strategic alliances, short-term contracts, and the shipment of components from many different international sources to as many different markets" (Glasmeier and Conroy 1994, 6).

Third, increasing global competition has come, in part, from technological changes and corporate restructuring. It in turn has resulted in a rapid increase in multinational firms, foreign direct investment, and international strategic alliances and production networks. Globalization provides opportunities for new foreign investment in U.S. rural areas so that foreign firms can have better access to U.S. markets. It also has the potential to lead to more rural branch plant closures by U.S. firms as they move overseas to seek new markets and lower their production costs.

Fourth, the American population is aging; people live longer, and the baby boom generation (people born between 1946 and 1964) is nearing retirement. Retirees generally do not leave the places where they spent their adult lives, but an increasing number of elderly people are seeking the amenities and low living costs of rural areas. During the 1980s, rural counties that attracted more retirees grew faster than other rural counties. Rural areas in 1990 had a larger share of people over 65 years of age (14.7 percent) than urban areas (11.9 percent). Rural areas also receive a larger share of personal income (18.8 percent) in retirement-related transfer payments (social security and government pensions) than urban areas (13.5 percent). Retirees generate income create a demand for special health care, housing, transportation, and recreational services.

Federal Policy

The federal government attempts to enhance economic activity both through national economic policies and through policies directed at narrower aspects of the public interest, such as maintaining the vitality of specific economic sectors or regions, or achieving specific social goals, such as the maintenance of minimum health and income standards (Reid and Long 1987).

The federal government has three sets of national economic policies through which it attempts to affect the overall level of economic activity in the country: monetary policy, fiscal policy, and trade policy. Through monetary policy, the federal government attempts to influence the money supply, the availability of loanable funds, and the interest rate. The principal tools of monetary policy are the discount rate (the interest rate charged by the Fed-

eral Reserve system on loans to banks), the reserve requirement (the amount of reserves a bank must have on deposit with the Federal Reserve), and the open market operations (purchases and sales of government securities) of the Federal Reserve system. Changes in the money supply, the availability of loans, and the interest rate affect the rate of investment (an important component of gross national product and a determinant of future economic health) and the rate of inflation (which affects the value of the dollar in international trade as well as the domestic standard of living).

Through fiscal policy, the federal government attempts to affect the overall level of national income and employment. The principal tools of fiscal policy are the level of taxation and the level of spending. By changing tax policy, the federal government can affect levels of savings and consumption; and by changing spending, it can affect the levels of overall demand and of employment.

Through trade policy, the federal government can adjust the levels of imports and exports, and thus, of national income and employment. The main tools of trade policy are tariffs (taxes on imports, making them less attractive to American consumers), import quotas (which restrict the supply of imports), nontariff barriers (such as requirements that imports pass certain tests or meet certain standards), and export embargoes (prohibitions of certain exports).

Monetary, fiscal, and trade policies are interrelated and work together to move the nation toward its economic goals of full employment, long-term economic growth, and price stability. The health of the rural economy clearly depends on the health of the national economy; therefore, the success of the federal government in advancing national economic goals is critical to the overall well-being of rural America.

Because of the characteristics of rural industries and population, however, the effects of changes in national economic policy may be felt disproportionately in rural areas. An increase in the interest rate reduces construction activity, which hurts rural economies dependent on sales of wood products. It also increases interest income, which helps rural areas with large concentrations of retirees. Cuts in the federal defense budget that led to military base closings hurt rural areas dependent on those installations. The reduction of trade barriers under the North American Free Trade Agreement and the General Agreement on Tariffs and Trade encourages the movement of low-wage, low-productivity manufacturing plants out of the rural areas of the United States (where they had congregated in recent decades) to foreign countries with lower labor costs (Glasmeier and Conroy 1994).

Some economic policies of the federal government are directed toward specific sectors, regions, or social objectives. These also affect rural economic activity. Sectoral policies attempt to improve the health of individual economic sectors. Agricultural policy, for example, regulates the supply, demand, and price of important farm commodities. Forest policy controls allowable harvest and reforestation on federal timberlands. Fishing policy determines the access to, and allowable harvest from, fisheries. By affecting the production and income of businesses in the natural resource industries on which many rural economies depend, these policies affect the economic health of rural America.

Regional policies attempt to stimulate economic development in specifically defined regions (such as the Tennessee Valley, Appalachia, or the Upper Great Lakes) or in noncontiguous areas with similar characteristics (rural and urban areas). The Appalachian Regional Commission, which administers a range of programs that fund infrastructure investments in Appalachia, is an example of the first kind of policy. The programs of the former Farmers' Home Administration (as a result of a U.S. Department of Agriculture reorganization in October 1995, the FmHA was subdivided into the Farm Services Agency and the Rural Development Agency), which helped finance housing, water, and sewer systems in rural areas, are examples of the second.

Social programs such as Medicaid, Social Security, and Aid to Families with Dependent Children also affect rural economic activity. With higher poverty rates than urban areas and higher proportions of the population over 65 years of age, rural areas can be greatly affected by national or state social program changes.

State and Local Economic Policy

Like the federal government, state and local governments spend, tax, and regulate economic activity, and they, too, can affect the economic health of their regions. In recent years, as economic competition between nations has intensified and corporate structures have become more multinational, states and localities have become much more aggressive in offering incentives to businesses for locating plants in their areas. The state of Oregon, for example, enacted a Strategic Investment Program in 1993 that allows local governments to substantially reduce property taxes on large new industrial investments. This program is credited with inducing several large semiconductor plants to locate in the Portland metropolitan area in the past several years. The size of the minimum investment that qualifies for this program ($100 million) makes it more likely to be attractive in urban areas than in rural ones. In 1995, the neighboring state of Washington enacted its own tax concession plan to attract high-technology investments across the Columbia River.

In a recent survey, Glasmeier and Conroy (1994, 11) found that rural communities offer "wide ranges of subsidized sites, training services, and plant construction, as well as abatement of taxes for long but varying periods of time [in spite of] a relatively strong consensus among both location theorists and development practitioners that the incentives now being offered by local governments may never be recouped in terms of direct and indirect benefits to the communities."

A National Rural Policy?

Many rural areas are economically healthy, but the average rural American has less income, a higher probability of being unemployed or in poverty, and less health care and schooling than the average urban American.

This has led some to suggest that the nation develop a comprehensive rural policy that attempts to reinvigorate rural economies, taking into account the unique characteristics and problems of rural areas. Others, pointing to the diversity of rural areas, the economic interdependence of rural and urban areas, and the increasing importance of state and local leadership in economic development, argue for a federal role limited to creating a healthy macroeconomy, fostering economic cooperation among jurisdictions, and ensuring adequate investment in people (Deavers 1987).

All Americans have a stake in the economic vitality of both urban and rural areas. Rural people depend on urban economies for many specialized goods and services and often move to urban areas in search of jobs and urban amenities. Rural areas are a source of much of the food, fiber, minerals, and water consumed in urban areas and are the places where many urban workers were raised. Urban residents enjoy recreation in rural places and often retire to rural communities.

People will continue to live in rural areas. Economic policy should recognize, therefore, that "it is in the nation's best interest to insure that those who do, and their children, do not become second-class citizens" (Stinson 1989, 7).

—*Bruce A. Weber*

See also

Agricultural and Resource Economics; Development, Community and Economic; Employment; Farm Finance; Financial Intermediaries; Foreclosure and Bankruptcies; Fringe Benefits; Income; Marketing; Natural Resource Economics; Taxes; Trade, International; Trade, Interregional; Workers' Compensation.

References

Browne, William P., and Louis E. Swanson. "Living with the Minimum: Rural Public Policy." Pp. 481–492 in *The American Countryside: Rural People and Places.* Edited by Emery N. Castle. Lawrence: University Press of Kansas, 1995.

Deavers, Kenneth L. "Choosing a Rural Policy for the 1980's and '90's." Pp. 17/1–17/17 in *Rural Economic Development in the 1980's: Preparing for the Future.* ERS Staff Report No. AGES 870724. Edited by David Brown. Washington, DC: U.S. Department of Agriculture, Agriculture and Rural Economy Division, Economic Research Service, July 1987.

Flora, Cornelia B., and James A. Christenson, eds. *Rural Policies for the 1990s.* Boulder, CO: Westview Press, 1991.

Glasmeier, Amy K., and Michael E. Conroy. *Global Squeeze on Rural America: Opportunities, Threats, and Challenges From NAFTA, GATT, and Processes of Globalization.* A Report of the Institute for Policy Research and Evaluation, Graduate School of Public Policy and Administration. College Park: Pennsylvania State University, 1994.

Reid, J. Norman, and Richard W. Long. "Rural Policy Objectives: Defining Problems and Choosing Approaches." Pp. 9/1–9/16 in *Rural Economic Development in the 1980's: Preparing for the Future.* ERS Staff Report No. AGES 870724. Edited by David Brown. Washington, DC: U.S. Department of Agriculture, Agriculture and Rural Economy Division, Economic Research Service, July 1987.

Stinson, Thomas F. "Toward a Federal Rural Policy." *Minnesota Agricultural Economist* 659 (October 1989): 5–7.

Weber, Bruce, Ron Shaffer, Ron Knutson, and Bob Lovan. "Building a Vital Rural America." Pp. 28–37 in *Focus on the Future: Options in Developing a New National Rural Policy.* Proceedings from four regional Rural Development Policy Workshops. College Station: Texas A&M University, Texas Agricultural Extension Service, May 1989.

Weber, Bruce A. "Extractive Industries and Rural-Urban Economic Interdependence." Pp. 155–179 in *The American Countryside: Rural People and Places.* Edited by Emery N. Castle. Lawrence: University Press of Kansas, 1995.

Policy, Environmental

The set of laws, programs, and administrative rules that guide the nation's environment-related actions. Many of the more controversial issues in rural America are in the area of environment. This entry examines a select number of critical areas of environmental concern and the policies and programs that affect them. While not comprehensive, the selection of issues forms a framework under which most environmental problems facing rural America fall.

Historical Background

In the nineteenth century, rural America underwent tremendous environmental change. Much of that change took place after the depression of 1897. These changes were accelerated by the development and use of the automobile. America was expanding in the period prior to 1897. Increased natural resource exploitation, agricultural development, and the establishment of regional community centers occurred, but in most cases, environmental change during this period was local. Regional environmental concerns, on which modern environmental policies are based, did not begin to emerge until the latter part of the nineteenth century.

As American society emerged from the depression of 1897, farmers began to realize increased prices for their goods, industries increased their demand for raw materials, and home construction expanded, driving up the demand for wood products and materials. With the onset of the twentieth century came mass production. Electrical energy came into being, and with it, increased demands for coal and oil. Agriculture began its transition from single-family farms to what became industrial agriculture—large-scale crop production. With the industrialization of agriculture and the chemical revolution of the mid- to late nineteenth century came a new generation of environmental concerns—nonpoint pollution and chemical contamination.

Loss of Agricultural Land

The American landscape is dynamic: Throughout the nation's history, people reworked, altered, and in many instances, permanently changed the character of the lands of rural America. Perhaps the most pronounced environmental changes in rural America occurred in the conversion of agricultural lands from one use to another (development) and in the associated results (such as soil loss).

The rate of conversion of agricultural lands in rural America remains under debate. In 1981, the National Agricultural Lands Study reported that 3 million acres of agricultural land were being lost to urbanization each year. In 1992, the Soil Conservation Service estimated a rate of conversion of 2 million acres per year. The true impact of this change has yet to be realized; but because much of this land was highly productive, its conversion has decreased our ability to produce food and fiber. Moreover, because the lands being converted are highly productive, agriculture is forced to bring marginally productive, environmentally sensitive lands into production. The

This billboard appeared one morning along a highway near Algodones, New Mexico. The message to prospective developers and buyers is a definite "stay out"—a clear response to the environmental threats posed to rural areas by development.

net results are poor yields and increased environmental impacts. The response to these changes came on a number of fronts with the central federal mandate embodied in the 1995 Farm Bill.

The 1995 Farm Bill

At present, the U.S. Congress devotes billions of dollars each year to subsidies that result in farmers applying large doses of pesticides and chemical fertilizers to their crops. Such practices contribute substantially to the contamination of drinking water, result in unnecessary pesticide residues on foods, and degrade the environment. At this writing, the 1995 Farm Bill is still being debated in Congress, and several major changes are being considered. Current policy discourages sound farm practices such as crop rotation to replace soil nutrients naturally rather than with chemical fertilizers. Further, the existing system denies farmers the freedom to decide what crops to grow, artificially manipulates the free-market price of crops, channels most of the benefits to a relatively small group of farm operations, and locks out many small family farmers.

The 1995 Farm Bill has several major objectives. The first is to advance environmentally sound farming by adopting a stewardship program to replace existing subsidy payments at no net additional cost to taxpayers. The stewardship program will create options for farmers to emphasize lower use of pesticides and chemical fertilizers and to reduce polluted runoff from farm land. In addition, the Farm Bill attempts to provide special incentives to small family farmers and those now excluded from farm programs to adopt environmentally sound farming practices that include such measures as wetlands conservation and endangered species protection. Finally, the Farm Bill will retain and improve existing environmental provisions, including the Conservation Reserve, Wetlands Reserve, Swampbuster, and Sodbuster programs.

Conservation Reserve Program

The Conservation Reserve Program (CRP) is a voluntary program that pays farmers to retire environmentally sensitive lands from production for 10 years. These lands include highly erodible areas, farmed wetlands, floodplains, and areas next to streams. Participating farmers receive an annual payment, plus cost sharing to establish a permanent cover of grass, trees, or shrubs. CRP was designed to reduce surplus crop production and to provide important environmental benefits including soil erosion control, improved water quality, wildlife habitat enhancement, and increased recreational opportunities. Since its authorization in 1985, 36.5 million acres have been enrolled in the CRP.

CRP is largely a grassland restoration program, because most environmentally sensitive, marginal cropland was converted from native prairie in the Great Plains and prairie region. CRP provided a stewardship opportunity to move away from farming unnecessarily on highly erodible, environmentally sensitive lands. Approximately 87 percent of CRP acreage was restored to grassland habitat, and about two-thirds is located in prairie regions.

Wetlands

There are roughly half as many wetlands in the contiguous 48 states today as there were 200 years ago. The rate of conversion was about 105,000 acres per year between 1987 and 1991, down from 500,000 acres annually between 1954 and 1974. Six federal agencies are primarily responsible for about 25 laws that provide for the regulation, acquisition, or protection of wetlands. The current distribution and quality of wetlands in rural America are the products of ever-changing wetland policies. These policy shifts are the result of increased understanding of the importance of viable wetlands in the landscape.

Wetlands were initially viewed in America as wastelands. These areas were believed to be unproductive, a nuisance, and a health hazard. In the Swampland Acts of 1849, 1850, and 1860, Congress granted 64.9 million acres of wetlands to 15 states in exchange for state promises to drain and convert them to farmland. The Reclamation Act of 1902 and the 1944 Federal Flood Control Act involved the U.S. Department of Agriculture (USDA) and the U.S. Army Corps of Engineers, respectively, in programs to promote wetland conversion. Other federal policies provided USDA cost-sharing for drainage. Tax laws allowed reimbursement by the government for drainage costs, and farm commodity programs encouraged the expansion of production.

During the 1940s and into the 1970s, messages to swampland owners became mixed following the adoption of policies that encouraged wetland protection. By 1962, USDA cost-sharing was eliminated for certain classes of wetlands. The Water Bank Program (implemented in 1972 in ten states) was the first USDA effort to encourage the protection of wetlands.

Federal Water Pollution Control Act Amendments in 1972 regulated the discharge of dredge and fill material into navigable waters. Executive Order 11990 (1972) stated that U.S. agencies should not be involved in any development activities that encouraged wetland conversion. By 1978, drainage cost-sharing had been eliminated.

Swampbuster provisions of the 1985 Food Security Act eliminated USDA farm program benefits for crops grown on wetlands converted after 1985 by tying farm program benefits to compliance with wetland protection measures. Swampbuster (legislation designed to protect wetlands) legislation was continued by the 1990 farm bill, with modifications including a switch in the timing of when swampbusting activities could take place from the time when the crop was planted to the time when conversion would make crop planting possible; an expansion of program benefits lost due to swampbusting; and the allowance of legal mitigation regarding specific swampbuster application in certain circumstances.

Much of the recent wetland controversy was focused on defining and delineating wetlands. Mainly there is disagreement concerning evidence of three wetland characteristics (soils, hydrology, and vegetation) needed to identify an area as a wetland. Wetlands regulated under sections 401 and 404 of the Clean Water Act (see below) were identified using technical criteria in the 1987 Corps of Engineers Wetland Delineation Manual.

The Clinton administration embraced the concept of no net loss as an interim goal in wetland protection, with the long-run goal of increasing the quality and quantity of the nation's wetland resource base. No net loss of wetlands is not a policy per se but is a policy goal specifying that loss of wetlands be balanced with a gain in wetlands elsewhere. The Natural Resource Conservation Service (NRCS) of the USDA has the responsibility to determine the extent of Swampbuster and Clean Water Act jurisdiction on agricultural lands.

Wetlands will continue as an important and controversial environmental arena in rural America. The unprecedented floods in the Midwest in 1993 and again in 1997 inundated millions of acres of farmland and led to an increased emphasis on the need for floodplain management. As a result, flood relief and floodplain management are used as the rationale to fund wetland restoration in the Mississippi Valley.

Section 404 of the Clean Water Act

The primary goal of the Clean Water Act (CWA), 33 U.S.C. §1251 et seq., is to "restore and maintain the chemical, physical, and biological integrity of the Nation's waters." In keeping with that goal, Section 404 of the CWA regulates the disposal of dredged and fill material in U.S. waters, including wetlands. Other activities that destroy wetlands, such as drainage, flooding, pumping, and burning, are not regulated under the CWA unless they entail discharges of dredged or fill material into U.S. waters.

Section 404 is administered jointly by the U.S. Army Corps of Engineers (Corps) and the U.S. Environmental Protection Agency (EPA). The Corps is authorized to issue or deny permits for fill in U.S. waters. Section 404(b)(1) of the CWA directs the EPA to develop guidelines for the Corps to use in assessing environmental impacts of proposed projects. The EPA also has veto authority over Corps permits. In addition, the EPA, the U.S. Fish and Wildlife Service (FWS), and the National Marine Fisheries Service (NMFS) may review and comment on permit applications, provide technical assistance to protect fish and wildlife resources, and mitigate project impacts.

Under §404(e) of the CWA, the Corps has authority to issue general permits on a state, regional, and nationwide basis for any category of activities involving discharges of dredged or fill material if the activities are similar in nature and will cause only minimal, individual, and cumulative adverse environmental impacts. General permits constitute an alternative to individual §404 permits. When landowners apply for individual §404 permits, the Corps gives each permit application a case-specific review. A general permit, on the other hand, operates like an exemption: If the proposed activity fits the category of activities authorized under a general permit, it is automatically authorized.

The Corps authorizes approximately 90 percent of proposed activities, or about 90,000 activities annually, through general permits. Only about 10 percent of projects or activities that affect wetlands are regulated through individual permits.

By 1995, the Corps had issued 39 nationwide general permits and many more state and regional general permits. Typical projects covered under general permits include navigation markers, utility line structures, bank stabilization projects, minor dredge and fill projects involving less than 10 cubic yards of fill material (not in wetlands), boat docks, and certain federally approved and funded projects.

Probably the single most controversial general permit is Nationwide Permit 26 (NWP 26), which authorizes discharges of dredged or fill material into wetlands that are either isolated or above the headwaters of a river or stream with average annual flow of 5 cubic feet per second or less. Isolated wetlands are those that are not adjacent to water bodies such as lakes or streams. An estimated 10,000 wetland acres were lost through Nationwide Permit 26 alone.

Under NWP 26, activities that fill less than 1 acre of wetland are automatically authorized without any meaningful environmental review. For fills between 1 and 10 acres in size, NWP 26 requires the discharger to notify the Corps before discharging by submitting a predischarge notification. The Corps will consider the proposed fill action and send a notice to the EPA, the FWS, and the NMFS to allow them an opportunity to comment. The agencies have 30 days in which to notify the discharger of any additional restrictions in the NWP 26 authorization. Otherwise, the discharger may proceed in compliance with the general conditions of the NWP 26 regulations. For fill activities that would destroy 10 or more acres of isolated wetlands or headwaters, an individual §404 permit is required.

Water

Water resources in rural America have been overused and misused. America's surface-water resources are truly immense. There are over a million miles of rivers and streams in America. The nation's inland water bodies encompass over 61,000 square miles, and there are an additional 94,000 square miles in the Great Lakes.

Surface water bodies serve as the drinking water supply for half of America's population. These systems are also the repository for wastes from 64,000 factories and sewage treatment plants. Of these dischargers, about 7,000 are considered major dischargers under federal legislation; billions of pounds of pollutants are released into the nation's waters every year from these point sources.

Groundwater faces similar problems. Since 1985, America, and in particular rural America, has increased its use of groundwater. Contamination of groundwater also has increased. Much of this contamination has come from chemical pollution: heavy metals such as mercury or cadmium; pesticides such as DDT and 2,4,5-TP; and organic chemicals such as PCBs and dioxins.

Water Policy

The goal of the federal Clean Water Act is that all waters be safe for fishing and swimming. To date, only 66 percent of the nation's waters meet this goal. To achieve this ambitious goal, Congress enacted a variety of programs attacking the many types of pollution entering the waters.

The Clean Water Act established a federal-state partnership to control the discharge of pollutants from large point sources. The EPA develops national guidelines for controlling industrial pollution discharges, based on the best available technology that is economically viable. These national standards regulate and apply to entire industrial categories.

Sewage treatment plants must meet basic levels of secondary treatment that use biological processes to transform disease-causing organisms into harmless matter. The federal government has provided billions of dollars in grants and loans to state and local governments to construct sewage treatment plants so that they can meet this standard.

All industrial and sewage treatment plants must obtain a permit that specifies the type and amount of pollutants they may discharge. The permits specify industrywide technology standards, state water quality standards, and sewage treatment standards that apply to that source. They are reviewed and renewed every five years to account for improvements in technology. Thirty-nine states run this type of permitting program, which holds dischargers accountable. The federal government, the state governments, and citizens can sue sources that violate their permits.

To ensure that waters stay safe for fishing and swimming, new sources of pollution are carefully reviewed to ensure they will not degrade the water body. Pristine waters, such as headwaters in our national parks or wilderness areas, can be designated by states to receive special protection.

Polluted runoff from agriculture, forestry, mining, and other sources is the largest remaining source of water pollution. Under current law, states are required to plan and use cost-effective, best management practices by landowners at the earliest practical date. Requirements for individual landowners who cause pollution are weak and unenforceable.

One source of water pollution that is becoming increasingly significant is the growth of large feedlots and factory farms. These concentrated animal feeding operations are responsible for phosphorus, pathogens, and nutrients from animal waste seeping into surface and groundwater. The EPA regulates these operations as point sources, but enforcement has been minimal.

Habitat and Species Loss

The rate of species extinction, although a natural process, has reached epidemic proportions in recent years. It is currently estimated that as many as 100 species are lost each day. By comparison, the rate of extinction before the appearance of humans was only about one species every 100 years.

Protecting the existence and variety of species (biological diversity) is essential, since all living species, including humans, are dependent on each other for survival. An astounding number of plant species provide over 40 percent of prescription drugs, including a possible cure for threatening diseases like AIDS and cancer. They provide sustainable food crops and consumer products like cotton and paper, clean the air and water, and give invaluable aesthetic and recreational experiences.

The acceleration of the extinction rate is directly linked with the human population explosion and the increased demands it places on the environment. More people mean more trash, buildings, roads, and highways, all factors that might endanger species survival. People alter or destroy habitats by drilling for oil, strip mining for minerals, or logging for timber, which often conflicts with species ability to find food and shelter and raise their young. Wildlife trade, pollution, and the introduction of nonnative species take their toll on indigenous ecosystems.

The Endangered Species Act of 1973 was an attempt to counteract the alarming rate of species extinction. The act provides a mechanism for conserving plants and animals in danger of extinction and protects the ecosystems necessary for their survival. Once a troubled species is identified, it is placed on a threatened or endangered species list. Either the U.S. Fish and Wildlife Service or the National Marine Fisheries Administration is then responsible for developing a plan to aid the species' recovery and for ensuring that government and citizen actions do not harm the species further. The act requires that a recovery plan be written for each species listed.

Congress periodically reauthorizes the Endangered Species Act by reviewing the law and making necessary changes. Funding authorization for the Endangered Species Act expired in 1992, but Congress has continued to appropriate funding annually for the act's programs. As of this writing, the Endangered Species Act has yet to be reauthorized.

Despite the continued overwhelming support of U.S. citizens, there are growing pressures from special interest groups to weaken the Endangered Species Act.

These groups, representing various members of the oil, timber, mining, livestock, and real estate development industries, see environmental laws as blocking their ability to do business.

Future Challenges
The environmental challenges that confront rural America are global in scope. The responsibility to protect and preserve environmental quality belongs both to individuals and to communities, here and abroad.

Ecological interdependence exists among nations; there is no boundary to our environment, so the issues facing rural America will involve individuals and communities from many nations and regions. How the rural American environment is treated ultimately will affect other parts of the world, including those guilty of its neglect or abuse. Current and future environmental concerns require that individuals think globally while acting locally. In agriculture, for example, cropping practices should be adopted that minimize the contaminants produced while providing sinks for those that are contaminating. There is a continuing need to merge environmental considerations with those of economics in decision making at the local and international levels in order to provide equitable solutions to problems. For agriculture, this implies providing technology, where appropriate, to help other nations overcome their problems. At the same time, social and cultural differences must be respected in any attempt to improve the human condition, in America's cities and rural areas as well as abroad.

—*William W. Budd*

See also
Agricultural Programs; Biodiversity; Conservation, Energy; Conservation, Soil; Conservation, Water; Environmental Protection; Environmental Regulations; Forestry Industry; Groundwater; Land Stewardship; Mining Industry; Natural Resource Economics; Parks; Policy, Agricultural; Soil; Water Use; Wetlands; Wilderness; Wildlife.

References
Petulla, Joseph M. *American Environmental History.* 2d ed. Columbus, OH: Merrill Publishing Co., 1988.
Plater, Zygmunt J. B., Robert H. Abrams, and William Goldfarb. *Environmental Law and Policy: A Coursebook on Nature, Law, and Society.* St. Paul, MN: West Publications, 1992.
Steiner, Frederick R. *Soil Conservation in the United States: Policy and Planning.* Baltimore: Johns Hopkins University Press, 1990.
Valente, C., and W. Valente. *Introduction to Environmental Law and Policy.* St. Paul, MN: West Publications, 1995.

Policy, Food
Government programs and regulations designed to help assure that all Americans have access to an adequate diet of safe food at a reasonable price. Food policy is consistent with investing in the health and productivity of people, especially the poor. This entry looks at the nature and extent of poverty in rural America, the food programs available to the rural poor, and how well they are served by these programs. For rural America, food policy was originally designed to uphold the income of farmers by purchasing surplus commodities and stabilizing farm prices and incomes. Redistributing surplus food, or the means to purchase food, provided food and nutritionally sound diets to about two-thirds of the poor and hungry. In the early twentieth century, it was perceived that rural people could grow their own food; thus, the distribution of food to alleviate hunger and help poor people maintain their health and lead productive lives was an urban program. However, the percentage of people living in poverty is greater in rural areas, and in modern times, they are little more likely to grow their own food than city people. Food assistance programs are at least as important for the rural poor as for the nonrural poor in America.

The Poor and the Rural Poor in America
Lack of food and inadequate nutrition are almost always results of inadequate income. The poverty level in America is defined by the ability to purchase a minimally nutritious diet. The number of Americans living below the official poverty level changed little between 1960 and 1993 (39.9 to 39.3 million), but the proportion of poor declined from 22.2 percent of the population (30.0 percent of the rural population) in 1960 to 15.1 percent of the population (16.8 percent of the rural population) in 1993. One-fourth of rural children live in poverty. For a frame of reference, a family of four was considered to live in poverty in 1993 if they had an annual earned income of less than $14,763. The median U.S. household income was $31,241 in 1993, whereas the median rural (nonmetropolitan) household income was $25,256.

Average incomes are lower in rural areas primarily because wages are lower. Over half of workers in rural areas earn low wages, if one defines low wages as an annual income beneath the federally defined poverty level. Between 1970 and 1986, the real (inflation adjusted) median income in metropolitan areas increased almost 4 percent, whereas it fell 1.4 percent in rural areas. As industry has moved out of rural areas, workers also have moved out, leaving behind housing that depreciated in value. This relatively inexpensive housing became attractive to the poor from other areas, where housing often absorbs more than 50 percent of total household income. This phenomenon tends to concentrate poverty in pockets of rural areas where people are poorer, older, less well-educated, more mobile, and less connected to the labor force than those who moved out. These tend to be people who are persistently poor, with long-term needs for food assistance and other aid programs. These poor people also tend to move more frequently in search of seasonal jobs or even cheaper housing. The elderly in rural areas are also more likely to be poor than the elderly in metropolitan areas.

About 27.5 percent of the U.S. population and 22 percent of households are in rural America; but only 2.4 percent live on farms. In spite of a general out-migration from rural areas, the proportion of rural nonfarm population has been fairly stable at 20 to 25 percent for nearly two centuries.

Characteristics of the poor in rural America are as diverse as they are anywhere; but their main distinguishing characteristic is that they are more likely to be working than are their urban or suburban counterparts. Two-thirds of the rural poor (42 percent of nonrural poor) are working and two-thirds have one worker per household; one-fourth have two workers. Low wages lead to twice as many rural working families being poor than urban working families. Eight percent of rural poor (5 percent of urban poor) are considered persistently poor. The rural poor are more likely to live in a household with two parents present; half of such couples are married. The rural poor are more likely to be elderly (14 percent versus 9 percent of nonrural poor) and/or White (73 percent versus 54 percent or nonrural poor). They have lower levels of education; over half of the rural poor live in the South. Although 20 percent of farmers reportedly live in poverty, rural poverty is not an agricultural problem. It is a problem for a broad range of people who do not earn sufficient income to be able to purchase enough food to have a nutritionally adequate diet on a regular basis.

Food Programs and Rural People

The first government food assistance programs were started during the Great Depression of the 1930s. Since hunger is largely caused by a lack of income, enhancing the incomes of farmers (25 percent of the population then) was one way to alleviate rural hunger. Distributing food to nonfarmers was a way to invest in the human capital of the country by trying to prevent hunger. Thirteen million people (5 percent of the population) were receiving food supplements by 1939. An early version of the Food Stamp Program was initiated at that time. Most of these early food programs were discontinued during World War II.

Increased demand for agricultural products and a strong economy brought food policy back to the political foreground in the late 1960s. Public attention was once again focused on the pressing problems of the poor, as evidenced by the widespread publicity given to a book titled *Let Them Eat Promises: The Politics of Hunger in America;* a CBS television documentary titled *Hunger, U.S.A.;* congressional fact-finding trips to the rural South; and various political protests. Although many food assistance programs, including the current Food Stamp Program, already had been established by the late 1960s, a White House conference was held in 1969 at which former President Nixon said it was time to end hunger in America once and for all. A Senate select committee on nutrition and human needs was established; spending on food programs reached $1.1 billion by 1969. During the 1970s, a major expansion took place in the Food Stamp Program, and federal expenditures on food assistance reached $35.5 billion by fiscal year 1993. The table lists many food and nutritional assistance programs that were in effect in 1993. Government spending for most programs rose in real terms over the 20-year period between 1973 and 1993. This is partly due to increased food costs and partly due to an increase in the numbers of eligible for these programs. In addition, there have been some absolute increases in the value of food stamps and in dollars allocated to purchase food for distribution.

Food programs serve rural people at least as well as they do those in metropolitan areas. Food program participants are overrepresented in rural areas: While 22 percent of all households are in rural areas, 30 percent of the households receiving food stamps are rural. Reports about the participation rates in the food stamp program vary by research organization or agency, but there seems to be a consensus that only about two-thirds of those eligible participate in both rural and urban areas.

Food stamps are, however, a relatively less important source of food aid in rural areas. Ignorance and pride often prevent people from using food stamps; and pride related to self-sufficiency is allegedly greater in rural areas, especially among farmers. Transportation to apply for, pick up, and use food stamps is also a greater problem in rural areas. The situation is exacerbated by the fact that many of the rural poor are elderly and may need to hire

USDA Food Assistance Program Costs

	Year Program Initiated	Cost of Program During Fiscal Year 1993 ($ millions)	1973 or First Full Year of the Program	Initial Annual Cost During First Full Year of Program in Constant 1993 Dollars ($ millions)	% Change 1973–1993 (or First Full Program Year, 1993)
Food Stamp	1961	23,605.0	1973	6,975.38	238.40
Nutrition Assistance[1]	1975–1982	1,043.9	1975	695.37	50.12
Food Donation Program[2]	1936	456.6	1973	890.80	-48.74
WIC	1972	2,818.5	1976	357.93	687.45
Commodity Supply Food[3]	1982	73.9	1987	70.81	4.36
Child Nutrition		7,047.3			
National School Lunch	1946	4,670.9	1973	2,787.00	67.57
School Breakfast	1966	866.0	1973	109.30[4]	692.05
Child & Adult Care	1968	1,218.4	1973	63.20	1,827.85
Summer Food Service	1969	210.4	1973	84.06	150.31
Other[4]		81.7			
Special Milk	1955	18.7	1973	286.93	-93.48
Food Program Administration		103.5			
TEFAP	1981	191.8	1983	1,437.41	-86.66

[1]The Nutrition Assistance Program began in July 1982 and includes block grants to Puerto Rico and to the Northern Marianas. Puerto Rico participated in the Food Stamp Program from FY 1975 to June 1982. Numbers for 1975 are costs for food stamps in Puerto Rico.

[2]Includes food distribution on Indian reservations, Nutrition Program for the Elderly (NPE), disaster feeding, soup kitchens, and food banks.

[3]Includes Elderly Pilot Projects (EPP). As of January 1987, also includes elderly participants in non-EPP projects.

[4]Includes commodities for schools, nutrition studies and education, and state administrative expenses.

Source: Food and Nutrition Service, *Food Program Update: Fiscal Year 1993* (Washington, DC: U.S. Department of Agriculture), p. 4 and updates; Food and Nutrition Service, *Annual Historical Review of FNS Programs: Fiscal Year 1989* (Washington, DC: U.S. Department of Agriculture).

someone to drive them to a county office to obtain food stamps, which might well cost them more than the value of the stamps. The high mobility of rural poor might make it difficult for them to receive food aid in the new location without reestablishing their eligibility. Other problems include a lack of literacy required to fill out forms, and an asset base that may be needed to do business (for example, farm equipment or other expensive vehicles) but that disqualifies a family for food assistance. Case workers who do not understand the different financial resources and assets in rural areas or who insult rural applicants may preclude some from participating although they are eligible. Additionally, average rural case loads often run higher than 250 per worker, making it very difficult to serve all clients well.

A larger percentage of rural children (80 percent) receive a school lunch than do city children (62 percent), and more than half of the Temporary Emergency Food Assistance Program (TEFAP) food distribution sites are located in rural areas. The elderly in rural areas are more likely to participate (50 percent) in feeding programs than are urban elderly (43 percent). The variety of food aid programs for the elderly, such as Senior Nutrition sites, where hot meals are served five days a week and food packages are provided to take home, or door-to-door meal delivery programs, make it relatively easy for

seniors to participate. In many communities attendance at the senior citizen center has become a noontime social event.

Food banks and other food distribution centers in rural areas are also frequented by the elderly. Many seniors report that they prefer to obtain food rather than food stamps. The food shelves are easier to access on an ad hoc basis, serving temporary food needs without much eligibility screening. Since many food stamp recipients run out of food before the end of the month, they also supplement their food supply with food from food banks, which have become an important part of the nutritional safety net.

Food assistance is not designed to lift people out of poverty. It does, however, provide basic nutrition and food for those who would otherwise go hungry. The monetary value of food stamps is about 20 to 30 percent of a poverty-level income for a family of four. The combination of food stamps with other related food and welfare programs can provide between 45 and 90 percent of the value of a poverty-level income. Most studies found that those who receive food stamps increase their overall food spending by about 20 to 30 percent (Senauer and Young 1986; Fraker 1993). One dollar's worth of food stamps frees 70 to 80 cents of cash that was previously used for food and that can then be spent on other goods and services. Food stamp recipients also eat more nutritious diets than nonparticipants who are eligible for the program.

The impact of food programs on farm incomes is negligible, even though initially many food programs were implemented to enhance farm incomes. However, farm prices have been estimated to rise less than 1 percent and farm income less than 1.8 percent for every dollar spent on food aid. Total food expenditures on food to be eaten at home increased less than 3 percent as a result of domestic food aid. Whereas the impact of food programs on individual recipients' health and well-being can be dramatic and society's investment in its human capital is rewarding on both productive and humanitarian grounds, food policy as implemented in the United States has had little impact on agricultural producers.

Over the years, food policy has graduated from the distribution of surplus commodities to supplement individuals' diets to a program of providing whole, nutritious meals, nutritional education, and in some cases, cash with which poor consumers can purchase whatever they deem most important to their livelihood. Recipients tend to prefer cash with as little administrative regulation as possible. Taxpayers tend to prefer highly targeted and monitored programs that ensure that their dollars are spent on nutritious food. This long-standing tension will play out in political and economic decisions as long as there are food and other welfare programs for people with low incomes.

—*Jean Kinsey*

See also

Consumerism; Food Safety; Home Economics; Homelessness; Nutrition; Policy (various entries); Poverty.

References

Devaney, B., and R. Moffit. "Dietary Effects of the Food Stamp Program." *American Journal of Agricultural Economics* 73 (1991): 202–211.

Duncan, Cynthia M. *Rural Poverty in America*. New York: Auburn House, 1992.

Fraker, Thomas. "The Effects of Food Stamps on Food Consumption: A Review of the Literature." (October). Alexandria, VA: U.S. Department of Agriculture, Food and Nutrition Center, Office of Analysis and Evaluation (a product of Mathematica Policy Research, Inc.), 1990.

Kinsey, Jean D., and David M. Smallwood. "Domestic Food Aid Programs." Pp. 135–152 in *Food, Agricultural and Rural Policy into the Twenty-first Century*. Edited by M. Hallberg, B. Spitze, and D. Ray. Boulder, CO: Westview Press, 1994.

Lane, Sylvia, John Kushman, and Christine Ranney. "Food Stamp Program Participation: An Exploratory Analysis." *Western Journal of Agricultural Economics* 8 (1983): 13–26.

Physician Task Force on Hunger in America. *Hunger in America: The Growing Epidemic*. Middletown, CT: Wesleyan University Press, 1985.

Senauer, Ben, and Jean Kinsey, eds. *Final Report by the Food and Consumer Issues Working Group, 1995 Farm Bill Project*. Washington, DC: National Center for Food and Agricultural Policy; St. Paul: University of Minnesota, Hubert H. Humphrey Institute of Agricultural Policy, March 1995.

Senauer, Benjamin, and Nathan Young. "The Impacts of Food Stamps on Food Expenditures: Rejection of the Traditional Model." *American Journal of Agricultural Economics* 68 (1986): 37–43.

Stewart, James B., and Joyce E. Allen-Smith, eds. *Blacks in Rural America*. New Brunswick, NJ: Transaction Publishers, 1995.

U.S. Congress. *Hunger in Rural America: Hearing before the Subcommittee on Domestic Marketing, Consumer Relations, and Nutrition of the Committee on Agriculture, House of Representatives*, 101st Congress, May 17, 1989, Serial No. 101-15. Washington, DC: Government Printing Office, 1989.

Policy, Health Care

The constellation of public actions and decisions, especially at the federal level, that influences the ability of rural people to receive needed health care services. This entry makes six major points. First, rural health issues and services are a long-standing national concern. Second, the federal government played a particularly important and helpful role during the past half-century. Third, despite this extended period of federal intervention, many historical issues and problems remain. Fourth, rural health issues and needs are not monolithic. Fifth, the historical context for thinking about rural health issues and rural policy may be of little value in the future. Sixth, it is important to make a connection or linkage between rural health considerations and broader rural development needs.

Health and health care services are not synonymous. Health is affected by a broad array of factors: parental genetics; societal violence; automobile safety and speed limits; drug usage, including alcohol and tobacco; and eating and exercise habits. Health care services are simply another input affecting health. However, these services are an expensive input. Specifically, in 1994, health care spending in the United States totaled nearly $1 trillion . Of this, $338 billion was spent on hospital care, $189 billion on physician services, $72 billion for nursing home care, and $78 billion for drugs and related items. The major focus of this entry is on health care services.

The History of Federal Policy and Programs

The traditional notion of rural locales as sources of strong, healthy people, both physically and mentally, was long ago brought into question. As early as 1862, President Lincoln's commissioner of agriculture called atten-

Cambridge Memorial Hospital, Cambridge, Nebraska. The size of this small rural hospital hints at the many challenges facing policymakers attempting to provide rural residents with high-quality health care.

tion to the high incidence of insanity and respiratory disease among farm people, and also noted that the longevity of farmers was not as great as the public supposed. However, it was not until the early twentieth century that the federal government became involved in any aspect of health care services, rural or urban. One of the first federal initiatives helpful in rural areas was the Sheppard-Towner Act of 1921. This act contributed to the strengthening of rural county health departments by providing federal grants to the states for maternal and child health services. Perhaps the most remarkable health service program directed specifically at low-income farm families was initiated by the U.S. Farm Security Administration (the forerunner of what later became the Farmers' Home Administration). This program offered loans and grants to families in the 1930s and 1940s, enabling them to enroll in prepaid medical care plans that provided physician, hospital, and sometimes dental and drug services. In 1942, the peak year, these subsidized, local health insurance plans served over 600,000 persons in 1,100 rural counties.

The national Hospital Survey and Construction Act of 1946 (also known as the Hill-Burton Act) was not designed exclusively for rural areas but had the effect of channeling billions of dollars into the construction or modernization of rural hospitals. Many of today's rural hospitals owe their existence to this particular piece of federal legislation.

During the 1960s' war on poverty, the laws creating Medicare and Medicaid were passed. Medicare was designed for the elderly, and Medicaid was a federal-state partnership that targeted the poor. Both programs provided public funds to help pay for medical services.

Because rural areas had a disproportionately large share of the elderly and poor, these programs were particularly helpful to those areas.

Providing the elderly and poor with an insurance subsidy was useless if medical services were unavailable. In the 1960s and 1970s, several federal programs were enacted to expand the supply of services. One example was the tremendous federal subsidy for medical education that began in the early 1970s. Along with the concern for increasing the number of physicians came growing concern over their geographic distribution, which led to the establishment in 1970 of the National Health Service Corps (NHSC). Selected physicians, dentists, nurses, and others were given financial support for their professional education, and they repaid this support by agreeing to practice for a certain number of years in federally-designated underserved areas. This program continues to operate and has proven to be especially helpful to inner cities and rural areas.

NHSC personnel are often located in federally supported community health centers (CHCs). The CHC program provides funds to establish and maintain primary care facilities and services in many underserved areas. A separate federal initiative provides basic medical services to the migrant farmworker population.

Two subsets of the rural population are served by health care systems that are owned and operated by the federal government, in contrast to the more common approach of providing incentives and subsidies to providers and consumers. One subset is served by the Veterans' Administration (VA), which operates hospitals, clinics, and other facilities for urban and rural veterans and their families. The other is the Indian Health Service (IHS), an entity that has been in existence since 1849.

A number of other important federal programs could be noted. For example, the area health education centers movement started in 1972, and the Rural Health Clinics Act became law in 1978. Both have proven to be invaluable in rural areas. Although we cannot describe these and other relevant programs in detail here, two observations are in order.

First, the historic thrust of the federal government's involvement in health care has been directed toward improving access to services. Rural areas benefited in two ways: from several programs that included both rural and urban populations (such as Medicare) and others that specifically targeted rural populations or underserved areas (such as NHSC).

Second, efforts by the federal government to

improve access, whether in rural or urban areas, generally take one of two distinct forms: demand-oriented or supply-oriented. Medicare and Medicaid are examples of demand-oriented programs in which individuals are subsidized in their purchase of medical services. With the supply-oriented approach, the federal government focuses on stimulating the supply of services. Examples include the NHSC and the CHC programs. Two very different mechanisms are incorporated into the supply-side approach. The most common mechanism involves the transfer of resources by the federal government to qualified state and local entities to provide services. The other mechanism is typified by the IHS and VA, with centralized federal ownership of the delivery systems.

Today's Issues and Problems

The various federal policies and programs have made a difference, but they have not entirely solved the problems that led to their inception. Some of the problems that continue to plague rural America are reflected in the following statistics. First, the physician-to-population ratio in nonmetropolitan counties is only slightly greater than half the metropolitan ratio. Second, more than three-fourths of all nonmetropolitan counties were designated health professional shortage areas by the U.S. Department of Health and Human Services between 1978 and 1995. Third, the rate of hospital closure during the past 15 years has been much higher among rural hospitals than among urban hospitals. Fourth, the proportion of the non-Medicare population without health insurance is somewhat higher among the rural population than the urban population. Fifth, in 1992, the average amount of Medicare expenditures per beneficiary was $3,937 for beneficiaries living in metropolitan areas, but only $3,191 for their nonmetropolitan counterparts. Finally, reimbursement rates to rural health care providers are typically much lower than those to urban providers. For example, one payment option under Medicare is called capitation. The capitated rate is what a provider will receive per month for agreeing to provide a comprehensive set of services to a Medicare beneficiary. The 15 lowest rates in 1992 were all in rural counties, ranging from $207 to $234. By contrast, New York City and Miami had capitated rates in the neighborhood of $700.

Rural Diversity

Whereas the differences between rural and urban areas noted above are of great interest and importance, the differences within rural America are of equal importance,

especially from the standpoint of rural health policy. For example, the rural health problem in the South is linked to ongoing repetition of a historical pattern of poverty and racism. For the most part, this is not the issue in the rural Great Plains and Intermountain West. In these regions, the sparsity of population leads to situations where people might be 100 miles or more from services and where it is economically difficult to provide a more even distribution of services, especially of complex health care services. In recognition of this, some health care policies and programs have targeted what are officially known as frontier areas (geographic areas with fewer than six persons per square mile). Differences in the availability of services within rural America are illustrated by yet another example: More than 100 nonmetropolitan counties do not have a single practicing physician. At the other extreme, one particular nonmetropolitan county has the highest physician-to-population ratio in the United States (either rural or urban)—Montour County, Pennsylvania, home of the world-renowned Geisinger Medical Center.

Separating the Past from the Future

The current and historical framework for thinking about rural health needs, issues, and policies is fundamentally obsolete. Several elements of impending change represent an unprecedented convergence of interrelated forces. First, the locus of public policy has been shifting from the societal goal of access to health care services toward cost containment. Many access-oriented programs of special importance to rural areas will likely have less standing in the public debate than they had in the past. Equity concerns, such as insurance coverage and distance to health care, are likely to become secondary relative to cost containment and efficiency concerns.

Second, largely in response to the concern with cost containment, the health care industry is experiencing an unparalleled shift toward managed care, of which the consolidation, integration, and coordination of services are foreseeable results. Some have speculated that in the not-so-distant future, a handful of national health care conglomerates may provide the bulk of the nation's health care services in both urban and rural areas. The norms of the free-standing hospital and the sole practitioner are quickly disappearing.

Third, pressures to control Medicare spending will continue to mount as the baby boomer generation draws nearer to retirement. Medicare is the single largest source of revenue both for physicians practicing in rural areas

(33.1 percent) and for rural hospitals (38.8 percent). These percentages are substantially higher than for urban providers.

Fourth, the locus of public policy is shifting from the federal level to the levels of states and locales. There has been serious discussion about ending Medicaid's status as an entitlement program and redesigning it as a block-grant program. Medicaid is the source of 16.1 percent of the revenue for rural physicians and 11.4 percent of the revenue for rural hospitals. Comparable figures are 10.5 percent and 12.9 percent, respectively, for urban providers.

Fifth, cost-effective, information-age technologies will lead to many changes. It will be more common for patients in remote rural areas to have certain specialized services made available to them through their local, attending physician. In addition, rural health professionals and administrators will experience less professional isolation as more information, collegial support, and continuing education opportunities are made available to them.

Sixth, even with increased efficiency and a decrease in federal health care expenditures, health services will be a growth industry, driven by the rapid increase in the number of elderly.

The Relationship to a Broader Rural Development Agenda

The historical concern over rural health services understandably focused on the need to provide care to those in need. However, the local health care sector also plays an important role relative to broader rural development needs. There are at least five dimensions to this role. First, health care services can influence health status, which in turn influences labor productivity, absenteeism, and quality of life. Second, high-quality services make a community more desirable and effective in attracting and retaining people and businesses. Third, the skills and abilities of health professionals and other health-service workers are available to the community to enhance the local pool of leadership talent. Fourth, the health services sector needs cash and short-term investments to meet payroll and other needs. Typically these funds are held in local financial institutions and become available for investment by others. Finally, the health services sector is an important local employer and purchaser of local goods and services.

Although the health care sector can legitimately be viewed as a growth industry, it is not likely that all locales will benefit from growth. The communities that are best positioned and most responsive in anticipating structural

and policy changes will capitalize on the potential of the health-service sector as a growth industry. Conversely, those communities and areas that cannot compete effectively in today's challenging environment will likely sustain economic losses tomorrow.

—Sam Cordes

See also

Food Safety; Health and Disease Epidemiology; Health Care; Nurses and Allied Health Professionals.

References

Beaulieu, Joyce E., and David E. Berry, eds. *Rural Health Services: A Management Perspective.* Ann Arbor, MI: Aupha Press, 1994.

Coburn, Andrew, Sam Cordes, Robert Crittenden, J. Patrick Hart, Keith Mueller, Wayne Myers, and Thomas Ricketts. *The Rural Perspective on National Health Reform Legislation: What Are the Critical Issues?* Prepared for the House Committee on Agriculture. Columbia: University of Missouri, Rural Policy Research Institute, 1994.

Frenzen, Paul D. *The Medicare and Medicaid Programs in Rural America: A Profile of Program Beneficiaries and Health Care Providers.* Staff Paper No. AGES 9604. Washington, DC: U.S. Department of Agriculture, Rural Economy Division, Economic Research Service, 1996.

Mott, Frederick D., and Milton I. Roemer. *Rural Health and Medical Care.* New York: McGraw-Hill, 1948.

Orloff, Tracey M., and Barbara Tymann. *Rural Health: An Evolving System of Accessible Services.* Washington, DC: National Governors' Association, 1995.

Osborne, Diana, and Lise Fondren, eds. *National Rural Health Policy Atlas* (March). Chapel Hill: University of North Carolina at Chapel Hill, Rural Health Research Program, Health Servies Research Center, 1991.

U.S. Congress, Office of Technology Assessment. *Health Care in Rural America.* OTA-H-434. Washington, DC: U.S. Government Printing Office, 1990.

U.S. Department of Health and Human Services, Office of Rural Health Policy. *Mental Health and Rural America: 1980–1993.* Washington, DC: U.S. Government Printing Office, 1993.

———. *Rural Health Research Compendium.* Washington, DC: U.S. Government Printing Office, 1989.

———. *Rural Health Resources Directory 1994.* Washington, DC: U.S. Government Printing Office, 1994.

Policy, Rural Development

The range of efforts to create wealth and to conserve natural resources, to enhance the capacity of rural people to identify and address their basic goals and needs, to provide basic social services, and generally to improve individual and community quality of life. With the notable exception of the farm commodity and conservation programs, rural policy has generally provided minimal assistance to rural areas and has been scattered in its efforts to reach goals. There has never been a coherent federal policy for the economic and social development of rural people and their communities. However, during the 1990s, this

Tourism is often promoted as a means of economic development in rural areas. This Oregon filling station made in 1947 from a B-17 bomber by a World War II pilot was a clever gimmick designed to attract tourists.

minimalist approach to rural development may be shifting toward a greater emphasis on economic and social infrastructure development through federal programs that give greater emphasis to local decision-making.

Twentieth-Century Rural Policies

Public and private sector development policy has varied from active intervention to intentional neglect. The historic emphasis of federal rural development policies has been on assistance to farming enterprises, characterized by much local input. An argument can be made that the New Deal agricultural policies coupled with rural electrification, the Tennessee Valley Authority (TVA), Civilian Conservation Corps, and the Works Project Administration represented an interventionist federal rural development policy. However, as the economic crisis of the Great Depression waned and as the economic base of rural America shifted from extractive industries such as farming, mining, forestry, and fishing toward manufacturing and service-sector employment, no corresponding shift in emphasis occurred among the myriad rural development policies until the mid-1990s, when fundamental changes in rural policy seemed to be under way.

Historically, federal rural development has not been the battlefield for partisan political party debates but rather has been subject to institutional political tensions between the legislative and executive branches. Congress determines the general guidelines for rural development programs and appropriates funds. Agencies of the executive branch interpret and manage these programs within the guidelines of congressional intent. In recent decades, Congress has been more likely to assign greater responsibilities to the states than to federal agencies.

Federal rural development policy has long been identified with the U.S. Department of Agriculture (USDA), particularly with farm programs born during the New Deal, when a majority of rural Americans earned their livelihood directly from agriculture or other natural resource–based industries. America's rural communities historically displayed great diversity in their economic activities, geography, culture, ethnicity, and other socioeconomic characteristics. Whereas some communities in the Plains continue to depend on farming, southern and midwestern communities tend to depend more on manufacturing and service jobs.

The development of broad-based national social policies during the New Deal, World War II, and the Great Society movement profoundly altered the relationship between American citizens and the federal government. Rural people, in particular, became reliant on Social Security, health, welfare, and other federal social services. National programs that had notable effects on rural socioeconomic development include the Eisenhower interstate highway system, social welfare programs of the New Deal and the Great Society eras, and national credit policy. If total federal expenditures are used as indicators of policy emphasis, then rural America may be more affected by policies administered by non–U.S. Department of Agriculture (USDA) federal agencies. These would include Health and Human Services (HHS), Housing and Urban Development (HUD), the Small Business Administration, the Economic Development Administration, and even the Department of Defense. Federal regional agencies, such as the Tennessee Valley Authority and the Appalachian Regional Commission, provide direct assistance to rural people. It is important to understand that rural public policies are much more than the programs authorized by successive farm bills and administered by the USDA.

Agricultural and Urban Biases

The main target of rural public policy has been the farm population. Approximately two-thirds of rural people were engaged directly in farming in 1935, the peak year for American farm numbers. Agricultural policy was a rural development policy. By the 1990s, less than 10 percent of rural people were directly employed in farming, though many communities in the High Plains continue to depend primarily on farming. During the middle decades of the twentieth century, rural America experienced a dual transformation with profound implications for its economic and social well-being. The economic base of most rural communities shifted from extractive industries to manufacturing and the service sector. This shift in economic base was accompanied by a change in social class. Whereas most farm families owned some part of the farming operation and were therefore to some degree self-employed, most rural people now work for someone other than themselves. Rural poverty continues to rival poverty rates in the inner cities. The jobs created during this transformation, on average, have not closed the income gap between metropolitan and nonmetropolitan counties. Yet farm policy continues to be thought of as rural policy by agricultural legislators.

Political science studies of agricultural policy and the U.S. Congress (Browne 1995) have emphasized a lack of interest by members of the Senate and House Agricultural Committees in nonfarm rural development. A policy consequence has been for federal rural development pol-

icy to reflect the interests of more politically powerful nonfarm groups, such as the rural banking and credit interests, rural electric cooperatives, and the rural housing industry. This pluralist political process yielded very specific, categorical grant programs (for example, water and sewer projects) that were distributed across USDA agencies. There was no coherent USDA policy to coordinate these categorical grant programs.

An ancillary consequence has been USDA rural policies that emphasize physical infrastructure (water and sewers) and employment (rural credit and economic development), giving little attention to enhancing social infrastructure and the capacity of rural communities to manage self-development efforts. The lack of coordination of USDA rural development programs led policy analysts to view federal rural development policy as "minimalist" or as de facto "community triage." The harsh criticisms implied by these labels are largely valid.

Rural social policy was relegated to other federal agencies, such as HHS and HUD. If the amount of funds transferred from the federal government to rural areas is used as a measure of policy importance, individual entitlement programs, such as Social Security, Medicare, and other social welfare programs, account for the great bulk of federal assistance and policy to rural people. But few if any non-USDA programs were designed specifically for the diverse experiences and needs of rural people. Although there is evidence that non-USDA agencies have begun to recognize the need to adapt programs to respond to rural experiences, it is unlikely these agencies will alter their existing urban biases in the near future. Therefore, while an agricultural bias existed in the USDA-administered rural development program, other federal programs have been characterized by a marked urban bias.

The Devolution of Government and the Emergence of Block Grants

Rural development policy at the federal level has been and will continue to be shaped by national political-economic forces. Whereas the period between 1930 and 1970 was characterized by the rapid expansion of interventionist federal programs and authority, the succeeding decades focused on a devolution of government responsibilities from the federal to the state and local levels. That is, national public policy recently attempted to reduce both the size and the authority of federal agencies. This movement toward a more restricted role for the federal government is referred to as the devolution, as opposed to the evolution, of government. The primary policy vehicle for the devolution of the federal government is the block grant, which has replaced the more restrictive categorical grant.

Block grants represent generic policy formulas that offer a framework for transferring a measure of authority and of resources from a higher to a lower level of government. In the case of rural development, this was principally a transfer from the federal to state and local authorities. Whereas categorical grants earmark funds for specific types of assistance (for example, sewer and water lines and telecommunications), block grants funnel money to state and local authorities, who then have considerable program authority. Three specific policy goals are often cited as favoring the use of block grants. First is the general concern to reduce the federal budget deficit. Block grants provide the option of reducing program funds (including administrative funds) while passing along much greater flexibility to the state governors. This permits a substantial reduction in budget. And if the history of community block grants is followed, most if not all of the funds can be eliminated in future sessions of Congress, since members will receive little if any political benefit from the block grant programs. Second, block grant programs require less federal bureaucracy to administer. Ironically, however, block grants can increase the total size of government by requiring states to increase their administrative bureaucracy. But this may be considered by members of Congress an acceptable political consequence. Third, proponents of block grants claim that increasing the flexibility of the states to administer a federal program brings substantial gains in program efficiency and effectiveness. However, this claim is unlikely to be universal among the states. Some states indeed may increase the efficacy of their programs, but there is no inherent guarantee.

There are three types of block grants. First, *restricted block grants* funnel funding and some authority to the states, but with specific regulations and guidelines for program expenditure. States are given some lee-way to adapt programs to their special circumstances. Second, *unrestricted block grants,* similar to the Community Development Block Grant program of the 1980s, come with fewer guidelines for state and local program targets and expenditures. Both restricted and unrestricted block grants have been used with varying degrees of success in rural areas.

Third, *competitive block grant* programs have been used less, but recently gained considerable policy legitimacy. Unlike many other block grant programs, competitive block grants do not necessitate either an entitlement or a guaranteed formula under which funding moves to the states or rural communities. Funding is based on a competitive process during which states or communities develop and forward their proposals. The Enterprise Community and Empowerment Zone (EC/EZ) program is a competitive grant program. Competitive block grant programs permit rural communities to create rural development programs that fit their specific circumstances as well as general federal rural development guidelines. In so doing, such programs promote federal and local development partnerships. The roles of the state government, subregional development organizations, private foundations, and other rural development providers are determined by the local grant proposal. However, competitive block grants are likely to be pursued by communities that are already well-organized and have access to the necessary technical assistance to write a competitive grant.

Renewed Interest in Local Self-Development

The political movement to restrict the authority of the federal government is often tied to a desire to make public policy more relevant to local circumstances. The United States has a long-term cultural suspicion of large, centralized government and a belief in local self-determination. The policy dilemma is the institutionalization of federal and local partnerships in which one partner has dramatically superior resources and political power. This is not a new policy dilemma. USDA farm programs historically required much local input and even governance. Since USDA farm programs historically were tied to local boards, USDA administrators may be able to draw on local-federal institutional partnerships to create new rural development programs.

The previous emphasis in local development was far less on a grand development model than on political realities. Local-federal partnerships reflected the great diversity of characteristics and needs of farm groups and their communities. This has been particularly true for agricultural commodity policies. American farm entitlement, conservation, and extension programs derived much of their political legitimacy by institutionalizing federal-local partnerships through local boards. The Agricultural Adjustment Administration Boards (later the Agricultural Stabilization and Conservation Service Boards, and now the Farm Services Administration Boards), the Soil and Water District Boards (now the Conservation District Boards), and the county-level Extension Councils are historic examples of rural federal-local partnerships.

Recent Policy Transformations

The 1995 reorganization of the USDA, coupled with the rural development title of the 1996 Farm Bill, may indicate a fundamental alteration in the USDA's rural development policies. The most innovative congressional initiatives are the establishment of the Rural Community Action Program (RCAP) and the Fund for Rural America (FRA). RCAP provides a framework for restrictive block grant programs to the states that are administered by the USDA rural development state directors, but it also mandates considerable local input aimed at strategic planning and development. FRA represents the first transfer of major funding from farm commodity programs to a more general rural development fund. FRA disbursements will go primarily for programs to enhance the creation of value-added agricultural industries and agricultural research and development. However, a portion of these funds will be applied also to broader measures toward rural economic and social development.

The reorganization of the USDA may have even greater implications for defining the federal role in rural development. For the first time, rural development has an agency status similar to the farm programs, Rural Development (RD). This agency has primary responsibility for nonfarm rural credit programs. However, since other USDA agencies have retained their own rural development programs, program coordination is necessary. A memorandum of understanding was signed by the Undersecretaries for Research, Education, and Economics (REE), Natural Resources (NR), and RD that established the Rural Economic Development Action Team (REDAT) to identify and address overlapping program areas. Unfortunately, interagency turf struggles may reduce the effectiveness and eventually the life of REDAT. In addition, Congress provided a general policy framework for the National Rural Development Partnership for Rural America to create institutional links among USDA and other federal programs and state rural development efforts. These legislative and bureaucratic transformations raised two critical policy questions that remain unresolved. First, will these changes make the USDA's role in rural development more relevant for rural communities? Second, how will these changes affect other rural development providers?

Consequently, the USDA's reorganization required its administrators to create new bureaucratic protocols for interagency cooperation (such as REDAT) and to generate performance criteria in an uncertain political environment (such as the Government Performance Review Act). The challenges of these new missions may be far greater for USDA than for other federal agencies, since the USDA administrators must enhance the agency's capacity to manage rural development programs at the same time that its rural development mission is being expanded and redefined and its professional workforce is being pared down. All of these new demands on a reorganized federal bureaucracy pose risks as well as opportunities.

A renewed commitment to rural America may emerge in the next few years, but the commitment is likely to be constrained by ongoing funding difficulties. It is unlikely that more federal funding will be allocated to the USDA's rural development programs. Rather, the programs' goals and outcomes are likely to be more specifically targeted. The agency's success in meeting its new opportunities will be determined to a great extent by how visions of cooperation and commitment are articulated and applied to institutional relationships. In essence, the present opportunity will be shaped not only by new programs and policy initiatives but also by the ability of the newly restructured USDA to provide a coherent though minimal rural policy in place of the scattered policy initiatives of the past. Success will depend equally on the long-term enhancement of human capacity, local economies, and basic physical infrastructures.

The devolution of the federal government generally has been characterized by a downsizing of federal agencies and a transfer of some administrative authority to the states. For most federal agencies this meant a movement from more centrally controlled and cohesive regulatory and funding programs and toward more minimal roles. This movement toward a more minimal role is consistent with the constraints imposed by bureaucratic downsizing. However, the USDA is something of a paradox where rural development is concerned. Historically, rural development at USDA has been characterized by fragmented programs (primarily categorical grant programs) scattered across several agencies. There was no coherent rural development policy tying these efforts together. The devolution of government required a reorganization of rural development programs at the USDA, which yielded a much more cohesive policy. The USDA is an exception to the rule also in that it is attempting to become more involved in rural development at the very time its bureaucracy is being downsized and reorganized.

The programmatic consequences for these changes will not be understood fully for years to come. The questions confronting rural development policy are formidable. Liabilities may reside in the inability of USDA agencies to overcome bureaucratic turf tussles, both within

USDA and with other federal agencies. Other liabilities may appear in the reorientation of USDA personnel to qualitatively different assignments as professionals. Still others may occur in how USDA field officers, those USDA professionals who work directly with the public, make the transition from treating the public as clients to working with rural communities and citizens as partners. Can sufficient authority be passed along to field office personnel to make the USDA's considerable resources effectively available at the local level? A great concern is whether or not liabilities will cause opportunities to be missed.

Although federal rural development policy never achieved a sustained presence at the local level, the New Deal farm and resource conservation programs were based on a federal-local partnership. This experience of more than a half-century of working with local boards can help make the newly emerging rural development initiatives locally relevant. The resource conservation and development program within the National Resource Conservation Service offers a readily available institutional example of an effective, locally relevant program. What seems apparent is that the opportunities to make the USDA a key player are greater now than at any other time in this century. At the time of this book's publication, rural public policies are undergoing their greatest changes since the New Deal.

—*Louis E. Swanson*

See also

Community; Decentralization; Development, Community and Economic; Government; Infrastructure; Policy (various entries); Public Services; Regional Planning; Taxes; Trade Areas; Urbanization.

References

Beaulieu, Lionel J., and David Mulkey. *Investing in People: The Human Capital Needs for Rural America*. Boulder, CO: Westview Press, 1995.

Browne, William P. *Cultivating Congress*. Lawrence: University Press of Kansas, 1995.

Browne, William P., Jerry Skees, Louis E. Swanson, Paul B. Thompson, and Laurian J. Unnevehr. *Sacred Cows and Hot Potatoes: Agrarian Myths in Agricultural Policy*. Boulder, CO: Westview Press, 1992.

Castle, Emery N., ed. *The Changing American Countryside: Rural People and Places*. Lawrence: University Press of Kansas, 1995.

Christenson, James A., and Cornelia B. Flora. *Rural Policies for the 1990s*. Boulder, CO: Westview Press, 1991.

Flora, Cornelia B., Jan Flora, Jacqueline D. Spears, and Louis E. Swanson, with Mark B. Lapping and Mark L. Weinberg. *Rural Communities: Legacy and Change*. Boulder, CO: Westview Press, 1992.

Rural Policy Research Institute. *Block Grants and Rural America: A Background Working Paper*. P95-4 (November). Columbia, MO: Rural Policy Research Institute, 1995.

———. *Opportunities for Rural Policy Reform: Lessons Learned from Recent Farm Bills*. P95-2 (April). Columbia, MO: Rural Policy Research Institute, 1995.

Policy, Socioeconomic

Policy relating to the conditions in a variety of dimensions of social life: economic dimensions (such as employment, income, and poverty); physical and mental health status; educational attainments; social disorganization (teenage fertility, substance abuse, accident rates, and crime); quality and quantity of local services, infrastructure, and housing; and environmental preservation and natural resource sustainability. Each dimension of socioeconomic well-being has its own literature and research tradition attached to it, so specific works on each topic should be consulted. Causes, consequences, and policies affecting socioeconomic well-being depend on the particular indicator used to define it. This entry gives an overview of the umbrella topic of socioeconomic well-being and the policy interventions that address it. Policy interventions can be seen as derived from underlying assumptions about the causal factors involved in socioeconomic well-being. Contrasts between rural and urban areas with regard to interventions to improve socioeconomic well-being are discussed.

Background to Research on Socioeconomic Well-Being

Several issues should be noted about research on this topic. The first is the analytical level to which studies refer. Studies examining socioeconomic well-being typically use individuals, households, or locales such as counties and communities as the unit of analysis. Contrasts between rural/nonmetropolitan and urban/metropolitan individuals, households, and locales are often made. Second, the topic of socioeconomic well-being is derivative of an older research tradition on the quality of life and social indicators, which was popular in the social sciences until the 1980s. This research tradition was concerned with developing indicators by which the quality of life of populations in different geographic locations could be compared (Land and Spilerman 1975). Focus on quality of life and social indicators was subject to criticisms of being atheoretical, ignoring the broader political economy, and imposing external, normative standards on local populations. Contemporary researchers on socioeconomic well-being are concerned with remedying these criticisms.

The extent to which rural individuals, households, and communities enjoy less socioeconomic well-being than urban ones is still an empirical question whose answer depends on the type of well-being considered as well as the time period, region of the country, and how comparisons are made with metropolitan populations. Extensive empirical work tends to confirm the generalization that nonmetropolitan people, households, and places have poorer economic conditions, lower income, and higher poverty rates than metropolitan ones (Rural Sociological Task Force on Persistent Rural Poverty 1993). Differences in unemployment vary over time: For most of the 1980s, rural unemployment exceeded metropolitan rates, but this trend seems to be reversing in the 1990s. Educational attainments among rural people historically have been lower than among urbanites. Beyond educational and economic indicators, the differences begin to blur. Some health status indicators such as infant mortality reveal higher rates for rural areas. Other indicators of poorer health status reflect problems associated with the higher proportion of elderly in rural areas. Although rural people have been assumed to have poorer mental health, some recent studies have not confirmed this. Certain types of substance abuse, such as alcoholism, and crime, such as trespassing, are thought to be higher in rural areas. The quality of rural infrastructure and housing is generally poorer.

Provision of social, educational, and health services is generally considered more problematic in rural areas for several reasons. Rural areas have lower population density, which complicates service delivery and makes it more expensive. Service organizations and agencies tend to be smaller and fewer in rural areas, where there is greater difficulty in attracting and keeping skilled professionals than in urban areas. A longstanding problem has been attracting physicians, whose training on high-technology medical equipment is difficult to transfer to rural practice, and whose lifestyle often centers around urban amenities. The composition of rural populations, with a higher proportion of elderly, fewer educated, and more poor people, presents additional barriers to service outreach.

Variations among Rural People

Any generalizations about the socioeconomic well-being of rural people must be tempered by a consideration of the extensive variations within rural areas and populations and between them and metropolitan areas and populations. Nonmetropolitan people residing in counties adjacent to metropolitan counties tend to have better socioeconomic conditions than their more distant rural neighbors. Rural people are differentiated by class, gender, race, and ethnicity, with those possessing greater social status experiencing a better quality of life. Finally, rural

people are not the only ones whose residential location jeopardizes their life chances. Comparisons of nonmetropolitan people with those of the urban core reveal striking similarities in terms of poorer economic conditions.

Policy Interventions: Overview

Policy interventions flow from assumptions about how differences in well-being are created. Following are two poles of a continuum into which interventions may be introduced. The first is from the supply side, and it involves human capital; it it motivated by the desire to empower rural people and upgrade their personal and community lives. To the extent that poorer well-being of rural people is due to their compositional characteristics (such as age, education, skill levels, and other personal attributes), interventions may be human-capital focused. Such interventions are centered on upgrading labor market quality through job training and programs and educational expenditures or on improving quality of life through social welfare interventions. Other supply-side interventions may take the form of improving local social capital or participatory initiatives that enhance community capacity for self-development.

The opposite pole of intervention is on the demand side. It assumes that well-being is increased through altering the economic and social institutions that surround rural people. Most economic development programs take this approach. They center on improving the quality of local industries and firms and expanding employment in them. Improving local infrastructure and social institutions (such as schools) and access to local services also can be seen as attempts to stimulate demand aspects of social and economic structure, which in turn may filter down to human capital upgrades.

Sociologists generally recognize the interrelationships between demand- and supply-side improvements but caution that the enhancement of human capital with better education and skills is not sufficient to improve well-being unless it is accompanied by demand-side expansions in local employment and wages. Also problematic in rural areas is local investment in education. Relative to urban areas, rural tax bases and hence local property tax support for schools are lower. People with higher education are more likely to out-migrate. Urban areas thus capture rural investment in education.

Policy Interventions: Issues and Problems

Analysts raise several policy intervention issues when considering rural areas. An important issue is the degree to which national policies are spatially biased. National policies are formulated in four major ways and each has outcomes that affect rural and urban people differentially (Rural Sociological Task Force on Persistent Rural Poverty 1993).

First, macroeconomic policies designed in response to global or national economic trends, such as deregulation or monetary and trade policy, differentially affect rural well-being. For example, deregulation of the transportation industry curtailed bus and air service to remote rural areas. The North American Free Trade Agreement (NAFTA) may have a more negative impact on rural employment, to the extent that it affects lower-wage industries (such as textiles, furniture, and food processing), which are traditionally based in rural locales.

Second, sectoral policies such as farm commodity programs are designed to affect specific industries, and thus have direct spatial effects. Farm policies have been considered major strategies of national government intervention in rural development, although promoters rarely make this intent explicit.

Third, policies and programs also might be directly earmarked for rural development or attached to primarily rural regions, such as those administered by Appalachian regional development agencies and the Tennessee Valley Authority. These programs have centered in particular on upgrading rural infrastructure.

Finally, national social welfare policies and programs have spatially varying effects depending on population composition. For example, the rural poor are more likely to be employed than are their urban counterparts. A lower proportion of rural people's incomes comes from means-tested income transfer programs (such as Aid to Families with Dependent Children [AFDC] and General Assistance). However, changes in AFDC, General Assistance, and in-kind assistance programs such as food stamps adversely affect the high-poverty populations found in some rural areas, such as Appalachia and the South. Similarly, changes to Social Security and Medicare will have greater effect on rural populations because they are older and depend more on these programs than do urban people.

Another issue affecting the performance of policy interventions in rural areas is the extent to which they are fragmented across policy domains and administrative units. Policies designed to improve the environment, for instance, may conflict with local employment goals, as illustrated by the case of Northwest logging. Local services for solid waste disposal, fire protection, ambulance services, and other types of social provisions may be supplied by multiple, overlapping administrative units, including a mix of public and private providers. Policies and programs set at the national or state level may be administrated differentially by lower levels of government. For example, state and federal guidelines for AFDC may be interpreted and applied informally in different ways by county social welfare services. Although urban areas face similar issues, coordination, coverage, and consistency are particularly problematic for smaller rural communities.

Recent efforts to decentralize federal programs and give greater control over social welfare spending to the states may have negative consequences for rural people, insofar as they further undermine the consistency of program and policy implementation. The states also vary in administrative capabilities and in the extent to which there is political support for helping the poor. Highly urbanized states of the Northeast, for example, tend to have more coordinated administrations to adequately service their populations, whereas predominantly rural states, such as those in the South, often lack service capability.

Delivery of social, health, employment, educational, and other services designed to improve local socioeconomic well-being is considered more complex for rural areas due to lower population density, lower tax base, more limited infrastructure, and the general characteristics of rural people. Multi-community or -county collaborations have been implemented particularly in the consolidation of local schools and hospitals. These types of collaborations increased markedly in the 1980s.

The characteristics of rural people make service outreach more problematic. A higher proportion of elderly and poor complicates service delivery. Farmers and other small business owners often fall outside eligibility requirements for food stamps, AFDC, and other means-tested programs. Lack of formal-sector employment creates health insurance and retirement savings barriers. Some analysts argue that farmers and other rural people have more individualistic attitudes about seeking help and are less likely to use formal mental health interventions. However, the extent to which rural people have different attitudes than their urban counterparts regarding the use of social services is not clear in the present case. Lack of use of social services results mainly from the social, economic, and demographic characteristics of rural residents and the conditions by which services are made accessible to rural people.

—Linda M. Lobao

See also
Decentralization; Dependence; Elders; Government; Housing;
    Policy (various entries); Public Services; Quality of Life; Rural
    Demography.
References
Barkley, David L., ed. *Economic Adaptation: Alternatives for Non-
    metropolitan Areas.* Boulder, CO: Westview Press, 1993.
Duncan, Cynthia M., ed. *Rural Poverty in America.* New York:
    Auburn House, 1992.
Flora, Cornelia B., and James Christenson, eds. *Rural Policies for
    the 1990s.* Boulder, CO: Westview Press, 1991.
Flora, Jan L., Gary P. Green, Edward Gale, Frederick E. Schmidt,
    and Cornelia Butler Flora. "Self-Development: A Viable Rural
    Development Option?" *Policy Studies Journal* 20, no. 2 (1992):
    276–288.
Land, Kenneth C., and Seymour Spilerman, eds. *Social Indicator
    Models.* New York: Russell Sage Foundation, 1975.
Lasley, Paul, F. Larry Leistritz, Linda M. Lobao, and Katherine
    Meyer. *Beyond the Amber Waves of Grain: An Examination of
    Social and Economic Restructuring in the Heartland.* Boulder,
    CO: Westview Press, 1995.
Lobao, Linda M. *Locality and Inequality: Farm and Industry
    Structure and Socioeconomic Conditions.* Albany: State Univer-
    sity of New York Press, 1990.
Rural Sociological Task Force on Persistent Rural Poverty. *Persis-
    tent Poverty in Rural America.* Boulder, CO: Westview Press,
    1993.
U.S. Department of Agriculture. *Education and Rural Economic
    Development: Strategies for the 1990s.* ERS Staff Report No.
    AGES 9153. Washington, DC: U.S. Department of Agriculture,
    Agriculture and Rural Economy Division, Economic Research
    Service, 1991.
Wagenfeld, Morton O., J. Dennis Murray, Dennis Mohatt, and
    Jeanne C. DeBruyn. *Mental Health in Rural America:
    1980–1993.* Washington, DC: National Institute of Mental
    Health, 1993.

Policy, Telecommunications

Public programs, laws, actions, and decisions, especially at the federal level, that influence the use of technology to communicate over long distances. Advances in technology and changing regulatory policies provide opportunities for rural communities to overcome the disadvantages of time and space and to become more integrated into the global information economy.

Introduction

Advances in communication and information technologies and radical changes in the way these technologies provide services have occurred along with the shift toward a more service-oriented economy. These developments hold considerable promise for rural areas. They reduce the importance of distance and space, two factors that typically have disadvantaged rural areas in the past. Equally important, they can provide the economic infrastructure that will allow rural communities to participate in, and reap the benefits of, an increasingly knowledge-based and electronically networked global economy.

For rural communities to benefit from these developments, however, they will need access to a modern network infrastructure. Ironically, just at the moment when communication and information technologies are beginning to play such a critical role, the regulatory structure that once assured rural access to communication technologies is rapidly coming unraveled. Under these circumstances, new and creative approaches to promote network deployment in rural communities must be found.

Barriers to Network Deployment

Rural communities typically have lagged behind urban areas in the deployment of communication technologies because of the high costs involved in providing service. Costs are higher in rural areas not only because of difficult terrain but also because of low-density populations and low-volume traffic dispersed over large areas, which makes it much harder to share costs. High costs, in turn, serve to increase the price of access and thus to reduce demand. They undermine the incentives that vendors and service providers may have to extend service to these areas.

Consider basic telephony, for instance. In rural areas, about one-half of all voice telephone service is provided by small independent telephone companies, with the Bell operating companies (BOCs) providing the other half. Few if any of the larger, more specialized providers are trying to enter or develop rural markets. Given the highly competitive postdivestiture environment, they are focusing their efforts on the more lucrative domestic and global business markets. With this goal in mind, for example, U.S. West, which services the largest number of remote areas and users, has begun to divest itself of some of those interests.

To appreciate the problem of rural deployment, one need only compare the average costs of providing urban and rural telephone service. For example, the BOCs, which service mostly urban areas, have approximately 10,000 lines per central office; their average costs are much lower than those of small, rural independent companies, which average about 2,500 lines per central office. Similarly, the BOCs have, on average, almost 130 subscribers per route mile of outside plant, whereas the small independents average only six. Equally important in terms of costs, the average length of a large company's subscriber loop (the wire between the central office and the user's premises) is about half that of the small independents (Office of Technology Assessment 1992).

Urban markets are also more lucrative than rural markets because they are comprised of a greater number of high-paying customers. Not only are per capita incomes generally lower in rural areas than in urban ones; so, too, is the density of business customers. Thus, whereas 33 percent of the BOCs' access lines serve business customers, only about 18 percent of small rural companies' access lines (using Rural Utilities Service borrowers as a measure) are dedicated to business usage.

A comparable situation can be found in the case of cable television, which provides the major source of video entertainment in rural areas. Most rural residents gain access to cable television through a headend receiving station, which receives video signals from satellites and distributes them via coaxial cables to receivers' homes. Although the cost of the headend is fixed, that of installing and maintaining the cable is generally proportional to distance, and thus to the number of houses receiving service. Cable penetration rates reflect this cost relationship; rates range from 60 percent in high density areas to 46 percent in communities with fewer than 3,000 residents. Where subscriber density falls below 10 percent, rural communities are unlikely to be served (National Telecommunications and Information Administration 1995).

Rural users also can gain access to television programming directly via satellite, but only if they are willing to bear most of the distance-related costs. To receive satellite signals, they must buy a television-receive-only (TVRO) satellite dish, which until the mid-1990s might have cost between $750 and $1,800. Thus, the number of TVRO owners is relatively few, ranging from 6 percent in the open country to 11 percent in rural mountain areas (Office of Technology Assessment 1992).

The deployment of modern information technologies and networked applications is likely to repeat this pattern, not only because of high costs and low demand but also because the rural infrastructure as it presently exists is unable to support a number of them, especially those at the high end. The poor quality of rural networks stems, in part, from the number of multiparty lines that can still be found in rural areas. Multiparty lines are unsatisfactory to transmit data because of interruptions. Long local loops diminish the quality of rural access. Loops exceeding 18,000 feet, for example, require special treatment, such as loading coils and range extenders, to maintain the quality of voice transmission. These treatments, however, can also introduce distortions in data transmission.

Recent studies show that the demand for many information-based services is quite high. Rural users are willing to pay as much as their urban counterparts, if not more, for equivalent services because they view them as essential. Networking technologies most in demand include telephone answering machines, fax machines, computers, cellular phones, and computer modems (Allen and Johnson 1996). Rural users also are interested in Internet access. In one recent study, 4 to 6 percent of those polled wanted to subscribe to Internet services, and 14 to 17 percent wanted additional information (Curran 1995).

In many of the more populated rural areas, the public switched telephone network (PSTN) can support such low-to-mid-speed data transmission services and some low-speed video services. However, accessing high-speed circuit-switched or fast packet-switched computer networks is impossible for the most part. High-speed networks require high-quality digital circuits that can support transmission at speeds of 56 kilobits or more. Such circuits are generally not found in rural areas (National Telecommunications and Information Administration 1995).

The lack of high-speed networks is a major shortcoming. Although many individual users may not need such high capacity, rural communities as a whole are increasingly likely to develop such a need. Without high bandwidth facilities, rural communities will be less able to take advantage of the growing number of community-based and business services such as electronic commerce, distance learning, and telemedicine, which could help them better compete in a knowledge-based global economy. As a result, rural communities may lag behind urban areas not only with respect to technology deployment but also in terms of overall competitiveness and economic growth.

The Impact of Technology Advance

The technical performance of all network components greatly increased, but costs fell precipitously. These advances can improve the economic viability of providing advanced communication services to rural areas. New technologies, however, are not a panacea. Although technology advance allows for enhanced services at lower costs, it also raises the standards that rural networks must meet just to keep up.

Technological advances in wireless systems, long the mainstay of rural telecommunications, are perhaps the most significant of all. Taking advantage of digitization and compression, wireless technologies now provide services that are increasingly comparable to wired systems. In areas where the costs of wired network installation are prohibitive, microwave, radio, and satellite facilities can provide access.

Microwaves can deliver high-capacity, long-haul and short-haul, analog, and digital services. One of the major advantages of microwave communications is its relatively low construction costs. Unlike terrestrial, wired technologies, microwave communications does not require cable placement; and rooftops, hills, and mountains often provide an inexpensive base for microwave towers. Today, unit costs of microwave service are falling as more high-powered systems expand the usable spectrum.

Like microwave technology, specialized mobile radio (SMR) can provide a variety of telecommunication and broadcasting services. However, its use for rural service has only recently been approved by the Federal Communications System (FCC). Providing short-haul telecommunication services, SMR can be used for the local loop in remote areas, greatly reducing access costs. Enhanced specialized mobile radio (ESMR) technology, which can provide video, voice, and data services, also is now available.

Advanced satellite technology can similarly reduce the costs of providing rural service. Because satellite-based signals are broadcast over a wide area, virtually any user within the satellite's "footprint" can access the network at the same cost. Moreover, mobile satellites now have sufficient power to enable the use of a larger number of small, mobile terminals on the ground. Portable units are self-contained and lightweight, capable of fitting on a company or family car. With these terminals, users can connect with private networks or the public telephone network for a variety of services, including facsimile, data, and voice communications.

The cost of wired services is likewise declining due to technology advances. Most important has been the introduction of loop carrier systems and digital remote electronics and switching technology. Loop carrier systems concentrate access lines by combining many customers into one or more shared trunks, reducing the need for each customer to have a dedicated loop. Digital switching reduces the amount of dedicated loop plant by allowing remote nodes to be connected to the host digital switch. Moreover, with remote digital switching, carriers can use fewer expensive host switches to provide advanced intelligent services, such as access to 1-800 telephone number databases.

Notwithstanding these technology advances, it is likely that telecommunications deployments in rural areas will continue to lag behind urban areas. One recent analysis suggested that assuming a cost of $1,000 per subscriber, it will be 10 to 20 years before narrowband digital service can be delivered to rural areas. Broadband capabilities could be available to business subscribers within 2 to 10 years, at a cost of $5,000 per subscriber. But it would take 10 to 20 years for residential users to receive broadband services, assuming the same costs per subscriber. Achieving parity between rural and urban areas will be even more difficult in the future, given deregulation and an increasingly competitive industry environment (Office of Technology Assessment 1992).

Deregulation: The Challenge of a New Regulatory Environment

Telecommunications deregulation, initiated in 1984 with the divestiture of the Bell system, culminated in January 1996 with passage of the Telecommunications Reform Act. The implications of deregulation for rural telecommunications are twofold. Competition and the loss of subsidies in rural areas may undermine the economic basis upon which rural networks traditionally have been deployed. At the same time, however, the regrouping of the communications industry in the wake of competition may afford rural providers new opportunities to share their costs across a larger number of providers, users, and applications.

In the past, government regulatory policy played a major role in assuring that communications technologies were deployed to rural areas. One major aspect of this policy was price averaging and cross-subsidization; another was the provision of low-cost loans to small, independent, and cooperative telephone companies through the government-established Rural Electrification Administration (REA), now the Rural Utilities Service (RUS).

Deregulation undermined the pricing structure that traditionally supported rural communications services. In a fully competitive environment, differences between costs and prices are untenable. When prices are kept artificially high to maintain subsidies, users will seek alternative, private solutions to meet their communications needs. Thus, to survive, communications providers must continue to price access close to real costs. Many subsidies are eliminated as a result.

The Federal Communications Commission (FCC) encouraged this development by shifting costs from interstate, interexchange service to local exchange service. At the same time, it tried to ensure affordable rural services by subsidizing some providers, using revenues drawn from a universal service fund. Under the new communications act, price averaging is mandated, and the FCC together with the states is charged to develop a plan to finance universal service in a competitive era.

The Communications Act of 1996, which significantly deregulated all segments of the communications industry, was intended to eliminate the remaining barriers to competition. Accordingly, the regional Bell companies are now permitted to enter the long-distance market, with FCC approval. Likewise, all cable rates are to be deregulated in the next three years, and in small communities, regulation ends immediately. Moreover, broadcasters are now permitted to enter a greater number of markets.

The new law poses a major challenge for rural providers. Not only must rural telephone companies operate at costs that are high relative to urban areas; they also must contend with potential competition. Providers that typically served urban areas may now find it profitable to extend service to many, and especially the most populated, rural areas. Free to provide voice, video, and data services, these competitive providers can now benefit from greater economies of scale and scope, and thereby more easily spread their costs.

On the other hand, under the new law, existing rural telephone companies can take similar steps. They can enter new business areas, join together to provide advanced services, and develop joint ventures, thereby extending their reach and sharing their costs more broadly. Many already have begun to do so. For example, a number of rural telephone companies are beginning to provide Internet access as well as cable services. Working jointly through the National Rural Telecommunications Cooperative (NRTC), others arranged with the direct broadcast satellite (DBS) consortium Sky Cable to distribute its basic programming, using relatively low-cost, fixed, 18-inch satellite dishes (Murphy 1995). In like fashion, members of ComNet, a consortium of 19 independent telephone companies in Ohio, cooperate to provide toll-free access to e-mail, bulletin boards, information services, and the Internet (Wetli 1994).

Even more promising for the future, a growing constituency is emerging to promote the deployment of advanced technologies in rural networks. Looking to communications technologies to support education, health care, and economic development, many state and local governments, community groups, and nonprofit organizations are getting involved. California State University at Chico, for example, linked up with a broad-based community partnership and Pacific Bell to establish the Northern California Regional Computer Network. In another effort, the International Internet Association (IIA) arranged with its partner, International Discount Telecommunications, to offer unlimited rural access to the Internet via a low-cost 1-800 dial-up number.

—*D. Linda Garcia*

See also
Electrification; Infrastructure; Technology; Technology Transfer; Telecommunications.

References

Allen, John C., and Bruce B. Johnson. "Telecommunications and Economic Development: A Study of 20 Rural Communities." *Rural Telecommunications* (July/August 1996): 28–33.

Curran, Steve. "Why Your Telco Can't Ignore the Internet." *Rural Telecommunications* (September/October 1995): 30–38.

Mayo, John W., and William F. Fox. "State Level Telecommunications Policy in the Post-Divestiture Era." *Survey of Business* (Fall 1992): 10–19.

Murphy, Beth. "Rural Americans Want Their DirecTV." *Satellite Communications* (March 1995): 30–32.

National Telecommunications and Information Administration. *Survey of Rural Information Infrastructure Technologies.* Boulder, CO: U.S. Department of Commerce, 1995.

Parker, Edwin B., Heather Hudson, and Don A. Dillman. *Rural America in the Information Age.* Boston: University Press of America, 1989.

U.S. Congress, Office of Technology Assessment. *Rural America at the Crossroads: Networking for the Future.* Washington, DC: U.S. Government Printing Office, 1992.

———. *Wireless Technologies and the National Information Infrastructure.* Washington, DC: U.S. Government Printing Office, 1995.

Wetli, Patty. "Rural Telcos Launch Subscribers from Main Street to Cyberspace." *America's Network* (December 15, 1994): 46–47.

Politics

Everyday public activities in which citizens and their formal and informal leaders address problems or issues and establish common goals and rules that often shape the direction of local governments. This entry examines rural issues at the national and local level. It explores the capacity of rural political communities to address their issues. The diffusion of power and role of local political units in decision making are discussed.

Introduction

Politics in rural areas is more than what government and politicians do. It is an everyday public activity that involves local citizens and nonelected leaders who attempt to address problems and issues, establish common goals and rules, and shape directions for local units of government. Rural politics is influenced by external forces from the region, state, national, and international arenas. These influences have economic, legal, environmental, and social components.

Rural politics in America has democratic roots that usually involve four major ideals. First, deliberation and debate are the ways that public issues and the trade-offs associated with choices are examined before a conclusion is reached about the common good or a common sense of direction. Second, elections are viewed as the proper means to select governmental leaders. Third, power is diffused. And fourth, the local unit of government is an instrument for the public to act collectively. The practice of these democratic ideals varies according to the issue, the external influences, the type of local government that predominates at the local level, and the people themselves.

Rural Issues at the National Level

Rural politics is extremely diverse and dynamic. However, state and national portraits of rural America often equate it with the business of agriculture and family farms or project an image of poverty and stagnation. Critics argue that these stereotypes do not portray rural issues accurately. Ninety percent of rural residents earn their livelihood from nonagricultural activities. The widely admired family farmer of today is more likely to own a million dollars in capital and be incorporated. Although poverty exists, it is no more representative of rural life than of urban life. Rural residents have lower income levels than urban residents but also have lower indices of inequality. Rural poverty is concentrated among the elderly, who live in disproportionately large numbers in rural areas.

The farm bloc, a potent bipartisan assortment of commodity organizations and other farm-related groups, received historically more national attention than any other rural group. The farm bloc has linked "rural" with family farming. National farm policy and expensive farm entitlement programs were justified on the grounds that they assisted financially strapped farmers and provided a cheap food supply for urban consumers. Other portions of rural America's heterogeneous economic base traditionally have received less national attention.

In recent years there has been an increase in nonfarm interests in agriculture and rural America. Environmental organizations and representatives of hired farm labor and other groups entered the fray with their concerns for environmental issues, worker and food safety,

Participation in local politics involves people of all backgrounds. Steve Beltz, mayor of Bagley, Minnesota, is also the town's pharmacist.

food distribution, sustainable agriculture, and rural development. Agroenvironmentalism emerged as a movement to address high rates of soil erosion and evidence of surface and groundwater pollution from chemicals used in farming. The rapid loss of medium-sized family farms led to questions about who benefits from farm policy. Given current federal budget deficits, there is growing interest in cutting back federal agricultural expenditures. These concerns often are integrated in U.S. farm policy discussions and legislation as well as in broader legislation such as the Clean Water Act. In spite of the declining influence of the farm bloc and growing interest in nonfarm rural issues, rural politics and corresponding legislation at the national level have been fragmented and disjointed. Rural America is not guided by a comprehensive federal rural development policy.

Politics at the Local Level

Some observers believe that rural politics is shaped by two different political economies, local and external. In the first, there is a distribution of power and wealth among local residents with minimal outside control. Politics is guided by ideological or economic interests. Some communities or key actors in this first situation have been fatalistic and unwilling to change, or they have been divided internally. However, other rural communities have mobilized grass-roots support to establish collective visions and carry out community-based agendas for action. Most of the available literature about local political economies is focused on the diffusion of power in them.

Diffusion of Power in the Local Political Economy. There is a history of disagreement about whether shaping local rural community policies and decisions involves a relatively diffuse power structure or whether that power is concentrated in the hands of a few elites. Pluralists tend to view politics as relatively open. From their perspective, people choose to get involved or not because of some grievance or issue; the interests of economic classes do not permanently dominate the agenda. Pluralists tend to see a fluidity of groups and classes nonparticipating or not participating in decision making.

The elitist argument suggests power is concentrated among economic elites who make it difficult for nonelites to reach the competition stage. For example, one study about voting among Mississippi African Americans discovered that nonvoting was marked by fear or vulnerability to local power elites. For the most part, this pluralist-elitist debate centered around the validity and reliability of research methods and findings. Recently the debate shifted to another level. Some observers (Gaventa 1980) have suggested that there is a more subtle use of power in which elites' interests are infused into the culture through the media or the powerful use of symbols, which encourages a false consensus, fatalism, and apathy. For example, some Appalachian industries moved mountains and reshaped the physical landscape to the point that the common person began to feel ineffectual. In other cases, values were reshaped by renaming local landmarks with foreign-sounding names, indicating that the local culture was not valued. The only attractive culture, it appears, is the culture and thinking of elites. Although there are case studies to strengthen such insights, this subtle component of power has been less well studied and understood than more direct power intervention by elites who often have vested economic interests in the status quo.

Another perspective, the interactional approach (Wilkinson 1991), suggests that leadership is multifaceted. There is a spectrum ranging from highly specialized leadership to more generalized community leadership. For example, highly focused economic activities are likely to be influenced by businesspeople, whereas more general activities, such as local government, are guided by generalized leaders with backgrounds that reflect local diversity. Some specialized leaders mature into generalized leaders over time. The number of generalized leaders varies from community to community. Openness to participation in community affairs is mixed and varies among localities. Several studies suggest that race may be a barrier to participation in leadership in many rural settings.

The Pulls of the External Political Economy. In recent years, social scientists noted the external barriers to a cohesive local political economy. They asserted that there is more external influence from corporations, national and international markets, or government and external communication networks. Hence, rural politics is pulled and tugged by competition between the interests of local residents and external factors.

For example, major coal, oil, or mineral interests in Appalachia, Wyoming, and western Colorado are dominant local employers and are more likely to influence rural political decisions than communities where power and wealth are relatively diffused. Rural politics also are influenced by external trade. At times, higher prices for rural-produced grains and energy products allow rural residents more purchasing power, but the cyclical nature of markets can also decrease rural incomes. Federal deregulation of the banking industry and the move toward bank consolidation in the 1980s opened up opportunities for urban-based banks to enter rural financial markets or to strengthen their presence there significantly. This trend may create new opportunities for rural communities, but it also may limit credit to credit-starved regions. These relationships influence how politics is discussed and carried out at the local level.

Federal and state governments play a significant role in rural politics. Unfunded state and federal mandates have strained local budgets and the problem-solving capacities of rural communities run by volunteer leaders. Federal rural development programs also have influenced rural political agendas and goal-setting because of the attractiveness of external funds. Federal investments during the 1960s through the 1980s led to improved transportation and communication systems for rural communities, which encouraged more interdependence between rural and urban areas. With improved access to major highways, many rural communities developed planning strategies to diversify their local economies in order to minimize economic and political dependence on external forces. In other cases, federal deregulation of transportation industries led to a cutback in bus, air, and railroad transportation.

Another force shaping rural politics is urban America. Urban dwellers often have moved into rural areas because they perceived a better environment and a higher quality of life. The urbanites tend to bring a high demand for public services that rural residents are often reluctant to fund. Urbanites view rural areas as prime recreation areas, where they often compete with rural recreation seekers or resource industries. Urban demand for water, energy, and other resources has contributed to environmental changes in rural America. Rivers are dammed and rural power plants are built to satisfy urban consumers' needs. Strip mining changes the landscape, and rural sprawl infringes on natural areas and wildlife habitats.

Another force is the changing function of rural communities and the sense of place. Rural communities are not necessarily fully functioning service, retail, and employment centers. In many cases, retail downtowns have been replaced by regional shopping centers. In some rural economies, the majority of workers commute to urban or other rural areas. Rural residents may identify with groups and organizations outside their community. Thus, politics takes on unique dimensions in these changing rural settings.

Most of the nation's environmental resources are in rural areas. Hence, growing environmental movements and federal environmental regulations often are aimed at rural communities. Conflicting environmental demands require communities to make trade-offs. Local decision makers question who will pay the costs of environmental stewardship or cleanup. Local firms and governments may wish to relax environmental regulations in order to create economic development opportunities for rural residents. In other cases, environmental protection is viewed as a necessity for rural viability. Competition for control of land resources among corporations, environmental groups, recreation users, government and other organizations often dominates rural political agendas. Some communities may be poorly equipped to handle these conflicts, and so community fragmentation is likely to occur.

Rural politics is also influenced by growing public concerns about farmland protection, historic preservation, main street revitalization, and maintaining viable rural communities. Land trusts and preservation groups have emerged in rural areas. Zoning and other types of local legislation are implemented to control the direction of rural growth.

Capacity to Address Rural Issues

Rural political communities tend to have a wide variation in their capacities to address issues. However, they have some commonalities. Rural peoples have many of the same problems as urban residents, such as poverty and environmental change. However, the scale of the problem and cultural traditions of problem solving may increase the potential for solving problems in rural areas if there are adequate resources and favorable policies. Rural communities face several unique obstacles to solving their problems. Rural leaders often serve in a volunteer capacity and lack the large, specialized technical support staffs

found in urban areas. They must draw on technical expertise from outside their communities. In contrast to urban areas, rural political communities tend to engage competitively rather than cooperate through inter-rural governmental units. As a consequence, rural communities find it difficult to benefit from economies of scale. Unrestricted intrarural competition leads to less effective and less efficient service delivery.

Modern politics changed rural areas. In the recent past, rural areas tended to dominate state legislatures when representation was based on areas rather than population. However, the Supreme Court's 1963 one-person, one-vote decision (*Gray v. Sanders*) lessened the legislative influence of rural areas in states where urban dwellers predominate. State and federal mandates tended to force rural communities to provide highly specialized services over more generalized, locally based services. The problem is exacerbated by rural citizens who are tied to unidirectional metropolitan communication linkages. As a result, rural communities find it difficult to communicate with each other. Some national and state policymakers have attempted to address these issues through incentives for locally based intercommunity cooperation in rural areas, or through inter-rural regional institutions, such as nonmetropolitan regional planning commissions. Cooperative extension services and major U.S. foundations have launched educational initiatives to strengthen the capacity of rural communities to address these issues and other complex problems.

Political Units

Rural politics shapes and is shaped by local political institutions. Counties are the primary level of government in 48 states. In Louisiana, the place is filled by parishes, equivalent to counties. Local government in Alaska is still evolving; settlements there can request the kind of government they want. Cities in Alaska, as elsewhere, are responsible for police and fire protection and sewer and water services. However, boroughs—which are equivalent to other states' counties—focus on planning and zoning, parks and recreation, tax collection, and schools. Rural Alaska also has "unorganized burroughs," where government functions are performed by the state.

County governments throughout the United States perform a number of important functions: law enforcement, judicial administration, road and bridge construction and maintenance, supervision of legal documents, and social welfare. State legislators tend to grant counties relatively broad powers, with anticipated supervision of smaller municipalities. However, whenever towns or cities win greater home rule (local political autonomy), power is counterbalanced with that of the counties.

Townships also may play a role in rural politics, depending on the region. Some states have townships while others do not. Most of the six New England states are divided into townships of about 20,000 acres, which perform traditional county functions. The government structure of these townships varies from direct democracy to representative town meetings to a council manager. Other townships have little local power. For example, townships in the Midwest only maintain small-town roads, provide fire protection, and serve as voting districts. In a few states, townships may provide for their own planning and zoning, whereas this function is confined to the counties and cities in most states.

Special districts are another type of rural government. If school districts are counted among them, special districts make up over half of the 80,000 governments in the United States. Special districts can be described as unifunctional, whereas counties, towns, cities, and townships are multifunctional in the services they provide. Each special district provides unique services such as water, sewers, roads, or drainage to small towns and unincorporated areas. Some are designed to protect lakes or other natural or human-made resources.

The American Indian Self-Determination Act of 1975 allowed federally entrusted tribal governments to become more independent. Tribal governments can impose taxes, create corporations, establish hunting and fishing regulations for their own members within their reservations, and regulate zoning and land use. They have the ability to develop their own community regardless of state and local regulations. Their autonomy is greater than that of other rural government entities, leading occasionally to disputes. For example, the creation of gaming and bingo parlors by tribal governments has been a source of friction between some rural municipalities and rural residents and the reservations. Others find that tribal self-determination offers limited resources and may lead to factional politics within the tribe.

Rural politics at the national level is diverse and fragmented, and it no longer concentrates exclusively on agricultural issues. Rural politics at the local level could be characterized as a tug-of-war between external factors and local perspectives. Rural communities, like urban ones, vary in their capacity to address their issues and problems.

—Ronald J. Hustedde

See also

Decentralization; Development, Community and Economic; Government; Leadership; Policy, Rural Development.

References

Brown, Ralph. "Rural Community Satisfaction and Attachment in Mass Consumer Society." *Rural Sociology* 58 (Fall 1993): 387–403.

Flora, Cornelia B., and James A. Christenson. *Rural Policies for the 1990s.* Boulder, CO: Westview Press, 1991.

Gaventa, John. *Power and Powerlessness: Quiescence and Rebellion in an Appalachian Valley.* Urbana: University of Illinois Press, 1980.

Korsching, Peter F., Timothy O. Borich, and Julie Stewart, eds. *Multicommunity Collaboration: An Evolving Rural Revitalization Strategy.* Ames, IA: North Central Regional Center for Rural Development, 1992.

Lapping, Mark B., Thomas L. Daniels, and John Keller. *Rural Planning and Development in the United States.* New York: Guilford Press, 1989.

Luloff, Albert E., and Louis E. Swanson. *American Rural Communities.* Boulder, CO: Westview Press, 1990.

Seroka, Jim, and Seshan Subramaniam. "Governing the Countryside: Linking Politics and Administrative Resources." Pp. 213–231 in *The Future of Rural America: Anticipating Policies for Constructive Change.* Edited by Kenneth E. Pigg. Boulder, CO: Westview Press, 1991.

Wilkinson, Kenneth P. *The Community in Rural America.* Westport, CT: Greenwood Press, 1991.

Poultry Industry

An important year-round source of reasonably priced egg and poultry meat products. This industry is one of the most efficient in agriculture and is often studied by other animal industries for its innovations and structure. The industry is highly integrated and concentrated. Both production and marketing costs remain low, contributing to the growth in use, particularly of broiler and turkey meat.

History and Status

The industry experienced many changes as it evolved into its present form. Chickens were brought to America with the first settlers, but they were not the primary poultry meat source, and were depended upon mainly for seasonal egg supplies. Wildfowl abounded. As settlements grew, chicken production was encouraged and turkeys were domesticated. The development of transportation encouraged the long-distance movement of eggs and live poultry. Later, refrigeration provided more help to the movement of eggs. Grain production in the Midwest led to the development of a large poultry production region, and that area remained the primary surplus region until well after World War II. Poultry production expanded in earlier days close to large consuming centers, and for many years there was a substantial amount of slaughtering and egg packing close to metropolitan areas. New York–dressed poultry (blood, feathers, and feet removed) was shipped in volume in frozen form over long distances until the mid-1950s. Then the eviscerated form, first frozen and then fresh, began to replace the New York–dressed form. Rapid truck movement from country points now permits quick delivery of poultry of higher quality. Egg quality is much higher than it once was because of more efficient cage operations and technology, which permit widespread country packing of eggs in consumer-ready form.

Today's poultry industry is commercialized, high-technology, large-scale, specialized, and vertically and horizontally integrated. The number of producing, marketing, and input-supplying units declined for several decades. Major items produced by the industry today are from large egg-laying flocks, year-round broiler enterprises, and single- to multiple-batch turkey enterprises. Resulting consumer products appear as fresh shell eggs, manufactured products containing eggs, fresh and frozen broilers, roasters, and turkeys, and processed products made from poultry meat. Only a small amount of non-commercial production is left to meet limited demand for local or specialized items, which tend to carry price premiums. Production of ducks, geese, and game birds is highly specialized and localized, and these fowl are sold as high-priced luxury items. Ducks are by far the most important of the latter group.

Baby chicks being fed at a chicken farm in New York State. Efficient production techniques have kept poultry prices low in comparison to those for other sources of protein.

Consumption and Uses

The consumption of eggs and poultry is substantial and diverse. Per capita annual consumption of broilers and turkeys more than doubled between the mid-1970s and the mid-1990s, with consumption of broilers reaching 80 pounds per capita per annum, and of turkeys, 18 pounds (dressed, ready-to-cook weight). Consumption of other mature chicken is two pounds per capita; all other poultry is less than one pound per capita. In contrast, egg consumption per capita per annum fell from nearly 300 to 234 in the past two decades. This decline was in consumption of fresh shell eggs due to changes in eating habits and to concerns with cholesterol and salmonella. Through 1993, the American Egg Board spent $94 million to counter adverse publicity, promote egg nutrition, and develop new products. Cholesterol levels in eggs are lower than earlier claimed, according to the latest government data.

Important shares of egg, broiler, and turkey production are used in manufactured or processed products, and by the away-from-home market (restaurants, fast-food outlets, hospitals, schools, and other institutions). A quarter of egg production goes into manufactured products, and a quarter of egg consumption takes place away from home. About half of broiler sales are to retail outlets, and about a third to institutional market outlets. Nearly half of the turkey output is used in further processing, and much of this, as well as some whole and cut turkey, goes to the away-from-home market. Over the last two decades, the proportion of broilers sold in cut-up form increased from one-third to over half, and nearly a third of turkey output is now sold in cut-up form. The use of broiler meat in processed products remained at 7 to 8 percent of output, since broiler meat tends to cost more than meat from mature chickens.

Inedible eggs and poultry are used in pet food production. Poultry by-product meal is manufactured from inedible carcasses and parts, offal, and some spent hens. Feathers from poultry processing are converted into feather meal. Both meals are recycled through poultry feeds. Some of the feathers from chicken processing are used in pillows, and waterfowl feathers and down are used to fill expensive sleeping bags and jackets.

Consumer Protection

The high quality of edible egg and poultry products is sustained by the federal and state system of inspection and grading. Mandatory inspection routinely takes place in poultry slaughtering, eviscerating, and processing plants and in plants producing liquid, frozen, and dried egg products. Nominal inspection exists in egg-packing plants, and grading of both eggs and poultry can be carried out under federal and state supervision. The U.S. Department of Agriculture (USDA) has federal responsibility for inspection and grading programs up to the retail and institutional levels. At those levels, responsibility rests with the Food and Drug Administration and various state and local agencies.

Efficiency and Costs

One reason why poultry and eggs have remained competitive protein sources in the marketplace is that growing efficiency in production and marketing kept prices low in comparison to other animal proteins. Laying hens, broilers, and turkeys are efficient converters of feed into finished products. It takes 3.75 pounds of feed to produce a dozen eggs. For broilers, two pounds of feed are required per pound of live weight, and for turkeys, three pounds or less of feed per pound of live weight. There have been substantial declines in the feed/product ratios in recent decades due to improved breeding and feeding and management. Additionally, the number of birds that can be handled per worker more than quadrupled because of mechanization and better housing facilities for the birds and the realization of substantial economies of scale. There have been substantial gains in productivity in marketing due to simplified marketing channels, economies of scale, and mechanization. Over two decades, the productivity of egg marketing increased 80 percent, that of broilers, 50 percent, and of turkeys, more than 60 percent. Intermediaries declined in importance; there is now more direct, plant-to-retailer or warehouse movement and less jobbing activity.

During 1994, the average cost to produce a dozen grade A large eggs was 46.8 cents per dozen, and the industry net return was 3.8 cents. The cost to produce a pound of live broiler during 1994 was 27.0 cents, and the net return was 6.0 cents in ready-to-cook equivalent. The

cost to produce a pound of live turkey in 1994 was 37.5 cents, and the net return was 2.8 cents per pound in ready-to-cook equivalent. The net return has been positive for each commodity for the past several years. In the longer run, broiler returns remained consistently positive, whereas returns from eggs or turkeys varied from positive to negative.

It cost 19 cents in 1994 to move eggs from the farm to the retail store. About one cent of this went toward assembly and procurement. (A unique feature of the egg industry has been the growth of "in-line" complexes. With production and packing at the same geographic location, eggs are conveyed from cages to the packing room by belts. Currently, over half of commercial production is of the in-line type, and this materially lowers average industry assembly costs.) Nearly 2 cents went for long-distance hauling; 12 cents for grading, packing, and cartoning; and four cents for wholesaling. The average annual retail markup on eggs ranges from 17 to 21 cents.

Costs of moving ready-to-cook broilers from producing areas to retail outlets were about 20 cents per pound in 1994. Nearly 4 cents went for assembly and hauling; 11 cents for processing; and about 5 cents for wholesaling. Retail markups range from 20 to 26 cents. For turkeys, costs from producing areas to the retail level were 24 cents per pound of ready-to-cook equivalent. Retail markups range from 20 to 26 cents.

Production and Pricing

Production of eggs and poultry is relatively widespread but tends to be concentrated more heavily in those states that have a comparative advantage or where individual entrepreneurs have been most persistent. Sixty percent of the nation's broilers are produced by the five leading states (Arkansas, Georgia, Alabama, North Carolina, and Mississippi); 82 percent by the top ten; and 95.5 percent by the first 20. Outside of the southern states, only California, Missouri, and Pennsylvania rank among the top 15 producers. The five leading turkey-producing states (North Carolina, Minnesota, Arkansas, California, and Missouri) produce nearly 54 percent; the top ten states, over 75 percent; and the 20 leading states, 85 percent. The five leading states in egg production (California, Georgia, Arkansas, Indiana, and Pennsylvania) account for about 36 percent of output; the top ten states produce nearly 60 percent; and the 20 leading states, over 80 percent.

Basic price levels on broilers, turkeys, and other poultry are determined primarily by sales to volume buyers in large consuming centers, with returns to plants and producers largely reflected by intervening costs of transportation. Sales to manufacturers of processed poultry products and to other institutions relate to basic price levels. Trading between producers and packing plants of gradeable nest run and graded loose eggs provides a base to which cartoning and movement costs to large markets can be added to fix prices for volume buyers. Trading of nest run breaking stock between producers, packers, and egg breakers and dryers largely determines the input costs for liquid, frozen, and dried egg products. In sales of these products to food manufacturers, long-term price contracts are common.

Market Movements

The bulk of poultry industry products go to domestic outlets, and the market for these is nationwide. While the local needs for each commodity often may be produced within a few hundred miles, large quantities must be moved greater distances to balance supplies with demand. The interregional movement of broilers and turkeys has trended upward for many years, and it may now be increasing on eggs. Only 14 southern states are surplus on broilers; all others are deficit, with as much as 40 percent moving interregionally. Less than 20 percent of turkey output moves interregionally. Long-distance hauling of eggs is increased by the need to obtain particular grades and sizes, even though eggs are produced to some extent in all states. In total, about a fifth of egg output moves interregionally.

Strong domestic price levels have been supported by growing and substantial export markets for broilers and turkeys, and to a lesser extent, for eggs. The major increases in exports began about 1990, with broiler exports rising from 4 to 10 percent of output by the mid-1990s, and turkeys from 2 to 11 percent of output. Egg exports rose from 2 to about 3.5 percent of output. Asia is our major export market for broilers, but exports to Russia (1.48 billion pounds in 1995) and Eastern Europe have been increasing rapidly throughout the 1990s, supplementing continuing increases in the Western Hemisphere and the Middle East. Mexico is our largest export market for turkeys (136 million pounds in 1995), followed by Russia (85 million pounds) and Korea (35 million pounds). The most important egg markets are Japan (55.6 million dozen in 1995), Hong Kong (43.5 million dozen), Canada (33.8 million dozen), and Mexico (23.3 million dozen), with the balance widely scattered geographically. The competitiveness of U.S. poultry and egg production, export promotion, and the federal export enhancement program have helped in expanding our export markets, as may recent trade pacts. But export sales remain vulnerable to political developments abroad (U.S. Department of Agriculture, 1996).

Integration and Concentration

The poultry industry exhibits a high and unique degree of vertical and horizontal integration, and increasingly is concentrated in fewer and fewer hands. Vertical integration began in the industry with various types of contractual arrangements between producers and packing plants, feed dealers, and marketing-oriented concerns. Over the years, contractual arrangements increasingly have been replaced by processor-owned farms, and the number of independent producers has declined drastically. Currently, only about 1 percent of broiler output is from fully independent farms. The proportion of non-commercial turkeys is estimated at 3 to 4 percent, whereas the volume of eggs being produced by independent farmers or marketed through true cooperatives is at 6 percent. Many large firms engaged in the egg, broiler, or turkey business are also involved with feed milling and distribution, processing, long-distance transportation, and wholesaling. Some are part of large conglomerates or have international branches.

There has also been a growing degree of concentration. The top ten broiler firms accounted for 59 percent of output in 1994; 52 firms for 99 percent. Many firms have more than one plant and are engaged in further processing. The top five turkey firms account for 48 percent of output; the top ten for 74 percent; and 28 for virtually all of the commercial production. In 1994, 57 firms owning more than 1 million laying hens accounted for 72.5 percent of the total. And 380 firms having 75,000 or more layers accounted for 94 percent.

Employment

The poultry industry furnishes substantial employment opportunities to rural America. But because of the decline in small independent output, employment in today's commercial egg and poultry enterprises is likely to be as a contractual or salaried worker. Even to become a commercial grower on the scale demanded by present companies requires capital investments of many thousands of dollars. Traditionally, catching and hauling live birds had low status and appeal, as did killing, picking, and eviscerating operations. Mechanization alleviated this to some extent. Nevertheless, poultry processing plants employing several hundred to a few thousand workers are valuable to local economies. Egg packing and processing jobs are more rewarding, but relatively fewer people are required. Related input supply and construction also help local employment. From the processing and packing operations forward, marketing activities tend to be more associated with urban areas, with the exception of local retailing and away-from-home facilities, and locally based hauling companies.

—*George B. Rogers*

See also

Agricultural Prices; Animal Rights/Welfare; Livestock Industry; Livestock Production.

References

American Poultry Historical Society. *American Poultry History, 1823–1973.* Madison: American Printing and Publishing, 1974.

———. *American Poultry History, 1974–1993.* Mt. Morris, IL: Watt, 1996.

Benjamin, Earl W., James M. Gwin, Fred L. Faber, and William D. Termohlen. *Marketing Poultry Products.* 5th ed. New York: John Wiley, 1960.

Lasley, Floyd Alvin. *The U.S. Poultry Industry: Changing Economics and Structure,* Agricultural Economics Report No. 502 (July). Washington, DC: U.S. Department of Agriculture, Economic Research Service, 1983.

Lasley, Floyd Alvin, William L. Henson, and Harold B. Jones, Jr. *The U.S. Turkey Industry.* Agricultural Economics Report No. 525 (March). Washington, DC: U.S. Department of Agriculture, Economic Research Service, 1985.

Lasley, Floyd Alvin, Harold B. Jones, Jr., Edward E. Easterling, and Lee A. Christensen. *The U.S. Broiler Industry,* Agricultural Economics Report No. 591 (November). Washington, DC: U.S. Department of Agriculture, Economic Research Service, 1988.

Rogers, George B. "Historical and Economic Development of the Poultry Industry, 1517–1950." Unpublished manuscript in Personal Papers of George B. Rogers. Beltsville, MD: National Agricultural Library, 1951.

———. "Poultry and Eggs." Pp. 148–189 in *Another Revolution in U.S. Farming?* Agricultural Economics Report No. 441, rev. ed. (November). Edited by Lyle Schertz. Washington, DC: U.S. Department of Agriculture, Economics and Statistics Services, 1980.

Sawyer, Gordon. *The Agribusiness Poultry Industry: A History of Its Development.* New York: Exposition Press, 1971.

Sykes, Geoffrey. *Poultry, A Modern Agribusiness.* London: Crosby, Lockwood and Sons, 1963.

U.S. Department of Agriculture. *Poultry Outlook: Supplement to Livestock, Dairy, and Poultry Situation and Outlook.* Washington, DC: U.S. Department of Agriculture, Economic Research Service, 19 June 1995, p. 5.

———. *Poultry Situation, Livestock and Poultry Situation, Poultry Outlook,* and *Poultry* (various issues). Washington, DC: U.S. Department of Agriculture.

Poverty

The lack of income or other resources needed to achieve a minimally acceptable standard of living. Poverty in the United States often is perceived as a principally urban problem, yet historically and today it is more prevalent in rural areas. Compared to the urban poor, the rural poor have somewhat different characteristics, face unique macroeconomic circumstances, and exhibit dissimilar economic survival strategies. Nevertheless, the popular perception and political concern about the poor often are shaped by images of inner-city poverty. The unique nature of rural poverty needs to be better understood in order to tailor realistic policy options for rural areas. This entry seeks to provide a rudimentary understanding. First, the definitions of and trends in poverty are detailed. Then, to help explain the rural disadvantage in poverty, the individual-level and structural causes of poverty are reviewed. Finally, rural-urban differences in the survival strategies of the poor are considered.

Definitions of Poverty

Absolute Poverty. Poverty can be defined in many ways. Absolute poverty occurs when people and their families lack the income or resources necessary to maintain a subsistence-level standard of living. The official definition of poverty in the United States follows this absolute approach. Developed in the early 1960s, it set the poverty threshold at three times the cost of a minimally adequate diet. To account for variation in needs across families of different types, multiple poverty thresholds were specified to adjust for family size, number of children, gender of family head, whether the head was elderly, and whether the family lived on a farm. Farm families were assigned lower poverty thresholds because it was assumed they produced some of their own food and therefore needed less income to get along. Other than adjusting annually for inflation, recent decades have seen only slight modifications to the official poverty thresholds (although the farm/nonfarm distinction is no longer made). In 1993, a family of four was defined as poor if their annual pretax income was less than $14,763.

Relative and Subjective Poverty. Two other less commonly used definitions of poverty are relative and subjective poverty. Whereas absolute poverty exists when a family has less than subsistence-level income, relative poverty is defined as an income that is much less than average. A typical relative definition is annual family income that is less than one-half the median annual family income. Trends in relative poverty rates are especially

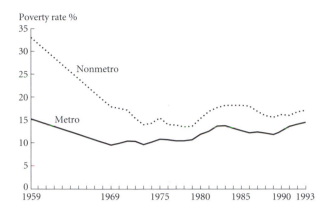

Poverty Rate by Residence, United States, 1959–1993

Source: U.S. Bureau of the Census P-60 series, 1974–1994; prepared by the Population, Labor, and Income Branch, Economic Research Service, U.S. Department of Agriculture.

sensitive to changes in the equality of income distribution, and these rates tend to be higher than the absolute poverty rates. Subjective poverty occurs simply when people define themselves as poor. Individuals might be asked what they feel is the minimum amount of income needed to buy the bare necessities, and then defined as poor if their income is below that level. Subjective poverty rates tend to be higher than official rates, suggesting that many people would define themselves as poor even though they are not poor by official standards.

Trends in Absolute Poverty

The figure shows absolute poverty rates among metropolitan and nonmetropolitan individuals for the period 1959 to 1993. The 1960s typify the postwar years as a period of steadily declining poverty rates, especially in nonmetropolitan areas. Since the early 1970s, poverty rates have been rising and falling in response to economic cycles, but generally have trended upward; in both metropolitan and nonmetropolitan areas, poverty rates were higher in 1993 than they were two decades prior. In every year, the nonmetropolitan poverty rate was higher than the corresponding metropolitan rate. For instance, the poverty rate in 1993 was 17.2 and 14.6 percent in nonmetropolitan and metropolitan areas, respectively. Thus, although the difference in poverty rates between urban and rural areas narrowed, poverty remains more prevalent in the nonmetropolitan areas, dispelling the myth that it is principally an urban phenomenon.

Rural poverty should not be regarded as homogeneous or uniform. Regionally, nonmetropolitan poverty is highly concentrated in the South, a fact that is only partly

attributable to the heavy concentration of nonmetropolitan Blacks in that region. Poverty rates also are higher in more remote nonmetropolitan counties. The 1989 poverty rate for residents of nonmetropolitan counties adjacent to metropolitan areas was 13.2 percent (or little different from the U.S. rate), but 19.4 percent were poor in nonmetropolitan counties that were not adjacent and had no city of at least 10,000 residents (U.S. Department of Agriculture 1993).

Explaining Rural Poverty

Studies of the causes of poverty differ in their emphasis on individual and family characteristics versus structural characteristics of place of residence. Both kinds of studies are helpful to understand why poverty rates are higher in nonmetropolitan America.

Individual-Level Explanations. At the individual level, the set of factors that influence poverty status is highly similar in rural and urban areas. In both places, for example, those with little education are more likely to be poor than those with more, as are Blacks or Latinos when compared to Whites. In seeking to understand and explain the higher poverty rate in rural America, social scientists explored rural/urban differences in both population composition and in the effects of specific variables on the likelihood of being poor.

Some differences in population composition work in favor of rural residents, which makes their higher poverty rate seem puzzling. Nonmetropolitan individuals are less likely to be members of racial or ethnic minority groups known to suffer much higher risks of poverty. When residential differences in poverty rates are examined within categories of race and ethnicity, the nonmetropolitan disadvantage appears that much worse. The 1990 population survey data show that the nonmetropolitan poverty rates for Whites, Blacks, Latinos, and Native Americans were even higher than those for their counterparts living in the central cities of metropolitan areas. An implication is that rural minorities rank among the poorest of all Americans. Compositional differences in family structure also benefit rural residents. Nonmetropolitan residents are more likely than metropolitan residents to be residing in families headed by a married couple, and they are less likely to be in female-headed families. Working against nonmetropolitan residents is the fact that they are more likely to be elderly—a compositional difference that is consistent with their higher poverty risks.

An important correlate of poverty is human capital. According to human capital theory, workers are remunerated in direct proportion to the bundle of skills they bring to the labor force. Those with human capital deficits, indicated by low levels of education or labor force experience, are at greater risk of poverty. Nonmetropolitan adults have completed fewer years of education on average and are more likely to have dropped out of high school than their metropolitan counterparts. There also is evidence that rural schools are of lower quality, and that rural high school students score lower on standardized tests of scholastic aptitude. There is less empirical support for a rural human capital disadvantage in work experience. When human capital is measured as total years of full-time work experience and the percentage of adult years worked full-time, rural household heads are relatively advantaged compared to urban heads. A related question is whether rural residents enjoy the same economic returns to human capital. For example, poverty rates could be higher in rural areas partly because additional years of education are less effective in keeping adults and their families out of poverty. Although education and work experience generally increase urban incomes more than rural ones, research on poverty per se has not revealed significant residential differences in returns to human capital.

Structural Explanations. In addition to the attributes of people and families, individual well-being will be shaped by structural characteristics of the places in which individuals live. These include the abundance and quality of surrounding economic opportunities and the permeability of local socioeconomic hierarchies. When rural poverty reached the national spotlight, structural explanations—most notably, dependence on extractive industries—are often invoked. It remains true that poverty rates are higher in counties dominated by farming and other extractive industries. For example, in 1989, the poverty rate for all nonmetropolitan counties was 16.8 percent, but was 18.3 and 22.0 percent in farming-dependent and mining-dependent nonmetropolitan counties, respectively (U.S. Department of Agriculture 1993). Often such places lack diversified economies, making them highly vulnerable to macroeconomic slumps and international competition. The farm crisis of the early 1980s, for example, contributed to the rise in rural poverty by hurting farmers and ancillary businesses that depend on a healthy farm sector.

Today, only about 7 percent of all nonmetropolitan workers are in agriculture-related industries, and 1 percent are in other extractive industries (U.S. Department of Agriculture 1993). To understand the structural causes of rural poverty, it is important to look beyond agriculture to other aspects of industrial structure. Local economies dominated by manufacturing tend to have lower poverty rates. Whereas metropolitan and nonmetropolitan areas are roughly equivalent in the percentage of workers in manufacturing, nonmetropolitan workers are more likely to be in the less lucrative nondurable goods manufacturing sector. Moreover, the slowly rising poverty rates in nonmetropolitan America over the past quarter-century can be attributed partly to the continued industrial restructuring away from manufacturing and toward services. Between 1980 and 1990, the nonmetropolitan workforce employed in manufacturing declined by 0.3 percent, while that in services grew by 21.9 percent (U.S. Department of Agriculture 1993).

Local industrial structure provides some clues to differential opportunity between places; however, analyses that control for it are still unable to explain completely the rural disadvantage in poverty (Brown and Hirschl 1995). Although controlling for prevailing wages can explain the nonmetropolitan disadvantage in poverty risks, this begs the question of why their wages are lower in the first place. Speculation includes smaller firm size, lower unionization rates, different phases of production that concentrate in rural areas, and lower costs of living, but there are no firm explanations.

In addition to industrial structure, individual opportunities are shaped by the permeability of local social hierarchies. In some instances the persistence of rural poverty is linked to highly ascriptive stratification systems. Certain families within rural communities may become pejoratively labeled and encounter blocked access to educational and occupational opportunities. Similar arguments explain persisting poverty among rural minorities. Minority individuals within communities can experience prejudice and discrimination in the pursuit of economic goals, just as minority communities as a whole can experience blocked access to societal resources.

An important reason to study structural determinants of poverty is that they can help account for individual-level disadvantages. For example, the comparatively low education of rural residents has been linked to poorer quality schools; a rural "brain drain," in which the best students migrate to opportunities found in more urban locales; and the possibility that rural residents, sensing a local economy that yields a low payoff to education, rationally underinvest in their own human capital. Similarly, while the increase in rural poverty in recent years may be blamed partly on family instability and the increase in the number of households headed by women, both of these phenomena in turn seem to result from industrial restructuring and constrained opportunities. The point is, individual-level explanations for poverty may have important structural roots.

Rural Economic Survival Strategies

The uniqueness of rural poverty is evident also in the economic survival strategies used by the rural poor. These strategies are consistent with the strong sense of individualism and self-reliance said to distinguish many rural areas. For example, compared to their metropolitan counterparts, poor nonmetropolitan families rely more on earnings from labor force participation and less on public assistance and other means-tested transfer programs (that is, they are more likely to be among the working poor). The higher labor force participation of the rural poor, along with difficulties of availability and accessibility to assistance programs generally, helps explain the lower rates of welfare use among the rural poor. There also is evidence that a greater sense of individualism in rural areas lowers welfare receipt both by making the rural poor themselves more averse to relying on the government and by making the negative stigma associated with welfare receipt stronger in rural America (Rank and Hirschl 1993).

Besides formal work and welfare, recent years have seen growing interest in informal or underground economic activities, which emerge as household survival strategies among the poor. The informal economy consists of unregulated economic activities that generate real or in-kind income. Such activities include under-the-table work for cash or other things of value, selling rummaged goods, and selling home-produced food or crafts. Several studies have shown that informal work is common in rural areas and can provide critical help to poor rural families, enabling them to survive through especially difficult periods.

This entry highlighted the distinctive nature of rural poverty and argued that its uniqueness needs to be borne in mind when dealing with the rural poor. Poverty policy proposals designed to strengthen the family and move the poor off welfare and into the workforce make somewhat less sense in rural areas, where the poor already are more likely to work and live in intact families. Instead, rural poverty would be ameliorated more by programs designed to generate employment opportunities and make work pay a living wage.

At the same time, significant areas of convergence need to be recognized. First, the nonmetropolitan disadvantage is not nearly as great today as it was 30 or more years ago (see figure, p. 573). Second, recent decades witnessed a substantial increase in the prevalence of single-parent families in rural areas, eroding the rural advantage in this regard and giving rise to an increase in child poverty. Third, over the past two decades there has been a significant decline in earnings and rise in public assistance as a percentage of poor family income. Although rural poor families still rely more heavily on earnings and less on government transfers than the urban poor, the residential differences are much less stark today. Moreover, rural areas are not immune to the many regrettable correlates of poverty, including drug and alcohol abuse, domestic violence, and homelessness, which is particularly disturbing since services often are lacking or inaccessible in rural areas.

—*Leif Jensen*

See also
Employment; Homelessness; Income; Inequality; Policy, Socio-economic; Underemployment.
References
Brown, David L., and Thomas A. Hirschl. "Household Poverty in Rural and Metropolitan-Core Areas of the United States." *Rural Sociology* 60 (1995): 44–66.
Duncan, Cynthia M., ed. *Rural Poverty in America*. New York: Auburn House, 1992.
Fitchen, Janet M. *Poverty in Rural America: A Case Study*. Boulder, CO: Westview Press, 1981.
Jensen, Leif, and David J. Eggebeen. "Nonmetropolitan Poor Children and Reliance on Public Assistance." *Rural Sociology* 59 (1994): 45–65.
Jensen, Leif, and Diane K. McLaughlin. "Human Capital and Nonmetropolitan Poverty." Pp. 111–138 in *Investing in People: The Human Capital Needs of Rural America*. Edited by Lionel J. Beaulieu and David Mulkey. Boulder, CO: Westview Press, 1995.
Lichter, Daniel T., and David J. Eggebeen. "Child Poverty and the Changing Rural Family." *Rural Sociology* 57 (1992): 151–172.
Rank, Mark R., and Thomas A. Hirschl. "The Link between Population Density and Welfare Participation." *Demography* 30 (1993): 607–622.
Rural Sociological Society Task Force on Persistent Rural Poverty. *Persistent Poverty in Rural America*. Boulder, CO: Westview Press, 1993.
U.S. Department of Agriculture. Appendix Tables in *Rural Conditions and Trends* 4 (1993): 64–102.

Public Libraries

Locally funded institutions that serve as the community's information center by acquiring, organizing, and disseminating information to meet customers' demands. This entry considers the nature of rural and small public libraries in the United States in light of the present opportunities for adult lifelong learning. Not reviewed is the active role played by the library in providing services to children, bookmobiles, or books-by-mail services, which currently are also popular strategies to serve rural constituents.

Rural Libraries

To discuss public libraries in the United States in an informed way, one must realize that 80 percent (7,118) of these institutions are located in population centers serving fewer than 25,000 people. Of this group, another 80 percent, or 2,656 libraries, provide services to communities of fewer than 2,500 individuals. The majority of rural libraries are staffed by one full-time person, have a collection of fewer than 10,000 books and serial volumes, and operate within a total budget of $21,000 (figures from the early 1990s) (Chute 1994). This situation prompted at least one author to write about the "genteel poverty" of the library. For the total budget figure given above must cover all expenses, from paying the utilities to staff salaries. This is very different from the situation in a school library, where salary costs come from a line item in the school's budget for personnel and the librarian's allocation is primarily for materials. Parenthetically, some rural libraries in the United States have no line item in their budgets for book purchases. In these instances, a variety of different means are used to raise funds, including donations for memorials to those who are deceased, or living memorials in recognition of someone in the town. Rural libraries have used the latter approach to obtain children's books donated by children themselves.

In comparison to the basic model of rural (population less than 2,500), in-service populations up to 25,000, the typical public library in the early 1990s had from two to four full-time staff persons available; the book and serial volume collection numbered 24,000; and the total operating budget was $117,000. While these conditions are an improvement over those facing smaller libraries, clearly they are not luxurious (Chute 1994).

Information Needs

Just as our country adjusted its institutions to accommodate the waves of immigrants in the nineteenth and twentieth centuries, the rural towns and townships that today are faced with accelerated demands for a wide variety of social and cultural services must cope with new challenges. Further, because the new rural residents bring with them expectations nurtured by urban living, unavoidable conflicts arise because of urban-acquired

Public library in Bagley, Minnesota.

value systems that cannot presently be supported by existing rural infrastructures. While the gap between rural and urban areas is closing politically and culturally, nonmetropolitan America continues to lag behind in relation to its economic base, health support, social services, and educational institutions.

Rural America faces many additional problems that are inextricably related to satisfying the information needs not only of private individuals but also of rural governmental officials, planners, and decision makers. Information needs must be satisfied for those who are transforming the rural economy from its agrarian and extractive beginnings to its current dependence on manufacturing and service industries. Information needs must also be satisfied for both the private and public sector as they develop new job training alliances, individuals and agencies responsible for the future of the rural family, and those who develop and execute telecommunications policy. Those involved in developing efficient ways to disseminate agriculture-related information also need information, as do those who develop agribusinesses near the place of farm production and those who live in rural America and wish to maintain a better life by access to timely information.

Planning Considerations

As decision makers contemplate avenues for lifelong learning at the community level, the following comments about rural library services must be considered. First, surveys among library managers about their most pressing issues would show finances as a leading concern. Throughout the country, some communities can provide a working budget for services and activities, and others cannot. Per capita expenditures in 1994 ranged from a high of over $30 to a low of $7 (Chute 1994).

Taxpayers often oppose raising assessments to pay for services, and prefer institutional activities to remain at present levels. Community leaders have been flexible in attempting to raise sufficient funds to support the local library. Fund-raisers that would have been used before to enhance endowments or provide for special programming are now being used to raise working capital to enable daily library functioning. As a result, a wide range of fund-raising events are held, ranging from selling stationery and used books to wine and cheese parties, dances, and direct solicitations to local community groups such as social and service clubs. At issue is the question of who is responsible to adequately fund America's rural and small libraries. The answer has many parts. Because of its varied services, the public library is one of the best economic values, which has not been emphasized enough.

Second, rural and small towns are traditionally conservative institutions. The statement "we never did it that way before" is an important attitude to recognize. Unfortunately, this attitude may also be shared by the library personnel and trustees/board members, who may see no reason to change the library's routines. The typical librarian has lived in his or her community an average of 17 years and has been the librarian for 10 years (Vavrek 1989).

Third, the most important factor limiting the present and future development of rural information services is the lack of academically trained staff. Only about 34 percent, or 3,452, of the full-time librarians in libraries in communities of less than 25,000 people have a master's degree from an institution accredited by the American Library Association (ALA); in communities of less than 2,500 people, the figure is 5 percent (86 individuals) (Chute 1994).

Reasons for this educational situation include attitudes such as: We've never had a trained librarian; why do we need one now? or What's the matter with a salary of $13,000? Additional reasons include the relatively few schools of library and information science that are serving a geographically dispersed population; the inability of individuals to leave their positions to participate in university coursework; and the attitude of staff persons who do not recognize their need to pursue formalized education. Some of these problems are being mitigated by enterprising institutions that aggressively offer long-distance educational opportunities to students in person or by satellite or cable.

The problem of providing training and education is not limited to the formal, credit-generating, degree-awarding programs but also includes continuing education. In addition to the schools of library and information science, library cooperatives, systems, regional libraries, and state library agencies are providing consumers with their wants and needs. Unfortunately, there are more library staff and trustees in need of continuing education, particularly in technology, than there are providers. Library staff need systematic training in order to fully utilize the advantages of electronic media and to better serve clientele in small towns, which are rapidly becoming "virtual communities" in cyberspace (Rheingold 1993).

Fourth, not only is trustee development key to future planning, it is a topic demanding action. States such as Nebraska have gone further than most to establish certification requirements for trustees who wish to remain active. But anecdotal information regarding trustees and librarians from around the country suggests that a "me versus them" mentality prevails. If libraries in rural communities are to prosper, they cannot make a routine of rolling over trustees, who hire and fire the librarian and are responsible for the library's financial solvency. The development that is needed to ensure that a library plans for the future, uses its resources wisely in consort with other agencies, and becomes a true community information center begins with mutual trust between library staff and trustees/directors.

Fifth, planners must be aware that typical rural public libraries probably have not conducted user surveys. Vavrek (1989) reported that only 22 percent of libraries, or 81, had conducted a community analysis during the previous five years, and 23 percent, or 86, had formulated multiyear plans. In the absence of data describing the library's use and the attitude of clients toward available services, planning is done in an ad hoc manner. Library personnel tend to use interpersonal methods to gather information rather than attempting systematic surveys, being under the impression that they are familiar with community members who use the library.

Sixth, despite the age of electronic access to information through a variety of networks, rural libraries are perceived primarily as bookshelves. Despite the wide variety of resources available in rural libraries, user studies suggest that requests for bestsellers and leisure reading materials outstrip the demand for informational and reference material in printed or other formats (Estabrook 1991;Vavrek 1990 and 1993). This tendency is accentuated by the fact that librarians were brought up in a cultural environment that encouraged a view of libraries as mere repositories of books. Although things are changing, the typical rural library has little money to invest in alternative media and services, and little time to spend on marketing or advertising the diverse services that they do make available. As a result, recent studies found that while about 70 percent of library users had heard or seen advertisements about their local libraries during the course of the previous year, over 40 percent of the general public had not (Vavrek 1990 and 1993).

Seventh, 70 percent of rural public library users are women (Knight and Nourse 1969; Doremus, Porter, and Novelli, Inc. 1987). Analysts have spent little time considering why this is so and what it means. It is the author's impression that women read more than men, and that despite an increasing number of women working outside the household and a growing number of men staying at home, the female member has the continuing responsibility to educate children, which includes trips to the library with the children for activities like story hours. When the Center for the Study of Rural Librarianship (CSRL) at the Clarion University of Pennsylvania reported that 70 to 80 percent of rural library users were women, some attributed this to women obtaining library items for members of the household. But in only 28 percent of cases were women in the library for reasons other than their own (Vavrek 1990). Whether this situation continues in the future is a matter of concern to library planners. With more women working outside of the home, their level of library use may diminish because of a lack of time. It is crucial that services be targeted at men as well.

Eighth, technology ranges on a continuum; to some it means that the library has a phone or conventional typewriter. Most librarians wish to use technology, but providing sufficient funds to accomplish this is a concern. The situation is improving. Because of the influence of cooperative library ventures, many libraries are included in online catalog access, statewide data bases, and Internet connections. About 30 percent of small libraries are connected to the Internet. Inhibiting growth of the newest technology is the lack of education and training. Although a growing number of rural libraries have adopted new technology, they typically do not have the infrastructure needed to support the routine use of new technology. To illustrate, a 1990 CSRL study of 317 libraries in populations of less than 25,000 found that each library had at least one personal computer, fax machine, and CD-ROM workstation. The computer was used for a variety of tasks, but word processing was the most popular. However, most libraries reported that they spent less than $500 annually to purchase technology-related items such as software, CD-ROM applications, and hardware.

The ninth topic relates to library and information services for Native Americans. The 1992 Federal Strategic Plan for the Development of Library and Information Services to Native Americans indicated that a lack of coordination among diverse federal agencies and a lack of overall leadership impeded the development of Native American library programs. Most states do not include tribal libraries in their statewide library network plans (U.S. National Commission on Libraries and Information Science [USNCLIS] 1992). This situation is unfortunate because reservation libraries are one of the best examples of multifunction facilities. For example, the community college libraries at the Standing Rock Sioux Reservation and the Devil's Lake Sioux Reservation in North Dakota function both as public and tribal libraries; similar facilities also exist in South Dakota and Montana.

The USNCLIS (1992) recommended several measures. First, develop consistent funding sources to support improved Native American library and information services. Second, strengthen library and information services training and technical assistance to Native American communities. Third, develop programs to increase tribal library holdings and to develop relevant collections in all formats. Fourth, improve access and strengthen cooperative activities. Fifth, develop state and local partnerships. Sixth, establish federal policy and responsibilities. Seventh, identify model programs for Native American libraries and information services. Eighth, develop museum and archival services to preserve Native American cultures. Ninth, encourage adult and family literacy programs and basic job skills training, and strengthen tribal community colleges. And tenth, encourage the application of newer information network technologies.

Rural Public Library and Adult Services

Rural public libraries traditionally have provided three types of products and services: educational, recreational, and informational. Although the public library always recognized the adult client as a major benefactor of activities, services for children received the highest priority. The library came to be perceived as a place for children and women. Summer story hours and other programs for children usually generate enthusiastic lines of young users.

Whereas services for children are burgeoning, programs for adults frequently generate few takers. As a consequence, librarians schedule few adult programs. When library staff consider marketing techniques to identify constituencies and their needs, they frequently lack the skills to conduct marketing programs. They develop sporadic efforts at public relations, and many staff members never organize any programs. Programming costs vary, and rural librarians have become adept at programming with low budgets. However, objectives cannot be accomplished with no money for programming.

Despite limitations, adult education is blooming. Public librarians recognize the need to expand adult programming and services. Activities range from great book discussions to computer classes, business programs, health services, higher education programs, activities associated with Black History Month, literacy services, travel-related events for retired persons/seniors, and genealogy. Continuing education is offered in public libraries for support staff through teleconferencing.

There are incidences of adult services offered in conjunction with other community agencies (such as literacy agencies, small business development centers, and cooperative extension services); however, few libraries have action plans for using these services. One example of cooperation was that stimulated by Arizona State Library in helping to develop economic development information centers (EDICs) in public libraries. These, in turn, initiated cooperative projects with other groups.

The present and future role of the rural public library as a source of lifelong learning, ongoing development, and application of technology must be assessed. The Internet is developing at such a pace that many people want access to it, including residents of rural communities. Wilkinson (1992) believes that technology has the potential either to rescue geographically remote areas from economic and social problems or to break their backs. Rural towns may cease to be communities with the capacity for development and growth and instead become nodes on a network. What is certain is that as the countryside merges with urban America, models of rural and small libraries will continue to change. Maintaining and supporting community libraries through such times of transition is not an act of romanticism or kindness; it is a way of supporting the American dream.

—*Bernard Vavrek*

See also
Education, Adult; Educational Facilities; Literacy; Literature; Technology; Telecommunications.
References
Chute, Adrienne. *Public Libraries in the United States: 1992.* Washington, DC: Government Printing Office, 1994.
Doremus, Porter, and Novelli, Inc. *Life Style Profile of the Library User.* Chicago: American Library Association, 1987.
Estabrook, Leigh. *National Opinion Poll on Library Issues.* Champaign-Urbana: University of Illinois, Graduate School of Library and Information Science, Library Research Center, 1991.
Knight, D. M. and S. Nourse, eds. *Libraries at Large: Tradition, Innovation, and the National Interest.* New York: R. R. Bowker, 1969.
Rheingold, Howard. *The Virtual Community: Homesteading on the Electronic Frontier.* Reading, MA: Addison-Wesley, 1993.
U.S. National Commission on Libraries and Information Science. *Pathways to Excellence: A Report on Improving Library and Information Services for Native American Peoples.* Washington, DC: Government Printing Office, 1992.
Vavrek, Bernard. *Assessing the Information Needs of Rural Americans.* Clarion: Clarion University of Pennsylvania, Department of Library Science, Center for the Study of Rural Librarianship, 1990.
———. *Assessing the Role of the Rural Public Library.* Clarion: Clarion University of Pennsylvania, Department of Library Science, Center for the Study of Rural Librarianship, 1993.
———. "The Rural Library: Some Recent Research." *Rural Libraries* 9 (1989): 85–95.
Wilkinson, Kenneth. P. *Social Forces Shaping the Future of Rural America.* Unpublished manuscript. Clarion, PA: Information Futures Institute, 1992.

Public Services

Public goods that modern societies have evolved to improve the quality of life, which are provided or controlled by local, state, or national governments and either paid for by taxes (as in the case of schools, roads, and police protection) or provided on a fee-for-service basis (as in the case of electricity, telephone, water, and health services). Discussed below are the role of government in providing services, the emergence of new governments created to provide new services, and methods that providers are using to serve dispersed rural populations at an affordable cost. Over time, the number of services has grown in response to new technologies and complexities of modern living. Providing and paying for the growing number of services has become a major challenge for rural governments.

The Rural Demand

Rural dwellers face the same issues faced by most people anywhere—housing, education, health care, transportation—problems that are sometimes complicated and sometimes simplified by the relatively low population density of rural areas. The challenges became greater during the past several decades, however, as many rural areas lost population while the demand for services grew at a pace at least equivalent to the growth in American real income and standard of living.

Americans expect a wide range of services. They increasingly define quality of life not only by their income level but also in terms of the quality and quantity of public and private services available to meet their needs and desires. Individuals who have access to high-quality services at a reasonable cost generally are considered to have a better quality of life than those who do not. Although rural residents today generally have access to the same range of services as urban residents, they may have to travel farther, pay more, or receive services of somewhat lower quality and less sophistication due to the lower population density in their areas of residence.

Rural public services range across a wide spectrum, from electricity, safe drinking water, telephones, and other services that reach the home, to the roads people take and the bridges they cross to reach the schools, hospitals, and other human services that have become necessities of life. A part of the value of services is that they have traditionally been provided close enough to home to enable rural consumers to have reasonable access at an affordable cost. Despite efficiencies of scale made possible by attempts to provide services to as large of a population as possible, some services must still be sought out of the local area because of relatively small numbers of users. Consequently, rural service providers are numerous and are dispersed in accord with the population. It would not be unusual in a typical rural county to find as many as 50 different agencies and organizations responsible for providing public services.

Municipal water tower and power plant in Volga, South Dakota.

Rural public services exhibit characteristics of a public good. Public goods are characterized by joint consumption and exclusivity. Joint consumption implies that consumption of the good by one person does not preclude its consumption by others. Many community services, such as schools, parks, sewer systems, and roads, fit that description, whereas others, such as electricity, water services, telephone, and health care, are provided on a fee-for-service basis. Exclusivity means that most services are provided by a sole local supplier.

The Role of Government

The public generally relies on the political process to determine the type and extent of services offered. Local governments (counties, municipalities, townships, school districts, and special districts) serve as political mechanisms for decision making about the types and quantities of services that should be provided. They also either serve as the direct provider of many of those services or contract with other organizations to provide them. Providing the services that each locality has grown to need and want, or that have been mandated by state or federal government, is a major reason for the existence of more than 83,000 local governments in the United States, 65 percent of which are located in rural (nonmetropolitan) areas. Because rural America includes 81 percent of the nation's land area but only 20 percent of the population, a much larger number of governments is required to serve the population. The ratio of population-to-government is only one-fifth as great in rural than in urban areas.

Because rural local governments and other service providers serve fewer people scattered over larger areas, services typically cost more per person than they do in urban areas. Because of the smaller rural economic and population base, paying for services places an added strain on rural local governments and consumers alike. In addition, the smaller size of companies also might affect the quality of services provided.

Adaptations to Provide Services at an Affordable Cost

Until about 1920, most rural services were provided by local governments. That was largely because few services were provided. Until then, federal and state governments played a minimal role in rural service delivery. Since then, technology has made new services available, and the provision of such services to rural populations as well as urban ones has come to be thought of as serving the national interest. As more services were offered and new technologies made more services possible, the number of providers of rural services grew, and various policies for sharing costs were adopted. In addition, rural populations adopted new strategies to provide services. Following are some of the adaptations that were made to provide accessible and affordable services.

Consolidations

Generally, the costs of providing public services are sensitive to economies of scale—the larger the number of consumers served, the lower the cost per consumer of providing the service. A U-shaped cost curve has been found for many public services, such as police and fire protection and public education. It is more expensive per person to provide the service to both extremely small and extremely large populations. Since the size of the population influences costs and the ability to provide a service, rural government officials and other decision makers employed various strategies to take advantage of economies of scale.

Significant among those has been consolidation—joining two or more service providers into a single organization to lower costs and expand services. The most widespread use of that strategy has been consolidation of public school districts. In 1930 there were 128,000 school districts in the United States, with a high percentage located in rural areas. Many of the rural districts offered only elementary education in one-room schools. By 1990, all but 14,000 of the school districts had been consolidated out of existence. Of the remaining districts, just over 7,000 are located in rural areas. The larger consolidated schools also offer a much greater array of educational services because of their greater size and the corresponding economic efficiencies. However, size alone does not affect the quality of service. Recent research showed that many small rural schools offer high-quality education, in part because their small size provides a supportive social environment and encourages the involvement of parents and other community members (Hobbs 1995).

A concomitant change in public policy greatly affected rural education. Until about 1920, virtually all the cost of public education was borne by the local school districts. Since an educated population is considered to further the state and national interest, state governments began to share educational costs with local school districts. Today, an average of more than 50 percent of the cost of public education is borne by state governments (more in some states, less in others). Local school districts and the national government bear about 45 percent and 5 percent, respectively.

Although health care services generally are offered by private providers, there has been great consolidation of rural health care services into larger regional towns and small cities, leaving most small rural communities without a physician. Population per physician is 2.5 times greater in rural areas than urban ones. Consolidation forced most rural residents to travel greater distances for health care services, adding to the cost they pay for the service. Despite this handicap, recent research finds little or no difference between rural and urban residents in number of physician visits per year (Hart, Pirani, and Rosenblatt 1994).

Despite extensive consolidation of education and health care services, there has been little consolidation of local governments. Virtually all the town and county governments of decades past remain in existence. Some towns and counties, in an effort to lower costs and improve services, share the provision of some services with other units of local government.

A Federal Role in Service Provision

Rural Americans today enjoy most of the same kinds of services available to urban people, but many changes were required to achieve that. As new technologies emerged, new and popular services became available, such as electric power, sewer and water systems, telephones, and motorways. Urban consumers were usually the first to enjoy these benefits, largely because of the economic efficiency in providing services to more densely populated areas. For the same reason, rural areas usually lagged behind. Extending services to rural areas often necessitated the creation of new methods and forms of organization. For example, early electrical services generally were provided to larger towns and cities by private, profit-making companies or municipalities. Rural electrification was initiated by the federal government with the establishment of the Rural Electrification Administration (REA) in the 1930s, because it was much more expensive, if not unprofitable, to extend electric power lines to individual farms. The REA facilitated the formation of consumer-owned (rather than investor-owned), local rural electric cooperatives to provide service to rural areas through the provision of low-interest loans. There are nearly 1,000 local rural electric cooperatives in existence today, providing about 10 percent of the electrical power consumed in the United States.

The federal government also began to establish agency offices in rural areas during this era, to provide direct services to farmers, including farm loans, soil conservation, commodity programs, and research and information services. These agencies have since expanded to provide loans for rural housing, community facilities, and rural development.

Special Districts

One reason for the large number of governments in rural areas is that many are recently created, special-purpose governments organized by groups of citizens to provide a single service. This strategy has been used widely by rural populations seeking to provide services not offered through other local governments. Among the most numerous types of rural special districts are those organized to provide fire protection, road extensions, parks, public water and sewer services, and ambulance and emergency medical services. State regulations govern the establishment of such districts. Thus, there is organizational variation among the states. Some special districts affiliate with other local governments, have independent taxing authority, and have the power to elect their own governing officials. The service is usually provided by fee-for-service payments when not supported by a taxing authority. There are nearly 30,000 special districts in the United States, more than half of them located in rural areas.

Human Services Expansion and Delivery Methods

The federal and state role in human service delivery at the local level increased significantly in the 1960s. Dozens of programs were enacted, providing funds to establish manpower training; Head Start centers; environmental, mental health, nutrition, transportation, and other services for the elderly; small business development centers; and family services. The development of new local organizations provided the service. Many of the new organizations were operated as nonprofit agencies. The funds to support these services were allocated by state or federal government, or a combination of the two. Local governments frequently played a role in awarding contracts to provide those services. The effect has been to greatly expand the number of services and service-providing organizations in rural localities.

New Technologies and New Possibilities for Delivering Services

Just as vehicle travel opened the practical possibility of consolidating of rural services, new developments in telecommunication technologies made it possible to reconsider how some services will be delivered in the future. Many rural services, such as health care and education, depend on the exchange of information. In the past, that exchange occurred by having the consumer travel to more distant schools or health care services. An increasing number of rural schools now offer a part of their curriculum through various forms of distance learning. A widely used practice involves the use of interactive television to provide specialized education services to clusters of small rural schools. Similar developments occur in telemedicine. It is cheaper and faster to transport information than to transport people. This causes rural officials and leaders to develop new approaches to service delivery.

The requirement for an information infrastructure limits the use of telecommunication technologies. Many rural areas lack the telephone and other information technologies needed for new methods of service delivery. The current telecommunications situation in rural areas is somewhat similar to the situation that existed with electricity 70 years ago.

The Complex Organization of Service Delivery

The complex structure of overlapping local, state, and federal agencies and public utilities provided rural people with an equality of services. Most service providers have different funding sources and are associated with different lines of authority. Each service has its own constraints and limitations. A wide range of services may be grouped under the same broad heading. However, they have different management and delivery problems because they are specialized and require different technical delivery capabilities.

Although the many services have produced great benefits for rural localities, the array of organizations that provide them has produced new challenges for rural leaders and decision makers. It is difficult for rural consumers to avail themselves of the combinations of services they need because services are dispersed among so many different organizations and agencies. The tasks of directing, managing, and providing public input for the service providers place a strain on limited rural leadership. It is not unusual to find rural leaders serving on many different service provider boards and commissions. One future challenge facing rural service delivery will be to provide better integration of services so that they may more effectively serve the cause of retaining and strengthening rural communities.

—*Daryl Hobbs*

See also

Education, Youth; Electrification; Government; Infrastructure; Municipal Solid Waste Management; Policing; Quality of Life; Taxes; Telecommunications.

References

Brown, David L. "Is the Rural-Urban Distinction Still Useful for Understanding Structure and Change in Developed Societies?" Pp. 1–7 in *Population Change and the Future of Rural America: Conference Proceedings*. Edited by D. Brown and L. Johnson. Washington, DC: U.S. Department of Agriculture, 1993.

Brown, David L., and Nina L. Glasgow. "A Sign of Generational Conflict: The Impact of Florida's Aging Voters on Local School and Tax Referenda." *Social Science Quarterly* 73 (1991): 786–797.

Dillman, Don A., Donald M. Beck, and John C. Allen. "Rural Barriers to Job Creation Remain, Even in Today's Information Age." *Rural Development Perspectives* 5, no. 2 (February 1989): 21–27.

Dooley, Frank J., Dean A. Bangsund, and F. Larry Leistritz. "Regional Landfills Offer Cost Savings for Rural Communities." *Rural Development Perspectives* 9, no. 3 (June 1994): 9–15.

Fox, William F. *Relationships Between Size of School Districts and the Cost of Education*. TB-1621 (April). Washington, DC: U.S. Department of Agriculture, Economics, Statistics, and Cooperatives Service, 1980.

Hart, L. Gary, Michael J. Pirani, and Roger A. Rosenblatt. "Most Rural Towns Lost Physicians After Their Hospitals Closed." *Rural Development Perspectives* 19, no. 1 (October 1994): 17–21.

Hobbs, Daryl. "Social Organization in the Countryside." Pp. 369–396 in *The Changing American Countryside: Rural People and Places*. Edited by Emery Castle. Lawrence: University Press of Kansas, 1995.

Jansen, Anicca. "Rural Counties Lead Urban in Education Spending, But Is That Enough?" *Rural Development Perspectives* 7, no. 1 (October–January 1991): 8–14.

Oarkerson, Ronald J. "Structures and Patterns of Rural Governance." Pp. 397–418 in *The Changing American Countryside: Rural People and Places*. Edited by Emery Castle. Lawrence: University Press of Kansas, 1995.

Reeder, Richard J., and Anicca C. Jansen. "Government Poverty Declines, But Spending Disparity Increases." *Rural Development Perspectives* 9, no. 2 (February 1994): 47–50.

South, Scott J. "Age Structure and Public Expenditures on Children." *Social Science Quarterly* 72, no. 4 (December 1991): 661–675.

Zimmerman, Joseph F. "The State Mandate Problem." *State and Local Government Review* 19 (1987): 78–84.

Quality of Life

The degree to which multifaceted human potential is reached on the individual, community, and societal levels. Individual- and society-level measures of quality of life are discussed in this entry, as are objective versus subjective measures of the concept.

Origins of Quality of Life Research

Much of the quality of life research on the individual level came from the medical community. Quality of life among the elderly and ill was studied intensively because these groups were the target populations of many large-scale government programs. This may explain the focus on the physical ability to do for one's self in many of the quality of life studies (Schuessler and Fisher 1985).

Morreim (1992) delineates two types of quality of life research. He calls the first "consensus quality of life," which is composed of shared societal values about what comprises the good life and what life conditions are to be pursued or avoided. Such measures yield terms like "quality adjusted life years" or "well years," which are used in economic analysis to rate the cost-effectiveness of proposed public policies. These measures are gathered from what healthy individuals view as important aspects of quality of life, and are used to forecast what might decrease it.

Another set of measures, "personal quality of life," focuses on individuals' judgments about their own life quality, particularly the effects of disease and therapy on ill persons. Thus, quality of life publications tend to focus on individuals' ability to tie their shoes, bathe themselves, fix their own meals, and feed themselves, which relate physical condition to personal self-sufficiency in a very basic sense. The self-sufficiency notion of providing for oneself is a basic aspect of quality of life measures implied in alternative agriculture and community development.

Personal quality of life is difficult to operationalize, since such measures are very difficult to validate. Yet quality of life research is important, despite methodological difficulties; it is the ultimate aim of much scientific advancement. In medicine, for example, the health care agenda is not simply to keep people alive, but to keep them alive with a good quality of life. Medicine's central goal also has been quality of life: easing pain, ameliorating handicaps, and providing reassurance and support.

It could be argued that the goal of economics is not simply to increase income but also to increase the means by which people can enhance their quality of life. Quality of life research is essential but difficult, since the material end of technology is but a means to a human end. Measures that come from the affected populations themselves are probably the most important and most accurate, as suggested by John Eyles (1990), who links quality of life to environmental quality.

Society-Level Measures

A range of aggregate measures of quality of life using secondary data sources with such things as infant mortality and per capita income divided by infant mortality were developed in the 1970s. A variety of secondary data sources were used to construct measures of quality of life for nations or states. Quality of life was examined in various dimensions, primarily based on spatial distribution, including physical and material well-being, social relations, social activities, personal development, and recreation. Research by geographers suggests that environmental quality and quality of life may be two sides of the same coin.

Subjective versus Objective Quality of Life

Not all researchers are comfortable with self-reported quality of life. Moum (1988), for example, believes that both systematic and random errors (for example, daily moods) may suppress, mask, or wash out statistical associations between objective, sociologically relevant indicators of well-being and self-reported quality of life. His data include Norwegian quality of life health measures, which he found were overestimated among older respondents, underestimated among well-educated respondents, and unstable among young female respondents. Some of his quality of life measures (such as satisfaction with oneself, lack of faith in oneself, a life worth living, a meaningless life, very good spirits, feeling depressed, and a composite score of factors related to depression) were phrased in terms of how respondents felt during the previous two weeks. Individuals also were asked about their use of sedatives and sleeping pills, trouble with sleep, and nervousness or fidgetiness in the previous two weeks. In contrast, research conducted among sustainable farmers in the Midwest used a much richer, complex set of dimensions to measure quality of life, including spirituality, communication, work, nature, love, and health (Coughenour and Swanson 1988; Wilkening and McGranahan 1978).

Most research since 1975 about the content of quality of life examines differences between objective and subjective indicators of quality of life. Objective quality of life indicators reflect observable environmental conditions such as per capita income and average daily temperature. These conditions are presumed to be causes of quality of life. Subjective quality of life indicators consist of responses to survey items measuring feelings of satisfaction (a general feeling about life as a whole), happiness, and domain-specific feelings (such as feelings about one's job). There is a certain tautology in some economic models of quality of life. It is assumed that higher per capita income automatically increases quality of life regardless of a wide variety of other factors. Various dimensions of quality of life may not necessarily be correlated with each other.

Schuessler and Fisher (1985) point out that the measurement problems related to quality of life exist because quality of life is a latent trait, not subject to direct observation. There is no clear consensus on which indicators to use. Many studies suggest that interpersonal rela-

tions are an important aspect, if not the most important aspect, of quality of life. For example, Wilkening and McGranahan (1978) found that change in interpersonal relations contributed more heavily to satisfaction with quality of life than did either socioeconomic status or social participation.

Schuessler and Fisher (1985) discuss various criticisms of quality of life measurements, but find that each can be adequately addressed. Quality of life measures must be examined at different levels of aggregation. Because quality of life measures can have policy implications, consistent, locally meaningful measures of the various dimensions of quality of life on the individual level must be developed.

Rural-Urban Differences in Quality of Life

There are many stereotypes that depict the quality of life in rural areas as superior to that in urban areas. However, very few subjective measurements support that stereotype. Using objective measurements, whether rural quality of life is better than urban depends on the specific measurement and the area being studied. For example, air quality, which is assumed to be associated with quality of life, is generally, but not always, better in rural areas. Poverty rates in rural areas are similar to those in central cities, although the rates in central cities are slightly higher. The terms "slower pace" and "less stress" are often, although not always accurately, related to rural areas.

Another set of stereotypes holds that urban quality of life is higher because of the ability to purchase a wider variety of goods and services. Rural development for many people has been oriented toward making rural areas more like urban areas by recruiting industry. Given the wide variation among rural areas, it is difficult to generalize about rural-urban differences in quality of life. Greater differences are found in both objective and subjective quality of life measures among rural places and rural people than between rural and urban places and people.

—*Cornelia Butler Flora*

See also
Elders; Health Care; Income.

References

Coughenour, C. Milton, and Lewis E. Swanson. "Reward, Values, and Satisfaction with Farm Work." *Rural Sociology* 53, no. 4 (1988): 442–459.

Evans, David R., Joan E. Burns, Wendy E. Robinson, and Owen J. Garrett. "The Quality of Life Questionnaire: A Multidimensional Measure." *American Journal of Community Psychology* 13, no. 3 (June 1985): 305–322.

Eyles, John. "Objectifying the Subjective: The Measurement of Environmental Quality." *Social Indicators Research* 22, no. 2 (March 1990): 139–153.

Morreim, E. Haavi. "The Impossibility and the Necessity of Quality of Life Research." *Bioethics* 6, no. 3 (1992): 218–232.

Moum, Torbjorn. "Yea Saying and Mood of the Day Effects in Self-reported Quality of Life." *Social Indicators Research* 20, no. 2 (April 1988): 117–139.

Schuessler, Karl F., and Gene A. Fisher. "Quality of Life Research in Sociology." *Annual Review of Sociology* 11 (1985): 129–149.

Wilkening, Eugene A., and David McGranahan. "Correlates of Subjective Well Being in Northern Wisconsin." *Social Indicators Research* 5, no. 2 (April 1978): 211–234.

Ranching

A social structure that evolved with unique economic and environmental conditions for large-scale herding following its inception during the mercantilist period (Galaty and Johnson 1990). Ranching was initiated as and remains a system of large animal production for economic exchange. The term derives from rancho, the Spanish word for small farm. The earliest ranches in North America were initiated in the Southwest out of colonial Spanish land grants of more than 1 million acres each. Small agricultural operations, villages, and towns were scattered throughout the land grants. Properties belonged to their users and were administered by the land grantee. Almost synonymous with cattle raising in the West, sheep and horse ranches are operated independently or as integral components in some outfits. The application of principles of private property govern American ranches. Some, like the fabled King Ranch, are multigenerational dynasties of huge, disparate properties (Slatta 1989). Ranching occupies a specialized economic and environmental niche. It can be interpreted from a variety of sociological perspectives. While facing environmental threats and social criticisms, its mythos survives among the small number of remaining ranchers and in the symbols of their way of life. Ranching can best be interpreted from a variety of sociological perspectives: functional, human ecological, interactional, and as a way of life.

Structures and Functions

Understanding the economic and environmental characteristics of ranching is essential, since they provide the parameters for the way ranching communities are organized and operate. Ranching is a major form of land use between the Mississippi and the Pacific, from Canada to Mexico. Early ranches resembled plantations in their production of a single product—sheep, cattle, or horses—with the intention of profiting on export. It relied, as it still does, on cheap local labor. It also requires massive shipping, initially along trails like the Chisholm, the Santa Fe, and the Bozeman (Wellman 1939). Operations had to be self-sufficient, since little assistance was available, given the size and resultant isolation of the ranches. Raising herds of large animals requires large acreages: As much as forty acres per animal unit (cow/calf) may be required. As a modern stage of pastoral herding, the ranch relies on naturally growing or at least minimally attended pasture or rangeland.

Ranching can provide relatively low-impact, sustainable food production, using land unsuitable for other agricultural purposes, especially nonirrigated mountain and arid areas (Savory 1988). It is a viable and efficient use of marginally tillable or untillable land, so long as there are no more profitable uses. Haying operations and some seasonal and supplementary feeding are nearly universal. As population increases and technologies become more sophisticated, there is continual pressure to convert ranch land to other uses, particularly agricultural, residential, recreational, and mining. Ranching may be regarded as a transitional economic stage, the primary form of production in areas only until more profitable uses of the land displace it.

The earliest ranching was on open range, made possible by few residents, few alternative uses, and seemingly boundless rangeland. As neighbors increased, property lines became clearer and fencing became increasingly common. Simultaneously, it was discovered that fencing was essential for more efficient production, because it allowed rotation of pastures and seasonal breeding. Open

Ranching makes efficient use of land that is unsuitable for the cultivation of crops. Here cowboys rope a calf at a ranch in Colorado.

range, such as on grazing associations and reservations, implies stock along the highways rather than totally unrestricted pasture. The disastrous winter of 1888, immortalized by Charlie Russell's *Last of the Five Thousand*, which shows a single emaciated survivor from a large herd, signaled the end of the open range (Russell 1890). Ranchers, too, have dwindled since the early twentieth century. Census data do not accurately distinguish farmers from ranchers. Many are both, arbitrarily calling themselves one or the other. A crude estimate is that of the roughly 4 million farmers who earn more than half of their income from agriculture, about 2 percent (80,000) own and operate a ranch.

Ranch work gradually has become less labor intensive than in its formative years (Gray 1968). Handling large animals from birth through shipping or slaughter remains difficult and dangerous work. Branding, docking, castrating, inoculating, dehorning, and other jobs requiring directly handling animals typically are performed with immobilizing chutes and other mechanical assistance. Less traumatizing techniques, such as elastra-

tors replacing knives for castrating and docking, are common. Motorized vehicles are usually used to drive and haul animals between ranches and markets. Horses and stock dogs are essential for broken terrain and rough ground. Mixed-animal operations are common, although the hierarchy is clear in the folk phrase "sheep for profit, cattle for prestige, and horses for pleasure."

Human Ecology of Ranching

Ranching from a human ecological perspective follows directly from attendant environmental and economic conditions. The social structure that evolved on the frontier—first ranches, then towns—existed primarily, if not solely, because of the production, sale, and transportation of animals, together with their service institutions and markets. Small towns grew and prospered during the era of settlement, while work was labor-intensive and expanding. Homesteading, often into areas unsuitable for farming, further stimulated growth. Between 1920 and 1970, most counties in ranch area continually lost population as homesteaders discovered making a living was impossible on their land and as technology gradually replaced labor. A bar, a gas station, and a few houses are all that remain of once prosperous towns with schools, churches, and main streets. The few remaining towns serve large trade areas. County seats commonly have fewer than 2,500 residents and serve areas the size of small eastern states. Even so, their markets have largely been replaced by the few metropolitan areas in the region where ranchers purchase machinery, vehicles, and household items.

Social Conflict and Ranching

The stratification system can as easily be understood from a conflict perspective as from a structural-functional perspective. Social class, prestige, and power overlap; they differentiate the haves from the have-nots, delineating their respective positions in the division of labor that persists from generation to generation. At the top of the stratification system are large, longtime owners and operators of ranches and businesses. The middle class is comprised of full-time employees with moderate wages and salaries, and smaller operators. The lowest class is made up of largely unemployed or seasonally employed laborers.

Across this spectrum, property ownership and residential stability are very important. Large, multigenerational ranches are owned by landed elites who exert local political, cultural, and economic influence. Some occupations are seasonal, such as sheep shearers or custom cutters. Others, like veterinarians, are local specialists. Their positions in the stratification system are commensurate with their skills, training, and earnings. Residents in ranch country frequently are residuals from a winnowing process that led most former residents to migrate. Those who remain often perform a variety of functions. Successful ranchers are trustees of financial institutions and members of influential committees. Professionals and business owners often own agricultural land. Conversely, lower-class residents are likely to be excluded from participation in formal organizations or voluntary associations. Outside ownership of ranches has always been common, both as an investment and as a place for escape. Outside owners, while a topic of conversation, are not part of the local stratification system, despite their obvious influence of the local economy.

Symbolic Interaction and Ranching

The realities described through the human ecological and structural-functional perspectives become more subjective when viewed from a symbolic interaction orientation. The meaning of ranching, both to ranchers and outsiders, is a composite, partially idealized and partially factual. Ranchers personify Frederick Jackson Turner's "rugged individualist." Survival in remote and challenging environments requires independence, self-sufficiency, and the ability to make do. Ironically, that very individualism makes ranching vulnerable, both directly and indirectly, to outside forces. External commodity markets and corporations for the most part determine the profits and losses on ranches. Locally, the opposition of ranches to collective activities such as planning and zoning often have made them vulnerable to land developments, resource extraction, and even religious cults.

The Mythos of Ranching as a Way of Life

A subjective mythos surrounds ranching. "Are you a real cowboy?" Debra Winger asks John Travolta in *Urban Cowboy.* The question is about the authenticity of a role type that captured imaginations internationally for over a century (Jobes 1986). As opposed to phony, drugstore cowboys, a real cowboy can do the tasks of ranching. Moreover, real cowboys have a mythical common character: They are soft-spoken, succinct, serious but of good cheer, and competent. They are husbands of the land (husbandry), frequently glorifying their concern with the environment. They are expected to believe in a Great Creator while acknowledging human weakness. Believing in God and yet occasionally acting like the devil are not mutually exclusive, especially for the young and unmarried. The roles are similar for single men and women ranchers. The role convention, however, is of the ranch family. Women are more often responsible for early childcare and food preparation. Men primarily perform machine maintenance. Beyond these tasks, other chores frequently require the participation of the entire family, making ranch life relatively egalitarian related to gender. Small operations increasingly require husbands and especially wives to work off the ranch for supplementary income.

The mixing of reality and fantasy, the mythos, is especially evident when friends and neighbors join together in ranch work that formerly was accomplished by the hand labor of large crews. Round-up presents such an occasion in some areas. Neighbors, remote family members, and friends converge to assist each other, whether they are really needed or not. Skilled hands are able to demonstrate their camaraderie and competence. Gemeinschaft is recollected. Tales of prior experiences are warmly shared. Copious amounts of food and hospitality further show the special skills of women. When the cap is removed from a whisky bottle, it often is symbolically tossed away. Roundup is but one of several such events that consciously demonstrate a way of life that all present universally agree is without equal in part because of its historical, almost atavistic, origins.

Ranching has its own unique recreation, based largely on the mythical perpetuation of such skills and values. In concept, rodeo events are created around the practical, essential tasks of being a cowboy. In fact, they are extremely specialized events, performed at the highest levels by trained athletes, who rarely, perhaps never, use their skills on a ranch for practical purposes. Many events, such as bull riding and bull fighting, have no practical functions. Women's events, particularly goat roping, have been established to demonstrate competence, although such activity may not exist on a ranch. Much of rodeo is a caricature of the noble qualities of ranch life, unabashedly glorifying ranch life. Participants, whether from Texas or Montana, California or New Jersey, dress, speak, and generally act in a single genre, again, reflecting the ideals of the way of life. Men and women are, deliberately and visibly, easy to distinguish as men and women. Deference is paid to God, free enterprise, family, and nature. Competitors help each other and share ideas and experiences. Competition is entirely individual, except for team roping and occasional idiosyncratic events held at a few rodeos. Winning, determined by time and style, is paid off directly in cash. No remuneration occurs for failure.

The mythos of ranching is currently under attack as environmentalists concerned with overgrazing of rangeland and destruction of riparian areas challenge ranchers' identity as husbands of the land. Animal rights activists such as Jeremy Rifkin (1992) have criticized the basis of their livelihood, claiming that killing is inhumane and that red meat is unhealthy. Recreationists treat ranchers as irrelevant or intrusive, since livestock interfere with recreational uses for the environment. The issues and problems delineating ranchers from others are more than a symbolic challenge to their way of life, although those are genuine and serious. They also affect food production and consumption—the very livelihood of ranchers.

Contemporary Problems of Ranching

Ranching is increasingly encountering complicated issues and problems, in large part because of the transitional stage it implies between early and later stages of environmental development. Restrictions concerning land and water uses continually pit outside interests against ranchers. In the West, where water is a particularly scarce and precious commodity, alternative uses of water allocations constantly are being proposed. Residential and industrial developments, frequently in distant states, may be the sources of such conflicts. Similarly, the availability of lands leased from government agencies such as the Bureau of Land Management and the Forest Service is a source of contention. Free-market advocates, symbolized by the Sagebrush Rebellion, call for the privatization of public lands. Other interests advocate establishing new priorities for water and land use that usurp the management prerogatives of ranchers. Rules controlling irrigation and noxious plants are obvious examples of very complex phenomena.

The control of land itself presents an overt threat to ranching. In some areas, land claims remain under dispute, particularly in traditionally Hispanic areas and Indian reservations. The position of ranchers as a cherished elite is challenged. From the perspectives of both users and ranchers, changes in the rules that previously governed accessible public and semipublic lands are problematic. Ranchers who previously allowed hunting increasingly do not, or do so for a fee. Government leases previously closed to the public now are open to them. The strains between ranchers and outsiders, recreationists, minorities, and government are extreme.

The transfer of land from one generation to the next presents a final problem to the ranchers. Decisions governing ranch operations generally are controlled by the older generation. Younger family members usually contribute increasingly disproportionate amounts of work with marginal increases in income or influence over the operation. This is a phase that is particularly vexing for spouses. The problem emerges in part because of the limited capacities of ranches to expand profits that could be redistributed to the younger generations. It also is a function of different notions of how the ranch should be run and who has the right to implement decisions.

In spite of contemporary pressures to undermine ranching, ranching will persist into the long foreseeable future. The human ecological foundations, established social structures and interactions, and way of life combine to create a persistent social system, in spite of both internal and external conflicts. Ranching also will continue to capture the imaginations of outsiders, as it has for over a century.

—Patrick C. Jobes

See also

Cowboys; History, Agricultural; Horse Industry; Intergenerational Land Transfer; Landownership; Livestock Production; Pasture; Policy, Environmental; Social Class; Values of Residents; Wool and Sheep Industry.

References

Galaty, John G., and Douglas L. Johnson, eds. *The World of Pastoralism: Herding Systems in Comparative Perspective.* New York: Guilford Press, 1990.

Gray, James R. *Ranch Economics.* Ames: Iowa State University Press, 1968.

Jobes, Patrick C. "Social Structure and Myth: Content and Form in Ranchland." *Studies in Popular Culture* 9, no. 2 (1986): 51–64.

Rifkin, Jeremy. *Beyond Beef: The Rise and Fall of the Cattle Culture.* New York: Dutton 1992.

Russell, Charles M. *Studies of Western Life, with Descriptions by Granville Stewart.* New York: Albertype Company, 1890.

Savory, Allan. *Holistic Resource Management.* Washington, DC: Island Press, 1988.

Slatta, Richard W. *Cowboys of the Americas.* New Haven, CT: Yale University Press, 1989.

Wellman, Paul I. *The Trampling Herd.* Philadelphia: J. B. Lippincott, 1939.

Recreational Activities

Leisure activity engaged in for the attainment of personal and social benefits. This entry begins with the definition of recreation and a short history of recreation in rural America, followed by a classification system for grouping rural recreation activities and some of the common benefits of recreation. The entry concludes with an overview of current issues and trends in rural recreation activities. Consideration of recreation activities in rural America invokes a variety of images associated with both social and natural landscapes. These images range from the traditional, socially oriented recreational activities associated with small-town life—church socials, country fairs, picnics, family reunions—to outdoor recreational activities such as hunting, fishing, camping, and hiking, which depend on the natural resource base of rural America. Recreational activities in rural America, like other aspects of rural life and human behavior, are constantly changing. Attitudes and participation patterns continually evolve.

Defining Aspects of Recreation

Recreation is leisure activity that is engaged in for the attainment of personal and social benefits. Rural recreational activities should include doing something desirable for participants and for society. Recreation is viewed as restoration from the toils of work. The word "recreation" comes from the concept of creating again, recol-

lecting, or reforming in the mind. The idea of refreshment of spirit and strength after toil led to the word being used to mean diversion, play, or amusement. Recreation is instrumental to work because it enables individuals to recuperate and restore themselves in order to accomplish more work. Recreation is related to an individual or group choice taking place during discretionary time.

Historical Perspectives on Recreation in Rural America

Foster Rhea Dulles's (1965) classic, *A History of Recreation: America Learns to Play,* compared the growth of recreation in the United States to a river, which adapts its course to the terrain through which it flows. As the United States evolved from a largely rural country to a largely urban country, recreational choices have evolved and been adapted based on changing technology. Dulles identified two factors that shaped recreation in America. The first is the continuing influence of Puritanism, both rising from and reinforcing a dogma of work born in economic circumstances that can be traced from the seventeenth century to the twentieth. Until recently, Puritanism devalued any activity that could be viewed as a waste of time. Some rural communities passed laws to prohibit activities on Sundays except those that were spiritual or essential for basic subsistence, and others forbade participation in specific activities such as card games, mixed dancing, and theatrical performances.

The degree to which Puritan taboos were observed and the nature of these restrictions varied considerably from rural area to rural area. The growing number of non-Puritan rural peoples became increasingly discontented and viewed these restraints as intolerable. Worn out by the endless work on their little farms, discouraged by poor harvests, fearful of famine and plague, they found release for pent-up emotion in drinking. Taverns sprang up as naturally as had meeting-houses, and the festive nature of the tap-room met a genuine need. Taverns were well patronized, and often provided opportunities to play cards or watch cockfighting, bear baiting, or boxing. Aside from the tavern sports, however, most rural recreational engagements made at least some pretense of serving socially useful ends. Rural residents commonly participated in hunting and shooting contests, in simple country sports, and in the communal activities of training days and barn raisings.

Contemporary observers agreed that there was a general lack of amusements in rural America in the late nineteenth century. Farm life varied greatly in different

Cross-country skiers enjoy the beauty of this snow-covered forest.

parts of the country; but in general, life in rural America could not offer recreational opportunities comparable to those in urban America. However, the isolated rural family may have had more enjoyment than did its urban counterpart engaging in passive, commercialized amusements. Many farm organizations, such as the Grange, fulfilled recreational needs and became the principal social gathering-places of the farm community. Women were admitted for the first time into full membership. The Grange organized lectures and concerts, held debates and spelling bees for youth, promoted singing school, and arranged evenings of general entertainment. The annual state or county fairs, which originated as educational vehicles, quickly were transformed into recreational opportunities. The annual county fairs and other special events (such as socials at the local schoolhouse, square dances, Fourth-of-July picnics, and circuses) were anticipated for months and remembered long afterward with continuing pleasure.

The second factor Dulles identified as of paramount influence on recreation was the gradual transformation of the economy from the simplicity of the agricultural era to the complexity of the machine age. By 1880, railroad fares decreased to the point that railroads provided rural residents an inexpensive form of recreational travel. New methods and machinery gave rural people more free time and better access to city amusements. Five years after the appearance of the nickelodeon in 1905, there were over 10,000 theaters around the country. Automobile ownership expanded dramatically in the 1920s and revolutionized transportation in rural America. Automobiles provided the opportunity for most rural residents to drive to a movie house or a community center for entertainment. The transition to the machine age also included the first major boom in the production and sale of manufactured items used primarily for recreation. Radio ownership went from 5,300 in 1920 to more than 5 million in 1924.

The stock market crash of 1929 and President Roosevelt's subsequent New Deal programs changed the number and types of rural recreational opportunities. Massive federal funding supported the design and construction of a wide range of public recreational facilities at all levels of government. The years following World War II brought widespread changes to rural recreation. The use of regional, county, state, and national parks and forests increased dramatically. The war effort developed four-wheel drive and off-road vehicles that became major forms of recreation for rural peoples. Car camping became popular during this period, with the development of thousands of campsites. Innovations in small engine technology have increased the use of personal, individual vehicles such as all-terrain vehicles, snowmobiles, and personal watercraft in the past two decades. The transition to the computer age likewise will lead to many changes in opportunities for recreation in rural Americans. Video stores already have replaced theaters in many rural towns and villages. Other developments in communication technology, including electronic bulletin boards, CD-ROM, and the Internet, are broadening the range of passive and educational recreational opportunities available to rural people.

Classification of Recreational Activities

Dumazeider (1967) developed a comprehensive classification with five major divisions, each with two subdivisions. This classification system identifies and specifies the more visible aspects of the rural recreational experience and how rural inhabitants use their free time. Physical recreation includes (1) physical activities, such as taking part in hunting and fishing, softball leagues, bridge club, and the like; and (2) travel activities, such as bus tours, Sunday drives, or driving for pleasure. Intellectual recreation includes (1) intellectual understanding, such as obtaining knowledge through formal or informal educational programs, how-to manuals, books or field studies, television programs, or lectures; and (2) intellectual production, such as being creative as an amateur writer, scientist, or philosopher. Artistic recreation includes (1) artistic enjoyment, such as listening to music; attending concerts, operas, or plays; visiting museums and art shows; and reading about the arts; and (2) artistic creation, such as taking lessons in the arts, singing, playing an instrument, painting, writing poetry or prose, dancing, acting, taking part in crafts as an amateur, or participating in community arts programs and organizations. Sociable recreation includes (1) sociable communication, such as oral communication for pleasure between two or more people in person, on the telephone, or through written communication by mail or the Internet; and (2) sociable entertainment, such as one-way communication from performers or the mass media to the consumer, as in the movies, newspapers, magazines, and books, and on television. Practical recreation includes (1) practical collection, such as personal hobbies that result in something to show for the effort of involvement in community collecting, preserving, and sharing, at museums, art galleries, and historic homes; and (2) practical transformation, such as activities that seek to change a thing (do-it-yourselfers), a person (gossips, advisers, amateur psychiatrists), or social institutions (political or service organization participants).

This classification system is one useful way to envision rural recreational activities and patterns of participation. Another approach is to examine the benefits of participation in recreation in rural America.

Benefits of Recreation

Assessing the benefits of participation in recreational activity is a very complex process. The benefits vary with the kinds of activity, the participants, the environment, and other factors. Kelly (1983) groups benefits of recreational participation into three overlapping categories: personal benefits, societal benefits, and economic benefits.

Personal benefits are those benefits associated with the individual. These have been inferred from studies of past rural recreation experiences and include excitement and relaxation. Many rural recreational activities are associated with environmental appreciation and immersion, learning and testing competence, developing famil-iarity with and exploring what is either new or old, and stimulating the mind and body. More long-term benefits may result from these experiences, such as self-enhancement through improved mental and physical health.

Societal benefits are outcomes that are related to social groups or collectives. These benefits relate to the support or enhancement of communities, families, and friendships that are central to life. Rural people's involvement with rural-based organizations and events partially extend their personal benefits; but in the long run, the benefits of recreational involvement associated with social institutions—family, church, government, school, and community—are societal rather than personal. They lead to increased social cohesion. Through recreational activities, rural people realize that they are part of a larger collective. County fairs and involvement in Grange activities do more than provide personal benefits; they reinforce the idea that rural people are part of a larger entity, and they reduce the feeling of isolation that many rural people experience.

Economic benefits are other outcomes of participation in rural recreation. These benefits include the contribution of resources to employment opportunities for rural people. The benefits may be primary, such as income-producing employment, or secondary, such as demand for goods and services in communities. A growing number of people in rural America depend on tourism and recreation for their livelihood. Given the wide range of benefits associated with participation in various recreational activities, it is important to consider recreational participation patterns of rural Americans relative to their counterparts living in urban and suburban areas.

Participation Patterns

Rural Americans find entertainment to a considerable degree in the same leisure and recreational activities as do urban and suburban counterparts. They watch many of the same television programs, read the same books, and watch the same movies. They, too, follow professional and college sports, go to conventions, and maybe save for a charter flight to Europe or Hawaii. Yet there are differences in their circumstances and environments. The country dweller lacks easy access to metropolitan museums, theaters, and concert halls, although the advent of cable and satellite antennas has brought many of these cultural events into their living rooms. The rural resident has easy access to many opportunities associated with undeveloped and abundant natural resources. It may be possible to fish or hunt close to home. Lower land prices may allow people to keep horses or other large pets and to grow most of their own fruits and vegetables. Many rural residents find it easy to have large pieces of recreational equipment on their land, such as motor homes, boats, workshops, or horse trailers. Rural people have higher participation rates than urban and suburban residents in camping, hiking, hunting, horseback riding, freshwater fishing, and snowmobiling.

Ruralness is an identity, a way of life, and a state of mind, but it is also about the pace of life. Residents of small places continually refer to themselves as rural people and their communities as rural places. Those who move from urban to rural places often say they have escaped the "rat race." Ruralness and recreation in rural areas has a great deal to do with the pace of life. Recreation remains an important defining characteristic of what it means to be rural. Rural people still participate in traditional rural recreational activities, and these activities will continue to contribute to the physical and social landscape of rural areas.

—*Robert A. Robertson and Rodney B. Warnick*

See also
Arts; Camps; Community Celebrations; Gambling; Games; Music; Parks; Public Libraries; Restaurants; Senior Centers; Sport; Theatrical Entertainment; Wildlife.

References
Chubb, Michael, and Holly R. Chubb. *One Third of Our Time? An Introduction to Recreation Behavior and Resources.* New York: John Wiley and Sons, 1981.
Dulles, Foster R. *A History of Recreation: America Learns to Play.* 2d ed. New York: Meredith Publishing Company, 1965.
Dumazeider, Josef. *Towards a Society of Leisure.* New York: Free Press, 1967.
Fisher, Ronald M. "Leisure Time: The Sharing of Happiness." Pp. 124–151 in *Life in Rural America.* Washington, DC: National Geographic Society, Special Publication Division, 1978.
Kaplan, Max. *Leisure Theory and Policy.* New York: John Wiley and Sons, 1975.
Kelly, John R. "Social Benefits of Outdoor Recreation: An Introduction." Pp. 3–15 in *Recreation Planning and Management.* Edited by Stanley R. Leiber and Daniel R. Fesenmaier. State College, PA: Venture Press, 1983.
Yu, Jih-Min. "The Congruence of Recreation Activity Dimensions among Urban, Suburban, and Rural Residents." *Journal of Leisure Research* 17, no. 2 (1985): 107–120.

Refugee Resettlement

Giving residence and provisions to people assigned refugee status. Rural America has long benefited from the labor force provided by refugees and immigrants from many corners of the world. A refugee, as defined in the Refugee Act of 1980, Section 101(a)(42), is: "any person who is outside any country of such person's nationality . . . and who is unable or unwilling to return to, and is unable or unwilling to avail himself or herself of the protection of, that country because of persecution or a well-founded fear of persecution, on account of race religion, nationality, membership in a particular social group, or political opinion. . . . The term 'refugee' does not include any person who ordered, incited, assisted, or otherwise participated in the persecution of any person." This is the most recent codification under which refugees may be resettled in the United States.

Oversight of Resettlement Efforts

The U.S. Department of State's annual refugee admissions program provides a legal mechanism to admit applicants who are among groups for which America has special concern or responsibility, who are eligible under applicable priorities, and who meet the definition of refugees under the Refugee Act of 1980, as determined by an officer of the Immigration and Naturalization Service of the Department of Justice. The need for resettlement, not the desire of a refugee to enter the United States, is the governing principle in the refugee admissions process.

Initial reception and placement of refugees in the United States is carried out largely by some dozen nonprofit organizations through cooperative agreements with the U.S. Department of State. These organizations are commonly known as voluntary resettlement agencies (or VOLAGS).

Shortly before the Refugee Act of 1980 was signed into law, former U.S. Coordinator for Refugees Julia Taft and her coauthors (1979, 38–39) wrote, "Since World War II the voluntary resettlement agencies have been the most eloquent and effective advocates for refugee admission. Throughout the years they have been the organizations in most direct contact with the refugees, as they have assumed responsibility for the day-to-day premigration counseling, reception, placement and other resettlement efforts. . . . The non-sectarian agencies [about half are] have normally relied upon sponsorship of refugees by individuals or community groups or have taken on the assignment of sponsors directly, relying upon a network of local offices [generally in urban areas] staffed by caseworkers. The religious-based agencies have normally linked refugees with their diocesan structures or local churches which provide direct services to refugees. . . . [T]his is, despite their common concern in

Refugee Resettlement in Rural U.S. Counties, 1983–1994

	Total State Population, 1995	Total Population in Rural Counties	Total Number of Refugees	Number of Refugees in Rural Counties	Percentage of Refugees in Rural Counties
AK	551,947	77,947	529	206	39
AL	4,062,608	1,090,893	3,167	335	11
AR	2,362,239	706,975	1,652	416	25
AZ	3,677,985	493,731	15,400	85	1
CA	29,839,250	848,753	346,693	3,968	1
CO	3,307,912	471,137	12,038	186	2
CT	3,295,669	0	13,225	0	0
DC	609,909	0	9,616	0	0
DE	668,696	0	444	0	0
FL	13,003,362	1,068,100	88,554	8,731	10
GA	6,508,419	2,386,438	25,524	1,815	7
HI	1,115,274	81,177	3,750	7	0
IA	2,787,424	1,547,373	9,564	1,531	16
ID	1,011,986	583,224	3,945	1,859	47
IL	11,466,682	1,915,882	48,153	2,688	6
IN	5,564,228	1,536,500	3,945	449	11
KS	2,485,600	831,673	8,142	3,151	39
KY	3,698,969	1,510,091	6,433	1,351	21
LA	4,238,216	1,436,440	16,915	9,980	59
MA	6,029,051	87,743	41,142	126	0
MD	4,798,622	504,779	21,328	250	1
ME	1,233,223	389,067	3,278	94	3
MI	9,328,784	1,737,423	23,676	598	3
MN	4,387,029	1,509,503	29,535	2,373	8
MO	5,137,804	1,426,011	16,661	900	5
MS	2,596,443	1,020,375	1,167	225	19
MT	803,656	421,900	778	613	79
NC	6,657,630	2,246,485	9,844	1,110	11
ND	641,364	470,706	2,942	880	30
NE	1,584,617	469,701	5,866	772	13
NH	1,113,915	264,504	2,441	230	9
NJ	7,748,634	251,990	25,012	256	1
NM	1,521,779	613,396	4,407	363	8
NV	1,206,152	106,150	4,461	156	3
NY	18,044,505	1,956,492	181,591	1,852	1
OH	10,887,325	1,948,495	18,244	634	3
OK	3,157,604	1,241,594	5,844	771	13
OR	2,853,733	922,444	20,203	1,010	5
PA	11,861,643	1,582,380	37,114	739	2
RI	1,005,984	136,053	5,242	24	0
SC	3,505,707	564,040	1,439	77	5
SD	699,999	424,699	2,492	478	19
TN	4,896,641	1,575,357	11,440	685	6
TX	17,059,805	3,233,439	64,917	4,147	6
UT	1,727,784	268,929	8,637	517	6
VA	6,216,568	1,628,451	23,294	2,401	10
VT	564,964	299,661	2,250	704	31
WA	4,887,941	907,194	49,209	3,717	8
WI	4,906,745	1,789,605	16,368	4,177	26
WV	1,801,652	908,799	345	143	41
WY	455,975	248,778	147	147	100
Total	249,579,653	47,742,477	1,259,003	67,827	5

refugee resettlement, a mixed collection of organizations, some much larger than others . . . [and] some with decades of experience."

Number and Characteristics of Refugees Resettling in Rural America

Since federal fiscal year (FY) 1989, the United States has resettled more than 100,000 refugees per year. The cumulative refugee admissions total for the period 1983 to 1994 is nearly 1,132,000. This number includes those granted refugee status, Cuban/Haitian entrant status, and Asian Americans and their family members. More than 6,000 refugees were resettled in rural counties of the eight states that have more than half their total population in rural counties (see table). These include the Great Plains states of North and South Dakota, Idaho, Montana, Wyoming, and Iowa.

Although refugee resettlement is a 50-state program, roughly 30 percent of all refugees have been initially resettled in California. In addition, refugees have migrated to California from the places of their initial resettlement in other states, thus increasing California's current overall share of the U.S. refugee population to about 40 percent. California's refugee population is basically as urban (99 percent) as its total population (97 percent). Yet about 35,000 Hmong from the mountains of Laos, along with refugees of various other ethnicities, are living in the rural agrarian areas of California's Central Valley. Many largely agricultural counties, such as Fresno County, California, are not defined as rural counties by the Census Bureau; thus, the number of refugees in rural counties noted for California on the table is only 3,868.

The prevalence of resettlement agencies with religious affiliations accounts in large measure for the number of refugee families that have been resettled in rural counties since the early 1980s. The U.S. Catholic Conference (USCC), Lutheran Immigration and Refugee Service (LIRS), and to a lesser degree, Church World Service (CWS), Episcopal Migration Ministries (EMM), and World Relief (of the National Association of Evangelicals) have strong rural resettlement capacity based on their local affiliate structures. Another VOLAG involved in rural resettlement is Iowa's Department of Human Services, Bureau of Refugee Services. Just under 40 percent of these refugees came from Southeast Asian nations. A similar number is from the area of the former Soviet Union. The balance is made up from similar size populations from Latin America, eastern Europe, other parts of Asia, and Africa. The latter have tended to arrive in waves based on political conditions in their home regions rather than in a steady flow.

The Federal Office of Refugee Resettlement (1994) found that about 35 percent of refugees aged 16 or over who have been in the United States less than five years were already employed, and nearly 20 percent of the households sampled were already financially self-sufficient. The average refugee arriving in 1994 had completed ten years of education, but over half spoke no English on arrival.

Earlier groups of refugees, such as many of those fleeing troubled countries of eastern Europe, became farmers in the American and Canadian West, whereas others, notably the Finns, worked in lumber camps in the nineteenth and early twentieth centuries. The rural work of post–World War II refugees has been different, as the frontier was long closed before their arrival. For example, many of the Hmong in California's Central Valley engage in intensive niche farming of cherry tomatoes and other specialty crops, where hard work is more important than massive capital. Many Vietnamese, African, and other refugees likewise do the rugged but vital work in the meat factories of the Plains and are prominent parts of the population in many rural counties as a result.

—AnnaMary Portz and Edward Sponga

See also
Community; Cultural Diversity; Culture; Ethnicity; Literacy; Migration; Policy, Socioeconomic; Rural Demography.

References
Office of Refugee Resettlement. *Report to Congress FY 1994: Refugee Resettlement Program.* Washington, DC: U.S. Department of Health and Human Services, Administration for Children and Families, Office of Refugee Resettlement, 1994. (These reports are published annually and include descriptions of the voluntary agencies that participate in resettlement.)
Taft, Julia Vadala, David S. North, and David A. Ford. *Refugee Resettlement in the U.S.: Time for a New Focus.* Washington, DC: New TransCentury Foundation, 1979.
U.S. Committee for Refugees. *Refugee Reports* (monthly).
———. *Refugee Voices* (multimedia service).
———. *World Refugee Survey* (annual).

Regional Diversity

The spatial mosaic of complex and varied natural and cultural environmental features, conditions, and patterns that give character to America's distinctive regional landscapes. This entry defines the concept of region and illustrates it with selected examples from both the natural and human environments. Many natural and cultural regional transitions may be imperceptible to the casual observer because they often occur on a macro rather than a micro scale. Within the nation's 3.8 million square miles can be found rural regional diversity unsurpassed by that of any other country.

The Nature of Regions

Rather than being random in their nature and distribution, America's rural features lend themselves well to regional expression, classification, and distribution. A region is an area of the earth that differs from other portions by virtue of possessing one or more homogeneous features or characteristics. Regions serve the same purpose for geographers and others that periods or eras do for historians; they function as organizational devices. The regional concept facilitates communication about places, their locations, and their characteristics. Midwest, for example, evokes a mental image of a specific spatial location (where it is), unique characteristics of a place (what is there), and spatial distribution (areal extent). Important information has been communicated about both place and space, yet details are vague. Geographers continue to argue about those features that make the Midwest and many other regions unique and where their boundaries should be drawn.

All regions are abstract; they are based on arbitrarily selected criteria. Some regions exhibit relative homogeneity of a single feature. Examples include a river drainage basin, soil type, area of single crop dominance, or zip code. Others, such as ecosystems, economic regions, and vernacular regions (for example, Dixie or the Sunbelt) are multiple-feature regions with many traits that set them apart from other areas of the country.

Geographers recognize three types of regions: formal, functional, and popular (vernacular or perceptual). Formal regions are areas with one or more trait in common, such as climate, landform, crop, ecosystem, and culture. Boundaries are poorly defined and often exhibit a broad transition, as is illustrated by lines separating the Middle West and West, the humid continental and dry continental climates, or the grassland and desert ecosystems.

Functional regions are defined by one or another predominant function. They are recognized both by the function that they perform and the nodal or control point from which their functions are coordinated. Examples include political units, infrastructure (such as transportation, utility, or irrigation systems), economic networks, and social units (for example, clubs, church parishes, schools, and cafes). Finally, popular regions are

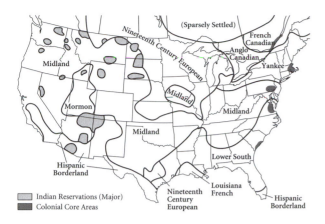

Traditional Formal Rural Culture Regions of North America

Source: Terry G. Jordan et al., *The Human Mosaic.* 6th ed. New York: Harper-Collins, 1994, p. 10. Reprinted with permission.

those widely recognized and used by the general population. Examples include Dixie, the Panhandle, East River/West River in South Dakota, and Delmarva or Eastern Shore (the peninsula lying east of Chesapeake Bay). Organizing geographical features and conditions, both physical and human, in a regional context can enhance understanding of their characteristics, distributions, and relationships.

Natural Regions

Because of its broad latitudinal range, from Hawaii's humid tropical conditions to Alaska's polar ice cap at high elevations, the United States includes within its territory all of the earth's climates and ecosystems. Landforms range from mountains to interior plains and coastal lowlands, with hills and plateaus also contributing to regional diversity. Water features (rivers, lakes, and groundwater) vary greatly from place to place in both quantity and quality. America's vast and diverse store of mineral resources (energy, metals, and nonmetallic) are distributed in countless regional patterns. Soil types and fertility also occur in marked patterns of regional variation.

Landforms are the most visible natural features. Most major physiographic provinces in the United States trend north-south. The Pacific mountain system includes California's fault-block Sierra Nevada (including 14,494-foot Mt. Whitney) and the volcanic Cascades, which extend northward from northern California into Washington. An Intermontane Plateau Province extends northward from western New Mexico into eastern Washington, with chief subregions including the Colorado Plateau, the Great Basin, and the Columbia Plateau. The Rocky Mountains extend from West Texas northward to Idaho and

western Montana. The Interior Plains extend from the Rockies to the Appalachians; subprovinces of this region include the Great Plains and Interior Lowlands. The Gulf–Atlantic Coastal Plain is a low-lying region with little surface configuration that extends from southern Texas to southern New Jersey. The Black Hills (South Dakota), Ozark-Oachita Highlands (Arkansas, Missouri, and eastern Oklahoma), and folded Appalachian Highlands (Alabama to Maine) contribute to the landform diversity of the central and eastern United States.

Atmospheric conditions are the primary key to environmental diversity. Weather and climate influence plant and animal life, the weathering and subsequent erosion of landforms, soil characteristics, and water features. Elements such as temperature, precipitation, growing season, and storms also present opportunities and challenges to human cultural adaptation, land use, and settlement.

Tropical climates occur in Hawaii (including the world's wettest spot, Mt. Waialeale, receiving an annual average 472 inches of precipitation), southern Florida (wet and dry tropical), and the southern margins of the desert Southwest (dry tropical). Subtropical climates occur in the Southeast (humid subtropical), the southern Great Plains and Southwest (dry subtropical), and coastal California (Mediterranean subtropical, unique because of its intense summer drought). Coastal Oregon and Washington experience a moist, mild climate (temperate marine). Much of the northern half of the country experiences a dry continental (west) or humid continental (east) climate, divided by the 20-inch isohyet, which coincides roughly with the 100th meridian. Most of Alaska lies within subarctic and polar climate regions.

Because of its varied climates, the United States includes all major ecosystems within its territory. Such diversity is significant because it contributes to diverse biomes, wildlife habitats, natural landscapes, and economic opportunities. Even the nation's history was somewhat influenced by natural vegetation. European settlers nurtured in woodland areas were unfamiliar with the vast grasslands of the country's interior. This region was the last to be settled and developed within the 48 conterminous states. Ecosystem diversity (climate, vegetation, soil, and animal life) also is an important factor in cultural ecology—that is, in how humans use land and resources. All of the world's crops and livestock, for example, can be raised someplace in the United States, and relatively large areas are well suited to growing such essential crops as grains, fruits and vegetables, oilseeds, and cotton.

Desert vegetation is dominant in the Southwest and

portions of the western interior. Steppe (short) and prairie (tall) grassland ecosystems dominate the non-desert western interior and Central Plains. Savanna grasslands occur in southern Florida. Needleleaf evergreen forests dominate the coastal lowlands of the Southeast, higher elevations of the western United States, the Pacific Northwest, and the taiga forests of Alaska. Broadleaf deciduous forests extend throughout much of the area drained by the Mississippi and Ohio Rivers. Mixed forests dominate the vegetation pattern in the Ozarks and Appalachians and in New England.

Climates and ecosystems occupy large areas, and the transition from one region to another often is both gradual and nearly imperceptible. Mountainous regions are an exception. High mountains in tropical Hawaii, for example, include nearly all of the earth's climates and ecosystems in micro scale, from humid tropical to polar, with corresponding changes in natural vegetation. Similar diversity, though not as extreme, occurs throughout the mountainous West. Diverse ecosystems create the varied natural habitats that support the country's broad array and considerable numbers of wildlife.

Soils are formed by a number of factors including parent material, climate, vegetation, slope, and time. Diverse geological, climatic, and vegetation conditions have contributed both to a diverse array of soil types and to vast areas of extremely fertile soils that constitute the natural foundation of the nation's unsurpassed agricultural productivity.

Water features also help to define regional diversity. The fact that the United States is bordered by two oceans, the Atlantic and Pacific, has contributed greatly to the nation's regional diversity. The oceans served as protective barriers as well as avenues of migration and trade. They exert a major influence on weather and climate, modifying temperatures and serving as the chief source of moisture. Many coastal areas turned to the sea for wealth, whether from fishing, off-shore petroleum development, or tourism, and developed a unique regional character in the process.

River valleys and fertile alluvial floodplains long have been choice sites for human settlement. The nation's heartland is drained by the Mississippi River and its many tributaries, including the Ohio and Missouri, which combine to create one of the world's finest inland waterway transportation networks. The Colorado River and the Rio Grande of the Southwest are of tremendous regional importance for electrical power generation and for irrigation. In the Pacific Northwest, the Columbia River is a source of energy, domestic and irrigation water, and salmon. Countless other rivers and river valleys played an equally vital role in the historical settlement, development, and character of their basins.

Most of the country's natural lakes lie in the glaciated area north of the Missouri and Ohio Rivers. The Great Lakes (Superior, Michigan, Huron, Erie, and Ontario) were created by the vast continental ice sheets that covered northern portions of the continent during the Ice Age. The Great Lakes are the most extensive system of freshwater lakes in the world. With several engineering assists in the forms of locks, canals, and channel improvement, the lakes form a shipping outlet that links America's agricultural and industrial heartland to the Atlantic Ocean.

Culture Regions

Regional diversity based on cultural differences is more pronounced and in many instances more apparent than are regional variations in rural America's natural environment. Within any natural region, a variety of human differences can be found. Whether economic, social, political, religious, or ethnic, these traits and characteristics contribute to a diverse mosaic of cultural traits and landscapes. Regional differences are so great, even on a micro scale, that a thriving service industry developed around the organization and use of demographic, economic, and social data within zip code areas.

Culturally, America's melting pot of racially and ethnically varied peoples and ways of life is becoming ever more diverse. Racial and ethnic diversity is becoming even more evident in many rural communities. It is not uncommon to find exotic foods on the shelves of rural or small-town grocery stores, available in response to the tastes of an ethnically changing population. Certain economic opportunities (for example, in agriculture and agricultural processing, fishing, and mining) attracted ethnic populations to many parts of the United States, and their cultural imprints became increasingly evident in many rural areas.

Demographic patterns in rural America also are changing. Some regions experience sharp population decline, whereas others undergo rapid population growth. Generally, recent movement has been from north to south (Rust Belt to Sun Belt), from interior to coastal, and from urban to suburban. The composition of the rural population also is changing. An aging population characterizes many agrarian areas that experience out-migration of the young as well as other areas that attract retirees.

Rural population decline in the United States has

been widespread since the mid-1930s, but it is currently taking place primarily in farming regions (for example, the Buffalo Commons of the Great Plains). Factors contributing to the farm population decline include increased mechanization that vastly reduced the need for human labor, lower fertility rates and smaller family size, and increasing farm size. The latter factor substantially reduced the number of rural families, and hence, the need for goods and services formerly provided by small rural communities. Improved transportation facilities simultaneously made it possible to conduct business in what became thriving regional centers.

Some of the rural population growth since 1995 has occurred in areas that formerly were negatively perceived. Examples include the Ozark and Appalachian highlands; the mountainous West, including many former mining camps turned ghost town; the Sun Belt, where effective air conditioning made living comfortable; and the coastal regions. Many urban residents have found rural America an attractive alternative to city living. The resulting urban-to-rural migration, with its concomitant economic, social, and political changes, can overwhelm small, homogeneous, traditionally conservative rural communities.

In terms of demographic, social, and economic change, regions that appear homogeneous on the surface can in reality be extremely diverse. For more than 300 years, perhaps the most distinctive and homogeneous rural cultural region in America has been the Hispanic heartland of northern New Mexico. During much of the twentieth century, small, economically impoverished rural communities in the region experienced population decline. As the century draws to a close, most of these are thriving once again, for a variety of reasons.

As land and housing values skyrocketed in Taos and Santa Fe, many local residents found themselves unable to afford to live in their own community. Surrounding towns grew as bedroom communities of the displaced, who now commuted to the cities for work. Others became amenity centers and grew because they attracted affluent residents seeking a serene, culturally exotic, country life. Elsewhere, a socially heterogeneous mix of "New Agers," mainstream drop-outs, religious cultists, and right-wing militants settled in communities shared by those with similar interests. Finally, many rural communities have began to grow as Hispanic Americans, many of whom left the area decades ago but never sold their property, returned to retire in their ancestral homelands. Each of the disparate groups imprints its own experience, interests, and values on the community in which it resides. In this way, a num-

ber of small micro-regions evolved in what once might have been the nation's most homogeneous culture region, the Hispanic heartland of northern New Mexico.

Economic areas are the best known and most widely recognized rural regions. The Corn Belt, Cotton Belt, Napa Valley, and Silicon Valley are examples of well-known formal culture regions based on a particular economic activity. Less well recognized but equally common and important are thousands of functional areas, each of which can be recognized by its node or function control center. Examples include trade or marketing areas, service areas, and transportation or communication networks. These can be based on a variety of factors, including the spatial distribution of a particular grocery, fast-food, or gasoline chain; the area from which an enterprise draws its customers; the area served by an electrical or natural gas company; the route map of an airline; or the broadcast area served by a radio or television station. Most functional areas begin in and are controlled from urban centers. Gradually, during the twentieth century, much of rural America was integrated into the majority of essential functions, and hence, includes functional regions.

Finally, America includes a great number of popular economic regions. These regions, illustrated by Washington State's Inland Empire; the Metroplex of Dallas, Fort Worth, and environs; North Carolina's Research Triangle Park; and northeast Mississippi's Golden Triangle, often are created and perpetuated by chambers of commerce. Strictly rural vernacular regions, emanating from traditional cultural roots, include the Mississippi Delta culture region of northwestern Mississippi and Alabama's fertile Black Belt.

Primary industries dominate the rural environment, where agriculture, mining, logging, and fishing contribute immeasurably to regional character and diversity. Each of these activities, in turn, has its own peculiar regional subtypes. In terms of rural landscape imprint, socioeconomic integration, and economic infrastructure, the wine industry of California's Napa and Sonoma Valleys, southern Florida's truck farming of vegetables for northern markets, and the Tobacco Belt of North Carolina are three extremely distinctive and diverse regions. Yet each specializes in a particular horticultural crop. Animal industries such as cattle ranching, dairying, and poultry raising also contribute to regional diversity.

Regional Change

Regions are fluid. Most if not all of them change through time. Change generally occurs most rapidly in regions delineated on the basis of such human characteristics as demographic, economic, political, ethnic, or social homogeneity. Natural regions also change, although generally at a much slower and less perceptible rate than do human regions. Few areas in America's contemporary rural environment remain stationary. An ability to adapt to changing conditions and regional affiliations is essential to the future well-being of rural America.

—*Charles F. Gritzner*

See also
Biodiversity; Culture; Desert Landscapes; Hydrology; Mountains; Settlement Patterns; Soil; Weather; Wetlands.
References
Allen, James P., and Eugene J. Turner. *We the People: An Atlas of America's Ethnic Diversity*. New York: Macmillan, 1988.
Garreau, Joel. *The Nine Nations of North America*. Boston: Houghton Mifflin Company, 1981.
Gastil, Raymond D. *Cultural Regions of the United States*. Seattle: University of Washington Press, 1975.
Gerlach, Arch C., ed. *The National Atlas of the United States of America*. Washington, DC: U.S. Department of the Interior, Geological Survey, 1970.
Glassborow, Jilly, and Gilliam Freeman, eds. *Atlas of the United States*. New York: Macmillan, 1986.
Graf, William L., ed. *Geomorphic Systems of North America*. Boulder, CO: Geological Society of America, 1987.
Hart, John Fraser, ed. *Regions of the United States*. New York: Harper and Row, 1972.
Rooney, John F., Jr., Wilbur Zelinsky, and Dean R. Louder, eds. *This Remarkable Continent: An Atlas of the United States and Canadian Society and Cultures*. College Station: Texas A&M University Press, 1982.
Weiss, Michael J. *Latitudes & Attitudes: An Atlas of American Tastes, Trends, Politics, and Passions*. Boston: Little, Brown and Company, 1994.
Zelinsky, Wilbur. *The Cultural Geography of the United States*. Englewood Cliffs, NJ: Prentice-Hall, 1992.

Regional Planning

Future-oriented studies and action programs undertaken by local governments (below the level of the state) or by subnational state governments. This entry provides an overview of regional planning in rural America. The first section discusses historical trends and their effects on planning. The second section summarizes the current status of various approaches to regional planning. The third and final section speculates on the future of regional planning in light of a broader set of social and technological trends.

Historical Experiences

There are really two rural Americas in the United States: the one that is declining and the one that is growing. The former tends to be distant—that is, it lies beyond and between metropolitan influences. The latter is typically located on the fringes of cities, but it might be more distant and have amenities, often recreational, that attract urban residents to it. Each of these types of rural regions has its own sets of planning problems and challenges. Distant areas need regional planning but engage in little of it because of disincentives to cooperate. Regional planning in areas that are growing seeks to centralize authority for land use and environmental management in order to promote efficiency, conservation, and social equity. But the future of regional planning of all types is uncertain. It is derivative of the larger political dialogue and is influenced by social forces such as renewed citizen activism and heightened conflict over private property.

The relationship of urban America to its rural regions might be characterized as ambiguous at best. On the one hand, there is the doctrine, traceable to neoclassical economic theory, that little, if anything, can or should be done to try to alleviate rural decline. Such decline is viewed as a product of powerful, rational economic and demographic forces that are beyond policy influence. Where public effort is expended, its target is the development of selected growth centers where manufacturing opportunities can congregate and to which rural residents can migrate. On the other hand, there is the view that rural regions are declining as a function of market failure. This view suggests that it is necessary and appropriate to intervene via regional planning and directed policy assistance. From this perspective, rural regions fulfill a social, economic, and cultural role, and their impoverishment is dysfunctional from the perspective of a larger, long-term economic calculus.

The United States first ventured into widespread experiments in regional planning during the 1930s. The rapidly changing conditions of rural America, as a function of the economic depression and widespread natural resource depletion (such as the "dust bowl" conditions in the Plains states), called forth creative responses by the national government. It was during this period that large-scale regional planning projects were implemented, the best known being the Tennessee Valley Authority (TVA). While ultimately the TVA became a power generation agency for the region, its original concept was to provide rural-based modernization throughout the Southeast. Also during the 1930s, the only national planning agency the United States has ever had, the National Resources Planning Board (NRPB), undertook several pioneering studies on the regional character of America and possible structures for regional planning. But little actually came of all this. The NRPB was disbanded, and the TVA and its cousins became agencies for the generation of inexpensive power, on the theory that this would attract economic enterprises to growth centers in distressed rural regions.

Regional planning for rural areas reemerged in the 1960s. As part of the social planning of the period, programs were developed to address the social and economic disadvantages of rural places relative to urban areas. These programs were regional in nature because it appeared administratively easier and more cost efficient to provide services on this basis. Few of these programs endured.

Contemporary Programs

The regional planning efforts that endured grew out of the need to manage rapid growth in rural areas on the urban fringes and in distant rural areas with recreational amenities. The tradition in these areas was one of fragmented, decentralized local control over growth and natural resources. In a selected set of states, such as Vermont, New York, Florida, Wisconsin, California, and Oregon, legislation was passed reasserting the state's authority over growth and natural resource management. This was reinforced by efforts at the federal level in behalf of selected natural resources, such as those along the coastal zones. The rationale in all of these cases was that the existing system of local control in rural regions was characteristically and inherently parochial, discriminatory, destructive of ecosystems, and socially irresponsible. Also, the tradition of local control, dating back to the turn of the century, was perceived as inefficient because local administrators had neither the technical knowledge nor the administrative capacity to respond to the complex problems of growth. In order to achieve greater rationality in land use and natural resource management and to fulfill a greater public good, it was proposed that more centralized administrative structures were necessary.

This approach to more centralized regional planning has expanded into the 1990s. There are now 13 states that have one or more programs for their rural areas oriented toward containing and controlling urbanization or toward preserving land uses that are considered socially significant, such as farmland and environmentally sensitive areas. These programs all share the characteristic of reducing the autonomy and authority of local government. For example, in Oregon a set of state goals exist that must be met in all local planning efforts. Local plans are reviewed at the state level for consistency with these goals. In Florida, environmentally sensitive areas must be identified in local plans, and local zoning is required to protect the integrity of such areas. Plans in one locality must be coordinated with the plans of adjoining localities, and efforts to provide public services must be organized in harmony with these plans. As in Oregon, there is also a state-level review of local plans for consistency with these requirements. New Jersey's approach emphasizes local areas developing plans and then meeting with each other to develop a consistent approach to land use and natural resource management. In all cases, local efforts to act autonomously have been preempted, and plans for rural locales have to be coordinated with those of related rural places and the region, and often the state.

While these comprehensive approaches to centralized planning are generally lauded by planning professionals, environmental protection advocates, and good government reformers, they have been adopted by only 13 states, and the majority of these states are on the east and west coasts. In general, the middle part of the United States either has not experienced the same types of growth pressures that prompted the centralized efforts, or has experienced actual population decline and severe economic restructuring.

As a result, regional planning between the coasts has taken on one of two forms. Some states have examined a form of rural triage. Prompted by concerns for the continued viability of all rural places, triage-style rural regional planning entails identifying those places with enough comparative advantage to survive successfully into the twenty-first century and then targeting centralized infrastructure and social investments at these places. This is a continuation of TVA-style regional planning.

The second approach is related, though more radical in concept. Known as the "buffalo commons" concept, it is regional planning writ large. The buffalo commons is a proposal for the future of the Great Plains, an area covering parts of ten states. It argues that the original settlement of this region was a historical error. Ecologically the region is ill adapted to extensive human settlement and intensive land uses such as agriculture. Instead, the best use of the region is as a grazing ground and national recreation area. The advocates of the proposal do not suggest the literal evacuation of towns, villages, and cities in the Great Plains region. Instead, they call for no extraordinary countermeasures to prevent what seems to be occurring as a result of economic, social, and demographic transition, and for conscious attention to reshaping the region as these transitions occur.

Because of the controversial nature of both approaches, neither has been adopted, and no alternative has emerged to fill the gap. As a result, little substantial regional planning occurs in nongrowth areas. In these places, the management of natural resources, such as farmland, forests, and wetlands, as well as the future structure of the economy, continues to be the domain of market forces and local planning, when planning exists.

Future Prospects

The future of regional planning is murky. All efforts to undertake public planning in the United States, regardless of geographic level or specific place, often become caught in the larger political dialogue. To the extent that market-oriented forces command the rhetoric of politics, public planning of all types is viewed with disfavor. It is seen as interventionist, disruptive, inefficient, and unproductive. To the extent that markets are perceived to be failing and the public interest and public benefits to be threatened, public planning can be undertaken, often being viewed as a possible solution.

Regional planning in the parts of rural America that are growing, or likely to grow, could continue along the route toward greater centralization. But even this is uncertain, given the renewed sense of localism across the country. While citizens can rationalize the basis for centralization, they are increasingly concerned about ceding control for land use and environmental management decisions to levels of government that can be difficult for them to access and influence. There are instances where they appear to prefer the anarchy of fragmented local control to the bureaucratization of centralized control.

With respect to distant rural areas, there is little reason to expect that they will not continue to decline. This will be especially true to the extent that their fate is left to market forces. In places where planning does exist, it will be local rather than regional in structure. In part, this will be due to the predominant underlying political and fiscal structures that favor interjurisdictional competition rather than cooperation.

Planning of all types is likely also to be shaped by several other social trends and forces throughout the United States. In addition to a renewed sense of localism, these include widespread citizen activism, the impact of new information technology, and heightened conflict over private property rights.

Citizen activism brings more people with more types of articulated interests into the policy and planning process. Increasingly citizens are convinced that their perspective on the public interest is the correct one, and they seem less willing to compromise, especially in an era of limited fiscal resources. The new information technology decentralizes access to specialized information resources, allowing citizen activists to develop more sophisticated analyses to support their positions and to challenge the official positions put forth by planning agencies. Together, widespread citizen activism and the new information technology make planning processes less and less dependent upon experts and more overtly political.

Heightened conflict over private property rights might turn out to be the most prominent social trend influencing regional planning in the 1990s. Proposals for regional planning are increasingly portrayed as attempts to diminish the private property rights of individual landowners. In turn, this is characterized as a threat to liberty and the structure of American democracy, as undermining the meaning of citizenship in the United States. To the extent that this representation of regional planning prevails, it will be difficult to undertake any planning of any substance anywhere in the country. Unless the concept of regional planning can be reinvented to position it as a defender of private property rights and a contributor to liberty and democracy, it may have little future in the United States in general, and rural America in particular.

—Harvey M. Jacobs and Edward J. Jepson, Jr.

See also
Community; Development, Community and Economic; Future of Rural America; Government; Policy, Rural Development; Settlement Patterns; Urbanization.

References
Friedmann, John, and Robin Bloch. "American Exceptionalism in Regional Planning, 1933–2000." *International Journal of Urban and Regional Research* 14, no. 4 (December 1990): 576–601.
Friedmann, John, and Clyde Weaver. *Territory and Function: The Evolution of Regional Planning.* Los Angeles: University of California Press, 1979.
DeGrove, John M., and Deborah A. Miness. *The New Frontier for Land Policy: Planning and Growth Management in the States.* Cambridge, MA: Lincoln Institute of Land Policy, 1992.
Jacobs, Harvey M. "The Changing Nature of Settlement Policy in the USA: A Theoretical and Case Study Review." Pp. 135–150 in *The Greening of Rural Policy: Perspectives from the Developed World.* Edited by Sarah Harper. London: Guilford Press, 1993.
———. "The Anti-Environmental, 'Wise Use' Movement in America." *Land Use Law and Zoning Digest* 47, no. 2 (1995): 3–8.
Lapping, Mark B., Thomas L. Daniels, and John W. Keller. *Rural Planning and Development in the United States.* London: Guilford Press, 1989.
Popper, Frank J., and Deborah E. Popper. "Great Plains: Checkered Past, Hopeful Future." *Forum for Applied Research and Public Policy* 9 (1994): 89–100.

Religion

Philosopher Emile Durkheim has defined religion as "a unified system of beliefs and practices relative to sacred things" (1947, 62). This entry will focus on religion in rural America and on the ways in which it has been altered by the general movement since the end of World War II of the rural population to cities and suburbs. This migration has resulted in a precarious situation for rural churches. Nonetheless, rural religion survives in a somewhat unique form, perhaps to witness a revival as postindustrial society deconcentrates into nonmetropolitan areas since the mid-1980s.

The Uniqueness of Rural Religion

Religion takes many varied forms in the countryside, from denominations to sects to cults. Rural religion and its varying forms were shaped by the transition of American society from an agrarian to an industrial one in the nineteenth century, and they are being reshaped today by the current shift from industrial society to a global-oriented, postindustrial one. Rural religion must continuously adjust to these far-reaching changes.

After reviewing the existing body of literature on rural religion, Goreham (1990) outlined the following thematic areas on which these sources have focused: (1) The economic, political, and social dislocations brought about by the industrial and urban upheavals in the United States since the turn of the century resulted in the decline of the rural church and its congregations. Church leaders at the denominational and congregational levels assisted both the broader society and the local country church to adapt to and respond to these social changes. (2) The responses of rural churches to this massive social change varied along ideological fault lines. Some groups advocated social activism in the face of negative change, whereas others called for a renewed evangelistic fervor. The growth in consciousness that came about in reaction to these social changes led churches to define themselves in terms of their distinctiveness: Some have been content to see themselves simply as the "church in the country," but others noted their responsibilities for stewardship of natural resources and the environment, for feeding the hungry throughout the world, and for ministering to a unique clientele. (3) Where this consciousness led to a unique role for the rural church, an accompanying development in theology and philosophy of the rural church, the land, agriculture, and rural life followed. These formulations ranged from seeing the land as a sacred trust to a need to protect and husband the land or to reduce world hunger and rural poverty. (4) Much of the writing on the rural church is devoted to methods and techniques of ministering to people in a rural setting. As such, this body of thought and research has been concerned with liturgy and the conduct of worship, education, youth programs, and the like.

A Short History of Religion in Rural America

Religion was established in the United States primarily as a small-town and rural phenomenon because of the rural nature of the original European settlers. Although Europeans came to the New World seeking religious freedom, it was not long before they established North American versions of the theocratic states from which they had fled. The War of Independence and the formulation of the American constitution set in motion forces that led to a struggle for souls fought largely on the emerging frontier. Thousands of churches sprang up in small towns and open countryside along the paths of exploration and settlement. After the home and family, religion and the church became the most influential components of the rural community.

While Protestants were establishing and reestablishing their denominations on the frontier, the Catholic Church was having a slow beginning in erecting its ecclesiastical structures in New England. However, Catholics following the Maryland model organized house churches, stations, and chapels. When priests could be secured, a central parish was established, with an itinerant priest. As did Protestants, Catholics moved onto the frontier of Kentucky and beyond after independence from England. Here they came into contact with Catholic faith communities already established by the French and the Spanish.

With the Civil War, both Protestantism and Catholicism had to brace themselves for the onslaught of urbanization, massive immigration, and the depletion of population and resources from the countryside. By the turn of the century, both religious traditions were ripe for a revitalization of their rural churches.

As the 1880s arrived, American denominations were becoming increasingly aware of the problems of building and maintaining rural congregations. An impetus to do something about these problems came from President Teddy Roosevelt's Commission on Country Life. This group felt that the problems of the country were basically moral and religious in nature and that the churches had a great potential power to deal with them. By the early twentieth century, the denominations had begun to organize themselves into a movement at the national and local

A woman is carried from the Ohio River in a state of ecstasy after being baptized at a tent revival.

levels, cooperating with each other and with governmental, agricultural, community, and educational institutions to become agents of spiritual, economic, social, political, and educational change. The agricultural land-grant colleges, and rural sociology as an applied academic discipline, were enlisted as trusted allies to remake the countryside. Various national organizations were formed to address rural concerns. For example, under the leadership of Bishop Edwin Vincent O'Hara, Catholics founded their own country church movement in the form of the National Catholic Rural Life Conference. This group worked to strengthen rural parishes and to keep Catholics on the family farm.

An Era of Social and Religious Change

All the while, the nation and the church were becoming more urban and suburban in orientation and approach.

Huge numbers of immigrants swelled the urban population of Catholics well beyond that of their Protestant counterparts. This migration of peoples left the Catholic Church with the perception that the need to attend to and to focus on the churches of town and countryside was greater than ever.

Not only Catholics but many other rural religious groups have been reacting for nearly a century against the trends symbolized by the dwindling number of retail and service outlets in local villages and towns in contrast to the shopping centers burgeoning in nearby cities and metropolitan areas. As the retail and in some cases the manufacturing functions of villages declined, residential functions increased. Outside of these villages, in the open countryside, there had long been a trend for rural neighborhoods to disappear in the face of improved transportation and for churches, schools, and stores to consolidate. Rising standards of living and increasing needs and wants turned rural people toward the outside world. Forms of association in the countryside changed from simple to more complex ones where wider contacts and interests were fostered by a broad variety of special-purpose organizations. The family evolved in such a way that its members associated as much with nonfamily as with family. There was at the same time a movement toward community segmentation and away from community wholeness. Although old neighborhoods in the vicinity of villages and towns were disappearing, new neighborhoods were appearing near cities and large towns, with a semisuburban, heterogeneous character. And although rural communities were once villages with attached, interdependent neighborhoods, today these communities tend to have ill-defined boundaries and often blend into the surrounding city. The development of modern transportation systems also accelerated the tendency for rural religious organizations to become centralized in villages and towns.

Rural Religion in Decline?

As the rural population decreased in proportion to the urban population, a decline in the rural church has been a constant threat for rural people. The open-country churches died more rapidly than the village and town churches. Changes in transportation and social organization of the countryside have made it more difficult for the open-country church to survive. Where open-country and hamlet congregations do survive, they tend to exist in stable farming neighborhoods and where population shifts have been minimal.

Today the overwhelming number of people attending rural churches are nonfarmers. Nonfarmer members of rural congregations do not always hold the same views as the farmer-members. There is thus a trend toward greater heterogeneity among the membership, and frequently conflict develops between traditional country churchgoers and newcomers. Other factors involved in the relative decline of the rural church in recent decades are overchurching (the establishment of too many competing churches), declining sectarianism (less particularistic ideology and theology given the growing secularism), competition from urban churches, and the loss of financial support from rural people. However, the long-term trend indicates that this situation might one day be reversed by a deconcentration of metropolitan population into nonmetropolitan areas. It is likely that two rural churches will emerge eventually; one in areas of rural out-migration

driven by the "politics of decline," and the other in areas of rural in-migration propelled by the "politics of growth." Churches facing the "politics of decline" often are marked by a quest for congregational survival, a concern to meet the needs of its present members as opposed to ministry in the community or world, and a perpetual fixation on their financial woes. Churches involved in the "politics of growth" must address questions of how to adjust their facilities, ministries, and programming to accommodate the needs of the newcomers, how to develop compromise among newcomers and long-term members regarding congregational dynamics, and how to integrate the long-term members who are likely to have a rural mindset with the newcomers with an urban mindset.

Chronic Problems

Typical problems encountered by rural and small-town churches include the inability to maintain adequate programs. There has been a strong movement in recent times to provide knowledge and help to small churches in providing and maintaining adequate programs. However, rural churches tend to do many things in informal ways. This often looks like inadequate programming to their urban and suburban denominational counterparts. Consolidation of churches and of programs between congregations often has been the solution to this problem. This is, however, not always a realistic possibility.

Another common problem encountered in rural churches has been inadequate financing due to small congregations and inconsistency of farm income. The every-member canvass, visiting each household in the congregation to explain the church's financial needs and to request a pledge to help support the church, and the Lord's Acre Program, allotting some portion of the crop or livestock to the church, are examples of attempted solutions.

Rural churches also have wrestled with getting, keeping, and training ministers knowledgeable of and sensitive to rural culture. Agricultural colleges, departments of rural sociology, town and country church departments of denominations, and sensitive seminary education have been used by some churches to overcome this difficulty in rural religious life.

An ongoing problem that most religious groups in the countryside must deal with is adjustment to change. The continuing movement of rural people to metropolitan, city, or town areas has left these groups in a state of near-constant transition. Likewise, more recent movement of urban or exurban populations into formerly rural congregations leads to successive new rounds of adjustments.

Roman Catholics and Protestants
in the Countryside

The Roman Catholic Church in nonmetropolitan areas has been called an "overlooked giant." This phrase applies equally well to rural and small-town Protestantism. Between 40 and 50 percent of all Catholic parishes and 25 to 40 percent of all Catholics live outside cities of 50,000 or their incorporated suburbs. Likewise, a study by the United Methodist Church (United Methodist Church 1992) has revealed that nearly two out of three Methodist congregations are small, and most are in rural areas and small towns. The same is true of many other Protestant denominations, which are generally more rural than Catholicism.

A study of Roman Catholic parishes and their parishioners (Burkart and Leege 1988) revealed a general tendency for congregational life, in whatever locale, to be affected by the culture of the surrounding area and for rural church membership to be increasingly heterogeneous. Other surveys have shown that rural churchgoers, particularly those who farm, have a particular orientation and lifestyle. Their closeness to the land affects their values regarding work, commitment, exercise and health, and religion.

A study carried out at Notre Dame, which is generalizable to rural and small-town Catholics in the United States and probably applies also to Protestants, found that rural religious people tend to be more moralistic in the way that they view God, God-given laws, human nature, morals, and ethics. This greater moralism, correlated with a greater conservatism, is reflected in attitudes toward change, the church and its policies and positions, and social issues. This would seem to indicate a greater religious orthodoxy as conceived of by sociologists who conducted this study, Charles Glock and Rodney Stark. Data from the Notre Dame study suggest that rural and small-town Catholics tend to view God more as a judge, unapproachable, mysterious, and strict. They see a God who is creative but who also has given humans clear-cut rules to follow. These same rural churchgoers are more inclined to relate directly to God as Father than to mediators such as Christ, the Church, or their fellow Christians. The greater presence of Protestant groups such as Baptists and Methodists in the countryside perhaps predisposes Catholics to view God in this fashion. The tendency to avoid open conflict and a greater propensity to focus on tradition and the past means the rural person is less disposed toward the sort of social activism that Glock and Stark were looking for. Finally, these data on rural and small-town Catholics showed individuals who said they experienced God less directly in their lives than did their urban or suburban counterparts. It is not known whether this would also apply to rural Protestants, as their religious ideology would predispose them more toward the validity of religious experience. Based on these findings, it would be possible to conjecture that rural religious individuals place more emphasis on religious (behavioral and ethical) codes rather than on experiencing God in deeper, more mystical ways.

Likewise, rural churchgoers probably experience a greater community through friendliness. The community may be a part of their religious experience or may be a part of their larger rural society. The closeness of their communities may account for a greater tendency toward ecumenism and boosterism. The stronger presence of community in the life of the rural resident usually manifests itself in a greater experience of informal social control. The impact of extended family and friends also is stronger in the religious experience of rural individuals. However, people living in rural areas and small towns are less patient with any form of human mediation apart from that of their families and friends. This manifests itself in less tolerance for any hierarchical structures (ecclesiology) in their religious life and a greater informality in leadership patterns and parish programming.

Rural congregations or parishes resemble small-scale organizations in their sociological dynamics. Tasks are less differentiated and structures of accountability less distinct. There are fewer positions and staff of all kinds, fewer formal programs, and a higher reliance on volunteerism. Thus, the rural church is not just a smaller version of the urban or suburban church. As people in the countryside are more affected by the seasons and by events that are closer to nature, they traditionally have been interested more in integrating with nature than in using it. Persons from small-scale communities have been nourished on stable and mutual relationships. Functional and personal roles frequently overlap in the countryside. Relationships involve many segments of life; they are broad in scope. Rural residents are different from their urban counterparts, and their religious expression differs accordingly.

Lastly, rural religion functions somewhat differently than religion in the city and suburb. It serves to integrate the rural individual into an already strong local nonreligious community. However, there is evidence not only of anomic rural communities but also of demoralized congregations. To the degree that a strong rural community already exists, those in the countryside use religion less for community-building functions than do their urban and suburban counterparts, who are more inclined to join religious organizations in an attempt to create a sense of community in an environment largely void of real community.

In a similar fashion, religious meaning is less salient to the person of town and countryside, as it traditionally has been supplemented by a secular culture that values most of the same things found in religion. This does not imply that religious meaning and belonging are unimportant to individuals who live in the country. As rural dwellers can find meaning and belonging more readily in their secular environments, rural religion functions more to underpin rural community life. With the spread of urbanism, the functions of religion in the countryside more closely approximate that of the average, urban resident. This fact sometimes gives rise to a fundamentalist backlash out of a concern over the pervading secularism of American mass society.

Fundamentalism

Rural religion often has manifested itself in movements, sects, and cults of various forms. One of the common reactions to the late-nineteenth-century integration of the country into the city and its industrial life has been religious fundamentalism. Fundamentalism is reinforced through reactions to the trend toward integration of the rural economy into the world economy. As noted above, rural religion tends to be conservative, while greater secularism and liberalism often are characteristic of urban religious groups. Accordingly, the strongholds of fundamentalism have generally been in rural areas and cities with a strong rural influence. To these groups the growth of science is often seen as occurring at the expense of the Bible. The alleged evils of the city, and more recently, the perceived dangers of a global economy, have fostered a more fundamentalist approach to religious faith and practice. An additional factor might be a longing for a more rural, community-based approach to religion found among many anomic urban transplants from the countryside. Finally, as rural places tend to have less educated inhabitants than urban places, fundamentalism is further reinforced. Contemporary groups such as state militias, the Posse Comitatus, farm fundamentalists (see Tweeten, 1989), and other apocalyptic groups often merge a religious fundamentalism with a strong political, economic, and social conservatism.

Sects

Elmer Clark (1949) studied American religious sects and delineated seven types of sectarian groups in his analysis. Various sectarian groups shall be mentioned here that have been prominent in rural American religion, using David Moberg's (1985) classification of Clark's typology of religious groups. First, the charismatic or Pentecostal sects seek special blessings and believe in manifestations such as speaking in tongues, visions, trances, dancing before the Lord, and other experiences. The "snake-handling" religious groups of the Appalachian region might be seen as another manifestation of this religious tendency. Mormons also would fit into this category. The Mormons and their splinter groups have had a significant impact on various rural regions, not only in America but around the globe; Mormonism today is one of the fastest-growing religions in the world, particularly in less developed countries.

Second, Clark's communistic sects are religious groups that have withdrawn from society to practice some esoteric religious and economic ideologies. Often such sects are possible only if removed to the countryside. The Oneida Perfectionists, the Shakers, and the Amana colonies are representative rural groups.

A final category of Clark's typology of sects relevant to our discussion of rural religion is the legalistic or objectivist sects. These groups stress some definite rites or taboos, usually derived from the Bible, around which the life of the religious adherents coalesces. Some rural representatives of these groups would be the Mennonites, the Amish, and the Hutterites. These groups in varying degrees managed to preserve the rural way of life and religious expression.

Rural religion is different from urban religion. It conforms, at least in part, to the dictates of rural culture and life, and manifests itself in a religious organization with smaller social scale and a personal religiosity that is less differentiated. Rural religion enriches rural culture and diversity with yet another variation on the theme.

—Gary Burkart

See also

Churches; Culture; Ethics; History, Rural; Land Stewardship; Music; Social Movements; Theology of the Land; Values of Residents.

References

Andrews, David. *Ministry in the Small Church*. Kansas City, MO: Sheed and Ward, 1988.

Burkart, Gary, and Patricia O'Connell Killen. "A History of the Rural Catholic Church in the U.S." Materials to accompany the video *The Rural Parish: Retrieving Our Future*. Los Angeles: Franciscan Communications, 1992.

Burkart, Gary, and David Leege. "Parish Life in Town and Countryside." Pp. 1–13 in *Report 13, The Notre Dame Study of Catholic Parish Life*. Notre Dame, IN: University of Notre Dame, 1988.

Clark, Elmer T. *The Small Sects in America*. Nashville: Abingdon, 1949.

Dudley, Carl, and Douglas Walrath. *Developing Your Small Church's Potential*. Valley Forge, PA: Judson Press, 1988.

Durkheim, Emile. *The Elementary Forms of the Religious Life*. Glencoe, IL: Free Press, 1947.

Goreham, Gary. *The Rural Church in America: A Century of Writings—A Bibliography*. New York: Garland, 1990.

Judy, Marvin. *From Ivy Tower to Village Spire*. Dallas: Southern Methodist University Printing, 1984.

Kephart, William, and William Zellner. *Extraordinary Groups*. 4th ed. New York: St. Martin's Press, 1991.

Moberg, David. *The Church as a Social Institution*. Grand Rapids, MI: Baker Book House, 1985.

Quinn, Bernard. *The Small Rural Parish*. New York: Glenmary Home Missioners, 1980.

Tweeten, Luther. *Farm Policy Analysis*. Boulder, CO: Westview Press, 1989.

United Methodist Church Report. *Strengthening the Church with Small Membership*. New York: General Board of Global Ministries, 1992.

U.S. Catholic Historical Society. "Catholic Rural Life." *U.S. Catholic Historian* 8, no. 3 (1989).

Restaurants

Eating and drinking establishments. Restaurants historically have played an important part in the social life of communities in rural America. They have served as places of nourishment for residents and travelers, and they have provided a forum where residents could convene to share informal news and take part in social events. Today, rural restaurants serve vital economic and social roles in their communities. Many of these communities owe their survival to the existence of their restaurants. Although rural restaurants' economic survival is often embattled, they continue to enrich the life of communities across the country.

History

Restaurants dot the American landscape. From the largest metropolitan area to the smallest unincorporated town, almost all feature some type of restaurant. Americans seem to have a special relationship with their restaurants. The restaurant industry is resourceful (Anonymous 1988). Diners will travel great distances to go to great restaurants, no matter where they are located (Anonymous 1994). Restaurants have been, currently are, and will continue to be an important part of the American social experience.

Restaurants historically played an important part in the founding of America. Eating and drinking places were among the first businesses to appear in early settlements. These early restaurants, although far different from today's establishments, served an important role in the social life of the community. Friends and neighbors gathered in them for social interaction and to exchange news. These early restaurants were a focal point for the operation of the early community. They brought people together to share topics of importance to the whole community.

When Americans began to move West, restaurants again played an important part in communities (Katsignis and Porter 1983). Inns and taverns developed along trails and rail lines that were used to open the country to westward migration. These establishments' immediate role was to provide meals and lodging to early pioneers. However, they also served as focal points of important social events and news dissemination.

Roles in Today's Society

Restaurants today look much different from their predecessors. They now are part of a large industry that supports the economic base of American society. Some establishments focus on quality food and quick service. At the other end of the spectrum are restaurants that provide a high level of personalized service and gourmet dining experiences. They focus on personalized service and a leisurely pace that pampers their guests. Between these two extremes are a multitude of other types of restaurants.

Today's restaurants play differing roles based on their location. Large city restaurants and rural restaurants are similar in providing basic products and services to their guests, even though the primary reason for going to a restaurant is to eat. However, beyond this, the roles played by the restaurants vary greatly. The remainder of this entry will examine the role that restaurants play in rural society.

The Role of Rural Restaurants

If businesses exist in a rural community, a restaurant also will likely exist. In 1988, 13.4 percent of the top 500 independent restaurants were located in rural areas. Since most rural restaurants would not qualify for this listing, the number of rural restaurants must be large. The number of customers frequenting these restaurants is currently growing (Anonymous 1988).

Why are restaurants present in rural communities? Why do restaurants prevail and grow in a community

Rural restaurants aren't just places to eat; they also serve as community centers. Here the Dakota Dairy Specialties Cooperative Board of Directors meets in a Hebron, North Dakota, restaurant.

where many retail segments have ceased to operate? There are at least three important factors that explain rural restaurants' existence and survival: economic, social, and survival factors.

Economic. The most obvious role of rural restaurants is to provide economic sustenance for various groups and individuals: restaurant owners and operators, restaurant employees, the community at large, and other retail outlets. The structure of operations in rural restaurants varies from that in many suburban and metropolitan ones, which generally are owned by a single individual and operated by a separate manager. While the manager derives his or her economic well-being from a particular restaurant, the owner usually is involved in more than one restaurant operation. Their economic base is diversified so that the success or failure of one restaurant does not determine economic survival or ruin. Rural restaurants usually are owned and operated by the same people. The owners/operators might be a husband and wife team, or perhaps a single individual. Where either a husband or a wife operates the restaurant, the other

spouse generally holds other employment. The economic success of the operator is directly tied to the restaurant. Operators are in business to make money. The rural restaurant's success will determine the economic status of its operators.

Just as the operators make a living from the restaurant, the same is true for restaurant employees. This is not universally true of rural restaurants, since some might be staffed solely by the owners or by nonpaid family members. However, for those who use paid employees, employees count on the restaurant for economic success. If the restaurant ceases to exist, their place of employment ceases to exist. With a chronic shortage of job opportunities, the economic impact may go beyond the individual employee to the community at large.

A third area of economic impact of a rural restaurant is the community in which it exists. The restaurant pays taxes to the community and helps support the economic infrastructure of the community. Fourth, a rural restaurant impacts the economic health of other retail establishments in the community. Many rural people have the unique characteristic of tending to support local businesses first. So retail businesses that provide necessary products and services to the restaurant are affected economically by the presence of that restaurant.

Restaurants play a significant role in the economic health of an area. Although a rural community is not totally dependent on a restaurant, blending its business with other rural businesses can enhance the economic well-being of the community. It can be argued that all restaurants play the same role in any community; however, the importance of this particular type of business is what sets it aside. Restaurants come and go in cities with little effect on the economic condition of the city. However, in a rural setting, the presence or absence of a restaurant has a larger economic impact.

Social. One of the unique roles of restaurants in rural settings is the social role. Although groups of friends may gather for social occasions in any restaurant, the social role of rural restaurants goes far beyond this function. Restaurants serve as the social "nerve center" of rural communities. Rural people might discuss any aspect of community life in the local restaurant, from political situations to social or personal situations. Although these individuals' and groups' discussions might be dismissed as local gossip, a closer examination would reveal at least two important functions for this activity. First, rural residents may be more independent and individualistic; they often shun organized meetings. Many of the formal meetings used to conduct the city's business will not work in a rural community. Informal gatherings serve as substitutes to inform and involve town members in town operation. Second, informal social groups serve as forums in which residents can exchange personal information. The rural community disseminates information through local newspapers and media and through conversation. Rural people are genuinely concerned about their neighbors, but might not see them on a regular basis. The social activities that occur in the restaurant can fill the role of providing this information.

It is unlikely that another business could fill this role as well as the rural restaurant, given people's nature. Many people converse more freely if food and drink are involved. Nearly all social meetings center around eating. The rural restaurant is the only business that can naturally fulfill this important function.

Survival. The third role of a rural restaurant is closely associated with the preceding two. Restaurants provide survival to many segments of the community.

Older patrons frequent the restaurant on a daily basis because they depend on the food for physical survival. Political rallies, field trips, and other formal social activities often are held in or in conjunction with the local restaurant. These formal functions are likewise important to the survival of the subgroups in the community. The survival of these various groups would be made more difficult if the restaurant were not there. Indeed, the entire community's survival might be jeopardized without the presence of a restaurant and its contribution to the community's financial well-being. Restaurants attract visitors and guests to the town, thus amplifying economic benefits. Even more important, however, is the role of the restaurant in providing a space in which community organization can take place. The restaurant serves as a centered focus for the community, a place where individuals can gather informally and formally to reaffirm their existence within the community.

—James L. Groves

See also
Community; Community, Sense of; Culture; Employment.
References
Katsignis, Costas, and Mary Porter. *The Bar and Beverage Book.* New York: Wiley and Sons, 1991.
Lundberg, Donald E. *The Hotel and Restaurant Business.* 4th ed. New York: Van Nostrand Reinhold, 1984.
Lundberg, Donald E., and John R. Walker. *The Restaurant from Concept to Operation.* 2d ed. New York: Wiley and Sons, 1993.
Nixon, Judith M. *Hotel & Restaurant Industries: An Information Sourcebook.* Phoenix: Oryx Press, 1988.
"Out-of-the-way Restaurants Have to Try Harder." *Nations Restaurant News* 28, no. 44 (1994): 11, 84.
"The Top 500 Restaurants." *Restaurant Hospitality* 12, no. 6 (1988): 101–156.

Retail Industry

Establishments engaged in selling merchandise and service for personal or household consumption. Migrations and changes in age distribution are processes that influence the evolution of rural retailing. Historically, in- and out-migration flows affected the viability of retailing in rural communities by changing the threshold level of demand for rural businesses. Currently, changes in the age distribution of the population affect the structure of retailing in rural communities by changing the resident's consumption habits.

Introduction

Rural America is continually adjusting to new circumstances and conditions in an evolutionary process. Much of rural America's history is a story of population movement—immigrants coming to America, people migrating to the new western frontiers, communities growing from the perpetual procession of new farms, and then community decline as rural peoples migrated into urban areas in search of opportunity. The perpetual shifting of population into and out of rural America affected the occupational mix, age composition, family organization, political character, and structure of retailing in rural communities.

The ever-changing nature of rural America is part of a natural progression of events that continues to affect the character of retailing there. Improved transportation made possible by hard-surfaced roads, trucks, and automobiles increased rural mobility and affected rural shopping patterns. More recent changes in the retail distribution system, exemplified by Wal-Mart, mark a trend toward larger retail outlets offering a broader array of goods at one store. The post–World War II changes in mobility and the retail distribution system are important recent supply factors that coincide with a longer-run demographic process affecting the demand for retailing in rural America.

Two preeminent demographic processes affecting rural communities are migration patterns and transitions in the age distribution. Both processes greatly affect the growth, stability, and decline of retailing activity in rural communities. Historically, in- and out-migration flows affected the aggregate level of demand for retailing in rural communities. Currently, changes in the age composition of the rural population are a principal demand factor affecting the structure of retailing in rural communities.

Historical Process

Two distinct periods characterized by diametrically opposed demographic processes can be identified in rural America. The initial period was one of a massive in-migration to rural America of a relatively young population of childbearing age. The subsequent period was one of a substantial out-migration from parts of rural America of people of childbearing age.

The initial period gave rise to a classic community in rural America, which lasted from the mid-nineteenth century to about 1940. The subsequent, postclassical period began about 1940 and has persisted into current times. The diametrically different migration patterns and age compositions between these two eras greatly affected the structure of retailing in rural communities.

The classical era was stimulated by the 1862 Homestead Act and other land laws designed to develop the largest portion of rural America. The total rural population in the country increased from 25.2 million to 56.5 million between 1860 and 1935. The increasing rural population provided the threshold level of demand necessary to develop thousands of viable family retail businesses. The classical era featured a viable rural economy, with thousands of intact communities of all sizes performing a total array of social and economic functions, including a bustling family-owned and -operated retail business district.

The postclassical era began with the Great Depression and accelerated during the post–World War II urban boom. The simultaneous rapid capitalization of rural agriculture and urban manufacturing stimulated a massive out-migration of the farm population, resulting in a decrease in the number of farm operators from 6.8 million in 1935 to less than 2 million in 1992. Although the total rural population stabilized at about 60 million, the spatial and demographic distributions of the rural population changed dramatically during this period.

Spatially, the apparent stabilization of the rural population occurred adjacent to urban areas. The total rural population in the United States increased by 3 million persons during the 1980s. Over one-third of the increase (896,805 persons) occurred in the 10 most urban states, as opposed to a 1 percent increase in the 10 most rural states.

Demographically, whereas the total number of persons defined as rural changed very little, there has been a significant change in the age distribution of the rural population. The number of children living in rural areas decreased by 25 percent from 23 million to 17 million during the postclassical era. Concurrent with the decrease in the number of school-aged children, the elderly population increased 70 percent from 4.4 to 7.5 million in rural areas. The tremendous exodus of childbearing adults and of children from rural America profoundly impacted the social and economic functions of rural communities.

The postclassical era for rural America is a period of sustained stagnation or deterioration for thousands of small communities. Two of the most obvious consequences have been school consolidations and stressed downtown retailing sectors. The rural population no longer provides the threshold level of demand necessary to sustain viable small, local schools or retail businesses in many communities. The postclassical era features rural communities that no longer fulfill the total array of social and economic functions performed during the classical era.

Implications for the Future

One of the most obvious national demographic trends is the growth in the number of elderly Americans. The number of persons 65 years of age and older increased from 3.1 million at the turn of the century to 31.1 million in 1990. The census bureau predicts a 14 percent increase in the number of persons 65 years of age and older by the year 2010.

The national trend toward an older population is accelerated in rural America. Nationally, 34 states gained rural population (2.7 million) and 18 lost rural population (0.5 million) during the 1990s. In the 18 states that continue to lose rural population, the population of persons over the age of 65 increased from 11 to 14 percent. Rural communities already reached the projected increase for the country in 2010 (14 percent), implying that rural communities are leading the nation in the demographic transition to an elderly population.

Not only is the elderly population rapidly increasing in rural areas that are losing population, but the spatial distribution of the elderly population is becoming more concentrated in smaller communities. The proportion of elderly is inversely related to city size, with urban places containing the lowest percentage, 14.8, and the smallest of communities, with 1,000 or less total population, housing the highest percentage, 22.3.

The continuing demographic transition to an older population will affect communities in rural America into the next century. Less than 2 percent of all elderly are expected to move out of the county of current residence and less than 1 percent are expected to move out of the state of current residence (Taeuber 1992). The expected increase in the elderly population in rural America will have a fiscal impact on local tax revenues and consequently an impact on local public service expenditures (Glasgow and Reeder 1990; Hoppe 1991).

Personal consumption expenditures among the aging population in rural areas will have a significant impact on the retail sector of community (Heinte 1976; Happel, Hogan, and Pflanz 1988; Miller 1993). The evidence indicates that as the rural population continues to age, the propensity to shop locally will increase in smaller communities (Henderson 1994). The implicit result is less relative retail and service business decline among the smallest communities (total population less than 1,000) in the future than during the initial phase of the postclassical era.

The impact on rural retailing can also be expected to differ by type of business. The relative frequency of different types of retail establishments within the retail distribution system will continue to adjust as the level and source of income (retirement versus wage and salary) continue to adjust in rural areas (Henderson 1990). Some rural businesses, such as drugstores, could flourish in the future, whereas others (for example, building materials) could continue to decline (Henderson 1994).

Implications for Retailing in Rural Communities

Historically, population size and age distribution influenced retail business activity in a community. All rural retail businesses have a threshold customer base necessary to cover costs and maintain a profit. During the classical era, in-migration translated into an increased customer base, excess demand, the creation of new retail businesses, and the growth of viable downtown retail business districts. During the postclassical era, out-migration resulted in a decreased customer base, insufficient demand, the dissolving of existing retail businesses, and the stagnation or decline of downtown retailing in many rural communities. Both processes continue in numerous contemporary rural communities.

Currently, the continuing demographic transition away from a family-based consumer patronage to an elderly consumer base is causing a change in the composition of the consumer shopping bundle—that is, the mixture of goods—demanded from rural retailers. The transformation in the consumption bundle directly affects the viability of the existing rural retail sector by changing the mix of goods and services demanded. Shifts in the total amount spent on each good in the consumption bundle and changes in the relative proportion of income spent on a particular good in the consumption bundle affect the viability of specific retail businesses offering the goods.

The table illustrates the difference between the consumption habits across various age groups for selected goods. The consumption habits vary by age cohort, which implies that a change in the age distribution of the consumer base affects the sales and profit level for individual rural businesses. Changes in sales and profits for individual businesses eventually will alter the structure of the rural retail sector by making some types of business more profitable than others. Preliminary research indicates that grocery stores, eating establishments, drugstores, home furnishing stores, and building material stores will be especially negatively or positively affected, depending on which age groups are growing or declining

Age Comparisons of Consumption Habits, in Dollars (1992)

	Under 25	25–34	35–44	45–54	55–64	65+
Food	2,621	4,218	5,218	5,233	4,354	3,198
Food at home	1,440	2,486	3,201	3,102	2,833	2,211
Food away from home	1,181	1,732	2,017	2,131	1,521	987
Alcoholic beverages	356	365	352	299	321	159
Housing	5,135	10,018	12,120	11,036	9,436	6,733
Shelter	3,148	6,132	7,215	6,299	5,105	3,241
Owned dwellings	363	3,146	4,926	4,406	3,514	1,978
Rented dwellings	2,656	2,817	1,901	1,313	1,016	1,039
Other lodging	129	169	387	580	575	223
Utilities	1,024	1,797	2,232	2,375	2,255	1,816
Natural gas	101	212	281	295	305	255
Electricity	384	688	899	959	892	725
Fuel oil	19	65	94	86	119	132
Telephone	469	648	698	753	652	465
Water	51	185	260	281	286	238
Household operations	141	579	664	393	374	474
Personal services	94	445	394	69	58	178
Other household	47	134	270	324	316	296
Housekeeping supplies	170	365	507	560	450	413
Laundry	65	111	137	162	116	94
Other products	57	158	228	247	210	201
Stationery	48	96	142	151	123	118
Household furnishings	652	1,145	1,502	1,409	1,252	789
Household textiles	48	86	109	116	101	75
Furniture	238	352	450	381	317	127
Floor coverings	2	45	82	57	61	125
Major appliances	67	127	163	160	150	138
Small appliances	45	70	87	120	136	55
Miscellaneous equipment	253	465	612	575	487	268
Apparel and services	1,267	1,842	2,210	2,245	1,631	882
Men and boys	273	504	588	672	395	185
Women and girls	483	606	894	902	708	425
Children under 2	121	138	91	53	53	22
Footwear	165	272	275	283	223	136
Other apparel	224	322	363	335	252	114
Transportation	3,622	5,376	6,228	6,755	5,684	3,290
Vehicle purchases	1,743	2,355	2,584	2,772	2,329	1,289
Gasoline and motor oil	649	994	1,165	1,269	1,046	621
Other vehicle expenses	1,086	1,772	2,155	2,364	1,945	1,122
Public transportation	144	255	324	350	364	257
Health care	416	1,053	1,570	1,646	1,993	2,474
Entertainment	928	1,569	2,041	1,896	1,587	754
Personal care	253	361	461	481	408	306
Reading	73	142	183	204	188	144
Education	833	305	533	809	282	93
Tobacco products	220	278	326	376	310	147
Miscellaneous	408	780	985	982	788	484
Total	17,258	29,554	37,196	37,427	31,704	20,616

Data are averages for the noninstitutional population and are out-of-pocket expenditures.

Source: U.S. Bureau of Labor Statistics, *Consumer Expenditures in 1992.*

in number in any particular rural community (Henderson 1994).

One conspicuous difference in the consumption bundle by age is that persons between the ages of 35 and 54 spend nearly twice as much per year as do persons 65 years of age or older. The rural cohort between the ages of 35 and 54 are predominantly families, complete with dependent children, which requires a higher level of aggregate family spending. The cohort of persons over the age of 65 typically belong to smaller households, of two or fewer, with a lower level of aggregate household spending. As rural America becomes an older population with smaller household size, the total expenditures per household can be expected to decrease. Less aggregate spending per household means decreased aggregate retail sales, declining retail business numbers, and continued stagnation or decline of downtown retailing in some rural communities. The negative effect of decreased aggregate household spending will be offset by the positive effect of the expected increase in local spending associated with elderly populations in the smallest rural communities.

Differences in the consumption bundle by age vary by category of consumption. Health care is the one part of the consumption bundle where the proportion of total expenditures increases with age. The proportion of the consumption bundle spent on health care monotonically increases from a low of 2.4 percent for persons under the age of 25 to a high of 12 percent for persons over the age of 65. Conversely, the proportion of the consumption bundle spent on transportation decreases from a high of 20.9 percent for persons under the age of 25 to a low of 15.6 percent of the budget for persons over the age of 65.

The total cumulative effect on retailing in rural communities will be significant, with millions of additional dollars being spent on goods in some sectors (such as health care) and millions less being spent on goods in other sectors (such as transportation). Continuing changes in the age composition of the rural population can be expected to change the composition of the consumption bundle of the consumer base, and to affect the sales and profit levels for particular rural businesses.

The future distribution of retail businesses by type in rural America can be expected to continue to adjust to the changes in rural consumers' expenditures and demands. At the regional level, the dynamic nature of the consumer base will continue to affect the choice of shopping destination, further supplementing the growth of larger rural retail centers adjacent to stagnating or declining smaller communities (Henderson 1992). At the community level, some business types will do better than others as the configuration of retail outlets in rural communities continues to adjust to changing rural market conditions. At the individual retail business level, the product mix of individual retailers also can be expected to adjust in accordance with changes in the rural consumption bundle associated with the aging rural population.

—*David A. Henderson*

See also
Consumer-Goods Advertising; Consumerism; Development, Community and Economic; Entrepreneurship; Service Industries; Settlement Patterns; Taxes; Trade Areas; Urbanization.

References
Glasgow, Nina, and Richard Reeder. "Economic and Fiscal Implications of Nonmetropolitian Retirement Migration." *The Journal of Applied Gerontology* 9, no. 4 (December 1990): 433–451.

Happel, Stephen K., Timothy D. Hogan, and Elmer Pflanz. "The Economic Impact of Elderly Winter Residents in the Phoenix Area." *Research on Aging* 10, no. 1 (March 1988): 119–123

Heinte, Katherine McMillan. *Retirement Communities for Adults Only.* New Brunswick: State University of New Jersey, 1976.

Henderson, David. "Rural Retail Sales and Consumer Expenditure Functions." *Journal of Agricultural Economic Research* 42 (1990): 27–34.

———. "Estimates of Retiree Spending in Retail and Service Sectors of Community." *Journal of the Community Development Society* 25 (1994): 259–276.

Henderson, David, Luther Tweeten, and Mike Woods. "A Multicommunity Approach to Community Impacts: The Case of the Conservation Reserve Program." *Journal of the Community Development Society* 23, no. 1 (1992): 88–102.

Hoppe, Robert A. *The Role of the Elderly's Income in Rural Development.* Rural Development Research Report 80. Washington, DC: U.S. Department of Agriculture, Economic Resource Service, 1991.

Miller, W. P. *Economic and Fiscal Impacts of Bella Vista Village, Arkansas.* Fayetteville: University of Arkansas, Cooperative Extension Service, 1993.

Taeuber, C. "Sixty-five Plus in America." *Current Population Reports.* Special Studies P23-178. Washington, DC: Bureau of the Census, 1992.

Rice Industry

Individuals and firms involved in the production, distribution, marketing, processing, and sale of rice and rice by-products to domestic and international consumers. This entry provides an overview of the rice industry. The key components of the rice industry discussed are production, government programs, marketing, economic impacts on rural economies, and current industry trends.

Introduction

Rice is one of the most important foods because it accounts for over 22 percent of global caloric intake. World per capita consumption averages approximately 140 pounds annually, but exceeds 300 pounds in some Asian countries. Rice is consumed primarily as a white milled grain but is also used in a variety of other forms (such as flour, noodles, breakfast cereals, beer, and animal feed). The United States produces less than 2 percent of the world's rice but is the second largest rice exporter. China and India produce approximately 68 percent of the world's rice, and all Asian countries account for 92 percent of the world's production and consumption (Parveen et al. 1994, 63–70).

Rice production ranks as the ninth highest value field crop in the United States, but it ranks in value among the top three field crops in Arkansas, Mississippi, and Louisiana. Other states that produce rice include California, Texas, Missouri, and Florida. Both long-grain (indica type) and medium-/short-grain rice (japonica) are produced in the United States. U.S. rice consumption increased rapidly in recent years, from 14 pounds per capita in 1984 to 25 pounds per capita in 1994. This growth has been driven by increasing dietary and nutritional concerns as well as rapidly growing Asian and Hispanic populations, who have a strong preference for rice. Higher-valued uses of rice and rice co-products (such as starch, proteins, oil, and fiber) are expanding rapidly. The baking industry uses rice starch, oil, and stabilized rice bran as food ingredients. Oil extracted from rice bran makes a superior cooking oil. Farmers use rice bran for animal feed, and rice hulls are used as fuel to generate energy, or for poultry litter. Rice-hull ash can be made into an excellent absorbent (used in cleaning oil and chemical spills) and kitty litter.

Only 4 percent of rice produced is traded internationally, compared to 18 percent for wheat. Thailand, the United States, Vietnam, China, India, and Pakistan are typically the major exporters of rice, and together they account for 70 percent of all rice exports. Major rice importers are the European Union, Saudi Arabia, Iran, Iraq, Brazil, Mexico, and sub-Saharan Africa. The United States exports about 50 percent of its rice, and consequently, U.S. rice prices are primarily determined by global supply and demand. Important customers for U.S. rice exports are Saudi Arabia and other Middle Eastern countries, Canada, Mexico, and Europe. The United States imports about 8 percent of its total rice consumption, of which most is scented or aromatic rice (jasmine or basmati).

Production

The location of rice production in the United States is primarily influenced by climatic and topographical requirements. Ideally, these requirements include adequate water, relatively high air and soil temperatures, adequate solar radiation, the absence of destructive storms, a moderately long growing season, relatively dry conditions during the ripening season, and land of which the surface gradient does not exceed one degree, with a subsoil hardpan that inhibits percolation. The latter facilitates uniform flooding and drainage as required during the growing season. The plentiful availability of either surface or groundwater for maintaining flood conditions on the rice land is the most important factor influencing the location of rice production. Flooded conditions provide benefits of weed control, improved water and air microclimates, and a root zone environment well-suited to rice culture. Rice typically needs 110 to 150 growing days, with abundant sunshine and average temperatures between 68 and 100 degrees Fahrenheit. Temperatures below 59 degrees Fahrenheit retard seedling development, slow tiller formation, delay reproductive growth, and consequently reduce grain yields.

From its beginning in early seventeenth-century Virginia, U.S. rice production spread slowly along the southern Atlantic coastal plain, across the Appalachians into Kentucky and Tennessee, along the Gulf Coast, and up the lower Mississippi River (Mississippi Delta). In the antebellum South, most slave-holding states grew some quantities of rice, with South Carolina accounting for the bulk of production. By the end of the nineteenth century, the Mississippi Delta, the prairies of southwest Louisiana, and the Gulf Coast of Texas produced most of the U.S. rice. Louisiana become the largest rice producer in 1890. Rice production began in the Central Valley of California in 1912. During much of the twentieth century, Arkansas, California, Louisiana, and Texas produced similar quantities of rice. Since the early 1970s, however, Arkansas has become the largest producer, with about 42 percent of production. Nearly all current production takes place in Arkansas and four other southern states (Louisiana, Mississippi, Missouri, and Texas), and in California's Sacramento Valley.

Rice has relatively high production costs per acre compared to other grains. The national average cost per acre in 1992 was $401, of which $296 were variable costs. Considerable differences exist for total costs across the production regions, from a high for California of $620 per acre to $357 for the nondelta, Arkansas region. However, yields in California are typically 25 percent higher than the U.S. average. This yield advantage helps California to be competitive on the basis of cost per hundredweight (cwt). Much of the higher production cost for rice compared to other crops is associated with irrigation, especially with creating and maintaining levees for continual flooding. In addition to equipment normally used for production of soybeans, a common rotation crop in the South, rice production requires a levee plow, levee gates, a landplane, grain carts, and additional trucks for hauling. Disease control is also a major cost because of the humid conditions caused by continual flooding. Aside from production costs, profitability or competitiveness is also determined by yields, prices, and alternative crops. Some areas, such as Texas and about 400,000 acres of land in California, have such impermeable soils that they are only suitable for rice production. Most southern states have a good alternative crop in soybeans.

Returns to rice producers have included market sales and direct government payments. Between 1991 and 1995, annual average market prices have fluctuated between $6 and $9 per cwt. Producers also received government deficiency payments (the difference between a target price of $10.71 per cwt and the higher of the market price or the government loan rate of $6.50 per cwt). Gross returns, including government payments, have averaged $617 per acre for the period between 1991 and 1995. Differences in gross returns result from different yields and prices received. Within any marketing year, prices received by individual farmers vary considerably depending on the rice type (long-, medium-, and short-grain), grade, and quality characteristics. Traditionally, long-grain rice received a premium over medium- and short-grain rice due to stronger market demand. However, the price premium has favored medium-grain over the past several years because of increased demand for japonica rice by Japan and South Korea as a result of the General Agreement on Tariffs and Trade (GATT) agreement to liberalize global rice trade. Quality attributes of rice affect its price. Rough rice (rice in hulls) grades are adjusted based on foreign matter, heat damage, red rice (weed), and chalky kernels. Milled rice is graded on the basis of the percentage of broken kernels, foreign matter, red rice, and chalky kernels, and on color.

Government Rice Programs

The U.S. rice farm program for the period of 1974 through 1995 contained three sets of policy instruments to support prices and incomes of rice producers. These included supply control mechanisms in the form of limitations on or incentives to reduce acreage planted in rice; price supports through a price floor, known as the nonrecourse loan rate; and income supports through deficiency payments. Due to relatively favorable target prices compared to market prices, participation in the rice program typically attracted over 94 percent of eligible rice production. Deficiency payments have been important to rice producers. The average annual cost of these payments since 1990 has been approximately $550 million. These payments have accounted for approximately 30 percent of the gross income of U.S. rice producers since 1990.

A comprehensive revision of the rice farm program was passed by the U.S. Congress and signed by President Clinton in April 1996. The new U.S. agricultural policy is titled the Federal Agriculture Improvement and Reform Act of 1996 (FAIR Act). This law significantly changes the price and income mechanisms for rice and other grains. Supply control mechanisms are essentially eliminated. Income support is decoupled from production of a specific program crop and replaced by a seven-year production flexibility contract that provides annual transition payments to producers who participated in the commodity programs for at least one of the previous five years. Nonrecourse loans continue to be made available to rice producers at a maximum rate of $6.50 per cwt.

The FAIR Act generally retains export assistance programs for rice and other grains. These programs include: (1) Export credit guarantee programs known as GSM, under the General Sales Manager in the Foreign Agriculture Service, U.S. Department of Agriculture (USDA), (2) Market access programs (MAPs), which assist commodity groups in export promotion, (3) Public Law 480 food assistance programs to alleviate hunger and poverty in foreign countries, and (4) the Export Enhancement Program (EEP), which subsidizes exports into markets as a countervailing policy to unfair export competition. Export programs have been important for the U.S. rice industry, as 20 to 40 percent of annual rice exports have relied upon these government programs.

Marketing and Consumption

Rice is harvested in the United States between August and November. The grain at harvest typically has a moisture content of 16 to 24 percent and must therefore be dried to a desired level of 13 percent. The harvested rough rice grain is dried in either on-farm drier facilities or in large, commercial drier elevators. Rough rice remains in storage until mill orders are received. Rice must be milled before it can be consumed. The dried rough rice is processed at the mill by cleaning, sorting by size, and removal of the hull and the bran layers. White milled rice is the most common form of processed rice; however, it can also be parboiled, precooked, or left as brown rice

with the bran layer intact. Once milling is complete, the rice and by-products (hulls and bran) enter domestic and export market channels.

Producers have several alternative pricing methods for their rough rice: cooperative pooling, private auction, direct contracting, and hedging on the futures market. Each producer chooses the pricing mechanism that best suits his or her payment and risk preference. Farmer cooperatives represent a significant segment of the U.S. rice industry. They are particularly important in Arkansas and California and are fully vertically integrated from the farm to the domestic and export distribution channels.

Domestic use of rice flows through three distinct channels. Direct food use by households, restaurants, and institutional kitchens accounts usually for 60 percent of domestic use. Processors of breakfast cereals, baby foods, package mixes, rice cakes, pet foods, soups, and candy use approximately 20 to 25 percent of the domestic shipments. The third domestic use is by the beer industry, which incorporates rice as a fermentable carbohydrate adjunct. The brewery industry traditionally has purchased 15 to 20 percent of the domestic market. The domestic processor and direct food use segments grew consistently during the 1990s, whereas beer use remained level. Dietary changes in the United States that favor complex carbohydrates such as rice, a growing demand for ethnic foods, and convenience in preparation are expected to be factors that contribute to further growth in the domestic rice market.

Exports of U.S. rice are important to the global supply and demand balance. Although the United States produces less than 2 percent of the world's rice, it has accounted for 18 percent of world rice exports since 1990. The United States has ranked second, behind Thailand, as the leading rice exporter for the past several decades. U.S. export shipments are made to over 80 countries, but the dominant customers include the Middle East countries, the European Union, Canada, and Mexico. As a result of the Uruguay Round GATT agreement on rice trade liberalization, Japan also has become an important buyer of U.S. rice. The world rice trade is a relatively small percentage of world rice production and consumption, compared with other grain markets. Total world rice trade accounts for only 4 percent of world grain production and consumption. Therefore, shortfalls and surpluses from year to year can result in extreme swings in the quantity traded and prices. For instance, a 25 percent shortfall in Japan's rice crop in 1993 caused U.S. rough rice prices to move quickly from $5.19 per cwt to over $10.20 per cwt. The volatility of rice trade and prices is caused by several key factors, including (1) the concentration of production in Southeast Asia, which is subject to an unpredictable monsoon climate; (2) protectionist trade policies in countries where rice is a main dietary staple, in order to achieve food security; and (3) market segmentation based on differences in rice types and qualities.

Economic Impacts of Rice Production

The concentration of rice production in the United States means that adjustments by the industry are vitally important to the local input markets, land prices, labor markets, and related marketing industries. Because rice production and processing are highly capital-intensive and specialized activities, changes in production can have pronounced effects on the local economies that depend on the rice industry.

Estimates of the economic impact of rice for the state of Arkansas have been recently developed (Department of Commerce 1994). Since Arkansas's production accounts for approximately 42 percent of the total U.S. output, these estimates are likely to represent the entire industry. The annual farm level value of rough rice sales in Arkansas averaged $750 million. Other economic activities associated with input, milling, and wholesale and retail sales account for an additional $1,150 million, resulting in a total economic impact on the state economy of $1.9 billion.

Trends in the Industry

The U.S. rice industry is dynamic, highly integrated, and specialized. Significant changes recently in government programs, international competition, and U.S. consumer diets are bringing about changes in the location, size, and economic characteristics of the rice industry. The rice sector traditionally has been dependent on government price and income supports. However, under the new FAIR Act, income supports have been decoupled from production decisions to allow farmers full flexibility in their planting decisions. The elimination of the relatively high price and income supports tied to rice production in the past is expected to result in a 10 to 20 percent reduction in the U.S. rice industry, with a larger impact expected in Texas and smaller reductions in California (Wailes et al. 1996). Due to the high cost of producing rice relative to alternatives, notably soybeans and feed grains, a reduction in rice production is expected in areas where these alternatives are competitive.

The domestic market is expected to grow and compete for the reduced domestic rice supply, thereby reducing U.S. rice exports. The competitive position of U.S. rice on world markets is expected to remain strong in high-quality markets such as Europe, the Middle East, and Japan. The expected downsizing also will affect farm input markets that are oriented toward rice production, such as the specialized equipment market. The U.S. rice milling industry, which operated in a very dynamic environment over the past two decades, also faces adjustments. The milling industry experienced a period of expansion during the 1970s, followed by periods of downsizing in the 1980s and of ownership restructuring in the 1990s. As the rice industry moves into an environment of even greater market orientation and less government intervention, the U.S. rice industry will experience further elimination of existing mills and a trend toward greater market concentration as fewer firms survive the challenges ahead. The industry must continue to improve efficiency if it is to maintain its share in the domestic and international markets.

—*Eric J. Wailes*

See also

Agricultural and Resource Economics; Agricultural Programs; Cooperatives; Irrigation; Marketing; Policy, Agricultural; Soil; Trade, International.

References

Dethloff, Henry C. *A History of the American Rice Industry, 1685–1985.* College Station: Texas A&M University Press, 1988.

Livezey, Janet. "Farm and Operator Characteristics as Sources of Cost Variation on U.S. Rice Farms." *Proceedings*, 26th Rice Technical Working Group Meeting. San Antonio: Texas Agricultural Experiment Station, 1996.

Luh, Bor S., ed. *Rice: Production and Utilization*, 2d ed. Vol. 2. New York: Van Nostrand Reinhold, 1991.

Salassi, Michael E. *Characteristics and Production Costs of U.S. Rice Farms, 1988.* AIB-657. Washington, DC: U.S. Department of Agriculture, Economic Research Service, 1992.

Setia, Parveen, Nathan Childs, Eric Wailes, and Janet Livezey. *The U.S. Rice Industry.* Agricultural Economics Report No. AER-700. Washington, DC: U.S. Department of Agriculture, Economic Research Service, Commodity Economics Division, September 1994.

Smith, R. K., E. J. Wailes, and G. L. Cramer. *The Market Structure of the U.S. Rice Industry.* Bulletin 921. Fayetteville: University of Arkansas, Arkansas Agricultural Experiment Station, 1990.

U.S. Department of Commerce. "Fact Sheet: Value of Rice Production to Arkansas." Mimeo. 1994.

Wailes, Eric J. "Rice." Pp. 8–9 in *Quality of U.S. Agricultural Products*. Task Force Report No. 126. Ames, IA: Council for Agricultural Science and Technology, 1996.

Wailes, Eric J., Gail L. Cramer, James Hansen, and Eddie C. Chavez. *Arkansas Global Rice Model: International Baseline Projections for 1996.* Fayetteville: University of Arkansas, Arkansas Agricultural Experiment Station, 1996.

River Engineering

The building of dams and other projects that facilitate navigation, flood control, pollution control, irrigation, recreation, and water supply. River engineering is the attempt to tame water in motion through dams, canals, jetties, dikes, and other construction projects. From the canal age of the 1820s to the modern era of dams, river engineering has transformed rural America and radically altered the way we perceive the natural world. The United States is an amazing hydrological system of more than 300 major rivers with tributary streams that extend about 3.6 million miles. Rivers are the lifeblood of the rural economy. Dredged and impounded for navigation, rivers are highways of commerce, the nation's first interstate transport system. Vital to agribusiness, rivers nationwide reclaim almost 58 million acres of farmland. Rivers are open sewers for agricultural runoff. They are hydro factories that produce a tenth of America's electrical power. Rivers are raging beasts and benign benefactors: here, rampaging floods, and there, the peaceful sites of boating facilities, wilderness areas, fisheries, and habitat for about 75 percent of all desert animal species. The stories of rural America and of the development of its rivers are inextricably intertwined.

Early River Projects

Construction on America's rivers long predated the civil engineering profession. About 700 years before Columbus, Hohokam Indians of the desert Southwest pioneered in irrigation, with an extensive network of ditches and dams. Prehistoric peoples in the Columbia basin narrowed large rivers with stones to harvest the salmon migration.

Europeans regarded rivers as thoroughfares of empire, yet the hazards of interior navigation—sandbars, shoals, snags (dead trees), rapids, and falls—were impediments to colonization. By the time of the American Revolution, the British army had drawn detailed maps of the most dangerous rapids. Builders aided navigation with dockyards, beacons, ice piers, and stationary winches to "warp" boats through gravel and mud. In 1785, George Washington organized a stock company that cleared rocks from the Potomac and canalled around Great Falls. Ambitious projects also developed on the Santee, James, Delaware, Susquehanna, Schuykill, and Merrimack Rivers. New York's Erie Canal, opened in 1825, was a 364-mile engineering sensation that made the Hudson-Mohawk a conduit of western trade.

The success of the Erie Canal fueled a pro-business, pro-union campaign to build a vigorous maritime economy through federal public works. Encouraged by the Supreme Court's outspoken nationalism in *Gibbons v. Ogden* (1824), a case that confirmed the federal jurisdiction over interstate river commerce, Congress pieced together omnibus waterway legislation with projects for every state. The U.S. Army Corps of Engineers supervised the largest federal projects. Ably assisted by steamboat pilots and the U.S. Topographical Bureau, the Corps and its contractors developed a fleet of machine boats to clear the log-infested Ohio-Mississippi system. In 1832 snag boat inventor Henry Miller Shreve, a federal river superintendent, cleared a 100-mile logjam on the Red River that blocked American access to Texas. Army builders and contractors also aided attempts to canal around treacherous rapids at Louisville on the Ohio, Des Moines on the Mississippi, Muscle Shoals on the Tennessee, and Sault Ste. Marie.

Federal Programs after the Civil War

After the Civil War the river program expanded with strong support from the South and the West. It was an age of innovation—of suction dredging, underwater explosives, steel lighthouses, concrete dams, and motorized locks that made rivers work like canals. One project dear to the heartland was the deep-water shipping channel that opened the Mississippi below New Orleans. In 1885 a movable dam at Davis Island below Pittsburgh became the first of the Ohio River's 46 locks and dams.

Dredging opened a 30-foot channel to Philadelphia and a 20-foot channel to Portland. Serious flooding in Louisiana, meanwhile, led to the establishment in 1879 of a levee oversight bureau called the Mississippi River Commission. That year John Wesley Powell of the U.S. Geological Survey advocated a public system of ditches and dams in a report that became a blueprint for reclamation in the 17 western states.

Powell preferred small government and local control but recognized, nevertheless, that large-scale reclamation efforts would require federal aid. Although Mormon irrigators had built impressive, church-sponsored projects without public assistance, state initiatives were rarely successful. Cautiously at first, Congress aided farmer cooperatives and irrigation districts through water and land-grant programs such as the 1877 Desert Land Act and 1894 Carey Act. In 1902, Congress extended federal financing through the U.S. Reclamation Service, later renamed the Bureau of Reclamation. Soon the bureau had astonished the nation with a string of spectacular proj-

Flooding of farms and residences has often been the impetus for large-scale river engineering projects such as dams that will regulate the flow of water.

ects: Roosevelt Dam on the Salt (1911), Arrowrock on the Boise (1915), and Elephant Butte on the Rio Grande (1916). Financial setbacks, however, crippled several grandiose projects. At Uncompahgre in Colorado, for example, a $1 million dam proposal ultimately cost three times that amount. Seldom in the history of federal dam-building have farm payments covered the cost of construction. According to a 1986 U.S. Department of Interior estimate, federal taxpayers footed the bill for 86 percent of the $19.6 billion appropriated for reclamation between 1902 and 1986 (Wahl 1989, 36).

Hydropower

Hydroelectric power sales helped the financially troubled projects recover some of their costs. Pioneered by the Edison Electric Company, the use of impounded water to generate electricity came of age in the 1880s and 1890s with American innovations such as power plants, voltage regulators, and long-distance transmission lines. Intense competition among private and public purveyors

prompted Congress to coordinate hydro development through the Federal Power Commission, established in 1920. Federal activity increased with the Wilson Dam and powerhouse at Muscle Shoals on the Tennessee River, a Corps project completed in 1925. Wilson Dam touched off a fiery debate between private power utilities and water conservationists such as Senator George W. Norris of Nebraska, a crusader for public power. In 1933, Norris sponsored the legislation that became a controversial experiment in federal planning, the Tennessee Valley Authority (TVA). Serving a seven-state region hard hit by the Great Depression, the TVA made the Tennessee River the most dammed and developed stream in the nation. Electricity, by 1950, reached 80 percent of the region's farms. Hydropower also reached America's farms through the dams and powerlines authorized by the Rural Electrification Administration (REA), an agency that began as a relief operation in 1936. By 1941, the REA served more than a million consumers.

Rural demand for electricity helped justify massive

construction. One engineering triumph was Boulder Dam (renamed Hoover Dam in 1947) on the Colorado River, finished in 1935. At 726 feet, the gravity-arch dam was the height of a six-story office building, nearly twice as tall as any existing dam. Federal engineers also broke construction records on the Columbia River at Bonneville Dam (completed in 1937) and Grand Coulee Dam (1941). Shasta Dam with its giant power plant, authorized by Congress in 1935, became the centerpiece of California's Central Valley Project, a vast network of dams and canals. With 475 miles of pipelines, 20 miles of tunnels, 22 pumping stations, and seven power plants, the Central Valley Project is the largest water conveyance system ever undertaken by a state.

Flood Control and Multipurpose Projects

Another catalyst to rural development has been the federal attempt to contain raging floods. For many years the Corps of Engineers believed that flood levees were the most effective way to control inundation, but catastrophic flooding along the Mississippi in 1927 shattered that conventional wisdom, forcing engineers to consider flood reservoirs and dams. The 1936 Flood Control Act greatly expanded the Corps' jurisdiction, with $310 million for some 250 projects. By 1952, Congress had spent more than $11 billion on flood-control levees and dams.

Flood control became a primary justification for basin-wide dam and canal projects that also developed rivers for hydropower and navigation. Disastrous flooding along the Missouri in 1943 interrupted the war effort and launched one of the Corps' most ambitious multipurpose projects, the Pick-Sloan Plan. The first large dam in the system was the $183 million project at Fort Randall, which created a giant slack-water channel for navigation, backing up the Missouri for 150 miles. Corps engineers also designed the 434-mile-long multipurpose McClellan-Kerr waterway along the Arkansas River to Tulsa. Featuring three large flood reservoirs and the Dardanelle Lock and Dam, completed in 1969, the waterway with its heavy barge traffic benefited farmers directly by dramatically cutting freight rates on fertilizers and grain.

The Mississippi system, meanwhile, has become one of the world's most sophisticated networks of multipurpose flood, hydro, and navigation projects, with more than 200 major dams. One critical part of the system is a navigation lock in the right bank of the Mississippi about 300 miles upstream from the mouth of the river. Built by the Corps in 1963, the lock prevents the river from shifting into the Atchafalaya floodway, bypassing New Orleans. In 1963 the Corps also completed the slack-water dam at the Chain of Rocks near St. Louis, thereby removing one of the last great hazards to barge navigation.

In all, about 75,000 large dams have been built in the nation's rivers. The Corps of Engineers has turned about 26,000 miles of river into channelized highways for barges. The Bureau of Reclamation has built at least 16,000 miles of canals, 1,500 miles of pipeline, and 355 storage reservoirs. Along the Colorado, the volume of water being stored for irrigation is six times the river's annual flow. Outside Alaska, only 42 rivers run free for more than 120 miles without locks or dams.

Opposition to River Projects

Even as engineering transformed the nation, there was seldom a time in the nation's history when dam builders worked without facing stiff opposition. Soon after the Civil War, the Corps was widely denounced as a pork-barrel organization, extravagant and corrupt. Again, in 1951, the New Dealer Harold Ickes called the Corps "the most powerful and pervasive lobby in Washington, . . . our highest ruling class" (Maass 1951, ix). Meanwhile, the Bureau of Reclamation was the target of an angry campaign to save part of Dinosaur National Monument from a high dam at Echo Park.

The Echo Park controversy built a nationwide base of support for antidam legislation such as the 1964 Wilderness Act and the 1968 Wild and Scenic River Act. Perhaps the most significant challenge to dam building was the 1969 National Environmental Policy Act, a law that required engineers see rivers not only as plumbing but also as parkland, raft runs, scenic vistas, and complex ecosystems. With the 1972 Clean Water Act came the recognition that slack-water projects often promote the swamplike eutrophication that clogs rivers with algae and pollutes drinking-water supplies. Although a few threatened streams have recovered—the Cuyahoga at Cleveland, for example, is no longer a fire hazard—the U.S. Environmental Protection Agency estimates that one-third of America's river mileage does not meet federal clean water standards.

Recent disputes over river construction often have a rural-urban dimension that forces governments to make difficult choices. On the Columbia and Snake Rivers, where sockeye and Chinook salmon are dangerously close to extinction, rural irrigators are pitted against urban-centered water conservation groups that are attempting to save the fish by releasing reservoir water. Meanwhile, thirsty consumers in Las Vegas, Phoenix, Los Angeles,

Albuquerque, Salt Lake City, and Denver tap into the Colorado, challenging the "first in time, first in line" doctrine of prior appropriation, a bedrock of western law. Thus, the rivers that touch every part of the nation are battlefields of raging debate over the human encounter with nature and the role that technology should play in shaping American life.

—*Todd Shallat*

See also
Conservation, Water; Environmental Protection; Groundwater; Hydrology; Impact Assessment.
References
Armstrong, Ellis L. *History of Public Works in the United States, 1776–1976.* Chicago: American Public Works Association, 1976.
Bartlett, Richard A. *Rolling Rivers: An Encyclopedia of America's Rivers.* New York: McGraw-Hill, 1984.
Maass, Arthur. *Muddy Waters: The Army Engineers and the Nation's Rivers.* Cambridge, MA: Harvard University Press, 1951; 2d ed. New York: Da Capo Press, 1974.
Palmer, Tim. *Lifelines: The Case for River Conservation.* Washington, DC: Island Press, 1994.
Shallat, Todd. *Structures in the Stream: Water, Science, and the Rise of the U.S. Army Corps of Engineers.* Austin: University of Texas Press, 1994.
Wahl, Richard W. *Markets for Federal Water: Subsidies, Property Rights, and the Bureau of Reclamation.* Washington, DC: Resources for the Future, 1989.
Wilkinson, Charles F. *Crossing the Next Meridian: Land, Water, and the Future of the West.* Washington, DC: Island Press, 1992.

Rural, Definition of

Although the idea of "rural" has widespread intuitive understanding, as with many scientific concepts, attempts at articulating a precise meaning have led to a tangle of arguments and counterarguments concerning the utility of a given definition. The major point of agreement among those involved in the debate has been that there is no singular or multifaceted definition that will suffice to satisfy the research, programmatic, and policy communities that employ the concept. With this unsettled situation in mind, this entry is divided into two major sections. The first section contains a summary of the origins of the concept, the interface of the concept of the rural with the concept of the urban, and finally, the issue of the dimensions of rurality. The second broad section provides an overview of various measures that have been employed to distinguish rural populations and places. These include the measures of rurality employed by the Office of Management and Budget, the definition of nonmetropolitan, and other categorizations and indexes that have been created.

The Rural-Urban Dichotomy and Continuum

Tracing the source of the word "rural" to its historical origins leads to the Latin word *rus,* which is interpreted as meaning "the country"; the Indo-European word *rewos,* meaning "space" or "wide"; and the Gothic word *rums,* meaning "room" or "space." Other words that often are used to specify rural areas or people include bucolic, pastoral, rustic, and provincial.

A key consideration in the concept of the rural is the recognition of an explicit or implicit definition or a delineation of the concept of the urban. Louis Wirth's (1938) classic work "Urbanism as a Way of Life" is perhaps the most widely cited binary juxtaposition of urbanism and ruralism. In this work, the rural way of life was characterized by stability, integration, and rigid social stratification. Urbanism, on the other hand, was seen as dynamic and unstable, fluid in terms of social stratification, and impersonal, with specialized social interaction and compartmentalized employment and family. Wirth's perspective was one of many that used societal level studies to describe and explain social changes as the country and the world became more industrialized and urbanized in the late nineteenth and early twentieth centuries. Other perspectives, including the societal contrasts of Emile Durkheim (mechanical and organic solidarity), Ferdinand Tönnies (*Gemeinschaft* and *Gesellschaft*), Max Weber (rational and traditional), Pitirim Sorokin (familistic and contractual), and Ernest Becker (sacred and secular), have been used to differentiate rural and urban ways of life.

Attempts to use rural and urban ways of life as empirical illustrations of these grand theories of societal change quickly proved that such binary conceptualizations were overly reductionist and inadequate to capture the diversity that exists within a society. Thus, led by the work of Redfield (1947), researchers proposed a continuum that arranged communities according to levels of rurality and urbanism. At one end of the continuum were very isolated, remote rural areas and at the other extreme were large cities, with transitional areas in between. The idea of the continuum provided a useful mechanism to empirically document differences and similarities between people and places in the United States. However, the findings have been mixed in documenting meaningful differences, and while the corporeality of the continuum is generally accepted, some regarded the importance of the differences as trivial (Dewey 1960) or incontinuously distributed across population aggregates (Duncan 1957).

Dimensions of Rurality

Inherent in the efforts to contrast rural and urban life has been the need to identify the dimensions along which distinctions are made. Although the specific delineation of rural populations varies depending on the research topic or the agency or institution that gathers the data, three dimensions—ecological, occupational, and sociocultural—have been at the core of historical and contemporary definitions of rurality (see Sorokin and Zimmerman 1929; Bealer, Willits, and Kuvelsky 1965).

The ecological component points to relatively sparse populations and relative isolation from urban areas. This spatial apportionment of the population has been the foundation of most academic and policy designations of the rural and the urban. The importance of the rural as an ecological characteristic lies in the cost of space (Kraenzel 1980), where distance and population sparsity are extraordinary factors in the availability, access, and costs of needed services and goods. Further, smaller size and relative isolation also affect both inter- and intra-locality personal contacts.

As for the occupational dimension, rurality historically has been associated with the predominance of extractive and production type industries, including agriculture and ranching, forestry, mining, oil and gas extraction, and natural resource–based tourism. Whereas the rural areas of the United States have a diverse occupational structure when considered in the aggregate, local economies of rural areas are likely to be much less diversified.

The sociocultural dimension of rurality, its most complex and least well articulated, generally refers to value structures or shared ideals that serve as the fundamental underpinnings of interactions. Rural culture has been variously described as socially conservative, provincial, fatalistic, traditional, hesitant to change, independent, prejudiced, ethnocentric, and intolerant of heterodox ideas (England, Gibbons, and Johnson 1979; Glenn and Alston 1967; Loomis 1950). However, empirical research has not served to substantiate these elements of the sociocultural domain as capable of distinguishing between rural and urban populations and has shown that heterogeneity of values rather than homogeneity characterizes rural America.

The concept of rurality includes a temporal aspect. It can be argued that development and population increases and dispersal limit the utility of certain components of the concept of rurality, particularly when time is included as a variable. When time is considered, the eco-logical approach to defining rurality has proven the most enduring in research and policy matters, in that distance and relative isolation, unlike the occupational and sociocultural components, are less immediately affected by the passage of time. In the past, rurality may have been highly correlated with sociocultural characteristics such as traditionalism and social conservatism, but changes in society, such as improved telecommunication and transportation and greater homogeneity in education, have weakened their association. Similarly, in the past, rurality was highly correlated with an agrarian and extractive occupational structure. However, decentralization of industry and mechanization and concentration of agriculture weakened the epistemic correlation between the rurality concept and an agricultural occupational structure. Although sociocultural differences remain and agricultural occupations still employ rural residents, some argue that the most salient contemporary differences in rural and urban areas are primarily a consequence of the spatial organization of the U.S. population (Wilkinson 1984).

Measures of Rurality

Numerous categories of rurality and entire continuums of residence have been devised to overcome the inability of a single indicator to depict the spectrum of rural characteristics (Farmer, Clarke, and Miller 1993; Hewitt 1989). The most often employed and most general classification schemes are provided by the U.S. Bureau of the Census and the Office of Management and Budget (OMB). In both cases the measures are based on delineating urban areas, with rural areas being the residual category. In other words, the rural is what is left over after the urban has been defined. In the case of the Census Bureau's definition, urban populations are those those people living in places with a population greater than 2,500, or residing within an urbanized area. Urbanized areas are defined by the existence of one or more central places and an adjacent fringe area that have a total population of at least 50,000. The fringe areas are required to have a population density of at least 1,000 persons per square mile.

A similarly sweeping measure, adopted by the OMB to delineate rural areas, employed counties as the analytic unit. In this scheme, a particular county is classified as either metropolitan or nonmetropolitan. Like the census bureau's definition, the OMB definition is a combination of population size and density. However, this classification also includes the additional element of economic

integration as defined by commuting patterns. Specifically, OMB defines a metropolitan area as either a county with a city of at least 50,000 people or an urbanized area that is part of a county or counties with a minimum of 100,000 individuals. When the traditional, dichotomous classification of an area as rural or urban is employed, the strategy results in rural areas being defined as counties that satisfy the threshold values for nonmetropolitan counties.

The efforts to make a dichotomous distinction between rural and urban and metropolitan and nonmetropolitan, although widely used, are severely reductionist and allow only the most crude comparisons. Recognizing the limited nature of these two approaches, researchers and analysts have developed a variety of other classification schemes and indexes that have been variously used to tap differences within and among rural and urban places and people.

One such approach, using OMB-designated nonmetropolitan counties and developed by McGranahan and colleagues (1986), incorporates the size of the nonmetropolitan county's urban population (using the Census Bureau's definition) and adjacency to metropolitan counties. In this case, adjacency is defined as a shared county boundary or the existence of a labor force commuting relationship. This strategy resulted in six categories of nonmetropolitan counties labeled as urbanized adjacent, urbanized nonadjacent, less urbanized adjacent, less urbanized nonadjacent, rural adjacent, and rural nonadjacent.

Another effort to classify nonmetropolitan counties employing the idea of adjacency distributes counties designated as nonmetropolitan among four separate categories. These categories are described as (1) adjacent rural areas, or those counties contiguous to or within metropolitan statistical areas; (2) urbanized rural areas, or those counties with populations of 25,000 or more but not attached to a Metropolitan Statistical Area; (3) frontier areas, or those counties with a population density of fewer than six persons per square mile; and (4) countryside rural areas, or the rest of the country not covered by metropolitan or other rural designations (Patton 1989).

Still another county-based approach uses adjacency to metropolitan counties and size of largest place within the county. This approach, used by Long and DeAre (1982), classifies nonmetropolitan counties according to four levels of settlement size (population less than 2,500; 2,500 to 9,999; 10,000 to 24,999; and 25,000 or more) and adjacency to metropolitan counties, thereby creating

eight classes of nonmetropolitan counties. This scheme also includes metropolitan counties, allocated according to size of largest place (under 100,000; 100,00 to 249,999; 250,000 to 499,999; 500,000 to 999,999; 1,000,000 to 2,999,999; and 3,000,000 or more). Thus, this approach creates a 14-category spectrum of counties.

A measure created by the U.S. Department of Agriculture (Bender et al. 1985) classifies nonmetropolitan areas based on economic dependencies. The seven classes of nonmetropolitan counties based on dependencies are: (1) farming dependent; (2) manufacturing dependent; (3) mining dependent; (4) specialized government; (5) persistent poverty; (6) federal lands; and (7) retirement. Yet another classification effort is based on the structure of the local area labor markets. This approach, developed by Pickard (1988), uses the ratio of resident workers employed in a county relative to the total employed workforce in the county (in other words, those that work in the county regardless of their place of residence). Pickard's strategy includes consideration of the proportion of the population classified as urban in combination with the size of the largest place and the total population of the county. This approach groups nonmetropolitan counties into six categories: nonmetropolitan center, nonmetropolitan satellite, nonmetropolitan commuting with center, nonmetropolitan small center, nonmetropolitan commuting, and nonmetropolitan rural.

There also have been attempts to create indexes incorporating multiple indicators into a single measure. Most recently, Cleland, Fontanez, and Williams (1994) created a measure of isolation and inability of residents to participate in programs of the larger society. Combining 11 equally weighted elements into a single score for each county in the contiguous United States, this index results in seven categories ranging from most rural to least rural.

As can be seen from the above discussion, those with an interest in rural topics have a wide variety of choices in terms of both conceptualization and measurement of rurality. Whereas the fundamental underpinnings of the concept and its measurement remain a topic for debate (Halfacree 1993) and there continue to be calls for standardization of the measurement of rurality, the diversity of purposes for which the measures have been and will be used will likely assure that no universally applicable definition or measurement will be developed. Indeed, there is an increasing call for recognizing that rurality is in large measure a social construct and connotes a variety of images ranging from the positive (friendly hamlets, productive farms, traditional values, and open space) to the negative (poverty, provincialism, and ignorance) (Willits, Bealer, and Timbers 1990). In order to construct a representational definition of rurality, one must first understand the popular and the academic images conjured up by the term (Halfacree 1993).

—*Frank L. Farmer*

See also

Community; Culture; Rural Demography; Rural Sociology; Town-Country Relations; Urbanization.

References

Bealer, Robert C., Fern K. Willits, and William P. Kuvelsky. "The Meaning of 'Rurality' in American Society." *Rural Sociology* 30, no. 3 (1965): 255–266.

Bender, Lloyd D., Bernal L. Green, Thomas F. Hady, John A. Kuehn, Marlys K. Nelson, Leon B. Perkinson, and Peggy J. Ross. *The Diverse Social and Economic Structure of Nonmetropolitan America.* Rural Development Research Report No. 49. Washington, DC: U.S. Government Printing Office, 1985.

Brown, David L. "Is the Rural-Urban Distinction Still Useful for Understanding Structure and Change in Developed Societies?" In *Population Change and the Future of Rural America.* Staff Report No. AGES 9324. Edited by Linda L. Swanson and David L. Brown. Washington, DC: U.S. Department of Agriculture, Economic Research Service, Agriculture and Rural Economy Division, 1993.

Cleland, Charles L., Will Fontanez, and Brian S. Williams. *Rurality Scores for U.S. Counties, 1994* (map). Agricultural Experiment Station Bulletin 689. Knoxville: University of Tennessee, 1994.

Dewey, Richard. "The Rural-Urban Continuum: Real but Relatively Unimportant." *American Journal of Sociology* 66, no. 1 (1960): 60–66.

Duncan, Otis Dudley. "Community Size and the Rural-Urban Continuum." Pp. 35–45 in *Cities and Society.* Edited by Paul K. Hatt and Albert J. Reiss, Jr. Glencoe, IL: Free Press, 1957.

England, J. Lynn, W. Eugene Gibbons, and Barry L. Johnson. "The Impact of a Rural Environment on Values." *Rural Sociology* 44 (1979): 119–136.

Farmer, Frank L., Leslie L. Clarke, and Michael K. Miller. "Consequences of Differential Residence Designations for Rural Health Policy: The Case of Infant Mortality." *Journal of Rural Health* 9 (1993): 17–26.

Glenn, Norval D., and Jon P. Alston. "Rural-Urban Differences in Reported Attitudes and Behavior." *Social Science Quarterly* 47, no. 4 (1967): 381–400.

Halfacree, Keith H. "Locality and Social Representation: Space, Discourse and Alternative Definitions of Rural." *Journal of Rural Studies* 9, no. 1 (1993): 23–37.

Hewitt, Marcia E. *Defining "Rural" Areas: Impact on Health Care Policy and Research.* Staff Paper, Office of Technology Assessment. Washington, DC: Government Printing Office, 1989.

Kraenzel, Carl. *The Social Cost of Space in Yonland.* Bozeman, MT: Big Sky Press, 1980.

Long, Larry, and Diana DeAre. "Repopulating the Countryside: A 1980 Census Trend." *Science* 217 (1982): 111–116.

Loomis, Charles P. "The Nature of Rural Social Systems: A Typological Analysis." *Rural Sociology* 15, no. 2 (1950): 156–174.

McGranahan, David A., J. Hession, F. Hines, and M. F. Jordan. *Social and Economic Characteristics of the Population in Metro and Nonmetro Counties, 1970–1980.* Rural Development Research Report No. 58. Washington, DC: U.S. Department of Agriculture, Economic Research Service, 1986.

Patton, L. "Setting the Rural Health Services Research Agenda: The Congressional Perspective." *Health Services Research* 23 (1989): 1005–1052.

Pickard, J. "A New County Classification." *Appalachia* 21 (1988): 19–24.

Redfield, Robert. "The Folk Society." *American Journal of Sociology* 52 (1947): 294–308.

Sorokin, Pitirim, and Carle Zimmerman. *Principles of Rural-Urban Sociology.* New York: Henry Holt, 1929.

Wilkinson, Kenneth P. "Rurality and Patterns of Social Disruption." *Rural Sociology* 49, no. 1 (1984): 23–36.

Willits, Fern K., Robert C. Bealer, and Vincent L. Timbers. "Popular Images of 'Rurality': Data from a Pennsylvania Survey." *Rural Sociology* 55 (1990): 559–587.

Wirth, Louis. "Urbanism as a Way of Life." *American Journal of Sociology* 44 (1938): 1–24.

Rural Demography

The study of the changing population and composition of rural areas. The key components of population change typically investigated are births (fertility), deaths (mortality), and migration. Analyses of population composition, however, are less focused and encompass a broad array of social and economic indicators (Shryock and Siegel 1976). This discussion of rural demography begins with the debate over the term "rural." Attention is directed first at differing interpretations of the term and then toward various contributions to their refinement. A brief history of population change in rural America follows. The remainder of the entry focuses on three key components of population change: migration, fertility, and mortality.

What Is "Rural"?

In the United States, the term "rural" frequently has several meanings (Fuguitt et al. 1989). The formal definition, as coined by the fact finders at the U.S. Bureau of the Census, views rurality from the perspective of city size. In brief, the United States is divided into rural and urban areas. From 1910 to 1950, "rural" described any residential area outside of an incorporated place of at least 2,500 people. However, as housing developments began to spread outside city limits in a process that is now called suburbanization, the concept of rurality took on a slightly different meaning. It was redefined to refer to places (including unincorporated areas) with a population of 2,500 or fewer and to urbanized areas (places with a population density of more than 1,000 persons per square mile). This city-based definition reflects the importance of cities in the residential growth and expansion of America. For example, the census of 1790 reported that 95 percent of Americans lived in rural areas. Only 24 urban places, which accounted for 201,655 people, were recorded in that census. In contrast, there were 8,510 urban places counted in the 1990 census, representing 187,053,487 persons, or over 75 percent of U.S. residents. The pattern of movement in America is clear.

Another word that frequently is used interchangeably with "rural" is "nonmetropolitan." This concept and its counterpart, "metropolitan," were introduced to more accurately encompass suburbanization. The definition periodically changes to capture urban sprawl. The major distinction, however, is that the definition is county-based (except in New England, where it is town-based). At present, "nonmetropolitan" means located in a county that does not contain either a place with a minimum population of 50,000 or a U.S. Census Bureau–defined urbanized area that has a total population of at least 100,000 (75,000 in New England). This county-based definition creates some confusion. For example, one can live in an urban city and still be defined as nonmetropolitan. Likewise, a farmer living in the countryside can be defined as metropolitan. Nonetheless, this definition is useful because it is not restricted to city boundaries. Modern commuting changed the pattern of living in rural areas, and this definition allows for a more accurate classification of residents. Unfortunately, because the definition of nonmetropolitan changed over time, longitudinal comparisons are difficult.

Analysts have continued to refine the term "rural." Three notable contributions in recent years came from Calvin Beale of the Economic Research Service of the U.S. Department of Agriculture (ERS-USDA), Charles Cleland at the University of Tennessee at Knoxville, and Lloyd Bender and colleagues at the ERS-USDA.

Beale (1975) expanded the dichotomous definition of metropolitan/nonmetropolitan to include nine categories, in order to explore more effectively the influence of urban areas on residential movement. Metropolitan counties were subdivided into three categories based on size. Nonmetropolitan counties were subdivided in two ways. First, they were classified as adjacent or nonadjacent to a metropolitan area. Second, within the adjacency classification, they were subdivided by size of largest city. This modification, known as the Beale Codes or the Rural-Urban Continuum Codes, shows the strong pull of large urban places. In 1990, half of the nonmetropolitan residents in the United States lived in counties adjacent to metropolitan centers. Furthermore, nearly half of those living in nonadjacent counties lived in a county with a city of at least 10,000 people.

Charles Cleland from the University of Tennessee at Knoxville further refined the definition of rurality by adding a new dimension, connectedness (Cleland 1994). The term attempted to capture the degree of isolation or limited access that rural areas have to other areas. A connectedness index was constructed to rank counties on a scale from 0 to 20. Cleland labeled this a rurality index. Indicators that comprise the scale encompass not only measures of physical isolation, such as low density, but also economic factors that act as barriers to accessing the larger society.

A third recent contribution to the term "rural" came from Lloyd Bender and his colleagues at ERS-USDA. They categorized rural counties by their major economic base, using a system that commonly called the ERS Typology or Dependency Codes. Seven distinct types of rural counties were identified, including counties that depend heavily on farming, manufacturing, and mining; counties specializing in government functions; persistently poor counties; federal land counties; and retirement settlements (Bender et al. 1985). These codes were more recently expanded and revised (Cook and Mizer 1994) to incorporate categories with special relevance for rural policy, such as counties that are dependent on commuting (at least 90 percent of the county's workers commuted to jobs in other counties) or government transfer payments (such as Social Security, unemployment insurance, Medicare, Medicaid, food stamps, government pensions, and welfare benefits).

Rural Population Change

The population of rural America has declined steadily since the turn of the century. Technological advancements, especially in farming, were a major reason for the exodus. Larger equipment, new seed varieties, and advances in chemicals, for example, expanded the production capabilities of farmers. Agricultural output per hour of farm work rose roughly 1,300 percent between 1940 and 1990 (Beale 1993). Productivity more than doubled per acre, whereas the number of acres of harvested cropland remained fairly constant. As a result of economies of scale, farm labor dropped dramatically. In the past four decades alone, farm employment declined from 8 million to slightly more than 3 million. Currently, farmers account for less than 8 percent of the rural workforce. Their proportion was nearly twice that in 1970. This translates into large rural population losses. For example, in 1940, the U.S. farm population topped 30 million, or one in four residents. At present, fewer than 6 million people live on farms, accounting for less than 2 percent of the total population. Neighboring rural towns have witnessed a similar population free fall. Residential losses in rural communities between 1940 and 1970 exceeded 50 percent due largely to lack of employment opportunities. Even greater losses occurred in the 1980s. In the farm-dependent counties of the Great Plains, small-town decline was over 80 percent between 1980 and 1990 (Beale 1993).

The diversity of rural America is reflected in very different population changes. Whereas farm-dependent counties continue to lose population, many other rural areas are enjoying significant population gains. The decade of the 1970s, known as the turnaround, found nonmetropolitan counties growing at a faster rate than metropolitan counties. Although this unique growth period was short-lived, many nonmetropolitan counties continue to expand. This is largely due to the movement of industries to rural areas, combined with a growing number of retirement settlements and extended commuting patterns.

Migration

Migration is the major reason for shifts in residential patterns. When people move, the place they move from loses population, while the place they go to gains population. In contrast, births and deaths, the other two main components of population change, affect the population size only of the place of residence. The United States has become a very mobile society. Over 42 million Americans moved between March 1992 and March 1993, which is about 17 percent of the total population. Recent estimates indicate that the average American will move nearly 12 times in his or her lifetime (Hansen 1994). However, the migration experience is very selective. Nearly one-third of all movers in 1993 were in their 20s; and 35.8 percent of all those between the ages of 20 and 24 moved in 1993, largely for reasons of employment or educational opportunities.

Net migration is determined by subtracting natural increase (births minus deaths) from the difference in the base population between two time periods. In general, nonmetropolitan areas have been net exporters of population. There have been notable exceptions, especially the decade of the 1970s. This period of rural revival was marked by widespread movement of people from large cities to rural areas, including those most remote from metropolitan counties. Nonmetropolitan counties grew at twice the rate of metropolitan areas, expanding by 3 million from net migration alone. The influx of metropolitan

movers accounted for nearly half the population growth of nonmetropolitan counties between 1970 and 1980. Numerous reasons have been cited for this unique change in the historical pattern including quality-of-life factors, decentralization of manufacturing, modernization of rural communities, retirement and recreational movement, and a general increase in rural employment (Fuguitt, Brown, and Beale 1989). However, the decade of the 1980s quickly reversed the short-lived trend. Between 1980 and 1990, net migration losses in nonmetropolitan counties topped half a million. But the latest *Current Population Survey* indicates that between 1992 and 1993, nonmetropolitan areas had net in-migration (Hansen 1994). Central cities lost an estimated 2.5 million people, while nonmetropolitan areas gained 317,000, and the remainder moved to the suburbs. This may signal another important shift in residential patterns that deserves close scrutiny.

Fertility

Women in rural areas historically have had higher rates of fertility. An analysis of the census of 1800 showed the ratio of children to women of childbearing age was more than 50 percent higher in rural areas than in urban ones (Grabill et al. 1958). The gap between urban and rural childbearing, however, has declined dramatically over time. The cumulative fertility of women 35 to 44 years old in 1980 was only 11 percent higher among rural women compared to urban women. In 1992, the rate of births per 1,000 nonmetropolitan women was 1,590, compared to 1,459 for metropolitan women. However, the average number of births that 1,000 nonmetropolitan women could expect over their lifetime was lower than it was for metropolitan women, at 2,231 to 2,253, respectively (Bachu 1993). Although differences exist in childbearing among rural women in nonmetropolitan areas versus those in metropolitan areas, the reversal in the long-term trend is notable.

The out-migration of young adults from nonmetropolitan areas has created a dramatic decline in births in those areas. As more young adults in their prime childbearing ages leave rural areas, fewer people are left to have children. The large out-migration of those in their late teens and early twenties between 1980 and 1990 reduced the number of children born in rural areas by nearly 500,000.

The composition of rural families also has changed. In 1990, the number of nonmetropolitan children living in homes with a single parent reached nearly 4 million, an increase of 1 million just between 1970 and 1990 (Ghelfi 1993). Significant regional differences exist in family composition in nonmetropolitan areas. For example, the South historically has had lower proportions of two-parent families. In 1990, over 30 percent of children in nonmetropolitan areas lived outside a two-parent home. In contrast, less than 20 percent of the children in nonmetropolitan areas of the Midwest did not live with both parents. Racial differences also are found in the composition of nonmetropolitan families. For example, in nonmetropolitan areas only 17 percent of White families with children are single-parent homes. In contrast, nearly half of Black families and one in four Hispanic families with children in nonmetropolitan areas are single-parent households.

Mortality

One of the most worrisome phenomena in America's rural areas today is natural decrease. Natural decrease occurs when deaths outnumber births. Historically, natural decrease seldom occurred in the United States. However, since the baby bust of the late 1960s, a growing number of counties have experienced natural decrease. By 1970, early 20 percent of all U.S. counties had experienced at least one year of natural decrease (Johnson and Beale 1992). Less than 10 years later, that proportion had jumped to 32 percent.

Natural decrease is predominantly a nonmetropolitan phenomenon. Over 95 percent of the counties experiencing natural decrease are nonmetropolitan. Many of the most rural counties are plagued by persistent decline. For example, nearly 46 percent of the nonmetropolitan counties that experienced natural decrease in the late 1960s had at least 10 years of natural decrease by 1990.

The major cause of natural decrease is protracted out-migration by young adults, which creates an imbalance between young and old. Even during the turnaround decade of the 1970s, nearly 300,000 young adults moved away from nonmetropolitan counties, creating a sharp decline in births in such counties. (For example, births declined by more than 12 percent during the 1980s in natural decline counties, compared to a 6 percent increase in births for the nation as a whole.) As the out-migration of those in their prime childbearing years reduces the likelihood of new births, so the corresponding increase in the proportion of elderly heightens the likelihood of increased deaths. The result is an ongoing natural decline in the rural population.

—*Richard Rathge*

See also

Adolescents; Elders; Health and Disease Epidemiology; Marriage; Migration; Rural, Definition of; Rural Women; Urbanization.

References

Bachu, Amara. "Fertility of American Women." *Current Population Reports*, P20-470 (June). Washington, DC: U.S. Bureau of the Census, U.S. Government Printing Office, 1992.

Beale, Calvin L. *The Revival of Population Growth in Nonmetropolitan America*. ERS-605. Washington, DC: U.S. Department of Agriculture, Economic Research Service, 1975.

———. "Salient Features of the Demography of American Agriculture." Pp. 108–127 in *The Demography of Rural Life: Current Knowledge and Future Directions for Research*. Edited by David L. Brown, Donald R. Field, and James J. Zuiches. University Park, PA: Northeast Regional Center for Rural Development, 1993.

Bender, Lloyd D., Bernal L. Green, Thomas F. Hady, John A. Kuehn, Marlys K. Nelson, Leon B. Perkinson, and Peggy J. Ross. *The Diverse Social and Economic Structure of Nonmetropolitan America*. USDA-ERS Rural Development Research Report No. 49. Washington, DC: U.S. Government Printing Office, 1985.

Cleland, Charles L. "Measuring Rurality." Paper presented at the annual meeting of the Southern Demographic Association, Atlanta, GA, October 1994.

Cook, Peggy J., and Karen L. Mizer. *The Revised ERS County Typology: An Overview*. USDA-ERS Rural Development Research Report No. 89. Washington, DC: U.S. Government Printing Office, 1994.

Fuguitt, Glenn V., David L. Brown, and Calvin L. Beale. *Rural and Small Town America*. New York: Russell Sage Foundation, 1989.

Ghelfi, Linda M., ed. *Rural Conditions and Trends: Special Census Issue* 4, no. 3. Washington, DC: U.S. Department of Agriculture, Economic Research Service, 1993.

Grabill, Wilson H., Clyde V. Kiser, and Pascal K. Whelpton. *The Fertility of American Women*. New York: Wiley, 1958.

Hansen, Kristin A. "Geographical Mobility: March 1992 to March 1993." *Current Population Reports*, P20-481. Washington, DC: U.S. Bureau of the Census, 1994.

Shryock, Henry S., and Jacob S. Siegel. *The Methods and Materials of Demography*. New York: Academic Press, 1976.

Rural Free Delivery

The daily delivery of mail to rural farm residents. This entry addresses the establishment of city free delivery of mail, the farmers' mail system before rural free delivery (RFD), experimental RFD, and RFD expanded and made permanent. It describes RFD under the postal corporation, the effect of RFD on rural America, the development of good roads on RFD, and the beginnings of rural parcel post. The entry concludes with a discussion of efforts to change RFD, and of RFD as an obstacle to privatizing the U.S. Postal Service.

Beginnings

Congress authorized the postmaster general to establish free delivery of mail in cities in 1864. The next year, it restricted this delivery to cities of 50,000 or more inhabitants; but gradually over the following years, it expanded service to reach towns of 10,000 (in 1887). Yet during that time, the postal system in rural America remained much as it had been before the Civil War.

Until the establishment of RFD, farmers received their mail from more than 70,000 small fourth-class post offices, to which Star Route mail carriers, under contract to the post office, brought the mail from rail or stagecoach centers, usually no more often than two or three times per week. Although this system provided farmers with an opportunity to visit neighbors, it often deprived them of postal services that their post offices were too small to offer. Moreover, it made subscription to a daily newspaper impractical. In 1896, however, the Post Office Department inaugurated an RFD service to alleviate rural isolation.

RFD of mail was not easily established. John Wanamaker, President Benjamin Harrison's energetic postmaster general, proposed creating an RFD service for farmers in 1891, but his term of office expired before his proposal could be adopted and implemented. Nevertheless, members of the Grange and Farmers' Alliance clubs, enthused by the publicity that Wanamaker had generated for the proposal, seized on the idea. Arguing that the government's mail service discriminated against them in favor of the cities, they swamped Congress in 1892 with petitions demanding an RFD of mail service.

Confronted by their demands, Congress appropriated $10,000 for an RFD experiment. Tom Watson, a Populist congressman from Georgia, was responsible for this small appropriation and ever after claimed to be the "father of the RFD."

In 1893, however, Grover Cleveland, the first Democratic president between the Civil War and 1900, returned to office, and appointed William Bissell, his friend from Buffalo, as postmaster general. Conservative and obdurate, Bissell refused to begin an experiment that he believed would bankrupt the government. But Congress, unwilling to accept this decision, continued to appropriate money for the experiment until 1896, when William L. Wilson, a former congressman from West Virginia, replaced Bissell as postmaster general and promised to begin the RFD experiment. On October 1, 1896, at Charles Town, Uvilla, and Halltown, in Wilson's home state, he established the first of what by spring 1897 would become 82 experimental mail routes in 28 states and the territory of Arizona.

The experiment had scarcely begun before the Republicans, less cautious about expanding the power of

Richard Audette, postmaster in Viking, Minnesota, in one of the many small post offices that provide mail service to rural dwellers.

the national government than the Democrats had been, returned to control both houses of Congress and the presidency in 1897. The fledgling RFD experiment fell into the hands of two politicians: Perry Heath, President McKinley's first assistant postmaster general, and August Machen, superintendent of free delivery. Driven as much by possible political advantage, perhaps, as by concern for the farmers, they saved RFD from an early death by cleverly inviting farmers to petition their congressman for a rural mail route if they wished to have their mail delivered to their farms. The farmers responded to this invitation with thousands of petitions, which led to the establishment of hundreds of rural mail routes and virtually forced Congress to make the experiment a permanent practice, which it did in 1902.

Political pressure, combined with a growing emphasis on saving farms and farmers, forced the rapid expansion of the service, until there were 45,318 rural mail routes (1926). After this, because of improved country roads and the mail carriers' substitution of the automobile for the horse and buggy, rural mail routes were gradually lengthened and reduced in number to 31,346 in 1970, the year Congress converted the post office to a government corporation.

Under the Postal Corporation

Virtually compelled to be self-sustaining by 1984, the new postal service's management sought to reduce expenses by replacing many small-town and village post offices with "heavy duty" rural mail routes on which carriers served large clusters of mailboxes. The reduction of post offices, however, necessitated an increase in the number of rural mail routes and mail carriers. In September 1995, there were 54,442 rural mail routes, 46,163 rural mail carriers, and 53,634 replacement carriers.

The national government developed few programs for farmers that had a more powerful effect than that of the free delivery of mail. It raised land values, eroded farm isolation, erased the discrimination between the urban and rural mail services, and became a daily reminder to farm families that the national government had not forgotten them. It gave farmers the daily market quotations and swelled the profits of publishers of daily newspapers, as thousands of farmers subscribed to their papers. True, RFD eliminated many little post offices that were the hubs of small communities, but it also made two inestimable contributions to rural life: good roads and a bona fide parcel post.

Because postal regulations required farmers to keep their roads passable if they wished to have their mail delivered, farmers began to improve their roads in the early 1900s as they never had before and became a vital part of the good roads movement of the era. Rural delivery also played a key role in the enactment of the Federal Highway Act of 1916. Because each road over which a rural route ran was obviously a post road, which Congress had the right to establish, members of Congress found in rural delivery the constitutional authority to give matching funds to the states to build roads over which the mail was carried or might be carried.

When rural delivery began, only packages weighing no more than four pounds were mailable. But when rural mail carriers began to pass farms with the mail each day, they themselves began to carry packages to farmers outside the mails for a small fee. When the Post Office Department stopped this service, parcel post enthusiasts argued for a parcel post that would permit the sending of large packages through the mails. Small-town merchants, who feared that farmers would use the parcel post to purchase their goods from mail-order stores, and the express companies wary of this postal competition, fought bitterly against an enlarged parcel post. But Congress, unable to ignore the practical use of RFD, created the present parcel post system in 1912, which began on 1 January 1913.

An Obstacle to Privatizing the Post Office

Rural free delivery was a costly service, but efforts to lower costs by contracting routes out to the lowest bidders failed, largely because Congress refused to give one kind of postal service to cities and another to farmers. Even the new postal service was unable to change the basic structure of rural delivery, although it substituted contract post offices for post offices that formerly had postmasters, and established highway contract routes in some areas, similar to the old Star Routes.

RFD recently has been the one greatest obstacle to privatizing the post office. Private contractors may be able to deliver the mail in cities more cheaply than the governmental postal service can and still make a profit. But this would be more difficult in rural America, where the mail service has never paid its way.

—*Wayne E. Fuller*

See also
Government; History, Rural; Infrastructure; Media; Public Services; Quality of Life; Town-Country Relations.
References
Aaberg, Gwendolyn M. *The RFD: Golden Jubilee, 1896–1946.* Washington, DC: n.p., 1946.
Fuller, Wayne E. *R.F.D.: The Changing Face of Rural America.* Bloomington: Indiana University Press, 1964.
Greathouse, Charles A. "Free Delivery of Mails." In *U.S. Department of Agriculture Yearbook.* Washington, DC: Government Printing Office (GPO), 1900.
May, Earl. "The Good Roads Train." *World's Work* 2 (July 1901): 956–960.
———. "Parcel Post at Last." *The Outlook* 102 (December 1912): 872–873.
Scheele, Carl. *A Short History of the Mail Service.* Washington, DC: Smithsonian Press, 1970.
Thrasher, Max Bennett. "Thirty Miles with a Rural Mail Carrier." *Independent* 55 (February 5, 1903): 311–317.

Rural Sociology

The study of social organization and social processes characteristic of communities and regions where population sizes and densities are relatively low. This entry begins with the history of rural sociology. Current research emphases, the organization of academic departments, and professional associations of rural sociologists are also discussed.

Introduction

While rural sociologists emphasize the study of social structures and processes of rural societies, they also recognize the fact that these structures and processes do not exist in isolation one from another or in a social vacuum. "Rural" is, in part, a reflection of the larger processes of the regional differentiation and allocation of populations, economic activities, and other human activities within a society as a whole, or increasingly within global economy and society. Rural social structures and well-being are greatly influenced by the formation and implementation of public policies in regional, national, and global political systems.

Rural sociology is predominantly an academic profession, with the bulk of its members being university faculty or researchers in government or private organizations. Rural sociologists serve rural areas and people through research and outreach in rural population, rural community, rural social stratification, natural resources and environment, sociology of agriculture, and sociology of agricultural science and technology. Rural sociologists are actively involved in international development and related work.

History

While rural sociology for most of its history has been closely associated with the land-grant university system, America's pioneering rural sociologists largely worked outside of that system. Notable examples of early rural sociological research included the work of W. E. B. DuBois of the U.S. Department of Labor on the well-being of Black sharecroppers in the Cotton Belt in the late 1890s, and that of F. H. Giddings of Columbia University during the first decade of the twentieth century, on agricultural communities in the Northeast.

There were two major impetuses to the establishment of rural sociology in the land-grant system. The first was the Country Life Commission, which was appointed in 1908 by President Theodore Roosevelt and chaired by Liberty Hyde Bailey of Cornell University. The commission's *Report,* published in 1909, was based in part on studies of 12 rural communities, which taken together constituted the first nationwide survey of the rural United States. The *Report* stressed that many of the problems of rural America were socioeconomic (for example, speculative land-holding, or single-crop plantation agriculture in the South), and recommended that the land-grant system invest in social science expertise to better understand and provide solutions to these problems.

The second and ultimately the most significant impetus to the establishment of rural sociology programs was the Purnell Act of 1925. The land-grant universities and the state agricultural experiment stations—institutions with which the majority of rural sociology programs have been affiliated—had been established through the Hatch Act of 1862 and the Hatch Act of 1887, respectively. Until the 1920s, however, federal agricultural research funding was very limited and did not involve social science. The Purnell Act of 1925 significantly expanded the federal commitment to experiment station research and for the first time allocated federal funds to agricultural economics, rural sociology, and home economics research. Within about 15 years after the Purnell Act was passed, most of the land-grant rural sociology programs that exist today were founded.

While the Purnell Act ultimately proved to be the principal stimulus to university-based rural sociology programs, government-sponsored rural sociological research, particularly that at the USDA, was the single most important component of the profession's work until the late 1930s. Spearheaded by the efforts of prominent rural sociologists such as Charles Galpin and Carl Taylor, rural sociology became institutionalized in federal agencies such as the Division of Farm Population and Rural Life of the USDA's Bureau of Agricultural Economics (BAE). Rural sociologists working at the USDA and elsewhere in government pioneered many research methods, such as rural community surveys, that later became standard approaches in the profession. Government-sponsored rural sociological research came to be particularly important in generating national-level data on social trends and conditions in rural America.

Rural sociology in its early years had a strong social reform ethic, and rural sociologists tended to be supporters of the New Deal. Rural sociologists therefore played a pivotal role in conducting research in the Rural Population Division of the USDA that later shaped the design and administration of New Deal programs. Rural sociologists also played prominent roles in New Deal agencies such as the Farm Security and the Resettlement Administrations. Rural sociology's role in government, however, would ultimately be substantially diminished. Conservative opposition to the New Deal led to the dismantlement of many New Deal agencies and the abolition of the BAE in the 1940s.

During the 1970s and 1980s there was a renaissance of the role of rural sociology in government, particularly within the Economic Research Service of USDA. USDA rural sociologists played a particularly important role during these decades in analyzing and disseminating aggregate data on rural social trends and issues.

Contemporary Rural Sociological Research

Modern rural sociology has seven major branches: rural population, rural community, rural social stratification, natural resources and environment, sociology of agriculture, sociology of agricultural science and technology, and sociology of international development. Each area has active theoretical and empirical research wings as well as applied research and practice wings (such as community development, technology assessment, social impact assessment, and rural poverty alleviation).

From the very inception of rural sociology, sociological analysis of rural population and rural community dynamics through census and social survey data has been central to the field. DuBois's early work on Black farming, for example, was based largely on population census data. The work of the Division of Farm Population and Rural Life of the BAE was pivotal in providing basic descriptive data about the rural population and in establishing rural population studies as one of the pillars of the field. Today virtually every major rural sociology program has one or more experts in both rural demography and rural community sociology.

Since the time of ancient societies and empires, there has been a tendency for rural people to suffer disproportionately from poverty, disadvantage, and political subordination. In modern industrial societies, rural people in aggregate tend to be poorer than urban or metropolitan people. For example, in the United States, non-metropolitan household average annual income is only slightly more than 70 percent of that in metropolitan counties (Rural Sociological Society Task Force on Persistent Rural Poverty 1993). The fact that rural people are particularly likely to experience poverty and inequality has thus made analyses of rural social stratification and inequality an important dimension of rural sociology. Studies of regional and labor market inequalities, rural gender inequality, and rural racial inequalities have been among the most important recent focal points of rural stratification research. These analyses have been extended to the global level and to metropolitan and corporate phenomena such as trade liberalization agreements and the globalization of agriculture and finance.

There has been a long, significant tradition of rural sociological scholarship on the relations among people, communities, and natural resources (Field and Burch, 1988). Rural sociologists were thus well positioned to play a prominent role in the emergence of environmental sociology during the 1970s and 1980s. Rural sociology continues to provide particularly strong leadership in applied areas of environmental sociology, such as social impact assessment.

The sociology of agriculture and the sociology of agricultural science and technology are both new labels for subjects that have been studied by rural sociologists for some time. Early twentieth-century rural sociology focused on the social structures of farming and rural communities. During the 1930s and 1940s, there was considerable rural sociological research on the implications of mechanization for farming people and rural communities, and in the 1950s and 1960s the adoption and diffusion of agricultural innovations was the single most important area of rural sociological research. These two areas have been revitalized over the past two decades. In addition to studying the social forces that affect family farming and farm labor utilization, the sociology of agriculture now places major emphasis on the globalization of agro-industrial systems. The sociology of agricultural science studies the social and economic influences on new technologies, such as biotechnology, as well as the social significance of indigenous or local agricultural knowledge.

Many of the most prominent American rural sociologists of the post–World War II period devoted major segments of their careers to encouraging the diffusion of rural sociology across the globe, particularly in the developing world. The postwar period was an emerging era of developmentalism (that is, an era of faith in the efficacy of planned social change and development in the decolonizing world). Rural sociologists made significant contributions to international development, but they were also among the early critics of the Green Revolution. Documentation of the shortcomings of the Green Revolution, particularly its tendency to exacerbate rural inequalities, proved highly influential in spurring the formation of new rural sociological specialties in the sociology of agriculture and sociology of agricultural science and technology.

Academic Departments

About 40 states have a university rural sociology program of some type, although about a dozen of these programs are very small, essentially confined to a single staff member. Most universities with rural sociology programs are land-grant universities, although there are several public and private non–land-grant universities that teach courses and train students in the profession. There are several different modes of organization of rural sociology programs. The most common structure, which prevails at about two dozen universities, is for rural sociologists to be members of a larger department of sociology or sociology/anthropology. In addition, there are six departments of rural sociology (or sociology and rural sociology), and an additional six departments of agricultural economics and rural sociology. Several additional programs consist of a single rural sociologist in a department of agricultural economics.

Training, Extension, and Public Service

Rural sociology traditionally has not been a significant undergraduate university major. Some university undergraduates, particularly in colleges of agriculture, receive exposure to rural sociology through a lower-division course. But rural sociology, much like sociology, is an area in which one must complete a Ph.D. to be considered a practicing professional. About 20 universities offer graduate degrees, usually both master's and Ph.D. degrees, in rural sociology.

Many land-grant rural sociologists have appointments, either part-time or full-time, in cooperative extension. Most extension rural sociologists are in community or rural development or rural population studies, although a growing number are specialists in the sociology of agriculture. Rural sociology tends to place a major emphasis on applied research and service, and thus rural sociologists, regardless of whether they have formal extension appointments, tend to give high priority to public service and policy involvement.

Rural Sociological Society (RSS) and International Rural Sociology Association (IRSA)

During the first two decades of American rural sociology, rural sociologists looked mainly to the American Sociological Society (later renamed the American Sociological Association) as their principal professional association. By the mid-1930s, however, rural sociologists felt increasingly uncomfortable within the American Sociological Society, as rural sociological research continued to be very applied and that of other sociologists became more theoretical. In 1936, the journal *Rural Sociology* was founded. *Rural Sociology* today remains the flagship journal of the profession in North America. In 1937, rural sociologists broke with the American Sociological Society and founded the Rural Sociological Society (RSS). The RSS today has about 1,000 members, is the publisher of Rural Sociology, and holds an annual meeting. The bulk of its members are either in academic positions or engaged in graduate studies. About 125 members are foreign citizens.

The International Rural Sociology Association (IRSA) was founded in 1966, mainly at the initiative of rural sociologists in the United States and Europe. IRSA is a federation of regional rural sociological societies, including the RSS and groups from Latin America, Africa, Asia, and Europe. IRSA holds a world congress every four years.

—*Frederick H. Buttel*

See also

Careers in Agriculture; Cooperative State Research, Education, and Extension Service; History, Rural; Land-Grant Institutions, 1862 and 1890.

Recommended Readings:

Busch, Lawrence, William B. Lacy, Jeffrey Burkhardt, and Laura R. Lacy. *Plants, Power, and Profit.* Oxford: Basil Blackwell, 1991.

Buttel, Frederick H., Olaf F. Larson, and Gilbert W. Gillespie, Jr. *The Sociology of Agriculture.* Westport, CT: Greenwood Press, 1990.

Buttel, Frederick H., and Howard Newby, eds. *The Rural Sociology of the Advanced Societies.* Montclair, NJ: Allanheld, Osmun and Co., 1980.

Field, Donald R., and William R. Burch, Jr. *Rural Sociology and the Environment.* Westport, CT: Greenwood Press, 1988.

Garkovich, Lorraine. *Population and Community in Rural America.* Westport, CT: Greenwood Press, 1989.

McMichael, Philip, ed. *The Global Restructuring of Agro-Food Systems.* Ithaca, NY: Cornell University Press, 1994.

Olsen, Wallace C., Margot A. Bellamy, and Bernard F. Stanton. *Agricultural Economics and Rural Sociology: The Contemporary Core Literature.* Ithaca, NY: Cornell University Press, 1991.

Rogers, Everett M., Rabel J. Burdge, Peter F. Korsching, and Joseph F. Donnermeyer. *Social Change in Rural Societies: An Introduction to Rural Sociology.* 3d ed. Englewood Cliffs, NJ: Prentice-Hall, 1988.

Rural Sociological Society Task Force on Persistent Rural Poverty. *Persistent Poverty in Rural America.* Boulder, CO: Westview Press, 1993.

Summers, Gene F. "Rural Sociology." In *Encyclopedia of Sociology.* Edited by E. F. Borgatta and M. L. Borgatta. New York: Macmillan, 1992.

Zuiches, James J. "Reinventing Rural Sociology." *Rural Sociology* 59, no. 2 (1994): 197–215.

Rural Women

Women who live in the open countryside, on farms and in nonfarm residences, and in villages and towns in nonmetropolitan counties. This entry presents a snapshot of the diversity of rural women. It pays disproportionate attention to women and farming because women's traditionally vital role in agriculture and rural community life had been underreported until the past few decades, when it received attention from scholars and farm women themselves. In contrast, more limited attention is given to the lives of rural nonfarm women, the majority of women in nonmetropolitan areas. One section explores women in rural labor markets and rural women in poverty.

Throughout human history, women have been associated with food production. In the horticultural societies of peoples indigenous to the United States, women were often principal food producers. Throughout U.S. history, women owned agricultural land and often farmed it. But at the end of the twentieth century, a small and steadily decreasing number of rural women (and rural men) in the United States are engaged in farming. These women are joined along country lanes and interstate highways by women whose work ranges from management responsibilities at corporate offices to night shifts caring for residents at local retirement centers; from irregular hours answering phones at communication centers of catalog companies to weekends caring for small retail businesses owned by neighbors. It includes women who, as single parents, work to support their children while studying at local colleges, and those who depend solely on public assistance. Accompanying the increased variations in the work of rural women are differences in educational and income levels, access to health care, and level and type of community participation.

Women and Farming

The transition in rural America from a predominantly farming population to a rural, nonfarm population is an uneven process resulting from capitalist relations in agriculture and spatial decentralization of industrial capital. Traditionally, a web of community ties connected farms and families together in rural neighborhoods. These patriarchal family farms depended on unpaid family labor and community-exchanged labor of women and men. Women played a vital role in rural survival through community building, home production, and making do, and in this manner not only increased their own share of farm resources but also added to communal resources available to farming men (Neth 1995).

However, in the twentieth century mechanization and agricultural policy led to farm consolidation, rural depopulation, and displacement of farm labor. Consumption replaced home production, and the need for cash increased. Modern agriculture fostered a gendered set of economic and social concerns. The business of farming was accentuated as efficiency of production took center stage, and family and community needs traditionally associated with women were progressively devalued over time. (Neth reports that at first, families were able to blend modern and traditional patterns.)

Capital penetration in farm input and product markets created business cycles that concentrated and differentiated farm structure (Buttel, Larson, and Gillespie 1990). In the past half-century, the number of farms declined from 6 million to 2 million, while the farm population decreased from 30 million to just under 4 million. At the beginning of the 1990s, farming operations included three major categories: traditional, medium-sized family farms, currently declining in numbers; a

Wava Haney—a rural woman at work, from farm wife to professor at a state university.

growing number of large-scale, industrialized farms operated by waged labor; and small-scale, part-time hobby or retirement farms, the numbers of which also are increasing.

Farm Women and Women on Farms

Most farm families still include a husband and a wife; the 1994 census data revealed that between 94 and 97 percent of farm-owning families were married couples. Whereas farm wives employed off the farm were less likely to do farm work, few of the farm women in a 1980 national sample (Rosenfeld 1985) indicated they did no farm work; most did a range of farm tasks. Many wives jointly owned the farm with their husbands and saw themselves as partners in its daily management. About one-half of the women considered themselves a major operator of the farm; nearly two-thirds said they were capable of operating the farm without their husbands.

Women's farm work and decision making was heavily dependent on the need for their labor, which varied by farm size, commodity, and off-farm employment of husbands. Women were more active in farm work and production decisions on livestock farms than they were on farms specialized in crops. On middle-income livestock farms of the upper Midwest, women were involved in management and record keeping. Joint decision making apparently was common for farm resource allocations. Recently, programs in livestock management for women sponsored by commodity groups and cooperative extensions encouraged their involvement in day-to-day production decisions.

Women's farm work on crop farms and on large farms with hired labor and management was more specialized in ancillary services like errand running. In contrast, women on specialty or small, limited-resource farms more frequently assumed major responsibility for field work and farm management, especially when men were working away from the farm. Some scholars (Feldman and Welsh 1995) believe that women's role in decision making on small farms may explain why some owners of small farms choose to adopt alternative agricultural technologies and techniques, but definitive research has yet to be done.

Independent Farmers. Some women have sole legal control over their land and farms. In 1982, just over 5 percent of the nation's farms were solely or principally operated by women. These independent women farmers tended to be older when they inherited small farms, and more were located in the South than in any other region. Independent farm women in the 1980 national sample reported the lowest incomes from farming. Despite their low farm incomes and a need for many of them to work off the farm to supplement those incomes, unmarried independent farm women reported that they were more satisfied with farming than other farm women. The largest group of women who owned farmland in 1987 were landlords. Women landlords are not as active as men in management decisions on the land they lease, but younger female landowners and those who also farm take a much more active role in production decisions of their tenants (Rogers and Vandeman 1993).

Agricultural Laborers. As classic family farming is replaced, the switch to industrialized agriculture has been selective by commodity, geography of the region, and the gender and type of labor supply (Padavic 1993). Corporatization of agriculture has had variable impacts on women's participation in the agricultural wage-labor force. The mechanization of several commodity systems decreased the demand for low-paid, low-skilled labor in much of the South in the 1970s. Women employed as farm laborers declined sharply as markets for labor-intensive crops employing women collapsed or as the work of women was mechanized. Many of these women shifted to jobs in the newly arriving light manufacturing industries or the service sector. In the West, a supply of undocumented immigrant labor in a labor market offering few alternatives favored industrial production of vegetables and fruit often using sex-segregated wage labor. When growers needed to recoup capital investments through lower wages, they could hire women at less than half the wage of the male workers who had done the task before mechanization.

Rural Women and Nonfarm Employment

Structural changes in agriculture in the 1970s and 1980s were accompanied by greater nonfarm employment of farm women. By the early 1990s, the nonfarm labor force participation rates of farm women approached those of rural nonfarm and urban women. Nonfarm income exceeds farm income on a majority of American farms today; the income of these women is an important part of that nonfarm income.

Accompanying the loss of farms have been relative declines in traditional secondary sector activities. Public and private services that are heavily dependent on population and income levels have become the dominant rural industries in many rural communities. But the economic bases of rural labor markets differ, as do job opportunities and wage rates. Traditional rural industries like mining and lumbering, typically employing only men, prevail in some areas, while industrial capital has relocated to others and employs women as well. Industrial restructuring produced home-based subcontracting and outsourcing arrangements employing primarily women in economically depressed rural areas to do piecework at low wages and without benefits.

Like women in the cities, rural women often find themselves in traditional female occupations such as those of office assistant, bank teller, nurse, primary school teacher, retail sales clerk, medical and dental assistant, guidance counselor, and social worker. For both women and men, human capital investments like education and skill development have an important impact on work stability and income. But the return on the same investment is greater for men in rural labor markets; earnings are lower and work is less stable for women with the same educational and skill levels as men (Tickamyer and Bokemeier 1988). National data for 1968 through 1991 show that earnings inequality between metropolitan men and women who worked year-round, full-time was declining, but in nonmetropolitan areas it was greater and remained constant (Tolbert and Lyson 1992).

Although the ratio of rural women employed is about the same as that of urban women, rural women have had difficulty finding stable, well-paid jobs commensurate with their education and skill. Like urban women, an increasing number of rural women have established small businesses. But studies show that small business is another area where rural women are disadvantaged in earnings and job security. The gender gap in small business sales has prompted some researchers (Tigges and Green 1994) to argue that women may be financially better off in management than in self-employment. But management positions are less often an option in rural areas, unless one commutes or telecommutes.

Limited job opportunities, job instability, and low wages in rural labor markets can account for poverty among rural women. Rundown farmhouses in the countryside, rental apartments in small towns and villages, and rapidly growing trailer parks house pockets of the rural poor, including the growing number of women who are single, divorced, or in fluid and fragile family situations (Fitchen 1991). A greater percentage of the rural poor than urban poor are employed steadily, although often at minimum-wage service jobs that, even if full-time or more than full-time, do not provide incomes above the poverty line. For others, disabilities, poor health, alcoholism, low self-esteem, and the need to care for other family members make getting a job difficult. Displaced homemakers from the lower class, like their middle-aged, middle-class counterparts, have limited job histories and lack the skills and self-confidence needed to acquire a good job. Fitchen (1991) and others also report a pattern of redistribution of poverty from urban and rural areas to depressed rural areas largely because of inexpensive rental housing that became available after plant closings and the loss of farms prompted a middle-class exodus. Many women living in such areas depend on various types of public assistance.

Rural Women and Community

Rural women's unpaid activities contribute to production and social reproduction. Traditionally, it was women's work to care for household members too young and too old to meet their own needs, and for those who were ill. They also provided for the daily needs of able-bodied adult members of the household and directed the education of the children. Laws and customs forbade their participation in the formal political process, but through church and family activities they built the networks of mutuality and reciprocity that undergirded rural communities. Over time these networks were formalized in women's organizations that tended to the general welfare of the community and its members.

Farm women joined agrarian movements (such as the National Farmers' Alliance) and many political parties, skillfully popularizing the plight of farm families through their poems, songs, and stories. In early surveys and public discourse, they advanced the relationship between the welfare of the family and that of the farm. Some farm organizations like the National Farmers Union, the Grange, and the Non-Partisan League integrated men and women into one organization; women also were members of separate auxiliaries of the American Farm Bureau and many commodity organizations (Haney and Knowles 1988).

In the past two decades, farm women have founded their own organizations: American Agri-women, Women in Farm Economics (WIFE), and Women for the Survival of Agriculture. Their approaches, policy positions, and membership characteristics vary, but their primary focus has been to improve farm income and to bolster family-based agriculture (Haney and Miller 1991). The 1980 national survey showed that many farm women belonged to a general farm organization but were not as likely to be part of either commodity associations or agricultural cooperatives. More farm women than men belonged to community organizations and participated actively on committees and boards, although not in elected or appointed positions in policymaking bodies.

Today, rural women more frequently are elected leaders in their communities. Some chair county boards, serve as mayors of small towns, and preside over previously all-male service organizations and over school and hospital boards; some rural businesswomen head chambers of commerce and other local economic development groups. Much agricultural policymaking, however, remains the domain of men.

—*Wava Gillespie Haney*

See also

Careers in Agriculture; Domestic Violence; Elders; Employment; Family; Labor Force; Landownership; Rural Demography; Underemployment; Voluntarism.

References

Buttel, Frederick H., Olaf F. Larson, and Gilbert W. Gillespie, Jr. *The Sociology of Agriculture*. Westport, CT: Greenwood Press, 1990.

Feldman, Shelley, and Rick Welsh. "Feminist Knowledge Claims, Local Knowledge, and Gender Divisions of Agricultural Labor: Constructing a Successor Science." *Rural Sociology* 60 (1995): 23–43.

Fitchen, Janet M. *Endangered Spaces, Enduring Places: Change, Identity, and Survival in Rural America*. Boulder, CO: Westview Press, 1991.

Haney, Wava G., and Jane B. Knowles, eds. *Women and Farming: Changing Roles, Changing Structures*. Boulder, CO: Westview Press, 1988.

Haney, Wava G., and Lorna Clancy Miller. "U.S. Farm Women, Politics and Policy." *Journal of Rural Studies* 7 (1991): 115–121.

Neth, Mary. *Preserving the Family Farm: Women, Community, and the Foundations of Agribusiness in the Midwest, 1900–1940*. Baltimore: Johns Hopkins University Press, 1995.

Padavic, Irene. "Agricultural Restructuring and the Spatial Dynamics of U.S. Women's Employment in the 1970s." *Rural Sociology* 58 (1993): 210–232.

Rogers, Denise M., and Ann M. Vandeman. "Women as Farm Landlords: Does Gender Affect Environmental Decision-Making on Leased Land?" *Rural Sociology* 58 (1993): 560–568.

Rosenfeld, Rachel Ann. *Farm Women: Work, Farm, and Family in the United States*. Chapel Hill: University of North Carolina Press, 1985.

Tickamyer, Ann, and Janet Bokemeier. "Sex Differences in Labor-Market Experiences." *Rural Sociology* 53 (1988): 166–189.

Tigges, Leann M., and Gary P. Green. "Small Business Success Among Men- and Women-Owned Firms in Rural Areas." *Rural Sociology* 59 (1994): 289–310.

Tolbert, Charles M., and Thomas A. Lyson. "Earnings Inequality in the Nonmetropolitan United States: 1967–1990." *Rural Sociology* 57, no. 4 (1992): 494–511.

Sawmilling

The conversion of logs into lumber. Sawmilling is an important national industry supplying large amounts of wood to construct houses, furniture, and other products. Softwood and hardwood sawmills differ considerably in raw materials processed, end products, capitalization, and size. Competition among sawmill firms, coupled with timber price increases, led to rapid improvements in sawing technology and application of computer technology in the lumber manufacturing process. Important regional differences in ownership of timberlands by forest products companies have a huge effect on sawmills. Wood products are an important part of life, and wise management of timberlands will allow use of these products without reducing the wildlife or recreational value of the timberlands.

Industry Structure

Sawmilling is an industry that supports the economy of many rural areas. Most sawmills are located in rural areas close to the timber resource on which they depend. In many western and southern states, forestry and the production of forest products are leading industries in total dollar sales and employment. U.S. sawmills employed a total of 140,000 workers with sales of $21 billion in 1992. Nationally, about 35 billion board feet of softwood lumber and 10 billion board feet of hardwood lumber are produced annually.

The sawmilling industry is composed of a large number of firms and is characterized by a high level of interfirm competition. This competition resulted in a steady decline in the number of sawmills in the years following World War II. There were 16,859 sawmills and planing mills in the United States in 1958. These decreased in number to 9,000 by 1977, and to 6,196 by 1992. Sawmill size increased at the same time that sawmill numbers declined; the total U.S. annual production volume increased from about 35 billion board feet in 1958 to 45 billion board feet in 1992. Increased sawmill size resulted in the ability to use greater amounts of capital to more efficiently manufacture lumber from logs.

Terminology

The forest products industry traditionally segregated the wood it processes into the two broad categories of hardwood and softwood species. Unfortunately, these two terms are somewhat misleading to those outside of the industry. The term hardwood does not mean that the wood is physically harder than that of a softwood, although this is often the case. The term hardwood refers to wood obtained from broadleaf deciduous trees (angiosperms), such as oak, elm, ash, hickory, and aspen. Softwood refers to the wood of coniferous trees (gymnosperms) that usually have leaves in the shape of needles. Examples are pine, spruce, hemlock, Douglas fir, and true fir. Note that the hardwood, aspen, is considerably softer than hemlock, Douglas fir, and most pine species, and is equivalent in hardness to the spruce and fir species.

Also confusing to those first exposed to sawmilling is the practice of measuring lumber in units termed board feet. A board foot is defined as 1 square foot of wood, 1 inch thick.

Hardwood Sawmills

Hardwood sawmills tend to be relatively small firms, with most producing less than 15 million board feet of lumber annually. The lumber sawed at hardwood sawmills is

Detail of saws used in sawmilling.

marketed primarily to furniture and pallet manufacturers. With the increase in the volume of goods shipped on pallets, the demand for pallet lumber grew to more than 50 percent of total hardwood lumber production.

Hardwood lumber is graded into quality classes by appearance because historically a large percentage of hardwood lumber was destined for furniture production. Consumers traditionally placed a high value on clear, defect-free parts on the exposed surfaces of wood furniture. For this reason, the hardwood lumber appearance grades primarily measure the percentage of clear area available to produce clear, defect-free parts.

Softwood Sawmills

Softwood sawmills differ considerably from hardwood sawmills in processing methods and size. The softwood timber resource is usually more concentrated geographically and trees require considerably fewer years to reach maturity. This decreases the haul distance to sawmills for softwood sawlogs and results in larger sawmills with higher capitalization. Most softwood sawmills produce between 50 and 125 million board feet per year.

Most softwood sawmill lumber production is consumed by the large U.S. housing market. Depending on the state of the economy, about 1 million single-family dwellings, half a million multiple-family dwellings, and one-quarter million mobile homes are produced annually. Preservative-treated wood for outdoor structures is another large softwood market. Southern sawmills have nearly all of the treated wood market because the southern yellow pine that they process is more easily treated with preservatives compared to other species. Over 50 percent of softwood lumber produced by southern sawmills becomes a treated wood product.

To remain competitive, nearly all softwood sawmills use computer automation in the lumber manufacturing process. Sophisticated scanners view the size and shape of tree-length logs, and computers determine the optimal lengths into which to cut the tree-length logs. Scanners and computer solutions are also applied to maximize lumber yield during the log sawing and lumber edging and trimming. Hardwood sawmills adopted some aspects of this computer technology. Many hardwood sawmills, however, are too small to devote the capital required to computerize to the same degree as have softwood mills.

Improved Sawing Systems

Saw thickness has decreased at both hardwood and softwood sawmills in the United States since the first sawmill was built on Manhattan Island in 1633. Early saws removed 0.5 to 0.75 inch of wood to produce each board. Kerf is the term used to describe the width of the sawpath in cutting wood. By 1840, sawing machine kerfs had been reduced to about 0.313 inch.

When the circular saw was introduced in the United States in 1814, its circular cutting action increased sawing speed, but kerf widths remained about the same. Bandsaw use began in the United States shortly after the Civil War. Advantages of bandsaws were reduced kerf width and the ability to saw logs of greater diameter. By the 1970s, the typical circular saw kerf width was 0.250 to 0.280 inch while the typical bandsaw kerf was about 0.180 inch. Sudden increases in U.S. stumpage prices in the 1970s stimulated efforts to further reduce sawing machine kerf. Bandsaw kerfs on some machines were reduced to 0.125 to 0.140 inch, while kerfs on small-diameter circular saws were reduced to 0.140 to 0.160 inch.

The continuing computer automation of softwood sawmills and kerf reductions on sawing machines in both softwood and hardwood sawmills during the 1970s and 1980s resulted in a significant increase in sawmill log-to-lumber conversion efficiency. U.S. Forest Service studies show that lumber conversion increased by about 16 percent between 1952 and 1985. Higher conversion efficiency allows more lumber to be produced from the same volume of trees cut. Therefore, less land can be devoted to timber production and more to such uses as forest recreation and wildlife habitat.

Industry Cycles

Both hardwood and softwood sawmilling are cyclical industries whose fortunes are closely tied to the vigor of the construction industry. When the economic cycle is at its peak and the housing industry builds many units, there is high demand and prices are higher for softwood lumber. When the economy is slow, the softwood lumber industry faces depressed markets and lower prices.

The hardwood lumber industry also follows the economic cycle, but the economic peaks and valleys it faces lag behind those of the softwood lumber industry. This is because hardwood furniture to furnish the new homes and offices is built some months following the new construction.

The United States is both an importer and an exporter of significant volumes of lumber. In 1986, the United States imported 14 billion board feet of lumber, about 30 percent of total U.S. production, while 2.4 billion board feet were exported. This large volume of imported lumber flowing into the American market increases the domestic lumber supply and acts to reduce prices to the consumer. Over 90 percent of U.S. imported lumber comes from Canada. Therefore, U.S. sawmills are under competitive pressure from Canadian sawmills in addition to domestic ones.

Ownership of Timberland

The pattern of timberland ownership in the United States has a great impact on the forest product industries. The figure shows that the forest industry owns a relatively minor portion of the nation's timberland holdings, ranging from 11.6 to 15.7 percent, depending on the region. The patterns of public and private ownership differ considerably by region, however, with private holdings in the eastern states at 69.8 percent, compared with 24.1 percent for the western region. Public holdings in the East are relatively minor, with 14.5 percent of the timberland being publicly owned, compared with the major public holdings of 64.3 percent in the West.

A result of these regional differences in timberland holdings between public and private owners is that western sawmills must obtain most of their sawtimber from public lands, and eastern sawmills need to obtain most of theirs from private owners. Thus, western sawmills are more influenced by public policy issues concerning the management of public lands than are eastern sawmills. In recent years, changes in public policy have had a dramatic impact on the western sawmilling industry.

In the East, sawmillers are much less subject to shifts in public policy regarding timberland management because they purchase their timber mostly on the open market from private timberland owners. Dependence on private timberland owners for sawtimber brings with it

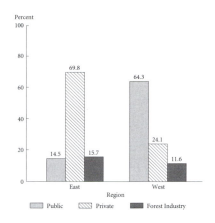

Percentage of Timberland in the United States by Ownership and Region, 1987

Source: K. L. Waddell, D. D. Oswald, and D. S. Powell. "Forest Statistics of the United States, 1987." Resource Bulletin PNW-RB-168. Portland, OR: U.S. Department of Agriculture, Forest Service, Pacific Northwest Research Station, 1989.

some problems for eastern sawmillers. Private owners may have goals other than timber production for their lands. An owner interested only in managing for wildlife or for recreation may not be interested in selling sawtimber. In addition, even those owners interested in timber production may lack forestry management skills themselves or the motivation to obtain professional forestry management advice. Thus, a significant portion of eastern private lands may be undermanaged for timber production, and sawtimber supplies may be less assured than the eastern sawmill industry finds desirable.

Since 1989, the harvest of softwood timber from national forests decreased from about 11 billion board feet per year to about 5 billion board feet per year in 1994. The reduction occurred mainly in the national forests in the West. Environmental and endangered species protection, such as for the spotted owl, has been the impetus for the reduced timber harvest. The reduced timber harvest in the West shifted some lumber manufacturing capacity to the southern United States. The reduced harvest of timber in the West resulted in many sawmills being closed and caused layoffs of large numbers of forest products employees. In addition, reduced timber supplies resulted in significant lumber price increases.

Many rural Americans own small, portable sawmills to produce lumber from trees harvested on their own land. The lumber produced is used for construction and other projects on their property or is marketed locally. Home sawmilling provides lumber at reduced prices for rural Americans. These portable sawmills typically use small bandsaws that are miniature versions of the large bandsaws in large sawmills. The kerf widths of these bandsaws are very thin, in the 0.040 to 0.060 inch range.

Wood Products in the Human Environment

Almost all U.S. houses are of wood frame construction. Writing paper, computer paper, tissues, and hand towels are wood products, many of which are manufactured from sawmilling residue. Recent studies of substitute materials for wood (steel, aluminum, concrete, and oil-based products such as plastics) have shown that production of these products has considerably more potential for environmental harm than wood products. This is due to the very large energy requirements to produce these substitute products. Wood products are also renewable resources, while steel, plastic, and other substitutes are from nonrenewable sources.

Waste disposal has become a problem for many industrial enterprises. For most sawmills this problem is less serious. Sawmills that dry their own lumber use the sawdust and bark to produce steam heat for their lumber kilns. Many sawmills market their planer shavings, log slabs, and board edgings for paper and composite board production. Charcoal and mulch are other products often produced from sawmill residue.

Although improper and indiscriminate timber harvesting can harm the environment, proper harvesting can enhance the use of forested areas by wildlife. Harvesting increases the use of forested areas by wildlife when timber diversity is maintained. Many rural families enjoy hunting, and most game populations benefit from proper harvesting. When harvesting is totally prohibited, the diversity of tree species is reduced. Shade-loving tree species replace sun-loving species. The shade-loving tree species are often not those that people and wildlife prefer most. For example, sugar maple and beech trees will predominate in our eastern hardwood forests if cutting is prohibited for long periods. Both people and wildlife appear to prefer a high proportion of oak trees in the forests. People like the oaks for aesthetic reasons, and wildlife like the acorns they produce.

—*Philip H. Steele*

See also
Forest Products; Foresters; Forestry Industry; Forests; Natural Resource Economics; Parks.

References

Brown, T. D. *Quality Control in Lumber Manufacture*. San Francisco: Miller Freeman Publications, 1982.

Denig, J. *Small Sawmill Handbook*. San Francisco: Miller Freeman Publications, 1993.

Steele, P. H., M. W. Wade, S. H. Bullard, and P. A. Araman. "Relative Kerf and Sawing Variation Values for Some Hardwood Sawing Machines." *Forest Products Journal* 42, no. 2 (1992): 33–39.

Steele, P. H., F. G. Wagner, and R. D. Seale. "An Analysis of Sawing Variation by Machine Type." *Forest Products Journal* 36, no. 9 (1986): 60–65.

———. "Comparison of Sawing Variables for Softwood Sawmills by Region of the United States." *Forest Products Journal* 38, no. 4 (1988): 19–24.

Steele, P. H., F. G. Wagner, Y. Lin, and K. Skog. "Influence of Softwood Sawmill Size on Lumber Recovery." *Forest Products Journal* 41, no. 4 (1991): 68–73.

Steele, P. H., F. G. Wagner, R. D. Seale, F. W. Taylor, and R. Bennett. "Kerf Width by Machine Type." *Forest Products Journal* 37, no. 3 (1987): 35–37.

Tooch, D. E. *Successful Sawmill Management*. Old Forge, NY: Northeastern Loggers Association, 1992.

U.S. Department of Agriculture, Forest Service. *An Analysis of the Timber Situation in the United States: 1989–2070.* General Technical Report RM-199. Ft. Collins, CO: Rocky Mountain Forest and Range Experiment Station, 1990.

Williston, E. M. *Computer Control Systems*. San Francisco: Miller Freeman Publications, 1978.

———. *Lumber Manufacturing*, revised edition. San Francisco: Miller Freeman Publications, 1978.

———. *Saws: Design, Selection, Operation, Maintenance*. San Francisco: Miller Freeman Publications, 1978.

———. *Small Log Sawmills*. San Francisco: Miller Freeman Publications, 1978.

Senior Centers

Community focal points where older adults come together for services and activities that reflect their experience and skills, respond to their diverse needs and interests, enhance their dignity, support their independence, and encourage their involvement in and with the community. As part of a comprehensive community strategy to meet the needs of older adults, senior centers offer on-site services and activities and link participants with additional resources offered by other agencies. Center programs consist of a variety of individual and group services and activities. The center also serves as a resource for the entire community, providing information on aging, support for family caregivers, training for professional and lay leaders and students, and development of innovative approaches to addressing aging issues (National Council on the Aging 1991).

Senior centers in rural areas play particularly important roles on behalf of older persons, their families, and the community. This entry provides an overview of the nature, operation, and programming of rural senior centers. It focuses on the availability of such centers, their resources, the activities they provide, and the characteristics of older persons who utilize them. We also consider the importance of such centers for the community at large and for serving elders with unmet health and social needs.

Availability

Recent estimates place the number of senior centers in this country at around 10,000 (Krout 1989). It is important to note that diversity is a key characteristic of senior centers. They span the gamut from small, volunteer-run programs to large, multipurpose, comprehensive service agencies. This diversity is found within as well as among rural and urban senior centers. Many senior centers provide a wide range of health, social, recreational, and educational services. Senior centers are well known to older persons, and research has shown that between 15 and 20 percent of the elderly in this country participate in center activities (Krout 1989).

A sizable number of senior centers can be found in rural areas across America. Krout (1983) used a 1982 National Council on the Aging list and found that one-half of the 4,000 centers from a 33-state listing were located in nonmetropolitan counties. Since service providers and sites generally are lacking in rural areas, senior centers are often the only service, information, and referral point for elders, and they also serve as a key link to the larger health and human services network. The general lack of availability and accessibility of rural services would suggest lower utilization rates for rural centers. However, research findings on this issue have been equivocal. Some rural community studies have found rates of as high as 25 percent, while others have rates of less than 10 percent (Krout, Williams, and Owen 1994).

Resources

National surveys conducted in the 1970s and 1980s found that rural senior centers have smaller facilities, lower budgets, and smaller numbers of volunteer and paid staff than urban centers. In the late 1980s, the majority of rural senior centers reported budgets of less than $20,000, although this figure may be misleading as space and even some staff are sometimes provided by outside agencies such as Area Agencies on Aging. Krout (1990) also found that rural centers were less likely than urban ones to have experienced budget increases during the 1980s.

Traditionally, senior centers in rural areas are located in self-standing facilities, often consisting of one or two main rooms and bathroom facilities. Sometimes they utilize space in community centers, churches, even fire halls; but centers without their own facilities often serve primarily as nutrition sites. Even so, some rural senior centers occupy more than 5,000 square feet of space and have facilities that can accommodate a wide range of programming.

The importance of adequate and affordable transportation for senior centers in rural areas cannot be stressed enough. Whether this transportation is provided by seniors themselves, relatives, friends, or neighbors, or by transportation programs funded by federal, state, or local dollars, it is essential for the survival of a community-based program such as a senior center. Generally, successful senior centers are integrated with, or administer and provide, transportation systems of one kind or another. Affordable and convenient access to rural senior centers is a necessity for success. Centers unable to provide transportation in one form or another to rural seniors are unlikely to prosper.

Activities and Services

The number and nature of programs offered by rural senior centers are closely related to the availability of financial resources and professional staff. However, it is important to note that even though rural senior centers support a smaller number of activities and services than urban centers, they still offer a wide range of programming. The author's research has found that even senior centers in communities of less than 2,500 persons reported offering a dozen activities and services on average (Krout 1990).

The nutritional function (congregate or in-home meals) is very important for all rural senior centers, and often serves as an anchor for other programming. Many times this other programming consists of socialization, recreation (card playing, bingo, trips), and education on a range of health, legal, and self-improvement areas. However, some rural senior centers offer a much broader range of services, including adult day care, case management, health screening, caregiver support, and housing assistance. It is important to recognize that many rural elders attend centers mainly for the social and recreational (and volunteering) opportunities, and because the center serves as a community that provides them with a sense of integration with others (Krout 1988).

Community Roles and Relationships

The relationships between rural senior centers and other community agencies are extremely important. Some rural centers are closely connected administratively and through planning and funding to Area Agencies on Aging

(AAAs), while others have minimal contact with these organizations. Some rural senior centers have a fairly high degree of interaction through referral and other activities with AAAs, hospitals, home health agencies, legal services, and other components of the community-based care system. These rural senior centers often are designated as official focal points by local AAAs. They can benefit from mutual marketing, referral of potential participants, and funding for services. These factors enhance the centers' ability to attract a wider variety of seniors and to provide a wider variety of programming.

Rural senior centers can serve as resources for the entire community as well as the elderly and can provide opportunities for residents to empower themselves and their communities. They provide a setting for rural elders not only to receive services and social support but also to contribute their skills and leadership qualities. For example, the Nebraska Department on Aging has developed a process by which rural senior centers work with an array of community interest groups to serve as focal points for community-service development, not just for elderly services. Although the degree of interaction with other agencies can be influenced heavily by factors such as financial and staff resources, terrain, population density, and availability and distance to service providers, it also reflects the orientation of center staff and participants. A rural center that is fairly isolated in terms of distance and terrain need not be isolated from other community-based services.

Characteristics of Senior Center Users

Research indicates that the participants of rural centers are somewhat older, poorer, and more likely to be White than the participants of urban senior centers. In addition, survey data suggest that participants in rural centers are more likely to have experienced "aging in place" during the previous decade, as indicated by increases in the ages of rural center user populations (Krout 1990). That is, fewer numbers of younger seniors are utilizing centers, and their user population is increasingly made up of older seniors who have been participants for many years.

Conclusions

The rural center participant profile suggests a greater need for a large array of income support programs (such as Supplemental Security Income, food stamps, home heating assistance, tax reductions, and supplemental earning opportunities) that senior centers could help provide. The centers could assist participants in identifying these programs and becoming involved in them through education

and referral activities. Health and wellness education and promotion (classes on nutrition, exercise, stress reduction, and drugs) as well as a wide variety of regularly scheduled health screening activities (dental, blood pressure, vision, dietary, and diabetes checkups) also appear to be particularly salient for rural center populations.

Unfortunately, many of the program needs noted above are generally less likely to be met adequately in rural areas because senior centers and the aging services network in general lack the dollars and health-service professionals to provide them. However, this does not mean that those program needs are impossible to fill, only more challenging and difficult. Training and resource materials can and should be developed to fit the needs of rural center participants and to build the capacity of rural centers to meet them. Traditional linkages with other agencies and the adoption of communications technologies, such as remote broadcast and videos, can help centers overcome resource gaps and accessibility problems.

—*John A. Krout*

See also

Elders; Mental Health; Mental Health of Older Adults; Nursing Homes.

References

Krout, John. *The Organization, Operation, and Programming of Senior Centers: A National Survey. Final Report to the AARP Andrus Foundation.* Fredonia, NY, 1983.

———. "Community Size Differences in Service Awareness among the Elderly." *Journal of Gerontology* 43 (1988): 528–530.

———. *Senior Centers in America.* Westport, CT: Greenwood Press, 1989.

———. "Community Size Differences in Senior Center Programs and Participation: A Longitudinal Analysis." *Research on Aging* 16, no. 4 (December 1994): 440–462.

Krout, John A., Peggy M. Williams, and Ollie Owen. "Senior Centers in Rural Communities" Pp. 90–110 in *Providing Community-Based Services to the Rural Elderly.* Edited by John A. Krout. Thousand Oaks, CA: Sage Publications, 1994.

National Council on the Aging. *Senior Center Standards: Guidelines for Practice.* Washington, DC: National Council on the Aging, 1991.

Service Industries

A diverse set of industries that includes business services, finance and real estate, health services, transportation, retail trade, and private household services. This entry presents definitions and classification schemes used to characterize service industries. Trends in the level and location of service industry employment are reviewed. The quality of service industry jobs and the implications of service sector growth for economic development are discussed.

Definitions and Trends

Over 65 percent of the employment in nonmetropolitan areas is in service industries—markedly less than that in metropolitan areas (Smith 1993). The quality of service industry jobs in nonmetropolitan areas is highly variable. The extent to which service industries can serve as a source of economic development for nonmetropolitan areas is a matter of debate.

Service industries traditionally have been classified as the tertiary sector, to distinguish them from the goods-producing industries (agriculture, forestry, fisheries, mining, construction, and manufacturing), which make up the primary and secondary sectors of the economy. However, collapsing a wide array of industries into a single residual group is unsatisfactory because of the considerable diversity among service industries with respect to activities, markets, and capacity for sustaining local and regional economies. Fortunately, several alternative classification schemes have been developed to characterize types of service industries. One useful categorization distinguishes producer from consumer services. Producer services provide inputs to other industries as an intermediary step in the production of a final good or service. These include finance, insurance, and real estate (FIRE), business services, legal services, and other professional services. Typically, producer service industries serve government agencies and business and manufacturing firms, and provide economic value by contributing to the competitiveness of another industry (Marshall 1988; Smith 1993).

Producer services typically locate in metropolitan areas that offer access to a skilled and educated labor force, a centralized location, and cost efficiencies associated with agglomeration (that is, cost efficiencies because a larger market permits greater economies of scale in production and greater specialization among firms). Data from the first half of the 1980s indicate that between 12 and 17 percent of metropolitan workers were employed in producer service industries, while less than 10 percent of nonmetropolitan workers were employed in this sector (Hirschl and McReynolds 1989; Miller and Bluestone 1988).

Nonmetropolitan areas are more likely to attract back-office than front-office facilities in producer services. Work production in back-office facilities tends to be routinized, labor-intensive, and poorly compensated. This contrasts with the less routinized, more administrative or managerial activities in front-office facilities, which tend to locate in more urbanized areas (Glasmeier and Borchard 1989). Such a propensity promotes a spatial division of labor within the service sector, particularly in producer services. However, some evidence indicates that certain producer service industries, such as data processing facilities, are decentralizing to a limited extent by locating in smaller population centers (Noyelle 1986).

On the other hand, consumer services typically serve private individuals, and their distribution across space follows the population distribution. Consumer services include retail trade, repair services, entertainment, recreation, and personal services. About one-fifth of nonmetropolitan workers are employed in consumer-related industries, with the majority in retail trade (Kassab and Luloff 1993; Miller and Bluestone 1988).

In addition to producer and consumer services, other types of services can be delineated based on the market or function served by the industry. These include distributive, social, educational, health, and government services.

Distributive services include transportation, communications, public utilities, sanitary services, and wholesale trade. These industries distribute goods and services within or among organizations, such as businesses and government agencies, as well as between organizations and consumers. Distributive service industries are connected to the goods-producing sector since they help sustain a network of organizations engaged in producer-related activities. Like producer services, distributive services tend to locate more in urban areas; fewer than 10 percent of workers in nonmetropolitan areas are employed in this sector (Kassab and Luloff 1993; Miller and Bluestone 1988).

The market for social, educational, and health services includes both government agencies and individuals. This sector constitutes a relatively important source of employment in nonmetropolitan areas. Of the 20 percent of nonmetropolitan workers employed in this sector, the majority are in education and health services (Kassab and Luloff 1993). The health sector is composed of hospitals, nursing homes, personal care facilities, and offices of physicians and other health care providers. The social services are a diverse group that includes job training and vocational rehabilitation, child day care, and adult residential care not involving nursing services. Educational services include elementary, secondary, trade, business, and vocational schools, as well as colleges, universities, and libraries.

The political process is a major factor affecting the level of employment in government services. Industries in this category include general government offices, justice, public order, and safety organizations. About 6 percent of nonmetropolitan workers are employed in this sector (Kassab and Luloff 1993).

Job Quality

Research indicates that discrepancies in job quality, particularly with respect to monetary compensation, are contributing to an increased economic polarization between metropolitan and nonmetropolitan areas. Average earnings for workers in nonmetropolitan areas tend to be lower than those for metropolitan workers employed in the same industry. For instance, average yearly wages for metropolitan workers employed in FIRE were estimated at nearly $17,000 per year (in 1982–1984 constant dollars) but only $12,000 for nonmetropolitan workers. Metropolitan workers employed in wholesale trade earned nearly $6,000 more than nonmetropolitan workers, while metropolitan workers employed in health and social services earned about $5,000 more than nonmetropolitan workers. Nonmetropolitan wages in retail trade came the closest to meeting metropolitan wages, although a gap of about $1,000 was evident (Kassab 1992). Furthermore, the financial status of households in nonmetropolitan areas has declined over time, compared with the status of households in metropolitan areas (Kassab, Luloff, and Schmidt 1995).

The quality of jobs in nonmetropolitan service industries varies widely in terms of monetary compensation and benefits. Research indicates that the highest paid nonmetropolitan service workers tend to be in distributive services. Wage and salary earnings for public utility workers averaged nearly $32,000 in 1990, and about $25,000 for transportation and communication workers. Average earnings in these industries were higher than those for nonmetropolitan workers employed in the goods-producing industries and government. For instance, employees in mining averaged $30,000 in 1990, while those employed in government and high-wage manufacturing industries, such as electronics, or stone, clay, glass, and concrete products, only averaged about $22,000 in 1990 (Kassab and Luloff 1993).

Wholesale trade is one of the lower paying industries within distributive services, with workers averaging $21,000 per year (1990 dollars). Even so, these relatively lower paid distributive service workers earned on average more than workers in low-wage manufacturing industries, such as textiles or apparel ($16,000). Although the level of pay in distributive services tended to exceed or approximate that offered in manufacturing, jobs in transportation and wholesale trade were less likely to offer health insurance benefits than jobs in either low- or high-wage manufacturing. About two-thirds of the nonmetropolitan workers employed in distributive services were employed in transportation or wholesale trade (Kassab and Luloff 1993).

The earnings distribution for nonmetropolitan producer service workers is bifurcated. Those employed in legal services, insurance, banking, and other finance services reported 1990 wages and salaries in the $20,000 to $26,000 range, but average annual earnings of those employed in real estate, business services, and other professional services were in the $13,000 to $17,000 range. The greater prevalence of part-time workers in this latter group of industries contributed significantly to the bifurcated earnings structure (Kassab and Luloff 1993).

Similarly, the quality of jobs within social, educational, and health services tends to be bifurcated. While average earnings for workers in the hospital and education industries ranged from $18,000 to $19,000 in 1990, average earnings for workers in nursing, personal-care facilities and social service facilities were $11,000. Moreover, hospital and education workers were more likely to have health insurance benefits than workers in the latter group.

Research indicates that compared with households in which the head is employed in traditionally higher paying industries (such as manufacturing, mining, or government), families whose heads are employed in higher paying service industries (such as the producer or distributive services) are more likely to experience economic hardship. Children in such households are less likely to have health care insurance. These differences most likely reflect the wide variability in earnings and the presence of marginal positions within these service industries, as contrasted with the relative homogeneity of higher-wage industries (Kassab et al. 1995).

Jobs in the consumer, health, education, and social services constitute an integral component of the nonmetropolitan economy, with about 40 percent of nonmetropolitan workers in 1990 employed in these sectors (Kassab and Luloff 1993). These industries continued to add workers (in other words, jobs) to the nonmetropolitan economy, as indicated by research covering the 1981–1986 period. Moreover, these sectors are expected to continue to grow at least until 2000. However, many of these new jobs require relatively few skills, and consequently, pay low wages (Porterfield 1990; Smith 1993). For instance, retail trade, entertainment, and recreation service employees averaged between $11,000 and $12,000 per year in 1990. Furthermore, workers in consumer services are among the least likely to have health insurance benefits. Two factors contributing to the low level of compensation are the prevalence of lower-level service occupations and part-time employment. However, discrepancies in job quality between these industries and traditional nonmetropolitan industries (such as agriculture, forestry, and fishery) are not large; workers in traditional nonmetropolitan industries earned about $13,000, on average, in 1990 (Kassab and Luloff 1993).

Implications for Economic Development

The promotion of jobs in higher-paying service industries, particularly in producer services, has been a focus of economic development efforts. In metropolitan areas, evidence indicates that this sector can constitute part of the economic base and serve as an autonomous force for generating economic growth. Services that are sold or exported outside of the local area to another region or city result in an influx of outside income (in other words, basic income). In addition, job growth in producer services has exceeded that in the goods-producing sector for some time (Smith 1993).

However, in nonmetropolitan areas, evidence regarding the capacity of service industries to grow independently of goods-producing industries is in conflict (Hirschl and McReynolds 1989; Miller and Bluestone 1988; Smith 1993). Furthermore, nonmetropolitan growth rates in producer services and in many other service industries traditionally have lagged behind those in metropolitan areas. In 1969, for instance, 68 percent of the wage and salary employment in metropolitan areas was in service industries; this increased to 80 percent by 1989. In contrast, nonmetropolitan employment in service industries increased only from 63 to 66 percent during the same period. Continued gains in the complement of service industries within nonmetropolitan areas would help diversify the local economy and promote economic stability (Smith 1993).

Disparities between metropolitan and nonmetropolitan areas with respect to the types of service industries comprising the local economy may mean that the mechanisms influencing service sector growth and development differ. Social, educational, and health services are more concentrated in nonmetropolitan than metropolitan

areas. These industries may be growing in nonmetropolitan areas in response to nonwork basic income, particularly income associated with the elderly, such as pensions and Social Security. In metropolitan areas, gains in service industries are more closely associated with basic income derived from work sources (Hirschl and McReynolds 1989). All the same, the predominance of low-wage/low-skill jobs in nonmetropolitan areas raises concerns about the capability of these jobs to adequately sustain the economic well-being of nonmetropolitan households.

—Cathy Kassab

See also
Employment; Home-Based Work; Income; Labor Force; Work.
References
Glasmeier, A., and G. Borchard. "Research Policy and Review 31. "From Branch Plants to Back Offices: Prospects for Rural Services Growth." *Environment and Planning* 21, no. 12 (1989): 1565–1583.

Hirschl, Thomas, and Samuel A. McReynolds. "Service Employment and Rural Community Economic Development." *Journal of the Community Development Society* 20, no. 2 (1989): 15–30.

Kassab, Cathy. *Income and Inequality: The Role of the Service Sector in the Changing Distribution of Income.* New York: Greenwood Press, 1992.

Kassab, Cathy, and A. E. Luloff. "The New Buffalo Hunt: Chasing the Service Sector." *Journal of the Community Development Society* 24, no. 2 (1993): 174–195.

Kassab, Cathy, A. E. Luloff, and Fred Schmidt. "The Changing Impact of Industry, Household Structure, and Residence on Household Well-being." *Rural Sociology* 60, no. 1 (Spring 1995): 67–90.

Marshall, J. N. *Services and Uneven Development.* New York: Oxford University Press, 1988.

Miller, James P., and Herman Bluestone. "Prospects for Service Sector Employment Growth in Nonmetro America." *Review of Regional Studies* 18 (1988): 28–41.

Noyelle, Thierry J. "Advanced Services in the System of Cities." Pp. 143–164 in *Local Economies in Transition.* Edited by Edward M. Bergman. Durham, NC: Duke University Press, 1986.

Porterfield, Shirley. "Service Sector Offers More Jobs, Lower Pay." *Rural Development Perspectives* 6, no. 3 (June–September 1990): 2–7.

Smith, Stephen M. "Service Industries in the Rural Economy: The Role and Potential Contributions." Pp. 105–126 in *Economic Adaptation: Alternatives for Nonmetropolitan Areas.* Edited by David L. Barkley. Boulder, CO: Westview Press, 1993.

Settlement Patterns

The spatial arrangement of people, enterprises, and infrastructure in the open countryside and in places of various sizes. The diversity of current settlement patterns grows out of human interaction with the physical landscape. Early settlers exploited geographical advantages and federal land disbursement initiatives to lay out property boundaries, town locations, and transportation networks. The regionally distinctive configurations that emerged are still with us today, despite major economic and technological changes. In the twentieth century, decreasing farm employment, increasing concentration of population and economic activity in metropolitan centers, and a near total reliance on the automobile for work and shopping lessened the importance of villages and towns as retail centers, although many continue to grow and thrive as residential communities.

Current Diversity

Rural and urban settlement patterns are highly integrated and cannot be viewed in isolation from one another. Almost half of the 62 million rural Americans in 1990 lived in metropolitan areas, consisting of counties with urbanized cores of 50,000 people or more and suburban fringes. Even though they live in rural settings, defined as open countryside or places of 2,500 or less, the vast majority of metropolitan-rural people lead lives that are better characterized as suburban. Because the U.S. settlement system is largely organized around metropolitan areas, the territory falling outside the range of daily metropolitan commuting, labeled nonmetropolitan, came to be equated with rural in the eyes of many researchers and policymakers (see Rural, Definition of).

In that context, the roughly 50 million nonmetropolitan Americans live in a diverse and regionally varied settlement structure. In 1990, half lived outside of nonmetropolitan places (including people living in unincorporated villages with fewer than 1,000 residents), 15 percent lived in villages with fewer than 2,500 people, and another 15 percent lived in towns with populations between 2,500 and 10,000. The remaining 20 percent lived in cities ranging in size from 10,000 to 50,000. Combining the first two categories above shows that almost two-thirds of nonmetropolitan residents lived in rural areas, with the remainder in urban towns and cities.

Nonmetropolitan territory averaged 18 persons per square mile in 1990, but wide regional diversity exists in both the number and arrangement of people on the landscape. Nonmetropolitan population densities range from 800 persons per square mile in parts of the highly industrialized Northeast to less than one in sections of the arid West. Ranching and mining in western states support a much smaller population in the open countryside, so that 132 counties lie beyond the frontier line of two people per square mile (Duncan 1993). Fifty percent of nonmetro-

politan residents in the West are urban, compared to just 30 percent in the Northeast. The South and Midwest fall between these extremes.

Settlement patterns are determined by physical environment, historical events, economic processes, and human initiative. Climate, topography, geology, and soils provide a framework within which economic, social, and technological factors operate to distribute and connect populations. The semiarid climate and flat topography of the Great Plains favor an economy of large-scale farms employing relatively few people; the population density in such farming-dependent counties is down to 10 people per square mile, and two-thirds of such counties are entirely rural, containing no town larger than 2,500 people. Mining-dependent counties, found largely in the Appalachian and Rocky Mountains, are more densely settled (30 people per square mile) and more concentrated into towns along valley floors separated by uninhabitable slopes and peaks. Density is highest where manufacturing prevails, such as near textile and furniture plants in Piedmont regions of the Southeast; counties dependent on manufacturing contain 60 people per square mile, with 80 percent of the population living in urban settings (Cook and Mizer 1994).

Early Settlement

Much of U.S. history is embedded in the landscape, because basic patterns of public and private ownership (such as land boundaries, town locations, and street patterns) are hard to change once they are established. Rural settlement patterns in the United States are largely North European (British Isles, Scandinavian, German, etc.) in origin (Meinig 1986). Spanish influences prevail in the Rio Grande Valley and other subregions; but during initial exploration and settlement, Spain favored strictly commercial enterprises in the New World, with small, mostly male populations. Settlers blazed trails, built roads, followed watercourses, surveyed and cleared land, laid out towns, established plantations and smaller homesteads, and built fortifications at strategic sites. The location and layout of these first settlements, and the farming and building methods initially employed, became the foundations for future expansion (Meinig 1993).

Colonial settlement was highly dispersed and lacked towns in many areas. Plantations along the rivers in Virginia did not depend on towns for marketing their agricultural products, and decentralization defined much of the rural South, where towns were difficult to establish. Authorities encouraged and sometimes required settlement in towns, to promote town-based commerce and to ease protection and taxation; but settlers hungered for land and rejected town living for individual farms (Lingeman 1981).

The Puritans of New England, whose settlement patterns reflected their religious purpose, followed a different scheme. Land was granted as a town to a group, which was responsible for distributing land to individuals and also keeping part of it as town land. Members lived in an organized community setting centered on the town and symbolized by the commons (large greens that still grace New England towns), but they owned their own land and valued enterprise and self-sufficiency. New towns were formed when older towns grew too large and needed to "halve off." Puritan town development ended in New England by the time of the Revolution, but these religious communities determined the pattern of rural settlement in much of the Northeast and sent their ideas about how a town should look and be organized west in subsequent migrations.

New England towns were irregular in shape, as were most rural parcels laid out along the Eastern Seaboard during the colonial period. Survey techniques employing "metes and bounds" created inexact boundaries that have been carried down to the present. The distinctive, rectilinear settlement pattern west of the Appalachian Mountains began with the Land Ordinance of 1785, a federal effort to ensure an orderly system of land distribution. Legal problems that plagued landowners in the East were lessened by sending surveyors to plot the six-square-mile townships and their component one-square-mile sections, often before settlement occurred. This township-and-range system was carried into most settled areas of the United States all the way to the Pacific, and was even employed in mountainous landscapes, where such grids were impractical.

Regional Diversification

Settlement proceeded unevenly from several Atlantic core areas (New England, Pennsylvania, Virginia, and South Carolina), each imprinting distinctive patterns on western lands. Settlers went first to high-quality land near transportation routes. Islands of settlement developed around mining and logging camps and army posts; but dispersed agricultural homesteads and trade centers were most prevalent. Cities grew up at strategic physical locations, such as the confluence of major waterways (Pittsburgh), where portage was necessary around falls (Louisville), or in the center of rich agricultural districts

(Lexington). In the northern tier of states destined to become the country's industrial heartland, investments in transportation (first roads, then canals, then railroads) lowered physical restrictions early on and bound the Midwest to Atlantic port cities in an integrated economic network.

Important insights into U.S. settlement geography come from central place theory, the predicted outcomes of which are most clearly seen in the Midwest. Settlements exist for their functions, many of which are ubiquitous (providing goods, services, and administration). Central place theory predicts the size and spacing of places based on thresholds (the minimum size of the trade area needed to support a given function) and ranges (how far people will travel to obtain these functions). In the nineteenth century, grocery stores, sawmills, and churches were lower-order functions (those that required small thresholds) found in hamlets spread thickly across the landscape, often at six-mile intervals in compliance with township-and-range geometry. People traveled farther to larger central places, fewer in number, to obtain higher-order goods and services (those functions that required large thresholds), such as hardware, clothing, financial help, and legal services. Assuming entrepreneurs located to minimize distance traveled by their customers, a nested hierarchy of hexagonal trade areas resulted, with higher-order centers containing all functions found in those of a lower order.

Physical barriers such as mountains and lakes, variations in climate and soils, and other environmental factors affecting the location of nonubiquitous functions such as mining, manufacturing, and transportation account for much of the deviation from central place patterns. Also, central place dynamics were weaker in different regional economic systems. Southern plantations (large, commercial enterprises dependent on the exploitation of large numbers of slave laborers) produced staples principally for export, and thus did not support complex patterns of commerce and trade. The planters themselves often lived in nearby cities, such as Charleston, Natchez, or Memphis, for comfort, security, and socializing, while Black slaves and overseers lived in concentrated rural settlements on the land being farmed. The majority of White southerners ran small farms, living and working on their land, often alongside the few slaves they may have owned. Stark economic and social contrasts developed between wealthy planter towns and most of the countryside. Towns serving small farmers were often meager, operating as seasonal marketplaces or county seats and providing the few services farmers did not perform for themselves (such as blacksmithing).

The Civil War changed settlement patterns in the South. A plantationlike economic system survived in the form of sharecropping, but Black families moved from clustered slave quarters to widely dispersed tenant farmsteads (Aiken 1985). Railroad expansion brought industry in the form of textile mills in the Piedmont, and lumber camps throughout the Coastal Plains. Towns and cities grew up around these activities and alongside the tracks every 6 to 10 miles, to serve as distribution and marketing centers.

The distinctly linear pattern of settlement associated with railroads can still be found throughout the country, perhaps most clearly on the Great Plains, where towns were laid out like beads on a string, often named in alphabetical order. East of the Mississippi River, settlement preceded the railroads and later conformed to it. In much of the West, railroads preceded settlement, and railroad companies operated as real-estate speculators, dispensing millions of acres of land and actively recruiting settlers from the United States and Europe to guarantee profits.

Like the mining towns in the Rocky Mountains and the Sierra Nevada, which sprang to life in an instant and just as quickly disappeared, Great Plains settlements suffered from volatile international markets and natural resource depletion. Railroad boosterism, aided by the Homestead Act of 1862, pushed population densities above the long-run carrying capacities of fragile prairie ecosystems. Many Great Plains towns disappeared shortly after being founded, and much of the area has experienced steady population loss since the late nineteenth century.

Twentieth-Century Changes

On the eve of the Automobile Age, Charles J. Galpin conducted a landmark study depicting the small scale of rural society in one midwestern county (Galpin 1915). Community life centered on 1 of 12 trade centers, "within which the apparent entanglement of human life is resolved into a fairly unitary system of interrelatedness" (p. 18). Ranging in size from 500 to 2,500, most of these centers contained their own bank, newspaper, milk delivery service, high school, and one or more churches. The average size of their trade areas, about 50 square miles, conformed to the speed of horse and wagon, the dominant mode of transportation at the time. Such communities were home to most Americans born before 1920, the

year in which urban residents outnumbered rural residents for the first time.

Since then, the automobile and other technological advances have rearranged settlement patterns, community life, and society in general. In the transformation from a rural to a metropolitan economy, the single most telling indicator was the displacement of farm labor. With productivity increasing 1,200 percent, the number of farm residents fell from 30 million in 1940 to 5 million in 1990, despite expanding farm output. During the same 50-year period, the number of farms dropped from 6 to 2 million and average farm size tripled. The proportion of farmers living off the farm jumped from 5 to 20 percent (Beale 1993). Few Black farmers had the financial resources or access to credit needed to mechanize and consolidate; thus, the rural Black population in the South reclustered into subdivisions and towns.

The automobile helped to trigger a convergence of rural and urban economic and social conditions, so that today's rural settlement patterns conform more to job commuting, retirement, and recreational businesses than to farming, mining, or logging. Many areas once entirely rural have been absorbed into metropolitan regions through suburbanization. Industrial deconcentration and growth in the service sector, including a growing number of information-oriented jobs that can be performed anywhere, greatly expanded rural commuting patterns.

Six-mile agricultural communities with 50-square-mile trading areas have been replaced by 30-mile "Wal-Mart towns" serving 5,000 square miles. Towns and villages left behind often continue to function and even thrive as residential centers. However, location within municipal boundaries seems to have become a disadvantage. Retail centers are moving to outskirts, where large tracts of undeveloped land allow larger stores and parking lots. Housing is following the same pattern, especially among higher-income populations.

Retirees and other migrants, many escaping urban ills, now populate former fishing villages, lakeside resorts, mountain hideaways, and other rural settings prized for their natural amenities. Such growth creates much-needed employment at the same time that rising property values push many long-term residents out and force lower-income workers to commute long distances. In amenity-rich areas such as the intermountain West and the South Atlantic coast, development has spread far beyond the confines of earlier settlements and increasingly consists of second homes, which stand empty much of the time. Such development increases the difficulties of preserving the amenities—unspoiled scenery, pristine air and water, rural ambience—that attracted newcomers in the first place.

—*John B. Cromartie*

See also

Community; History, Rural; Migration; Plantations; Regional Diversity; Regional Planning; Rural, Definition of; Rural Demography; Trade Areas; Urbanization.

References

Aiken, Charles S. "New Settlement Patterns of Rural Blacks in the American South." *Geographical Review* 75 (1985): 383–404.

Beale, Calvin L. "Salient Features of the Demography of American Agriculture." In *The Demography of Rural Life.* Edited by David L. Brown, Donald R. Field, and James J. Zuiches. University Park, PA: Northeast Regional Center for Rural Development, 1993.

Cook, Peggy J., and Karen L. Mizer. *The Revised ERS County Typology: An Overview.* Rural Development Research Report 89. Washington, DC: U.S. Department of Agriculture, Rural Economy Division, Economic Research Service, 1994.

Duncan, Dayton. *Miles from Nowhere: Tales from America's Contemporary Frontier.* New York: Viking, 1993.

Fuguitt, Glenn V., David L. Brown, and Calvin L. Beale. *Rural and Small Town America.* New York: Russell Sage, 1989.

Galpin, Charles J. *The Social Anatomy of an Agricultural Community.* Wisconsin Agricultural Experiment Station Research Bulletin Number 34. Madison: University of Wisconsin, 1915.

Lingeman, Richard R. *Small Town America: A Narrative History, 1620–The Present.* Boston: Houghton Mifflin, 1981.

Meinig, Donald W. *The Shaping of America: A Geographical Perspective on 500 Years of History.* Volume 1: *Atlantic America, 1492–1800.* New Haven, CT: Yale University Press, 1986.

———. *The Shaping of America: A Geographical Perspective on 500 Years of History.* Volume 2: *Continental America, 1800–1867.* New Haven, CT: Yale University Press, 1993.

Sheep

See Wool and Sheep Industry

Signs

Devices, fixtures, placards, or structures that use any color, form, graphic, illumination, symbol, or writing to advertise or announce the purpose of a person or entity, or to communicate information of any kind to the public. This entry discusses the purposes and common uses of both public and private signs. It reviews the different types of signs. Public efforts to regulate private signs and the practical and legal issues involved in such regulation are examined.

Context and Types of Signs

Signs can be sources of valuable information, essential tools of commerce, or blights on the landscape. The effect of a sign depends in part on its nature and location. To some extent, however, the effect also depends on the perspective of the viewer. The fast-food restaurant operator and the environmentalist have different views on the subject. Furthermore, the environmentalist with a screaming child in the back seat who can be calmed only by a special meal served under golden arches might have quite a different perspective from that of the same environmentalist in a more abstract discussion about signs.

Although signs can be intrusive in an urban environment, they are more noticeable in rural areas, where they amount to a larger percentage of the human-built landscape. Advertising and other private signs are the subject of most public concern involving signs. Through appropriate regulations, local governments can and do manage the number, size, height, and location of such private signs.

Most signs in the rural United States are oriented to roads. Although there are small signs in store windows, signs inside shopping malls, and signs in locations to identify restrooms, such signs are beyond the scope of this discussion. Signs along bicycle and hiking trails are similar in purpose to the road-oriented signs described below, although the signs aimed at bicyclists and pedestrians are generally smaller than those intended for high-speed traffic, and thus less intrusive.

There are three basic categories of signs in the rural United States: public signs, quasi-public signs, and private signs. Public signs are those determined by public agencies to be essential or at least important to the functioning of society or to governmental operation. Such signs include speed-limit and other traffic regulation signs; signs giving distances to the next city and other important travel information; signs identifying historic landmarks, scenic overlooks, and other points of interests; and official notices announcing elections, public hearings, and other formal matters.

Quasi-public signs include street addresses and other signs necessary or useful for public purposes but generally placed on private property. Street numbers are required by many local governments to assist public safety officials. Other quasi-public signs may identify driveway entrances and exits, public telephones, handicapped parking spaces, and other directions and facilities on private property. Although these signs are not as essential to public business as street addresses and speed limits, they are a great convenience to the public and fulfill public purposes. For these reasons, local governments often require some quasi-public signs (particularly street

A typical collection of signs along a rural highway.

numbers) and allow or encourage others without much public regulation.

Private signs include everything from the smallest FOR RENT sign to the largest billboard. The most numerous private signs are those located on business properties, identifying the businesses and advertising their services and goods. Private signs also include noncommercial signs, such as those urging the reader to vote for a particular candidate or to support a particular cause or issue. Most controversy and serious public discussion about signs involves such private signs.

Regulation of Sign Placement and Design

Some signs are clearly essential to the life of a complex society, particularly one that moves on four wheels at high speed. Questions involving signs focus on how many signs of what size and design should be allowed where.

Most public signs providing traffic directions, warnings, and information conform to U.S. Department of Transportation standards, which are based on considerations of safety and visibility. Such signs are a familiar part of the highway landscape and their design is likely to remain unchanged except as these national standards evolve. Other public signs, such as official notices, are typically so nonintrusive on the visual environment that they are often not even noticed by their intended audiences.

Quasi-public signs vary somewhat by region, but they are generally relatively small and nondescript. Occasionally a rural subdivision may be identified by a large structural entrance marquee or a family farm may be identified with a barn-sized sign painted on the roof, but those are atypical. Quasi-public signs erected by private individuals become most problematic when erected in

the public right-of-way, interfering at times with road maintenance and even with visibility and highway safety.

Most of the actual and perceived intrusion of signs on the rural landscape involves private signs, erected to attract the business or attention of the motoring public. Burma Shave pioneered the use of such signs, placing catchy verses on series of small signs along highways in rural areas. Other early signs in rural areas consisted of metal logo signs, often located at businesses, and advertisements for soft drinks and tobacco painted on the sides of barns.

As highway traffic grew, so did the advertising directed at it. Signs grew both in number and size. The increase in the number of signs is in part a function of an increase in population and the related increase in business activity. It is also a function of the significant increases in the number of miles that people drive. As people drive more, they spend more time in their car, and that time becomes a sort of prime time for advertisers in a different medium.

Billboards initially proliferated along major highways. One policy aimed at controlling the impact of billboards succeeded in reducing their numbers but increasing their size. Under the Highway Beautification Act adopted during the 1960s, new billboards were significantly restricted within a specified distance of federally subsidized highways. The result of that program was a gradual reduction in the number of billboards, as old signs were removed and not replaced. Because of the restrictions on new signs near the highways, however, the billboard industry developed supersized billboards, designed to be located outside the federally regulated zone of 660 feet from the pavement and easily read from that greater distance. The other significant change in sign design along rural roadways was the effort of some businesses, notably fast-food franchises, to reach highway traffic with very tall signs located at the site of the business but designed to be read or recognized from a highway many hundreds of feet away.

Local governments can and do regulate sign numbers, size, height, and location. Most local governments that adopted zoning also have sign regulations of some sort. Typical local sign regulations specify the number of freestanding signs that may be located on a single property, as well as their size, height, and the distance at which they must be set back from a roadway or property line. Some communities also regulate sign lighting and even the colors and materials used in signs. Lighting restrictions are common, particularly on signs in or near residential areas. Regulation of colors and materials is most common in historic districts, but such regulations are also found in a number of tourist communities and exclusive suburbs. Other communities have the legal authority to regulate sign design, but many choose not to expend the political capital necessary to regulate business beyond basic standards on number, size, height, and location.

Often much of the visual impact of signs comes from sign clutter, a proliferation of different types of signs in front of one or more businesses. A convenience store may have a professional pole sign with its name and logo, a changeable marquee with gas prices, a banner announcing a new food special, a sandwich board promoting a brand of cigarettes, and several paper window signs promoting food specials. Communities address this visual clutter both with limits on the number of signs and with significant restrictions on such temporary signs as banners and sandwich boards. Several communities ban trailer-mounted readerboards with flashing lights that may confuse motorists, although some allow that type of sign without the lights. Some communities prohibit or severely restrict such promotional devices as beacons, spotlights, large balloons, flapping pennants, and moving signs.

Many local ordinances regulate on-premise signs (advertising goods and services offered on the same property) and off-premise signs (which are usually but not always billboards) differently. That distinction raises some significant constitutional and other legal problems. The safer approach to sign regulation is to regulate signs based on their location and physical characteristics, not on their messages. In many communities sign regulations vary by zoning district, imposing the most restrictive regulations in residential areas and the least restrictive ones in some commercial areas, with industrial and agricultural areas falling somewhere between the two.

Small paper signs, often used to promote political candidates or issues or to advertise yard or tag sales, pose interesting practical and theoretical challenges in sign regulation. Users often place those signs in the public right-of-way. Such use of public property for private activity typically requires complex lease negotiations and extensive bonding, insurance, and indemnification arrangements. Unwilling to confront good-hearted citizens who are simply trying to empty their attics or promote good government, many local governments look the other way and tacitly allow such signs to exist, even on the right-of-way. A few communities developed regulatory schemes specifically to allow such signs for limited peri-

ods of time. Others have aggressive enforcement programs and regularly remove such signs, even on weekends.

Regulating signs is one of the most significant political challenges that a community can face. Consideration of a new sign ordinance is often contentious, even dividing the business community. Only a community-wide rezoning is likely to be more hotly debated. Thus, adopted local sign regulations might start from sound planning suggestions such as those outlined here but evolve through the planning process into something much more complex and much less ideal. Anyone attempting to evaluate local sign regulations should always recognize the political and legal context in which they were adopted.

Just as the flashing lights, neon tubing, and readerboard marquees of 42nd Street are an integral part of that urban streetscape, so are signs part of the rural landscape. Increases in the number and size of signs during the 1960s made them more intrusive on the rural landscape and thus the subject of greater public concern. The greatest intrusions are by the very large signs that are targeted at distant or high-speed roads. Although some people may propose banning many signs as a solution to visual blight, the more appropriate response is typically to use sign regulations to manage the number, size, height, and location of signs. Through such regulations, local governments can keep signs in scale with the buildings and activities of a particular streetscape, thus making them again a vital part of the rural community, rather than an intrusion into it.

—*Eric Damian Kelly*

See also

Consumer-Goods Advertising; Environmental Regulations; Government.

References

Fleming, Ronald Lee. *How Corporate Franchise Design Can Respect Community Identity.* Planning Advisory Service Report No. 452. Chicago: American Planning Association, 1994.

Fraser, James. *The American Billboard: 100 Years.* New York: Harry N. Abrams, 1991.

Greene, Frederick Stuart, Robert Moses, Lithgow Osborne, and Rexford Tugwell. *The Billboard: A Blot on Nature and a Parasite on Public Improvements.* New York: New York Roadside and Safety Improvement Committee, 1939.

Kelly, Eric Damian, and Gary J. Raso. *Sign Regulation for Small and Midsize Communities.* Planning Advisory Service Report No. 419. Chicago: American Planning Association, 1989.

Mandelker, Daniel R., and William R. Ewald. *Street Graphics and the Law.* Chicago: Planners Press, 1988.

"Signs of the Times." *Planning* 57, no. 11 (November 1991): 32.

Venturi, Robert, Denise Scott Brown, and Steven Izenour. *Learning from Las Vegas.* Rev. ed. Cambridge, MA: MIT Press, 1977.

Williams, Norman. "Scenic Protection as a Legitimate Goal of Public Regulation." *Washington University Journal of Urban and Contemporary Law* 38 (1990): 3–24.

Social Class

A categorization of people based primarily on their occupation of similar economic positions in a stratified social system. The discussion of social class in rural America may be described in terms of two distinct approaches. First, there are analyses that focus on gradations within the social hierarchy, or social strata, and the process by which they emerge and interrelate, or social stratification. Second, there are analyses that focus on the social relationships that people enter into during the process of economic production. These are more strictly understood as social classes. Both types of analysis will vary further, depending on whether the population in question is composed entirely of farmers or encompasses a broader rural community. The following discussion will refine this definition of class and stratification analysis, then turn to an examination of trends in this tradition within rural sociology. Finally, basic characteristics of rural class and stratification structures, drawn from the 1990 census, will be presented.

Rural Stratification

Stratification analyses of rural communities or regions follow largely the same pattern as stratification analyses of society as a whole. There are exceptions, however, stemming from the fact that the assignment of status in the everyday lives of rural people is bound less tightly to occupation than is that of their urban counterparts. Since anonymity is less prevalent in rural communities, the assignment of status is, on the one hand, more likely to be grounded in individual achievement (within a particular occupation). On the other hand, status is also more likely to be based on ascribed characteristics derived from the individual's association with his or her family (nuclear and extended), when the latter are known to the community. Apart from these differences, the study of stratification in rural communities examines all of the same factors that would be examined in any stratification study of the larger society: occupational status, income, education, and wealth. However, even within each of these categories variations between rural and urban values might be observed. For example, some occupations, such as farming, might be assigned a higher status by rural residents than by urban ones.

Stratification analyses of the farm population might include specific indicators or combinations of indicators to determine the number of strata. Farm size in acres or sales volume, net farm or family income, net worth, educational attainment, and tenure status are common variables used to determine an individual's location within a particular stratum among a farming population.

Rural Class

The analysis of class focuses on social relationships constructed in the production process, especially relationships between direct producers and nonproducers. For example, analyses of class in antebellum America would involve study of the relationship between plantation owners as nonproducers and slaves as producers. In modern capitalism, it would involve study of the relations between, for instance, farm wageworkers and farm owners. California fruit and vegetable production exemplifies a historical dependence on this type of class structure. Similarly, to the extent that a rural region has undergone industrialization, a class analysis examines the relationship between owners of rural industries and wageworkers.

This class analysis is rather indistinct from the study of class in urban settings. More distinctive is the relationship between producers and nonproducers in what often appears as "the family farm." Most family farmers engage in social relationships with nonproducers in the process of production. Many borrow heavily from banks or other credit institutions. Others rent land, making payments to landowners in the form of cash or a share of the crop. In some commodities, especially where there is a regional monopolization on processing facilities, farmers sign contracts with processors that rather strictly specify labor and price conditions. These relationships can, at times, approximate those of wageworkers. Each of these cases can constitute class relationships insofar as control over production and the distribution of economic returns (value) to labor and capital are contested.

The Study of Rural Class and Stratification

Early twentieth-century studies in rural sociology focused on class and stratification issues in the context of a community studies orientation. These studies focused on the overall stratification structure of rural communities. For example, were they "diamond-shaped" (that is, having a large middle class with a small elite and small, impoverished lower strata) or were they "triangular" (with a small elite and a large underclass)? During and after the Great Depression, rural sociological studies of class structures sometimes met with political opposition. Now-classic studies, such as Goldschmidt's (1947) research on class structure in post–World War II California, met with attempts at suppression, while others, such as an analysis of sharecropping conditions in the South, were completely censored (Hooks 1986). Some of these studies have been lost altogether.

Sewell (1965) wrote that rural sociology maintained consistent interest in stratification issues throughout the mid-twentieth century, although he noted that these interests were generally subordinated to other concerns of the discipline. In the post–World War II era, stratification variables were often embedded in the study of the diffusion and adoption of agricultural innovations. In the late 1960s and early 1970s, rural sociologists and the mass media increasingly examined issues related to rural poverty and to migratory farm labor.

By the late 1970s, a qualitative shift had emerged in rural sociology that made class analysis a focal point of the discipline, especially in what came to be labeled the new sociology of agriculture (Buttel, Larson, and Gillespie 1990). The first wave of these concerns was associated with the study of the relationships between family farms and capitalist enterprises at the input and output levels. These studies tended to reflect both a populism and a functionalism, or a grounding in the literature on complex organization. Heffernan (1972), for instance, studied vertical integration, emphasizing the contractual relationship between poultry producers and processors. Rodefeld (1974) developed a typology of farmers based on categories associated with ownership and control of land, labor, capital, and management within agricultural production.

A more explicit class analysis of agriculture in the advanced capitalist societies developed in the late 1970s and early 1980s, fueled by an infusion of interest in Marxist theory. Initially, many of these studies took a rather orthodox or structuralist Marxist approach. This view contended that agricultural class structures would eventually come to parallel the class structures of the larger capitalist society. Mann and Dickinson (1978), for instance, followed Marx in contending that the transformation of the class structure of agriculture was dependent on the specific logic of capital. This logic was said to be shaped by the distinctive nature of agriculture. It was contingent, first, on the perishability of agricultural commodities, and second, on the disjuncture of labor time and production time in the production of agricultural commodities. These obstructed capitalist penetration, but eventually the obstacles would be overcome.

Other forms of class analysis took a more historical orientation. By examining specific agricultural regions, a number of scholars demonstrated the necessity of developing a historically informed analysis of U.S. agriculture.

Pfeffer's (1983) study of regional variations in agricultural class structures compared corporate farming in California, sharecropping in the South, and family farming in the Great Plains. This study illuminated the role of land tenure and labor relations in the emergence of diverse class structures. Pfeffer showed the inadequacy of linear models. Rather, distinct class structures emerge from historical struggles over the distribution of wealth between producers and nonproducers.

Adapting Wright (1978) to an exploration of agricultural class structure, Mooney (1983, 1988) focused on the contradictory class location of many farmers. Mooney challenged the view that agriculture must be transformed eventually into wage labor. He showed that instead, capital might continuously and more effectively appropriate surplus value from agricultural producers in the form of rent, interest, contract production, and part-time farming. This left control over the agricultural production process socially contested between farmers on the one hand and landlords, bankers, and processors on the other. The strength of cooperatives in the agricultural economy was a manifestation of this contest for control of capital and surplus value between farmers and nonproducers. Further, cooperatives reflected an institutionalized form of this contradictory class position of farmers. The class analyses performed by scholars like Pfeffer and Mooney thus emphasized regional traditions, social structures, and historical legacies over the abstract logic of capital.

A more concrete and more historical analysis is also seen in Friedland, Barton, and Thomas's (1980) analysis of agriculture (See also Thomas 1985). Their commodity systems approach is an analysis of class embedded in the social relations of production that are present in any given commodity production and distribution chain. As this approach diffused within the sociology of agriculture, attention to class and status variables varied considerably with the particular focus of individual researchers. The most recent developments in the sociology of agriculture focus on issues associated with globalization processes. Most of this research retains a central, though nonsystematic, class-analytic interest. Class structures in this tradition tend to be viewed on a global scale, transcending the boundaries of nation-states.

The Class and Stratification Structure of Rural America

Although official data reflecting urban and rural differences are often inadequate (and government sources increasingly neglect this variable), it is possible to describe, with some basic information, stratification as it varies within the rural population and between urban and rural populations. Data on class categories are much more difficult to obtain, outside of specific surveys generated to analyze class structure (as in Mooney 1988). Such surveys often are limited to single points in time and specific regions. The following discussion provides basic data on self-employment, income distribution, poverty, and educational attainment.

Self-Employment. Historically, rural America has been perceived as a haven for the self-employed and petty bourgeois classes, whether in town or on the farm. This popular image is a fiction insofar as there always has been greater use of wage labor and presence of absentee capital than it acknowledges. Nevertheless, self-employment declined in rural areas over time, and small, family-owned enterprises gave way to regional or national retail chains in hardware stores, groceries, and restaurants. Further, a process of rural industrialization has taken place largely during the 1970s and 1980s in many parts of rural America. According to the 1990 U.S. census, 7 percent of the total U.S. population (employed persons 16 years and older) were classified as self-employed. In urbanized areas, the proportion was smaller (5.8 percent), while in rural areas, 10.1 percent of the population was self-employed. Eighty-one percent of this rural self-employment was in agriculture. Among those employed, rural males were more likely (17.9 percent) than rural females (6.7 percent) to be self-employed.

Income. The use of income data can be problematic in comparing rural and urban standards of living, since certain costs of living, such as housing, can be much lower in rural areas. In 1989, the median income for U.S. households was $30,056. In urbanized areas, the median income was $32,002, while the total rural median income was $27,460. The figure shows a comparison of income levels among rural and urbanized populations. There are slightly smaller percentages at the lower end of the income distribution for urbanized populations than for rural ones. A similar pattern shows slightly higher percentages at the upper income levels for urbanized areas than for rural regions. However, overall the figure shows remarkable similarities in distributions of income among both populations. Greater differentiation can be found by examining income distribution within the rural population. While the median income for rural farm households was $29,505, the median income of rural townspeople in places of less than 1,000 was only $20,917.

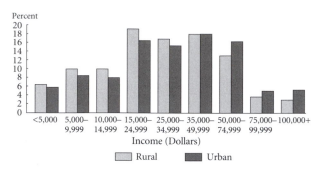

Comparison of Rural and Urban Income Levels

Source: U.S. Department of Commerce, Bureau of the Census. *1990 Census of Population: Social and Economic Characteristics: United States.* 1990 CP-2-1. Washington, DC: U.S. Gvoernment Printing Office, November 1993, Table 23.

Poverty. The percentage of people living in poverty does not differ dramatically between rural and urban areas. Throughout the United States, 13.1 percent of individuals live below the poverty level (data from the early 1990s). In urban areas, 12.6 percent live below poverty level, whereas in rural areas the percentage is slightly higher (13 percent). However, there is considerable regional variation in poverty among rural areas, with pockets of persistent poverty (Lyson and Falk 1993; Rural Sociological Society Task Force 1994). Within rural areas, the highest levels of poverty are located in small towns. In places of less than 1,000 people, 17.1 percent of persons are living below the poverty level. This was comparable to the 17.9 percent of persons who live below poverty level in central cities. The proportion of the rural farm population living below the poverty level was 11.6 percent. Elderly people in rural areas were more likely to live below the poverty level than were their urban counterparts (15.3 percent and 10.1 percent, respectively). However, the poverty rates for rural children were lower than for urban children (12.1 percent and 14.1 percent, respectively).

Education. The rural population (25 years and older) is less likely (67.9 percent) to have completed a high school education than the U.S. population as a whole (75.2 percent) or than those residing in urbanized areas (81.5 percent). The metropolitan population was twice as likely (22.5 percent) to have completed a bachelor's degree as the rural population (11.1 percent). Within the rural population, women were slightly more likely than men to have completed high school (69.0 percent compared with 66.8 percent). There are indications that the differences in educational attainment between rural and urban populations are diminishing. Among younger rural males (between the ages of 25 and 34), 77.5 percent had received a high school diploma, compared with 83.6 percent of the metropolitan population. Similarly, 82.6 percent of rural females had completed high school, compared with 86.0 percent of metropolitan females. Considerable gaps, however, persist between urban and rural populations with respect to the completion of a college degree.

Stratification and class structures of rural communities vary considerably by region and sometimes even by the predominant commodity mix in either agriculture or in the other rural resource-based extractive economies of lumbering, fishing, and mining. Such variations might often be more significant than variations between urban and rural populations.

—Patrick H. Mooney and D. Wynne Wright

See also

Homelessness; Income; Inequality; Migrant Farmworkers; Plantations; Poverty; Quality of Life; Social Movements; Underemployment.

References

Buttel, Frederick, Olaf Larson, and Gilbert Gillespie. *The Sociology of Agriculture*. Westport, CT: Greenwood Press, 1990.

Friedland, William H., Amy E. Barton, and Robert J. Thomas. *Manufacturing Green Gold*. New York: Cambridge University Press, 1981.

Goldschmidt, Walter. *As You Sow*. New York: Harcourt, Brace and Co., 1947. Reprinted Montclair, NJ: Allanheld, Osmun and Co., 1978.

Heffernan, William D. "Sociological Dimensions of Agricultural Structures in the United States." *Sociologia Ruralis* 12, no. 3/4 (1972): 481–499.

Lyson, Thomas A., and William W. Falk. *Forgotten Places: Uneven Development in Rural America*. Lawrence: University Press of Kansas, 1993.

Mann, Susan A., and James M. Dickinson. "Obstacles to the Development of a Capitalist Agriculture." *Journal of Peasant Studies* 5, no. 4 (1978): 466–481.

Mooney, Patrick H. "Toward a Class Analysis of Midwestern Agriculture." *Rural Sociology* 48, no. 4 (1983): 563–584.

———. *My Own Boss? Class, Rationality and the Family Farm*. Boulder, CO: Westview Press, 1988.

Pfeffer, Max J. "Social Origins of Three Systems of Farm Production in the United States." *Rural Sociology* 48, no. 4 (1983): 540–562.

Rodefeld, Richard. *The Changing Organizational and Occupational Structure of Farming and the Implications for Farm Work Force: Individuals, Families and Communities*. Unpublished Ph.D. dissertation. Madison: University of Wisconsin, 1974.

Rural Sociological Society Task Force on Persistent Rural Poverty. *Persistent Poverty in Rural America*. Boulder, CO: Westview Press, 1993.

Sewell, William H. "Rural Sociological Research, 1936–1965." *Rural Sociology* 30, no. 4 (December 1965): 428–451.

Thomas, Robert. *Citizenship, Gender and Work*. Berkeley: University of California Press, 1985.

Wright, Erik Olin. *Class, Crisis and the State*. London: New Left Books, 1978.

Social Movements

"Collective challenges by people with common purposes and solidarity in sustained interaction with elites, opponents, and authorities" (Tarrow 1994, 3–4). Definitions of social movements vary from subtle variations within a certain perspective to strong differences among perspectives. One particularly important difference lies in the degree to which the role of ideology is emphasized versus the role of material resources. A related distinction has to do with the degree of emphasis on informal association as opposed to formal organization. This discussion emphasizes social movements that tend toward more formal organization and focuses on the resource mobilization model of social movements. Specifically, three types of social movements in rural America will be analyzed and compared, giving special attention to the history of each. Changes in the character of U.S. agriculture have led to and have been caused by historical changes in the nature of rural social movements. The basic forces of technology and market conditions in interaction with the interests of rural people will continue both to shape and to be shaped by rural collective action.

Types of Social Movements

Social movements in rural America may be divided into three distinct types. The first two types are associated with agricultural production—specifically, either with the interests of family farmers (the first type) or with the interests of hired farm workers (the second type). A third type of movement involves the more general pursuit of rural interests rather than of specific agricultural interests.

Farmers' movements in the United States have a long and fascinating history. In some ways, these movements can be said to differ from one another across time as the nature of agriculture changed. In other ways, however, the elites, opponents, and authorities that farmers challenged in their mobilizations have been somewhat constant. Bankers, landlords, middlemen, government officials, and land-grant colleges most often have been identified by farmers' movements as antagonists. Although the specific persons involved may have changed, their roles and the conflict generated by such roles lends some continuity to agrarian mobilization in the United States.

Historical Overview of Farmers' Movements

As early as the colonial period, farmers mobilized to pursue specific interests in a variety of conditions. The Hudson River Valley of New York State has a long history of rebellion by farm tenants against their landlords that stretches from the colonial era to the mid-nineteenth century. The North Carolina Piedmont region was home to the colonial-era Regulator movement, which sought greater political representation (and less taxation) for farmers as against the interests of the coastal elite. Shortly after the Revolution, Admiral Shays's Rebellion was fought against the creditors and courts that sought to collect cash payments on debts in a rural economy that was still based largely on barter. This rebellion, centered in Massachusetts, helped sway elites to adopt the Constitution, as it demonstrated the need for a centralized army, given the inability of local militia to put down the rebellion. The Whiskey Rebellion involved Pennsylvania farmers' opposition to a tax on the sale of the whiskey that they distilled from their corn crops as a means to produce a less perishable and more easily transportable commodity.

However, after mass migration westward over the Appalachian Mountains began, agrarian discontent was more likely to lead to individual or familial geographic mobility than to collective action. The exception to this was the existence of localized squatter associations protecting their claims to land they had developed. Throughout this period, there were also hundreds of relatively isolated rebellions staged by slaves engaged in agricultural production across the South (Aptheker 1988).

The closing of the frontier and the end of slavery after the Civil War corresponded with a new wave of farmers' movements. Two elements stand out with respect to the post–Civil War farmers' movements: the development of pressure on political parties to better represent the interests of farmers, and the emergence of cooperatives to meet the economic needs of farmers in the face of what were seen as increasingly monopolized markets. Depending on the relative competitiveness of the party structure, farmers attempted to exert pressure on the hegemonic party, to take over and strengthen the weaker party, or to develop a third party. The farmers' movements of the late 1800s are the most well-known attempts to challenge the American party system, although the culmination of these efforts in the elections of 1896 often is viewed, perhaps incorrectly, as an example of the cooptation and ultimate failure of the farmers' movements. In addition to pursuing a political agenda, the movements also experimented with formal economic cooperation.

The Grange, founded shortly after the Civil War and modeled largely on the Masonic Order, engaged in political activity largely oriented to reform and regulate the railroads. The Grange developed several cooperative enterprises that, even if often failing, served to teach valuable lessons to future generations of cooperators.

The Northern and Southern Alliances turned to political solutions in the form of populism; but in many regions, suballiances formed the basis of a cooperative movement. The apparent failure of most efforts to build agricultural cooperatives in the late nineteenth century may have been due mostly to a lack of the capital needed to withstand the opposition mustered by private sector agribusiness firms. This situation changed in the early twentieth century; nearly two decades of relative prosperity provided farmers with the capital resources to firmly establish cooperative economic institutions as a mainstay of the American agricultural economy. The National Farmers' Educational and Cooperative Union (Farmers' Union) and the Society of Equity were other key farmers' movements that built cooperative enterprises in the early twentieth century.

A more radical strand of the cooperative movement was embodied in an agrarian socialism that became quite strong in the upper Midwest and Great Plains in the early twentieth century. The Nonpartisan League of North Dakota is the most famous and successful manifestation of this cooperative socialism. The Nonpartisan League temporarily gained control of the government of North Dakota between 1916 and the late 1920s and continued to influence politics in the northern Plains for decades. The success of farm cooperatives in this era and the threat from these more radical socialist movements facilitated the passage of the Capper-Volstead Act in 1922, which more firmly secured agricultural cooperation in law. The threat of these agrarian socialist movements stimulated countermovements by elites designed to co-opt or preempt the organization of farmers around leftist ideology, politics, and economics. The most important of these countermovements was the American Farm Bureau Federation. The Farm Bureau was organized through the efforts of USDA personnel with the financial resources of agribusiness interests such as banks, railroads, Sears, International Harvester, and the U.S. Chamber of Commerce (all of which, up to that point, had been seen traditionally as the opponents of most farmers' movements). Using cooperative enterprises as the basis of selective economic incentives toward membership, the Farm Bureau pushed an increasingly conservative ideology. By the post–World War II era, it had become a powerful political and ideological opponent of the Farmers' Union in advocating a laissez-faire orientation toward agricultural production at the farm level (as distinguished from government subsidization of research and development projects through USDA and the land-grant college complex).

The Depression era generated important mobilizations of farmers. In the Midwest, the Iowa-based Farmers' Holiday Association organized a farm strike to obtain better prices. This movement provided the networks of farmers that served as the basis for the famous "penny auctions," in which farmers forcefully disrupted the sale of foreclosed farms. In the South, the Southern Tenant Farmers' Union, centered in Arkansas and Delta cotton regions, sought greater rights for both Black and White sharecroppers, such as entitlement to a share of the crop subsidies provided by New Deal agricultural policy. Founded in the last days of the old cotton sharecropping system, which soon would be replaced by mechanization, chemicalization, and to some extent, soybeans, this latter movement in a way established a precedent for the civil rights movement that later blossomed in the South.

In the post–World War II era, the National Farmers' Organization (NFO) emerged out of the Iowa-Missouri region as a movement to develop collective bargaining for farmers. As had groups that previously attempted to control farm production, the NFO often found itself opposing the use of violence against free riders who benefited from price increases without bearing any of the costs incurred by those engaged in farm commodity holding actions. The shift to the use of economic rather than political power may be seen as a function of the dramatic demographic declines in farm population after World War II. The NFO remains, along with the Farm Bureau and the Farmers' Union (and the Grange in some regions), one of the more influential general farm movement organizations.

The most recent farmers' movement is the American Agriculture Movement (AAM). Centered in the Wheat Belt, the AAM talked of a farm strike during the "farm crisis" of the 1980s, but primarily has engaged in political protest activity to increase the federal government's support of farm prices. The AAM was, for a short time, successful in manipulating media (especially television) coverage. Otherwise, the legacy of the AAM may lie primarily in its networking function within the broader rural social movements that coincided with the agricultural and rural crisis of the early 1980s.

The New Rural Social Movements

Perhaps the most important precursor to more broadly based rural social movements, as distinct from farmers' movements, was the Country Life Commission of the early twentieth century. Danbom (1979, 144), among oth-

ers, contends that the Country Life Movement, which derived from the more general progressive movement of the early twentieth century, was primarily ban-based and "concerned with the social and economic difficulties an unindustrialized agriculture created for urban-industrial society, identifying them as rural problems despite the fact that farmers did not see them as such."

More recently there have been new movements associated with the interests of the larger rural society. Many of these movements may deserve the label "new social movements." Although the notion of new social movements is heavily contested with respect to its most useful definition, in general new social movements tend to exhibit a greater concern with cultural or lifestyle issues beyond economic or production matters. In this sense, they strive to change values, norms, and beliefs in civil society, rather than invest all of their resources into traditional forms of political influence via governmental action. Participants in new social movements also generally make a conscious effort to resist formal and hierarchical organizational structures and to incorporate strong democratic participation from the grass roots upward.

Most of the research on new social movements has focused on their urban manifestations. However, by the early 1970s, several local groups coalesced to form a coalition known as Rural America. New Deal agricultural policy, formulated around specific commodities, led to the rise of commodity associations—particularly powerful players in the formulation of agricultural policy. This piecemeal approach impeded the development of a holistic policy attending to the total fabric of rural life. Rural America represented an attempt by rural citizens to develop such a policy. The primary drive behind Rural America came from rural churches, cooperatives, the Farmers' Union, and especially younger rural residents, many of whom constituted a portion of the rural population turnaround of the early 1970s, returning to or staying in rural communities after attending college or serving in the war in Vietnam in the 1960s. This organization provided important networks to develop the many local movement centers that arose during the farm crisis of the 1980s. These latter movements tended to be concerned about rural society as a whole even though the crisis was grounded in the credit-based agricultural economy. Most striking about these newer rural social movements was the explicit incorporation of strong elements of environmentalism, feminism, and civil rights issues (Mooney and Majka 1995). The traditional dichotomy between farmers and environmentalists was eroded, giving way to a movement focused around the development of a sustainable agriculture coincident with the family farm and similar types of agriculture. Women took much stronger leadership roles in these newer rural social movements and facilitated the development of this broader, more inclusive agenda. These movements expressed more concern for issues of civil rights (such as access to land by minorities, and Native American rights) than had been characteristic of farmers' movements in the past.

Farmworkers' Movements

Farmworkers' movements have been largely a twentieth-century phenomenon, generally corresponding to the development of large, capitalist agricultural production. These movements primarily have originated in California and the Southwest, although more recently a mobilization of farm workers has taken place in the so-called eastern stream (that is, among migrants from the southeastern United States who travel to Michigan, Ohio, Wisconsin, and other states in the Midwest). Many obstacles impede the mobilization of farmworkers. First is the often abundant labor supply for farmwork, leaving workers very little leverage for the sale of their labor. This impedes their ability to strike, a weakness that is exacerbated by the succession of various ethnic groups one after another to farm labor in the West (Chinese, Japanese, Filipinos, Mexicans, and Anglos). Ethnic identity has fostered solidarity within each ethnic group but often has been the basis of conflict between these workers as a class.

This problem, in turn, reflects the relative lack of resources available to farmworkers for mobilization. Sometimes these workers do not even have citizenship to use as political clout. The conditions of migratory labor obstruct the building of ties and networks with other members of communities and political representatives. The fact that agricultural labor has not been covered by basic labor legislation can be seen as both a cause and a consequence of farmworkers' lack of resources for political mobilization. These conditions force farmworkers to depend on external resources to support their movements. But even here, what would seem likely allies, such as organized labor, have proven highly unreliable and even antagonistic at times. Thus, the fortunes of farmworkers' movements depend largely on the political opportunities offered by periods or cycles of protest that are generated in the larger society. Not surprisingly, the Depression and the late 1960s and early 1970s have been their moments of greatest success. The 1970s, for example, saw the United Farm Workers (UFW) rely heavily on the support of consumers in the form of boycotts of certain growers to exert pressures they alone could not exert.

The organization of the UFW itself depended on the political opportunity afforded by the termination of the U.S.-sponsored Bracero Program (1942–1964). Under the Bracero Program, the state organized the importation of 5 million guest workers from Mexico, thwarting the tactical efficacy of the labor strike as a means to improve wages or working conditions. The UFW emerged subsequent to the end of the Bracero Program and borrowed heavily from the ideology and practices of the larger civil rights movement taking place in society. It is unclear (and often debated) whether the recent death of César Chávez (1927–1993), the longtime charismatic leader of the UFW, will deepen the deterioration that the movement has suffered in the 1980s and 1990s or provide opportunity for a resurgent mobilization generated by a new leadership.

The Farm Labor Organizing Committee (FLOC) spun off the UFW efforts but focused on negotiating contracts primarily in Ohio and Michigan. The relative success of this movement perhaps hinged on the triadic, rather than dyadic, nature of the negotiations. These farmworkers engaged in negotiations with both processors (such as Campbell's or Heinz) and smaller, family-type producers. This is a different situation from that in California, where grape growers, for example, are also the producers of wine.

Both the UFW and FLOC focused on issues of wages but also on issues of control over the labor process. The latter included hiring criteria, methods of pesticide application, grievance procedures, rest breaks, access to cool drinking water, and the use of various tools or machinery to reduce the drudgery of the labor.

The Near Future

The influence of social organizations on the direction of change in rural America will likely continue to be determined largely by the relative power of the commodity associations to influence governmental policy with respect to specific commodities. Trends toward government downsizing may mitigate this latter effect to some extent. Two particular developments will shape the character of future rural social movements: globalization and biotechnology. Although rural America has always been embedded in a global market, the recent acceleration of the process of globalization (led by initiatives such as the General Agreement on Tariffs and Trade and the North American Free Trade Agreement) will demand that farmers and other rural people think in global terms, even if they are capable of acting only at the local level. Similarly, technological development has long driven the structure of agriculture and rural society. However, recent developments in genetic engineering promise revolutionary changes in the production and marketing practices of farm and rural people. Control over the uses and abuses of this technology will certainly be a focus of rural social movements in the future. The growing movement for a sustainable agriculture and sustainable rural communities must contend with opposing elites and authorities whose interests do not coincide with local or regional sustainability. In this sense, rural movements will demand external alliances with sympathetic consumers and environmentalists in order to challenge these powerful opponents in an increasingly global and high-technology market for both agricultural commodities and rural labor.

—*Patrick H. Mooney*

See also

Agricultural Law; Cooperatives; History, Rural; Latinos; Town-Country Relations.

References

Aptheker, Herbert. *Abolitionism: A Revolutionary Movement.* Boston: Twayne Publishers, 1988.

Danbom, David B. *The Resisted Revolution: Urban America and the Industrialization of Agriculture, 1900–1930.* Ames: Iowa State University Press, 1979.

Majka, Linda C., and Theo J. Majka. *Farm Workers, Agribusiness and the State.* Philadelphia: Temple University Press, 1982.

McConnell, Grant. *The Decline of Agrarian Democracy.* Berkeley: University of California Press, 1953.

Mooney, Patrick H., and Theo J. Majka. *Farmers' and Farm Workers' Movements: Social Protest in American Agriculture.* New York: Twayne Publishers, 1995.

Saloutos, Theodore, and John D. Hicks. *Twentieth-Century Populism: Agricultural Discontent in the Middle West, 1900–1939.* Lincoln: University of Nebraska Press, 1951.

Tarrow, Sidney. *Power in Movement: Social Movements, Collective Action and Politics.* Cambridge, UK: Cambridge University Press, 1994.

Taylor, Carl C. *The Farmers' Movement: 1620–1920.* Westport, CT: Greenwood Press, 1953.

Socioeconomic Policy
See Policy, Socioeconomic

Sociology
See Rural Sociology

Soil

Naturally weathered earth, including inorganic and organic matter, that supports plant growth by supplying elements, water, and a medium for anchorage. Despite the above definition, soil means different things to different people. Some define soil as a medium for plant growth, but this tells little of its nature. Others say that soil is weathered rock, but a good definition needs to include the strong impact living things have on the nature of soil. Soil has been studied extensively both because plants grow in it (the field of edaphology) and for its own nature (pedology). An edaphologist might define soil as a mixture of mineral and organic materials capable of supporting plant growth. A pedologist might say that soil is a natural product formed by biochemical weathering of mineral and organic materials. Many qualifications could be added to either definition. This entry will consider the physical, chemical, and biological nature of soil, and how these properties influence its use for growing plants

Soil covers nearly all of the earth's land surface. Soil and plants rooting in it are almost everywhere unless human efforts have displaced them with buildings, roads, or other structures. People grow plants in soil, dig in soil, walk on soil, build on soil, and sometimes build with soil. Some soil gets in the wrong place and is called "dirt." Hands, clothes, houses, and machines get dirty. Soil is so prevalent and commonplace in life that it often is ignored, but it is vital to the earth's life-support system.

Soil Profiles and Pedons

Soil is extremely variable. Farmers know that sandy soils store less water and nutrients for plant growth than loamy soils, and that clay soils are harder to work than other soils. They also know that erosion changes the nature of soil by exposing subsoil layers. The layers that occur in a soil are often so distinct that an engineer considers them different soil materials for construction purposes. For example, a subsoil layer may be suitable for holding water in a pond, while the topsoil above it would be too porous for this purpose.

The soil layers at a particular site are so related to each other that a soil scientist considers the assemblage as a soil. A vertical section through these layers is called a soil profile. Each profile includes some combination of the following O (organic) horizons:

I. A horizons, which are generally higher in organic matter and therefore darker colored than the deeper-lying layers;

II. E horizons, lighter in color because eluviation (loss of small solid particles) and leaching have removed materials from them;

III. B horizons, which contain a higher percentage of clay than the rest of the profile (partly because of illuviation, deposition of the particles eluviated from above); and

IV. transitional horizons.

Whatever combination of these horizons happens to be present is called the solum (meaning true soil). Underlying, unconsolidated material lacking the influence of living things is called parent material or C horizon, and bedrock is designated as the R layer (see figure).

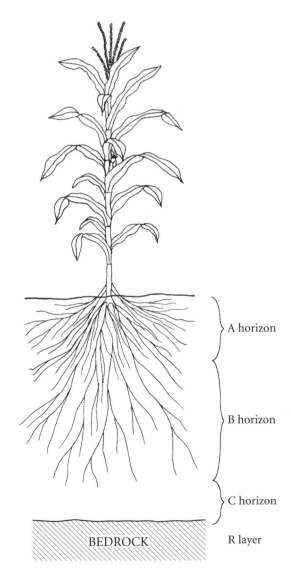

A horizon

B horizon

C horizon

BEDROCK   R layer

A typical pedon has a surface area of about one square meter and is as deep as the soil profile. It can encompass the root zone of a medium-sized plant such as corn.

A soil profile with enough surface area to grow a medium-sized plant (usually about one square meter) is called a pedon. A contiguous group of similar pedons is called a polypedon. Soil surveyors name, classify, and map soils in the field. Soil maps accompanied by descriptive and interpretive materials are published in soil survey reports.

Plant Growth Media

Plants can root in many kinds of media, including water cultures and various mixtures of solid materials, but no other medium competes with soil for the number and variety of plants grown. Food and fiber products that support human life are grown mostly in soil.

Soil is versatile, but it is seldom a perfect growth medium. Plant growth usually can be increased and improved in quality by adding fertilizer and either adding water to a dry soil or removing water from a wet soil. Soil amendments, such as lime to neutralize excessive acidity or gypsum to remedy alkalinity, can dramatically improve plant growth. Organic materials, such as plant residues or manure added to soil, are generally favorable for plant growth. Microbes decomposing organic materials may tie up nitrogen for a time, but they make the soil more porous and workable and ultimately release plant nutrients. Tillage or other manipulations can alter the soil structure and pore space, and thus influence water and air movement, seed germination, and root growth.

Varieties of Soil

Soil scientists have described and named thousands of different soil series, each of which has its own set of profile characteristics. Five factors influence the nature of the soil that forms in any particular place. These are climate, living organisms, topography, parent material, and time. Climate and living organisms are active factors, providing the weathering environment that converts rock into parent material and parent material into soil. Topography exerts a strong local effect by influencing water movement both on and in the soil and affecting temperature through the angle of the sun's rays. Weathering processes are slow but persistent, so changes continue over long periods of time.

Climate and living organisms are interrelated in that certain types of plants and animals live in certain climates, but their actions are too varied for these two factors to be fused. In general, the large-scale soil patterns of the world are controlled by the climatic factor, and the local soil patterns are strongly influenced by topography. For example, a particular group of soils commonly occurs repeatedly in a geographical area, with each soil occupying a specific topographic portion of each landform in the area.

Soil Classification

Several systems have been devised to arrange the thousands of known soil series into higher units of classification analogous to those used for plants and animals. The current U.S. system is known as soil taxonomy. It has six categorical levels: Soil series are classified into families, subgroups, great groups, suborders, and orders. Soil series are most useful when detailed soil information is needed, usually at a local level. Higher levels are useful when more generalized information is needed, such as the preparation of a world or national soil map. At its highest level, soil taxonomy groups all soils into 11 orders (see table).

Physical Properties of Soil

The usefulness and behavior of a soil depends greatly on its physical properties. Depth, texture, structure, porosity, color, and temperature are all significant physical properties. Soil depth is equivalent to the zone from which plants can extract water and nutrients. Depth is easy to measure where the solum directly overlies bedrock, gravel, or some other contrasting layer, but is less precise where the underlying material is loess, alluvium, or other material that resembles soil. The solum still coincides with the root zone, but the bottom of the root zone can be diffuse and difficult to identify precisely.

Soil texture characterizes the sizes of mineral particles in the soil. A textural analysis begins by either measuring or estimating the percent by weight of sand, silt, and clay in the soil. The U.S. Department of Agriculture (USDA) divides mineral material into clay particles less than 0.002 mm in diameter, silt particles between 0.002 and 0.05 mm in diameter, and sand particles between 0.05 and 2 mm in diameter. Particles larger than 2 mm in diameter are called gravel and stones. Laboratory measurements are made with sieves to separate the very coarse, coarse, medium, fine, and very fine sand sizes, and settling rates in water are used to separate the silt and clay. Field estimates are made by feeling the hardness, grittiness, stickiness, and plasticity of the soil. Texture names such as silty clay loam include various combinations of sand, silt, clay and loam. The word loam describes a mixture exhibiting the properties of all three size ranges approximately equally. It should be noted that a loamy soil contains less clay than sand or silt; clay exhibits its

The Eleven Soil Orders in Soil Taxonomy

Order	Abbreviated Description
Alfisols	Soils with grayish-brown colors and significant clay accumulation in their B horizons; most Alfisols form under forest vegetation.
Andisols	Soils containing high contents of glass and/or extractable iron and aluminum compounds; most Andisols form in young volcanic ash materials.
Aridisols	Light-colored soils that generally have alkaline reactions; Aridisols form in arid regions.
Entisols	Soils that have little or no horizon differentiation; Entisols are very young soils, at least in appearance.
Histosols	Soils whose properties are dominated by organic matter (>20 to 30 percent); Histosols form in wet and/or cold conditions.
Inceptisols	Soils with some soil profile development but without significant clay illuviation; Inceptisols form in humid climates under forest vegetation.
Mollisols	Soils with thick, dark-colored upper horizons; Mollisols form in temperate climates under grass vegetation.
Oxisols	Soils that are very highly weathered and low in natural fertility; Oxisols form in tropical climates.
Spodosols	Intensely leached soils with bright colors, strong acidity, and low fertility; Spodosols form under evergreen trees in cool, humid climates.
Ultisols	Strongly weathered soils with redder or yellower colors and more acidity than Alfisols; Ultisols form under forest vegetation in warm, humid climates.
Vertisols	Soils with high clay contents that form deep cracks at least 1 cm wide when dry; Vertisols form in high-clay parent material in climates with wet and dry seasons.

properties very strongly because clay particles have a very large surface area per gram.

Soil structure is the arrangement of individual soil particles into aggregates and peds. Soil tilth, the ability of a soil to be tilled easily, is related to structure. Small, loosely packed clumps of soil forming granular structure give good porosity, permeability, and tilth to the surface horizons of many soils. Denser peds that fit more tightly together form blocky structure that may occur at any depth. Many subsoils have cracks that bound the vertically oriented peds of prismatic structure. The E horizons of some soils have platy structure, with horizontal surfaces. Each kind of structure influences the movement of water and air and the growth of plant roots.

Soil structure may be disturbed by tillage. For example, working a wet soil may produce clods, and traffic can compact the soil. Compaction is favorable for building a roadbed or in a dam, but it is generally unfavorable for plant growth and soil tilth. Fortunately, natural forces such as freezing and thawing and the activity of living things tend to regenerate soil structure and tilth.

A favorable soil for plant growth has a wide range of pore sizes. The continuity of the pores larger than 0.1 mm is important for aeration and soil permeability. Microscopic pores hold water against gravity, but plant roots can withdraw roughly half of this water for plant use. Water available to plants may occupy 15 to 20 percent of the volume of a porous soil with loamy texture, but the percentage decreases in sandy soils as the surface area of the particles decreases. Some dense clay soils have no large pores and therefore may be permanently saturated with water.

Soil color has little importance of its own, but it indicates other properties such as organic matter content, which darkens soil color; excess salts or free lime, which may lighten soil color; or oxidized iron coatings, which redden soil color. Poor soil drainage is indicated by rust mottles in the soil, and long-term saturation is indicated by the bluish-gray colors of reduced iron compounds.

Cool soil temperature may slow or prevent seed germination, and hot temperatures may cause soil water to evaporate rapidly. Temperature also influences the rate of weathering of soil minerals, the decomposition of organic materials, and the release of plant nutrients.

Chemical Properties of Soil

Sand and silt are chemically inert, but clay and humus (the organic matter remaining after decomposition slows) have electrical charges that attract ions to their surfaces. The large surface area of these small particles makes colloidal chemistry very important in soils. The ions held in temperate regions are dominantly calcium and magnesium; but lesser amounts of potassium, sodium, and micronutrient cations are also held. The attraction is strong enough to resist leaching but weak enough to permit exchanges to occur and for plants to obtain nutrient ions. Plants often exchange hydrogen ions for nutrient ions, thus causing the soil to become more acidic.

Weathering and leaching cause the soils of humid regions to lose fertility over long periods of time. Highly weathered tropical soils lose cation exchange capacity as well as plant nutrients, so it is more difficult to maintain good soil fertility in the tropics than in temperate regions. Crop removal and nitrogen fertilizers cause soils to acidify much more rapidly than they would naturally. The

remedy is to apply lime periodically to keep the soil pH suitable for the crop being grown.

Inadequate leaching causes salinity in some soils of arid environments, especially where a water table provides upward moving water carrying soluble salts toward the surface. This condition applies to many houseplants as well as to arid climatic regions. Excess salts form a white crust on the high points of the soil whenever it dries out. The remedy is to increase downward movement by drainage and leaching. A soil amendment such as gypsum must be applied before leaching if the accumulated salts are high in sodium. Otherwise, leaching can produce a sodic soil that is too alkaline and impermeable to grow plants.

Biological Properties of Soil

Soil supports a remarkable population of living things. Plant roots constitute the largest living mass in the soil, and bacteria are the most numerous inhabitants. A single gram of fertile topsoil may contain billions of bacteria. Fungi, actinomycetes, protozoa, nematodes, insects, earthworms, rodents, snakes, and many other living things are also at home in soil. The decomposition of the dead remains of plant and animal life is an important activity in soil. Plant nutrients are recycled thereby for future generations of plants.

Soil is made porous by the tunneling of earthworms, insects, and other animal life and by the growth of plant roots. Gummy substances produced during decomposition processes improve soil's structural stability, keeping it porous. Materials such as cellulose and protein are decomposed in a few weeks or months of warm weather, but more resistant materials are left to accumulate as soil humus, which takes years or even centuries to decompose. Prolific plant growth, cool temperatures, and wet conditions that reduce soil aeration favor the accumulation of several percent of organic matter in the upper part of a soil. Dominantly organic peat and muck soils are produced in saturated bogs or in cold climates such as in Alaska. Organic matter contents are usually less than 1 percent in tropical soils because the organic matter decomposes rapidly there, in desert soils because little organic matter is produced there, and in subsoils because plant roots diminish with depth.

Using Soil for Growing Crops

Annual crops will be emphasized here, although perennial grasses and trees also can be crops. Until recently, annual cropping began with tillage to eliminate weeds and produce a seedbed. The current trend is toward less tillage, the ultimate being no tillage, in which the only soil disturbance is that caused by planting. Pesticides can control weeds and other pests, and many soils make suitable seedbeds without tillage. Fertilizer is still needed to make up for nutrient deficiencies caused by crop removal. Also, the soil pH should be monitored and lime or gypsum applied when needed.

Soil conservation efforts have benefited greatly from reduced tillage. Undisturbed soil is less easily eroded, and crop residues left on the surface absorb the impact of raindrops and wind. Even so, proper management of sloping soils involves choosing crops that provide good cover and/or mechanical practices such as terracing or contour tillage to reduce runoff.

Soil organic matter contents usually decline in cropped soils, and practices such as reduced tillage, which cause slower decomposition, are generally beneficial. It is important to return as much organic matter to the soil as possible, especially if the soil tilth needs to be improved. Crop residues, manure, and green manure all provide beneficial organic matter. Gardeners have found compost to be good for improving both fertility and tilth. The composition of compost varies, but it generally includes layers of soil, manure, and grass clippings or other organic materials. Nitrogen fertilizer and lime are often added. The mass is kept moist so that microbes will decompose (compost) the organic materials. The pile may be mixed and turned periodically, and applied to a garden after some weeks or months of composting (the process is generally too labor intensive for use on field crops).

—*Frederick R. Troeh*

See also
Agriculture, Hydroponic; Conservation, Soil; Cropping Systems; Regional Diversity; Tillage.
References
Brady, Nyle C. *The Nature and Properties of Soils.* 11th ed. New York: Macmillan, 1996.

Fanning, Delvin Seymour, and Mary Christine Balluff Fanning. *Soil Morphology, Genesis, and Classification.* New York: Wiley, 1989.

Foth, Henry D. *Fundamentals of Soil Science.* 8th ed. New York: Wiley, 1990.

Soil Survey Staff. *Soil Taxonomy: A Basic System of Soil Classification for Making and Interpreting Soil Surveys.* Agriculture Handbook 436. Washington, DC: U.S. Department of Agriculture, Government Printing Office, 1975.

Troeh, Frederick R., J. Arthur Hobbs, and Roy L. Donahue. *Soil and Water Conservation.* 2d ed. Englewood Cliffs, N.J.: Prentice-Hall, 1991.

Troeh, Frederick R., and Louis M. Thompson. *Soils and Soil Fertility.* 5th ed. New York: Oxford University Press, 1993.

Special Education
See Education, Special

Sport
A competitive physical activity guided by established rules and motivated by a combination of intrinsic and extrinsic rewards. The history of sport in America is examined from the colonial era through the 1800s and into the modern age. Particular attention is given to rural America's historical contributions to sport and to the importance of sport for modern rural communities.

Introduction
Sport is pervasive in American society. Three levels of sport—informal, organized, and corporate—can be distinguished. Informal sport is primarily for the enjoyment of the participants, who determine and enforce the rules. Organized sport involves formal organizations (for example, leagues, teams, and sponsors) and a regulatory agency that establishes and enforces rules. The basic function of the organizations is to benefit the participants in sport. Corporate sport is dominated by economics and politics. Organizations at this level of sport are less concerned with the participants' interests than with benefiting consumers (fans, owners, and alumni), generating profits, and maintaining a high concentration of power. In general, rural communities are directly involved in informal sport and organized sport and indirectly involved in corporate sport.

Sport can be viewed as a mirror of society that reflects the social structure and the changes society experiences. This is evident in the history of American sport from colonial times to the present, as society shifted from a rural, agricultural context to an urban, industrialized context. Guttman (1978) has asserted that modern sport did not come into existence until the late 1800s, as a result of the industrial revolution and urbanization. Although colonial sport was primarily a rural activity, the evolution of American society shifted the predominant context of sport to urban centers. Nevertheless, sport continues to play an integral role in rural America.

Sport in the Colonial Era
Sport in the colonial era reflected religious influences and living conditions of the colonists. Puritan and Protestant religious influences inhibited sport participation. Lucas and Smith (1978, 8) note "That everyone should have a

Harold Darnold of Burlington, Pennsylvania, shows the winning form in the eighteenth annual horseshoe tournament at the 1976 Mississippi Valley Fair in Davenport, Iowa.

calling and work hard at it was a first premise of Puritanism. . . . Not leisure and enjoyment but activity only served to increase the glory of God." As a result, local laws prohibiting many sporting activities were enacted. The struggle for survival and severe living conditions of the colonists left little time for leisure activities. Further, the sparse population of the frontier inhibited the pursuit of many of the folk games that were part of European culture.

Although officially prohibited in most colonies, certain sporting activities took place during this period. Popular sports included horse racing, footraces, jumping contests, fistfighting, wrestling matches, eye-gouging, shooting matches (rifles and pistols), and hunting contests. The Dutch introduced kolven, a game similar to golf, and gander pulling, a contest in which participants attempted to jerk the head off a live goose. Other sporting activities involving animals were cockfighting and rat baiting (dozens of rats were placed in a ring with a ratting dog, and spectators wagered on the number of rats the dog would kill in specified period of time). Bear-baiting (large dogs turned loose on a chained bear) and dog fights were also common recreational sports during this era. Taverns often served as social centers where sporting activities such as cards, dice, billiards, skittles (a precursor to bowling), and shooting matches took place.

Sport activities were more common in areas less influenced by Puritan religion traditions, such as in the southern colonies and on the frontier. Sport activities increased during the later years of the colonial period. Most of the sports were informal activities or organized by sponsors such as county fairs, communities, and taverns. They also often occurred as part of holiday festivals, or during militia training. In the South, the gentry established jockey clubs for thoroughbred horse racing. The wealthy generally had more time for recreation and could afford to engage in more expensive sports.

Sport in Nineteenth-Century America

Sporting activities of the colonists continued after they gained independence. In rural and frontier areas, sport continued to be informal or loosely organized around community festivals. However, American society and sport began to change during this period. Racing became a popular mass entertainment, with horse racing as one of the biggest attractions. Other racing activities involved trains, sailing boats, and steamboats. Their promoters—for example, railroad companies—organized the races to increase profits. Racing events were often scheduled in remote places accessible by rail. Spectators not only paid admission to the event, but also paid to travel on the trains carrying them to the event. Although it was illegal, rail and steamboat companies also promoted prizefighting. Sporting activities increasingly catered to an urban clientele and focused on profit making.

American society experienced a transformation during the mid-1800s, as industrialization and urbanization increased. During this transformation, the focus of sport moved from rural areas to urban centers. Informal sport still operated in rural America, but urban-based corporate sports emerged to dominate the nation's attention. Baseball was a sport that epitomized this transformation. Baseball emerged from a variety of games, such as town ball, rounders, and One Old Cat, played in urban areas like New York City and Boston. The formal rules of baseball were established in 1845 by Alexander Joy Cartwright. Although formal baseball began as an urban, upper-class activity, it soon spread to the middle and working classes and rural areas. Professionalism in baseball gradually developed and became concentrated in urban areas. However, many rural communities sponsored baseball teams that played in loosely organized leagues.

Other sports, such as football and basketball, followed a development path similar to that of baseball. They were primarily urban in origin, initially played by middle- and upper-class athletes, and later spread to rural areas. However, football and basketball were more strongly linked to college sports. Like baseball, these sports became professionalized around the late 1800s. They were eventually dominated by a corporate sports orientation, and sports organizations and universities increasingly concentrated on the commercial aspects of these activities.

Sport in the Modern Age

The twentieth century witnessed the emergence of the sport hero in American culture, and rural sports made significant contributions by providing many star athletes. Examples of athletes with rural backgrounds who became baseball stars include Grover Cleveland Alexander, Ty Cobb, Dizzy Dean, Lefty Grove, Gil Hodges, Carl Hubbell, Walter Johnson, Connie Mack, Mickey Mantle, Roger Maris, Jackie Robinson, and Cy Young. Football stars, such as Red Grange, and famous Olympians, such as Jesse Owens and Jim Thorpe, also came from rural areas. Boxing stars like Jack Dempsey and Joe Louis likewise had rural origins. Legendary coaches hailing from rural areas included Paul "Bear" Bryant, John J. McGraw, Branch Rickey, and Adolph Rupp.

The linkage of sport with secondary public education was an important development. This linkage developed at the turn of the twentieth century and was aided by two major factors: First, popular collegiate sports were diffused to high schools, first in metropolitan areas then in rural ones. Second, the population shift from rural to urban areas accelerated during the 1900s, causing disruptions and crisis in rural communities. Local high school sports programs became a source of community identity and cohesion during this period. School sport in rural communities promoted parental, alumni, and community support for the school.

Since the 1970s, high schools have faced numerous issues involving gender equity in boys' and girls' sports programs, pay equity between men and women coaches, and increasing costs of equipment and travel. The organization of high schools within each state also has been an issue as smaller rural schools were pitted against larger, urban schools in state tournaments. Most states resolved this equity issue by instituting a classification system based on school size. As late as 1996, however, Indiana high school basketball still operated under a single class system.

Little League baseball was established in 1939, with roots in rural America. Carl Stolz of Williamsport, Pennsylvania, organized the league with initial support from Floyd A. Mutchler of Lycoming Dairy Farms. Little League grew from its humble beginnings to sponsor a national tournament in 1948 (Lock Haven, Pennsylvania, defeated St. Petersburg, Florida). Stolz received corporate support for the tournament from the United States Rubber Company, which made a long-term commitment to support the organization after receiving positive publicity. Today, Little League Baseball, Inc. has more than $11 million total assets and consists of more than 7,000 leagues and more than 48,000 teams. Most rural communities have a Little League team. Further, more than 8,000 international leagues in more than 40 countries are affiliated with Little League Baseball, Inc.

Currently, corporate sport dominates athletics. However, informal sport can be found throughout the nation. Rural areas continue to produce athletes who gain national recognition and superstar status. Although sport will most likely continue to be dominated by urban-based corporate sport organizations, rural sport will continue to be an important component of rural communities. From high school sports to Little League, community-based softball leagues, Pop Warner League football, tennis, swimming, and other athletic activities, sport will continue to provide recreation opportunities in rural areas and serve as a source of rural community identity and pride.

—*Duane A. Gill*

See also

Community, Sense of; Culture; Educational Curriculum; Gambling; Games; History, Rural; Horse Industry; Recreational Activities; Stock Car Racing.

References

Eitzen, D. Stanley, and George H. Sage. *Sociology of North American Sport.* Dubuque, IA: Wm. C. Brown, 1993.

Fine, Gary Alan. *With the Boys: Little League Baseball and Preadolescent Culture.* Chicago: University of Chicago Press, 1987.

Guttmann, Allen. *From Ritual to Record: The Nature of Modern Sports.* New York: Columbia University Press, 1978.

Krout, John Allen. *Annals of American Sport, The Pageant of America Series.* New Haven, CT: Yale University Press, 1929.

Lucas, John A., and Ronald A. Smith. *Saga of American Sport.* Philadelphia: Lea and Febiger, 1978.

Noverr, Douglas A., and Lawrence E. Ziewacz. *The Games They Played: Sports in American History, 1865–1980.* Chicago: Prentice-Hall, 1983.

Radar, Benjamin G. *American Sports: From the Age of Folk Games to the Age of Televised Sports.* Englewood Cliffs, NJ: Prentice-Hall, 1990.

Spears, Betty Mary, and Richard A. Swanson. *History of Sport and Physical Activity in the United States.* Dubuque, IA: Wm. C. Brown, 1978.

Twombly, Wells. *200 Years of Sport in America: A Pageant of a Nation at Play.* New York: McGraw-Hill, 1976.

Stock Car Racing

A form of automobile racing using modified standard American cars on oval, usually paved, tracks. Beginning as speed competitions among moonshine runners, stock car racing developed into a nationally recognized American sport in the middle of the twentieth century. Bill France spearheaded the National Association for Stock Car Auto Racing (NASCAR) in 1948, organizing and legitimizing the races. Professional drivers today make it a family affair, involving several generations. The mostly southern sport courted corporate sponsorship from the beginning, and it attracts fans from throughout the country.

From Moonshine Runs to Racetracks

On the back roads of the Deep South and mountain roads of Appalachia, young men delivered moonshine liquor to the Piedmont and Tidewater Flatlands during the 1930s. The hardscrabble existence in the mountain regions afforded the residents few opportunities. The soil supported few cash crops besides corn and grain. Converting them into moonshine liquor made these crops easier to haul to market than the bulky harvest. Despite the federal

Stock car racing, which developed out of informal daredevil driving in the rural South, now attracts a national following as well as major corporate sponsorship.

government's insistence on controlling liquor production through taxation, the local independent-minded moonshiners continued to produce their wares with a free-enterprise mentality; they believed it their right to make a living as they had been doing for years. To outrun and outmaneuver local sheriffs and the federal revenue agents determined to stop the flow of untaxed alcohol, the drivers modified and improved their cars' performance. Junior Johnson and Curtis Turner became legends for their skill in implementing a "bootleg turn"—rapidly reversing the direction of their speeding cars. Johnson once commented, "I always think someday I'm gonna look in my mirror on the race track and see a flashing blue light. I got caught at the still [in 1955]. I never got caught on the road. They never outrun me" (Wilkinson 1983, 12; Bledsoe 1975, 43). The competitive daredevil drivers, proud of their driving ability and cars, inevitably began to race each other to prove who had the fastest car.

From one-on-one speed contests on back roads and in cow pastures and clearings, the participants moved to old fairgrounds horse racetracks. Using only American-made standard or stock cars modified for racing, the blue-collar, predominantly southern drivers proved which car was fastest on dirt and paved racetracks. Corporate sponsors watched the cars circle the track as rolling advertising billboards for their products. Throughout the 1930s and early 1940s, racing remained a local event, often disorganized and run by shady promot-

ers who sometimes absconded with the gate receipts before the race ended. The racing boom exploded with returning World War II veterans. The red clay in the foothills of the Appalachian and Blue Ridge Mountains offered an excellent natural racing surface. Farmers easily cut out a quarter- or half-mile oval, hammered together wooden grandstand seating, and created a racetrack. Stock car racing became the fastest growing spectator sport, eventually attracting drivers and fans from other regions and economic classes.

Bill France Creates NASCAR

The home of land-speed racing, Daytona Beach, Florida, became the site of the first organized and sanctioned stock car race in March 1936, when the American Automobile Association, the owner of the timing equipment, sponsored a race of a specified length and purse. Sig Haughdahl, a motorcycle and car racer, cut two passes through the sand dunes to form an oval beach roadcourse for the race. Although it failed because of the deep sand and infighting among the local politicians, one of the drivers, Bill France, Sr., saw the potential; within two years he promoted races over the beach course. Drivers from as far away as the red clay ovals of Atlanta, Georgia, traveled to Daytona Beach to race, often generating more excitement along the way than when they arrived. France continued to hold weekend races. In the 1940s, along with several other racers and promoters, he created NASCAR to bring the sport respectability and profit.

In December 1947, Bill France, Sr. and Bill Tuthill, a promoter of midget car and motorcycle races called a meeting with other promoters in the lounge of the Streamline Hotel in Daytona Beach, Florida, to discuss organizing stock car racing. Within two months, France and Tuthill drafted the plan for NASCAR, a name suggested at the December meeting by Red Voght, an early builder of some of the fastest Atlanta stock cars. France brought in one of his service station's customers, attorney Louis Ossinsky, to handle legal issues and problems. They incorporated NASCAR on February 21, 1948, with France holding 50, Tuthill 40, and Ossinsky 10 shares of stock. NASCAR set and enforced rules, ensured that promoters paid purses, paid bonuses to top drivers based on a points-earned system, and sought insurance for drivers. The first year began slowly with only nine races, mostly promoted by France. The following year, France's novel idea to hold a new car race catapulted stock car racing into the limelight.

The new race used regular cars directly from showrooms, thus the term "stock." Spectators finally were able to see which American-made cars that the average person drove were the fastest. The fans could more easily identify with the Fords, Chevrolets, Pontiacs, Hudsons, and Plymouths, among others, than the nondescript modified lightweight cars with big engines previously run in stock car races. The June 19, 1949, race on a 75-mile dirt track in Charlotte, North Carolina, attracted over 13,000 paying fans and instituted NASCAR's Grand National Division. This track evolved into the Charlotte Motor Speedway, a 1.5-mile track completed in 1960. In neighboring South Carolina, Harold Brasington, a construction worker and heavy-equipment owner, built an Indianapolis 500–type, oval, 1.25-mile speedway for stock cars in Darlington in the summer of 1950. To overcome the deep sand that bogged down the cars on the Daytona Beach course, France built a 2.5-mile triangular oval off the beach, where he staged what would become, after the Indianapolis 500, the second most attended car race—the Daytona 500.

Bill France, as president of NASCAR, made stock car racing a national sport. France actively courted politicians, to prevent interference with his tracks and to thwart unfavorable legislation that might ban racing. As a self-styled benevolent dictator, he kept the reputation of the sport uppermost, often to the disgruntlement of owners and drivers seeking an edge. When one car manufacturer modified a model to gain an advantage, France placed restrictions on it to bring all cars back to parity. Driver Bobby Allison, often frustrated with constantly changing rules, recognized that "Big Bill knew there were a lot of people who wanted to see those cars on the track, and he knew that having them look like the ones at home in the driveway was important. He made the rules where there wasn't anyone who could run away and hide. Another thing he did was keep the rules where it didn't take a young fortune to get started." But France also ruled with an iron fist. Allison remarked, "There were no arguments, no back talk, no nothing. If you were going to race in NASCAR, you were going to do it his way and not say anything until you were asked" (Glick 1992, C2). In the 1950s, when Curtis Turner and Tim Flock tried to form a drivers' union, France suspended them from NASCAR racing for four years. When France retired as president of NASCAR in 1972, his son Bill France, Jr., assumed control of the organization. The elder France continued as the head of the International Raceway Corporation, which operates Daytona International Speedway and Alabama International Motor Speedway at Talladega (the 2.66-mile track constructed in 1969), until his death in 1992.

The Drivers

Before stock car racing succeeded in Daytona and blue-collar, working-class White men entered stock car racing as owners, drivers, mechanics, and fans, upper-class men had dominated motor sports in America. As the sport branched out from the South, drivers from northern and western states began to win their share of races. Except for Wendell O. Scott, who raced full-time between 1949 and 1973, African Americans have lacked a presence in NASCAR. Women also have remained on the sidelines, unlike drag racing's Shirley Muldowney, as relatives or race queens; the male network does not welcome women drivers or mechanics.

The mainstay of NASCAR remain the tiers of racing that bring the sport to short dirt tracks (for the Modified, Sportsmen, and other lesser divisions) near small, rural towns in the South (like the old three-eighths-mile clay Lanier Raceway in north Georgia), short paved tracks under one mile (like Richmond), and to the speedways of Charlotte and Atlanta for the Winston Cup Grand National Circuit. From the 10 races run in 1949, NASCAR increased the number to 40–60 races each year through 1971. The modern era of 30–33 major races began in 1972. Among its 11 divisions, NASCAR sanctions about 2,000 stock car races annually. Fans in Martinsville, Virginia, Jennerstown, Pennsylvania, Loudon, New Hampshire, and Indianapolis flock to what NASCAR claims is the fastest growing spectator sport in America. The France family–run organization fosters loyalty from the drivers, who earn bonuses in special NASCAR programs. Successful drivers such as Richard Petty and Darrell Waltrip never considered racing Formula One cars in the Indianapolis 500; Cale Yarborough and Bobby Allison briefly attempted to cross over to Formula One but soon returned to stock car racing.

NASCAR is a family affair in more than its organizational control. Three generations of the Petty family—father Lee, son Richard, and grandson Kyle—successfully race stock cars. Other racing families include the Bodine brothers (Geoff, Brett, and Todd); fathers and sons Ralph and Dale Earnhardt and Ned and Dale Jarrett; and brothers Terry and Bobby Labonte, Dale and Michael Waltrip, and Rusty and Mike Wallace. Kyle Petty remarked that since racing is a time-consuming sport, with racing from February through the middle of November and building and testing cars in January, "If you're going to hang out with your family, you have to hang out at a racetrack. So when you grow up in that environment and look for something for your children, you say: 'Well, it wasn't too bad when I was growing up; it can't be too bad for them, either.' So you bring them along" (Denlinger 1995, C3).

The sport also attracts families as fans. As the race car craze outgrew its southeastern roots, northern, midwestern, and western middle-class families flocked to the racetracks and watched televised coverage. Compared with other sports heroes, stock car drivers make themselves accessible to their fans for autographs, pictures, and personal contact. The fans, in turn, root not for a particular car, but its driver. They identify with the human in control rather than the brand name of the car or its sponsors.

Sponsors

Long before baseball erected billboards or colleges sought corporate tie-ins, stock car racing depended on sponsors to underwrite the costs of running the expensive machines. In exchange for financial support, the owners emblazon corporate logos on the cars and drivers' uniforms. Initially supported by beer and tobacco companies such as R. J. Reynolds, which lends its product name to NASCAR's primary series, the Winston Cup, stock car racing appealed equally to other corporate sponsors, who recognized the advertising potential in having their product visible on every lap of a televised race. Sponsors include McDonald's, Budweiser, Valvoline, and their product competitors Burger King, Miller Genuine Draft, and Pennzoil. Even country music performers see the benefit of sponsoring a rolling billboard.

When R. J. Reynolds backed the sport in 1971, Bruton Smith saw a wise investment future in stock car racing. He developed the Charlotte Motor Speedway into a well-respected, and perhaps the finest, racing oval in the country. Smith constructed condominiums overlooking the track in 1984. When he purchased the Atlanta Motor Speedway in 1990, he vowed to convert it into a world-class speedway that would attract fans from among the over 3 million people in the countryside surrounding Atlanta, and return the NASCAR to its roots in the Atlanta area.

—*Susan Hamburger*

See also
Community Celebrations; Recreational Activities; Sport.
References
Black, James T. "The South's Fastest Sport." *Southern Living* (May 1990): 12–14.
Bledsoe, Jerry. *The World's Number One, Flat-Out, All-Time Great, Stock Car Racing Book.* Garden City, NY: Doubleday, 1975.
Chapin, Kim. *Fast as White Lightning: The Story of Stock Car Racing.* New York: Dial Press, 1981.
Denlinger, Ken. "NASCAR and the Crew." *Washington Post* (August 1, 1995): C1 and 3.
Glick, Shav. "France: Benevolent Dictator." *Los Angeles Times* (June 12, 1992): C2.
Pillsbury, Richard. "A Mythology at the Brink: Stock Car Racing in the American South." *Sport Place International* 3 (1989): 2–12.
"Scott Legacy: Overcoming Racism." *Atlanta Journal and Constitution* (December 25, 1990): E12.
Wilkinson, Sylvia. *Dirt Tracks to Glory: The Early Days of Stock Car Racing as Told by the Participants.* Chapel Hill, NC: Algonquin Books, 1983.

Sugar Industry

The production of raw sugarcane and sugar beets and their transformation into marketable sweeteners. This entry will address international and U.S. governmental issues related to the sugar industry before focusing on production and processing of sugarcane and sugar beets in the United States. Implications of the industry for labor and the environment are then discussed.

Sugar and International Relations

Most sugar produced worldwide is consumed domestically, often at government-controlled prices. A large portion of the world sugar trade is conducted under bilateral agreements and preferential terms, such as the European Community's Lomé Agreement. As a result, slight shifts in total world production or government policy can have a substantial impact on prices. Governments can block exports in times of scarcity and dump surpluses in times of excess production. Price variability, in turn, increases risk, particularly to producers who do not have mechanisms available to smooth price variations.

The United States traditionally has maintained domestic sugar prices both for producers and consumers at or above world market prices since the mid-1930s, a practice followed in many countries due to the great fluctuation annually in sugar production worldwide. Price maintenance has been accomplished by limiting sugar supplies.

U.S. Sugar Legislation

Until the 1900s, sugar tariffs were a major source of revenue for the federal government. Refiners wanted to import raw sugar as cheaply as possible, but imports provided competition for U.S. growers. The Sugar Act of 1934 (also known as the Jones-Constigan Act) was intended to isolate domestic U.S. sugar production from price-depressing conditions. The U.S. secretary of agriculture determined the nation's sugar consumption requirements each year. Those requirements were divided among U.S. production areas and foreign countries by assigning a quota to each. The 1937 Sugar Act added an import tax. Nonquota sugar, raw or processed, could not be imported. The quota provisions were suspended with World War II and the disruption of normal agricultural production, but were reintroduced after the war through the Sugar Act of 1948. The act was similar to previous legislation, but provided greater detail. It was amended in 1951, 1956, 1962, 1965, and 1971.

The Food and Agriculture Act of 1977 provided support for the 1977 and 1978 sugarcane and sugar beet crops through loans or purchase over twice the world market price. These loan provisions helped to shift power within the industry away from the growers, which were favored under the initial New Deal legislation, to the processors. Loans are made to processors rather than to growers.

The Food Security Act of 1985 mandated a price-support program for domestically produced sugarcane and sugar beets at not less than 18 cents per pound. However, the Dole Amendment to the 1985 farm bill stipulated that the sugar program must be conducted at no cost to the U.S. Treasury, which meant that no Commodity Credit Corporation (CCC) forfeiture was permitted. The 1996 Farm Bill continued to protect sugar growers, with domestic sugar prices still protected above world market prices.

Growing Sugar

The regional structure of the U.S. sugar industry changed markedly between 1960 and 1990, shifting from small farms in the West and North Central region to large sugar plantations in the South. Sugarcane is grown in Florida, Louisiana, Texas, Puerto Rico, and Hawaii. Florida's sugarcane production increased significantly when the United States stopped importing sugar from Cuba in 1960. The owners of the Cuban sugar mills moved to southern Florida and purchased the organic soils along the southern and southeastern shore of Lake Okeechobee. By the mid-1980s, Florida was the largest U.S. cane producer, with 50 percent of the acreage and 43 percent of the production.

The number of farms producing sugarcane declined steadily. For example, in Louisiana, a major cane-producing state, there were more than 2.500 sugarcane growers in 1960, but only 750 by 1990. The largest farms are in Florida, averaging 3,339 acres compared to the national sugarcane farm average of 765 acres. Owner-ship of sugarcane production is highly concentrated, particularly in Florida and Hawaii, where relatively few landowners, who are also processors, control most of the sugarcane production.

Sugar beet production in the United States is much more widespread than sugarcane production, with nearly nine times as many growers. Further, the number of farms producing sugar beets has actually increased, although the location of production has shifted among the states where it is grown. Because of the greater productivity in sugar beet growing, more efficient processing, and the sugar support program, sugar beet production became more profitable than other crops. Currently, California is the largest producer of sugar beets, followed by Minnesota, Idaho, North Dakota, and Michigan. The average area for sugar beets harvested per farm was 131 acres.

The current distribution of sugar production in the United States from beets versus cane was locked in place through the imposition of allocations in July 1993. This meant the increasing entry of family farmers into sugar beet production was blocked, and the concentrated cane industry guaranteed its current market share, although if cane processors buy into beet processing, they can maintain their quota and shift their locus of operation.

Sugar Processing

Sugar processing requires enormous capital investments. Growers cannot process sugar individually except at very inefficient levels. There is no market unless there is a processor. Sugar processing is generally most efficient and profitable if done near the place of production.

After sugarcane or beets are processed into raw sugar, it is further refined. The number of sugar refiners in the United States declined drastically, from 24 in 1980 to only 12 in 1990. Refining volume declined as the amount of raw sugar imported declined. Some of the refiners are integrated with sugarcane acreage and beet and cane processing facilities.

Neither sugar beets nor sugarcane can be marketed directly after harvest. They are relatively heavy crops in relation to their value and must be processed prior to sale even to wholesalers. Both cane and beet growers depend on processors not only to add value to their crop, but to sell it as well. Thus, power in the sugar industry is centered in the hands of the extractors and processors. Whereas many growers can produce sugarcane or sugar beets, such production is worthless unless there is a nearby processor. For example, in the Red River Valley of North Dakota and Minnesota, those who are not members of the sugar beet processing cooperative are totally shut out of the profitable sugar beet production.

Costs to process sugarcane in the United States are high by world standards, averaging 7.88 cents per pound in 1987 and 1988. The range was from 6.29 cents per pound in Florida to 10.59 cents per pound in Hawaii. For the 1987–1988 sugar beet crop, the total cost to produce one pound of sugar from beets (net of by-product credits, which totaled 2.87 cents per pound) was 18.18 cents.

The number of sugar beet processing factories in the nation has declined steadily from a peak of over 50 in the 1960s to 8 in 1994. Without a nearby processor, producers go out of business. The closing of a sugar beet–processing cooperative in Kansas in the mid-1980s destroyed sugar beet production in that state.

The number of sugar processors decreased as the industry became more consolidated and concentrated between 1973 and 1982, the time period when sugar prices were highest and most volatile. The decrease affected markets for growers to sell their raw products. Smaller cane producers quit production, and more sugar factories produced their own sugarcane. Processing efficiency (the amount of time a sugar mill can operate at maximum capacity during the year and the volume of cane it can control) determines profitability. Thus, as sugarcane expanded more rapidly than sugar beets between 1973 and the early 1980s, a decreasing number of individuals received an increasing proportion of the sugar dollar.

Labor

Both cane and beet sugar in the United States have been labor intensive, although there is increased mechanization to harvest and plant sugarcane and to thin sugar beets. In a few parts of Louisiana and most of Florida, sugarcane is harvested by hand due to the composition of the soil, which will not support large harvesting machinery such as the combines used in Texas or the bulldozers and cranes used in Hawaii. Cane cutting is dirty, hot, dangerous work. Almost all of the labor used to cut sugarcane is brought into the United States by a contractor under special agreement with the Immigration and Naturalization Service using specific laws passed for that purpose. Sugar growers provided powerful pressure in the face of congressional investigation to maintain an immigrant labor stream. Either the contractor or the plantation owner must provide housing for the workers, who must leave the country when their contract expires or their work is completed. Workers are reportedly charged for a bewildering number of goods and services provided by their contractors and employers, often reducing their paychecks to nearly nothing.

Sugar processing is capital intensive. Investment tax credits during the 1980s encouraged the substitution of capital for labor in U.S. processing mills. In the late 1980s, the U.S. Commerce Department estimated that it cost $76,000 to save one job in the sugar industry. The high price of U.S. sugar allowed producers to mechanize their operations and sharply reduce their labor needs. For example, Louisiana cut its sugar workforce from 15,000 to 4,000 between 1979 and 1989.

The Environment

Sugarcane is grown in monoculture. This has implications for biodiversity and increased input use; pests become resistant and soils exhausted. Sugarcane growing is therefore a major user of chemical inputs and has had negative environmental impacts in the United States. However, some argue that it is the best agricultural use for the Florida Everglades.

Agricultural pollution as a result of sugarcane production brought about major destruction in the Everglades. There has been excessive phosphorus runoff. In addition, the capture of water from the Everglades for sugarcane production decreased the flow of water. The consequences of the externalized environmental impact of sugarcane production threaten many plant and animal species, South Florida's water supply, tourism, and fishing.

Sugar beets, in contrast to sugarcane, are grown in three- to five-year rotations with other crops, reducing their vulnerability to pests. Nevertheless, they are vulnerable to bad weather and disease. The major environmental impact of sugar beets is that they encourage intensive use of inputs. Because they are much more profitable than other crops that can be grown in the area, land prices are driven up. High land costs, in turn, encourage high input use to recoup the increased investment in purchase or rent necessary to gain access to land.

—Cornelia Butler Flora

See also
Agriculture; Labor Force; Trade, International.
References
Barry, Robert D., Luigi Angelo, Peter J. Buzzanell, and Fred Gray. *Sugar: Background for the 1990 Farm Legislation*. Staff Report No. AGES 9006. Washington, DC: U.S. Department of Agriculture, Economic Research Service, Commodity Economics Division, 1990.
Buzzanell, Peter. *Latin America's Big Three Sugar Producers in Transition: Cuba, Mexico and Brazil*. Agricultural Information

Bulletin (September). Washington, DC: U.S. Department of Agriculture, Economic Research Service, 1992.

Buzzanell, Peter, and Ron Lord. *Sugar and Corn Sweetener: Changing Demand and Trade in Mexico, Canada, and the United States.* Agriculture Information Bulletin Number 655 (April). Washington, DC: U.S. Department of Agriculture, Economic Research Service, 1993.

Christy, Ralph D., Brian A. Chapman, and Arthur M. Heagler. *Structural Changes and Economic Efficiency within Louisiana's Sugarcane Processing Industry.* DAE. Research Report No. 685, Baton Rouge: Louisiana State University, Department of Agricultural Economics and Agribusiness, 1990.

Economic Research Service. *Sugar and Sweetener: Situation and Outlook Yearbook.* USDASSRV18N2 (June). Washington, DC: U.S. Department of Agriculture, Economic Research Service, 1993.

Messina, William A., Jr., and James L. Seale, Jr. "U.S. Sugar Policy and the Caribbean Basin Economic Recovery Act: Conflicts Between Domestic and Foreign Policy Objectives." *Review of Agricultural Economics* 15, no. 1 (January 1993): 167–180.

Westfall, Donald W. "Prospects for Sugar Use." *Agriculture Outlook '93: Prospects for Cotton, Sugar and Tobacco.* Washington, DC: U.S. Department of Agriculture, 1992.

Wilkinson, Alec. *Big Sugar: Seasons in the Cane Fields of Florida.* New York: Alfred A. Knopf, 1989.

Taxes

Mandatory payments to governments, unrelated to the amount or value of government services received by the taxpayer. This entry discusses elements of the property tax and the individual income tax that have distinct implications for rural America.

Introduction

Rural residents pay property taxes, sales taxes, income taxes, and a host of minor taxes and fees to support their local, state, and federal governments. Most tax issues are national and of equal importance to rural and urban taxpayers, but some concerns have a distinctly rural focus. Much of the local tax base in rural America is land used in resource-based activities, and this property (farmland, forests, and mineral deposits) poses particular assessment problems. Special income tax provisions for defining farm income also disproportionately affect rural residents.

Property taxes are the most important source of tax revenue for rural America's local governments. The individual income tax provides the bulk of rural revenues for the federal government, whereas state receipts come in varying proportions from sales and income taxes.

In counties with populations below 50,000, the property tax is the most important tax, accounting for $15 billion (nearly 85 percent of local tax revenues) in 1987. Local governments in more populous counties, where local income and sales taxes are more widely used, obtained about 72 percent of their tax revenues from property taxes. Although the use of local sales and income taxes has expanded since 1987, the property tax remains the primary source of local government tax revenue in rural counties.

Property Tax

The tax levied on each piece of property is computed by multiplying the taxable value of that property by a tax rate. Tax rates are set locally by each local government with authority to tax property located within its boundaries. Most often tax rates are expressed in mills (dollars per thousand dollars of taxable value). The property tax bill reflects the sum of the property taxes levied by all local governments with power to tax that particular parcel. Thus, properties located outside the city limits pay less in property taxes than identically valued properties inside city boundaries because no city taxes can be levied. Typically, property owners receive a single tax bill for each parcel of property. Local tax revenues are usually collected at the county level and then distributed to the appropriate local governments.

Real property (land and buildings) is the largest component of the local property tax base. In some states personal property (equipment, farm machinery, breeding stock, and inventories) is also subject to the property tax. Motor vehicles may also be subject to a personal property tax at the state and sometimes the local levels.

The fair and true market value, or estimated market value, of each piece or parcel of property subject to tax is determined by local assessors. State officials then compare local assessments against actual market values determined by recent sales of property and adjust or equalize the assessed values to ensure a consistent ratio of assessed value to market value across the state. Without this process, localities systematically underassessing property could unfairly increase the amount they receive from state aids, such as school aid, which are dependent on the value of the local property tax base.

Taxable property value, the value actually subject to

tax, is computed in one of two ways. In most states taxable value is established by law at a single, fixed, uniform percentage of the estimated market value for all types of property. That percentage is often less than 100 percent of market value. In these uniform property tax systems, $100,000 of commercial property and $100,000 of agricultural property would each have a taxable value of $100,000, assuming an assessment rate of 100 percent. If the local tax rate were 150 mills, both the agricultural and commercial property would face a tax levy of $1,500.

In some states the statutory ratio of a property's taxable value to its full and true value depends on the type, or class of property under consideration. In states with classified property tax systems, the effective tax rate—the tax as a percentage of full and true value—varies depending on the type of property. For example, if the class rate for commercial property were 100 percent and the class rate for agricultural property 50 percent, the taxable value for the commercial property in the example used above would remain at $100,000, but that for the agricultural property would fall to $50,000. With this classified system, the tax levied on the commercial property would continue to be $1,500, but that on the agricultural property would fall to $750, and the effective tax rate on agricultural property would be one-half that on commercial property, even though the tax rates set by local governments were the same. Owners of residential homesteads and agricultural property are the most frequent beneficiaries of a classified property tax system.

Assessors set the fair and true market values for most types of real property by comparing sales prices of similar properties or by capitalizing expected net income from the property. Much land in rural America, however, requires special treatment. Sales of farmland, timberland, and mineral rights are often insufficient to support use of the comparable sales method. Capitalizing net income can be inconclusive or misleading due to problems in determining the true income-producing potential of the property.

Some states responded by adopting alternative methods to assign assessed values for these resource-based properties. For mineral lands, the full extent and value of deposits are unknown, so accurate assessments of fair and true property values are impossible. Most states where mineral values are important replaced the property tax on mineral lands with a severance tax levied at a fixed rate on either the quantity or value of the mineral extracted each year.

Timberland creates a different problem for the property tax. Levying an annual tax on the value of an unharvested forest resource creates a cash-flow problem for the owner, encouraging premature harvest and conversion of timberland to other land uses. Privately owned timberland is exempted from the property tax in some states and replaced with a severance tax levied at the time of harvest.

By 1988, all states had provisions allowing assessment of farmland at their agricultural value, and not at their value for alternative uses. Some states went further, basing their assessment of farmland on soil quality indices or other measures of farmland productivity, and not on estimates of market value or comparable sales.

Assessing farmland in areas on the fringe of residential development poses additional challenges, since the farmland in question might have a higher value for residential development but the owner might wish to continue farming the land. In extreme cases, valuing the land for tax purposes at its highest and best use could drive that land out of agriculture. States developed several alternative approaches to deal with that problem while limiting windfall gains to real-estate speculators. One approach requires that any land currently used for agriculture be assessed only on its agricultural value until the land is converted to a nonagricultural use. Other states require establishment of a dual assessment roll, with all farmland assessed at its value for both agriculture and its highest and best use. Taxes are levied only on the agricultural value of the parcel; but at the time of sale and conversion to nonagricultural uses, foregone taxes plus interest for a predetermined number of past years comes due.

Some states use restrictive zoning agreements. By definition, when zoning prohibits nonagricultural uses, the land has no value other than for agriculture, so assessments must be based solely on the parcel's agricultural value. Properties zoned agricultural typically cannot be converted to nonagricultural uses for several years after a change in zoning is approved. During those intervening years, assessments may be gradually increased to reflect the nonagricultural value of the land. In some states, notice of intent to change zoning classifications must be given as many as ten years in advance.

Farm real-estate taxes averaged $5.78 per acre in 1992, according to the USDA. State averages ranged from $54.38 per acre in Rhode Island to $0.41 per acre in New Mexico. In 17 states the average tax per acre was less than $3, while 18 states had average taxes exceeding $10 per acre. The variation among states is due to the degree of local reliance on the property tax and to the value of farmland. Taxes per acre are much higher in New England and the mid-Atlantic states and lower in western states, where a larger proportion of the farmland is low-value grazing land.

When expressed as a proportion of full market value, tax levels were more uniform. The national average in 1992 was $0.84 per $100 of full market value. In Alabama, Delaware, New Mexico, and West Virginia, taxes averaged less than $0.20 per $100 of full market value, whereas in New York and Wisconsin they were slightly more than $2 per $100 of full value. In Michigan, the tax per $100 of full value exceeded $3.

Total taxes levied on farm real estate increased by one-third during the 1980s. Taxes per $100 of full market value grew by 59 percent.

Income Taxes
The income of individuals actively participating in farming is reported for federal income tax purposes on Schedule F. In 1992, 2,288,000 filers reported income on that schedule. Not all of those filing Schedule F live in rural areas, however, for there is agricultural activity in all but the most densely settled urban counties. Income received by individuals who lease land to others on either a cash or a crop share basis and take no active role in the production of crops or care of livestock is reported on Form 4835. Nearly 635,000 filers reported farm rental income in 1992.

Farmers reported a net loss for federal income tax purposes of $12.6 billion in 1992. Much of this loss was reported by filers with large nonfarm incomes. Just over $2 billion in farm losses was reported by individuals whose federal adjusted gross income (AGI), after their farm loss, exceeded $100,000. An additional $2.3 billion of farm losses were reported by filers with negative AGI. Some filers reporting negative AGI may have offset relatively large nonfarm incomes with even larger farm losses. The importance of off-farm income to farm households is shown by the fact that while 1.4 million of the 2.3 million Schedule Fs filed showed a loss, all but 102,000 of those filers reported positive AGI.

Income reported on Schedule F is not considered a good measure of farm income. Federal tax law allows farmers to use cash basis accounting rather than accrual accounting for tax purposes, so reported income does not reflect changes in farmer-owned inventories of products and inputs. In addition, since sales of breeding stock are considered to be sales of capital assets and reported on Schedule D as a capital gain, Schedule F income under-

states actual farm income. The combination of cash basis accounting and capital gains treatment for some forms of farm income made it possible to create tax shelter investments offering large, currently deductible operating losses, offset by future capital gains taxable at a lower tax rate. The tax reform act of 1986 eliminated much of the tax benefit available for agricultural investments.

—Thomas F. Stinson

See also
Agricultural and Resource Economics; Agricultural Law; Farm Finance; Government; Income; Land Values.
References
Aiken, David. *State Farmland Preferential Assessment Statutes.* RB31. Lincoln: University of Nebraska, Department of Agricultural Economics, 1990.
DeBraal, J. Peter. *Taxes on U.S. Agricultural Real Estate, 1890–1991, and Methods of Estimation.* SB-866. Washington, DC: U.S. Department of Agriculture, Economic Research Service, 1993.
Stinson, Thomas F., and George Temple. *State Mineral Taxes, 1982.* Rural Development Research Report No. 36. Washington, DC: U.S. Department of Agriculture, 1982.
Wunderlich, Gene, and John Blackledge. *Taxing Farmland in the United States.* Agricultural Economics Report No. 679. Washington, DC: U.S. Department of Agriculture, 1994.

Technology
Tools, knowledge, skills, and procedures that help people create, utilize, and accomplish useful things. Although technology pervades all aspects of life, this entry specifically addresses technologies used in rural America's production systems—that is, in the extraction of raw materials and the production and distribution of food, fiber, manufactured goods, and services. The discussion includes the nature of technology; how technology is developed; the use of technology in the production and distribution of goods and services; the social and economic impacts of technology on rural society; the movement toward development and use of more sustainable forms of technology; and the importance of assessing the potential impacts of new technologies.

The Nature of Technology
Human populations use technology to adapt to the environment, to modify the environment to make it more hospitable, and to obtain means of existence from the environment. Although technology usually is thought of as the physical or hardware aspect of culture—that is, the tools, implements, instruments, and machines—in a

broad sense, technology also includes the software or the knowledge needed to apply the tools toward practical ends. This software includes the social organization necessary for the use of complex technologies. The useful trait is not inherent in the technology but is socially defined by the members of each specific culture. Rural technologies range from the mammoth earthmovers used in strip mining, to the computer expert systems used by farmers to make decisions on crop and livestock production, to sonar systems used by fishing trawlers to locate schools of fish, to scouting for insects by grape growers for vineyard integrated pest management, to the basic hand hoe used to cultivate home gardens.

Technology Development

Traditionally, technologies were developed through trial and error and the accumulated experiences of users in crafts and trades. During the past two centuries, however, the development of new technology became closely associated with progress in science. America's strong faith in science and science's perceived effectiveness in addressing and solving society's problems augments its perceptions of the usefulness and benefits of technology.

America's faith in science and technology is evident in the primary institution that develops and disseminates production-oriented technology in rural areas, the land-grant university system. Congress established the land-grant system with the Morrill Acts of 1862 and 1890 to provide states with resources to teach the agricultural and mechanical arts. The system was developed further through the Hatch Act of 1886 and the Smith-Lever Act of 1914, which established state agricultural experiment stations and state extension services, respectively. The work of this system is funded by the states and by other federal agencies within and outside of the USDA. Much of the new technology research and development of private industry is accomplished through private industry's grants to scientists in the land-grant universities.

Land-grant university scientists shared America's faith in science and technology and saw their products as overwhelmingly positive. The leaders of those institutions pressed forward with programs based on scientific knowledge to improve the conditions and welfare of rural people, especially in production agriculture. Much scientific research during the first half of this century resulted in technologies that greatly increased agricultural production, but few concerns were raised about the decreasing farm population and the declining rural communities.

Technology and Production

Agricultural technologies and the technologies of other extractive industries (fishing, forestry, mining, oil extraction, quarrying) are part of the treadmill of production. The treadmill involves two processes: first, expansion of technological capacity, resulting from reinvestment into the production system of surplus values (profits) from previous production, and second, the preference for economic growth even when decision makers know that adverse effects will result (Schnaiberg and Gould 1994). To maintain the accelerating treadmill, technology increases in size, power, capacity, and speed. The pulpwood industry uses a large, tractorlike machine with a hydraulically powered clipper to harvest pulpwood trees quickly; strip miners use gigantic excavating and earthmoving equipment with many cubic yards of capacity to move overburden and extract coal; and farmers use combines that can cut a swath 36 feet wide to harvest grain such as corn, soybeans, or wheat.

Some new technologies have the potential to affect the structure, organization, and operation of entire industries or all of rural society. Two such technologies are biotechnology and computer/telecommunications technology. Biotechnology is any technique to improve plants or animals by changing their genetic structure, or to use living organisms to make or modify products. It includes the artificial production of enzymes necessary to produce hormones, vaccines, and feed additives; artificial reproduction or growth of cells such as in cloning or growing tissue cultures; and genetic engineering, altering the genetic structure of the cell. Much controversy has centered around one biotechnology product alternatively known as bovine somatotropin (BST) or bovine growth hormone (BGH), a hormone that substantially increases a cow's milk production. One issue of the BST controversy is public concern over the hormone's potential presence in milk from BST-injected cows, and thus the milk's safety for human consumption. A second issue is that increased milk production may lead to a further decrease in the number of dairy farmers, with impacts on the viability of rural communities and the milk-processing industry.

The computer/telecommunications technology complex, also called telematics, is "the joining together of telecommunications, broadcast media, and computer technologies into a single infrastructure for developing, sending, receiving, sorting, and utilizing information" (Dillman 1991, 292). Telematics has the potential to break down distance barriers in the production and delivery of goods and services, and thus it is seen as a tool to return isolated rural areas to mainstream American social and economic activity. Expanding the telematics infrastructure to rural areas is particularly cogent in a society with an increasing role for information and its storage, retrieval, and transmission in social and economic functions. Jobs such as credit card account processing, telemarketing, data entry and processing, and copy and manuscript editing all can be done through telecommuting from a computer cottage. Will rural areas benefit significantly from telematics? The outcome is uncertain. Much of this type of work can be transferred from rural America to other places that already have the infrastructure and have lower labor costs, such as Latin America or the Far East.

Impacts of Technology

Impacts of technology and the technology treadmill on rural people and communities are profound. Advancements in technology relieve much of the drudgery and long hours related to extractive occupations. But rural areas also suffer from the negative effects of technological advancement. One potential effect is a restructuring of industrial sectors. Implementation of advanced technology creates the need for increased income to pay for the investments in the technology. Existing production units (such as farms, fishing fleets, and logging firms) are reorganized and consolidated into larger operations to compensate for declining prices resulting from increased production. The investment in technology and formation of larger operations makes much of the labor and management workforce superfluous, creating a stream of rural out-migration. The loss of population in turn leads to the restructuring of rural communities' commercial and institutional sectors, as there are fewer individuals, families, businesses, and organizations requiring their goods and services. Thus, businesses close, schools and churches consolidate, and many rural towns become virtual or actual ghost towns.

A second negative impact of the technological treadmill on rural areas is that technology tends to benefit urban areas over rural areas. Most new technology has urban origins. Research and development, whether conducted by private corporations or public educational institutions, tend to be urban activities. Examples of urban research and development centers are the high-technology research parks such as North Carolina's Research Triangle (North Carolina State University in Raleigh, Duke University in Durham, and University of North Carolina in Chapel Hill) or Massachusetts' Route 128 in and around Boston. Initial new technology beneficiaries are urban areas, with rural areas benefiting as the technologies diffuse, a process sometimes called the "trickle-down effect." Some rural areas cannot take advantage of new technologies because they lack the supporting infrastructure. The information highway bypasses many rural communities because local telephone companies lack fiber optic lines and digital switching. Other rural areas are on the technological forefront. The early establishment of telephone and electricity services in the 1930s is a prime example. However, these services were promoted by a specific government policy through the Rural Electrification Administration. Generally, early rural implementation of technology is atypical.

Not only do urban areas reap early benefits of technological advancement, but the externalities, the indirect and long-term costs of using technologies, often fall to rural areas. The dumping grounds for waste materials of the technological treadmill, including nuclear and other hazardous waste, are primarily rural. Rural communities with no other prospects for economic prosperity may accept such wastes in local dumps for a fee. Some rural communities have landfills and hazardous waste sites thrust upon them with little or no local involvement or control in the siting decision. Other rural communities have their landscapes ravaged and soil and water polluted from strip mining, which provides the raw materials for industrial growth.

Sustainable, Appropriate, and Indigenous Technology

In reaction to problems created by the technological treadmill, sustainable technology has emerged as part of the larger sustainability movement. The values of sustainability promote technologies that are ecologically sound, economically viable, socially just, and humane. One major component of sustainable technology is appropriate technology. "Appropriate" indicates a favorable judgment as to the effects of a technology on its social, cultural, and environmental context. Barbour (1980) suggested five characteristics of appropriate technology. First, intermediate scale technology is more efficient than traditional tools or methods, but sufficiently inexpensive to promote wide adoption and use. Second, to promote retention of a gainfully employed population, technology should be labor intensive rather than capital intensive. Third, a relatively simple technology promotes easy adoption, self-help in operation and maintenance, and thus independence. Fourth, a technology that is relatively simple and small in scale and that does not rely on outside experts or large supporting organizations or infrastructure promotes self-reliance, self-determination, and local control. And finally, a technology that is environmentally compatible promotes low energy use, minimal pollution, renewable resource use, and the integration of functions. Although any specific technology considered appropriate may not embody all of these characteristics, some examples of rural appropriate technologies are wind and solar electricity generators, hedgerows to prevent soil erosion and block heat-robbing wind, and a simple kit that allows farmers to test fields for the amount of nitrogen fertilizer required.

Indigenous knowledge, a concept closely related to sustainable technology and appropriate technology, is knowledge unique to a given society or culture. It is the information base for decision making, sometimes simply called local knowledge. Research and development involving indigenous knowledge reverses the roles of technology developers and technology users. Technology users share their fund of viable traditional tools and methods with the technology developers. Minimum tillage, a cultivation practice that retains protective amounts of residue on the soil's surface to prevent erosion, was first used by farmers, who often also built their own special tillage equipment. The practice was later embraced and promoted by university scientists and government agencies. Often spurned in the past as being outdated, unproductive, or unscientific, indigenous technologies and methods are being reevaluated. Organizations of users have emerged that conduct their own research and work collaboratively with scientists to merge the best of new and traditional technologies.

Much of the impetus for incorporating indigenous knowledge comes from Third World areas. Lacking scientific methods and sophisticated instruments, technology users develop their fund of knowledge based upon what they observe and the meaning they attach to it. Therefore, indigenous knowledge tends to be organized around what is conspicuous and culturally important. This provides the basis of a strategy for incorporating indigenous knowledge into technology development (see Bentley 1992 for additional information). For phenomena both important and conspicuous, the technology developer can learn from the user. For phenomena either not important or not easily observed, the developer and user work cooperatively to learn together. And for phenomena neither easily observed nor important and thus ignored by the user, the user can learn from the developer.

Technology Impact Assessment

Potential impacts of new or emerging technologies on rural people or communities can be examined through technology assessment. Although benefits of new technologies are often evident immediately, technology assessment can provide early warning of potentially negative impacts that may be delayed, remote, and cumulative. Technology assessments helped to raise the public consciousness and affected state and federal policy on new technologies such as bovine somatotropin, large-scale confinement operations for raising hogs, the siting of nuclear waste facilities, and the development of offshore fisheries. The federal government has an active role in technology assessment through the establishment in 1972 of the Office of Technology Assessment (OTA). With the mandate to provide early indications of the probable beneficial and adverse impacts of the applications of technology, OTA has supported a variety of assessment research projects and commissioned many papers on technologies affecting rural areas.

Although technology is pervasive in all aspects of life, it does not in itself determine the direction of change and development in rural America. The creation, development, and use of technologies is based on choices made by government, scientists, engineers, manufacturers, marketers, users, and benefiters. The benefits received and costs incurred are trade-offs resulting from these choices.

—*Peter F. Korsching and Michael M. Bell*

See also
Agriculture, Alternative; Biotechnology; Computers; Cropping Systems; Electrification; Land-Grant Institutions, 1862 and 1890; Mechanization; Policy, Telecommunications; Technology Transfer; Telecommunications.

References
Barbour, Ian G. *Technology, Environment, and Human Values.* New York: Praeger Publishers, 1980.
Bentley, Jeffrey W. "Alternatives to Pesticides in Central America: Applied Studies of Local Knowledge." *Culture and Agriculture* (1992): 10–13.
Busch, Lawrence, and William B. Lacy. *Science, Agriculture, and the Politics of Research.* Boulder, CO: Westview Press, 1983.
Dillman, Don A. "Telematics and Rural Development." Pp. 292–306 in *Rural Policies for the 1990s.* Edited by Cornelia B. Flora and James A. Christenson. Boulder, CO: Westview Press, 1991.
Milbrath, Lester W. *Envisioning a Sustainable Society.* Albany: State University of New York Press, 1989.
Molnar, Joseph J., and Henry Kinnucan, eds. *Biotechnology and the New Agricultural Revolution.* Boulder, CO: Westview Press, 1989.
Schnaiberg, Allan, and Kenneth Allan Gould. *Environment and Society: The Enduring Conflict.* New York: St. Martins, 1994.
Summers, Gene F., ed. *Technology and Social Change in Rural Areas.* Boulder, CO: Westview Press, 1983.

U.S. Congress, Office of Technology Assessment. *A New Technological Era for American Agriculture*. OTA-F-474. Washington, DC: U.S. Government Printing Office, 1992.

Warren, D. M. "Linking Scientific and Indigenous Agricultural Systems." Pp. 153–170 in *The Transformation of International Agricultural Research and Development*. Edited by J. Lin Compton. Boulder, CO: Westview Press, 1989.

Technology Transfer

An exchange of information between technology developers and technology users that involves identifying and using new tools to solve new problems or to address existing problems better. This entry summarizes traditional models of technology transfer and presents new network and community approaches to transfer. People once believed technology transfer was like going to the store; they looked over available products and processes and decided what to buy (in other words, what to adopt). Technology is the source or hub from which spokes, or transfer agents, diffuse information to independent adopters. But this understanding of technology accounts for only part of technology transfer in rural communities. In particular, many technologies require the direct involvement of participants working in informal networks. The transfer of such system technologies involves more complexity, beyond that of one-on-one contacts between technology sources and independent adopters.

Promoting Adoption and Diffusion through Information Access

The traditional adoption and diffusion perspective promoted a five-stage model of technology transfer (Rogers 1983): (1) awareness, (2) interest, (3) evaluation, (4) trial, and (5) adoption. Although the progression is not always completely linear, the order of the stages is approximately accurate. For example, a user must first become aware of and interested in a new tool in order to evaluate it, and subsequently try it and decide to adopt it. Therefore, from the user's perspective, each successive stage of the model provides additional information about the new technology or tool. However, virtually no technology is universally acceptable or accepted at the adoption stage, and additional modifications are often necessary long after adoption. This model emphasizes education and the flow of information to rural communities.

Channels for Technology Transfer. Media (advertising on new machinery, extension circulars on health hazards, and videos on waste management systems) make rural communities aware of new ideas. Impersonal channels (radio reports on endocrine disrupters and magazine coverage of aquifer problems) and interpersonal sources (field days on calf management and satellite conferences on market opportunities) help deepen an interest in technologies and their impact.

An enduring approach used with increasing creativity is the demonstration project, a hands-on way to evaluate a technology through a local trial. Mobile vans have been used to demonstrate technologies, such as Pennsylvania's forage testing program, to farms or communities. Permanent training sites combine seminars, field visits, and experimental use of new systems, as does Texas's Stiles Farm Computer Training Center. Joint programs of public agencies and farm associations use multiple sites to systematically adapt and demonstrate new technologies, as has Michigan's program on the new system of high-density fruit production. In short, when rural people get together to define and directly contribute to their goals, field trials can be very useful.

Type of Information Needed for Technology Transfer. In the traditional literature, the type of information needed for technology transfer is assessed in terms of profitability, compatibility, and trialability (that is, it can be tested or tried on an experimental basis). These three concepts state that information on a new technology should describe it, relate each of its components to existing practice, and explain how the components interact in producing an overall benefit. The description should be complemented by thorough statements of the resources (capital, time, and management effort) required and benefits accrued from implementing each component as well as the entire system. Decision makers also need to know of difficulties and failures encountered by other adopters and the extent of continued interest among their peers.

Technology transfer has been studied by experts from several disciplines (see Gold, Rosseger, and Boylan 1980, for an economics approach; Tornatzky and Fleischer 1990, technology management; and Saltiel, Bauder, and Palakovich 1994, sociology). Profitability plays a central role in the findings of most such studies. For example, Griliches (1960) determined that profitability explained much of the variation in adoption rates for hybrid corn. However, the prediction of profit is often complicated by factors outside the technology itself. Government programs and economic wherewithal can constrain or augment profit from use of a technology. New technologies often replace existing methods, and it is a principle of technological change that new technologies stimulate improvements in old ones. The most reliable vacuum tubes ever made were developed after the invention of transistors (Cooper and Schendel 1976). Changes in the prices of economic factors and the availability of ancillary technologies may also affect the profitability of old and new technologies. For example, the profitability of the tractor was sharply increased by increased labor costs and the invention of a universal hitch that allowed tractors to pull carts, spreaders, and reapers (Sahal 1981).

Social Interaction and Technology Transfer

It is often true that the best way to move technology is to move people. Therefore, most studies of technology transfer emphasize interaction between adopters in complex social networks. At times, opinion leaders influence a wide segment of their community. In other cases, people are informally allied with competing subgroups (such as those advocating diversified, single-crop, and organic agriculture) that favor alternative technologies. Whether leaders encourage bridge building among competing subgroups can determine whether this competition is productive or adversarial. In other cases, intermediaries play a strong role, such as in the case of an irrigation association that aids in the formulation and dissemination of safety standards for irrigation systems. The basic message is that people need to interact with others who have accumulated experience and data on a technology and its impact.

The more that technology developers such as corporations, agencies, and universities know about the needs of rural communities, the better they can help them. Technology management studies have shown that technology transfer works best when developers and users (1) mutually define a problem; (2) interact to interpret data from pilot programs and share in defining next steps; and (3) disseminate information and the technology through preexisting networks of users (Wolek 1985).

Rural communities will benefit from knowing their needs and cooperating to satisfy them. This means that rural communities face the challenge of building a capability to define problems in technical terms and to lobby technologists to work with them on solutions.

Systems Technologies and the Creation of Community Infrastructure

Technologies such as integrated pest management (IPM), dairy herd management, soil and water conservation, and sustainable agriculture have multiple components. We call such technologies "systems" (*see* Agriculture).

Local Situation Requires Systems. Albrecht and Ladewig (1985) documented the impact of local soil and water quality on the value of a technology. They showed that irrigation technologies (for example, furrow diking, soil moisture detection, center pivot, and return pits) are more readily adopted on farms having lower lifting costs because more groundwater is available. Technologies must be adapted to local application. In some situations, such as in Texas where early market cantaloupes are grown, the local adaptations are extensive. Such adaptations will not occur and there will be nothing of value to transfer unless local people play a strong role.

The components of a system generally interact to provide a greater total impact; in other words, they are synergistic. People can adopt some components and not others, as they do with IPM and soil conservation (Nowak 1987). Ridgely and Brush (1992) showed that fruit farmers adopted relatively low-cost components of IPM technology (insect monitoring and using economic thresholds) before adopting the more costly components (orchard treatment). IPM components such as using beneficial insects as substitutes for insecticides were less frequently adopted because the market placed a high price on blemish-free fruit. In short, "whatever works for you" seems to be the rule in system transfer.

Building Innovative Communities. Most technological systems require action on the part of a supporting infrastructure. For example, although air transport existed for several decades, it did not expand much until the mid-1950s. Aircraft technology had improved, but even more important was the existence of an infrastructure of trained pilots, mechanics, airports, a supply system, and experienced air travelers, all brought about by World War II.

Systems innovation may be conceived of in three stages: (1) initial application of the technology to existing tasks (early movies were of familiar images such as plays); (2) development of an infrastructure to service the technology (mobile camera crew); and (3) expansion into new applications by the people staffing the infrastructure (action movies filmed on location). The importance of building a supporting infrastructure presents a challenge for communities to cooperate with one another toward achieving mutual benefit. An infrastructure was what a group of citrus farmers in Arizona developed when they sought to raise the price of their fruit through higher quality. They had to commit to public standards of quality, support an independent testing organization, find and negotiate with a market outlet (a California cooperative grocer), and employ a fruit shipper that would maintain the quality fruit they grew. In sum, it is essential for rural communities interested in transferring useful technologies to develop local networks that will adapt technologies to local conditions and to build the infrastructure required for the practical operation of the needed system.

Power Structures and Technology Transfer

Models of technology transfer are politically potent. In the 1700s, Dutch farms were the leading source of red dye (madder) used in Europe. By the 1800s, their market was under serious attack from a French factory technology. The Dutch refused to transfer the new technology because they saw the central issue as one of who was going to control the dye industry (manufacturers or farmers). For a while, the Dutch lost market share, until farmers and government cooperated to develop a new technology that not only kept farmers in charge but also provided significantly better quality at lower cost.

A central issue in rural technology transfer is whose future welfare is primary—rural communities', academics', government policymakers', or agribusinesses' (Heffernan 1984). Rural people who cooperate to form innovative communities will establish the conditions they need to make their own futures.

—Francis W. Wolek and Cathy A. Rusinko

See also
History, Agricultural; Land-Grant Institutions, 1862 and 1890; Technology.
References
Albrecht, Don E., and Howard Ladewig. "Adoption of Irrigation Technology: The Effects of Personal, Structural, and Environmental Variables." *Southern Rural Sociology* 3 (1985): 26–41.

Cooper, Arnold C., and Dan Schendel. "Strategic Responses to Technological Threats." *Business Horizons* 19, no. 1 (February 1976): 61–69.

Gold, Bela, Gerhard Rosseger, and Myles G. Boylan, Jr. *Evaluating Technological Innovations*. Lexington, MA: Lexington Books, 1980.

Griliches, Zvi. "Hybrid Corn and the Economics of Innovation." *Science* 132, no. 3422 (July 29, 1960): 275–280.

Heffernan, William D. "Constraints in the U.S. Poultry Industry." *Research in Rural Sociology and Development* 1 (1984): 237–260.

Nowak, Peter J. "The Adoption of Agricultural Conservation Technologies." *Rural Sociology* 52, no. 2 (1987): 208–220.

Ridgely, Anne-Marie, and Stephen B. Brush. "Social Factors and Selective Technology Adoption: The Case of Integrated Pest Management." *Human Organization* 51, no. 4 (Winter 1992): 367–378.

Rogers, Everett. *Diffusion of Innovations*. New York: Free Press, 1983.

Sahal, Devendra. *Patterns of Technological Innovation*. Reading, MA: Addison-Wesley Publishing, 1981.

Saltiel, John, James W. Bauder, and Sandy Palakovich. "Adoption of Sustainable Agricultural Practices: Diffusion, Farm Structure, and Profitability." *Rural Sociology* 59, no. 2 (Summer 1994): 333–349.

Wolek, Francis W. "The Transfer of Agricultural Technology." *Journal of Technology Transfer* 9 (1985): 57–70.

Telecommunications

The communication of any single message form or mix of message forms in text, graphics, images, moving images, computer code or a variety of command signals over an electrical conduit, fiber optic strands, or in a variety of electromagnetic broadcast forms such as microwave, television, radio, cellular telephone, or satellite.

Telecommunications has a special role in rural America—or in any rural environment—because it overcomes distance and the other challenges of the lack of population density. The public often associates telecommunications with the public telephone system, radio, or television. Less visible to the public are data networks linking banks, large corporations, military installations, and university computer centers, among other establishments. The newly popular Internet is an amalgam of computer-based telecommunications data networks that are able to communicate with one another.

"Distance Penalty" in Rural America

Rural sociologists and economists note the "distance penalty" of living or doing business in a rural area. Rural areas traditionally have been underserved in many types of business or public service because less densely populated markets offer less potential for return on investment and the distribution of services over the relatively greater distances involved in rural areas as compared to urban ones is more costly. Many rural retail businesses are fewer, farther apart, and carry less inventory than their urban counterparts, which was one of the primary reasons for the growth of catalog marketing. Rural schools typically are underfunded and offer far fewer educational opportunities than urban ones. Rural physicians tend to be general practitioners rather than specialists, often must serve patients over large geographic areas, and often do not have the services of nearby modern clinics or hospitals. Although rural manufacturers might have lower labor and land costs, this advantage is often offset by the penalties of distance to gather raw materials or ship finished products. Emergency medical, fire, or police services either have far longer response times or are virtually nonexistent.

Many people accept the challenges of these distance penalties in order to enjoy the space, natural environ-

The satellite dish is an increasingly common sight in rural areas, as residents exploit technology to overcome the disadvantages of physical isolation.

ment, lack of congestion and crime, and other benefits of the rural lifestyle. Fortunately, advances in telecommunications may lessen these penalties by offering more alternatives for information, education, entertainment, and economic development.

Improvements in Rural Telephone Services
Telecommunications in rural America has benefited greatly from the U.S. tradition of promoting inexpensive, quality access to public telephone service. Although many small or isolated rural communities traditionally depended on small, independent or cooperative telecommunications utilities, after World War II, services from these groups improved remarkably. A major reason was the expansion of the Rural Electrification Administration (REA) into low-interest loans for rural telephone development. In some instances these gave small independents or cooperatives an edge over the Bell System or larger independents because of the lower-interest financing. High-cost pools also were developed, from which funds were drawn away from more lucrative parts of the tele-

phone business to subsidize the relatively high costs of low-density networks. These practices kept basic telephone rates reasonable for the rural customer. REA funds have been very much a part of the development of American rural telephony from the 1950s through the 1980s.

Multiparty lines have been steadily reduced, line quality increased, and local calling areas expanded. Finally, rural telephony leaped ahead with the arrival of cellular services, which greatly expanded in the 1990s. Ironically, many regulators thought that cellular telephones would be of no particular interest to the rural areas, and less profitable, so the designation of rural service areas for cellular phones was slower in coming than to urban areas. On the contrary, there was remarkable growth in rural cellular usage, and much of it could have been predicted by using common sense: Farmers, for example, are not usually at desks where there are telephones, so they see great advantages to telephones that can be accessed from different farm buildings, or from the tractor while plowing or harvesting.

Radio was a communications staple for the rural household, particularly from stations that could greatly extend their broadcast range ("clear channel") during the evening hours. Beginning in the late 1950s, when television stations became economically feasible in the smaller cities or towns of America, their range also extended to the rural dweller. The greatest expansion in broadcast communication services to rural America came with the availability of the home satellite dish. Satellite-delivered broadcast services freed the rural consumer from the penalty of distance. Practically speaking, the satellite makes distance largely irrelevant. In the 1980s and 1990s, the number of broadcast alternatives that can be received from the transponders of a single satellite expanded. In 1995, digital satellite broadcasting exploded onto the scene across the United States. It offered more channels, better fidelity, and eventually lower costs than the larger satellite dishes that can be seen in the yards adjacent to country homes.

Telecommunications and
Rural Businesses and Farms

Telecommunications has been a boon to many rural American businesses. In the heyday of catalog sales, particularly in the years after World War II, it became much more common to order merchandise by telephone than by mail. It became especially convenient for farmers to order feed grain, seed, fertilizers, or equipment repair parts, or to get help from a dealer or repair station for equipment problems. Small businesses in rural America found the telephone an increasingly handy means to communicate with their wholesalers or suppliers, or in the case of franchisees, their supervising offices.

After the breakup of AT&T in 1984, states realized that they had more control over the destiny of intrastate telecommunications regulation, and they soon saw the relationship between activities in this area and their aspirations for economic development. Many arguments regarding revisions of state telecommunications regulation in the late 1980s and early 1990s were cast with economic development goals in mind. The strategy was that enhanced telecommunications capabilities, less regulation, and low tariffs would make it possible for many rural businesses to expand. Small manufacturers, for example, could stay in touch with their suppliers and their customers through use of telephone and data communications. Studies in the 1980s showed the rise of businesses in rural areas that could not have existed but for telecommunications. This included businesses that conducted

area-wide marketing through long-distance telephone, businesses that were small-scale suppliers of subcomponents for large manufacturers, and even marketing businesses that made exclusive use of the telephone for customer contact (telemarketers and 1–800 numbers).

During the 1980, the rise of the personal computer that could be linked by modem to the telephone system greatly enhanced many of the these capabilities. Complex inventory retail businesses, like drugstores or hardware outlets, could maintain inventories on their local personal computers, and then, with the use of special software, call their suppliers and automate the restocking process. Service and transportation businesses could plan their schedules better by using computer software and connections, and many even kept in touch with their moving units by cellular telephone. The remarkable growth of Wal-Mart was due in part to the company's innovative uses of telecommunications for inventory management.

In the 1980s and 1990s, small businesses, farms, and cattle operations with access to data networks found themselves in a newly advantageous position to solicit bids for cattle feed, seed, fertilizer, or other supplies. Many rural feedlots (where cattle are brought to fatten for market) have management offices that look like computer centers. Managers track the feeding schedules of cattle, check on weight gains, survey wholesale feed availability for the best prices, and examine their own marketing possibilities to get the highest price for the cattle. The value-added chain is made much more productive and profitable through rural information services.

Although data communications services are still relatively expensive for small businesses, the Internet is opening up a new range of possibilities for rural dwellers and business persons. The Internet not only makes it possible for the resident or client to have better access to financial acquisition and marketing services but also promises to extend their reach globally. It is possible for the farmer to check grain production, say, in Russia, in order to assess whether conditions are propitious for the import or export of grain to that market. New data on global commerce and services appear monthly on the Internet.

Telecommunications in Rural
Social Services and Medicine

Telecommunications continue to benefit social service delivery in rural America. Distance education can bring highly skilled classroom lectures via satellite to the rural school. Two-way video systems also can link schools and classrooms—for example, a high school calculus class at a rural school to one in a nearby city. Telecommunications can be used by rural schools to download new curriculum materials, to support voice calling or electronic mail for troubleshooting, and to integrate their administration much more closely with their school district and state education agencies. There are numerous examples of how rural teachers have been able to confer with one another. For example, a biology teacher in a remote rural school can confer with biology teachers in other rural schools and with experts at the state university.

Distance education systems also offer many continuing education alternatives to farmers and rural businesspersons. They provide a variety of opportunities for individuals to upgrade their education on new farming methods, to participate in small-business seminars, or to improve their technical education for manufacturing jobs.

Rural medical practice also has benefited from telecommunications, which provides increasing opportunities for rural health care providers to exchange diagnostic information with urban clinics or hospitals. Through video telemedicine, a rural patient might even be seen by a physician in an urban clinic. Telecommunications is used extensively by rural clinics and physicians to take and analyze electrocardiograms. Medical applications of radiology are already an accepted part of telemedicine. In the years to come, we can expect that an increasing number of diagnostic and medical advice telecommunications services will link rural and urban medical facilities and allow them to interface directly with rural homes on demand.

Modern telecommunication carries many social implications for rural America. Some of the previously penalizing aspects of rural living have been eliminated or partly alleviated by the availability of telecommunication services. Rural dwellers need no longer be in isolation from neighbor to neighbor, from town to town, or from rural area to city. Connection is as close as a phone call. Rural dwellers in the United States watch much of the same television fare as their urban counterparts. In many cases, rural dwellers with satellite services have more television program alternatives than urban residents have over their cable or over-the-air broadcasting. Perhaps most intriguing is the concept of the "new rural society" envisaged by Peter Goldmark (1972), the inventor of one form of color television and of the long-playing record. Goldmark thought that by using telecommunications to "stretch the links," many of the services available to the urban dweller could be delivered to the rural business or household. As this becomes possible, people have more

choices as to where they can live or do business. It may no longer be necessary to give up fresh air, clean water, and a beautiful environment for the problems of the city in order to make a good living and have access to state-of-the-art education and other social services.

—*Frederick Williams*

See also
Computers; Development, Community and Economic; Education, Youth; Electrification; Health Care; Infrastructure; Media; Policy, Telecommunications; Technology.
References
Bollier, D. *The Importance of Communications and Information Systems to Rural Development in the United States.* Report of an Aspen Institute Conference. Turo, MA: Aspen Institute for Humanistic Studies, 1988.
Dillman, Don A. "The Social Impacts of Information Technology in Rural North America." *Rural Sociology* 50, no. 1 (1985): 1–26.
Dillman, Don A., and Donald M. Beck. "Information Technologies and Rural Development in the 1990s." *Journal of State Government* 6, no. 1 (1988): 29–38.
Glasmeier, Amy K. *The High-tech Potential: Economic Development in Rural America.* New Brunswick, NJ: Rutgers University, Center for Urban Policy Research, 1991.
Goldmark, P. C. "Communication and the Community." In *Communication: A Scientific American Book.* San Francisco, CA: W. H. Freeman, 1972.
———. "Tomorrow We Will Communicate to Our Jobs." *The Futurist* 6, no. 2 (April 1972): 55–58.
Hudson, H. E. "Ending the Tyranny of Distance: The Impact of New Communications Technologies in Rural North America." In *Competing Visions, Complex Realities: Social Aspects of the Information Society.* Edited by Jorge Reina Schement and Leah A. Lievrouw. Norwood, NJ: Ablex, 1984.
Office of Technology Assessment. *Critical Connections: Communications for the Future.* Publication OTA-CIT-407. Washington DC: U.S. Congress, Office of Technology Assessment, 1990.
Parker, Edwin B., Heather E. Hudson, Don A. Dillman, Sharon Strover, and Frederick Williams. *Electronic Byways: State Policies for Rural Development through Telecommunications.* 2d ed. Washington, DC: The Aspen Institute, 1995.
Schmandt, Jurgen, Frederick Williams, R. H. Wilson, and Sharon Strover, eds. *Telecommunications and Rural Development: A Study of Business and Public Service Applications.* New York: Praeger, 1991.
Strover, Sharon, and Frederick Williams. *Rural Revitalization and Information Technologies in the United States.* Report to the Ford Foundation. New York: Ford Foundation, 1990.
Williams, Frederick. *The New Telecommunications.* New York: Free Press, 1991.

Temperate Fruit Industry

Production, marketing, sales, and related businesses associated with fruit grown in temperate climates. The fruit industry in recent years has grown substantially, changing products and production and marketing practices, becoming an intensively managed, highly technical enterprise. This entry addresses each of these issues.

The internationalization of the modern fruit industry means that U.S. cherry growers may be competing against orchardists in New Zealand.

Temperate Fruit Production

Commercial temperate fruit and nut production in the United States ranged from 13 to 15 million tons per year in the 1980s. This figure does not include many locally grown and consumed products, nor does it include citrus or other subtropical crops. Of the temperate fruit crops, wine, juice, and table grapes represented (percentage of total tonnage) 36.7, apples 31.6, peaches and nectarines 9.0, pears 5.7, plums and prunes 5.6, sweet and sour cherries 1.8, strawberries 3.6, and cranberries 1.1. Nut crops (almonds, walnuts, and pecans) collectively accounted for nearly 5 percent, and small fruits other than grapes and strawberries accounted for less than 1 percent. All these fruits, including grapes and apples, are considered minor crops compared to corn, wheat, and soybeans.

Temperate Fruit Crops

Before Europeans arrived in the New World, Native Americans cultivated some native fruits, but mostly harvested wild fruits. These included raspberries, blackberries, dewberries, and strawberries in many parts of North America. Wild grapes grew throughout Eastern America; blueberries and cranberries grew in the North, mulberries and persimmons in the South, and plums, crabapples, and cherries in every part of the country from Canada to the Gulf. Like the natives, early settlers frequently used indigenous plants, and some of these, including corn, soon became dietary and economic mainstays. In the case of fruits, however, settlers more often relied on European introductions, making little effort to domesticate and improve native species.

Most of the deciduous tree fruits now common in America such as apple, pear, quince, peach, sweet and sour cherry, plum (both European and Asian), and apri-

cot, are Old World species cultivated there since ancient times. All are native to temperate regions, which provide an essential winter chilling period (extended exposure to temperatures of 4° to 7° C), and where most can withstand mild to moderate, if not severe, winters. These species came to North America with the Europeans and were common features of colonial farms and settlements. They were quickly adopted by Native Americans who relied extensively on cultivated fruits and vegetables in their diets. As American agriculture developed, fruit orchards of all types were soon planted, and nearly every early farmer in the northern United States maintained an apple orchard. Apples were grown for cider, a common drink of both rich and poor. Cider was as much a local agricultural mainstay as were butter and eggs, and along with applejack and peach brandy, it was also exported to the southern states and the West Indies.

Grapes, the most widely planted deciduous fruit crop in the world, were not important in the eastern United States until attempts to cultivate relatively cold-tender and disease-susceptible European *Vitis vinifera* varieties were abandoned in favor of more cold-tolerant and pest- and disease-resistant American varieties from *V. labrusca* and *V. rotundifolia*. European grapes did well in California and continue there today as the mainstay of table grape, raisin, and wine production. Large-scale wine and champagne production did not become important in either the East or California until after the Civil War and then grew steadily until Prohibition. Since then, per capita wine consumption, especially of California-grown *V. vinifera* products, has increased, although the last few years have seen intermittent declines.

Commercial fruit production, which initially followed settler populations, has more recently expanded where favorable climates provide advantages. Significant production is limited to relatively few areas, where latitude, elevation, or proximity to large bodies of water results in appropriate climatic conditions. California, with its moderate winters, accounts for half of U.S. deciduous fruit production, including more than 90 percent of grapes. Other important areas are the Pacific Northwest, the eastern shores of the Great Lakes, a narrow belt along the eastern slopes of the Appalachians, and some areas in the northeast and the southwest. Since the continental United States has few frost-free areas, subtropical species, including those only slightly frost tolerant (such as citrus, olive, pomegranate, avocado, and fig) are restricted to the milder climatic regions of California and Florida.

Growing, Propagating, Grafting

Cultivars, or named varieties (the result of vegetative propagation from cuttings or grafting), were uncommon in colonial America. Early settlers and missionaries distributed seeds and seedlings that were not likely to come true to type. In the late 1700s, budded and grafted apples and pears became familiar in New England, and nursery-grown trees were available. In Virginia most trees were grafted. Some early varieties remain in cultivation. The Montmorency tart cherry is several hundred years old, as are several common European pears and wine grapes. The native cranberries and blueberries underwent little improvement since their prehistoric use by Native Americans. However, although more than 2,000 apple varieties have been developed in America and over 100 have been imported from Europe, few remain in cultivation. Only 13 relatively recent varieties now account for 90 percent of the apples grown in America, but the relative popularity of the most commonly grown cultivars is changing (O'Rourke 1994).

The use of vegetatively propagated rootstocks is now nearly standard in tree fruit production. There are several reasons: growth control (dwarfing effects), induction of precocious (early) flowering, disease and pest resistance, anchorage, lack of suckering (root sprouts), and resistance to drought and flooding. Unfortunately, although some rootstocks are widely used, none provides all these characteristics, and some tree fruits are still grown on rootstocks that lack many of these characteristics.

Trees

Orchard practices have changed dramatically in the past century. Pruning and training were rare practices in early America, except to keep fruit out of the reach of livestock. Johnny Appleseed reportedly believed that pruning and grafting were wicked. Orchardists now endeavor to develop maximum bearing potential per unit land area in a minimum of time and to expedite pest control and harvesting. To achieve these goals, orchards are planted at much higher densities than even a generation ago. Density is obtained by using dwarfing (growth-controlling) rootstocks coupled with extensive pruning and training (sometimes relying on support with posts and wires) to drastically limit overall tree size. For example, apples previously grown on nondwarfing rootstocks at a density of 70 or fewer trees per acre may now be on fully dwarfing rootstocks at 1,000 or more trees per acre.

Trees are trained to improve light interception, distribution, and penetration into the leaf canopy. Shaded leaves are inefficient; a shaded interior produces inferior fruit of poor color. Efficiency requires maximizing light interception. Balancing these requirements while considering spray coverage for pests and diseases and convenience in harvesting to reduce labor costs results in a wide variety of highly specialized training methods and cropping systems for nearly all deciduous fruit crops. Barritt and van Dalfsen (1992) refer to this as the orchard system puzzle, where tree arrangement, spacing and density, variety selection, tree quality, support system, pruning, training, and site selection must all fit together.

Pest and Disease Control

There were no effective disease and pest controls until the late 1800s. When diseases and pests threatened, crop loss, tree removal, and orchard abandonment were the only alternatives. Life histories of insect pests only began to be understood early in the 1800s. Even less was known about diseases. Early settlers, however, did not have as many problems. Fruit growing was less concentrated and consequently so were the pests. Many of today's most serious diseases and insects are relatively recent introductions from other parts of the world, and in colonial times, fresh market quality was less important. Consumers were less demanding, and faulty fruit still made good cider and brandy.

Fruit growers now rely extensively on a variety of chemical and biological controls. Broad-spectrum chemicals are still the control mainstays, but chemicals for insect mating disruption (pheromones), "soft" pesticides (insect growth regulators), biopesticides (biologically derived chemicals), and releases of insect parasites (such as wasps) are becoming more common. The efficacy of these alternatives often remains to be determined, and both the technical expertise required for implementation and costs are higher.

Pest resistance to conventional chemicals is a continuing problem. As alternatives are developed to handle single pests, nontarget species may become problems that require more conventional controls. New sprayer designs eliminate drift and are much safer for applicators, but their use is confined to high-density orchards and vineyards where trees and canopies are limited in size. Organic production using only natural pesticides is being tested, but it will be difficult to achieve in perennial crops that cannot be rotated to new fields as high pest and pathogen populations develop.

Currently, regulatory agencies debate about how to implement programs that reduce pesticide risk or use.

Technological advances—mainly a better understanding of pest biology, coupled with research to conserve beneficial insects and mites in apple orchards—have enabled some reductions in pesticide rates. Just as significantly, with development of smaller trees and widespread adoption of dwarfing rootstocks, spray coverage is now more efficient, requiring less water and less pesticide. Pest management builds on improvements in both biological understanding and orchard technology. If the industry is to progress in pest management, policymakers must recognize the importance of the relationship between growers' understanding of pest ecology and their ability to adopt new technology.

Fruiting and Harvesting

Most fruit-producing plants will set more fruit than necessary for a full crop. Thinning (partial removal of fruits by hand or chemically) is often essential for quality purposes, to increase average fruit size, and to improve color. Thinning is often necessary to stimulate flower initiation for the next year to avoid alternate bearing (heavy crops alternating with no crop or with light crops).

Harvesting deciduous fruits may be highly mechanized, as in the case of grapes, cherries, blueberries, raspberries, and some cling peaches destined for processing; but fruits intended for fresh markets are usually hand harvested to avoid surface damage and bruises, which reduce consumer acceptance and accelerate deterioration and decay. Hand harvesting, however, presents problems that increase costs and social issues associated with the availability and use of migrant labor.

Grading, Packing, Storage, and Processing

New equipment, technology, and computers now allow packing houses to sort fruit efficiently by grower source, cultivar, size (weight), and color. The entire packing process is highly automated. Fruit may be graded for firmness and for sugar and acid content. These factors relate to maturation or degree of ripening, which affects potential for long-term storage. Harvest quality affects quality after storage: If picked at the right stage of maturity, some apple varieties may be stored for 6 to 12 months with no loss of quality. Some pear varieties require an extended chilling period before they can complete maturation and ripening.

Controlled atmosphere (CA) storage, which relies on modifications of the humidity, carbon dioxide, and oxygen in the air surrounding stored fruit, can extend the storage life of some fruit. Most apple growers rely on CA technology to market a high-quality product well beyond harvest. Although nearly all major apple-growing areas have expanded CA capacities, the technology is not yet applicable to most other fruit species. Nonetheless, advances in storage, shipping, and handling transformed much of the industry, with the trend often being the concentration of production in places where growers have climatic advantages.

As indicated, apples and other tree fruits were once grown predominantly to produce ciders and brandies. Fresh products could not be shipped, and processing technology had not developed except for dried products. Use of apples for processing grew steadily between World War II and the early 1970s. Total apple production, which dropped sharply after World War II, began a long-term upward trend in 1952. But in the mid-1970s, per capita consumption of almost all processed fruits and vegetables began to decline. Sliced products are still important in processing, especially for pies; but apple processing and juice markets today generally offer relatively low profits, especially with a fivefold increase in the 1980s of imported concentrated frozen juice. Processing is often only a means to salvage otherwise low-value (cull) fruit. Grapes, however, are primarily grown for juice and wine production; many other fruits are grown predominantly for processing into jams and juices.

Regional Differences

Consumer preferences in the past varied significantly from region to region. Varieties grown and marketed locally often reflected these preferences. Today these differences are frequently offset by consumer preference for fresh products year-round and centralization of marketing by chain stores. Other factors include growers who have regional climatic advantages and are located some distance from markets. They tend to rely on fresh market varieties that can be stored and shipped without significant loss of quality. Processing quality, however, is a different marketing consideration. It is often difficult to substitute fruit varieties and maintain processing quality. With grapes, for example, varietal characteristics are critically important in determining wine quality and type.

Economics

Trends in orchard and vineyard numbers and acreages generally reflect trends in agriculture. Total fruit production is up, although acreages have stabilized or even declined. Contrary to the trend, in Washington State, which leads in apple production, acreages have increased continuously over the past 30 years; but even there, orchard numbers declined, especially in the 1960s. Small orchards (less than 25 acres) have been declining steadily since the 1970s almost everywhere, but corporate operations remain rare. Although most of the acreage is managed by full-time producers, many orchards and vineyards are operated part-time. The number of young people in the fruit industry, either part-time or full-time, is quite small. Studies in both Michigan and Washington have shown that 50 percent or more of full-time operators are over 55.

Other economic factors include changing consumer preferences, demographics, and lifestyles. These have increased per capita consumption and also demand for greater variety and novelty of fresh fruits and vegetables. Items almost unknown in 1980, such as kiwi, star fruit, or Granny Smith apples, were known to most consumers by 1990. Retailers responded by devoting an increasing share of ever larger stores to fresh produce. Keeping shelves stocked on a 12-month basis requires retailers to draw supplies from many parts of the world. European and eastern U.S. wholesalers are now as likely to negotiate for fresh apples with suppliers in Chile or New Zealand as in nearby producing regions. The entire fruit industry is responding by learning to identify markets and consumer preferences.

Demands by retailers place pressure on warehouses to carefully monitor their product composition. Larger orchard operations with more available fruit and the potential for more consistency, grades, sizes, and varieties have distinct advantages over smaller operators. Consequently, demand for locally grown products from small growers often becomes insignificant in marketing channels.

Imports and Exports

More than half the apples in New Zealand are exported to compete in the off season with U.S. and other Northern Hemisphere fruit from storage. Air transportation means that sweet cherries harvested in New Zealand and blueberries from Chile are only one or two days from U.S. markets, just as U.S. producers ship sweet cherries to Tokyo and blueberries to Europe.

Although only 3 percent of U.S. apple production is exported, this is changing. With approval of the North American Free Trade Agreement (NAFTA), apples are exported to Mexico. An agreement signed in 1993 allows import of U.S. apples into China, if exporters meet phytosanitary requirements (certifications that fruit are free of pests and diseases). So far, few growers and shippers are part of such certification programs. Phytosanitary measures became a major impediment to U.S. apple and other fruit exports over the past decade at the same time as trade barriers, import quotas, bans, and high tariffs were reduced or eliminated by trade agreements such as NAFTA and the General Agreement on Tariffs and Trade (GATT).

Although consumption of fresh fruit and fruit products is increasing, production has more than kept pace, especially in the past decade. With more domestic and foreign competition, more fruit products, and an increasingly demanding consumer, America's fruit industry is changing. It is better integrated, has larger operators, and places more focus on promotion, quality, product image, and export market development. Efficiencies are increasing, and the entire industry is far more mechanized and computerized. Access to quality and diversity of fruit and fruit products throughout the year has never been better.

—Wayne Loescher

See also

Aquaculture; Greenhouses; Horticulture; Trees; Vegetable Industry.

References

Barritt, Bruce H., and K. Bert van Dalfsen. *Intensive Orchard Management: A Practical Guide to the Planning, Establishment, and Management of High Density Apple Orchards.* Yakima, WA: Goodfruit Grower, 1992.

Faust, Miklos. *Physiology of Temperate Zone Fruit Trees.* New York: John Wiley and Sons, 1989.

Hedrick, Ulysses P. *A History of Horticulture in America to 1860.* Portland, OR: Timber Press, 1950.

Kader, Adel A., ed. *Postharvest Technology of Horticultural Crops.* Oakland: University of California, Division of Agriculture and Natural Resources, 1992.

O'Rourke, A. Desmond. *The World Apple Market.* Binghamton, NY: Haworth Press, 1994.

Ryugo, Kay. *Fruit Culture: Its Science and Art.* New York: John Wiley and Sons, 1988.

Westwood, Melvin N. *Temperate-Zone Pomology, Physiology and Culture.* 3d ed. Portland, OR: Timber Press, 1993.

Textile Industry

Manufactures woven, knitted, and nonwoven fabrics for apparel, home furnishings, automobiles, hospitals, and a variety of other end uses. This entry reviews the history and development of the textile industry and explores its importance to the rural economy.

History of the Rural Textile Industry

In colonial rural and urban areas, needed textiles often were produced at home. Fluctuating availability and the cost of textiles contributed to the home manufacture of cloth, typically of homegrown flax or wool. Yarn spinning

Workers in a textile plant.

was the most likely process to be undertaken at home. Rural women and children spun for their families and purchased yarn and cloth from local women. In prosperous farming regions, many ordered textiles from local craftspeople or purchased imports. Weaving operations were less likely to be undertaken in the home. Looms were larger and more expensive than spinning wheels. Paying skilled weavers yielded products of higher quality and greater complexity.

However they were secured, textiles had to be transformed into functional garments and items for the home. Sewing was women's work, requiring knowledge of how to cut and piece garments together and fit them to the body. Coarseness of fabric and inadequacy of styling and fit indicated low economic status. In the seventeenth and eighteenth centuries, rural families commonly wore unfashionable, loose-fitting garments to accommodate their busy and changing lives. Textile products were often used and reused. Clothing was patched, remade, and passed along to others. Tailors were employed by those with the financial means to create fashionable garments of finer fabrics. Commercial manufacture of common textiles was not a reality in North America until the late 1700s and early 1800s, and even then it was limited.

Access to imported textiles depended at first on the arrival of ships and later on the development of transportation and distribution networks.

As the nineteenth century progressed, more factory-made textiles became available from the growing textile industries. Home production declined slowly in rural areas. Expansion of the U.S. cotton and wool textile industries focused primarily on production of commonly used fabrics for consumers in rural and urban settings and on ready-to-wear clothing. Rural Americans with access to stores or itinerant merchants could purchase woven textiles such as sheeting, shirting, duck, flannel, cashmere, and denim.

New England companies led the textile industrialization. Large mills turned first to young farm women to supply much of the labor. Textile workers coming off the land were significant sources of labor also for southern textile mills. Large cotton mills became part of the rural landscape in the South. Small midwestern woolen mills often were located at rural sites to better sell products locally (Dublin 1979; Hall et al. 1987).

More apparel was being manufactured for the marketplace as ready-to-wear. Reliance on construction by family members or custom production by tailors, dressmakers, and seamstresses lessened. Industrial development in menswear was urban-centered, but basic sewing tasks sometimes were put out to rural seamstresses. By midcentury, any necessary item of men's clothing could be purchased.

The expansion of mail-order retailing targeted at rural Americans substantially increased access to textile products. Rural women had options to purchase ready-made articles such as outerwear, undergarments, skirts, and waists (blouses). They had more products to aid their home sewing. Full-size patterns for women's garments were first marketed in the 1860s. Broad distribution of sewing machines by the 1870s made construction much easier and relieved some of the tedium of the mending required to make continued use of items.

Before a full range of ready-to-wear was available, women had to sew or find a dressmaker. Although the most talented were probably in cities, women earning a living or augmenting family income through sewing also were present in rural areas. Rapid expansion of the women's ready-to-wear industry in the 1890s made more types of apparel available. By 1915, catalogs still provided the greatest merchandise options for rural women who could access fashion news through magazines. Within a decade this changed, as cars and roads proliferated.

Until the twentieth century, textile production was confined to natural fibers such as cotton, wool, silk, and flax. Advances in chemistry and physics brought the creation of human-made fibers, including nylon, polyester, acetate, rayon, and others.

The Textile Industrial Complex Today

The present U.S. textile industrial complex is composed of over 28,000 companies employing almost 2 million people in the creation of natural and man-made fibers and their transformation into home furnishings, apparel, and industrial products. Fiber manufacturers include both agricultural producers and chemical corporations. Fabric manufacturers provide spinning, weaving, knitting, dyeing, and finishing. Garment manufacturers design and create the patterns, samples, and finished garments. Retail operators include specialty stores, mass merchandisers, department stores, and mail-order companies.

The U.S. textile industry is one of the largest in the world and is the single largest employer of women, minorities, and immigrants. As of December 1994, the textile industry employed 673,000 workers in over 6,500 plants, and the apparel industry employed 969,000 workers in over 22,000 plants (*Textile Highlights* 1995). Some 70 to 80 percent of these employees were women and most were not college educated.

The industry is still highly labor intensive and not as automated as other industries, with most of the profit going toward salaries and wages. Wages for sewing operations in many apparel plants are still paid on a piece-rate basis. The more products employees produce at a determined level of quality, the more money they earn. This system provides incentives to improve throughput and quality of production. Higher-skilled jobs, such as pattern making, grading, and cutting, are paid an hourly rate. Workers in textile plants are primarily paid by the hour. The average weekly wage in 1995 was $380 (*Textile Outlook International* 1995).

Apparel and textile plants can be found in every one of the United States. These plants are often small companies located in rural communities that rely solely on the success of the textile industry for their economic stability. Seventy-seven percent of all textile employees and 34 percent of all apparel employees reside in seven rural southern states: Alabama, Georgia, Kentucky, North and South Carolina, Tennessee, and Virginia (*Textile Highlights* 1995). The 1992 total U.S. gross product for the textile and apparel industries was $51,449,000 (*Textile Highlights* 1995). More than 51 percent of this figure was contributed by these seven states.

Imports and Exports

Recently, relationships between producers and retailers have been increasingly strained. Domestic producers, particularly those in small rural communities, now are feeling the impact of lost sales as more retailers are going overseas to satisfy consumer demand. In 1960, 96 percent of apparel purchased in the United States was produced domestically (Sheldon 1988). In 1991, only 40 percent of all apparel sold in U.S. retail stores was produced by U.S. manufacturers. The reasons for this increase in imports include more competitive costs, better quality, better sourcing (obtaining materials from available sources or distributors), and greater flexibility. Their ability to obtain goods cheaply and easily overseas allows retailers to make demands on domestic manufacturers regarding quality standards, prices, and delivery dates. Smaller manufacturers with only modest financial and technological resources often are unable to meet the needs of their customers. Domestic producers who are unable to respond to market demands are closing their plants and placing thousands of employees out of work.

In 1994, the North American Free Trade Agreement was passed. This agreement was implemented to create a free-trade zone between the United States, Canada, and Mexico by reducing tariffs and restrictive trade practices. Year-end figures for 1994 indicate that "U.S. exports of textiles and apparel to Mexico increased 28 percent over 1993 to reach $2.1 billion" (*Textile World* 1995, 16). In addition, exports to Caribbean nations such as Honduras and El Salvador increased an average of 42 percent. Overall, exports of textiles and apparel increased 11 percent in 1994, hitting a record $11.9 billion. However, imports also set a record in 1994, with $45.9 billion worth of textiles and apparel unloaded at U.S. ports of entry (*Textile World* 1995). This resulted in a record trade deficit of $34.1 billion and accounted for 22 percent of the total 1994 U.S. trade deficit.

The Role of Unions

The textile and apparel industries have long had strong labor union support. The International Ladies' Garment Workers' Union (ILGWU) was founded in 1900 by the American Federation of Labor. The roots of the present Amalgamated Clothing and Textile Workers' Union (ACTWU) date back to 1891 and the United Garment Workers' Union. The initial role of these unions was to combat extremely poor working conditions in the urban Northeast and the lowest wages in the manufacturing sector. Activities of the unions expanded to include establishment of adult education programs, health centers, day-care facilities, and pension and welfare funds in rural and urban areas. The unions generously contributed to philanthropic and labor causes. Both the ILGWU and the ACTWU worked hard to fight high unemployment in both rural and urban areas and to seek favorable legislation concerning imports, the minimum wage, and occupational safety (Douglas 1986).

In the 1970s, the ACTWU organized several attempts to unionize textile and apparel plants and reduce anti-union sentiment in the rural South. The ILGWU launched one of the most successful advertising campaigns, "Look for the union label," in 1975. This campaign was aimed directly at curbing the purchase of imported textile and apparel products by the American public.

Since the 1980s, the unions have chosen a rather quiet labor-management relationship as technological revolutions (such as improved communications, transportation, data processing, and materials handling) created turbulence, including continuing globalization of production. Membership in the ILGWU shrank from almost 500,000 in 1964 to 125,000 in 1994 (Tyler 1995). The membership of the ACTWU likewise decreased in number from 500,000 in 1976 to about 230,000 in 1995. In 1995, the Amalgamated Clothing and Textile Workers' Union and the International Ladies' Garment Workers' Union merged to form the Union of Needletrades, Industrial & Textile Employees (UNITE), resulting in a new membership of over 355,000 workers. A new organizing drive, including workers outside the textile and apparel industries, was begun. UNITE also continues to concentrate on influencing U.S. trade policy and international labor conditions.

Legislation of the Industry

The textile and apparel industries are governed primarily by legislation and regulations concerning consumer product safety. Since 1954 the Flammable Fabrics Act has guided the setting and revising of standards on the flame resistance of textiles for apparel and interior environments. Concern for children's safety led to specific standards for sleepwear in 1972 and 1974. Regulations are regularly revised to address changing product characteristics and risk assessments. Violation of these standards results in a $5,000 penalty per violation and can go as high as $1.25 million for a series of violations.

Textile and apparel plants must meet strict guidelines for environmental protection. In rural areas in particular, dumping of waste from dyeing plants and emission of toxic gas from chemical fiber development have been heavily restricted. Plants in rural areas have had to rebuild or restructure to meet these environmental standards.

Future projections for the industry now include computerization to the extent that each manufacturer will be part of a network linked to a common database. Computer technology will allow the industry to meet consumer demand at the highest quality standards while lowering prices and remaining in rural areas. The use of computers will improve the quality of life of rural employees by offering them the opportunity to gain new marketable skills.

—Lisa A. Shanley, Pamela V. Ulrich,
and Dianne T. Koza

See also
Clothing and Textiles; Employment; Labor Unions; Manufacturing Industry; Trade, International; Wool and Sheep Industry.

References

Douglas, Sara U. *Labor's New Voice: Unions and the Mass Media.* Norwood, NJ: Apex Publishing Co., 1986.

Dublin, Thomas. *Women at Work: The Transformation of Work and Community in Lowell, Massachusetts, 1826–1860.* New York: Columbia University Press, 1979.

Hall, Jacqueline D., J. Leloudis, R. Korstad, M. Murphy, L. Jones, and C. B. Daly. *Like a Family: The Making of a Southern Cotton Mill World.* Chapel Hill: University of North Carolina Press, 1987.

Sheldon, Gwendolyn J. "The Impact of Technology on Apparel Designer Training." *Clothing and Textiles Research Journal* 6, no. 4 (Summer 1988): 20–25.

Textile Highlights. Washington, DC: American Textile Manufacturers Institute, 1995.

Textile Outlook International (September 1994).

Textile World 145, no. 3 (March 1995).

Tyler, Gus. *Look for the Union Label: A History of the International Ladies' Garment Workers' Union.* New York: M. E. Sharpe, 1995.

Theatrical Entertainment

Dramatic presentations ranging from melodramas and Shakespeare's plays to nonscripted events, such as vaudeville, medicine shows, and chautauqua. This entry examines the variety of theatrical and related performance events found in rural America during the rapid expansion of the country following the Civil War. An explanation of likely performance spaces and of the variety of events that used the expanding railroad system shows a breadth of experiences beyond formal drama from the 1870s into the 1920s, such as tent rep (drama in a tent), chautauqua, medicine shows, variety, and vaudeville. Even with a single auditorium in a rural community accommodating all these events (which was often the case), the calendar was a mosaic of entertainments that filled the social and cultural needs of the community. The impact of mass entertainment forms such as film, radio, and television, and the loss of the road (chains of theaters networked across the country) meant the almost complete loss of live entertainment to rural America by World War II.

The Development of Theater in Rural America

In the late nineteenth century, an increasing number of performance entertainments followed the rail lines out of the large cities. The large population base needed to repeatedly fill a theater often could be obtained only by moving the performers from location to location. This economic incentive to develop the road was enhanced by new communities springing up at certain points along the way that provided a performance space for use by these troupes. This pattern of development was particularly evident in the western states following the Civil War,

whereas in eastern states, theatrical sites became additions to established communities. Glenn and Poole (1993) documented over 300 existing structures in Iowa and estimated that four times that number originally existed. This author once located over 400 sites in North Dakota; only 5 percent of these structures survive today.

Active construction of theaters from the 1870s into the 1910s resulted in four distinct types or stages that in many cases reflected the relative economic success of the community. Some of these included (1) a general-utility hall on the second floor of a commercial establishment; (2) a second-floor, theatrically equipped space with specific theater seating and support areas, often elaborate; (3) a single-story building with a stage and flat floor for multiple uses; and (4) a large, multistory, ornate grand opera house. Because these buildings became gathering places for the community, they served many social functions. It was not uncommon to find them housing kitchens; and reports exist of meals served in conjunction with a performance. Schools rarely had auditoriums, and churches often had proscriptions against entertainments; so the immediate community could converge on the opera house for more than a cultural experience. The buildings became the hub of many fraternal, religious, business, athletic, professional, and amateur entertainments. Often, as communities grew, so did the number and size of these spaces. Local and regional historical societies and museums continue to document and preserve mementos of these cultural and social centers.

Community leadership wished to emulate the cultural values of the professional theater found in larger cities. As the railroads spread, so did the touring companies, taking large and small troupes doing Shakespeare, *The Count of Monte Cristo*, or *Ten Nights in a Bar Room*, and stars such as Sarah Bernhardt, to all stops along the rails. These troupes were booked across national circuits from New York City; and smaller, regional circuits developed from important regional cities such as Chicago. In the first decade of the twentieth century, there were between 230 and 420 troupes on the road (Poggi 1968). Of some 3,000 theaters serving a national population of around 76 million, more than 1,000 theaters had an audience capacity large enough to generate sufficient revenue and the necessary staging support for the top touring productions (Lewis 1973). Resident acting companies in larger cities (Durham 1987) had smaller counterparts throughout the countryside that brought most Americans into contact with mainstream theater. To many observers of the day, this was not necessarily a positive development. Even the highest pretensions of culture might be deflated by sentiments such as those expressed in "A Lecture on Amusements": "It is a fair objection to the theater, that, as an amusement, it is too exciting.... To older persons it may not be so hurtful; but for the young man, I do not know of any habit . . . which is more injurious, or more fraught with serious danger, than that of theatergoing. It stimulates the imagination too strongly" (Lewis 1973). Such attitudes, then and now, drive discussions about the role of entertainment in the value-system of a small community. The movement to document the history of popular culture has revealed additional entertainment forms that contributed to the discussion about appropriate entertainments for American audiences.

Beyond the Drama

Parallel to the legitimate theater, troupes of variety and vaudeville performers began to develop into circuits. Although not bound by a dramatic script, these entertainments often repeated a similar pattern of acts. A combination of performers with physical skills such as juggling or knife throwing, comic patter like that of George Burns and Gracie Allen, singing by the likes of Al Jolson, or trained animal acts gave a predictable evening of entertainment. Variety shows, although similar to vaudeville, often carried a tarnished image and appealed to a rougher, predominantly male crowd. Vaudeville's claim to wholesome family entertainment meant easy booking into the opera house.

Another social hub in many communities was the saloon. Less refined performances could move easily from specialized saloon theaters in large cities into a circuit of performances in smaller cities. Other troupes, such as companies like the British Blondes (a burlesque show introduced in the United States in 1868), could perform their musical numbers, with high-stepping chorines, in the largest opera house in the county—or be forced into one of the less desirable saloon theaters by a battle of community standards. These minimally scripted spectacles and troupes of specialty performers became enormously popular, as did the omnipresent minstrel company. The musical and dance numbers of the minstrel show, the racy song-and-dance couplet of variety, and the trained pig act opening a vaudeville evening meant live entertainment to audiences of merchants and farmers everywhere. Another of the entertainments that moved into town for a day or two would be the medicine show. Sometimes presented in the opera house, this combination of performance and salesmanship often came in a

vehicle that allowed a quick setup and takedown. The entertainment, a small troupe doing comedy and music routines, was geared toward assembling a crowd in order to sell the merchandise—patent medicine.

Culturally more refined presentations—though they were not as theatrical in nature—also were available, through lyceum circuits and speakers' bureaus devoted to all forms of education and self-improvement. The Boston Lyceum Bureau (later the Redpath Lyceum Bureau), booked such luminaries as Mark Twain and Julia Ward Howe. In summers throughout the 1910s and 1920s, tent chautauqua was a principal source of edification to communities across the country. National and regional circuits as well as independent chautauqua sites maintained a high moral tenor with religious and political speakers, musical performers, inspirational messages from the Women's Christian Temperance Union, elocution and dramatic readings, and addresses by the likes of William Jennings Bryan.

The Decline of Hometown Entertainment

The delivery of entertainment to rural America significantly changed following World War I. The impact of film, radio, and improved highways began to erode the core social function of the opera house. The number of legitimate theater companies on tour went from 339 in 1900 to 22 in 1935 (Lewis 1973, 209). For the most part, only the largest theaters could generate the income needed to maintain touring companies. Improving highways meant the small-town opera house closed down, while the audience drove to larger cities for theatrical entertainment. National weekly radio shows and a motion-picture distribution system brought the best vaudeville and stage stars into the home or the movie house (usually the old opera house, with a screen and a balcony converted into a projection booth). The mass distribution of entertainment was not necessarily tied to live performers and a community center in every town. New school auditoriums often provided better spaces for theater and musical events and served community talent needs as the professional entertainers were seen or heard via the new technologies.

Tent Entertainments

"Ladies and gentlemen, children of all ages!" and similar bombast was heard throughout the land by the late nineteenth century, when circus troupes of all sizes traversed the countryside. Not all of these skilled entertainments were housed in large tents at major cities. Smaller troupes, often dog and pony shows, played in smaller tents, in the open air, or on theater stages, and did not require the large entourage associated with the Barnum & Bailey or the Ringling Brothers circuses. The carnival, a commercial venture engaging its patrons in activities of thrill-seeking rides and games of skill and chance, also made the rounds of communities, mostly in tents. The circus tent virtually disappeared in lieu of the large arenas in midsize and larger cities. Today, carnivals mostly follow the state and county fair circuit.

A unique form of tent show, which began in the last half of the nineteenth century, continued into the 1950s. Prior to World War I, acting troupes, carrying all their own staging paraphernalia, brought their tent theaters to communities to present what William Slout called rep shows, tent rep, rag opries, and tent shows. Over 400 tent shows crossed the United States by the mid-1920s. In part, the tents allowed companies to go to communities without theaters and to places where indoor theater was impossible with the heat of summer. Often bound to specific regions, hundreds of tent shows returned year after year, bringing most of the dramatic forms found on indoor stages. Interrupted briefly by World War I, tent shows continued into the 1930s, while an offshoot of the form, called the Toby Show, continued into the 1960s. Toby, the freckle-faced yokel with red hair and many rural manifestations in dress and demeanor, would figure in performances and playlets as the tent show played several nights in one community before moving on. Caroline Schaffner, a driving force in preserving the heritage of Toby and the tent repertoire tradition, established the Museum of Repertoire Americana in Mount Pleasant, Iowa, which preserves this uniquely rural entertainment form.

Today's Venues

Although the decline of the road meant an increasing loss of professional entertainers, many communities created their own little theater or community theaters. By 1910, the Drama League was born, with the stated desire to bring better plays to small towns. Leaders in theater higher education across the country, such as Frederick Koch at the University of North Carolina, Hubert Heffner at Stanford, E. C. Mabie at the University of Iowa, and others linked their expertise to the increasing numbers of small-town drama clubs. Today, most states have their own community theater associations. There are regional affiliations such as the Southeastern Theater Conference, Inc.'s Community Theater Festival each year and the national American Association of Community Theaters. The latter provides connections between 6,500 commu-

nity theaters across the country, linking large and small communities in the production of dramatic works.

Currently there are 84 outdoor companies affiliated with the Institute of Outdoor Drama, many of which are major summer tourist venues that enrich rural economies. In 1995, *Unto These Hills* in Cherokee, North Carolina, brought 92,061 viewers to 63 performances, and the Black Hills Passion play had 56,880 attending 40 performances. The Utah Shakespearean Festival in Cedar City was the subject of a detailed study by the Utah Office of Planning and Budget in the mid-1990s, which reported that the festival provided employment for 268 people and earned a total of $3.4 million (*U.S. Outdoor Drama* 1995). There is no agency to assess the economic impact of, or the additional revenues produced by, the hundreds of summer stock theater companies found in tourist sites across the country; but the greater effects of these once-yearly entertainments might be significant for many rural communities, helping to build local civic pride (as suggested by Glassberg 1990). While mass-produced entertainments and newer technologies have reduced the live professional troupes to a trickle, there are still many thriving, locally produced theaters, pageants, festivals, and summer stock companies bringing rural communities a cultural identity and a reminder of an earlier, more abundant tradition.

—*Lawrence J. Hill*

See also
Arts; Community Celebrations; Culture; Films, Rural; History, Rural; Music; Recreational Activities.

References
DiMeglio, John E. *Vaudeville U.S.A.* Bowling Green, OH: Bowling Green University Popular Press, 1973.

Durham, Weldon B. *American Theater Companies, 1888–1930.* New York: Greenwood Press, 1987.

Glenn, George D., and Richard L. Poole. *The Opera Houses of Iowa.* Ames: Iowa State University Press, 1993.

Hoh, Lavahn. *Step Right Up: The Adventures of Circus in America.* White Hall, VA: Better Way, 1990.

Lewis, Philip C. *Trouping: How the Show Came to Town.* New York: Harper & Row Publishers, 1973.

McNamara, Brooks. *Step Right Up.* New York: Doubleday, 1976.

Morrison, Theodore. *Chautauqua: A Center for Education, Religion, and the Arts in America.* Chicago: University of Chicago Press, 1974.

Poggi, Jack. *Theater in America: The Impact of Economic Forces, 1870–1967.* Ithaca, NY: Cornell University Press, 1968.

Slout, William L. *Theater in a Tent: The Development of a Provincial Entertainment.* Bowling Green, OH: Bowling Green University Popular Press, 1972.

U.S. Outdoor Drama (Summer 1995): 1–4.

Wilmeth, Don B. *Variety Entertainment and Outdoor Amusements: A Reference Guide.* Westport, CT: Greenwood Press, 1982.

Theology of the Land

An effort to describe land in relationship to God, which implies that human beings should relate to the land in a way appropriate to God's relationship to, and purposes for, land. This entry identifies four conceptions of land; offers an extended overview of the biblical theological themes by which the Judeo-Christian tradition has understood land in relation to God; and outlines relevant contemporary issues surrounding land. Theology is a human effort to understand aspects of life from the perspective of an ultimate center of value. Thus, a theology of land is subject to all the contingencies that influence men and women. A theology of the land written by theologians in some lands, say the former Yugoslavia or South Africa or Brazil, will be very different from that written in the rural United States. It will also differ by time period: Imagine, for example, how much more complex such a theology would have been in 1900, when many U.S. citizens had a visceral appreciation for how interdependent their lives were with that of the land.

Conceptions of Land

Currently, political conflicts are common between ethnic and national groups over land issues, population and development pressures, and the ecological destruction that accompanies present lifestyles, especially in affluent countries. These are vitally affected by an understanding of land and by the empirical facts of land dynamics. The way in which land is conceived of in public policy and church debates will determine whether all the concerns of all the parties necessary to sustain the land are addressed.

Theology has defined land in several ways. First, land can be defined scientifically as earth—topsoil, subsoil, bacteria, water drainage, grub worms, humus, and tilth—all very concrete ingredients of land. Second, land can be used in a sociopolitical sense to indicate boundaries and geographic borders. That carries two connotations: one is merely geometric; the other includes the full range of values and identifications that accompany ethnic and national loyalties. A third definition looks at land as a possession or commodity. Land in this sense can symbolize all of one's material properties and even status. Fourth, land can be defined as nature and the environment itself (the earthly habitat), and thus, as a component of every human activity and choice. Although each of these conceptions of land adds its weight to a more complete picture of land, this entry will focus on the fourth, more holistic one.

Judeo-Christian Themes for Interpreting Land

One metaphor comes close to comprehending the themes by which the Hebrew scriptures, the New Testament, and the Christian theological tradition interpreted the significance of land: The earth is home, God's home, home for humankind, and home for animals and other living things. The earth, therefore, is the place where human beings find their identity and purpose. God does not dwell only in the heavens; the incarnation of God in the man Jesus Christ established that God's home is also with humankind. This theme suggests that while the land is not itself sacred, it is intrinsically valuable to God as well as essential to human, animal, and plant life. The incarnation of Jesus Christ adds another wide spectrum of meaning to this earth as home to God and to humankind. The Christian faith affirms that the whole creation is full of God; some have suggested that the Holy Spirit might be identified as God in creation (Moltmann 1985). (For a fuller description of the metaphor of land as home, see Jung 1993.)

The theme of land as God's home carries three other, more explicitly biblical themes: the land is God's gift to all living things; the land is God's covenantal promise to human and other kinds (plants, animals); and the land is God's challenge to humans. (The best summary of these themes is Brueggemann 1977.)

The Land as God's Gift to All Living Things. The Christian and Jewish faiths affirmed as one of their cornerstones that "God created the heavens and the earth" (Genesis 1:1), and that the whole earth continues to be God's (Psalm 24:1). Throughout Scripture the entire cosmos that God created is described as "very good." God gives the land to human beings to care for and to enjoy. This is one clear source of the stewardship of creation ethic (*see* Land Stewardship).

The Hebrew author called the Deuteronomist saw land as a gift from Yahweh (God), the same Yahweh that delivered the slave band from Egypt, the same Yahweh who promised land to Abraham and Sarah, the Creator Himself. This gift implies accountability to the Creator. Similarly, Jesus Christ over and over again in his parables and natural figures pointed to the giftedness of nature. Over and over he praised the beauty and fittingness of the land as a gift from God. In the same way, although to an even greater degree, Jesus Christ was the expression of the incarnational love of God, the gift of God to humans and other kinds in the land.

The centrality of the Creator image of God is evident in its placement in the First Article in the Apostles and

Nicene Creeds. Most traditions maintain that the creativity of God still continues in the natural and also the human world. Rural peoples find this cyclical and continual creativity easy to understand and see in their fields and the surrounding countryside.

Several characteristics with clear moral import are evident in the theme of land as gift: the life of the world as God's life; the interconnection of all life; the land as a living, creative organism; and the limitations of createdness. These understandings find expression in many farmers' feeling that they have the land "on loan," as they say. The world and all that is in it remain God's, but some farmers and other rural residents feel their interconnection with God through the land. Because of God's gift, they have gifts to pass on.

The Land as God's Covenantal Promise to Human Beings and Other Kinds. Covenants that Yahweh made with Hebrew leaders, described in the Bible and the holy books of Israel, enable Jews and Christians to see the land as God's promise. These covenants involved the promise of land—indeed, a Promised Land. The covenant God made with Noah after the flood was also made with "every living creature"; especially mentioned are "the birds, the cattle, and every beast" (Genesis 9:10). These covenants underscore God's love and care for his home.

Christians perceive Jesus Christ as the culmination of the promise/covenant tradition, but debate whether the new covenant in Jesus Christ supersedes the older covenants involving land. Another biblical theme expresses God's promise in a way that can reconcile such debate, the blessing tradition. This tradition emphasizes the everyday, routine way in which God is active in cosmic history.

Jesus Christ is portrayed as the reconciler who articulated God's continuing love for the people and the whole creation. "For in him the fullness of God was pleased to dwell, and through him to reconcile all things" (Colossians 1:19–20). The most compelling vision of land is one that is crystallized in Jesus Christ as the carpenter of Nazareth and Son of God. In bringing together the images of creation and redemption, Jesus Christ expressed the concrete intention of God to produce *shalom. Shalom* refers to the way in which the whole created order functions in symbiotic interdependence; it implies an ecological smoothness, harmony, or enjoyment in which there is an abundance for all. All are living and acting as they were created to.

Ideas with clear moral implications emerging from the theme are: the redemption of the land along with humankind; a presumption in favor of solutions that benefit all life rather than only human life; a view of the world as a kinship system; and a warning not to forget that land is always populated, and that humankind counts as part of the whole. Humankind is called to find ways to live that respect, and indeed restore, all other life forms. There is a hint that only in this way can the human species find the fullness of *shalom.*

The Land as God's Challenge to Humankind, to Work for Justice in the Whole Creation. This theme should be understood in the context of the other two, as the three are interrelated. The land is a gift from God and a covenant with God, and as such it involves human responsibility. God challenges human beings to care for the land as part of the task of sustaining God's home in a way that will allow all life to flourish. The way that men and women respond to God's goodness is through worship and responsibility.

God challenges humans to take care of the land. God, as Scripture points out, is present in land, actively delighting in the created order, watching out for the sparrow and lily, as well as enjoying the whales and mountain goats. God calls humans to live with *sadek,* righteousness. Humans are to embody justice by maintaining the right relationship or balance that God created between human need, plant life, and animal flourishing. Humans have the land only in trust; they are shop stewards.

This challenge is directed not only toward ecological health but also and interrelatedly toward political and economic health for people. Humankind is one of the species for whom the land was created. God challenges them to create structures that enable all peoples to realize justice, to participate in shaping their future, and to live so as to sustain an equitable and sufficient distribution of the earth's bounty among all creatures.

The land is home for all life. There is something wrong, from God's point of view, when political, economic, and environmental structures prevent the land from being a good home for every species. The land seen as God's challenge expresses the moral vision of the earth as one community. It is intended to foster communion among all beings. The only way that can happen is through establishing structures that make for justice; furthermore, the more just those structures are, the more likely the possibility of communion, or the development of relationship between God and humankind. (For examples of how human beings can "live lightly on the land" in ways that can be sustained even in the midst of great pressures, see McKibben 1995).

Emerging Theological and Social Issues

The press of environmental degradation and the specter of global conflicts has made Christian theologians and ethicists more aware of the need to understand land issues and to incorporate a sympathy for the land and other beings into our way of life. What is emerging is an appreciation of the physical and material roots of life. Theology is overcoming its dualistic treatment of bodies as inferior to minds/spirits and is balancing its appreciation of history with an appreciation of nature.

Church-Based Response. In the last 15 to 20 years, a torrent of books and articles have been issued on the environment. Many denominations wrote social statements on the need to attend to ecology, among them Lutherans, Methodists, Presbyterians, Roman Catholics, and the World Council of Churches. A number of seminaries are understanding that the churches they represent have a stake in land issues. After all, a majority of Protestant and Roman Catholic churches are still located in rural areas. The Center for Theology and Land at the University of Dubuque (Presbyterian and United Methodist) and the Wartburg (Lutheran) Theological Seminary in Iowa was instituted to explore land questions theologically and to strengthen rural churches and their communities. The National Catholic Rural Life Conference and many other church-sponsored programs see land-related issues as priorities.

The rural base of many of these issues stimulated a collaborative text on *Rural Ministry: The Shape of the Renewal to Come,* in which a team of nine are writing a theology of rural life and ministry for local congregations. That book takes land issues as a central concern. Some of the theological themes lifted up there are the presence of God, a sense of place, a love of community, dealing with suffering and decline, and reclaiming power.

Unless concern about land is translated into an appreciation of land locally—the quality of the places where people live—those concerns will remain general and abstract. Theology has not yet de-universalized its message. Definitely moving in that direction have been feminist, African American, Central American, and Asian calls for contextual theology, a recognition of social context. That context sometimes recognizes land and environmental issues (May 1991), and sometimes does not.

There simply is not yet a systematic theology of land. Such a theology would need to recognize the interconnection of human and ecological issues in a way that also comprehends political and economic structures and the power relations contained in any system of land distribu-

tion. Such a theology would need to start with a theory of how human beings are themselves spatial, physical beings, and interpret that theologically. It would need to see land issues as part of the agenda of every contextual theology. It would also have to leap the gap between individual physicality and corporate, socioeconomic structures.

Societal Issues. Societal issues provoke theological response. Among the issues that are emerging in rural America, one that has quite pernicious consequences is the growing concentration of food-supply enterprises. For example, many rural communities are experiencing the placement of large-scale hog production facilities in their backyards. Although the hog production industry is only integrated at 45 percent (the top four companies control 45 percent of the market) and many other industries are far more concentrated (such as sheep, poultry, ethanol), the same eight or ten companies control most of the agricultural commodity markets. This has implications for democratic participation in rural areas; economic implications for all food eaters; destructive consequences for rural community life in towns where production is located; and very negative environmental impacts. It threatens to erode democratic participation throughout the United States. It fails to recognize the "giftedness" of land.

A second issue is the lack of any serious attention to rural development policy and funding. In comparison to Zimbabwe or Nicaragua or many other developing countries, the United States has neglected its rural communities. U.S. economic policy has disadvantaged small and medium-sized farms for years, and the effect of that has been a shrinking of the number of farm families and the quality of life in rural America. The "farm crisis" of the 1980s became a community crisis in the 1990s. Both farmland and community land are fragile. Like other centers of community life, many rural churches are finding it difficult to afford a minister. While there are instances of amazingly creative local efforts at revitalizing communities, many other local efforts will fail for lack of assistance. Rural areas do not receive services in proportion to the taxes they pay; one impact of this is the rate of poverty found in rural communities, which now exceeds that in city centers. That can affect land issues, especially if low-cost labor attracts industries and businesses that exploit both the land and rural people without returning community or individual benefits. Such destruction of community and such human impoverishment are not in keeping with the covenantal promises of Yahweh.

A third land issue connects the conflict afflicting

U.S. urban centers to international and intranational relations. Group violence and conflict has a physical or land basis that is intermixed with racial, ethnic, religious, and class differences. Our society needs research into environmental designs that reinforce mutual, reciprocal benefit and neighborliness rather than adversarial, competitive relations. Land issues are not only rural; they include the design of cities and interior layout of institutions. The theology and ethics of land remain God's challenge to all people and will demand considerably more attention in coming decades.

—*L. Shannon Jung*

See also

Animal Rights/Welfare; Churches; Community; Community, Sense of; Culture; Environmental Protection; Ethics; Future of Rural America; Land Stewardship; Religion; Values of Residents.

References

Brueggemann, Walter. *The Land: Place as Gift, Promise, and Challenge in Biblical Faith*. Philadelphia: Fortress Press, 1977.

Evans, Bernard, and Greg Cusack, eds. *Theology of the Land*. Collegeville, MN: Liturgical Press, 1987.

Jung, Shannon. *We Are Home: A Spirituality of the Environment*. Mahwah, NJ: Paulist Press, 1993.

Jung, Shannon, Pegge Boehm, Deborah Cronin, Gary Farley, Dean Freudenberger, Judy Heffernan, Sandy LaBlanc, Ed Queen, and Dave Ruesink. *Rural Ministry: The Shape of the Renewal to Come*. Nashville: Abingdon Press, forthcoming 1997.

Krause, Tina B., ed. *Care of the Earth: An Environmental Resource Manual for Church Leaders*. Chicago: Lutheran School of Theology, 1994.

May, Roy. *The Poor of the Land: A Christian Case for Land Reform*. Maryknoll, NY: Orbis Books, 1991.

McFague, Sallie. *The Body of God: An Ecological Theology*. Minneapolis: Fortress Press, 1993.

McKibben, Bill. *Hope, Human and Wild: True Stories of Living Lightly on the Earth*. Boston: Little, Brown and Co., 1995.

Moltmann, Jurgen. *God in Creation: A New Theology of Creation and the Spirit of God*. San Francisco: Harper and Row, 1985.

Mortensen, Viggo, ed. *Region and Religion: Land, Territory and Nation from a Theological Perspective: International Consultation, Imigrante, Rio Grande do Sul*. LWF Studies No. 4. Geneva, Switzerland: The Lutheran World Federation, 1994.

Oliver, Harold H. "The Neglect and Recovery of Nature in Twentieth-Century Protestant Thought." *Journal of the American Academy of Religion* 60, no. 3 (Fall 1992): 379–404.

Warren, Karen. "The Power and the Promise of Ecofeminism." *Environmental Ethics* 12 (Summer 1990).

Tillage

Any one of several types of mechanical manipulation of soil primarily for seedbed preparation and weed control. Tillage has been an integral part of agricultural production. As the technology evolved, tillage expanded to include many aspects of soil and crop residue management and evolved into different tillage systems, each with their own objectives. Equipment used in these systems is briefly described. Improved soil management practices are described that minimize agriculture's impact on environmental quality while maintaining the soil resource.

Introduction

Agriculture is one of the foundations of rural America and has a major influence on components of industry, world trade, and global ecology. Traditional agricultural production involves at least five separate operations: (1) tilling or preparing the soil; (2) planting; (3) cultivating; (4) harvesting; and (5) processing, transporting, and storage before consumption. Tillage is first on this list because it has been an integral part of the production process. New technology is redefining and combining some of these operations, such as where tillage and planting are combined (no-till) and where mechanical cultivation is being replaced by herbicides.

The moldboard plow, historically, was an essential tool used by the early pioneers to settle the prairies of the central and western United States. From its rudimentary origins as a glorified hoe many years ago, the plow has been the principal tool to open land for planting, to destroy weeds, and to bury crop residue. The moldboard plow allowed farmers to create a soil environment in which grain crops could thrive. The use of the plow was unquestioned, and the ritual performed every year shaped the culture and rhythm of the rural community. The moldboard plow left a clean, neatly furrowed field that reflected farmers' pride in their property and management skills. The plow has been a significant symbol of agriculture over the last 150 years, but it is now being reevaluated, as new, conservation tillage techniques are developed and researched. Tillage practices evolved continually around the best crop systems limited by soil and water resources for a given geographical location. Tillage is thought of as the mechanical manipulation of the soil. Tillage is needed to prepare the seedbed, that is, to develop an area where crop seeds can be planted, sprout, take root, and grow to produce grain. Tillage loosens the soils, kills the weeds that compete with crop plants for needed water and nutrients, and improves the circulation of water and air within the soil. Tillage can release soil nutrients that enhance crop growth for a short time. It can enhance pest and disease control by covering or stirring residues. It can be used to enhance soil temperature by covering reflective residues and increasing solar heat absorption in the cooler seasons. These are the main rea-

Advances in mechanization have provided farmers with many options in equipment used for tilling the soil. Here chisel plows prepare a field for planting on an Ohio farm.

sons for clean tillage and moldboard plowing in the dark soils of the Northern Corn Belt.

Description of Tillage Systems

The concept of tillage systems combines various aspects of tilling, planting, managing residue, and applying pesticides and fertilizers. Because of the number and diversity of tillage system components, it is difficult to give any one system a meaningful name or very precise definition. Systems can be identified according to their ultimate objective, whether it is conventional or conservation tillage; and sometimes they are described by the primary tillage implement used (for example, a moldboard plow or a chisel plow). The naming problem often is compounded because the definitions differ among geographic regions. Different names may be used to identify a similar tillage system in different parts of the country. Listing all of the operations in the system results in the most accurate description.

Conventional Tillage. Conventional tillage is a sequence of operations most commonly used in a given geographic area to prepare a seedbed and produce a given crop. Because the operations vary considerably in the different climatic, agronomic, and other field conditions, the definition of conventional tillage varies from one physiographic region to another. Conventional tillage is often thought of as two major operations: primary tillage and secondary tillage. Primary tillage is more aggressive, deeper, and leaves a rougher surface relative to secondary tillage operations. Primary tillage tools are the moldboard plow, chisel plow, and various types of subsoiler implements designed to disturb the soil to greater depths.

Secondary tillage varies widely in the type and number of operations and generally works the soil to a shallower depth, provides additional soil breakup, levels and firms the soil, closes some of the air pockets, and kills some of the weeds. Secondary tillage equipment includes disk harrows, field cultivators, spring- and spike-toothed harrows, levelers, drags, and various types of packers.

Conservation Tillage. Conservation tillage is a general term that encompasses many different types of tillage and planting that maintain at least 30 percent or greater residue cover after planting. The objective is to provide a means of profitable crop production while minimizing soil erosion caused by wind and water. Although specific operations may vary, the emphasis is on conserving soil, water, energy, labor, and equipment.

No-Till (Slot Planting). The soil is left undisturbed from harvest to planting except for fertilizer injection. Planting or drilling is accomplished in a narrow seedbed or a slot created by a coulter, row cleaner, disk opener, in-row chisels, and sometimes small rototillers. Weed control is accomplished primarily with herbicides.

Ridge-Till. The soil is left undisturbed from harvest to planting except for nutrient injection. Planting is completed in a seedbed prepared on ridges four to six inches higher than the middles built the previous season with an aggressive cultivation. About one-third of the soil surface is tilled with various types of sweeps, disk openers, coulters, or row cleaners. Weed control is accomplished with a combination of herbicides and cultivation.

Strip-Till. Similar to the ridge-till, strip-till leaves the soil undisturbed from harvest to planting except for nutrient injection. Tillage in the row is done by in-row chisel, a row cleaner, or a rototiller that disturbs about one-third of the soil surface. Weed control is accomplished with a combination of herbicides and cultivation.

Mulch-Till. The total soil surface is disturbed prior to planting to various depths. Tillage is accomplished by chisels, field cultivators, disks, sweeps, or blades to varying depths and degrees of mixing. Generally there is more than 30 percent residue cover after planting. Weed control is accomplished with a combination of herbicides and cultivation.

Reduced-Till. Less intensive tillage types are accomplished with various tillage tools that leave 15 to 30 percent residue cover after planting and during critical erosion periods. Weed control is usually accomplished with a combination of herbicides and cultivation.

General Description of Tillage Implements

Moldboard Plow. The moldboard plow has been used extensively in the United States since about 1775. Many other tillage tools were invented to replace them but the moldboard plow is still used by many farmers as the primary tillage tool in areas receiving medium to high rainfall. The moldboard plow cuts, lifts, shears, and inverts the furrow slice to break up tough sod and turn under green manure crops on heavier soils. Moldboard plows are equipped with one or more bottoms of various cutting widths.

Chisel Plow. The chisel plow is a primary tillage implement that breaks or shatters the soil, leaving it rough with residue on or near the surface. Its general operating depth ranges from 6 to 12 inches. It consists of multiple rows of staggered curve shanks mounted either rigidly or with spring cushions or spring resets. Their interchangeable sweeps with chisel spikes and shovel tools are attached at each shank. Working width is increased by adding wings to the main unit.

Subsoiler. The subsoiler is a primary tillage tool similar to a chisel plow in that it is typically designed to operate from 12 to 22 inches deep. Subsoilers are used primarily to alleviate soil compaction and therefore are used when the soil is dry, for maximum effectiveness. Subsoiling leaves as much residue on the surface as does chiseling, or more. Coulters are often used to cut residue, to minimize clogging.

Blade or Sweep Plows. The blade plow or sweep plow is used primarily in the drier areas of the Great Plains to cut the roots of the weeds, and it leaves most of the residue on the soil surface. The V-shaped sweeps range from 2.5 to 6 feet wide, and are mounted on standards attached to a toolbar. The typical operating depth varies from 2 to 5 inches. The wider the sweep, the greater the soil depth needed to operate the equipment.

Rotary Tiller. Rotary tillers are used as once-over tools designed to produce a finished seedbed in one operation. They are operated by the power takeoff from the tractor, and they simultaneously till the soil and incorporate fertilizers and pesticides. Planter units occasionally are attached to the rotary tiller, making tillage and planting a one-pass operation. Some rotary tillers only till narrow strips, while others till the entire surface area. Residue remains on the surface between the strips for erosion control, and herbicide can be incorporated within the strip.

Rod Weeder. Rod weeders are used in the western Great Plains and the Pacific Northwest primarily for weed control during the summer fallow period and prior to seeding. A rod shaft is mounted on bearings and either rotated by ground driven wheels or left free to turn due to soil forces acting on it. The rotating rod is operated just under the surface to pull the weeds by the roots and flip them onto the soil surface to dry them out. Most of the residue remains on the surface after the rod weeder.

Disk Harrow. The disk harrow is used as a primary or secondary tillage implement. When used as a primary instrument, its large-diameter, concave disks mounted on a common shaft form a gang that turns the soil. The tandem disk harrow has two opposite gangs that throw the soil outward from the center of the implement followed by two gangs that throw the soil back toward the center. The disk cuts, throws, and loosens the surface soil at a depth of 3 to 6 inches, and is used primarily to break up large clods and cut some residue into the surface. The result is a rougher surface than other forms of secondary tillage, but multiple passes can result in a fine surface for seedbed preparation.

Field Cultivator. A field cultivator is a secondary tillage tool that is similar to a chisel plow but lighter in construction and designed for less severe conditions. Field cultivators generally have three or four ranks of equally spaced, flexible shanks. The shanks are spaced 24 to 40 inches apart, and provide effective soil disturbance at depths of 3 to 5 inches.

Harrows. Harrows are used as a secondary tillage tool to level the soil surface, redistribute surface residue to enhance moisture retention, pulverize clods, and disturb germinating weed seeds. The most common harrows are the spring-tooth harrow (thin wire teeth with a coil spring to allow flexibility) and the spike-tooth harrow with round, wire teeth on a rigid mount. These harrows often are attached to the rear of disk harrows. They perform the final operation prior to planting.

Culti-Packer. The culti-packer is especially useful to compact and level freshly plowed soil. It pulverizes clods, firms up the surface to a depth of 2 to 4 inches, but has little effect on the lower half of the furrow slice. The surface of the rollers is ridged rather than smooth, as a smooth roller presses stones into the soil surface. Rollers and packers can consist of one or two smooth or shaped in-line gangs of rollers.

Combination Implements. Combination implements consist of a wide variety of components commonly found as parts of other tillage tools, that are adjustable to vary the residue cover left after tillage to fit the definition of conservation tillage. For example, a combination implement may have two single-acting disk gangs in front, followed by three or four rows of field cultivator shanks and shovels, followed by a multirow, spike-tooth harrow or possibly subsoiler shanks. Combination implements often are used for one-pass incorporation of chemicals. Most combination implements operate in heavy residue conditions without clogging. They often require the greater horsepower available in today's modern tractors.

Tillage and Environmental Issues

Concern over soil erosion and increased pressure to farm land too steep or dry for conventional practices led to the development of reduced tillage and residue management systems that conserve crop residues on the soil surface. Within the past three decades the merits of reduced or no-tillage management systems have been recognized throughout the United States. Increased interest in conservation tillage arises from advantages these systems offer over conventional tillage practices.

Surface residue prevents erosion by absorbing raindrop impact and by slowing both water runoff and wind erosion. Conservation tillage techniques reduce soil erosion losses and increase use of land too steep to farm by conventional tillage methods. Other advantages include improved timing of planting and harvesting, increased potential for double-cropping, conservation of soil water through decreased evaporation and increased infiltration, and a reduction in fuel, labor, and machinery requirements. With conservation tillage, most residues are left on the soil surface, and only a small portion is in intimate contact with the soil moisture unavailable to the microorganisms. As a result, the residue decomposes more slowly. These advantages occasionally are offset by several disadvantages that limit crop production when compared with conventional systems. Disadvantages include cooler soil temperatures, which in temperate and cold climates impede germination and early crop growth. Other management concerns are an increase in potential insect and disease damage to crops and an increased need for more precise management of soil fertility and weed control.

Although moldboard plowing and other forms of intensive tillage have done much to increase crop production in the past 150 years in the United States, the increase in production has not been without some unseen costs in decreased soil quality and environmental impact (Schlesinger 1985). The unseen, unmeasured costs that result from intensive tillage include loss in soil organic matter due to enhanced oxidation and depletion of soil fertility reserves. The organic matter in many of the prairie's soils declined from 40 to 60 percent of that present under virgin conditions. The magnitude of these effects depends primarily on the intensity of tillage, that is, the type and frequency of tillage and the quantity and quality of crop residue returned to the soil. Intensive tillage, primarily moldboard plowing, decreases soil carbon in virtually all crop production systems. Differences in soil carbon decrease were related to various crop rotations and residue return in a given management system.

Recent studies involving tillage methods indicated major loss of gaseous soil carbon immediately after intensive tillage (Reicosky and Lindstrom 1993), which might be contributing to global climate change. They measured the effects of fall tillage methods on carbon dioxide flux in the Northern Corn Belt. Measurements immediately after tillage showed differences in the carbon dioxide loss were related to soil fracturing, which facilitated the movement of carbon dioxide out of and oxygen into the soil. The moldboard plow treatment buried nearly all the residue and left the soil in a rough, loose, open condition, resulting in maximal carbon dioxide loss. Considerably more carbon was lost as carbon dioxide from the plowed plots than from the area not tilled. Moldboard plowing now appears to have two major effects: to loosen and invert the soil, allowing a rapid carbon dioxide loss and oxygen entry, and to incorporate and mix residues to enhance microbial attack. The moldboard plow perturbs the soil system and causes a shift in the gaseous equilibrium by releasing carbon dioxide, enabling oxygen to enter the soil, and soil organic matter thus to be oxidized more rapidly.

Soil organic matter is the foundation of sustainable agriculture and is highly dependent on management decisions on the intensity of tillage and the amount and placement of residues. Conservation tillage or no-till systems have increased soil organic matter within 10 to 12 years of consistent use. The increase in soil organic matter depends on a delicate balance between the residue inputs of the previous crops and the tillage intensity associated with establishing the next crop. Farmers are faced with serious decisions with respect to the environmental consequences of maintaining sustainable production and managing this delicate balance.

—*Don C. Reicosky*

See also

Agricultural Engineering; Agriculture, Alternative; Agronomy; Conservation, Soil; Cropping Systems; Land Stewardship; Mechanization.

References

Alimaras, R. R., P. W. Unger, and D. W. Wilkins. "Conservation Tillage Systems and Soil Productivity." Pp. 357–411 in *Soil Erosion and Crop Productivity*. Edited by R. F. Follett and B. A. Stewart. Madison, WI: American Society of Agronomy, 1985.

American Society of Agricultural Engineers, Cultural Practices Equipment Committee. "Terminology and Definitions for Agricultural Tillage Implements." Pg. 310–319 in *ASAE Standards, 1986*. Edited by Russell H. Hahn and Evelyn E. Rosentreter. St. Joseph, MI: American Society of Agricultural Engineers, 1986.

Carter, Martin R. *Conservation Tillage in Temperate Agroecosystems*. Boca Raton, FL: Lewis Publishers, CRC Press, 1994.

Griffith, D. R., J. F. Moncrief, D. J. Eckert, J. B. Swan, and D. D. Breitbach. "Crop Response to Tillage Systems." Pp. 25–33 in *Conservation Tillage Systems and Management, Crop Residue Management with No-Till, Ridge Till and Mulch Till*. Midwest Plains Service, MWPS-45, First Edition. Ames: Iowa State University, Agriculture and Biosystems Engineering Department, 1992.

Journal of Soil and Water Conservation 32, no. 1 (1977): 3–65. Special issue on conservation tillage in different geographic regions of North America.

Phillips, Ronald E., and Shirley H. Phillips, eds. *No-Tillage Agriculture: Principles and Practices*. New York: Van Nostrand Reinhold, 1984.

Reicosky, Don C., W. D. Kemper, G. W. Langdale, C. L. Douglas, Jr., and P. B. Rasmussen. "Soil Organic Matter Changes Resulting from Tillage and Biomass Production." *Journal of Soil and Water Conservation* 50, no. 3 (May–June 1995): 253–261.

Reicosky, Don C., and Michael J. Lindstrom. "The Effect of Fall Tillage Methods on Short-term Carbon Dioxide Flux from Soil." *Agronomy Journal* 85, no. 6 (November–December 1993): 1237–1243.

———. "Impact of Fall Tillage and Short Term Carbon Dioxide Flux." Pp. 177–187 in *Soil and Global Change*. Edited by R. Lal, John Kimble, Elissa Levine, and B. A. Stewart. Chelsea, MI: Lewis Publishers, 1995.

Schlesinger, W. H. "Changes in Soil Carbon Storage and Associated Properties with Disturbance and Recovery." Pp. 194–220 in *The Changing Carbon Cycle: A Global Analysis*. Edited by J. R. Trabalha and David E. Reichie. New York: Springer-Verlag, 1985.

Soil Science Society of America, Terminology Committee. *Glossary of Soil Science Terms*. Madison, WI: Soil Science Society of America, 1987.

Tobacco Industry

A complex, tumultuous, long-term relationship among farmers, leaf dealers, and manufacturers that contributed significantly to the development of the nation. Since the earliest colonial settlements, development of the tobacco industry paralleled the development of the United States. Tobacco production is very labor intensive, but the high value per acre contributes significantly to farm income in tobacco-producing states. Government policy toward the industry has been to raise revenue from excise taxes on the sale of tobacco products and to make the growers and leaf buyers responsible for any price-support program.

Development

Tobacco has a deeply rooted and storied history in the United States and contributed much to its cultural and monetary development. The recorded history of tobacco in the United States began with a related species, *Nicotiana rustica*, which was being grown by Native Americans when European settlers first arrived. This high-nicotine, harsh-tasting tobacco was smoked, chewed, and used as snuff for medicinal, religious, and ceremonial purposes. The Spanish introduced the milder *Nicotiana tabacum* from South America into the Caribbean Islands.

Despite the success of antitobacco campaigns in the 1980s and 1990s, the tobacco industry remains the economic backbone of many rural areas.

John Rolfe obtained seeds of this species from Cuba and planted it at Jamestown in 1612. The first shipment of tobacco leaf from the colonies went to England in 1613. The demand for tobacco grew rapidly in England and the tobacco economy of the colonies provided an impetus for development of lands west of the Eastern Seaboard. Tobacco was an instant source of income for the British government and became a surrogate currency in the colonies. Tobacco served as collateral for loans for the colonies to help finance the American Revolution and has been a significant part of American culture and an important source of government income ever since.

Today tobacco is grown in at least 18 states as well as in Puerto Rico. However, North Carolina and Kentucky produce 65 percent of the total, with Georgia, South Carolina, Tennessee, and Virginia producing another 26 percent. The high value per acre of tobacco, averaging $3,750 in 1993, makes it significant to the growers and to the economies of the producing areas. Tobacco is the nation's sixth-largest cash crop, with an annual farm value of $3 billion. The high value per acre is somewhat misleading, since tobacco farms are relatively small, averaging only about 120 acres, with less than 6 of those acres in tobacco. Tobacco acreage per farm nearly doubled since the mid-1950s, as the number of tobacco farms decreased to 115,000. This trend is expected to continue if U.S. tobacco is to remain competitive in world markets.

Production

Tobaccos in the United States are grouped into seven classes and 28 different types. The most significant are the flue-cured and light air-cured types. Burley tobacco is the most important of the light air-cured group. Flue-cured tobacco production is centered around North Carolina, and Kentucky produces the majority of burley tobacco. The flue-cured and light air-cured tobaccos are used primarily in cigarette production, and account for the vast majority of total production and value of U.S. tobacco. The other classes are used mostly for cigar manufacture and smokeless tobacco products.

Tobacco production requires 125 to 250 hours of labor to produce one acre. The lower end of the range is for flue-cured tobacco, with much more mechanization in the harvest and curing process, and the high end of the range is for stalk-cut, fire-cured tobacco. The very small seed and slow seedling development necessitate transplanting young plants to the field. Traditionally, seeds are sown on top of soil beds three months prior to transplantation. This early seeding requires the seedbeds to be covered with cotton cloth to protect the young seedlings from the freezing temperatures that occur in early spring. At transplanting time, individual plants are pulled from the seedbeds and transplanted to the field. More recently, the seeds are sown in multicelled trays that can be handled as multiple-plant units in greenhouses. Each cell is filled with a soilless medium, and the trays are floated in nutrient solution. Advantages of the greenhouse system include faster plant development and reduced labor requirements. Transplants may be set by hand, but most often they are planted mechanically with the aid of a one- or two-row transplanter. These operations may require 50 hours of labor per acre.

When the plants begin to flower, the entire apical meristem is removed (in a process called topping) to maximize leaf yield and quality. Topping also allows growth of axillary buds to form suckers that must be removed or inhibited. Suckers may be removed from the plants by hand or more commonly the plants are treated with a growth modifier that prevents the further development of the axillary buds. Tobacco harvesting is a physically demanding task, especially for air-cured tobacco, which requires about 65 hours of labor per acre evenly divided between cutting the plants, impaling them on a stick, and hanging the sticks in the curing barn.

Growing tobacco is a management-intensive process; but curing the leaf is the most important operation for determining the quality of the product. Flue-cured tobacco is so called because it describes the heating system used in early curing barns. Bulk-curing barns with forced-air heat replaced the older barns with flues and convection heat. The initial step in curing is harvesting the ripe leaves. Flue-cured leaves are primed, removed individually from the stalk, starting at the bottom of the plant as the leaves ripen. At each harvest, three to five leaves are removed from the stalk at approximately weekly intervals. Leaves are placed into bulk-curing barns in racks or boxes directly from a mechanical harvester, thus greatly reducing labor input. During the first stage of curing, conditions are maintained at approximately 95°F and 85 percent relative humidity to cause yellowing, destruction of the chlorophyll, and simultaneous hydrolysis of many leaf constituents. After yellowing is completed, in 36 to 48 hours, the temperature is raised to about 125°F to dry the leaf lamina and allow oxidation of constituents formed in the first phase of curing. The temperature is further raised to 160°F to dry the leaf midrib and stop any remaining biological reactions. The entire process takes about four to seven days; then the leaves must rehydrate to become pliable for preparation and transport to market.

Air-cured tobaccos are harvested by cutting the stalk and hanging the whole plant in a curing barn; consequently, all the leaves are harvested at the same time. Barns for air-curing tobacco have large vents on the sides to allow for humidity control around the leaf during curing. Best curing conditions are when the temperature ranges between 60° and 90°F and the relative humidity averages between 65 and 70 percent. Relative humidity is the critical factor, because if it is too low the leaves dry too fast and the biological and chemical changes that are required for high-quality cured leaf do not occur. If the relative humidity is too high, microorganisms begin to grow on the tobacco and damage the leaf. Air-curing is dependent upon the ambient conditions, but is usually completed in 8 to 10 weeks.

Dark fire-cured tobaccos are stalk-cut and air-cured through the yellowing process and drying of leaf lamina, then the barn is filled with wood smoke to put a finish on the leaf. Loss of barns and tobacco to fire is a hazard of this curing process. This tobacco type is in demand for use in smokeless tobacco products, and is produced mainly in western Kentucky and western Tennessee.

After the curing process is completed, the leaves must be separated into grades, usually two to four grades based on color and visual assessment of quality. Prior to grading leaves of stalk-cut, air-cured tobacco, the plants must be taken down from inside the curing barn and leaves removed from the stalk. These tasks require an additional 85 hours of manual labor. The leaf is now ready for market.

Manufacture

Approximately 95 percent of the tobacco produced in the United States is flue-cured and burley for use in cigarettes. U.S. consumption of cigarettes has declined over the past 30 years, but about 700 billion cigarettes are still manufactured annually in the United States. Of this total, more than 25 percent is exported, making the United States the world's largest exporter of manufactured tobacco products. Tobacco leaf production for domestic consumption has been adjusted to conform not only to decreased per capita use but also to the decreased weight of leaf used per cigarette. The amount of tobacco in each cigarette was reduced because of decreased cigarette size and changes in technology. Cigarette circumference decreased, and with the shift to filter cigarettes, the portion containing tobacco decreased. Improved technology to make sheet tobacco from leaf midribs and scrap pieces of leaf, and the expansion or puffing of the leaf, also decreased the amount of tobacco required to fill a cigarette.

Prior to 1890, the manufacture and sale of tobacco products were performed mainly by small, local companies using locally produced tobacco. Standard manufacturing and marketing techniques were begun in the latter half of the nineteenth century, when Bull Durham brand was one of the first widely recognized brand names in America. In 1883, James Bonsack patented a cigarette-making machine that allowed mass production of uniform-quality cigarettes. James Duke obtained exclusive use of this machine for what eventually became the American Tobacco Company. By 1910, American Tobacco controlled 86 percent of the cigarette market, and cigarettes quickly became the primary tobacco product sold. Farm prices of tobacco plummeted during this time, and the battles of words and violence between growers and manufacturers were known as the Tobacco Wars or Black Patch Wars. In 1911, the Supreme Court ruled that the American Tobacco Company was in violation of the Sherman Anti-Trust Act, and the company was divested. Dominance of cigarettes as the product of consumer choice was greatly enhanced by the development of the blended cigarette, Camel, introduced in 1913. The blended cigarette contained about 60 percent flue-cured tobacco, 30 percent burley, a small amount of Turkish tobacco to enhance flavor, and light, air-cured Maryland tobacco for better burning quality. Burley tobacco has the unique property among tobaccos of absorbing and holding additives such as sweeteners and flavorings. The use of additives in the manufacturing process allows more stringent quality control for each cigarette brand, as taste and aroma are not dependent entirely on the raw leaf used.

Policy

Attempts to regulate supply and price have been initiated by growers since the beginning of tobacco production in the early 1600s. In the long term, these actions were unsuccessful. In the economic depression of the early 1930s, the federal government initiated a price-support program to farmers in return for regulation of production quantity, which has continued to this day. Present price-support programs cover 97 percent of total tobacco grown. All producers of tobacco types covered by a program must participate in the program. Initially, the price support received by the farmer was based on an acreage allotment that each producer was permitted to grow; but more recently, the quota is based on total poundage that may be sold annually by each producer.

Other significant changes to the government tobacco program include no net cost to taxpayers, production quotas based on intended purchases by manufacturers, and the lease or sale of quotas between farms. To finance the no-net-cost program, the producer and the purchaser are required to pay equal amounts toward expenses incurred to operate the program, plus the expense to purchase the tobacco that is not sold to a primary purchaser. Importers of flue-cured and burley tobacco are required also to pay fees toward the no-net-cost program. Tobacco purchased by the program is stored and is often sold at prices that recover the initial cost plus interest.

Previously, quotas were established on estimated disappearance of tobacco stocks. However, now export disappearance and reserve stocks are more minor considerations, and intended purchases by manufacturers is the single most important factor in the calculation of quotas. The statutory right to lease or sell quotas between farms increased the average quota size and has increased the potential for tobacco income by individual farmers. Also contributing to the implementation of the right to transfer quotas has been the replacement of older farmers by younger farmers with a desire for greater income potential, and the trend toward using hired, often migrant, labor. The consolidation of quotas may allow greater use of technology and increased economy of scale, and thus, greater competitiveness in the world market.

—Lowell Bush

See also

Agricultural Programs; Greenhouses; History, Agricultural; Policy, Agricultural.

References

Akehurst, B. C. *Tobacco.* 2d ed. New York: Longman, 1981.

Axton, W. F. *Tobacco and Kentucky.* Lexington: University Press of Kentucky, 1975.

Bush, L. P., and M. W. Crowe. "Nicotiana Alkaloids." Pp. 87–107 in *Toxicants of Plant Origin.* Edited by Peter R. Cheeke. Boca Raton, FL: CRC Press, 1989.

Clauson, A. "Costs of Producing and Selling Burley Tobacco: 1991, 1992, and Preliminary 1993." *Tobacco Situation and Outlook* (1993): 46–48.

Clauson, A., and D. Glaze. "Costs of Producing and Selling Flue-cured Tobacco: 1992, 1993, and Preliminary 1994." *Tobacco Situation and Outlook* (1994): 32–34.

Grise, V. N. "The Tobacco Program: A Summary and Update." *Tobacco Situation and Outlook* (1994): 34–37.

Tobacco Institute. *Tobacco: Deeply Rooted in America's Heritage.* Washington, DC: Tobacco Institute, 1981.

Tso, Tien-Chioh. *Production, Physiology, and Biochemistry of Tobacco Plant.* Beltsville, MD: Ideals, 1990.

U.S. Department of Agriculture. *Tobacco Situation and Outlook Yearbook.* Commodity Economics Division TBS-229 (December). Washington, DC: U.S. Department of Agriculture, Economic Research Service, 1994.

Town-Country Relations

The forms of conflict and cooperation between, and contrasting attitudes toward, town and country. These relations constitute a spatial opposition of deep economic and cultural significance, one of the great axes along which social life is organized and understood. This entry describes how this axis is manifested in the images, social identities, communities, patterns of migration, economic development, and power relations of rural and urban America.

Images of Town and Country

"Fuscus, who lives in town and loves it, greeting from one who loves the country, and lives there!" With these words, written in the year 20 B.C., the Roman poet Horace began one of his many works advocating country living (Raffel 1984, 215). Horace's writings, along with Aesop's ancient fable of the town mouse and the country mouse, show that relations between town and country have been an issue for at least 2,000 years. Probably for as long as there have been towns and surrounding countryside, the residents of both have pondered their attitudes toward each other and the interests that sometimes unite and sometimes divide them.

Yet for all their ancient significance, town and country are notoriously ambiguous terms. In America, "town" can refer to a city or an urban settlement as well as to a "small town"—a settlement perceived as culturally and economically rural, despite its concentration of population and businesses. By contrast, British usage marks "town" as clearly urban and the term "village" as descriptive of most of the places Americans call "small towns." Americans also use the term "village" at times, but for them the term "town" can cover both a village and a city—and sometimes even the "country," as in the use of "town" and "township" to demarcate local political boundaries in rural areas. The term "country" is no less indefinite. English speakers use it to refer to the open country of the wilderness, the farms and small towns of the rural countryside, and sometimes the quasi-rural landscape of exurbia and suburbia.

Despite these spatial and conceptual ambiguities, town and country do have distinct meanings, ultimately drawn from the opposition between culture and nature so central to Western thought. This distinction, imprecise and contradictory as it often is, has been a central prop for many moral arguments. "Those who labour in the earth," wrote Thomas Jefferson (1984 [1787], 290), "are the chosen people of God . . . whose breasts he has made his peculiar deposit for substantial and genuine virtue." The Jeffersonian faith in the pastoral, natural, and democratic virtue of country folk has, however, often jostled uneasily against what Raymond Williams (1984) called the "counter-pastoral" image of the countryside. Rather than a deposit of genuine virtue, the counterpastoral sees the countryside as a repository of backwardness, isolationism, and small-mindedness.

Like those of country life, the values of town life have been both elevated and denigrated in American thought. The town has been praised as the seat of progress, civilization, and a sophisticated and open-minded lifestyle. And from Thoreau onward, it has also been regarded as a constraining jungle of laws, rules, greed, and competitiveness. Both town and country have been seen as the true site of individual freedom, freedom from social convention on the part of the country, and freedom from country gossip on the part of the town. As well, both have been seen as the essential condition for real community, from the ethnic solidarity of "urban villages" to the helpfulness and neighborliness of country life.

Social Identity and Community

Given this range of available meanings, the distinction between town and country remains a valuable boundary upon which to establish a sense of identity. Many Americans continue to identify themselves as a "small-town person" or a "city person," and to take pride in the distinction. Part of the power of this distinction derives from people's sense of its naturalness (Bell 1992). The sheer physicality of place makes the country-town distinction an appealingly authoritative one. Moreover, the widely held notion that country places are closer to nature than urban areas, combined with the increasingly positive associations given to being closer to nature, makes a country identity especially secure and sought-after.

This spatial identification is central to what Hummon (1990, 11) called community ideologies, "systems of belief that legitimate the social and psychological interests of community residents." For example, a person who can claim to be "a local" may gain both a rooted sense of self and greater political legitimacy in local conflicts. A commitment to a spatial locale also may serve as the principle around which an economic and social solidarity may be constructed. As Allen and Dillman (1994) document for the small town of Bremer, Washington, a strong local community is possible even in an age in which information technologies have shattered so many spatial boundaries.

Many scholars, however, have argued that the distinction between country life and town life in the modern world is, in the oft-quoted words of Richard Dewey (1960, 60), "real, but relatively unimportant." Earlier scholarship argued for the existence of a rural-urban continuum, using Ferdinand Tönnies's (1940 [1887]) famous distinction between *Gemeinschaft* (a community based upon shared sentiments) and *Gesellschaft* (a community based upon interdependent interests). A host of community studies have challenged the idea that *Gemeinschaft* is more typical of rural communities and *Gesellschaft* of urban ones. But despite these scholarly challenges, the American popular imagination still finds the distinction between country life and town life a fruitful one to make. To the extent that people still act on this distinction as a source of identity and ideology, it remains both real and important, at least in its consequences. In any event, commitment to the local community remains high in many rural and urban locales.

Migration

The turnaround in the historical decline of the rural population in the United States and most western European countries is in part a consequence of the belief in town-country distinctiveness. The positive connotation of a country identity grew sharply following World War II. Beginning around 1970, the century-old pattern of rural population loss reversed itself, and nonmetropolitan (that is, rural) counties grew at a faster rate than metropolitan (urban) ones. This rural turnaround was associated with both suburban and exurban growth, which although it was defined as urban in census statistics, may have been motivated by similar community ideologies. In many instances, rural, exurban, and suburban growth resulted in an influx of wealthier residents, driving longer-term and poorer residents out, a contentious process that sociologists sometimes refer to as rural gentrification.

Migration between town and country, however, depends upon more than ideology. A number of technological and economic changes were important facilitating factors in the rural demographic turnaround. Better transportation, rural electrification, electronic media, and the shift to a more mobile and service-oriented economy made rural living both more practical and more desirable for many Americans. These changes are complex, geographically uneven in extent, and ongoing. For example, even at the height of the rural turnaround, many rural counties continued to decline. Then, in the 1980s, the rural turnaround itself turned around, and rural population decline resumed in most areas of the country, due largely to the farm crisis. Recent studies suggest that the rural population began growing once more after 1990, now that the farm economy has improved, but at a slower rate than in the 1970s (Johnson and Beale 1994). Throughout this period, exurban and suburban growth remained high.

Town and Country as an Isolated State

These changing trends in America's rural population show how crucial the patterns of economic development and technological change are to understanding town-country relations. In 1826, in *The Isolated State*, Johann Heinrich Von Thünen suggested a simple but powerful thought experiment about these patterns. Imagine an isolated world in which a single city sits in the midst of the hinterland from which it draws its resources. Such a city would be surrounded by concentric circles in which "with increasing distance from the Town, the land will be progressively given up to products cheap to transport in relation to their value" (Von Thünen 1966 [1826], 8). Perishable products (such as dairy, fruit, and vegetables) are expensive to transport, and so must command a high price and be produced close to town. This will raise the value of the land (what Von Thünen called "land rent") on which these products are produced. Cheaper products easier to transport will be produced on lower-valued land, farther from the town.

The real world, of course, is more complex. Cities and towns are not isolated from each other. Moreover, modern transportation technology greatly changed the economics of moving goods from Von Thünen's day, resulting in interregional agricultural specialization. A ham-and-cheese sandwich with lettuce and tomato served in New York City might have cheese from Duchess County, some 50 miles away, as Von Thünen would have expected. The ham, however, probably came from Iowa, the wheat for the bread from South Dakota, and in an inversion of Von Thünen's zones of production and land rent, the lettuce and tomato from California. The cheese might have come from California too. Yet, seeking the origin of real-world departures from an isolated state remains a valuable way to understand the dynamics of interregional competition and cooperation, the growth and decline of urban and rural populations, and the direction that technological change has followed in the industrial period. Town-country relations have been greatly affected by efforts to get around the economic realities indicated in Von Thünen's model.

Yet despite these efforts, the general pattern of primary production (that is, agriculture, forestry, and quarrying) still follows Von Thünen's model. Eighty-five percent of America's fruits and vegetables are produced in metropolitan or metropolitan-influenced counties (American Farmland Trust 1993). Goods like grain and timber (which are relatively nonperishable, and therefore easier to transport) remain lower valued and produced farther from cities on lower-valued land, such as the grainfields of Iowa, the Dakotas, and Nebraska, and the forestlands of Montana, Oregon, Alabama, and Maine. The generally depressed rural economies and continued rural population decline of these states reflects these lower values. Deborah and Frank Popper (1987) made the highly controversial suggestion that in some western states, this amounts to a re-creation of the frontier, in which there is little population or economic activity.

Von Thünen's model, however, presupposes the existence of a town. Walter Christaller sought to explain the town's origin with his Central Place Theory. A town, said Christaller (1966 [1933], 19), derives from the need for central goods and central services, goods and services "produced and offered at a few necessarily central points in order to be consumed at many scattered points." These goods and services are mainly those provided by government, industry, marketplaces, and the media. "Produced and offered" is actually an "and/or" connection For example, government services such as public education tend to be both centrally produced and offered; a newspaper, on the other hand, is centrally produced but offered at spatially dispersed points. Other goods and services may be produced at dispersed points but offered centrally, like vegetables in a supermarket. Christaller argued that there is a regional hierarchy of higher-order and lower-order central places, like satellites around a great planet.

Power Relations between Town and Country

The ideas of both Christaller and Von Thünen were incorporated into the more comprehensive theory of human ecology, the study of competition among human populations for scarce space and other resources. By analogy with the ecology of nonhuman populations, writers in this research tradition noted that human communities are interconnected, despite their competitiveness with each other. Differentiation of function, however, leads to inequality in a community's relative power. The hierarchy of places described by Christaller thus promotes urban dominance over the countryside.

From the ideas of Von Thünen, Christaller, and the human ecologists, it is a short theoretical jump to the observation that wealth tends to flow to the town. This is one of the essential insights behind the urban growth machine theory of Logan and Molotch (1987). The other insight is that this wealth flow is not merely the outcome of systematic economic and ecological forces, operating in a quasi-natural way; human agents are actively involved in structuring these flows. In order to maximize return on fixed capital, such as buildings and machines and the relatively fixed capital of human resources, urban economic and political elites advocate pro-growth policies that circulate as much mobile capital as possible through cities and towns. The size and centrality of cities give urban elites a political advantage when lobbying to create economic structures that will direct capital flows in their direction. The result is that despite the frequent objections of local citizens, elites operate cities and towns as economic vacuum cleaners, drawing capital and population from each other and from the hinterlands.

Industrializing the countryside is one way that urban interests gain control over rural capital, with important consequences for rural areas. In one of the most famous works of rural sociology, Walter Goldschmidt (1978 [1947]) argued that the structure of agriculture has a large impact on poverty and community life in farming-dependent counties. Based on a case study comparison of two California farming communities, Goldschmidt developed what has come to be called the "Goldschmidt hypothesis": that industrial farming leads to the deterioration of community well-being. Subsequent research generally upheld this conclusion, with the important caveat that rural poverty, the retention of rural social institutions, such as churches and schools, and rural depopulation depend on other factors as well.

Given these economic patterns, it is perhaps unsurprising that country people often feel a general hostility toward town people and town things. These tensions emerge in the centuries-long debate over whether the structure of the U.S. political system gives too much power, or not enough, to rural interests. These tensions are probably also largely responsible for the continued salience many people find in claiming a town or a country identity. The distinction between town and country is, in the final analysis, a mental construction that people choose to make. The likely persistence of economic tensions between central places and their hinterlands suggests that this is a construction that many people will continue to find significant to their lives.

—Michael M. Bell and Peter F. Korsching

See also

Community; Community, Sense of; Development, Community and Economic; History, Rural; Rural Demography; Rural, Definition of; Settlement Patterns; Trade Areas; Urbanization.

References

Allen, John C., and Don A. Dillman. *Against All Odds: Rural Community in the Information Age.* Boulder, CO: Westview, 1994.
American Farmland Trust. *"Farming on the Edge: A New Report on the Importance and Vulnerability of Agriculture near American Cities."* Washington, DC: American Farmland Trust, 1993.
Christaller, Walter. *Central Places in Southern Germany.* Trans. Carlisle W. Baskin. Englewood Cliffs, NJ: Prentice-Hall, 1966. Orig. ed. 1933.
Dewey, Richard. "The Rural-Urban Continuum: Real but Relatively Unimportant." *American Journal of Sociology* 66 (1960): 60–66.
Goldschmidt, Walter. *As You Sow: Three Studies in the Social Consequences of Agribusiness.* Montclair, NJ: Allanheld, Osmun, and Co., 1978. Orig. ed. 1947.
Hummon, David M. *Commonplaces: Community Ideology and Identity in American Culture.* Albany: State University of New York, 1990.
Jefferson, Thomas. *Writings.* Edited by Merrill D. Peterson. New York: Literary Classics of the United States, 1984.
Johnson, Kenneth M., and Calvin J. Beale. "The Recent Revival of Widespread Population Growth in Nonmetropolitan Areas of the United States." *Rural Sociology* 59, no. 4 (1994): 655–667.
Logan, John, and Harvey Molotch. *Urban Fortunes: The Political Economy of Place.* Berkeley: University of California Press, 1987.
Popper, Deborah Epstein, and Frank J. Popper. "The Great Plains: From Dust to Dust." *Planning* 53 (1987): 12–18.
Raffel, Burton. *The Essential Horace.* San Francisco: North Point Press, 1983.
Tönnies, Ferdinand. *Fundamental Concepts of Sociology (Gemeinschaft und Gesellschaft).* Trans. Charles P. Loomis. New York: American Book Company, 1940. Orig. ed. 1887.
Von Thünen, Johann Heinrich. *Von Thünen's Isolated State.* Ed. Peter Hall. Trans. Carla M. Wartenberg. Oxford: Pergamon, 1966. Orig. ed. 1826.
Williams, Raymond. *The Country and the City.* New York: Oxford University Press, 1973.

Trade Areas

The geographical areas to which residents are attracted to shop at a trade center. Trade centers are locations with an assortment of businesses that sell goods and services to consumers. Early trade areas in the United States origi-nated with Native American settlements but changed over the years, as nonnatives settled the country. As the country become more mechanized, local residents gained mobility and started shopping farther from home, thereby changing the size and shape of trade areas. Academics developed theories of trade areas and various methods of measuring them. Individual merchants can determine the size of their own trade areas by analyzing data gathered from consumers. Regional variations of trade area size and shape are brought about by differences in topography and population density. Dominant businesses within a community can enlarge the trade area, whereas weak businesses can decrease it.

History

The first trade areas in what is now the United States were developed by Native Americans, who lived primarily in tribes. Tribes in different parts of the country had access to different raw materials and natural resources and developed different handicraft skills. Tribal members could improve their well-being by trading with members of neighboring tribes—thus, the beginning of trade areas. The early nonnative settlers in the United States tended to settle in the vicinity of streams and wooded areas, since they needed the streams for transportation and water, and the wood to construct buildings and provide fire. Consequently, the early businesses in the country consisted of trading posts around these settlements, which became trade centers for the newly settled territories.

In the mid- to late 1800s, railroads played a large role in settling the rest of the country. Railroads provided a leap over horses and oxen in the transportation of both people and goods. There was great competition to entice the railroads to come through various settlements. The lucky settlements that got a railroad station tended to become trade centers, and their populations grew rapidly. Meanwhile, transportation for pioneer farmers was poor, consisting primarily of horses and oxen traveling over rough trails. For many pioneer farmers, making trips to the railroad trade centers was a formidable task. Therefore, intermediate trade centers sprang up between the railroad stations, and initially were successful because of the immobility of rural residents.

Despite their limited mobility, some early settlers made occasional trips to larger towns and cities by animal power or later by train to shop for items not locally available. However, the first major challenge to rural retailers occurred in the late 1880s, when Montgomery Ward and Sears, Roebuck began mail-order operations. At its peak,

Sears, Roebuck offered over 100,000 items through its catalog. Mail-order firms offered great convenience to rural residents by allowing them to order by mail and receive shipment within several weeks. The mail-order companies captured trade from many rural retailers.

Automotive vehicles appeared in the early 1900s. However, it was some time before roads and highways were sufficiently developed to allow easy travel to larger trade centers to shop. By the end of the 1930s, both motor vehicles and highways had been improved considerably, but the Great Depression of the 1930s kept most rural residents shopping close to home because they did not have the money to travel or shop.

The United States mobilized for World War II from 1941 to 1945. Severe rationing of retail goods and gasoline caused most rural residents to stay close to home to shop. After World War II, the combination of relative prosperity and great pent-up demand caused rural consumers and others to go on shopping sprees, creating the first widespread migration from rural areas to larger trade centers to shop. At about the same time, rapid mechanization of farms meant that fewer and fewer people were needed in agriculture, thus causing many people to leave the rural areas and to seek opportunities elsewhere. This out-migration was the beginning of severe depletion of the trade areas of rural retailers.

Shopping malls began to appear in larger trade centers in the 1950s and 1960s, and spread rapidly across the country in the 1970s and 1980s. Consumers were attracted to shopping malls in large numbers because of their large selections, ease of access, free parking, controlled climate, and extended shopping hours. Rural residents flocked to the malls, thus further eroding the trade areas of rural retailers. The 1980s and 1990s saw the expansion of many mass merchandiser chains, such as discount general merchandisers and specialty superstores. More and more these chains congregated around larger trade centers and accelerated the capture of retail trade from the rural areas.

The trends of continual consolidation in farming and retailing continue today and are responsible for shrinking rural trade areas and multiplying problems for small-town retailers. For example, studies in Iowa have shown that towns of 500 to 1,000 people lost over 45 percent of their retail trade between 1983 and 1993.

Theories of Trade Areas
Central Place Theory. In the early 1900s, sociology, geography, and economics scholars began to express interest in the theory of trade areas and the measurement of their size. Two German scholars, Walter Christaller and August Losch, were responsible for the first major developments of a theory of retail trade, called Central Place Theory, although some believe that the French scholar, J. Reynaud, originated the idea in the mid-1800s.

Central Place Theory is the theory of the location, size, nature, and spacing of business communities. It is an attempt to explain the function and spacing of different size trade centers and to develop a hierarchy. In more recent times, various researchers have designated the hierarchy of central places as *minimum convenience, partial shopping, complete shopping,* and *primary regional.* For example, a minimum convenience trade center might have only a convenience store, service station, hair salon, and restaurant, and draw customers from a five-mile radius. Conversely, a primary regional trade center might have a complete assortment of businesses and draw customers from a 100-mile radius.

Early researchers experimented with several variables to explain the relationship between trade center size and spacing. For example, the number of telephones in a community was used to designate a place in the hierarchy when mainly businesses had telephones. In later years, nearly everyone had a telephone. It became obvious that variables such as this could quickly become obsolete. Others used the number of businesses and the relative size of the businesses in formulae designed to develop a ranking of central places. Most of these variables were difficult to acquire and impractical to use. This led to the use of a simpler, generalized theory, called Reilly's Law of Retail Gravitation.

Reilly's Law of Retail Gravitation. In 1929, William J. Reilly of the University of Texas developed a simple equation to determine the breaking point between two competing trade centers where consumers theoretically would be indifferent as to which trade center they shopped in. In other words, the boundaries of a trade center's trade area could be computed. Reilly's point of indifference can be expressed algebraically as

$$Dab = \frac{d}{1 + \sqrt{\dfrac{Pb}{Pa}}}$$

where Dab = limit of town A's trade area, measured in miles along the road to town B;

d = distance in miles between towns A and B;
Pa = population of town A;
Pb = population of town B.

For example, if Town A of 40,000 population and Town B of 4,000 population were 25 miles apart, the point of indifference would be derived by the equation:

$$Dab = \frac{25 \text{ (that is, 19 miles from Town A and 6 miles from Town B)}}{1 + \sqrt{\dfrac{4,000}{40,000}}}$$

Functional Economic Areas. In 1965, Karl Fox of Iowa State University published his first article on functional economic areas. It was his premise that individuals generally did not care to work, shop, or go to school more than an hour's drive from their home, which he deduced to be about 50 miles. He found that by superimposing a grid of 50-mile squares on a map of Iowa, centered on the larger trade centers, and by rotating the grid 45 degrees, the functional economic areas could be depicted. The squares fit nicely together and covered about 80 percent of the state and accounted for 90 percent of the population. In other words, he found that the natural trade areas for the larger cities extended about 50 miles. The concept came to be known as "Fox's boxes."

Measurement of Trade Area Size

Researchers had discovered ways to measure the theoretical size of trade areas; but businesspeople still needed practical ways to determine the size of their trade areas. Some of the more common ways are consumer surveys, check and credit card receipts, and pull factor analysis.

Consumer Surveys. Trade areas can be delineated fairly well by conducting a consumer survey. A random sample of consumers within a generous radius of a trade center is selected and respondents are queried about where they shop for various goods and services. The approximate trade area then can be defined based on consumer responses.

Check and Credit Card Receipts. Individual merchants can determine their own trade area by analyzing their check and credit card receipts periodically. The findings can be plotted on maps to show primary and secondary trade areas.

Pull Factor Analysis. Pull factor analysis is a precise way to show the relative size of a trade area, but not the exact geographic boundaries. The pull factor, developed by Stone and McConnon (1980), is derived using sales data, usually gathered from state sales tax reports. A pull factor is merely a town's per capita sales divided by the state's per capita sales. For example, if a town had per capita sales of $15,000 and the state per capita sales were $7,500, the pull factor would be $15,000 divided by $7,500 = 2.0. The interpretation is that the town is selling to 200 percent of the town population in full-time customer equivalents (the amount customers would have spent if they made all their purchases in that town). The pull factor is very useful in comparing trade area size over time, since it adjusts for price inflation, population change, and changes in a state's economy.

Regional Variations

Many of the studies on trade areas have occurred in the Midwest, where the terrain is fairly uniform and there are few barriers to transportation. In these areas, it is easy to predict trade area size for various trade centers.

Geographical Differences. In mountainous areas, where travel is more difficult, it is possible for smaller trade centers to pull trade from a large geographical area and to remain viable. Certain parts of the High Plains and desert Southwest have very sparse populations. Small trade centers remain robust because larger trade centers are too distant to attract business away from them.

Dominant Businesses. There are many small trade centers across the country that are blessed with one or more superior businesses. For example, it is common to see an outstanding restaurant in a small town that draws business from a large area. Other towns may have an outstanding furniture store, a large building materials store, or a large automobile dealership, any of which can draw an inordinate amount of traffic.

In recent times, many factory outlet malls have been opening in small towns adjacent to major highways. These centers draw traffic not only from the highway, but sometimes become shopping destinations for customers from 100 or more miles away.

The Future

The continued concentration of large, mass-merchandiser stores in larger trade centers and the continued out-migration of people from rural areas does not bode well for most smaller trade centers. The residents of these smaller towns are greatly inconvenienced in that they must travel somewhere else to transact a large share of their business.

The development of electronic interactive mail order along with tremendous improvement in delivery services holds some promise for changing the retail equation in the future. It may be possible in the years to come to browse through an electronic mail-order catalog, get expert product information, make a selection, order, and receive the merchandise within a very short time. This will not appeal to everyone; but it holds the potential to change retailing so that place no longer matters. People in the most rural areas may be able to shop for virtually anything in the world from the comfort of their homes. Conversely, small-town merchants with unique products will not be constrained to their local trade areas but will be able to market to the world.

—*Kenneth E. Stone*

See also
Community; Community, Sense of; Development, Community and Economic; History, Rural; Regional Planning; Rural Demography; Settlement Patterns; Town-Country Relations; Trade, Interregional; Urbanization.

References

Anding, Thomas L., John S. Adams, William Casey, Sandra de Montille, and Miriam Goldfein. *Trade Centers of the Upper Midwest: Changes from 1960 to 1989.* CURA 90-12. Minneapolis: University of Minnesota, Center for Urban and Regional Affairs, 1990.

Berry, Brian J. L. *Geography of Market Centers and Retail Distribution.* Englewood Cliffs, NJ: Prentice-Hall, 1967.

Borchert, John R., and Russell B. Adams. *Trade Centers and Trade Areas of the Upper Midwest.* Minneapolis, MN: Upper Midwest Research and Development Council, 1963.

Fox, Karl A. *Urban-Regional Economics, Social System Accounts, and Eco-Behavioral Science.* Ames: Iowa State University Press, 1994.

King, Leslie J. *Central Place Theory.* Beverly Hills, CA: Sage Publications, 1984.

Mahoney, Tom. *The Great Merchants.* New York: Harper and Brothers, 1955.

Martin, Paul S., George I. Quimby, and Donald Collier. *Indians before Columbus.* Chicago: University of Chicago Press, 1947.

Stone, Kenneth E. *Competing with the Retail Giants: How to Survive in the New Retail Landscape.* New York: John Wiley and Sons, 1995.

Stone, Kenneth E., and James C. McConnon, Jr. "Retail Sales Migration in the Midwestern United States." Paper presented at the American Agricultural Economics Association annual meeting, University of Illinois, Urbana, 1980.

Trade, International

The commercial exchange of goods, services, or capital across national frontiers. Growth in the volume and scope of international trade is having a tremendous impact on rural areas. The extent of that impact, and whether it is positive or negative, varies considerably by product, region, and historical point in time.

Introduction

International trade is one of the numerous forms of cross-national social interaction that are increasing in frequency and intensity. The various configurations that international trade can take, and the ways in which it can be integrated with local social, economic, and political activities, makes it extremely difficult to assess accurately the microlevel impacts of trade on people and communities. In addition, long-term impacts are more difficult to detect than short-term ones. Finally, comparatively little research has been done on the local impacts of international trade because it is generally assumed that the benefits of trade outweigh the costs. Thus, whereas there have been numerous studies evaluating the positive and negative consequences of international trade for regional and national economies, comparatively fewer studies investigated whether growth in trade improved job situations and the quality of life for people in specific communities. Nonetheless, it is possible to identify some of the impacts that international trade has had on rural people and communities. Assessments of whether these impacts have been, on balance, beneficial to rural areas of the United States vary considerably.

Trade and Prices

One of the more direct impacts that the expanding volume of international trade has had on rural areas is the increased volatility of commodity prices. As agricultural commodities and raw materials from extractive industries are traded more and more on global markets, they become increasingly subject to fluctuations in global prices for those commodities. In cases where worldwide supplies of a commodity are low, rural areas that produce these commodities can experience substantial jumps in income. However, the opposite is also true. As more regions around the world produce and market the same or substitutable commodities, or as demand for a commodity falls due to changes in tastes or declines in purchasing power, prices for these commodities can fall. Some scholars have argued that increased international trade, along with technological improvements, is a primary reason for the general decline in world commodity prices over the past 20 years. Thus, whether a community benefits or not from growth in international trade will depend in part on whether it produces a commodity that is in short supply or great demand in various parts of the world, as well as on other global financial conditions, such as volatility in currency exchange markets.

Trade and Labor

Another impact of expanding international trade on rural America has been to place rural labor within a global labor market. As international movement of goods and services becomes easier due to improved transportation and telecommunication technologies, firms are increasingly able to locate production facilities in whatever country provides them with the least expensive labor force of a particular quality. Thus, just as the prices of commodities produced in rural America have become increasingly coupled with global prices for comparable commodities, wage rates in the rural United States are being affected by overseas wage rates. This can serve to suppress wage rates for jobs that can be exported while creating new employment opportunities for individuals and firms that produce goods and services that are in short supply globally.

Many rural communities in the United States have been adversely affected by shifts in where multinational firms source labor because they are dependent on low-skill manufacturing jobs. During this century, and especially after the end of World War II, many rural areas became less dependent on agriculture and more dependent on manufacturing for employment. This was made possible by the fact that rural labor was less organized and less expensive than urban labor. Thus, rural communities, particularly those in the southeastern states, became attractive places for urban firms to relocate, particularly those that depended on cheap labor. However, in recent years, many firms found it profitable to leave rural America and relocate to overseas locations where labor is relatively plentiful and inexpensive. Thus, many researchers now believe that manufacturing will not support the future development of the rural United States.

However, trade opportunities also can contribute to the creation of jobs in rural areas of the United States. For example, increased food product exports, particularly of processed and semiprocessed foods, contribute to the growth of food processing firms, many of which are located in rural regions that are centers of agricultural commodity production. However, these employment opportunities often are not found in the same communities that experienced job losses due to the overseas transfer of jobs. Nonmetropolitan areas of the United States generally are less diversified economically and more dependent on goods production than are metropolitan areas. As a result, many communities that hosted manufacturing industries that are being exported as a result of free trade regimes have suffered, while other communities benefited from the opportunities provided by increased international trade.

Estimating the number of jobs generated by increased trade opportunities is extraordinarily complicated. Economists generate multipliers that can be used to estimate the number of jobs generated by an increase in exports of a particular good or commodity. However, these figures can be based on very broad assumptions, and they do not always capture the complexity of the economic situation facing particular firms. Without both domestic and overseas orders, many firms are unable to achieve the efficiency levels needed to stay in business. In other words, whether the jobs generated by a firm are attributable to domestic or overseas sales is debatable because a firm's financial health might decline if sales in any of its markets declines.

Finally, observers sometimes overlook the job generation benefits that can result from increased imports of capital investments, finished goods, or product parts that are used or sold in domestic markets. An interesting example of such a case is the economic growth experienced by rural regions that became home to Japanese automobile manufacturers. Certainly, the continued viability of many rural firms, and the socioeconomic well-being of the communities where they are located, has become dependent in large measure on international trade activity, just as other communities experienced socioeconomic decline for the same reason.

Trade and Environment

Another kind of trade effect that is not mentioned very often is the effect on the environment. However, Stevens (1993) has discussed some of the possible positive and negative impacts of international trade on the environment. On the positive side she lists increased trade in environmentally sound production inputs and technologies, increased wealth and subsequent financial support for environmental programs, and the global reallocation of economic activity according to environmental endowments. On the negative side are increased trade in dangerous chemicals and hazardous waste, increased trade in endangered species, faster depletion of natural resources due to economic growth, and transfer of production to environmentally incompatible areas. Arguably, the negative environmental impacts of increased international trade are falling disproportionately on poorer countries. Just as low wage rates in these countries attracted many firms to relocate some of their manufacturing facilities overseas, less stringent environmental regulations have been a compelling reason for some companies to move plants outside the United States. In any case, research on the environmental effects of international trade is just beginning, and further studies are needed to determine whether increased international trade is, on balance, good or bad for the environment.

Conclusion

Undoubtedly, international trade is growing and is affecting rural America. For example, in fiscal year 1994, U.S. agricultural exports totaled $43.5 billion, and agricultural imports were $26.4 billion. The comparable figures for fiscal year 1984 were $38.0 billion and $18.9 billion, respectively. Although one can find examples of decline from year to year as well as of growth, the overall trend in recent decades has been for expansion in both exports and imports, in agriculture as in most other sectors of the national economy. This trend is expected to continue.

Whether this growth will, on balance, have a positive influence on rural life will depend not only on the region and the community but also on how individuals living in rural areas adjust to the challenges presented by globalization. National governments are currently under tremendous pressure to agree to bilateral and multilateral trade agreements that lower trade barriers and permit a freer exchange of goods, services, and capital throughout the world. A difficulty that local communities face as this situation develops is that their residents tend to be inwardly focused, while firms, particularly multinational firms, are active in a multitude of local places and consequently have more options at their disposal. Despite the reporting of export and import statistics by country, virtually all international trade is managed by, takes place between, and is for the benefit of, private firms. An understanding of how firms interact with rural communities in an integrated global political economy will be crucial to rural residents' success in adapting and prospering in the twenty-first century.

—*Raymond A. Jussaume, Jr.*

See also

Agricultural and Resource Economics; Manufacturing Industry; Marketing; Markets; Policy, Economic; Trade, Interregional; Value-Added Agriculture.

References

Falk, William W., and Thomas A. Lyson. *Rural Labor Markets.* Research in Rural Sociology and Development. Greenwich, CT: JAI Press, 1989.

Fitchen, Janet. *Endangered Spaces, Enduring Places.* Boulder, CO: Westview Press, 1991.

Freudenburg, William R. "Addictive Economies: Extractive Industries and Vulnerable Localities in a Changing World Economy." *Rural Sociology* 57 (1992): 305–332.

Fuguitt, Glen V., David L. Brown, and Calvin L. Beale. *Rural and Small Town America.* New York: Russell Sage Foundation, 1989.

Gaston, Noel, and Daniel Trefler. "The Role of International Trade and Trade Policy in the Labor Markets of Canada and the U.S." *The World Economy* 17 (1994): 45–62.

Jussaume, Raymond A., Jr. "Agricultural Trade, Firms and the State: Extrapolations from the Case of Japanese Beef Imports." *International Journal of the Sociology of Agriculture and Food.* (forthcoming).

Jussaume, Raymond A., Jr., and Martin Kenney. "Japanese Investment in California and Washington Agriculture." *Agribusiness* 9 (1993): 413–424.

Leach, Belinda, and Anthony Winson. "Bringing 'Globalization' Down to Earth: Restructuring and Labour in Rural Communities." *Canadian Review of Sociology and Anthropology* 32, no. 3 (1995): 341–364.

Stevens, Candice. "The Environmental Effects of Trade." *World Economy* 16 (1993): 439–451.

Trade, Interregional

The exports and imports of a region. Measurement and meaning complicate the application of the term "interregional trade" to rural areas. The first factor in the equation is the measure of gross exports, the out-shipments of goods and services to producers and consumers outside the region. The second is the measure of gross imports, the in-shipments of goods and services for the use of economic units inside the region. Apropos to both measures is the concept of the region itself. In an economic sense, a region is a collection of local labor market areas or the commuting areas of central places that are the areas' trade centers. The export-producing businesses of an area define its economic base and that of the region.

The trading region includes the infrastructure of commerce as well as the export-producing businesses, workers, and production facilities, and a host of residential activities catering to these businesses and their workers and households. All are important participants in the initiation and support of interregional trade, the inevitable result of businesses and workers exercising their particular comparative advantage through remunerative product specialization (Krugman 1991). We therefore address the topic initially by defining and measuring trade within and between trading regions, and finally, by accounting for the variability and value of interregional trade with the product specialization of its export-producing businesses and industries.

Trading Regions

A trading region is a mixture of urban and rural areas that transcends state boundaries. The areas are both metropolitan and nonmetropolitan. Each region has a center, or metropolitan core area, and a periphery. The metropolitan core area is also an air node in the U.S. air transportation network of air nodes and connecting cities within each region. A trading region is defined by the proximity of its contiguous labor market, or daily commuting, areas to the metropolitan core area. Figure 1 delineates a system of 29 air node regions (that is, regions served by a large, central airport) based on (1) the 29 U.S. air nodes, excluding Alaska and Hawaii, and (2) the daily commuting areas, using the proximity criterion. The daily commuting area of a resident population also represents the geographical boundaries of the local labor market. The nonmetropolitan labor market areas (LMAs) lack even one place with a population of more than 50,000. While the majority of counties in the United States are classified as nonmetropolitan, 252 of the 382 LMAs are metropolitan-centered. They contain one or more of the 184 metropolitan statistical areas, that is, individual counties or groups of counties, each containing one or more places with a population of at least 50,000.

Figure 2 illustrates the use of individual counties as building blocks for the labor market areas by focusing on Region 10, the Minneapolis–St. Paul air node region. Of the 281 counties in the Minneapolis–St. Paul region, based on the 1980 commuting area delineations (Tolbert and Killian 1987), 32 are included in 13 metropolitan statistical areas (MSAs). Thirteen of the counties are in the Minneapolis–St. Paul MSA and are also part of the 16-county Minneapolis–St. Paul LMA. An additional 94 non-MSA counties are part of the remaining 12 LMAs that include the MSA counties outside the metropolitan core area. Even a dominantly rural region like Minneapolis–St. Paul, with 155 counties in 13 entirely rural LMAs, forms a highly integrated trading region with much internalization of trade between metropolitan and nonmetropolitan areas. The metropolitan core area is of critical importance to the rural areas with an expanding industrial base because of its market and nonmarket linkages to the core area producer services and transportation infrastructure (Glasmeier 1993; Kravis 1985; Ohmae 1995, 117–140). Also important are the secondary core areas. These include the endogenous growth centers, characterized by their increasingly diverse local labor markets (Hansen 1993). The commuting areas of both the primary and the secondary core areas also serve as the functional economic community for solving areawide problems by strengthening and extending the "networks of civic engagement" that facilitate flows of information about technological developments, employment and entrepreneurial opportunities, and related factors affecting the competitive position of export-producing businesses in their respective markets (Putnam 1993, 163–185).

An excess of local jobs over resident jobholders identifies the central place of a labor market area. This definition of a central place focuses on the critical resource of most regional economies, a diverse and dynamic labor market and its daily commuting area (Saxenian 1994, 133–159, 161–168). The in-commuting of nonresident jobholders overcomes the deficit in resident jobholders for the central places. This accounts for the varying concentrations of economic activity, depending on type and size of the LMAs and their location relative to the metropolitan core area (Maki and Reynolds 1994). The University of Minnesota Impact Analysis for Planning (IMPLAN) regional database and modeling system illustrate the meaning and use of the several measures of interarea and interregional trade among labor markets. The regional database includes a common 1990 data set of industry and commodity exports and imports, as well as industry and commodity sales and industry employment and value added, for all U.S. counties.

Product Specialization

By definition, a positive balance of trade exists when gross commodity exports exceed gross commodity imports. Interregional trade is, thus, a measure of the competitive advantage of a region's export-producing

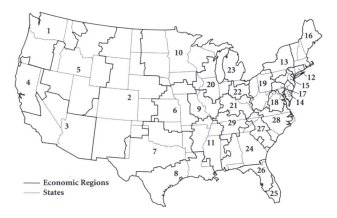

Figure 1. Economic Regions, U.S. Air Node Proximity

Source: C. M. Tolbert and M. S. Killian. *Labor Market Areas for the United States.* Staff Report AGE 870721. Washington, DC: U.S. Department of Agriculture, Economic Research Service, Rural Economy Division, 1987.

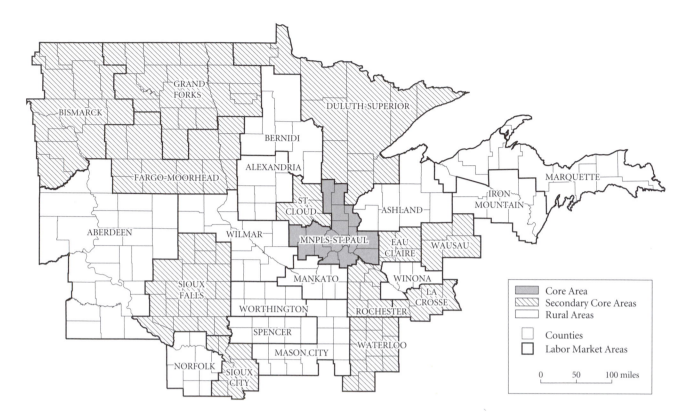

Figure 2. Minneapolis–St. Paul Region, U.S. Air Node Proximity

Source: See source for Figure 1.

industries. A region may experience a positive balance of trade, however, and still lag in economic growth behind another region that is experiencing a negative balance of trade. For example, a disproportionately large share of the export earnings may leave the first region immediately, without benefiting regional residents. On the other hand, a large share of the gross imports of the other region may be capital goods. These could be purchased by local private investors acquiring financial resources from outside the region. The first region, with positive exports, lacks profitable investment opportunities, while the second region at least has the perception of profitable investment opportunities. A region consisting largely of declining rural areas typically falls into the first category of a positive trade balance. A region consisting largely of rapidly growing urbanizing areas falls into the second category. Interregional trade has various measures, each with its particular meaning for the two types of trading regions.

A leading measure of gross exports is the propensity to purchase locally produced goods and services—that is, goods and services produced within the area or region of measure. A leading measure of gross imports is the propensity to import. The primary difficulty in the use of

these two measures is the lack of any accurate monitoring of commodity or product flows from one area or region to another. We have only indirect measures of these two indicators of actual shipments from a variety of data sources, including the U.S. censuses of transportation that show the gross out-shipments and in-shipments of industries in each state. Once we have the estimates of gross out-shipments using the indirect measures, we can then estimate gross in-shipments, given the total production in the area or region.

Table 1 presents estimates of gross out-shipments, or exports, of local industry production for the core area and six clusters of LMAs in the Minneapolis–St. Paul region, including parts of North and South Dakota, northeastern Nebraska, the northerly counties of Iowa and Wisconsin, the Upper Peninsula of Michigan, and all counties in Minnesota. Inclusion of the core area of 16 counties provides comparison of its external trade with the external trade of the more rural areas of the region. These are net exports, that is, gross industry out-shipments less gross industry in-shipments, for the industry groups in each of the seven subregions. Industry groups with net out-shipments vary from nine for the core area

Table 1
Net Exports of Specified Industry by Subregion, Minneapolis–St. Paul Economic Region, 1991 ($ million)

Industry	Minneapolis–St. Paul Core Area	North[1] Region LMAs			South[1] Region LMAs		
		East	Central	West	East	Central	West
Agriculture	472	244	435	1,211	297	554	862
Agricultural Services, forestry, fish	71	7	-3	-28	24	-21	-13
Mining	94	1,332	26	232	37	151	57
Construction	-2,232	-731	-580	-633	-836	-1,021	-1,094
Manufacturing, total	15,327	2,076	1,294	935	3,879	5,660	5,427
Transportation, communication, utilities	475	-143	113	47	-348	-415	-388
Wholesale trade	2,022	71	60	183	137	186	239
Retail trade	158	-201	-23	-138	-210	-355	-278
Finance, insurance, real estate	1,154	-47	78	-85	-168	-35	-13
Private services	1,416	-542	-230	-288	-602	-316	-485
Government	-134	-99	-14	-21	-55	-109	-104
Total	18,824	1,968	1,155	1,415	2,155	4,280	4,209

Source: University of Minnesota IMPLAN System.

[1] North refers to the 74 counties in nine labor market areas (LMAs) (from Marquette westward to Bismarck) north of Minneapolis–St. Paul, whereas South refers to the remaining 191 counties in 17 LMAs, largely in South Dakota, southern Minnesota, and central Wisconsin, including the Iron Mountain LMA. The 26 LMAs aggregate to the following: Northeast combines Duluth-Superior, Ashland, and Marquette; North-Central combines Bemidji, Alexandria, and St. Cloud; Northwest combines Bismarck, Grand Forks, and Fargo-Moorhead; Southeast combines Eau Claire, Wausau, Winona, LaCrosse, Rochester, and Waterloo; South-Central combines Willmar, Worthington, Spencer, and Mankato; and Southwest combines Aberdeen, Sioux Falls, Sioux City, and Norfolk.

to four for the south-central and southwest LMA clusters. Construction and the services-producing industry groups consistently show net in-shipments for the LMA clusters outside the core area. Construction, of course, is the most highly import-dependent industry group. However, the aggregation of many individual industries into broader categories such as manufacturing obscures the sharply contrasting composition of exports of the core area and its surrounding LMAs. The additional data would more clearly identify opportunities for the internalization of interarea trade within the region.

Applying the share of total employment engaged in producing the exports of each industry to the industry's total employment yields a measure of the industry's contribution to the local economic base. Using this measure, manufacturing accounts for 50 percent or more of the economic base of all but the north-central and the north-west LMAs of Minnesota and North Dakota. Agriculture is dominant in the northwest LMAs, accounting for 46 percent of the subregion economic base. Exports thus become the means to acquire an in-flow of dollars into the area for purchasing, in large measure from its own metropolitan core area, the many imported goods and services sought by local producers and consumers.

Each industry produces one or more commodities. Use of commodity, rather than industry, measures of exports and imports would reveal the balance of trade among individual commodity groups for each of the combined LMAs. Measures of net commodity exports, for example, would show the excess of individual commodities produced within the area over their total imports. They also would show the purchases of commodity imports by individual producing and consuming sectors and the extent to which each sector contributes to any trade deficits. The proportion of net exports accounted for by each locally produced commodity is an alternative measure of an area's economic base.

Table 2 presents estimates of the import-dependency of each of the 11 industry groups in each of the 7 subregions. The dominant basic industry groups are also the dominant import-dependent industry groups, except for the construction industry. Export growth means import growth because of the corresponding increases in demand for the imported intermediate production inputs. As an area grows and diversifies, however, import replacement occurs for both intermediate inputs and final purchases. Imported finished goods and services dominate total imports in the periphery of an economic region, while imported intermediate goods and services are dominant in its core area. Again, the import dependencies of the core area contrast sharply with those of the periphery, which, of course, is a measure of the opportunities for internalizing the export trade of individual LMAs within the region.

We validate the indirect measures of gross exports and gross imports with a variety of auxiliary measures of local economic activity and structure. First, product specialization and localization measures show the relative

Table 2
Import Share of Total Outlays in Specified Industry by Subregion, Minneapolis–St. Paul Economic Region, 1991 ($ million)

Industry	Minneapolis–St. Paul Core Area	North[1] Region LMAs			South[1] Region LMAs		
		East	Central	West	East	Central	West
Agriculture	34	53	74	32	58	39	23
Agricultural Services, forestry, fish	16	62	81	69	70	43	33
Mining	16	38	46	45	49	15	37
Construction	27	39	71	86	44	45	46
Manufacturing, total	27	43	64	31	40	41	49
Transportation, communication, utilities	13	20	32	42	20	20	22
Wholesale trade	1	2	3	2	2	2	2
Retail trade	5	11	17	15	12	11	11
Private services	6	21	34	22	21	18	19
Government	2	3	4	3	2	3	3
Total	$13	$23	$38	$24	$25	$24	$23

Source: University of Minnesota IMPLAN System.
[1]See note to Table 1.

importance of the product in the region and the nation and its geographic distribution within a region. Second, the central place and its local labor market measures link the geographic localization of production within a region or area to its industry structure. Third, regional advantage measures show the propensities to trade, both export and import, of the individual, geographically differentiated regional industries.

An additional measure of product specialization is the localization index, or location quotient. This ratio ranks all industries in a region for comparison with other regional rankings. A ratio of 1:1 for all regions would mean that the industry is ubiquitous on a regional scale of measurement, a possibility only for the frequently purchased items that lack large economies of scale in their production and distribution. An alternative form of the localization index is its absolute version. If the industry measure were employment, then the absolute measure would show the excess employment for the region, that is, the employment in excess of the amount based on a localization index of one. For both measures, the most detailed industrial and geographic breakdown of the regional economy yields the most accurate representation of product specialization and localization.

—*Wilbur R. Maki*

See also
Agricultural and Resource Economics; Marketing; Markets; Trade, International; Trade Areas.

References
Glasmeier, Amy K. "High Tech Manufacturing: Problems and Prospects." In *Economic Adaptation: Alternatives for Non-metropolitan Areas.* Edited by David L. Barkley. Boulder, CO: Westview Press, 1993.
Fox, Karl A. "Delimitation of Regions for Transportation Planning." Pp. 97–117 in *Urban-Regional Economics, Social System Accounts, and Eco-Behavioral Science: Selected Writings of Karl A. Fox.* Edited by James R. Prescott, Paul Van Moeseke, and Jati K. Sengupta. Ames: Iowa State University Press, 1994.
Hansen, Niles. "Endogenous Growth Centers: Lessons from Rural Denmark." In *Economic Adaptation: Alternatives for Non-metropolitan Areas.* Edited by David L. Barkley. Boulder, CO: Westview Press, 1993.
Kravis, Irving B. "Services in World Transactions." In *Managing the Service Economy.* Edited by Robert P. Inman. Cambridge, UK: Cambridge University Press. 1985.
Krugman, Paul R. *Geography and Trade.* Cambridge, MA: MIT Press, 1991.
Maki, W. R., and P. D. Reynolds. "Stability Versus Volatility, Growth Versus Decline in Peripheral Regions: A Preliminary U.S. Application." Pp. 27–42 in *Northern Perspectives on European Integration.* Edited by Lars Lundqvist and Lars Olof Persson. Stockholm, Sweden: Nordiska Institutet för Regionalpolitisk Forskning, 1994.
Ohmae, Kenichi. *The End of the Nation State: The Rise of Regional Economies.* New York: Free Press, 1995.
Otto, Daniel M., and Thomas G. Johnson. *Microcomputer-Based Input-Output Modeling: Applications to Economic Development.* Boulder, CO: Westview Press, 1993.
Putnam, Robert D. *Making Democracy Work: Civic Traditions in Modern Italy.* Princeton, NJ: Princeton University Press, 1993.
Saxenian, Annalee. *Regional Advantage: Culture and Competition in Silicon Valley and Route 128.* Cambridge, MA: Harvard University Press, 1994.
Tolbert, Charles M. III, and Molly Sizer Killian. *Labor Market Areas for the United States,* Staff Report AGE870721. Washington, DC: U.S. Department of Agriculture, Economic Research Service, Rural Economy Division, 1987.

Transportation Industry

The collection of firms that move goods from one location to another, including railroads, truck lines, airplanes, barge lines, and pipelines. A series of congressional acts in the late 1970s and early 1980s deregulated the transportation industry. This entry discusses the events leading to transportation deregulation, the subsequent adjustments made by the transportation industry and their customers in rural areas, and the current deregulated transportation environment.

Importance of the Rural Transportation Industry

Transportation is very important to the economic well-being of rural America. A rural area generally ships a relatively limited range of goods that is dependent on the mix of available regional resources. Typical shipments from rural areas include crops, processed foods and other agricultural products, forest products, mine and quarry products, and products of light manufacturing. Modern rural communities likewise require a full range of consumer goods and manufactured and raw materials such as fertilizers and fuels. Because of the volumes and distances involved, low-cost, reliable transportation is critical to rural communities. Since the passage of the Interstate Commerce Act in 1887, rural residents have depended on government, primarily the Interstate Commerce Commission (ICC), to ensure adequate and reliable transportation from the transportation industry.

The transportation industry in rural areas, as elsewhere, is composed of different methods or modes, including rail, motor vehicles, air, water, and pipelines. Railroads were the primary method of rural transportation of both goods and people from the Civil War era until the widespread adoption of automobiles. Although trucking has captured a significant share of intercity freight traffic, rail still dominates. In 1994, the railroads' share of intercity ton-miles was 39 percent, while the motor carrier share was 28 percent.

Barges on inland waterways, although not serving many rural areas directly, are very important, as they are generally the low-cost mode. Excluding seacoasts and the Great Lakes, there are over 25,000 miles of navigable rivers and canals in the United States. The Mississippi River and its tributaries make up about half of the navigable waterway mileage. Barges are used to move bulk commodities, such as grains and feeds, coal, fertilizer, chemicals, and petroleum products, at least part of the way to and from rural areas. The waterways are especially important to move grain and agricultural products to export ports. The waterway share of 1994 intercity ton-miles was 15 percent.

In recent years, intermodal transportation, which uses two or more modes for a single shipment, increased in importance. Examples of intermodal movements include trailers on flatcars (TOFC), other containers on flatcars (COFC), or trucks. Air cargo grew rapidly but remains a specialized market. Pipelines are very important in transporting natural gas, petroleum, and petroleum products to rural areas. The transportation industry underwent significant changes in recent years, both as a result of deregulation and due to technological changes in transport and in the general economy.

The Regulatory Era

The ICC played a major role for many years in ensuring that rural areas received fairly priced and reliable transportation services from railroads and later from trucking and busing firms. The ICC was established by the Interstate Commerce Act of 1887 in response to pressures from rural shippers and communities. When the act was passed, railroads were the dominant and often the only means of passenger or freight transportation throughout much of America. Congress desired to protect the public from monopoly abuses and from discriminatory practices of railroads at the time.

The Interstate Commerce Act made explicit the legal principles that were already embedded in common law. It required that rates be reasonable and just, and it prohibited discrimination against shippers and undue preferences among regional areas, and charging more for a short haul than a longer haul. The ICC established numerous precedents, being the first independent federal regulatory agency established to enforce the law on a continuing basis. It had to develop the procedures for economic regulation almost on a trial-and-error basis. The ICC eventually was given regulatory power over rail mergers and the control of entry and exit of both routes and service into and within the industry.

Concurrent with the development and evolution of the ICC, the motor vehicle industry was developing. Roads and highways were built to accommodate this new and highly flexible mode. By the 1930s, the monopolistic power and financial health of the railroads had been severely eroded by competition from trucks and passenger vehicles. Partly to protect the railroads from motor competition, Congress passed the Motor Carrier Act of 1935, which gave the ICC broad powers over interstate shipments and rates charged by the motor carriers. Similarly, with the Civil Aeronautic Act of 1938, Congress created the Civil Aeronautics Authority (CAA), which had powers similar to those of the ICC to make rates and control entry and exit of routes in the airline industry. The CAA eventually became the Civil Aeronautics Board (CAB).

Increased regulation was unable to ensure both reliable, low-cost transportation service and financial health for all modes of rural transportation. Competition from trucking and barges reduced or eliminated railroad profits. Trucking firms were able to selectively capture the rail traffic with profitable rates, whereas barges successfully competed for low-valued commodities on the basis of cost.

The interstate highway project and other federal expenditures on highways encouraged trucking expansion and the use of automobiles for passenger traffic. The federal government paid the capital costs to develop the modern inland waterway system by the Army Corps of Engineers (COE) during the 1930s. The federal government continued to finance waterway improvements and operations and maintenance expenses. It even subsidized barge operations to encourage the barge industry's development in the 1940s and 1950s.

Problems of Regulation

Regulation prevented or discouraged the railroads from competing effectively, especially in rural areas. Other factors, including high labor costs, restrictive work rules, and questionable management choices, also contributed to the railroads' financial problems. Consequently, by the 1960s, large portions of the railroad industry, and especially those serving rural areas, faced serious problems. Although competition from the other modes eroded markets, making much trackage obsolete and many services unprofitable, the ICC limited route and trackage abandonments. The railroads were allowed to stop their unprofitable intercity passenger services in 1970, when Congress established Amtrak. However, the railroad problems continued, resulting in the bankruptcies of many lines serving rural areas, and unprecedented numbers of applications to abandon trackage and service were made to the ICC. The miles of railroad track decreased to 179,000 miles in 1980, down from 206,00 miles in 1970 and 218,000 miles in 1960. Rail mileage peaked at 254,000 miles in 1916. Most of the abandonments were low-volume branch lines serving rural areas.

Congress attempted to assist the railroad industry in 1973 by passing the 3R Act (Regional Rail Reorganization Act) to reorganize the bankrupt railroads, but this was insufficient. In 1976, the 4R Act (Railroad Revitalization and Regulatory Reform Act) made fundamental changes in railroad regulations. However, the changes actually implemented by the ICC did not adequately free the railroads, improve their financial condition, or allow

much improvement in service. Consequently, in 1980, Congress deregulated the railroads with the Staggers Act of 1980.

Effects of the Staggers Act of 1980

These actions (Staggers Act of 1980, 3R Act of 1973, and 4R Act of 1976), along with ICC rulings during the 1970s, transformed railroads from one of the most regulated American industries to a market-oriented system. The Staggers Act (1) relaxed controls over rates, (2) allowed railroads to contract for specific services to individual firms and to enter into long-term contracts, and (3) made mergers between railroads and the abandonment of unprofitable branch lines easier. Railroads were not completely deregulated immediately, as the ICC retained the ability to regulate maximum rates and other oversight powers. By the early 1990s, however, more than three-fourths of rail traffic was not subject to rate regulation either because rates were below threshold levels or because the ICC had exempted the traffic entirely. Exempted classes important to rural areas included boxcars, piggyback and container traffic, perishable agricultural products, lumber, wood, and transportation equipment. A major change from the long-standing principle of public and nondiscriminatory tariffs was the ability of the railroads to enter into confidential, binding contracts for both rates and services. These contracts must be filed with the ICC but are not made public. Many grain companies and other rural shippers took advantage of contracts to obtain improved or guaranteed services.

Railroad freight rates declined at an average rate of 1.5 percent annually between 1980 and 1994. However, there were significant differences in rate changes across commodities, with many rates increasing after deregulation because of the greater market power of the railroads. However, by 1988, deregulation resulted in lower rates for most commodities, suggesting that increases in productivity and competition generally overcame the initial rate increases due to railroad market power.

Major benefits to rural areas from rail deregulation included not only rate reduction but also service improvements and increased reliability. Although railroad abandonments were of major concern to rural communities and shippers prior to, and immediately after, deregulation, most observers felt that rationalization of branch line track and service generally improved most rural rail service. The railroads abandoned thousands of miles of track, but the number of smaller railroads increased from 212 in 1980 to 550 in 1994. Many of these regional or short-line railroads that serve rural areas have done well financially because of regulatory reforms. Labor can be paid at local and not national wage levels, and work rules are relaxed so employees can do multiple tasks. This resulted in both reduced rail rates and fewer railroad employees. In addition, the regional and short-line railroads are more responsive to local service needs that the urban-based, nationally oriented railroads tended to ignore.

The rail crisis of the 1970s resulted in a growing realization of the failure of economic regulation to keep up with changing technologies in a competitive economy. Consequently, several other deregulation bills for other transportation modes were passed prior to and after the Staggers Act. These included the Air Cargo Deregulation Act of 1977, the Airline Deregulation Act of 1978, the Motor Carrier Act of 1980, and the Bus Regulatory Reform Act of 1982. Although all of these had some impact on rural transportation industries, the most significant was the Motor Carrier Act of 1980.

Effects of the Motor Carrier Act of 1980

Trucking rates, service, and regulation had not received much attention in rural areas during the 1970s for two reasons. First, unlike railway service, the availability of trucking service was not declining and trucks were frequently competing for the railways' declining traffic base. The interstate highway system enabled trucking companies to lower costs and improve their reliability. Second, grain and unprocessed agricultural commodities truckers were exempt from ICC regulation. Back hauls to rural areas in exempt trucks were also exempt in many instances.

The Motor Carrier Act of 1980 (MCA) followed substantial liberalization of trucking regulations by the ICC in the late 1970s. Changes in regulation included reducing entry barriers, loosening restrictions on contract carriers, and allowing unregulated agricultural carriers to carry regulated commodities on back hauls. The MCA went further and allowed applicants to enter the industry when the service was found to meet a useful public purpose, reversing the previous burden of proof from the entrant to the existing carriers. The MCA permitted common carriers to raise and lower rates 10 percent annually without regulatory interference, and it granted the ICC discretionary powers to permit even greater price freedom in the future. Antitrust immunity for voting on rates was reduced and eventually eliminated.

A major concern prior to motor truck deregulation in the United States was the possible loss of service to small communities. However, early studies showed little change in quality and availability of service and small benefits in lower rates. Eventually, the results of trucking deregulation proved substantial and far-reaching. Many new carriers entered the industry; the number of trucking firms increased nationally from 16,000 in the mid-1970s to over 49,000 in 1992. Many of these new carriers were formed to provide services to small and medium-sized communities and markets. Previously, major firms ignored small-volume rural markets but always maintained that they were being adequately served. These established carriers protested against new applicants at ICC hearings and typically won, maintaining their status as monopoly carriers. Many of the recent entrants are freight forwarders, brokers, or other third parties who expanded services to rural communities and provided innovative services such as small package pickup, package express, or air cargo.

Studies identified substantial cost reductions due to trucking deregulation through lower labor costs, route rationalization, and better equipment utilization. For example, Winston et al. (1990) found that lower operating costs for private trucking nationwide generated $3 billion annually in benefits to shippers and $4 billion in rate reductions by commercial carriers. In addition, shippers received benefits in the form of more responsive and dependable service as a result of the new market discipline imposed by competition. These benefits allowed shippers and customers to develop just-in-time inventory management by transporting smaller shipments more frequently, substantially reducing inventories and inventory carrying costs. This is especially important to shippers and firms in rural areas, who never would have received the improved service under the old regulatory regime.

The Barge (Inland Waterway) Industry

The barge industry that operates on the inland waterway system is very important to rural America. Approximately 60 percent of U.S. grain and oilseed exports are shipped from Mississippi River terminals after traveling 700 to 1,200 miles by barge from the U.S. agricultural heartland. Since these distances are three to five times greater than those from international competitors' grain-producing areas to their ports, low-cost water transportation has been a major factor in maintaining exports of U.S. agricultural products and bulk commodities. Waterway transportation is also important in moving bulk commodities like fertilizer, ores, and petroleum products from coastal areas to rural areas served by river terminals.

Unlike other modes of transportation in the United States, barges were not subject to extensive economic regulation. The Transportation Act of 1940 placed inland waterway barge transportation under the regulatory authority of the ICC but kept private carriage, most bulk carriage, and liquid cargo exempt from regulation. Consequently, shipments of bulk commodities such as grain, coal, chemicals, and petroleum products were all generally exempt from rate regulation, and although barges were technically deregulated in 1980, deregulation had few direct effects. The barge industry was, however, immediately affected by competition from the deregulated railroads: By the early 1980s, it had been financially devastated by increasing competition from railroads, combined with a slowdown in U.S. grain and coal exports; and it did not recover until the end of the decade.

In spite of its low cost and energy efficiency, in recent years barge transportation in the United States has had the disadvantage of being under continual attack by environmentalists, resulting in increased industry costs but limited environmental improvements. Fuel-user charges for commercial barges were instituted in 1980 as part of a compromise of the barge industry, shippers, and the U.S. Army Corps of Engineers (COE) with the railroads and environmentalists in order to remove a major bottleneck between the Upper Mississippi and Illinois Rivers and the Lower Mississippi. The commercial navigation fuel-user charge gradually increased to $0.20 per gallon in 1995, reducing the cost advantage of water transportation over rail. Other compromises between the barge industry, the COE, and environmentalists on topics such as channel maintenance and dredging added to the industry's operating costs and underlying cost structure.

Summary

The transportation services available to rural America have been expanded and improved in recent years. Deregulation of the transportation industries generally has been considered a success. In 1995, Congress passed the Interstate Commerce Commission Termination Act. Most ICC functions pertaining to rural transportation were assumed by the new Surface Transportation Board (STB) in the Department of Transportation. Rural areas ship a variety of goods and receive a full range of consumer goods and raw materials. Because of the volumes and distances required, a healthy transportation industry providing low-cost and reliable transportation on a well-maintained infrastructure is a necessity for rural America.

—Jerry E. Fruin

See also

Grain Elevators; History, Agricultural; History, Rural; Infrastructure; Public Services; River Engineering; Trade, International; Trade, Interregional.

References

Glaskowsky, Nicholas A., Jr. *Effects of Deregulation on Motor Carriers.* 2d ed. Westport, CT: Eno Foundation for Transportation, 1990.

Harper, Donald V. *Transportation in America: Users, Carriers, Government.* 2d ed. Englewood Cliffs, NJ: Prentice-Hall, 1982.

Lieb, Robert C. *Transportation.* 4th ed. Houston, TX: Dame Publications, 1994.

Locklin, D. Philip. *Economics of Transportation.* 7th ed. Homewood, IL: Richard D. Irwin, 1972.

Muller, Gerhardt. *Intermodal Freight Transportation.* 3d ed. Lansdowne, VA: Eno Transportation Foundation and Intermodal Association of North America, 1995.

Smith, Frank A. "Historical Compendium 1939–1985." *Transportation in America: A Statistical Analysis of Transportation in the United States.* Westport, CT: Eno Foundation, 1989.

Teske, Paul, Samuel Best, and Michael Mintrom. *Deregulating Freight Transportation: Delivering the Goods.* Washington, DC: AEI Press, 1995.

Wilson, Rosalyn A. *Transportation in America: Statistical Analysis of Transportation in the United States.* 13th ed. Lansdowne, VA: Eno Foundation, 1995.

Winston, Clifford, Thomas Corsi, Curtis Grimm, and Carol Evans. *The Economic Effects of Surface Freight Deregulation.* Washington, DC: Brookings Institution, 1990.

Trees

Perennial woody plants having one dominant vertical trunk with many branches and generally a minimum mature height of 10 feet. Trees are a major part of nature's infrastructure. They provide shelter, food, and cover to wildlife and humans in native forest stands, planted farmstead windbreaks, and home landscapes. Trees' value appears static, but it is dynamic in the rural American lifestyle.

North American Forests

Trees are among the largest living plants on earth. A forest can be compared to a building or enlarged house; the vertical trunks form the walls or partitions, and the canopy forms the ceiling, with irregularly shaped skylights between the tree canopies. The forest floor is made of various types of mosses, growing on fallen tree trunks and branches. Herbaceous plants grow dependent on the patches of sunlight moving along the floor. Some plants prefer the shade and cool, moist conditions. In the fall, leaves drop to the floor, decay, and form organic matter. Seeds are produced in the canopies and fall to the moist organic floor, germinate, and perpetuate the next forest. To complete this house, organisms move in and out by foot across the floor, in running water of woodland streams, or flying among the tree branches.

The forests of North America can be divided into four general vegetation/forest regions. These include the eastern forest, the northern boreal forest, the prairie forest of the Great Plains, and the western forest.

The eastern forest covers the area from the east coast of Canada and the United States west to the Mississippi River. The eastern forest is subdivided into several subforest types, of which each is a community of related tree species, plants, and animals that coexist due to similar macro- and microclimatic conditions: moisture, temperature, and soil types. Primary eastern forest types and species include mixed deciduous (sweet gum, yellow poplar, ironwood, sugar maple, white oak, basswood, ash, and buckeye); oak-hickory (various oaks, mocknut and shagbark hickory, butternut, and sycamore); southern deciduous (yellow poplar, sycamore, black locust, sugar maple, black cherry, and white ash); southern pinelands (longleaf, loblolly, slash, and Virginia pine, white and live oaks, sweet gum, bald cypress, magnolia, and eastern red cedar); and subtropical (loblolly, longleaf, and slash pine, saw palmetto, turkey oak, and bald cypress).

The northern boreal forest covers a large area from near the east coast of the northeastern United States and Canada to the Great Plains and up into northwestern Canada and Alaska. These forests are the northernmost in North America and meet the Arctic tundra. The main tree species found in the northern boreal forest include quaking aspen, balsam poplar, various birches, maple, oak, white and black spruce, and white cedar (arborvitae). In transitional zones between the northern boreal and eastern forests, yellow birch, sugar maple, and balsam fir are prevalent.

The prairie forest of the Great Plains in the United States and Canada is often glossed over because of the insignificance of its woodland acres relative to its predominant grassland vegetation. These native forests, although small in area, are important in their location along streams and rivers and in highly erodible sandy soils. Trees grow and survive best on the semihumid plains, where there is moisture near rivers and in soils with a high or perched water table. Tree stands generally did not move out from these moist areas because prairie fires encouraged grassland development. However, two species—quaking aspen and bur oak—did succeed in expanding their ranges. The bur oak has a thick bark that insulated the tree from fire injury; and aspen sucker regrowth from the roots was stimulated by fire. Common species along rivers (riparian forests) include American and red elm, green and black ash, hackberry, bur oak, American linden (basswood), ironwood, various willows, and cottonwood. These forests are critical to streambank stabilization, sediment and erosion control, and filtration of water runoff into rivers or lakes. These islands of woody plants provide a haven to wildlife from the wind, the sun in summer, and the cold in winter. Leaves, bark, berries, and roots provide browse and winter stores for deer, elk, moose, grouse, and turkey.

The western forest extends from the eastern edge of the Rocky Mountains to the west coast. The native ranges of tree species in the West resemble spots or pockets of forest; they are divided physically by mountain ranges and climatically by cold temperatures in upper altitudes. There are several forest types and associated species of the western forests: northwestern coastal (Douglas fir, coastal redwood, various hemlocks, red cedar, spruce, fir, rhododendron, bigleaf maple, and alder); Sierra-Montane (ponderosa pine, Douglas fir, white and red fir, black oak, incense cedar, various hemlocks, and red cedar); Rocky Mountain (ponderosa and lodgepole pine, Douglas fir, grand and noble fir, Colorado spruce, and quaking aspen); and woodlands (white and bur oak, limber pine, Rocky Mountain juniper, and madrone).

Trees' large size often dwarfs human-made structures. The sequoias (*Sequoiodendron giganteum*) and coastal redwoods (*Sequoia sempervirens*) are among the largest and oldest living things on earth. The sequoias grow in the arid Sierra Nevada in eastern California, while the redwoods prefer the moister northern coast of California. The General Sherman sequoia for many years was considered the largest living thing at 275 feet tall and 26.5 feet in diameter; its age was estimated to be between 2,500 and 3,000 years old (which means it was a seedling during King Solomon's reign). General Sherman's top was broken off in a storm in 1993, and a taller sequoia replaced it in height and diameter. The world's tallest tree is a redwood, at 313 feet. The oldest tree can also be found in California's White Mountains. These trees are estimated to be 4,000 years old—seedlings in the days of Abraham.

Trees and American History

Native Americans lived in harmony with forests. They cleared openings in the forests to provide enough sun-

Prairie windbreak planting with field windbreak and native river trees in the background on a North Dakota farm.

shine to raise vegetable and fruit crops in the moist forest floor. The trees protected the crops from drying winds. Garden culture produced high-yielding crops such as corn, squash, tomatoes, peppers, potatoes, fruiting vines, and shrubs on small patches of ground. Trees were tapped for maple syrup, food, and medicinal saps. Tree bark, leaves, and fruit, along with native herbs, were harvested for medicine. The wildlife that used the forest for cover, shelter, and food provided meat for the Native Americans. They taught these skills to early European colonists as basic survival skills.

The forest was a storehouse of natural resources—lumber, tars, maple syrup, fruit, wild game, and freshwater fish. Pitch pine provided charcoal for smelting, tar and pitch as a wood preservatives for boats, ships, and wharf piles, turpentine as a disinfectant, lumber for barn floors, bridges, and mill waterwheels, pitch for torches, and axle grease for carts and wagons.

Trees and their by-products played an important role for explorers and trappers. Canoes were made from hollowed logs, or birch or larch bark. Frames of snowshoes were made from birch. Wagons and carts were built for the move west across wooden bridges, roadways, and barges. Steam engines ran on white pine rails. The clipper ships that sailed goods and passengers around South America to California were built with several species of pine.

The cider presses of the seventeenth and eighteenth centuries, used to extract juice from apples, were also made of wood. Apple seeds were not damaged by this process, and it was from the debris of cider mills that John Chapman collected his seeds. Chapman was born in a log cabin in Leominster, Massachusetts, in 1774. At the age of 18 years, Johnny moved west to Pennsylvania and Ohio, planting apple seeds wherever he traveled. The seeds were planted in small nurseries scattered across Ohio, Indiana, and Illinois. Chapman tended the nurseries and distributed apple seedlings to settlers moving west. Johnny Appleseed, as settlers called him, died in Indiana in 1845 of pneumonia he caught while traveling to one of his nurseries to fix a broken fence. His final will began with the words "I, John Chapman (by occupation a gatherer and planter of apple seeds)."

Forests became a hindrance to settlers as they traveled west to build settlements and establish farms. The forest soils were shallow and not highly productive for long-term grain, cotton, and tobacco farming. Settlers continued to move west until they reached the Great Plains. In his book *The Great Plains,* historian Walter Prescott Webb wrote that there were three distinct characteristics of the region: an expansive, comparatively level surface; insufficient rainfall for intensive agriculture common to lands in humid climates; and a treeless, unforested area. Ironically, it was in the Great Plains that a new attitude toward trees began. The settlers' impressions of this open sea of grass were almost agoraphobic (fear of open, unenclosed places). Trees were a rare occurrence, a landmark, and a place to hang onto in the wide-open spaces. This was a quite different land from the forested East.

In the Interest of Trees

J. Sterling Morton, a Nebraska newspaper editor, disagreed with the idea that the Great Plains should be perceived as the Great American Desert. He believed in the productivity of the land and its people, and thought that tree planting was the key to survival under the West's harsh environmental conditions. Morton, along with his newspaper colleagues, promoted the first Arbor Day observance on April 10, 1872, and he is now credited as the founder of Arbor Day. An estimated 1 million trees were planted in Nebraska on that first Arbor Day. One man alone planted 10,000 cottonwood, silver maple, Lombardy poplar, box elder, and yellow willow near Lincoln, Nebraska, that day. Nebraska Governor Furnas officially recognized Arbor Day as a holiday on April 8, 1874. All 50 United States and overseas possessions, as well as many other countries, now recognize a day for planting trees.

The Timber Culture Act of 1873, sponsored by Nebraska Senator Phineas W. Hitchcock, encouraged tree planting to grow more timber, benefit the soil, and influence the climate. The act included provisions to award 160 acres of land to settlers if they planted 40 acres of trees and cared for them for ten years. The tree acreage later was reduced to 10 acres, and the act was repealed in 1891.

The Clarke McNary Law in 1924 provided programs for fire protection of forests, distribution of tree seedlings, and planning assistance to landowner-cooperators on new tree plantings, woodlots, and shelterbelts. Many states had tree bounty programs that paid landowners to plant and care for trees on their land. Some states' laws reduced landowners' taxes instead of paying a set bounty per tree. New cities recognized the importance of trees.

Hope, North Dakota still has an ordinance requiring that all grazing animals be fenced to prevent feeding on young shade and boulevard trees.

Hedgerows and Windbreaks

The concept of planting trees at close spacing in multiple rows for windbreaks has been credited to immigrants of various heritages. These windbreak groves were first planted in England and Europe, where they were referred to as "hedgerows." Germans took this technology to the Russian steppes, and later carried it to the plains of Canada and the United States in the early twentieth century. Dense plantings delineated property lines, and hedgerows of thorny tree species acted as fences for livestock. Hedgerows in France, Belgium, and Holland were infamous during the world wars as a hindrance to invading Allied troops, costing many lives.

The adaptation of hedgerows or windbreaks to North American agriculture provided many benefits, especially in the Great Plains. The drought of the 1930s and poor farming practices, such as continuous cropping, allowed the soil to blow. When dust storms were seen at the Capitol in Washington, D.C., President Franklin Roosevelt became concerned and lent his support to the Prairie States Forestry Project, the goal of which was to plant millions of windbreaks in the Great Plains. Many tree plantings extend from North Dakota to Texas today as a result of this program. Trees planted in windbreaks became a valuable conservation tool.

Local soil conservation districts were organized after the Great Depression. They provided trees for forest plantations and windbreaks to conserve soils, water, and wildlife resources. The Agricultural Conservation Program and Conservation Reserve Program are recent governmental programs that provide a cost-share incentive to landowners interested in tree planting. The American Forests Association started the Global Releaf Program, with the goal of planting 100 million trees. The National Arbor Day Foundation has several programs that encourage tree planting in rural and urban settings. Many private wildlife organizations also provide cost-share incentives.

Windbreaks provide a barrier against prevailing winds and create zones of protection on the leeward side of the tree planting. The winds are forced up and over the zone of protection. Soils are not exposed to wind erosion or desiccation within the zone of protection. More soil moisture is available to the crops in the zone, and yields are higher. However, crop yield is reduced immediately next to the windbreak. This zone of competition extends to a distance of only two to four times the height of the tallest trees. Yields dramatically increase from the zone of competition, and continue to the distance of 12 to 20 times the tree height. Past the zone of protection (or zone of increased crop yields), production gradually decreases to an average yield. The yield increase from windbreak protection in the zone of protection more than compensates for the yield loss in the zone of competition. Therefore, overall yields are higher in protected fields. Trees also provide protection to crops from wind damage, lodging, and sandblasting.

Windbreak designs are based on tree density and number of tree rows. Single-row windbreaks are designed with one row of trees, and are planted for field crop production. This windbreak design is highly valuable in winter; it allows snow to be blown evenly across fields. Farmers have fewer difficulties with snow pockets or wet areas at seeding time in the spring. The snow melt is more evenly distributed, adding more soil moisture to the field.

Multirow windbreaks are planted around farmsteads, and commonly are called shelterbelts. Multirow windbreaks collect snow in the tree planting and keep more snow out of the farmyard, driveways, and working areas. The farmstead windbreaks reduce windchill factors and improve working conditions in the farmyard for people and animals. Energy costs to heat homes, barns, and workshop buildings can be reduced by 20 to 40 percent with north and west protection by tree plantings. Livestock also need windbreak protection in winter, or they will expend more energy to grow. This energy use is translated into increased feed requirements and weight loss. According to one Montana study, cattle protected by windbreaks gained an average 34 to 35 pounds more than those maintained in an open feedlot. During severe winters, protected cattle maintained 10.6 more pounds over unprotected cattle. Dairy cattle respond to lack of wind protection by lower milk production and increased feed requirements. Health can be reduced by cold temperatures along with freezing injury to reproductive parts and death in young animals. Swine are especially poorly adapted to cold temperatures and require protection for weight gain and breeding.

Community Forests

Trees play a major role in small rural and suburban communities similar to their role on rural farmsteads. Trees, through their height and density, force winds up and over neighborhoods and the community as a whole. Many rural communities in the Great Plains established multirow windbreaks on the north and west sides of their limits to assist in wind protection and snow control. Wind control reduces heat loss in the winter and improves working and play conditions outside of the homes. City snow management costs are reduced by collecting more snow outside the city and reducing ground drift that creates hazardous travel conditions. Tree plantings, or living snow fences, cost less than structural fences, and pay through reduced snow removal costs, improved travel conditions, and saved lives.

Community tree plantings offer other benefits by acting as a greenway in and around the town or suburban development. A greenway provides aesthetic beauty by using a wide variety of plant materials for colorful foliage (maple, buckeye, sweet gum), fragrant flowers (linden, lilac, cherry), edible fruits (juneberry, apple, peach), various textures (hackberry, cork tree, arborvitae), and unique sounds (shimmering poplar leaves or whispering pine boughs in the wind). Wildlife use plantings for food habitat, cover, and travel lanes also benefit hunters and wildlife enthusiasts. Potential for recreational experience in these tree plantings is very high. Tree plantings provide wind protection for bike/hiking trails, camping, active sport fields, playgrounds, and outdoor school classrooms.

Trees around homes and on boulevards that are not planted in dense windbreaks also are effective in providing the benefits described above. Additionally, shade trees planted on the east and west sides of houses reduce summertime cooling costs. The use of a single tree to shade an outdoor air conditioner can save as much as 10 or 15 percent in cooling costs. Trees in parks provide valuable shade, and if properly placed, can screen unsightly views. And they can screen traffic noises and glare from the sun around ball fields and camping areas. The mixture of individual and group plantings in the collective yards of residential neighborhoods provide a wide variety of flowers, foliage, fruit, and form for year-round aesthetic beauty and interest.

Tree-lined boulevards are similar to the rows of trees planted around fields. Public trees are a tradition brought over with European immigrants during early settlement. Thomas Jefferson planted poplar trees along Pennsylvania Avenue in the new capitol, Washington, D.C. He was a man of horticultural and architectural understanding, who believed that humans and nature belonged together. Trees separate residential homes from the hurried pace of traffic.

Country Meets City

Trees in rural American can provide a unique rural-urban interface. Tree crops can open new ways to market and harvest natural products. Pick-your-own fruit tree or shrub orchards offer opportunities for urban dwellers to experience the country. Many pick-your-own orchards have special weekend activities, such as apple grading demonstrations, juice and cider making, pie eating contests, and sack races. Such experiences with nature can be shared by adults and youth alike.

Another type of tree product marketing is the choose-and-cut Christmas tree operation. Urban families travel into the country to find their own tree, cut it, and bring it home—the start of a new family tradition. Nearby warming houses provide hot apple cider and fresh-baked cookies; Christmas shops sell tree accessories, stands, wreaths, garlands, candles, and floral and green arrangements. Misshapen or unsalable trees are salvaged for use as wreaths, garlands, and door swags. Christmas trees and fruit orchards require intensive cultural measures such as pruning, weed control, and insect and disease control. There is much work in providing the pick-your-own or choose-and-cut product, including advertising and marketing, hiring personable employees, and providing a rewarding experience to customers.

It is difficult to place a monetary value on the benefits people derive from trees. The price of a tree purchased at the nursery is based on the labor, materials, transportation, and maintenance costs expended to produce it. Other factors involved in tree valuation include legal fees, insurance settlements, property value, timber value, and historical and sentimental values. A shade-tree valuation formula was developed by the International Shade Tree Conference and National Arborists Association in 1951, and later tested and revised several times to meet new challenges. Today, the International Society of Arborists provides a handbook and teaching materials to assist tree assessors.

—Vernon C. Quam

See also

Conservation, Soil; Forest Products; Forestry Industry; Forests; History, Agricultural; History, Rural; Land Stewardship; Parks; Sawmilling.

References

Droze, Wilmon. *Trees, Prairies, and People*. Denton: Texas Women's University, 1977.

Grey, Gene W., and Frederick J. Deneke. *Urban Forestry*. New York: John Wiley and Sons, 1978.

Olson, James C. "Arbor Day: A Pioneer Expression of Concern for the Environment." *Nebraska History* 53, no. 1 (1972): 1–14.

Platt, Rutherford. *This Green World*. 2d ed. New York: Dodd, Mead and Company, 1988.

Quam, Vernon, John Gardner, James Brandle, and Teresa Boes. *Windbreaks in Sustainable Agricultural Systems*. EC91–1772-X. Lincoln: University of Nebraska Extension Service, 1991.

Quam, Vernon, LaDon Johnson, Bruce Wight, and James Brandle. *Windbreaks for Livestock Operations*. EC94-1766-X. Lincoln: University of Nebraska Extension Service, 1994.

Quam, Vernon, and Bruce Wight. *Protecting Fields with Windbreaks*. F-1054 (August). Fargo: North Dakota State University Extension Service, 1993.

Quam, Vernon, Bruce Wight, and Harvey Hirning. *Farmstead Windbreak*. F-1055 (May). Fargo: North Dakota State University Extension Service, 1993.

Randall, Charles, and Henry Clepper. *Famous and Historic Trees*. Washington, DC: American Forestry Association, 1977.

Rupp, Rebecca. *Red Oaks and Black Birches*. Pownal, VT: Storey Communications, 1990.

Schlebecker, John. *Whereby We Thrive: A History of American Farming, 1607–1972*. 4th printing. Ames: Iowa State University Press, 1978.

Webb, Walter Prescott. *The Great Plains*. New York: Grosset and Dunlap, 1931. Reprinted New York: Ginn and Company, 1977.

Welsch, Roger L. *Of Trees and Dreams: The Fiction, Fact, and Folklore of Tree-Planting on the Northern Plains*. 2d printing. Lincoln: University of Nebraska Press, 1982.

Underemployment

Inadequate employment, or employment-related hardship, such as employment that is less than full-time (including unemployment), or employment that does not fully utilize an employee's training and skills and/or provides inadequate compensation (Lichter and Costanzo 1987). This entry will characterize the underemployed, offer explanations for underemployment, and discuss the connections of underemployment to poverty and to the wider economy. The particular issue of gender and underemployment will be discussed. Last, methods of measuring underemployment will be described.

Who Are the Underemployed?

Nonmetropolitan areas are characterized by higher rates of underemployment than metropolitan areas. The most prevalent types of economic underemployment in rural areas are unemployment and employment with very low wages. A complex set of factors influence underemployment, including individual, family, structural, and spatial characteristics. Underemployment directly affects the economic resources of many rural families and can disrupt family interaction processes, leading to increased stress and loss of community ties.

The level of underemployment in the United States in 1990 was about 22 percent of the civilian labor force. About 13 percent of the civilian labor force were economically underemployed. Although the level of economic underemployment in rural areas in 1990 had decreased compared to that in 1980 (Lichter and Costanzo 1987), it remained slightly higher than that of metropolitan areas. About 13 percent of nonmetropolitan workers in 1990 were economically underemployed, compared to 12 percent in metropolitan areas. In rural areas, four out of ten full-time workers in rural areas in 1987 earned wages below the poverty level (Deavers and Hoppe 1992). On farms, three out of four workers had poverty-level earnings (Gorham 1992).

Women workers in nonmetropolitan areas are more likely to experience economic underemployment than their metropolitan counterparts. They are more likely than men to work part-time in the absence of full-time jobs. Among those underemployed, men are more likely than women to be unemployed and to work for poverty-level wages. Younger workers (less than 25 years of age) are more susceptible to unemployment than those 25 or older. In contrast, workers aged 25 and over are more likely than younger workers to be underemployed due to low income. Nonmetropolitan, nonwhite residents are more likely than whites to be unemployed, to work for poverty-level wages, or to work part-time in the absence of full-time jobs.

Agriculture and extractive industries in rural areas have higher proportions of underemployed workers than manufacturing and service industries, and particularly of workers earning less than poverty-level wages. In manufacturing industries, most underemployed workers are working poor and unemployed. In service industries, the working poor and those working part-time for economic reasons are the most frequent categories of underemployed.

The South is more likely to experience greater underemployment compared to other regions. The South has higher levels of unemployed and working poor compared to other regions. The Northeast has lower rates of economic underemployment. The West and Northeast have higher levels of underemployment by occupational mismatch. The essential questions remain: Why is underemployment so prevalent in nonmetropolitan areas, and what social, economic, political, and other factors have contributed to its higher levels in those areas?

What Explains Underemployment?

Research on rural underemployment has examined the demographic, industrial, and occupational positions of the underemployed by focusing on workers' characteristics, and has neglected structural, institutional, and organizational bases of underemployment. The challenge is to integrate individual, family, structural, and spatial variations with multilevel analytical approaches, to explain the social, economic organizational, and spatial aspects of underemployment.

Determinants of rural underemployment include a limited opportunity structure, which is the outcome of past social and economic development policies as well as of the current economic transformation. Many rural areas lack stable employment, opportunities for upward mobility, investment in local communities, and diversity in the economy and other social institutions. Moreover, levels of underemployment are shaped by family organizations and individual characteristics. Finally, they are exacerbated by the fact that rural areas are increasingly isolated socially and spatially given the depopulation of some regions and particularly vulnerable to adverse effects from structural economic change.

Personal qualifications such as skills, education, and work history are important in that they represent investments in self-enhancement that are rewarded in the marketplace. Rural workers on the whole suffer from deficits in education, cognitive skills, and work experience. In addition, job skills and education are poorly rewarded in rural areas, where the underemployment level is higher for each level of education than it is in metropolitan areas. The disadvantages are considerably higher among women and minorities (Swanson 1988).

Differences in earnings returns to education and workplace experience account for the largest portion of metropolitan-nonmetropolitan differences in earnings (McLaughlin and Perman 1991). Although individual characteristics, especially educational factors, determine who receives low-paying or part-time jobs as opposed to adequate employment, these characteristics alone cannot explain the persistent high poverty, unemployment, and underemployment in rural areas or the poor rewards and persistent wage differentials in rural areas, especially among women and minorities (Lichter et al. 1993). The low skills and education of rural workers do not attract

high-skilled jobs, so employment growth and industrial restructuring are not likely to benefit rural workers. Underemployment results from the skills gap between rural workers and available jobs as well as from a lack of good jobs available to rural workers.

Underemployment varies by demographic structure (age, sex, and race) and by demographic processes, particularly life course, family structure, birth cohort, and migration. Also, the demographic composition of the labor force has changed substantially since World War II. Metropolitan and nonmetropolitan differences in underemployment in part reflect differences in demographic composition by age, sex, and race of their workforces.

Wages and employment are the main economic reasons for migration from nonmetropolitan areas. Those with higher human capital levels tend to migrate. Yet many who remain in nonmetropolitan areas also have higher education and continue to experience negative returns on their human capital investment. This suggests that noneconomic factors might influence the decision not to migrate—such as the fact that rural communities provide residents with feelings of security and stability, along with strong ties to family and friends.

Poverty and Underemployment

Demographic evidence of poverty, unemployment, and underemployment, especially in urban areas, has shaped the debate about persistent poverty and its relationship to family structure and policy, especially welfare. The popular perception is that the poor in the United States are Black, urban, underclass, and female-headed households. Poverty in female-headed households, especially for children, is much higher and lasts longer than that in married-couple households. Yet changes in family structure have less causal influence on poverty than is commonly thought. In rural areas, traits often associated with families of urban poor—female-headed households, marginal parental attachment to workforce, and welfare dependency—are less in evidence (Lichter and Eggebeen 1992). But poverty in female-headed households is increasing in rural areas, and the growing problem of rural poverty cannot be disassociated completely from changing family structure (Duncan and Tickamyer 1988).

Childhood poverty and deep poverty both remain prevalent, especially in nonmetropolitan areas. Increasing rates of child poverty attributable to higher prevalence of female-headed households more than offset the economic improvements attributable to increases in female employment and rising levels of parental education. Black children continuously living in two-parent families were as likely to experience poverty as White children in female-headed households.

Economic Organization and Underemployment

Underemployment is a structural problem that cannot be understood by reference to individual characteristics alone. The economic organization perspective, or new structural perspective, focuses on the nature of opportunities within the workplace, including the quantity and quality of employment, but mainly on the organization of work. Large work organizations offer higher wage rates. The relatively low earnings of rural workers are due in part to the disproportionate share of small firms in rural areas. The paternalistic organization of rural work may provide benefits such as personal loans for home improvements or automobile purchases, or to meet sudden financial crises. However, while paternalism implies commitment to reciprocal social relations between employers and loyal employees, the structure of interpersonal relationships involves unequal exchanges (Doeringer 1984). Workers who quit their jobs generally have difficulty finding reemployment in the area because quitting is seen as evidence of disloyalty and unreliability. Opportunities for informal employment in rural areas offer low wages and can only supplement other sources of income. Low levels of remuneration for most informal work result because the products of such work are sold in highly competitive markets marked by uncertain demand.

Rural occupations offer lower earning potential. Farmers, for example, have very low earning potential, as do workers in rural services and semiskilled manual jobs (Spenner, Otto, and Call 1982). Thus, the persistence of rural poverty seems partially due to the prevalence of career lines in rural areas with limited earning potential. For rural workers employed either in farming or in service occupations, the option to switch careers in order to improve their earning potential becomes more limited as they get older. The high poverty of many rural workers results from limitations in the earning potential and exit portals of their career lines (Bloomquist et al. 1993).

The increased informalization of work is a strategy to reduce labor costs not only in terms of wages but also in terms of benefit packages, maintenance of health and safety standards, and other production costs related to the state regulation of economic organizations. Few analysts of informal activities besides Gringeri (1994) have focused on rural social contexts in the United States or on the resurgence of homework. Homework usually is paid by the piece or unit of production rather than by labor time, and it offers limited if any fringe benefits or job security.

Studies of the spatial division of labor focus on the competitive advantages of places of various sizes for the location of particular sustenance activities or industries. The advantages of rural areas from an ecological perspective are the relatively low costs of land and labor, and the ready access to natural resources and rural amenities (Bloomquist et al. 1993). Generally, rural areas serve as sites for routine, low-skilled work activities. In most industries, routine production is located in rural areas, while managerial and professional-technical jobs are concentrated in large metropolitan areas. The increase in rural working poor is related to these routine production jobs, which pay low wages.

New industries attracted by rural areas' low labor costs and absence of labor unions bring new jobs with low wages in peripheral and secondary sectors (Tickamyer 1992). Few of these industries have greatly assisted local economic growth and major financial transactions. Industries that require higher skills and offer better-paid jobs generally have hired outside labor. In addition, many rural plants tend to suddenly relocate their operations in areas of cheaper labor. Despite the fact that industrial growth in rural areas, particularly in depressed areas, improves the amount of employment opportunities and the distribution of income across different groups, levels of underemployment may remain high. New jobs in peripheral industries and the secondary sector might merely create new forms of working poor (Tickamyer and Duncan 1990).

Gender and Underemployment

Feminists have noted that women's economic opportunities are conditioned and shaped by their disadvantages in the wage-labor market; by their high level of participation in informal and unpaid labor, both productive and reproductive; and by state policies toward women, work, and welfare (Tickamyer et al. 1993). Gender plays a central role in enabling, sustaining, and integrating relations of production and reproduction in various ways. First, without women's domestic labor in social reproduction, wage labor geared toward production could never take place. Second, women engaged in wage labor are exploited not only as members of a particular class but also as women. Rural women increasingly join the paid labor force. Yet rural women have higher levels of underemployment than their urban counterparts. Underemployment among rural women has been a significant aspect of employment-related hardship in nonmetropolitan areas since the 1970s. One of every three rural female workers today experience some form of economic distress (Lichter 1989). Women are less likely than men to become or stay adequately employed—a gender effect that cannot be explained by differences in human capital, job characteristics, or spatial location (Lichter and Landry 1991). Joblessness and low wages are the greatest barriers for females seeking an adequate job. Overall, women are especially vulnerable to tight labor markets and limited opportunities (Tickamyer 1992).

In formal employment, women tend to be concentrated in secondary occupations and peripheral industries with low wages and less prestige. Despite the increase in women's participation in the nonagricultural labor market, sex segregation has increased in rural communities. Women have much more limited employment opportunities and flatter earnings curves in areas dominated by agriculture and mining (Tickamyer and Bokemeier 1988). Women's wages and incomes are often the resources that sustain both family and farm in times of severe economic need. Yet family ties are more likely to constrain women than men; men are more likely to change jobs in order to improve their employment situation, while women are more likely to change employment for reasons related to marriage, family, or personal circumstances (Tickamyer and Bokemeier 1989).

Women have always contributed to the survival of the family through paid and unpaid work in and outside the home. Rural women spend much time in domestic work, with major responsibility for child rearing and household chores, work on farms and in gardens, and other activities to sustain their families. Women's work both in the informal economy and in households limits their opportunities to generate income, especially through jobs in the formal sector. Within many rural areas in the United States, exploitative informalization has resulted in the development of unregulated enterprises and home-based industries targeted specifically at women workers (Gringeri 1994).

Measuring Underemployment

The most commonly used indicator of economic hardship and employment marginality in prior research of labor market conditions has been the official unemployment rate. However, the unemployment rate ignores workers who are marginally employed because it measures job seeking rather than true joblessness or job inadequacy. Clogg and Sullivan (1983) have developed more sophisticated underemployment indicators in their labor

utilization framework, which includes the following categories: (1) not in labor force; (2) subunemployed, including discouraged workers who are either (a) persons not currently working because they were unable to find work or (b) part-year and seasonal workers who are currently out of the labor force but looking for full-time work; (3) unemployed, including (a) persons without work who are seeking employment and (b) employed persons in the process of job transition or layoff; (4) underemployed by low hours, the involuntary part-time and officially part-time for economic reasons who are working less than 35 hours a week but who desire a full-time job; (5) underemployed by low income, the working poor, including those with earnings less than 1.25 times the individual poverty threshold; (6) underemployed by occupational mismatch, referring to workers in a particular occupation who have completed schooling that exceeds the educational levels typical of persons in that occupation; and (7) adequately employed workers who are employed but not in any of the preceding categories. Voluntarily part-time workers are included among the adequately employed. The sum of categories 2, 3, 4, and 5 provides a composite measure of economic underemployment because of its direct link with individual labor-market earnings (Lichter and Costanzo 1987).

Underemployed individuals are affected by changes in their economic resources and by their feelings about those changes or losses. In families where one spouse is underemployed, both spouses may experience trouble in their communication, increasing conflicts and stress. Families adapt various employment strategies to survive: seeking more than one job, increasing the number of earners, having irregular jobs, spending additional time in working activities, or opting for informal activities both legal and illegal. Family adaptive strategies require close-knit kinship and community structure based on solidarity.

—*Janet L. Bokemeier and Jean Kayitsinga*

See also
Division of Household Labor; Employment; Home-Based Work; Income; Labor Force; Migrant Farmworkers; Policy, Rural Development; Policy, Socioeconomic; Poverty; Quality of Life; Social Class; Work.
References
Bloomquist, Leonard E., Christina Gringeri, Donald Tomaskovic-Devey, and Cynthia Truelove. "Work Structures and Rural Poverty." Pp. 68–105 in *Persistent Poverty in Rural America*. Edited by the Rural Sociological Society Task Force on Persistent Rural Poverty. Boulder, CO: Westview Press, 1993.
Clogg, Clifford C., and Teresa A. Sullivan. "Labor Force Composition and Underemployment Trends, 1969–1980." *Social Indicators Research* 12 (1983): 117–152.

Deavers, Kenneth, and Robert Hoppe. "Overview of the Rural Poor in the 1980s." Pp. 3–20 in *Rural Poverty in America*. Edited by Cynthia Duncan. New York: Auburn House, 1992.

Doeringer, Peter B. "Internal Labor Markets and Paternalism in Rural Areas." Pp. 272–289 in *Internal Labor Markets*. Edited by Paul Osterman. Cambridge, MA: MIT Press, 1984.

Duncan, Cynthia M., and Ann R. Tickamyer. "Poverty Research and Policy for Rural America." *American Sociologist* 19, no. 3 (1988): 243–259.

Gorham, Lucy. "The Growing Problem of Low Earnings in Rural Areas." Pp. 21–39 in *Rural Poverty in America*. Edited by Cynthia M. Duncan. New York: Auburn House, 1992.

Gringeri, Christina E. *Getting By: Women Homeworkers and Rural Economic Development*. Lawrence: University Press of Kansas, 1994.

Lichter, Daniel T. "The Underemployment of American Rural Women: Prevalence, Trends and Spatial Inequality." *Journal of Rural Studies* 5, no. 2 (1989): 199–208.

Lichter, Daniel T., and Janice Costanzo. "Non-metropolitan Underemployment and Labor-Force Composition." *Rural Sociology* 52, no. 3 (Fall 1987): 329–344.

Lichter, Daniel T., and David J. Eggebeen. "Child Poverty and the Changing Rural Family." *Rural Sociology* 57, no. 2 (1992): 151–172.

Lichter, Daniel T., and David J. Landry. "Labor Force Transition and Underemployment: The Stratification of Male and Female Workers." *Research in Social Stratification and Mobility* 10 (1991): 63–87.

Lichter, Daniel T., Lionel J. Beaulieu, Jill L. Findeis, and Ruy A. Teixeira. "Human Capital, Labor Supply, and Poverty in Rural America." Pp. 39–67 in *Persistent Poverty in Rural America*. Edited by the Rural Sociological Society Task Force on Persistent Rural Poverty. Boulder, CO: Westview Press, 1993.

McLaughlin, Diane K., and Lauri Perman. "Returns vs. Endowments in the Earnings Attainment Process for Metropolitan and Nonmetropolitan Men and Women." *Rural Sociology* 56, no. 3 (1991): 339–365.

Spenner, Kenneth I., Luther B. Otto, and Vaughn R. A. Call. *Career Lines and Careers: Entry into Career Series*. Volume 3. Lexington, MA: Lexington Books, 1982.

Swanson, Linda. "The Human Dimension of the Rural South in Crisis." Pp. 87–98 in *The Rural South in Crisis: Change for the Future*. Edited by Lionel J. Beaulieu. Boulder, CO: Westview Press, 1988.

Tickamyer, Ann R. "The Working Poor in Rural Labor Markets: The Example of the Southeastern United States." Pp. 41–62 in *Rural Poverty in America*. Edited by Cynthia M. Duncan. New York: Auburn House, 1992.

Tickamyer, Ann R., and Janet L. Bokemeier. "Sex Differences in Labor Market Experiences." *Rural Sociology* 53, no. 2 (1988): 166–189.

———. "Individual and Structural Explanations of Non-metropolitan Men and Women's Labor Force Experiences." In *Research in Rural Sociology and Development*, Volume 4. Edited by Falk W. Lyson. Greenwich, CT: JAI Press, 1989.

———. "Alternative Strategies for Labor Market Analyses: Micro/Macro Models of Labor Market Inequality." Pp. 49–68 in *Inequality in Labor Market Areas*. Edited by Joachim Singelmann and Forrest A. Deseran. Boulder, CO: Westview Press, 1993.

Tickamyer, Ann R., Janet L. Bokemeier, Shelly Feldman, Rosalind Harris, John Paul Jones, and DeeAnn Wenk. "Women and Persistent Rural Poverty." Pp. 201–229 in *Persistent Poverty in Rural America*. Edited by the Rural Sociological Society Task Force on Persistent Rural Poverty. Boulder, CO: Westview Press, 1993.

Tickamyer, Ann R., and Cynthia M. Duncan. "Poverty and Opportunity Structure in Rural America." *Annual Review of Sociology* 16 (1990): 67–86.

Unions

See Labor Unions

Urbanization

The conversion of rural land to urban uses, which directly affects agriculture and other rural uses of land. This entry looks at the rates of conversion of rural land to urban uses. It compares the areas of major land uses in the United States and the shifts between uses.

Population Growth: Rural-to-Urban Migration

Urbanization is the process of population expansion into rural areas. Urban expansion uses agricultural land, rangeland, forestland, and other rural land. The quantity and rate of urban conversion affect national food and fiber production, rural economies, and environmental quality. Public concerns about urbanization include maintaining open space and retaining natural systems and processes. Other concerns include controlling public infrastructure costs, preserving local economies, protecting rural lifestyles and ethnic patterns, maintaining local specialty crops, and conserving energy. State and local measures adopted to protect rural land uses include current use value assessment for property tax purposes, purchase or transfer of development rights, and agricultural districts. Right-to-farm laws, large-area land use planning, and exclusive agricultural zoning also may serve to protect rural land (Vesterby and Buist 1994).

Population growth and demographic change are the primary forces shaping changes in land use. The percentage of people living in urban areas has increased over time because of migration from rural areas to urban ones. In 1950, the U.S. population was 151 million people, 64 percent of whom lived in urban areas. By 1990, the U.S. population was 249 million people, with 187 million (75 percent) living in urban areas, which comprise less than 3 percent of the total U.S. land area. Increases in population result in more housing, schools, shopping centers, offices, roads, recreational areas, utilities, and other infrastructure, which translates into demand for more land for urban uses (Frey 1983; U.S. Department of Commerce 1989, 1993, and 1994a).

Population and Household Increases Compared

Population growth provides the major impetus for urban land-use change. Most rural-to-urban conversions are for residential use. These conversions directly relate to household formation and migration. Households make decisions that affect urban land use. Socioeconomic characteristics such as age, marital status, and income influence housing preference. These characteristics are more easily understood in terms of households than by general population characteristics. With smaller households at the same density, more land is needed per capita, since more housing units must be built to serve the same number of people.

Household numbers increased by a greater percentage than did overall population during the decades of the 1960s, 1970s, and 1980s, due to decreases in the number of persons per household. Average household size decreased from 3.40 persons per household in 1960 to 2.66 in 1990 (Vesterby, Heimlich, and Krupa 1994).

Rates of Urbanization and Urban Encroachment

Urban area increased significantly during the 1950s, 1960s, and 1970s. By the 1980s, the increase over the decade in urban area had slowed to 18 percent, about one-half of what it was for the previous three decades (see Table 1). However, despite large percentage increases in urban area, the corresponding decreases in rural area were small, about one-half of 1 percent for each decade. Rural area is much larger than urban area, which explains the difference in percentage changes.

The amount of urban land used per household in 1990 was 0.6 acres per household, a slight increase over previous decades (it was 0.49 in 1960). Urban land includes not only residential lots but also streets, shopping centers, urban parks, recreational areas, and all other

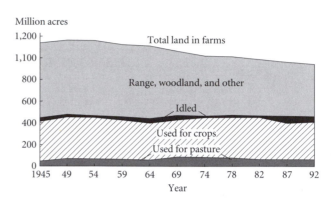

Use of land in farms, 1945–1992

Sources: Daugherty 1995; Krupa and Daugherty 1990.

nonrural land. Accounting for all urban uses, the average amount of land used by each household has remained under one acre.

Land Use

Of the almost 2.3 billion acres of U.S. land, 2.6 percent, or 59 million acres, was in urban uses in 1992 (see Table 2). Land area used for cropland or pasture is nearly eight times larger than urban land area and is about one-fifth of all rural land. Rural land is primarily in forest, range, and other uses.

About 946 million acres are classified as land in farms. Less than one-half of all farmland is cropland and pasture (435 million acres in 1992). While land in farms declined by 17 percent (196 million acres) since 1945, land used for cropland and pasture remained remarkably stable, about 460 million acres (see Table 2). Most of the farmland decline was from farm woodland, range, and other farmland uses, not from cropland. Woodland and forest, range, and other rural uses replaced much of the cropland lost to urbanization, illustrating the dynamics of shifting land uses.

Table 1
Rural Land Conversion

Year	Million Acres Urban Area	Million Acres Rural Area	Total	Percentage Urban Area Increase	Percentage Rural Area Decrease	Urban Land Area as Percentage of Total Acres	Urban Acres per Household
1950	18	2,251	2,269	—	—	0.8	—
1960	26	2,240	2,266	39	0.48	1.2	.49
1970	35	2,229	2,264	36	0.49	1.6	.56
1980	47	2,218	2,265	37	0.49	2.1	.58
1990	56	2,207	2,263	18	0.49	2.5	.60

Sources: Frey, 1983; U.S. Department of Commerce 1957, 1989, 1993, and 1994a.

Table 2
Major Uses of Land in the United States, 1992
(in million acres)

Major Land Use	Land in Farms[1]	Other Land	All Land
Urban	0	59	59
Rural	946	1,259	2,204
Range	411	180	591
Cropland and pasture	435	25	460
Farmsteads and roads	6	0	6
Forest[2]	74	663	737
Other rural land[3]	19	391	410
Total U.S. land	946	1,318	2,263

Sources: Daugherty 1995; U.S. Department of Commerce 1994b.

[1]"Land in farms" is land that generates at least $1,000 in product sales per year.

[2]Included are timberland and reserved timberland, federal and nonfederal lands, parks, wildlife areas, and other special use areas.

[3]Included are swamps, military reservations, roads, parks, deserts, and barren areas.

Distinction between Rural Land Uses

Rural land includes agricultural land, forestland, farmland, rangeland, and all other nonurban land. Agricultural land, farmland, and cropland are terms that often are used interchangeably, when in fact, each has a different meaning. Agricultural land includes farmland, nonfederal rangeland, and any land not in farms that is used for crops or pasture, such as portions of wildlife refuges. Agricultural land excludes nonurban rural forestland, parks, roads, and wildlife refuge areas not in crops or pasture.

Farmland consists of land in farms, including cropland, pasture, and lands that are part of a farm but not used for producing crops or livestock. Cropland and pasture (95 percent), rangeland (69 percent), and some forestland (11 percent) constitutes "land in farms." Other (nonfarm) rural land includes public rangeland and forestland grazed on a permit basis and managed by the Bureau of Land Management and the Forest Service. Some cropland and pasture is in wildlife refuges and is not classified as land in farms. Urban land includes residential, commercial, industrial, institutional, transportation, communications, utilities, and other development and building uses.

Acres Converted between Major Uses

While most land stays in the same use over time, some land shifts between major uses. The number of acres that shift varies by use and by the length of the period under investigation. Shifts between cropland, rangeland, and forestland tend to be dynamic in the sense that increases and decreases occur to and from these major uses. Shifts

to urban uses are usually smaller and more permanent. Urban areas give up very little land to the other major uses, although there is some shifting within the urban categories.

A study of land-use change during the 1970s found that net percentage increases in urban categories were large, as much as 50 percent for residential areas. Corresponding net decreases for rural areas were small, 2 percent for cropland and pasture, 5 percent for rangeland, and 3 percent for forestland. Conversions from other major uses such as rangeland and forestland largely replace cropland lost to urban uses. Although urban uses gained 2.3 million acres, they lost only 49,000 acres to other major uses.

Dynamic shifts occurred between the agriculture, forest, and range categories, which both gained and lost during the decade. Cropland and pasture gained 975,000 acres and lost 1.5 million acres, for a net loss of 548,000 acres. Rangeland gained 695,000 acres and lost 1.9 million acres, for a net loss of 1.2 million acres. Forestland gained 357,000 acres and lost 1 million acres, for a net loss of 683,000 acres. Major nonurban categories of land not only lose to other uses but also gain from other uses. Greater shifts in land use occurred between cropland and pasture, rangeland, and forestland, than between any of these uses and urban land. Percentage net urban conversions from rural uses during the 1970s ranged from 2.8 percent from forestland to 6.1 percent from wetlands.

Despite the seemingly large changes in land use, most land remains in the same use. Ninety-three percent of cropland and pasture (21.5 million acres) stayed in the same use from the beginning to the end of the decade. Forestland remained 95 percent in the same use, rangeland 92 percent, and the urban category, 98 percent (Vesterby et al. 1994).

Urbanization of Prime Cropland

The study of the 1970s fast-growth counties showed that urbanization does not develop prime cropland faster than nonprime cropland. Prime cropland is regarded as best suited to producing food and fiber. Forty-three percent of all cropland was classified as prime in fast-growth counties (compared to 49 percent nationally), but only 40 percent of cropland urbanized was prime (Vesterby et al. 1994).

Regional Differences in Land Use

Urbanization and population growth go hand in hand. Increases in population spur the demand for land to convert to urban uses. In the study of fast-growth counties in

A typical housing development in Leesburg, Virginia, encroaches on agricultural land.

the 1970s, the most rapid population increases occurred in the southeast and southwest. The largest groups of counties meeting the fast-growth definition were in Florida, California, Texas, and Arizona. Other concentrations of fast-growth counties occurred in the coastal states, particularly along the west coast. There were none in the Central Plains states.

The largest expansion in urban area in the 1970s was in the Southeast (875,000 acres) and the Southwest (815,000 acres). Northern counties' urban areas expanded by 337,000 acres. Urban area in the Pacific region grew by 434,000 acres. Acres per new household were also greatest in southern states; 0.54 acres per household in the Southeast and 0.49 acres in the Southwest. The Pacific region averaged 0.40 acres per household (Vesterby et al. 1994).

Average and Marginal Urban Acres per Household

Households averaged 0.87 acres per household in the 1970s fast-growth counties. By the early 1980s, the aver-age had decreased to 0.71 acres per household. Results were similar for fast-growth counties of the 1960s. Marginal rates were about the same for both the 1960s and the 1970s, 0.47 acres per new household added during each decade. However, differences were observed between residential and nonresidential urban uses (primarily commercial, industrial, and institutional uses). During the 1960s, marginal nonresidential categories used 0.18 additional acres per added household. These categories decreased to 0.10 acres per household in the 1970s, a 44 percent decline. Thus, fewer nonresidential acres sup-ported newly developed residential land in the 1970s than in the 1960s. These coefficients may vary by locality depending on previous urbanization, land costs, and infilling of urbanized areas.

Popular accounts of urbanization may prompt some to conclude that urban encroachment is converting all of the U.S. cropland and pasture to housing lots, shopping centers, and office parks. However, studies of land-use change show that urban conversion of cropland is no threat to U.S. food and fiber production. Large increases in urban areas represent proportionately small decreases in rural areas. These studies have shown that total cropland and pasture in the United States have remained almost constant since the early 1940s. Conversions from other major uses, such as rangeland and forestland, largely replaced cropland lost to urban uses. During the same period, agricultural productivity per acre more than doubled and continues to increase. Fifty million acres were set aside by commodity programs and the Conservation Reserve Program (CRP) in 1994. Many of these idled acres will again be used to grow crops. In addition, one-third or more of some major U.S. crops are exported, depending on the year and on market supply and demand (Vesterby et al. 1994).

Although urban encroachment is no threat to U.S. food and fiber production, there are many reasons to control urbanization at the local and regional levels. These include maintaining open space, maintaining traditional economic activities, preserving water and air quality, and conserving locally important farmland and specialty crops. Many different kinds of programs address farmland preservation, including use value assessment for property tax relief, zoning, agricultural districts, right-to-farm laws, and purchase of development rights.

—*Marlow Vesterby*

The views expressed in this entry are the author's and do not necessarily represent policies or views of the U.S. Department of Agriculture.

See also

Community; Future of Rural America; Impact Assessment; Landownership; Migration; Policy, Rural Development; Rural, Definition of; Rural Demography; Settlement Patterns.

References

Daugherty, Arthur B. *Major Uses of Land in the United States: 1992.* AER-723. Washington, DC: U.S. Department of Agriculture, Economic Research Service, 1995.

Frey, H. Thomas. *Expansion of Urban Area in the United States: 1960–80.* Staff Report AGES830615. Washington, DC: U.S. Department of Agriculture, Economic Research Service, 1983.

Krupa, K. S., and Arthur B. Daugherty. *Major Land Uses.* No. 89003 (computer file). Washington, DC: U.S. Department of Agriculture, Economic Research Service, 1990.

U.S. Department of Commerce, Bureau of the Census. *County and City Data Book, 1956.* Statistical Abstract Supplement. Washington, DC: U.S. Government Printing Office, 1957.

———. *Statistical Abstract of the United States: 1989.* 109th edition. Washington, DC: U.S. Government Printing Office, 1989.

———. *Population and Housing Unit Counts, United States, 1990 Census of Population and Housing.* CPH-2-1. Washington, DC: U.S. Government Printing Office, 1993.

———. *Statistical Abstract of the United States: 1994.* 114th edition. Washington, DC: U.S. Government Printing Office, 1994a.

———. *1992 Census of Agriculture.* AC92-A-51. Washington, DC: U.S. Government Printing Office, 1994b.

Vesterby, Marlow, and Henry Buist. "Land Use Planning in Agriculture." *Encyclopedia of Agricultural Science* 2 (1994): 645–655.

Vesterby, Marlow, Ralph E. Heimlich, and Kenneth S. Krupa. *Urbanization of Rural Land in the United States.* AER-673. Washington, DC: U.S. Department of Agriculture, Economic Research Service, 1994.

Value-Added Agriculture

The production, processing, and packaging of raw agricultural commodities in order to enhance marketability and profit. This entry addresses several questions connected with value-added agriculture: One concerns the desirability and feasibility of building a manufacturing base in rural regions to process agricultural crops and livestock; this question, in turn, demands a consideration of location economics and vertical integration. Another issue is that of developing close economic ties between agricultural industrialization and the new generation of farmer-owned cooperatives. Still another question is that of switching from crops traditionally grown to niche market crops, or developing new commercial uses for crops and livestock.

The Scope of Value-Added Agriculture

Value-added agriculture is widely acclaimed as a key strategy to revive and strengthen rural economies. Politicians from both parties and most farm organizations view value-added agriculture as the means for rural development and new job creation. Despite its broad appeal, there is no simple interpretation of value-added agriculture. This discussion of value-added agriculture includes its scope, rural economic development, industrial uses of crops, alternative crops, vertical integration, and location economics.

The U.S. Commerce Department has classified the food manufacturing system into 49 industrial sectors. These sectors are classified as higher or lower value-added, based on how much value is added by processing. Higher value-added sectors manufacture retail-ready, packaged, brand-name consumer products of which at least 40 percent of the value is added by manufacturing.

Since 1988, the average annual growth rate for higher-value agricultural sectors has been 3.6 percent, compared with only 2.1 percent for lower value-added agricultural sectors. Although both sectors employ around 500,000 workers, those in the higher-value sector earn on average $11.87 per hour, compared with $9.26 per hour in the lower-value sector.

Approximately half of the food industry shipments are of higher-value agricultural products. In 1991, the three largest higher-value agricultural sectors by industry shipments were soft drinks ($25.2 billion), breads and cakes ($17.3 billion), and malt beverages ($15.9 billion). The top three sectors for lower-value agricultural products were meat packing ($49.3 billion), poultry slaughtering ($21.7 billion), and milk ($21.1 billion).

The "percent value-added" measures how much of an industry's final shipment value is added in processing. A higher value in this category means that more value is added during processing. The top three sectors in terms of percent value-added are breakfast cereal (72.7 percent), cookies and crackers (61.6 percent), and breads and cakes (61.5 percent). The lowest three sectors are meat packing (13.0 percent), vegetable oils (19.5 percent), and prepared animal feeds (21.5 percent).

Rural Economic Development

A second dimension of value-added agriculture is aimed at developing more processing industries in rural America that are high value-adding. A major impetus for such an approach is to further rural economic development. In the Great Plains, recent development efforts along these lines have been led by an upsurge in new farmer-owned cooperatives, along with involvement by rural electric cooperatives.

There are at least three reasons for the renewed efforts at rural development of value-added agriculture: First, rural development strategies that promote job creation are seen as critical to replacing jobs lost in farming since the 1970s. Providing additional opportunities for the youth in rural America reduces their incentive to migrate to metropolitan areas. In addition, these jobs are critical to maintaining and expanding the client bases for retail businesses on the main streets of rural towns and cities. Second, the creation of new value-added agriculture results in a more diversified economy, reducing rural states' historical reliance on primary agricultural production for tax revenues. Finally, the Freedom to Farm Act will likely lead to reduced farm price supports. Thus, value-added agriculture is viewed as an important replacement for the expected decline in federal payments.

Industrial Uses of Crops

A third dimension of value-added agriculture lies in expanding the industrial uses of crops. Such expansion efforts include inventing new uses for traditional crops, such as corn and soybeans, as well as introducing new crops, such as crambe, jojoba, and guayule. Besides the new uses in food products, certain crops also are being used to produce newsprint and ink, pharmaceuticals, cosmetics, food colorings, plastics, and lubricants.

Corn historically has been grown as livestock feed. Yet in 1994, 20 percent of corn was used in food, seed, and industrial applications. The annual growth rate for industrial uses of corn is relatively high, at 6 percent. Examples of food and industrial uses of corn include ethanol (fuel alcohol), high-fructose corn syrup, dextrose and glucose, and starch. In part, the industrial uses of corn reflect societal efforts to reduce pollution. Ethanol reduces air pollution, and corn starches are used in biodegradable plastics. Research at land-grant universities is investigating alternative uses for other traditional crops as well. Examples include using soybeans for ink, sunflower pectin in jelly, and wheat in ice cream.

Other public and private sector research is developing new industrial crops as substitutes for existing manufacturing inputs. One estimate places the market potential for alternative industrial crops at $15 to $20 billion per year, or about 10 percent of U.S. agricultural production. Criteria for successful new industrial crops include (1) replacing an existing industrial input by being less expensive or more effective; (2) meeting a specific market niche requirement; (3) being compatible with the existing farming system; and (4) meeting quality standards and being produced in volumes sufficient to meet buyer requirements.

Alternative Crops

Another dimension of value-added agriculture suggests that different crops should be raised. Instead of growing commodities such as corn, wheat, or soybeans, individual producers might shift to specialty crops for niche markets. Two difficulties may prevent this from becoming a viable strategy for many producers. First, the machinery complement designed for 1,000 acres of wheat probably is not adaptable to growing 20 acres of carrots or garlic. Similarly, the agronomic methods to raise alternative crops may require completely different production practices. Second, there may not be an established market for some alternative crops, and the amount of that commodity becomes critical. Until a certain minimum quantity is grown, building a processing plant is not feasible. Nevertheless, agricultural trade shows are filled with displays featuring niche market products, ranging from mustard to ostrich eggs to organic foods.

Vertical Integration

A fifth dimension of value-added agriculture in the movement toward processing in rural America is a form of forward vertical integration. That is, farmers are taking ownership in forward assets, such as pasta plants, ethanol plants, or buffalo slaughterhouses. These efforts are driven largely by farmer-owned cooperatives and individual farmer entrepreneurs. Their motivation is to capture the profit or value earned farther up the supply chain. Since production agriculture is a mature industry with slow growth, these new ventures become attractive ways of building profits from year to year.

Some large food companies, such as ConAgra or Budweiser, are backward vertically integrated. Reasons for vertical integration include capturing the profits or value in different stages of the supply chain and ensuring a supply of critical raw materials. For example, Budweiser contracted with farmers to grow malting barley. The malting barley is then processed in malting plants owned by Budweiser. The malt is then shipped to Budweiser breweries. In contrast, Miller Brewing concentrates on producing beer. Instead of vertically integrating, Miller buys all of its malt from independent suppliers such as Cargill or ADM.

Vertical integration is not without its difficulties. Studies in strategic management identify four disadvantages of vertical integration. First, vertical integration

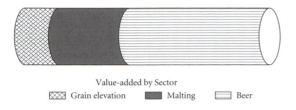

Value-added by Sector
▨ Grain elevation   ■ Malting   ▭ Beer

Value Added by Sector in Beer Supply Chain

concentrates a firm's investment in a particular industry. Large, vested investments make it more difficult to exit the industry or adopt new technology. Second, vertical integration may reduce flexibility in sourcing raw materials by linking the firm to particular suppliers. This is especially worrisome for farmer-owned cooperatives. Third, balancing capacity at each level of the supply chain might be difficult. For example, although a farmer-owned flour mill may be at an optimal size, its milling capacity may be more than is required at the next level of processing, say baking. Thus, the vertically integrated firm may be forced to sell its primary product to competitors. Finally, different business activities may require management with vastly different skills and business capabilities. Being a low-cost processor does not make one an effective manager of logistical or marketing issues.

Location Economics

Developers of value-added agriculture face pressure to build new processing plants in rural areas. Traditional locational analyses suggest that weight-losing agricultural processes should locate near producing regions, whereas weight-gaining processes should locate near consuming regions. However, this simple rule is complicated by a rail rate structure that traditionally favors the movement of multiple-car shipments (25 to 100 rail cars) of bulk commodities. In contrast, processed products typically move in smaller rail shipments or by truck. The transportation cost difference can be enormous.

Thus, when promoting rural economic development, issues of altering the traditional description of firm objectives must be addressed directly. Under traditional economic analysis, the objective is maximum profit, not location. However, a farmer-owned cooperative may opt for a lower return on investment in exchange for the additional economic development in their community.

A final locational factor for the developers of new value-added agriculture is how far to extend the definition of community. Large-scale value-added agriculture projects might require capital, labor, and raw materials that

can only be generated at a regional level. Their developers might need to view several towns or even counties as their home base, rather than a specific town. Although all may benefit from cooperation, it might be difficult for communities to put aside rivalries of many years standing.

Value-added agriculture gives rise to new hope for the future of rural America. The many sides of value-added agriculture make its introduction complex and difficult. Yet as U.S. agricultural policy increases its reliance on free markets and reduces government price support programs, new value-added agriculture will likely increase in importance.

—Frank J. Dooley

See also
Agricultural and Resource Economics; Agro/Food System; Cooperatives; Development, Community and Economic; Manufacturing Industry; Marketing; Markets; Policy, Rural Development.
References
Boehlje, Michael. "Industrialization of Agriculture: What Are the Implications?" *Choices* 11, no. 1 (First Quarter 1996): 30–33.
Dicks, Michael R., and Katharine C. Buckley, eds. *Alternative Opportunities in Agriculture: Expanding Output through Diversification.* Agricultural Economic Report No. 633. Washington, DC: U.S. Department of Agriculture, Economic Research Service, 1989.
Drabenstott, Mark. "Industrialization: Steady Current or Tidal Wave." *Choices* 9, no. 4 (Fourth Quarter 1994): 4–8.
Flaskerud, George. "Corn Is More Than Feed." *Market Advisor.* Fargo: North Dakota State University Extension Service, January 5, 1994.
Nelson, Paul N., James C. Wade, and Julie P. Leones. "The Economics of Commercializing New Industrial Crops." *Agribusiness: An International Journal* 11, no. 1 (1995): 45–55.
Thompson, Arthur A., Jr., and A. J. Strickland III. *Crafting and Implementing Strategy: Text and Readings.* 6th ed. Chicago: Irwin, 1995.
Urban, Tom. "Agricultural Industrialization: It's Inevitable." *Choices* 6, no. 4 (Fourth Quarter 1991): 4–6.
U.S. Department of Commerce. *U.S. Industrial Outlook, 1994.* Washington, DC: Internal Trade Administration, 1994.

Values, Land
See Land Values

Values of Residents

In general, those things thought to be good, whether abstract or concrete. Personal security, for example, is a value that is abstract but often is associated with the material aspects of life, such as adequate food, shelter, and clothing. But security has a psychological aspect as well. Some people can feel quite secure with much less wealth than others. This entry discusses some of the historically distinct values associated with rural American life and begins with a brief contrast to those experienced by people living in urban settings. Then two kinds of values are discussed in order to explain why some values are thought more important than others. In American literary and historical myth, values are reflected in moral character traits attributed to rural Americans. In turn, these rural values and virtues have been associated with broader community virtues and with the movement to achieve a sustainable agriculture. But these same American values also underlie economic efficiency and trends toward technological expansion, which often result in a decline in the quality of life in rural America.

Rural versus Urban Values

The moral and aesthetic values of people who live in rural areas are commonly thought to differ from those of their metropolitan or suburban counterparts. Certainly, the challenges and benefits of the two lifestyles differ so much in the United States today that people who move to small towns from large cities or vice versa almost always experience some culture shock associated with differences in tempo, intimacy, and personal visibility in day-to-day life. The question of whether core values are unalterably different among populations who are raised and remain in rural areas from those more urban is a matter of continuing controversy and empirical uncertainty. But it is safe to say that the situations in which humans find themselves in rural versus urban settings contrast enough so that people behave differently in each setting. This means that in a rural setting certain values and virtues become more apparent, but those same values or virtues might recede to the background in urban living.

Nevertheless, some values are thought to be more important than others regardless of the setting in which people live. To distinguish these more important values, usually a means-ends criterion is proposed, where ends are the values most important to humans and means are the various ways used to achieve those ends. Thus, values are divided into those that are good intrinsically and those that are good instrumentally. The former are sometimes described as "good in themselves" or "ends in themselves." Various intrinsic goods have been proposed, among them happiness, security, self-realization, enlightenment, nonviolence, love, and oneness with nature. Instrumental goods are desirable only because they help us to reach a more ultimate good. The linguistic usage of

This New Englander gathering sap from maple trees seems to exemplify the solid virtues thought to characterize farmers—hard work, efficiency, self-reliance, and independence.

the term "instrumental" implies that such values are less important than the intrinsic ones. While intrinsically good things are desirable—that is, people want them— not everything desirable is intrinsically, or even instrumentally, good. In assessing the values of rural Americans, then, part of our task is to think about whether the values associated with rural life are ultimately good for their own sakes or are good in certain contexts and situations as a means to some higher, unspoken value that is shared by rural and urban people alike.

Values and Virtues

Moral virtues are associated with values that are instrumentally and/or intrinsically good. A virtue is a character trait such as honesty, fidelity, courage, compassion, justice, or self-reliance. People who are honest or faithful, brave or compassionate have a certain disposition to behave in recognizable ways and they also are motivated for good and virtuous reasons to do what they do. A virtuous person will exhibit most or all of the good character traits and none of the bad ones.

Virtues often serve individuals or society by helping

them to achieve an ultimate, more intrinsic good. So a society of people who tell the truth, keep their promises, admit mistakes, defend themselves against aggressors, and attend to the feelings of others would arguably be well on its way toward achieving the higher ends of peace, harmony, and security. Virtues are not solely instrumental, however. Becoming a virtuous person is an end that no one could attain by seeking to be honest, faithful, self-reliant, and courageous only as a means to virtuous integrity. In many instances, honesty, fidelity, justice, and most other virtues are thought to be intrinsic goods, desirable as character traits of a truly good and happy person.

Virtues and American Mythology

Until the past few decades, the majority of the U.S. population lived in rural areas. Historically, American values were rural values. Most rural dwellers described in literature and research were farmers, ranchers, loggers, fishers, and others who harvested renewable crops and owned small businesses that were family operated. Writing in Revolutionary times, Thomas Jefferson believed that a strong democracy depended on maintaining a nation of small landowners who made their livelihood from the land. According to Jefferson, such a populace would naturally exhibit the self-reliance, independence, and efficiency that are essential to a democratic way of life. Mythic tales about figures such as Paul Bunyan, Johnny Appleseed, the Lone Ranger, Davy Crockett, and Daniel Boone also signify the persona of hardiness that is closely associated with ideals of courage, liberty, and individualism as American values. Henry David Thoreau articulated the virtue of self-reliance in his writings and life at Walden Pond in the nineteenth century, and his ideas still symbolize the way many Americans believe we ought to view ourselves and our relationships to others.

Today, most Americans live in cities; but our cultural history and values are still rooted in the images, stories, and virtues of rural life. The stories that have been recorded and repeated and the virtues that are admired reflect only part of that rural culture. Although farmers, ranchers, loggers, fishermen, and other small business owners live in rural America, large numbers of others live there, too. Most Native American populations live in rural areas. Many African Americans lived there as slaves, sharecroppers, or tenant farmers in the South during and after the Civil War. Chinese laborers were brought in to build the railways in the West, and immigrants from Mexico have been a staple in the labor force of southwestern farms and orchards since territorial days. The values of

rural women have been assumed to be identical to those of the men in their families. Until recently, the contributions of these and other groups to the quality of community life were downplayed or not recorded. Their values might be quite different from what many Americans perceive as central to the American way of rural life (see *Agriculture and Human Values,* Summer 1985, for a series of discussions).

Rural Values and Sustainable Agriculture

The values reflected in the mythology of pioneering America are largely those of people of European descent. With that vision in mind, recent commentators have claimed that the passing of traditional family farms signals the loss of important moral values from American life. Most urgent among them is community. The loss is both abstract and concrete. Small towns are disappearing as small farms sell out to larger farms and conglomerates. The sense of community has been lost, it is argued, and the quality of life thereby degraded. By this, writers usually refer to the feeling of trust and relationship, interdependence and unity that is prevalent in small towns. Small family farms have been extolled as places where these values arise. The land itself is sometimes said to be of intrinsic value. Small farmers should value a sustainable agriculture and should have better motivation to be good stewards than large profit-making corporations, which have no intimate connection to the land and its communities.

The idea that small farmers are preservers of important American values has been criticized in several ways. Most commonly, small farmers who must sell their farms to their neighbors because of debt load or low profit margin are said to be simply inefficient and by implication deserve to lose out because they have not worked hard enough or well enough. Efficiency and hard work are values these critics hold as more important than other values that might accompany the existence of small and medium-sized family farms, such as better communities and family integrity. Countering that attack, some economists note that economies of scale work to the advantage of medium-sized farms, many of which are family operated. Large farms are not necessarily better farms or more efficient farms.

Economic and Technological Impacts

Concerning the implication that inefficient farms somehow deserve their fates, many scholars point out that small farms are vulnerable to the technological treadmill. As new technologies are introduced to make farms more efficient, the earliest adopters benefit most from the cost savings that permit profits. Larger farms are more likely to be capable of adopting such technologies and thus reap the technological rewards. By the time small farmers are able to afford the innovations, commodity prices have dropped because the technology permits more production. If they adopt the innovations, their profit margin decreases because the technology is expensive and the drop in commodity prices only enables them to stay even or lag somewhat behind. If they do not adopt the technology at this later time, they face lower and lower returns on the crop or herds, which eventually will force them out of business. Thus, small and medium-sized farmers have not earned their losses but instead are victims of a system that has been arranged to benefit those who already have more wealth and power. Part of the system is funded by the public, and an affirmation of equality requires restructuring the system to benefit all citizens.

Many other aspects of the social restructuring of American life from rural to urban majorities have contributed to the loss of rural community values. During the farm crisis of the 1980s, medium-sized farms operated by a family or extended family on a full-time basis tended to disappear at an alarming rate. The causes of the decline lay in broad trends and policies that were not in themselves immoral or irresponsible. Mechanization, hybrid seed technology, chemicals, commodity programs, and a general tendency of Americans to encourage big business have been cited as primary causes. The decline in world food production of the 1970s encouraged the United States to expand production to help feed the world. Farmers invested heavily in machinery and equipment and bought more land in a time of inflation. Bankers encouraged farmers to take high-leverage loans, but then the Federal Reserve raised interest rates to attack inflation, thereby increasing costs of production. Then exports began to decline and land values fell, pushing many family farmers into insolvency.

Rural community values were once believed to foster conservationist virtues. Some scholars proposed that owners who lived on and personally worked the land developed a personal relationship to the land and would be more motivated to preserve the land as a bequest to their offspring. In actuality, however, farmers on the brink of ruin are less likely to exercise the restraint and self-sacrifice needed to ensure good stewardship; they might need to plow every available square inch, and be unable to exercise the conservation practices needed to preserve the quality of the soil.

Self-Defeating Values?

Ironically, the values encoded in the traditional mythology of the American persona—independence, self-reliance, and individualism—may themselves be driving the decline in quality of rural life. Independence and individualism may lead to a so-called tragedy of the commons, wherein each person seeking his own good or self-interest is a collective cause of collapse of a community or common good. For example, each cattle rancher who places a herd along a river can reason that this single herd will do no irrevocable damage to the river, the fish population, or the habitat of other animals. Each rancher abutting the river reasons that he or she has a right to use the water flowing by for the herds. But if each rancher reasons as if no other rancher matters or exists, then the river will be polluted, spawning beds destroyed, and habitat lost.

Paradoxically, new champions of rural community as a lost value see interdependence as important. Some writers point to the Amish as exhibiting this kind of community where one could rely on one's neighbors in times of need. But in our culture, the writings traditionally taught in American literature, the heroes of American history, and the scions of American economics and politics have lived and admired independence and self-reliance and discouraged interdependence. Perhaps it is simply the small numbers living in rural towns that engender the trust and interdependence that people feel in living there. It is a condition of human life that each person can know only a limited number of people well enough for trust. A common theme in criticisms of urban life today involves loss of safety and the longing to see a familiar face in the endless crowds, for extended family and circles of friends with shared beliefs, among whom each of us can feel safe. In praising rural community virtues and values, their opposites are thereby logically excluded. Individualistic self-reliance and interdependent community are likely to be mutually exclusive in the American context.

—*Kathryn Paxton George*

See also
Animal Rights/Welfare; Culture; Ethics; Land Stewardship; Religion; Theology of the Land.

References
Agriculture and Human Values. Special Issues: "Agrarianism, Agricultural Development, and the Farm Crisis." 2, no. 2 (Spring 1985); "Agriculture in the U.S.: Its Impact on Ethnic and Other Minority Groups." 2, no. 3 (Summer 1985); "The Land, the Agrarian Tradition, and the Common Good." 2, no. 4 (Fall 1985); "Agriculture and the Social Sciences." 4, no. 1 (Winter 1987); "Ethical Values and Public Policy." 6, no. 4 (Fall 1989); "Agrarianism and the American Philosophical Tradi-

tion." 7, no. 1 (Winter 1990); "Rural Economic Development." 8, no. 3 (Summer 1991).

Berry, Wendell. *The Unsettling of America: Culture and Agriculture.* San Francisco: Sierra Club Books, 1977.

Comstock, Gary, ed. *Is There a Moral Obligation to Save the Family Farm?* Ames: Iowa State University Press, 1987.

Critchfield, Richard. *Trees, Why Do You Wait?* Washington, DC: Island Press, 1991.

Deaton, Brady J., and B. R. McManus, eds. *The Agrarian Tradition in American Society: A Focus on the People and the Land in an Era of Changing Values.* Proceedings of a Bicentennial Forum, June 16–18, 1976. Knoxville: University of Tennessee, Institute of Agriculture, 1976.

George, Kathryn Paxton. "Do We Have a Moral Obligation to Practice a Sustainable Agriculture?" *Journal of Sustainable Agriculture* 1, no. 1 (1990): 81–96.

———. "Sustainability and the Moral Community." *Agriculture and Human Values* 9, no. 4 (Fall 1992): 48–57.

Goldschmidt, Walter. *As You Sow: Three Studies in the Social Consequences of Agribusiness.* Montclair, NJ: Allanheld, Osmun and Co., 1978.

Montmarquet, James A. *The Idea of Agrarianism: From Hunter-Gatherer to Agrarian Radical in Western Culture.* Moscow: University of Idaho Press, 1989.

Pollack, Norman. *The Populist Mind.* Indianapolis, IN: Bobbs-Merrill, 1967.

Thoreau, Henry David. *Walden and Other Writings of Henry David Thoreau.* Edited by Brooks Atkinson. New York: Random House, 1937.

Zube, Ervin H., and Margaret J. Zube. *Changing Rural Landscapes.* Amherst: University of Massachusetts Press, 1977.

Vegetable Industry

A group of individuals and firms involved in the production, marketing, processing, handling, selling, or storage of vegetable plants grown primarily for human consumption. Vegetables are defined, in this entry, by their common, culinary usage rather than their formal botanical meaning. For example, tomatoes, peppers, and eggplants are botanically classified as fruits, but many consumers, producers, distributors, and industry analysts classify them as vegetables. Similarly, potatoes, sweet potatoes, melons, and mushrooms are frequently listed as vegetables, so the broad definition of vegetables will be assumed in this entry (for a complete list of vegetables included, please see various issues of the USDA's *Vegetables and Specialty Crops: Situation and Outlook Report*). This entry examines trends that helped redefine the vegetable industry of the 1990s. Important structural and organizational differences between the fresh market and processing sectors of the vegetable industry are noted and discussed. Production and marketing challenges that the vegetable industry faces as it approaches the twenty-first century also are discussed.

For many Americans, an obvious link with an agrar-ian past is planting a vegetable garden. The perishability of vegetables and the just-harvested taste of fresh produce motivate some individuals to spend hours planting and nurturing their gardens. For the modern nuclear family, however, it is more common to drive to a local supermarket, select vegetables from the 100 or more types usually available, microwave a portion for that evening's meal, and repeat this process every few days. Problems with out-of-season shortages, limited selection, and exorbitant prices are often memories rather than constraints to buying. Sophisticated advances in genetics, production technology, and transportation provide shoppers with a variety of high-quality vegetables throughout the year. Increased availability and heightened consumer awareness about health, diet, and nutrition cause the average American consumer to eat nearly 425 pounds of fresh and processed vegetables each year.

Trends

The first and perhaps the most visible change for U.S. consumers was the year-round availability of fresh market vegetables in grocery stores in the 1950s. Technological advances in transportation, storage, refrigeration, and communication systems permitted retailers to obtain regular supplies of high-quality vegetables from distant suppliers. During the low supply periods of early spring, late fall, and winter, supermarkets obtain fresh vegetables from milder climates in the United States, Mexico, Chile, and Spain. Consumers have expanded and diversified their tastes and buying habits for vegetables. Health, diet, and nutrition considerations motivate many consumers to experiment with new and different items, such as yellow bell peppers and exotic mushrooms. Producers respond to changing consumer preferences by expanding the set of traditional vegetables grown to include many specialty vegetables. The result is steady growth in the vegetable industry.

From the mid-1970s through the mid-1990s, harvested acreage of vegetable crops increased 12 percent, total vegetable output expanded 70 percent, the amount of vegetables imported to the United States increased 170 percent, and U.S. per capita consumption increased nearly 30 percent. Acreage and output increases were realized despite a 20 percent decline in the number of commercial vegetable farms in operation. Greater output per farm was achieved through better utilization of resources and crop specialization in geographic areas where producers had a comparative advantage in growing vegetables. Off-farm industry changes also influenced the

A young shopper examines locally grown vegetables in a North Dakota grocery store.

domestic vegetable industry. Successful completion of the Uruguay round of the General Agreement on Tariffs and Trade (GATT) and implementation of the North American Free Trade Agreement (NAFTA) reduced trade barriers, allowing easier access to foreign-grown vegetables and reduced procurement costs. Attempts to reduce barriers to trade were enormously important for rural vegetable farmers and residents. Although reductions in trade impediments made local vegetable producers more susceptible to foreign competitors (particularly fresh-market imports from Mexico), lower-cost producers will have additional opportunities to export vegetables. Economic growth associated with increased vegetable exports could expand small-town employment, keep more people in the rural service base, and fund needed upgrades in rural services and infrastructure.

The second major industry-wide trend has been heightened consumer and producer sensitivity to environmental issues and the need to use resources wisely and in more sustainable ways. Whereas vegetable output increased, growers reduced usage rates of synthetic fertilizers and chemical pest controls. Handlers and retailers developed new methods to protect vegetables and recycle shipping containers while also reducing in-transit losses. Organically grown vegetables and other specialty vegetables were available to consumers in locations throughout the United States. Many sustainable methods were incorporated into the vegetable industry during the past decade, but new and better ways to grow, handle, and prepare vegetables are still needed.

The third major trend in the vegetable industry is the widespread adoption of new technology. Biological and genetic advances have allowed producers to incorpo-

rate desirable features in vegetable plants. Computer and communication advances now provide distant growers with up-to-date information concerning market prices, supply availability, and buyer needs. Widespread use of refrigerated trucks created opportunities to ship perishable items over long distances without significant losses in quality and spoilage. The improved efficiency offered by truck transport reduced grower and buyer reliance on trains, so that trucks now haul about 85 percent of all fresh-market vegetables in the United States. The convenience and ease of using trucks, however, did reduce an advantage that many smaller-scale, rural vegetable farmers had in providing vegetables to local grocers. Distant growers were able to provide fresh vegetables at competitive prices with local suppliers. Increased competition reduced market access for many rural vegetable growers and limited the profit potential offered by vegetable production. Improved postharvest handling capability resulted in larger-scale production, more centralized growing locations, and riskier marketing prospects for rural growers. Growers located in concentrated areas in California, Texas, and Florida were competitive suppliers to rural midwestern, southern, and east coast growers.

Although significant changes occurred in the U.S. vegetable industry, consumers remain dependent on rural American vegetable growers because rural areas offer relatively inexpensive, high-quality land on which to grow crops, an adequate labor supply to cultivate and harvest crops, and rural agribusinesses that can provide farm operating inputs. Hundreds of smaller industries compose the U.S. commercial vegetable industry, including producers of 30 or more different crops, packers, shippers, sales agents, brokers, transporters, intermediate handlers, and retailers. Despite this fragmentation, however, collectively vegetables remain an important and vital part of the domestic food system. Each year, consumers typically spend about 10 percent of their grocery bill to buy fresh, frozen, dehydrated, and canned vegetables, about twice as much as the average consumer spends on poultry or milk products. Each vegetable has its own unique supply and demand conditions, its own specialized production, marketing, and handling requirements, and its own specialized business deals.

Fresh Vegetables

Production and Consumption. Today, commercial fresh vegetable production is concentrated mostly in California, with growers and grower associations supplying 55 percent of all fresh-market vegetable output. Growers

Top Five Fresh-Use Vegetables Measured in Terms of Shipments and Per Capita Consumption in the United States, 1993

Vegetable	1993 Volume Shipped (tons)	U.S. Per Capita Consumption (pounds per person)
Potatoes (table stock)	8,400,000	51.9
Lettuce (iceberg)	2,606,000	24.6
Onions (dry)	1,837,000	16.2
Tomatoes	1,790,000	16.2
Watermelons	1,123,000	16.0

Source: Vegetables and Specialty Crops Yearbook: Situation and Outlook Report, USDA, ERS, TVS-263, July 1994.

in Florida (12 percent), Arizona (7 percent), and Texas (5 percent) also are important suppliers of fresh vegetables, primarily during the fall, winter, and spring. Growers and shippers located in Oregon, Washington, Michigan, and Georgia are seasonally important suppliers of fresh vegetables, but collectively they provide less than 15 percent of commercially grown vegetables. Approximately 30 fresh-market vegetable crops are grown commercially; the five most important vegetables measured by the amount shipped to market and per capita consumption are listed in the table.

Concerns. Fresh vegetables are expensive crops to grow and harvest. Although field corn or soybean production costs often range between $175 and $300 per acre, vegetable production costs typically range from $700 per acre for watermelons to nearly $10,000 per acre for fresh-market staked tomatoes. Major expense categories include specialized machinery and equipment costs, hybrid seed or plant costs, disease and pest control, and harvesting expenses. Most fresh-market vegetables must be harvested by hand, using hired workers or seasonal migrant laborers. Hand harvest expenses frequently account for 30 to 40 percent of total premarketing expenses. Because many vegetables are perishable and require extensive use of labor, most growers plant fewer than 50 acres of fresh-market vegetables (although plantings can exceed 10,000 acres in certain states). This decentralized production often results in insufficient volume for one grower to access mainstream marketing networks. Often, local marketing options such as direct selling to consumers through community farmers' markets or pick-your-own operations are the best marketing methods available to small growers. Alternatively, some rural growers identified windows of opportunity where market niches exist before or after vegetables are available from growers in competitive regions. The successful marketing of the crop is the greatest challenge to most rural vegetable growers.

Marketing. After harvest, activities shift from the field to central packing and shipping facilities. Although some crops such as lettuce are packed in the field, most vegetables are transported to nearby packing sheds. Commodities are washed, sorted, graded according to size, maturity, and quality features, and placed into standardized shipping containers. Most shed operators also arrange transportation to market and are identified as packer-shippers. Shippers usually remove excess field heat from vegetables prior to market shipment. Cooling vegetables maintains their field quality, preserves freshness, and extends shelf life. Facilities can be owned by an individual grower or a group of growers such as a cooperative or marketing association. Alternatively, services can be provided by a firm that performs these activities for a fee per unit. Often fee-based packers sell product for growers, providing payment to growers after the sales price is negotiated with a buyer and various service fees (for packing, boxing, and selling) are deducted. Most vegetables are packed, graded, and sold from facilities owned by growers or groups of growers.

After loading, the market destination is determined by the buyer or buyer's agent. If the buyer represents a chain store or wholesale company, the shipment will go to the company's central receiving warehouse. After arrival, vegetables are reinspected to ensure they meet company quality standards and then re-sorted into smaller units for store distribution. If the buyer's agent is a broker or distributor, vegetables are shipped to a central market facility located in an urban area. It is difficult for rural, small-volume growers to access the chain, wholesale, and urban market networks because buyers desire large quantities of product from relatively few sources. Use of few supply sources tends to reduce paperwork, procurement costs, and handling time. For most rural growers, viable marketing options are limited to niche sales to local supermarkets and direct marketing to consumers such as pick-your-own, roadside stand, and community farmers' markets. Successful niche and direct marketing strategies ensure profits to farmers.

Processed Vegetables

Situation. The average American consumes nearly 210 pounds of processed vegetables each year, with processed potatoes (85 pounds per person), processed tomatoes (73 pounds per person), and processed sweet corn (20 pounds per person) among the most popular items. Canned or frozen vegetables are preferred by many consumers because of their stable shelf life and their convenience. Despite rapid increases in the amount of frozen vegetables consumed each year by Americans, the average consumer still eats nearly five times more canned vegetables than frozen. Nearly two-thirds of all U.S. vegetable production for processing is raised in California. For some commodities, such as processing tomatoes, California growers supply nearly 90 percent of domestically grown product. Growers in other states are seasonally important suppliers of processing vegetables. The bulk of the processed green beans, sweet corn, sweet peas, and potatoes (for fries) are grown in Wisconsin, Michigan, Minnesota, Oregon, and Washington.

Procurement. Processing firms obtain vegetables in three principal ways. First, they can grow their own vegetables. Second, they can purchase vegetables on the open market; that is, at harvest time, they can make an offer to buy a grower's vegetables. And third, prior to planting, processors can contract with an individual grower to purchase all or a portion of the grower's crop for a pre-arranged price. Most processors elect to acquire vegetables under the terms of a bilateral contract between the processing company and the grower or growers' association. Contract terms typically include items such as planting dates, varieties planted, cultural practices, and a method for determining the price to be paid for the crop. Since processors require a consistent, steady flow of product to maintain efficient plant operations, contractual arrangements are advantageous. Vegetable processors perform many different tasks such as preservation (freezing broccoli), transforming raw product (making catsup or tomato paste or juice), and blending multi-ingredient food packages (canned soups or frozen dinners). In addition to processing vegetables for sale under their own brand names, many processors also freeze or can private label products such as store brands or cost-cutter brands. There are fewer than 900 vegetable processing plants operating today.

Contracts. Because the exact terms of a production contract are important to the success of both processors and growers, intense bargaining occurs. Contract terms are negotiated in two ways: (1) directly between an individual farmer and the processor or (2) between the processor and a bargaining association that represents growers. Examples of successful bargaining associations include a group of processing tomato growers in central California and a group of sweet corn growers in central Washington. Contracting provides growers with relative price certainty and a definite sales outlet. In return for these advantages, however, negotiated prices for growers are usually below fresh market prices. Since most vegeta-

bles cannot be used in raw form directly (for example, potatoes must be peeled and sliced for chips), processors often send raw product to preparation plants. Specific activities at prep facilities vary by location and the needs of the processor, but generally the raw product must be washed, topped, skinned, cut or diced, and bulk-packed so they can be preserved in a shelf-stable form. Soup stock items such as celery and carrots, potatoes for chips, grapes for juice, and apples for sauce are prepared in this way. After commodities are frozen and bulk-packed at the prep plant, the commodities are stored for transport later to the final processing or blending facility.

Future Issues. Consumer concerns about environmental preservation, food safety, and pesticide residues on vegetables will continue to change basic production and distribution practices. Integrated pest management, sustainable production methods, and environmentally friendlier packages will be used more extensively by vegetable growers and marketers. The internationalization of markets will reduce the significance of borders and will motivate growers to examine efficiency, cost, and resource use. Because Americans buy vegetables primarily on the basis of visual appearance, American farmers use some pesticides simply to maintain a vegetable's "eye appeal." Other factors, such as price, packaging, and health and safety concerns, are equally important to shoppers in European and South American countries. To the extent that pesticide use is motivated by the desire to maintain eye appeal, enhanced international sales opportunities may permit some American growers to be less concerned about consumer attitudes toward pesticide use and other environmental factors.

Enhanced internal sales opportunities benefit the American vegetable industry by increasing sales volume, allowing expansion into untapped markets, and reducing downward domestic pressures. However, export sales also mean increased time and effort in locating buyers and dealing with unfamiliar business practices, complex government regulations, foreign currency, and complex transportation logistics. Since foreign consumer preferences and uses for vegetables may differ from American ones, U.S. vegetable growers must acquire new information about foreign market sales requirements. Rural farmers will provide the expertise, land, and entrepreneurial spirit needed to expand and diversify the mix of vegetables available to consumers. Rural communities and businesses will provide other critical resources such as labor, operating inputs, and the financial capital to increase output. In the past, rural vegetable farmers discovered that the harder they worked, the more success they realized. In the future, accomplishments will similarly depend on hard work and the ability to work more intelligently.

—*Edmund A. Estes*

See also
Agriculture, Hydroponic; Biodiversity; Food Safety; Greenhouses; Horticulture; Marketing; Organic Farming; Temperate Fruit Industry.

References
Cook, Roberta L. *North American Free Trade Agreement: Fruit and Vegetable Issues,* vol. 4. Park Ridge, IL: American Farm Bureau Research Foundation Project, 1991.

Claytor, Diana L., ed. *Bibliography of Fruit, Vegetable, Tree Nut, and Ornamental Publications*. U.S. Department of Agriculture handout prepared for the 1994 Produce Marketing Association Convention and Exposition, San Antonio, TX, October 1994.

Estes, Edmund A., ed. *Look through the 90's: The U.S. Fruit and Vegetable Industry*. Proceedings of the S-222 Regional Research Committee Workshop on the U.S. Fruit and Vegetable Industry. Overland Park, KS: The Packer, Vance Publishing, June 1990.

Gibson, Eric. *Sell What You Sow: The Grower's Guide To Successful Produce Marketing*. Carmichael, CA: New World Publishing, 1994.

Lucier, Gary, ed. *Vegetables and Specialties: Situation and Outlook Report*. TVS-263 (July). Washington, DC: U.S. Department of Agriculture, Economic Research Service, 1994.

McLaughlin, Edward W., and D. J. Perosio. *Fresh Fruit and Vegetable Procurement Dynamics: The Role of the Supermarket Buyer*. Cornell Food Industry Management Program publication RB 94-1 (February). Ithaca, NY: Cornell University, Department of Agricultural, Resource, and Managerial Economics, 1994.

The Packer. *1994 Fresh Trends: A Profile of Fresh Produce Consumers*. Overland Park, KS: Vance Publishing, 1995.

Panyko, Frank. *Food Retailing Review: 1994 Edition*. Fair Lawn, NJ: Food Institute Information and Research Center, 1994.

Powers, Nicholas J., *Marketing Practices for Vegetables*. Agricultural Information Bulletin No. 702 (August). Washington, DC: U.S. Department of Agriculture, Economic Research Service, 1994.

Voluntarism

Unpaid activity typically performed outside the home. Voluntarism has long been recognized as a hallmark of rural American life. The approach taken in this entry will be to provide a brief overview of the functions and dimensions of voluntarism within the larger society, followed by discussions of the rural voluntary tradition and contemporary issues and trends.

Dimensions

In the 1830s, the French scholar Alexis de Tocqueville returned from the United States convinced of the importance of the democratic experiment under way there. At the core of this new nation, he believed, was a commitment to the principle of voluntary association, which functioned not only as an efficient and egalitarian mechanism to organize communal life but also as a bulwark against the potential excesses of government. He wrote: "Americans of all ages, all stations in life, and all types of dispositions are forever forming associations. There are not only commercial and industrial associations in which all take part, but others of a thousand different types—religious, moral, serious, futile, very general and very limited, immensely large and very minute. . . . In every case, at the head of any new undertaking, where in France you would find the government or in England some territorial magnate, in the United States you are sure to find an association" (Tocqueville 1969, 513).

Voluntary activity continues to attract Americans today. Recent estimates are that some 38 million citizens, or just over 20 percent of the adult population, perform some type of unpaid service beyond their own homes and families (Hodgkinson and Weitzman 1986). Most, although not all of this effort, occurs through organizations, with religious groups, schools, political or civic clubs, health care facilities, social welfare agencies, and sporting and recreational associations providing the primary outlets. All told, the value of this donated labor is estimated at more than $100 billion annually. Although such participation is widespread, it tends to occur disproportionately among certain segments of the population, notably among those with higher levels of income and educational attainment and among those between 35 and 54 years of age, and more among women and Whites than among men and members of minority groups. For present purposes, it should also be noted that small towns and rural areas often have been effective incubators of the voluntary spirit, and more precisely, that nonmetropolitan residents have higher levels of voluntary participation than do city-dwellers and suburbanites.

The Voluntary Tradition in Rural Life

From colonial times onward, farmers and their neighbors relied on one another to carry out the routine tasks of the agrarian or village calendar and to provide assistance in the wake of disaster. Barn raisings, state and county fairs, agricultural cooperatives, harvest festivals, and volunteer fire companies remain among the best known of these rural traditions.

During the nineteenth and early twentieth centuries, the rural ethos of self-help and mutual aid provided the foundation for dozens of formal organizations regional or national in scope. Among the most influential of these groups was the Grange. Founded in 1867, the Grange gathered and disseminated information about promising agricultural practices and provided a framework for representation of the political and economic interests of small farmers. Granges were among the first organizations to welcome the participation of women. Largely through the efforts of farm wives, the local Grange was often a focal point for social, cultural, and recreational activity.

Later organizations that served broadly similar functions included the Farmers' Alliance, the Farmers' Union, and the Farm Bureau. Farmers and other rural groups also provided support for both mainstream and radical political reformers, including the Populist movement, which dominated the north-central states at the turn of the twentieth century. More recently, farmworkers' unions were formed to advance the interests of agricultural employees, many of whom are itinerants close to the bottom rung of the national income ladder. Similarly, when falling crop prices and rising interest rates combined to throw small farm owners into financial crisis in the 1980s, protests and self-help efforts were mounted across the country, including the Farm Aid benefit concert.

Education is another institution with deep roots in the rural voluntary tradition. Prior to the establishment of the modern public school system in the mid-nineteenth century, families and churches were the principal sources of instruction for rural children and youth. In the more prosperous rural areas and townships, district schools and academies depended on a mixture of private and public support, and parents' donations to the local church often made it possible to employ a single man in the combined capacities of schoolmaster, church custodian, and gravedigger. The enactment by Congress of the Morrill Act of 1862 gave rise to the land-grant university, which in turn provided the impetus for several voluntary organizations for rural youth, notably the 4-H Club and the Future Farmers of America. In addition, land-grant universities pioneered the cooperative extension movement, which offered professional and voluntary outreach activities in agriculture and related fields. During the 1930s, the federally organized Civilian Conservation Corps (CCC) trained thousands of young men to protect the natural environment. Although it ended with the onset of World War II, the CCC inspired some of the youth and adult environmental organizations that are now well-established across rural America.

Contemporary Issues

Rural voluntarism today faces a variety of uncertainties, some of which stem from the ongoing decline of the rural population, and others of which are rooted in cultural and demographic transformations within the larger society. Most fundamentally, the migration from outlying regions to metropolitan areas poses the threat of nonsustainability for organizations that require a substantial recruitment base. In the case of service-oriented organizations, an additional difficulty is the enrollment of prospective clients. Compounding the rural organization's woes are the challenges that now confront voluntary associations everywhere. Several of these are consequences of the changing social roles of women, who have been the traditional mainstays of voluntarism in the United States. Some feminist theoreticians, for instance, argue that voluntarism exploits women by denying them payment for their work and stigmatizing their efforts as lacking in economic value. A related and more basic obstacle is the long-term erosion of workers' purchasing power, which forced many women to take paid employment who might otherwise prefer voluntary community service. Other demographic developments with crucial implications for voluntarism involve groups at opposite ends of the age spectrum. Older people represent the fastest-growing segment of the American population. Insofar as most no longer hold full-time jobs, they conceivably represent a fruitful source of recruits for voluntary organizations. On the other hand, the limited physical capacity and restricted financial resources that some senior citizens experience translates into a lower rate of volunteering and a greater reliance on the services provided by voluntary organizations. Young people ranging in age from 16 to 24 also have been comparatively reluctant to volunteer. One factor militating against their participation is the steady increase in the proportion of college and high school students now holding full- or part-time employment.

The challenge for rural voluntarism will be to make maximum use of dwindling human resources. Because they have been underrepresented thus far, the elderly and the young, together with the poor and the handicapped, are logical targets of any future recruitment drives. One set of obstacles that dependent populations encounter anywhere but especially in rural areas are physical isolation combined with a lack of adequate transportation facilities. Assuming, however, that technological advances continue to drive down the cost of telecommunications, it is possible to envision that voluntary activity increasingly will be conducted through computers, fax machines, and satellite and cable broadcasts rather than in person.

Another question that will impact the future of rural voluntarism involves the role of government. During the late 1980s and early 1990s, Congress passed a series of laws providing federal funding for community service activities. The most far-reaching of these was the National and Community Service Trust Act of 1993 (NCSTA). Although the NCSTA is broad in scope, its centerpiece is AmeriCorps, an initiative that offers volunteers health benefits, a stipend, and an education voucher worth $4,725 that can be used to cover the costs of higher education or job training. To qualify for funding, projects must address at least one of four areas of human need: education, health care, public safety, and environment. Several rural-based voluntary action programs, including those associated with the Cooperative State Research, Education, and Extension Service and 4-H, have been funded through AmeriCorps.

Rising concerns about budget deficits and the scope of government authority have cast a large shadow over AmeriCorps and other federally sponsored outreach efforts. Accordingly, the future of rural voluntarism ultimately will depend not on laws passed by governments but on the actions of ordinary citizens. Until fairly recently, the most common basic motive for voluntary participation was the well-developed sense of obligation that most women and men felt to their communities, the nation, humanity, or God. Although fulfillment of duty continues to be a driving force for many volunteers, recent studies conducted both among college students and adults indicate that it has been superseded by an ethos of self-fulfillment (Serow 1991; Wuthnow 1991). In other words, participating in various forms of voluntary activity permits some individuals to achieve personal goals that cannot be fulfilled through work, school, or family life. The desires to live a complete, well-rounded life and to make the most of one's talents are not necessarily incompatible with a sense of neighborly obligation. Rather, organizations, particularly those drawing on relatively sparse population bases, should be prepared to take this new, more psychologically informed motivation into account when recruiting, training, and evaluating their volunteers.

—*Robert C. Serow*

See also

Adolescents; Churches; Community; Community, Sense of; Cooperative State Research, Education, and Extension Service; Elders; Labor Force; Movements, Social; Quality of Life; Rural Women.

References

Coles, Robert. *The Call of Service: A Witness to Idealism.* Boston: Houghton Mifflin, 1993.

Daniels, Arlene Kaplan. *Invisible Careers: Women Civic Leaders from the Volunteer World.* Chicago: University of Chicago Press, 1988.

Ellis, Susan J., and Katherine H. Noyes. *By the People: A History of Americans as Volunteers.* San Francisco: Jossey-Bass, 1990.

Hodgkinson, Virginia Ann, and Murray S. Weitzman. *Dimensions of the Independent Sector: A Statistical Profile.* 2d ed. Washington, DC: Independent Sector, 1986.

Serow, R. "Students and Voluntarism: Looking into the Motives of Community Service Participants." *American Educational Research Journal* 28 (1991): 543–556.

Smith, David Horton, and Burt R. Baldwin. "Voluntary Associations and Volunteering in the United States." Pp. 277–305 in *Voluntary Action Research.* Edited by David Horton Smith. Lexington, MA: Lexington Books, 1974.

Tocqueville, Alexis de. *Democracy in America.* Paris: C. Gosselin, 1835–1840. Garden City, NY: Doubleday, 1969.

Wuthnow, Robert. *Acts of Compassion: Caring for Ourselves and Others.* Princeton, NJ: Princeton University Press, 1991.

Waste Management
See Municipal Solid Waste Management

Water Use
Occurs when water is employed as an input to activities or products that people enjoy, including withdrawals from ground- or surface water sources for use elsewhere or the enjoyment of water where it is found, such as in fishing or boating on a stream or lake. This entry provides an overview of rural water use and associated economic values. Several concerns related to rural water management are described and key policy questions are raised.

Water Use in Rural America
Water is important to the vitality of families, businesses, and communities in rural America. It is crucial to rural citizens' health and quality of life. Access to water is a key determinant of where rural people live, opportunities for employment, and enjoyment of recreation. Agriculture and many other rural businesses and industries depend on the availability of a high-quality water supply for their survival and growth.

Although water is clearly important to almost every aspect of rural life, less than ideal information is available concerning its use and importance in different regions of the country. Major, regularly tracked rural water uses include domestic uses that are self-supplied by wells or other sources, livestock watering, and irrigation of agricultural lands. The most recent effort to estimate water use in the United States (Solley, Pierce, and Perlman 1993) indicates that about 42.8 million people, or about 17 percent of the nation's population, had their own individual water supply systems and withdrew about 3.4 billion gallons of water per day. Almost all (96 percent) of this water was taken from groundwater. Second, water used by livestock includes that associated with traditional products (such as meat, poultry, eggs, and milk) and animal specialties, primarily fish farming. Such water use amounted to 4.5 billion gallons per day. About 60 percent of these withdrawals were from underground supplies. More than two-thirds of the water used for livestock purposes was used for consumptive purposes and not returned to water bodies. Third, an estimated 137 billion gallons of water per day were used for irrigation purposes. Irrigation water use includes all water artificially applied to farms and water use in horticultural facilities and golf courses, which might not be located in rural areas. Sixty-three percent of this water came from surface water sources. Irrigation use was highest in the West, followed by the lower Mississippi River and southern Gulf regions.

Rural Water Infrastructure
Water is important to rural residents for drinking and irrigation and for disposal of domestic waste. Based on the 1990 census, almost 50 percent of households in rural areas (places with 2,500 or fewer people) used individual drilled or dug wells to obtain water. Forty-six percent of rural households received their water supply from a public or community water system, many of which were small and lacked economies of size in water treatment and distribution.

Generally, rural residents consume more water on average than their urban counterparts. This may be due to differences in needs (for example, larger yards or gardens), lifestyles, or lower rural water costs. Many smaller public systems in rural areas do not meter customers' usage. Metering and price increases are effective ways to increase residential water conservation. Several water

Sprinklers providing irrigation for grapes. In many rural areas competition for scarce water resources pits farmers against users in urban areas.

demand studies have shown that rural customers are more sensitive to price changes than those in urban areas.

In addition to directly withdrawing water from ground or surface sources, rural residents and businesses use ambient water to dispose of or dilute their liquid wastes. In 1990, about three-quarters of rural households used a septic system or other individual method to treat sewage and other domestic wastewater. Collective or public sewer treatment of wastewater was used by the remaining rural households before discharge into waterways.

The Value of Water

The actual or expected use of water gives rise to its value. The values of water are often not reflected in its price, due to imperfect or nonexistent markets. Important rural water uses include domestic (either self-supplied or through a community/municipal system), agricultural (livestock and irrigation), industrial, and recreational uses. Analysis of residential demand for water indicates that the value of water varies greatly among regions within the United States. For example, Gibbons (1986) found that households were willing to pay as much as $5 more per year to avoid a 10 percent reduction in water use. For larger possible reductions, willingness to pay more was found to be much greater. More recently, researchers documented the value of quality attributes of water supplies. A 1991 study conducted in rural Massachusetts, New York, and Pennsylvania communities found that households were willing to pay between $42 and $81 per year to protect their groundwater supplies (J. Powell, as cited in National Research Council, forthcoming 1997).

Most water use for agricultural purposes occurred on irrigated farms in the western states. Researchers who assessed the extra value added to crop production from irrigation found values ranging from $0 to $100 per acre-foot, according to the geographic area and the crop produced. This wide range of values indicates that scarce water has different productivity levels in different agricultural activities. Institutional arrangements that allow shifting water to higher-valued uses do not exist or are not functioning well. Legal and institutional barriers often prevent water reallocation and protect inefficient water uses. As markets for water develop and water rights become more transferable, it is likely that higher-valued uses will bid away water from lower-valued ones. In some populated areas of the West, municipal users purchased the rights of agricultural users, leading to reduced irrigation.

The value of water for industrial use depends on the quantity and quality needs of the particular industry. Some industrial users in rural areas, such as power-generating plants, consume large water quantities and have the potential to infringe on other uses, such as recreation on rivers and streams. In addition, contamination of water affects industries that require high-quality supplies.

There are possible values of water that exist beyond current actual uses. People may have values for potential future use, or option value, of a water resource. In addition, some individuals are willing to pay to protect a water resource although they have no intention of using it themselves. This category of value is called existence value. Option and existence value for rural water resources may be held by both rural and urban residents.

Current Concerns and Issues

Drinking Water Availability and Safety. Many rural residents lack complete water facilities in their homes and reliable access to a safe water supply for domestic use. Information about rural water conditions is fragmented, so it is difficult to get an accurate overall picture of the problem. The U.S. Department of Agriculture (USDA) estimates that more than 500,000 rural households do not have complete indoor plumbing. Many such households are located in the poorest and most isolated areas of the United States, including Appalachia, the lower Mississippi Delta, along the U.S.-Mexican border, and in several American Indian reservations and Alaskan villages. Problems include the needs for technical and financial resources to develop water supplies and for cheaper, more innovative water treatment approaches. The USDA initiated a program in 1994 to coordinate and focus public and private efforts on this problem with the goal of providing all rural residents with a reliable supply of clean water by the end of the century.

Rural residents, whether they have their own wells or are connected to a public water system, generally encounter more water-quality problems than do urban water consumers. Private wells are generally shallower and often not as well-built as public wells, leading to contaminants from the surface entering the well. In addition to substances, such as iron and manganese, that occur naturally in groundwater, several important categories of human activities can contaminate well water. These include waste disposal, storage and handling of oil and other materials, mining and oil and gas production, and agricultural practices. The most common contaminants from human sources found in well water are bacteria and nitrates. Assessments of rural drinking-water wells found that as many as 40 percent of private individual wells are contaminated with coliform bacteria, often due to improperly located or constructed wells. Based on a 1990 nationwide survey of water wells, the U.S. Environmental Protection Agency (EPA) estimated that 4.2 percent of rural domestic wells had levels of commonly used agricultural chemicals that were detectable but generally did not exceed health standards for the 10 most commonly used pesticides. Nitrates were present in more than half of the well samples, but only in 2.5 percent of cases did the levels exceed health guidelines (EPA 1992).

Rural residents who receive water from public systems also face water-quality and -reliability problems. Community systems that serve rural residents are smaller, older, and in many cases, lack the funds and expertise needed to be properly run and maintained. In a national assessment of rural infrastructure needs, nearly one-third of rural systems were found to have unacceptable levels of coliform bacteria (Stinson et al. 1989). Based on its 1990 survey, the EPA estimated that 10.4 percent of rural community wells have detectable levels of pesticides and about 50 percent contain nitrates. Only a very small percentage of wells exceeded the health risk standard for these contaminants.

Affordability. A major issue facing rural residents is the rising cost of water supply and sewage disposal. The 1986 amendments to the federal Safe Drinking Water Act created an expanding list of national safety standards that must be monitored by local water suppliers. These and other requirements pushed the costs of supplying water upward across the nation. The financial costs of compliance with these rules is greatest for small rural systems that lack economies of size and often have management and financial constraints. For example, customers of small water systems can expect to pay $360 to $600 more per year to filter surface water, compared to only $72 more per year for customers of large systems. Through the end of this century, small water systems are expected to incur costs of more than $3 billion to comply with new regulations and an additional $20 billion to refurbish and expand infrastructure to deliver safe drinking water (U.S. Government Accounting Office 1994). Many small communities also will have difficulty upgrading wastewater collection and treatment facilities to meet federally established water-quality goals contained in the federal Clean Water Act.

State and local concerns about the high costs to implement some federal laws give rise to local complaints about unfunded mandates. Affordability concerns are central to the debate over reauthorization of several national environmental laws, and they also influence the decisions of the EPA, USDA, and other agencies. Efforts to revise the federal Safe Drinking Water Act have been made. Some of the proposals included increasing infrastructure financing through a state revolving loan fund; allowing greater flexibility to states with respect to monitoring and use of alternative treatment technologies; targeting financial and technical assistance to needy problems areas; promoting consolidation of small systems; and preventing new systems that are too small to be economically viable from being formed.

Protecting Water Resources. As the cost of mistakes in water-resource management has become evident, scientists and water resource managers have developed more proactive, comprehensive strategies to better manage the nation's water assets. Such approaches are aimed at both ground- and surface water protection.

Several attributes of groundwater have proven economically advantageous and have allowed people to live and work in rural areas. Groundwater can be obtained at the point of use, such as the farm or home. Unlike surface water, no expensive pipes are needed to transport groundwater from the source to the point of use. Also, groundwater has been pure enough, at least in the past, to be used for drinking and cooking purposes with little or no treatment. In many cases, these advantages of groundwater were recognized too late, often only after the resource became contaminated. Actions by individuals who are widely dispersed can degrade groundwater, although contamination events also may be concentrated at a specific locale. Prevention is a much wiser management approach since cleaning groundwater is very costly, and in some cases, impossible. Policies have emerged to change practices that degrade groundwater as awareness of the costs of mistakes in managing groundwater has increased. U.S. policy for groundwater quality protection at present is decentralized and largely voluntary in nature, although the EPA has encouraged states to develop comprehensive groundwater protection programs. It has encouraged public water suppliers in rural areas to delineate recharge areas for their wells and to manage land use within these areas through the EPA's promotion of wellhead protection programs. A critical challenge is the development of collaborative arrangements among local jurisdictions, which are needed to protect groundwater resources since water flow does not respect political boundaries.

Water resources protection efforts are moving in the direction of being more proactive and comprehensive. One important development is the attempt to manage resources on a watershed basis. The existence of many autonomous jurisdictions is a barrier to such a strategy. But efforts like the Chesapeake Bay Program indicate that progress can be made to address water resources problems at a more comprehensive, systemic level. A second way water management is becoming more comprehensive is the emergence of consideration of in-stream and extractive water uses in public decisions. In the past, water managers emphasized protection of uses that involved withdrawals of water from surface or underground sources, such as municipal or agricultural uses. In-stream water uses, such as recreational lake fishing or viewing wildlife that depend on wetlands habitats, recently are being recognized. These uses were overlooked because the products or services are often not marketed; therefore, prices are not readily available. Conflicts can occur between users who withdraw water and alter its condition or consume large quantities and those who enjoy in-stream water uses. Those who withdraw water have an advantage in these conflicts because of earlier usage and because such uses are easier to monetarily quantify. A significant challenge for public agencies and institutions is the development of management approaches to balance the interests of traditional, extractive users with those of people who enjoy the in-stream benefits of water resources.

Key Policy Questions

Several underlying questions reappear in rural environmental debates. What should be the resource management goal (in other words, How clean is clean?) What is the appropriate role of government? Who bears the cost and who enjoys the benefits, and who decides? The answer to each question will change as rural areas change or public values toward natural and environmental resources shift (Batie and Diebel 1990).

Defining the Management Goal. A question at the center of the rural water quantity and quality debate involves the desirable amount of water protection or conservation. In terms of water quality, how pure should water supplies be? In the case of water allocation issues, how much water should each user category be allowed when supplies become scarce? Since human health effects become a consideration in ground- and surface water management and water infrastructure decisions, discussions of management goals translate into the difficult area of defining acceptable risk.

Role of Government. What is the appropriate role of government in rural water resource management? In a society that places a premium on individual rights and relies on markets to allocate goods and services, this is a central question. The question is perhaps more to the point if restated in the following terms: Do individuals' and firms' actions in response to incentives within the existing market result in the best resource use for society? If not, then there might be a role for government in altering public policies and practices to make them more consistent with broader societal goals. The extent and degree of governmental action to protect water supplies must be balanced against a loss in individuals' rights to use land or water.

Who Bears the Cost? Few good things can be obtained without a price, and the protection and conservation of rural water resources are no exception. If rural water supplies are to be protected from farm chemical contamination, changes in agricultural practices will be required. It can be expected that such changes will have a cost, in most cases. Should farmers bear the costs of changes in practices to protect water supplies? If so, what will be the effect on rural businesses and neighbors, should the added costs cause the farm to go out of business?

Who Decides? Rural water-management policies will be influenced by the participants involved in the policy-making process. The level of government that takes action affects who influences decisions. It determines whether the advantages of basin or watershed management on a more comprehensive basis are realized. Federal officials previously took the lead in setting standards for drinking water provided by public water systems and guidelines for discharges into the nation's water systems. Other programs, such as the EPA's program to protect groundwater, put state and local authorities in the lead position. In the 1990s, the trend is toward giving more responsibility for decision making to the state and local leaders. In many cases, an attempt is made to balance the influence and interests of various publics and decision makers. Gradually, with changing circumstances and new information about impacts of government programs that affect water, the sharing of decision-making authority will be renegotiated. The choice of which agency will make decisions about program details is crucial. This decision affects how water resource are used and determines resultant benefits and burdens for various rural, and in many cases, urban interests.

—*Charles W. Abdalla*

See also
Agriculture, Hydroponic; Aquaculture; Conservation, Water; Environmental Regulations; Groundwater; Hydrology; Irrigation; Natural Resource Economics; Policy, Environmental; Recreational Activities; River Engineering; Wetlands.

References
Batie, Sandra S., and Penelope L. Diebel. "Key Policy Choices in Groundwater Quality Management." *Journal of Soil and Water Conservation* 45, no. 2 (1990): 194–197.

Committee on Valuing Ground Water, National Research Council. *Valuing Ground Water.* Washington, DC: National Academy Press, 1997.

Gibbons, Diana C. *The Economic Value of Water.* Washington, DC: Resources for the Future, 1986.

Solley, Wayne B., Robert R. Pierce, and Howard A. Perlman. *Estimated Use of Water in the United States in 1990.* Circular 1081. Alexandria, VA: U.S. Geological Survey, 1993.

Stinson, Thomas F., Patrick J. Sullivan, Barry Ryan, and Norman A. Reid. *Public Water Supply in Rural Communities: Results from the National Rural Communities Facilities Assessment Study.* Staff Report No. AGES 89-4. Washington, DC: U.S. Department of Agriculture, 1989.

U.S. Bureau of the Census, *1990 Census of Housing, Detailed Housing Characteristics.* Washington, DC: U.S. Department of Commerce, Bureau of the Census, 1993.

U.S. Environmental Protection Agency. *Another Look: National Survey of Pesticides in Drinking Water Wells (Phase 2 Report).* Report No. 570/9-91-020 (January). Washington, DC: U.S. Environmental Protection Agency, Office of Water, 1992.

U.S. Government Accounting Office. *Drinking Water: Stronger Efforts Essential for Small Communities to Comply with Standards.* Report No. US GAO/RCED-94-40. Washington, DC: U.S. Government Accounting Office, 1994.

Weather

A set of global atmospheric phenomena that in many cases are of great importance to the biota of the rural United States. This entry includes a general description of atmospheric science, weather prediction, climate change and air pollution, biometeorology and agricultural meteorology, microclimatology, and severe and unusual weather. Weather prediction, agricultural meteorology, and biometeorology are emphasized because these topics are especially relevant to rural areas.

Atmospheric Science

Numerous variables are used to quantify atmospheric science and describe the phenomena of weather, such as temperature, precipitation type and amount, humidity, radiation, and others described below. The study of fluid dynamics and mechanics is used to describe and predict atmospheric flow patterns that determine day-to-day weather. The interaction between atmospheric flow patterns, heating and cooling of the earth's surface by radiation, and evaporation and condensation of water is complex and still not fully understood. Supercomputers are needed to predict even simplified aspects of weather. Severe weather conditions such as tornadoes and hail can affect agricultural activities, as can less spectacular phenomena such as extremes in temperature and precipitation. Finally, human activities can result in alteration of the atmospheric composition, commonly thought of as air pollution, which can impact rural regions.

The major variables used in atmospheric science are temperature, humidity, wind velocity (speed and direction), pressure, precipitation amount and type, radiation, sky cover, evaporation, and composition of the atmosphere. In the United States, temperature is frequently measured in units of degrees Fahrenheit (°F), humidity in units of dew point temperature (°F) or percent (relative humidity), precipitation and evaporation in inches falling on or evaporating from the ground, and radiation in Watts falling on a meter squared. International scientific convention uses the metric units of degrees Celsius (°C) for temperature and dew point temperature, and millimeters or meters for precipitation and evaporation (Ahrens 1982).

Weather is composed of (1) the fluid dynamics of the atmosphere, coupled with (2) the thermodynamics of evaporation, condensation, and precipitation, and (3) heating and cooling by radiation. Evaporation uses some of the radiative (solar) energy gained by the earth's surface. This energy is later released to the atmosphere when condensation occurs. Pressure differences, which are associated with differential heating by radiation (such as land-ocean differences), drive the wind patterns of weather.

Weather Prediction and Recent Technological Advances

Complex calculus equations (partial differential equations), which may be solved by computers, may be used to describe fluid flow (Meyers and Paw U 1987). The numerical solution of equations describing the three main types of processes mentioned in the previous paragraph are used to predict weather. Predictions are made for a range of times, from a few hours to hundreds of years in the future. The accuracy of such predictions, when made for less than a week in the future, is excellent. It improved over the past quarter century, as computers and satellites played an increasing role in the gathering and analysis of data. However, because precipitation is highly variable for any particular location, errors may occur, even when regionally accurate forecasts are made.

Recent technological advances include Doppler radar, that is, the National Weather Service's NEXt general RADar (NEXRAD) program, which has the capability to accurately observe precipitation and the wind velocity field. This capability allows NEXRAD radars to provide unprecedentedly accurate tornado warnings.

Several general methods are available to nonatmospheric scientists for predicting weather based on the type of information commonly available from the media. The first prediction method is based on assuming the weather tomorrow will be the same as today's; this method is called persistence forecasting. A related method is to assume that weather systems, which generally move from west to east, will continue to move at the same speed as they have in the past; this method is called continuity. Both these methods suffer from inaccuracy caused by the increase or decrease in intensity of pressure systems, which are not accounted for. Another popular method in rural areas is to use historical climatological records to predict the weather of any particular day.

The numerical forecasts made up to a week in advance and disseminated by the National Weather Service are generally more accurate than climatology. Forecasts made for longer periods in the future, by numerical methods or by individuals, are generally no more accurate than climatological predictions. Mathematical chaos theory indicates that limits exist on the ability of computers to predict weather too far into the future.

Climate Change and Air Pollution

Atmospheric pollution occurs mainly because of combustion processes and other human activities. The main pollutant problems in rural areas arise from secondary pollutants, which are transformed from the primary pollutants directly emitted into the atmosphere. Rural areas may be affected by acidic precipitation (acid rain), high near-surface ozone (O_3) concentrations, and elevated

Biometeorological instrument tower in the Mariani Brothers walnut orchard, Winters, California, which was used in a 1989 University of California–Davis study measuring carbon dioxide, water vapor, and heat exchange between the orchard and the atmosphere.

particulate levels. Stratospheric ozone depletion by chorofluorocarbons also impacts biota by letting in more damaging ultraviolet radiation. The stratospheric ozone depletion is greatest in high latitudes.

Computer simulations of the world's climate show that if the concentration of certain gases, such as carbon dioxide (CO_2) and methane (CH_4) continue to increase, the average temperature of the air near the surface of the globe will increase by several degrees Celsius (IPCC 1990). Specific rural localities may have much greater temperature changes, or little change at all, because of the complexities of local climatology and the statistical variability of weather. In general, it is predicted that the U.S. grain belt will become warmer and Canadian rural locations will become a more ideal location for certain crops. Some plants could increase their growth because of increased CO_2 concentrations, but it should be noted that the competition between weed and agricultural species may be altered with increased CO_2 concentrations, and plants may also adapt to the concentration increases such that there is no net increase in plant growth (Rosenberg, Blad, and Verma 1980; McKenney, Easterling, and Rosenberg 1992).

The models used in these global climatic simulations are called general circulation models (GCMs). When used to simulate current climatology, these models have yielded reasonable distributions of temperature and pressure and less accurate distributions of precipitation. They are based on very large numerical grids, such that only a few grid points are used to describe even a state as large as California. Therefore, topological effects and localized climatology are not well described by such models.

Biometeorology and Agricultural Meteorology

The intimate interaction between biota (animals and plants) and the atmosphere is called biometeorology. For several millennia, people have recognized the importance of weather and climate in controlling the location and abundance of plants and animals available for food, building material, and tool sources (Tromp 1980). It is generally recognized that atmospheric composition and its mean temperature have been influenced by biotic evolution. Atmospheric oxygen (O_2) is mainly the result of photosynthesis, and the greatly reduced carbon dioxide concentration compared to Venus is to some extent caused by photosynthetic activity. The net result is a moderate temperature ideal for life on earth.

The importance of biometeorology led to an extensive mythology in virtually all cultures. Some myths are not truly myths because they contain elements of scientific observations in them. One example is the counting of cricket chirps to obtain temperature, which is relatively accurate when calibrated for a particular cricket species. Other myths have little scientific support, such as Groundhog Day's usefulness for predicting spring's arrival, and woolly caterpillars having more fur before a harsh winter. Although many animals, including insects and small mammals, prepare for winter in a variety of physiological ways, this preparation is dependent on seasonality rather than on some innate predictive ability.

Biometeorological indices that are used in rural regions include growing degree days (GDD), which represent the linear integration of mean temperature above some threshold, with respect to time measured in days. GDDs are used to analyze and predict the stage (phenophase) of crop and plant growth and yield. A form of GDD is used by entomologists to predict the timing of insect plant pests and their populations. A related measure, heating degree days, is used to determine energy usage in buildings. Other temperature-related indices include the first date of frost and thaw based on climatological records or long-term climatological predictions.

The hours of sunshine and the intensity of visible light are linked closely to photosynthetic rates, and therefore to plant growth. Areas where the growing season is relatively cloud-free, such as the Central Valley region of California, present opportunities for large crop yields. Solar radiation in the ultraviolet range can be harmful not only to some plants but also to plant diseases and pests.

The photoperiod of plants and of certain animals is the duration of daylight hours, or a change in the duration of daylight hours, that forewarns these organisms of changes in season. The accumulated night length (scotophase) is biochemically measured by the plant chemical phytochrome. A long-day plant is one that senses a day is longer than some threshold, and a short-day plant is one that senses a day is shorter than some threshold.

Some biometeorological indices are used to gauge the health of plants and animals. The potential evapotranspiration, defined as the water loss by evaporative processes from a short-grass plant canopy with no water stress, is used to measure evaporative demand in rural areas, and therefore, to aid in irrigation scheduling and water management. Combined temperature and humidity indices are used to quantify the thermal stress to humans and animals. Increased thermal stress to animals, for example, can lead to reduced weight gain, increased morbidity and mortality, and reduced milk production.

One biometeorological index used for humans is the windchill index (WCI) and its offshoot, the windchill equivalent temperature (WCET). The WCI is a dry heat (energy) loss index, indicating wind conditions under which metabolic rate cannot keep up with advective heat loss, resulting in frostbite and other detrimental cold damage to exposed human extremities. The WCET represents the temperature to which a thermostat in an almost wind-free room would have to be set in order for the heat loss from a human extremity to match the heat loss occurring for a human exposed to a wind at the ambient air temperature. The WCI and WCET do not account for radiational effects or phase changes effects such as evaporative cooling of the skin (Steadman 1971).

Microclimatology

The microclimatology of an immediate locality is frequently unique. Wind speed, air temperature, humidity, and radiation may follow a similar diurnal pattern each day of a season in an immediate locality, or may change because of changes in plant cover and atmospheric variables.

Microclimate modification may be accomplished to improve plant productivity. Irrigation is one of the oldest methods of modification, providing water where precipitation is insufficient. Another well-known method is that of windbreaks, which shield crops from adverse wind speeds, and reduce eolian soil loss. Mulches are used to cover soil and crops to suppress weed formation and water loss. Frost protection methods use large fans, combustion heaters (smudge pots), sprinkler systems, and soil flooding and compaction (Rosenberg et al. 1980). The drift of aerial applications of agricultural chemicals represents modification of the local atmospheric chemistry.

Severe and Unusual Weather

Severe weather and unusual events seriously affect agricultural operations in the rural United States. High winds associated with severe storms, hurricanes, hail, and tornadoes may damage crops, blow trees over, and damage rural buildings. Unseasonal frost damages crops and trees. Excess precipitation floods some regions, making the soil too wet for agricultural operations and damaging plant organs at critical phenophases, such as the flower-bud stage. Too much snow can break the branches of orchard or other trees. Excessive snow may also damage telephone lines and prevent driving on unplowed roads. Too little precipitation may cause serious damage also, when droughts are lengthy enough to cause plants to be stressed or even die. Lightning is the leading cause of weather-related deaths in the United States and also causes forest fires.

—*Kyaw Tha Paw U*

See also
Climatic Adapability of Plants; Drought.
References
Ahrens, C. Donald. *Meteorology Today*. 4th ed. San Francisco: West Publishing Company, 1991.
Intergovernmental Panel on Climate Change (IPCC). *Scientific Assessment of Climate Change: The Policymakers' Summary of the Report of Working Group I to the Intergovernmental Panel on Climate Change*. Geneva, Switzerland: World Meteorological Organization/United Nations Environmental Programme, 1990.
Jones, Hamlyn G. *Plants and Microclimate: A Quantitative Approach to Environmental Plant Physiology*. 2d ed. New York: Cambridge University Press, 1992.
McKenney, Mary S., William E. Easterling, and Norman J. Rosenberg. "Simulation of Crop Productivity and Responses to Climate Change in the Year 2030: The Role of Future Technolo-
gies, Adjustments and Adaptations." *Agricultural and Forest Meteorology* 59, nos. 1–2 (15 April 1992): 103–127.
Meyers, Tilden P., and K. T. Paw U. "Modeling the Plant Canopy Micrometeorology with Higher-order Closure Principles." *Agricultural and Forest Meteorology* 41 (1987): 143–163.
Oke, Tim R. *Boundary Layer Climates*. New York: Wiley, 1978.
Rosenberg, Norman J., Blaine L. Blad, and Shashi B. Verma. *Microclimate: The Biological Environment*. 2d ed. New York: Wiley, 1983.
Steadman, Richard G. "Indices of Windchill of Clothed Persons." *Journal of Applied Meteorology* 10 (1971): 674–683.
Tromp, Solco W. *Biometeorology: The Impact of the Weather and Climate on Humans and Their Environment (Animals and Plants)*. London, UK: Heyden Publishing, 1980.

Wetlands

The wide variety of areas from the shallow edge of open waters to areas that are often dry but are subject to seasonal flooding such as river bottoms and sloughs. After a history of developing these areas for commercial uses, policymakers have begun to understand the importance of wetlands to the earth's ecological balance. Many federal and state programs have been established to promote the protection of wetlands and to reverse years of damage. Although there is little controversy over the goal of protecting wetlands and the functions they provide, a renewed public debate emerged in the late 1980s over the question of how much wetland acreage is needed, how to balance economic and ecological priorities, and how best to restore previously damaged areas.

Overview

Wetlands are a significant component of our rural landscape. They played an important role in forming the geography of our settlement patterns by serving as a source of food, water, and rich land that could often be easily brought under cultivation. It has been estimated that there were originally 220 million acres of wetlands in the 48 contiguous states and another 200 million acres in Alaska. As the country developed, approximately 53 percent of the original wetlands in the 48 states was converted to other uses such as farms, home sites, roads, and ports. It was estimated that during the 1960s and 1970s, more than 11 million acres of wetlands—an area twice the size of New Jersey—were drained and developed for various purposes (Thompson 1983).

Wetlands have been viewed as wastelands that serve no beneficial purpose and as critical natural resources deserving protection. The understanding of the importance of wetlands has increased, but there is still controversy over how they should be managed.

Wetlands form a transition between sites that are permanently wet and those that are generally dry, and although they may have characteristics of both, they cannot be classified exclusively as either aquatic or terrestrial. There is no consensus on a particular, unified set of characteristics defining wetlands. This is because wetlands encompass such a wide variation in their physical and hydrologic characteristics and in the types of plant and animal communities they support (Finlayson and Moser 1991). In general, they include the following six types:

Marshes are among the most productive ecosystems in the world. There are three major groups: freshwater marshes, tidal salt marshes, and tidal freshwater marshes. Collectively these account for over 90 percent of the wetlands within the contiguous 48 states. Dominant plants often include reeds, sedges, and rushes. They are used by a variety of waterfowl, muskrats, beavers, turtles, fish, and fur-bearing animals.

Swamps differ from marshes in that they have saturated soils or are flooded for most of the growing season. They are dominated by woody plants such as the red maple in the northeastern states and the bald cypress and tupelo in the South.

Peatlands occur most often in shallow lake basins, along sluggish streams, and on flat uplands. They support a spongy ground cover of mosses, horsetails, sedge, and rushes. Their shape, thickness, and dominant plant material varies widely, depending in part on the hydrology and the latitude.

Floodplains are the low areas bordering rivers and streams, which are subject to periodic flooding, particularly during the spring.

Estuaries and lagoons are areas at the mouths of rivers that form a boundary between fresh and marine environments. The deltas that form from sediment-rich rivers provide necessary environments for spawning and feeding of many marine species of fish as well as habitat for shorebirds and waterfowl.

Lakes are wetlands that characterize the shallow margins of many large and deeper lakes, or the entire area of shallow bodies of open water. The types of wetlands and their productivity vary according to the water depth and shoreland gradient.

Functions

Wetlands of virtually all varieties have been subjected to alterations to make them more adaptable for grazing or cultivation, or by filling for roads, railways, buildings, and other developments. It is possible to fly over coastal salt marshes and see the herringbone patterns of trenches that were dug in the 1800s in order to drain the soil, making it easier to harvest the grasses and other marsh plants for animal feed. Although wetlands were not ideal for development, they were relatively flat and easy to fill. For roughly the past 100 years, federal and state policies encouraged the alteration and development of wetlands to provide services more highly valued by society at that time. Agricultural use is estimated to make up over 80 percent of the conversions (Weller 1985).

Over time the important ecological and social functions that wetlands provide in their natural state have been better understood. The loss of coastal wetlands to development and pollution has been linked to population declines in important fisheries that use them for spawning and nursery areas. The extensive damage caused by the flooding of the Mississippi River in 1993 was attributed in part to the reduction in wetlands that traditionally served to retain and slowly release floodwaters. In addition to providing wildlife and fishery habitat and flood protection, wetlands serve to stabilize shorelands and reduce soil erosion. They retain and absorb nutrients from surface runoff and thereby protect lake and river water quality. They often serve as a hydrologic link between surface waters and groundwater, at times as a source of recharge for depleted groundwater or as a discharge of groundwater to surface waters to maintain critical rates of stream flow. They may have forestry or agricultural potential in their natural state. Examples of commercial products from wetlands include cranberries and wild rice. Many people enjoy wetlands for their educational and recreational value.

Although wetlands vary significantly in size and character, each provides at least one or more of the above functions. The further conversion of wetlands entails a loss of their natural productive attributes. The type and magnitude of the impact will vary from site to site. Policies to protect wetlands have been difficult to establish and administer because of conflicting priorities. Most of the functions performed by wetlands are recognized as valuable to society and the environment, but they are functions that are not easily expressed in terms of market value. On the other hand, a wetland site that is converted to another use—roads, homes, or cultivated cropland—will produce products that are more readily valued in a market economy. History demonstrates that Americans give greater weight to market-based alternatives. Only recently have significant efforts been made, largely because of an increase in public understanding of the ecological importance of wetlands and the increasing political will to act, to develop policies and regulations to preserve or protect wetlands.

Regulation

Congress began to make the protection of wetlands a priority with the 1972 Water Pollution Control Act and the 1977 Clean Water Act. Section 404 of the Clean Water Act gave the U.S. Army Corps of Engineers the authority to regulate activities that affect wetlands through a permit process. Some have argued that because agriculture and forestry are exempted from this process, there is a significant gap in the protection provided by the Clean Water Act. Others have asserted that the Corps has overstepped the bounds of its authority under the act (Wakefield 1982).

Many worried that wetlands would continue to disappear, because agriculture was exempted from the Section 404 provisions and other federal programs provided incentives for conversion of wetlands to agricultural uses. This led to the Swampbuster (the term commonly used for the wetland provisions) provisions of the 1985 Farm Bill, or the Food Security Act. The Swampbuster provisions sought to remove any incentives for the agricultural conversion of wetlands by denying farm program benefits to producers who filled, drained, or otherwise converted wetlands for cropland use (McCullough 1985; Heimlich and Langer 1986). It made farmers ineligible for price-support payments, crop insurance, disaster payments, and insured or guaranteed loans for any year in which the crop was produced on lands that had been converted from wetlands. It did not prevent further conversions, but it removed significant incentives that previously existed.

More recently, President Bush expressed a policy of "no net loss." This goal was based on the view that the point was reached where it was important to make every effort to protect all remaining wetlands. In those cases where it was determined to be essential to convert an area of wetland, the policy allowed the activity only if it was offset with the construction or rehabilitation of another site into a stable and functioning wetland comparable to the site that was being lost. This technique is commonly referred to as mitigation. The degree to which such efforts are technically successful or adequately replace the functions of the natural site remains very controversial.

Many but not all states have established regulatory controls over wetlands that go beyond the protection afforded by federal programs. A recent survey of state programs indicates that most states have enacted additional regulatory controls. Some states rely on an additional permit review process or a combination of other requirements, such as mitigation or the permanent dedication of another wetland site by the developer to its natural state through acquisition or easements. Much progress has been made, but there is more to be done to ensure that wetland regulations are effective and targeted at the appropriate level of protection.

Information about local wetlands can be obtained from the water resources institute at each state's land-grant university. Further information about regulations of wetlands may be obtained from the state's department of natural resources or environmental protection.

—Gregory K. White

This entry was supported by the Maine Agricultural and Forest Experiment Station and is publication MAFES #2131.

See also

Agricultural Programs; Conservation, Water; Environmental Protection; Environmental Regulations; Groundwater; Hydrology; Natural Resource Economics; Policy, Environmental; River Engineering; Wildlife.

References

Heimlich, Ralph E., and Linda L. Langer. *Swampbusting: Wetland Conversion and Farm Programs.* Agricultural Economics Report No. 51. Washington DC: U.S. Department of Agriculture, Natural Resource Economics Division, Economic Research Service, 1986.

Klinko, Deborah, and J. Bergstrom. "The Value and Regulation of Wetlands in the United States: A Review." Unpublished manuscript. Athens: University of Georgia, Department of Agricultural Economics.

Larson, J. S. "North America." Pp. 57–84 in *Wetlands.* Edited by Max Finlayson and Michael Moser. Oxford, UK: International Waterfowl and Wetlands Research Bureau, Facts on File, 1991.

Maltby, E. "Wetlands and Their Values." Pp. 8–26 in *Wetlands.* Edited by Max Finlayson and Michael Moser. Oxford, UK: International Waterfowl and Wetlands Research Bureau, Facts on File, 1991.

McCullough, Rose, and Daniel Weiss. "An Environmental Look at the 1985 Farm Bill." *Journal of Soil and Water Conservation* 40, no. 3 (May–June 1985): 267–270.

Thompson, Roger. "America's Disappearing Wetlands." *Congressional Quarterly Editorial Reports* 11 (1983): 615–632.

Wakefield, Penney. "Reducing the Federal Role in Wetlands Protection." *Environment* 24 (1982): 6–13, 30–33.

Weller, Milton W. "Reports on Reports." A review of "Wetlands of the United States: Current Status and Recent Trends" and "Wetlands: Their Use and Regulation." *Environment* 27 (1985): 25–27.

Wheat Industry

All individuals and companies involved in the production, transportation, marketing, and sale of wheat to domestic and international consumers. This entry provides an overview of the wheat industry, one of the most important sectors of U.S. agriculture. Individual sections discuss wheat production, marketing, selected government programs, supply and demand, economic impacts of wheat on rural economies, and recent industry trends.

Introduction

Wheat ranks with rice as one of the world's most important food crops. Adapted to a variety of growing conditions, wheat has excellent storage qualities and is consumed worldwide in a variety of forms (such as bread and baked goods, cereals, noodles, and pasta). The United States is a major wheat-producing country, with production exceeded only by China, the former Soviet Union, and the European Union.

In recent years, wheat has ranked second among U.S. field crops in terms of planted acreage (behind corn) and third in terms of gross farm receipts (behind corn and soybeans). Wheat is the primary food grain for U.S. consumers. Domestic demand has grown steadily for milled and baked products, fueling the expansion of diversified processing industries. Wheat is also a major export crop. About half of U.S. wheat production is exported (a larger fraction than for corn or soybeans). As a result, the wheat sector is influenced strongly by external market forces, with U.S. prices moving in response to shifts in global supply and demand.

U.S. wheat production is concentrated in the Great Plains, although significant quantities are also grown in other regions. Wheat has five separate classes, each with unique characteristics and suitability for different end products. Hard red winter (HRW) wheat accounts for about 40 percent of total production and is grown primarily in the Central and Southern Plains (Kansas, Oklahoma, and Texas). HRW is principally used to make bread flour. Hard red spring (HRS) wheat accounts for about 25 percent of production and is grown primarily in the Northern Plains (North Dakota, Montana, Minnesota, and South Dakota). HRS wheat is valued for high protein levels, which make it suitable for specialty breads and blending with lower-protein flours. Soft red winter (SRW) wheat (15 to 20 percent of total production) is grown in Missouri, Illinois, and Ohio and is used for cakes, cookies, and crackers. White wheat (10 to 15 percent) is grown in Washington, Oregon, and Idaho and is used for noodle products, crackers, and cereals. Durum wheat (3 to 5 percent) is grown primarily in North Dakota and is used for pasta.

Production

Production practices vary throughout the United States, due to differences in seasonal cropping patterns, growing conditions, and farming systems (for example, organic, no-till, and conventional). Agronomic conditions are responsible for much of the regional variation. In the Northern Plains, where winters are harsh, HRS and durum wheat are planted in the spring and harvested in the fall of the same year. In the Southern Plains, where winters are generally mild, winter wheat is planted in the fall and harvested midway through the following summer. In response to dry conditions found in the western Dakotas and western Kansas, farmland is often summer-fallowed, a practice of idling portions of land each year to conserve top moisture and nutrients. Wheat production practices in other parts of the United States are influenced by general farming systems, such as double cropping and rotational considerations for row crops.

Farms in the Great Plains raise primarily small grains and tend to be larger than farms raising only row crops. In Kansas and North Dakota, top wheat-producing states, wheat accounts for half of all planted acres. In other regions of the country, particularly in the Corn Belt and the southeastern states, wheat is secondary to row crops, often raised to add flexibility in crop rotations and to provide enterprise diversification.

U.S. wheat production is highly mechanized. Preplant tillage operations include the use of disks, harrows, and field cultivators to prepare the soil and apply fertilizer and preemergence herbicides. Wheat is usually planted using a grain drill. Some farming systems apply postemergence herbicides to control weeds, and some require occasional treatments to combat insects and plant diseases. Wheat is typically harvested using a combine, either alone in a process called straight combining (a combine cuts and threshes in one operation) or in conjunction with a swather. Swathing cuts and places unthreshed wheat into windrows to be combined later. At harvest, wheat normally is hauled directly to storage facilities either on the farm or at local elevators. Depending upon farming systems, postharvest tillage will involve the use of disks, chisel plows, or moldboard plows.

Yields vary according to agronomic factors such as soil type, temperature, amount and timing of precipitation, plant pests, wheat variety limitations and nutrient

Combining wheat.

availability, and management-related factors such as seeding rate, time of planting, fertilizer use, weed control, and harvest efficiency. Wheat yields in the Southern Plains average 28 bushels per acre, while yields in the Northern Plains average 32 bushels per acre. Yields in the Corn Belt and southeastern states average about 40 bushels per acre, with the highest yields, 52 bushels per acre, occurring in the Pacific Northwest.

Revenues from wheat production generally consist of cash crop sales and (for participating producers) payments from government programs. Most wheat is sold as cash deliveries to local elevators at harvest or stored and delivered in the months following harvest. Prices received by producers vary depending upon crop quality, global supply and demand, and seasonal factors. Gross revenues, not including government program payments, range from under $100 per acre in the Southern Plains to $200 per acre in the Pacific Northwest. Gross revenues from wheat production in the United States average about $115 per acre. Variable cash expenses average about 40 to 45 percent of gross revenue in the Northern Plains and up to 75 percent of gross revenue in the Southeast. Generally, fertilizer and fuel/lubrication expenses comprise the greatest portion of variable costs, followed by machinery repairs, pesticides, and seed expenses. Fixed cash expenses average about 20 percent of gross revenue, with remaining returns applied toward noncash expenses.

Marketing

The marketing chain for wheat sometimes is described as the physical flow of grain from producers to processors. Seen in this way, the chain begins with the delivery of wheat (by truck) from farms to country elevators. The country elevators assemble grain for shipment (by truck or rail) to larger facilities, called subterminal or terminal elevators. From these elevators, the wheat can be shipped (by truck, rail, or barge) to domestic millers or to port elevators, where it is loaded onto ocean vessels for export.

Alternatively, the chain can be identified with changes in ownership as wheat moves through the marketing system. The distinction is important because changes in physical location need not imply a purchase or sale. Some wheat-handling firms are highly integrated, owning elevators both at points of origin (wheat-producing regions) and points of destination (terminal markets or ports). Further, wheat may be bought or sold (and resold) well in advance of actual shipment. In this light, the market chain comprises a sequence of transactions linking producers to handlers and merchandisers, domestic millers, and foreign buyers.

Wheat prices are determined in individual transactions between buyers and sellers. This may occur through private negotiations or through public and semipublic trading mechanisms. Prices received by producers are generally those bid by local elevators. These reflect quality factors (such as protein content, test weight, and dockage), costs of shipping to alternative markets, and daily changes in market conditions. In general, elevators and merchandisers seek to add value through blending and conditioning activities, grain storage, and efficiencies in shipping and handling.

Commodity futures play an essential role in the wheat marketing system. Futures are highly standardized contracts calling for the delivery of fixed quantities (5,000 bushels per contact) at specified times and locations. Wheat futures contracts are traded on the Chicago Board of Trade (CBT), the Kansas City Board of Trade (KCBT), and the Minneapolis Grain Exchange (MGE). Prices at these three exchanges reflect locational differences and other differences in delivery specifications. MGE wheat futures pertain to HRS wheat, and KCBT futures to HRW wheat. CBT wheat futures are more widely traded, with less restrictive delivery specifications (admitting several classes of wheat). Hence, the Chicago futures price provides the best barometer of national market conditions.

Futures provide standard reference prices for buyers and sellers. Grain traders commonly express their bids or offers in terms of basis values (cents above or below a specified futures price). Futures also provide a mechanism for reducing price risk via hedging. Producers, trading firms, and processors can use futures contracts to establish a price in advance of an intended sale or purchase. This eliminates much of the risk associated with holding grain stocks, for example, or pending sale commitments. Relatively few wheat producers trade futures directly. However, elevators often act as intermediaries for producers. By using futures (or options based on futures) to offset their commitments, elevators can offer forward contracts to producers or other contracts that offer more pricing discretion.

Government Payments and Programs

The U.S. Department of Agriculture (USDA) has played a significant role in the wheat sector for several decades. Policies have changed intermittently along with farm legislation, which has been subject to renewal or revision roughly at five-year intervals.

Through the early 1990s, the government has sought to support incomes of wheat farmers through a target-price mechanism. The target price for wheat (fixed at $4 per bushel since 1990) is an administrative device used to calculate payments to producers who participate in the program. Producers collect deficiency payments, equal to the difference between the target price and the national average wheat price, multiplied by qualifying production. Participation is voluntary but often has required producers to idle part of their base acreage. Acreage restrictions under the program have been used by the USDA to influence domestic supplies, wheat prices, and (hence) the costs borne by taxpayers.

Participation rates have been high for the wheat program, averaging 86 percent of all U.S. wheat producers between 1991 and 1994. The average yearly cost of the deficiency payments program was $1.67 billion, equivalent to 22 percent of the market value of wheat sold during that period. Apart from the budgetary cost, critics of the program have pointed to a skewed distribution of benefits. Most wheat deficiency payments are collected by larger-scale producers because payments are tied to base acres, which vary enormously across farms.

A number of other government programs have provided benefits, directly or indirectly, to wheat producers. One of the most significant since 1985 has been the Export Enhancement Program (EEP), which provided export subsidies for U.S. wheat, flour, and other selected commodities in targeted foreign markets. EEP is designed to combat the subsidies of competing exporters (such as the European Union) and to stimulate U.S. exports. In recent years, most U.S. wheat exports have been officially subsidized. The EEP program has raised U.S. domestic prices relative to subsidized export markets.

Factors Affecting Wheat Supply and Demand

Market fundamentals are essential to understanding wheat prices and how they change from year to year. U.S. supplies of wheat consist of current production, beginning stocks (wheat in storage), and imports (usually negligible). Production levels reflect producers' planting decisions, which in turn depend on farm program parameters, expected returns from alternative crops, and anticipated

A train loaded with wheat at a grain elevator.

market conditions at the time of harvest. Weather conditions during the growing season can cause upward or downward revisions in expected production, with immediate impacts on futures and cash prices.

Demand for wheat can be divided into domestic use, exports, and ending stocks. Domestic use includes demand for food (use by millers and processors) and demand for livestock feed. Food use usually accounts for 75 to 80 percent of domestic use, and it shows little variation in its long-term upward trend. Feed use can vary markedly from year to year, depending on crop conditions and prices of alternative feed crops. Feed use is a residual market for wheat, becoming important only with excess production or substandard crop quality. Exports accounted for half of the total use between 1991 and 1994. Shifts in export demand due to changes in market conditions or to the availability of U.S. subsidies can have pronounced price effects, particularly when stocks are low relative to total use.

Beyond these aggregate factors, wheat prices reflect other, more detailed market relationships. Buyers prefer different classes and grades of wheat for different end products. Prices are quoted for individual classes and grades, and most buyers apply premiums or discounts for specific quality factors, such as protein. The availability of different classes and qualities changes over time, due to growing conditions and transitory demand pressures. Quality-related price differences are a critical feature of grain merchandising, and to varying degrees, they are reflected in the net revenues of most wheat producers.

Economic Impacts of Wheat Production

Although wheat is produced throughout the United States, production is concentrated in a few regions. This concentration has important economic implications. In several of the Great Plains states, wheat production comprises a substantial share of the economic base. Economic base activities bring new dollars into a region and generate personal income, retail sales, gross business volume, employment, and tax revenue. Because there are few viable alternative crops in the Northern and Southern Plains, the dependence of these regions on wheat is accentuated.

Several studies have identified the economic contribution of wheat production to rural, agriculture-based economies (for example, Bangsund and Leistritz 1995). Economic impact estimates have included industry-wide expenditures and revenues associated with wheat activities, and estimates of the spending and respending of industry outlays and returns. Results from recent studies of the wheat sector in North Dakota and Minnesota are indicative: Total annual impacts from wheat production in these two states were estimated at $5.8 billion. Crop sales alone accounted for $1.9 billion annually. Other impacts in North Dakota and Minnesota included the indirect support of 65,000 full-time jobs and the generation of nearly $200 million in economy-wide tax revenue annually. Unquestionably, the wheat industry plays a similar role in other major wheat-producing states, such as Kansas, Oklahoma, and Washington.

Trends in the Industry

Significant changes are under way in the industry. Among these are changes or pressures for change in production practices, which have traditionally relied on intensive chemical applications. As environmental and food-safety concerns play a larger role in regulations and policy guidelines, wheat producers are being pressured to consider alternative farming methods.

In recent years, firm concentration in the wheat handling, merchandising, and processing sectors has increased. Throughout the wheat-growing regions, grain handling is dominated by a small number of private firms and cooperatives. Similar trends are evident in the wheat export business, where a handful of integrated companies with elevators at ports and interior locations account for most U.S. export shipments. As a result of this consolidation and because of improved efficiency in grain transportation and logistics, there are fewer links in the wheat marketing chain (in other words, fewer transactions between buyers and sellers). A parallel phenomenon has been the decline of centralized markets where cash grain may be traded (for example, in Minneapolis).

These trends pose a long-term challenge to market participants, including wheat producers, who rely on publicly disseminated price information.

Government programs for producers of wheat and other commodities are increasingly viewed as an unnecessary burden on taxpayers. In successive rounds of congressional farm legislation, changes have been implemented to reduce the outlays for crop subsidies and restore a market orientation in the decision making of wheat producers. Future reductions in farm subsidies appear likely and could have significant effects on wheat producers. The exit of smaller, less efficient producers from the industry might be accelerated, and wheat production could become more concentrated. The move toward larger farms has long been evident in wheat, as in other sectors of U.S. agriculture.

Changes in the global marketplace will also affect the U.S. wheat sector. As a result of treaty obligations under the General Agreement on Tariffs and Trade, the United States and other wheat-exporting countries have begun to reduce their export subsidies. Another important development has been the movement toward market reform in many importing countries, such as Russia and Mexico, where grain trade formerly was controlled by state monopolies. In this new trading environment, U.S. wheat exports will depend more heavily on competitive market forces.

—*D. Demcey Johnson and Dean A. Bangsund*

See also

Agricultural Prices; Agricultural Programs; Crop Surplus; Dryland Farming; Futures Markets; Grain Elevators; Grain Farming; Marketing; Markets; Mechanization; Policy, Agricultural.

References

Bangsund, Dean A., and F. Larry Leistritz. *Economic Contribution of the Wheat Industry to the North Dakota Economy*. Agricultural Economics Report No. 332. Fargo: North Dakota State University, Department of Agricultural Economics, 1995.

Bangsund, Dean A., Randall S. Sell, and F. Larry Leistritz. *Economic Contribution of the Wheat Industry to the Minnesota Economy*. Agricultural Economics Report No. 312. Fargo: North Dakota State University, Department of Agricultural Economics, 1994.

Cramer, Gail L., and Eric J. Wailes, eds. *Grain Marketing*. 2d ed. Boulder, CO: Westview Press, 1993.

Hickman, John, Jeff Jacobsen, and Drew Lyon. *Best Management Practices for Wheat: A Guide to Profitable and Environmentally Sound Production*. Washington, DC: Cooperative Extension Service and National Association of Wheat Growers Foundation, 1994.

Hoffman, Linwood A., Sara Schwartz, and Grace V. Chomo. *Wheat: Background for 1995 Farm Legislation*. Agricultural Economics Report No. 712. Washington, DC: U.S. Department of Agriculture, Economic Research Service, 1995.

U.S. Department of Agriculture. *Economic Indicators of the Farm Sector: Costs of Production, 1993-Major Field Crops and Livestock and Dairy*. Report No. ECIFS 13-3. Washington, DC: U.S. Department of Agriculture, Economic Research Service, 1995.

———. *The Physical Distribution System for Grain*. Agricultural Information Bulletin No. 457. Washington, DC: U.S. Department of Agriculture, Office of Transportation, 1990.

———. *Wheat Situation and Outlook Report*. Washington, DC: U.S. Department of Agriculture, Economic Research Service, various issues.

Wilderness

Land retaining its primeval character and influence, without permanent human habitation, which is protected and managed so as to preserve its natural conditions. This discussion of wilderness is divided in two sections. First, the history of the concept of wilderness as it emerged in Europe and the United States is examined. The second section addresses the current status and amount of land devoted to wilderness in the United States.

The Wilderness Idea in Europe and the United States

American ideas about wilderness are like a surprising, mutant grain, new but deeply rooted. They combine and modify several Western traditions. For most of their recorded history, European people have not regarded wilderness highly. Traditional Judeo-Christian thought portrayed wilderness as a dangerous place, home to savage and even demonic beasts, and no place for moral people. Many early Christians believed Cain had been banished from Eden to the wilderness, and wilderness still was home to Cain's infernal descendants. The Bible explicitly contrasts alien wilderness with the blessed and domesticated Garden of Eden ("The land is the Garden of Eden before them, and behind them a desolate wilderness" [Joel 2:3]). If a seventeenth-century European or American had trekked into the wilderness for enlightenment or pleasure, most contemporaries would have responded with puzzlement and some derision.

The past 250 years witnessed a radical transformation in the values Europeans attached to wilderness. This transformation, which is still going on, is one of the most dramatic turnabouts in the history of ideas. For Americans in the twenty-first century, it is also one of the most important.

The modern idea of wilderness has evolved through three phases. The first phase occurred in the late eighteenth and early nineteenth centuries, when nature came to be viewed as a teacher. In England, this phase was called romanticism. Writers like Edmund Burke, William Wordsworth, and Lord Byron portrayed wild nature as a source of sublime awe, delight, and inspiration. In France, it was known as primitivism. Jean-Jacques Rousseau wrote of the noble savage, innocent of the corruption of court and city. In America, intellectuals absorbed both doctrines, romanticism and primitivism, and added a third from the Far East; seafaring Yankees brought home new ideas about the sanctity of nature. The "Boston Brahmins" stirred all these doctrines together to produce the heady brew of transcendentalism. For transcendentalists, God dwelt in nature, and the natural world was a reliable guide to enlightenment. Two great American writers, Ralph Waldo Emerson and Henry David Thoreau, took up the transcendental torch, with revolutionary results. They turned the theology of two millennia upside down. With Yankee brashness in his 1851 essay "Walking," Thoreau announced, "In wildness is the preservation of the World" (p. 275). Nature was not the problem, but the solution. Thanks largely to Thoreau and Emerson, transcendentalism has influenced ideas of wilderness ever since.

In the first phase—romantic, primitivist, and transcendental—Anglo-Americans prized wilderness as a source of moral elevation. In the second phase, they saw more businesslike values. Scientists and other thinkers began to describe the practical benefits of wilderness, such as watershed protection. They argued that people had a responsibility to protect those benefits. George Perkins Marsh led this group with his brilliant, influential book, *Man and Nature* (1864). Marsh admonished that humans had a responsibility to care for nature, not simply consume it. He developed the important idea that civilization had fallen because of the waste of resources. As an example of practices that had brought down great civilizations in the past, he pointed to indiscriminate logging. With the Adirondacks in mind, he argued that Americans should preserve large areas of undeveloped land. Economics joined aesthetics as a category of wilderness values. The modern wilderness movement had begun its erratic course.

Marsh's ideas were timely and influential. Other Americans agreed that the conservation of natural resources was good policy, and the United States began to protect special places. Usually, the reasons given were a mixture of aesthetic, spiritual, recreational, and practical. For all those reasons, in 1872, President Grant set aside 2 million acres in northwestern Wyoming as Yellowstone, America's first national park. Largely for watershed pro-

tection, the state of New York established the 715,000-acre Adirondack Forest Preserve in 1885.

Still, the marriage of economics and aesthetics was not completely congenial. The transcendental gene was strong, and advocates of preservation for its own sake demanded to be heard. By far the most forceful was the naturalist John Muir. The first official act of preserving wilderness for its own sake was the creation of Yosemite National Park in 1890, thanks to John Muir's writing and organizing. Yet the struggle was just beginning.

In the third phase, the United States developed a unique, extensive system of protected wilderness areas and a complex set of laws and institutions surrounding them. In 1891, Congress gave the president authority to create forest reserves, which were later renamed national forests. President Harrison immediately created 15 reserves, comprising more than 13 million acres. Yet the act left the purpose of the reserves unclear and opened the door for disagreement between those who advocated restricted timber production and those who wanted complete preservation. That issue was raised almost immediately and is still a matter of intense debate.

Wilderness preservation came into its own as a twin to the idea of conservation. Gifford Pinchot defined conservation as the wise use of natural resources for the long-term benefit of society. With Pinchot, conservation became a key element of the Progressive movement's credo. Well into the twentieth century, this utilitarian view of humankind's relationship to the rest of the natural world dominated virtually all official policy with regard to U.S. public lands. Meanwhile, however, John Muir and a few like-minded visionaries slowly began to develop the protocols of another way of thinking. Building on transcendentalism, they held that wild country had a value transcending any human use and deserved preservation for its own sake. This was not a sentiment that the average public-lands bureaucrat found appealing. People like Muir, the utilitarians said, were naive romantics.

Ironically, the two men most responsible for beginning the long crusade that ultimately made wilderness preservation public policy were both veterans of the U.S. Forest Service, the definitive federal land-management bureaucracy: Aldo Leopold and Robert Marshall. Both men had discovered in wild country values that deserved the respect, love, and protection of human beings. Leopold persuaded his superiors to set aside more than half a million acres of wild lands in New Mexico as the first official federal wilderness area in 1924. Marshall helped to formulate forest service regulations that established a system of protected primitive areas in the country's national forests—the beginning of today's National Wilderness Preservation System. In 1930, Marshall called for "an organization of spirited people who will fight for the freedom of the wilderness" (p. 149). In 1935, Leopold and Marshall joined with a handful of other preservationists to found the Wilderness Society.

Two more veterans of the federal bureaucracy, Olaus Mure and Howard Zhaniser, led the Wilderness Society as it joined with other organizations such as the Sierra Club and the Izaak Walton League to engineer the wilderness idea's most important triumph. In 1964, after one of the longest and most sophisticated environmental campaigns ever launched, Congress passed the Wilderness Act. The act established the National Wilderness Preservation System and thereby validated an idea once dismissed as impossibly romantic.

Current Status and Extent of Wilderness in the United States

Today, more than 103 million acres of federal land in 44 states are protected as wilderness under the 1964 Wilderness Act. Only Connecticut, Rhode Island, Delaware, Maryland, Kansas, and Iowa, states that have little federal land, do not currently have designated wilderness areas within their boundaries. Well over half of these protected lands (57 million acres) are located in Alaska, while only 4 million acres are located in states east of the Mississippi River. National parks account for 43 million acres of designated wilderness, followed by 34 million acres of national forests, 21 million acres of national wildlife refuges, and just 5 million acres of Bureau of Land Management lands, the largest manager of federal lands in the U.S. government. There is no inventory or reliable estimate of the area of federal land that could still be eligible for wilderness designation under the terms of the 1964 act.

The Wilderness Act defines wilderness as land where "man is a visitor who does not remain." Going further, the act states, "an area of wilderness is further defined to mean in this Act an area of undeveloped Federal land retaining its primeval character and influence, without permanent human habitation, which is protected and managed so as to preserve its natural conditions." These definitions have given rise to the view held by many that a federal wilderness designation removes lands from human use and thus renders them of little economic value; and therefore, that the wilderness designation can be significantly detrimental to local communities. The facts are quite different, however. Wilderness

Designated Wilderness by State (in acres)

State	National Forests	Wildlife Refuges	National Parks	Bureau of Land Management	Total
AK	5,788,637	18,676,311	32,979,397	0	57,444,345
AL	33,231	0	0	0	33,231
AR	119,011	0	10,529	0	129,540
AZ	1,345,102	1,343,646	443,700	1,406,180	4,538,628
CA	4,362,622	9,031	5,975,068	3,699,855	14,046,576
CO	2,599,912	2,560	52,730	0	2,655,202
FL	74,499	51,271	1,296,500	0	1,422,270
GA	113,859	362,107	8,840	0	484,806
HI	0	0	142,370	0	142,370
ID	3,958,193	0	43,243	720	4,002,156
IL	30,316	0	0	0	30,316
IN	12,953	0	0	0	12,953
KY	17,437	0	0	0	17,437
LA	17,025	0	0	0	17,025
MA	0	2,420	0	0	2,420
ME	12,000	7,392	0	0	19,392
MI	93,485	25,309	131,880	0	250,674
MN	1,086,954	6,180	0	0	1,093,134
MO	63,627	7,730	0	0	71,357
MS	6,046	0	3,202	0	9,248
MT	3,371,669	64,535	0	6,000	3,442,204
NE	7,794	4,635	0	0	12,429
NC	103,854	0	0	0	103,854
ND	0	9,732	29,920	0	39,652
NH	102,932	0	0	0	102,932
NV	786,227	0	0	6,458	792,685
NJ	0	10,341	0	0	10,341
NM	1,391,737	39,908	56,392	130,340	1,618,377
NY	0	0	1,363	0	1,363
OH	0	77	0	0	77
OK	15,968	8,570	0	0	24,538
OR	2,089,257	495	0	16,543	2,106,295
PA	8,938	0	0	0	8,938
SC	16,847	29,000	15,000	0	60,847
SD	9,826	0	64,250	0	74,076
TN	66,345	0	0	0	66,345
TX	71,048	0	46,850	0	117,898
UT	777,815	0	0	22,600	800,415
VT	59,598	0	0	0	59,598
VA	87,658	0	79,579	0	167,237
WA	2,587,488	838	1,728,138	7,140	4,323,604
WI	44,447	29	0	0	44,476
WV	80,852	0	0	0	80,852
WY	3,081,047	0	0	0	3,081,047
U.S. total	34,496,256	20,662,117	43,108,951	5,295,836	103,563,160

Source: The Wilderness Society.

in America provides substantial social and economic benefits. These values are reflected by industries associated with wilderness recreation, such as outfitters and guides. In addition, wilderness is increasingly used for personal growth, therapy, education, and leadership development by businesses, educational organizations, and a variety of nonprofit groups. Some have estimated that commercial uses of wilderness generate over $100 million in revenues annually to entrepreneurs and even more to local communities as those dollars are respent in local businesses.

Wilderness lands, though protected from commercial logging, are open to commercial grazing and mining interests. Many grazing allotments exist in designated wilderness areas, and hardrock mining claims remain in force, although few mines are active—primarily due to low prices. Prospecting for new claims was ended with legislation passed in 1983.

Other economic values of wilderness include its contribution to property values of private land adjacent to designated wilderness areas. Studies in the northern Rockies, for example, have shown that population growth among counties along the front range of the Rocky Mountains is fastest in those with a greater concentration of designated wilderness. That growth contributes to the value of local property and fuels the local economy. Yet given its economic, social, and biological importance, wilderness management continues to receive little attention. The U.S. Forest Service, for example, spends just 1 percent of its total land management budget on wilderness management, even though 20 percent of the lands that it is charged with managing is wilderness. The situation is the same or worse at other federal agencies charged with wilderness management.

Today a broad consensus in the United States supports wilderness preservation. People's motives for preservation differ, but four values are common. First, Americans support protecting rare species and communities of species. The most common cause of extinction is the loss of habitat, and preserving wild land is essential for habitat protection. Second, Americans recognize the need to protect useful natural systems and processes. For example, the most efficient way to provide clean water is often the protection of natural watersheds. Third, wilderness provides unique opportunities for recreation and spiritual renewal. Fourth, many people accept an ethical responsibility to what Leopold called the "land community." He argued that the idea of community should be expanded to include other species on whom humans depend, and ethical responsibilities to the larger community should be recognized.

—*G. Jon Roush and Jeffrey T. Olson*

See also

Biodiversity; Camps; Desert Landscapes; Environmental Protection; Forests; Mountains; Natural Resource Economics; Parks; Policy, Environmental; Values of Residents; Wetlands; Wildlife.

References

Fox, Stephen. *John Muir and His Legacy.* Boston: Little, Brown, 1981.

Leopold, Aldo. *A Sand County Almanac and Sketches Here and There.* New York: Oxford University Press, 1949.

Marsh, George P. *Man and Nature; or Physical Geography as Modified by Human Action.* New York: Charles Scribner, 1864.

Marshall, Robert. "The Problem of Wilderness." *Scientific Monthly* (1930): 142–148.

Nash, Roderick. *Wilderness and the American Mind.* 2d ed. New Haven, CT: Yale University Press, 1973.

Thoreau, Henry David. "Walking." In *The Writings of Henry David Thoreau*, Volume 9. Boston: Houghton Mifflin, 1893.

Wildlife

Living creatures not directly under human control. The term usually excludes fish, being associated with larger animals such as birds, mammals, and reptiles. Wildlife was historically, and remains today, a source of rural-urban conflict. It is especially important to rural areas, as it provides recreational opportunities, economic benefits and costs, and symbolic meaning.

Historical Background

Rural people through the mid-nineteenth century, and in some isolated locations even today, depend on some species of wildlife for subsistence. Until recently, predator species were vilified and targeted for extermination because they represented potential economic loss through damage to livestock, competition for subsistence species, and potential harm to humans. Many of these species (such as the wolf, grizzly bear, and mountain lion) had been extirpated from many areas of the continental United States by the early twentieth century.

As a societal response to scarcity, urban sportsmen led the fight for scientific, state-centered wildlife management (Tober 1981). These interests demanded controlled hunting seasons, limits on hunting techniques deemed unsporting, prohibitions on the commercial sale of game, and hunting licenses. Whereas some of these regulations proved useful for the maintenance of wildlife populations, they marginalized the experience and interests of the poorer, more subsistence-oriented rural people. Although spectacularly successful for maintaining and increasing the populations of species valued by sport hunters (such as white-tailed deer and Canada goose), this approach often did not prevent the extirpation of large predator species perceived to be in conflict with game species.

Wildlife Recreation

Wildlife recreation can be broadly classified as consumptive (the goal of which is to pursue or capture an animal) and nonconsumptive (to observe, photograph, or feed). The great majority of both types of recreation takes place in rural areas.

Nonmetropolitan residents were more than twice as likely as the general population to have hunted in 1991 (15 percent and 7.4 percent, respectively). In contrast, only 4 percent of those living in a large metropolitan statistical area (MSA) of 1 million or more hunted. Because so many Americans live in cities, however, 54 percent of all hunters come from metropolitan areas. Regions of low population density, even if classified as urban, also have higher levels of hunting participation. For example, the Rocky Mountain and west-central regions show hunting participation rates of 11 percent and 13 percent, respectively. In contrast, only 4 percent of the population hunts in the heavily populated New England region.

Higher hunting rates in rural areas are fostered by greater opportunity, a more dominant hunting culture, and active parental socialization (the process by which knowledge, attitudes, values, skills, and motives are learned and internalized by youth). Males who grow up in a rural area, whose fathers hunted, are much more likely than other demographic groups to begin and continue hunting. Some researchers suggest that two types of hunters exist based on contrasting socialization mechanisms linked to urban versus rural areas. First, traditional hunters are socialized in rural areas by family members at a young age. This group obtains a broad base of satisfactions from their participation, is provided extensive social support, and is committed to continuing participation. In contrast, the late adopter is socialized by friends at an older age and is more likely to have an urban residence. This type of hunter has less social support, is less committed to hunting, and is more likely to cease participating.

The U.S. Fish and Wildlife Service (USFWS) classifies primary nonresidential, nonconsumptive recreation as travel one mile or more from the residence with the specific purpose of observing, feeding, or photographing wildlife. Sixteen percent of the total U.S. population participated in this activity in 1991, making it twice as common as hunting. Rural people were only slightly more likely to participate. Nineteen percent of those living outside an MSA participated, compared with 13 percent of people living in a large MSA. Nonconsumptive recreation does not depend strongly on the rural socialization variables associated with hunting; participants are more likely than hunters to be self-initiated at older ages.

Wildlife in Rural Economies

Wildlife can have an important positive or negative effect on rural people. Economic value is not distributed evenly among wildlife species. Those that are important to recreation or subsistence provide much-needed redistribution of monies to rural areas. Hunting expenditures related to consumptive use of animals (hunting) totaled $12.3 billion in 1991. Of this amount, $3.4 billion (28 percent) was spent on trip-related expenses, including food and lodging ($1.8 billion) and transportation ($1.3 billion). Many of these revenues go directly to rural areas. To the degree that they are spent by urban dwellers in rural areas, they serve to redistribute income from urban to rural areas.

Leasing and fee hunting are an increasingly important part of wildlife-related income. Although wildlife in the United States is owned by the state, the private landowner can regulate access and charge a fee if he or she wishes. One in every 15 hunters hunted on leased land in 1990; the average price for leases was $660 per year. Great regional variation exists in these figures: Leasing was most prevalent in the southeast and south-central regions of the United States. Over 50 percent of leasing took place in only six states: Texas, Georgia, Louisiana, Virginia, Alabama, and Mississippi. The prevalence of leasing and fee hunting is influenced by the relationship between buyers, sellers, and the amount and quality of game available. For example, if the rural landscape is characterized by small, dispersed parcels, or if regulations severely limit the amount of game that can be harvested, an individual landowner cannot command a high price.

Nonconsumptive wildlife-oriented recreation (such as bird-watching trips) accounted for even greater levels of expenditures than consumptive activities. Primary nonresidential recreationists spent $18.1 billion on trip-related expenses in 1991. Of these, food and lodging alone accounted for $4.4 billion (59 percent) and transportation accounted for an additional $2.6 billion (35 percent). Wildlife-oriented tourism is increasing, and wildlife is a significant factor in people's decisions to visit certain rural areas. The potential for capturing revenue from this land use depends on the appeal and presence of the species, compatibility with other income-generating activities, and local sociocultural traditions.

Wildlife on rural lands is an economic double-edged sword. Wildlife can have negative economic effects through various types of property damage, or can even represent a physical hazard through direct contact with humans. There are estimates that more than 1 million deer-auto collisions occur every year (725,000 are reported), with an average estimated auto repair bill of $1,500 per reported incident. The cumulative economic impact of reported incidents alone is $1.1 billion. In addition, Conover et al. (1995) have estimated that roughly 29,000 human injuries (over 200 fatalities) occur per year from these incidents. The USDA National Agriculture Statistics Service's national survey estimated total wildlife-related losses to agricultural production at $533 million in 1989, including $160 million to livestock and poultry and $274 million to field crops.

A variety of mechanisms exist to compensate farmers for wildlife damage to crops. However, filing claims and obtaining compensation may be complicated and time-consuming, and the resultant compensation might prove inadequate to cover damages. The extent or cause of damage might be disputed. For example, although there are pools of federal and state money to compensate ranchers for livestock killed by wolves, such claims might be disputed (was the animal killed by a wolf, or was the wolf merely feeding on an animal that had died of other causes?). These problems have policy implications; surveys in many states show that those who are actively involved in farming or ranching are strongly opposed to wolf repopulation.

Theoretically, the financial losses that rural people, particularly agriculturists, suffer from wildlife damage are offset by the revenues that wildlife provide to rural areas. In reality, with the exception of income from leasing and fee hunting, wildlife-related revenues do not accrue to the same people who suffer losses but instead go to local business owners. A study in the Horicon Marsh area of Wisconsin (Heinrich and Craven 1992) estimated annual damages to crops from Canada geese at approximately $1,000 per farmer, representing a total net loss of income of $1.6 million. The Horicon Marsh is a major destination for wildlife viewing, generating over 10 percent of local income to restaurants, motels, taverns, and gas stations. However, virtually none of this income is captured by the farmers who sustain the costs of maintaining a large goose flock. Mitigating wildlife damage and redistributing revenues to those who suffer economic damage is important, if high populations of wildlife are to be maintained in rural areas.

Symbolic Importance of Wildlife

There are strong differences in attitudes toward wildlife between urban and rural residents. Traditional rural residents are more likely than other groups to see animals as resources that can provide material, utilitarian benefits to humans, or to see humans as superior to animals, with animal-human interactions providing opportunities for the exercise of human skill. These attitudes are manifested most strongly in traditional rural occupations; farmers are especially strong in these orientations. In contrast, urban residents are of two primary types. First, those scoring high on moral or humanistic scales express concern with the welfare and suffering of individual animals, based either on affection or on general philosophical principles. Another type of urban orientation is neutral or negativistic; people of this orientation score high on scales that measure irrelevance, avoidance, or intolerance of wildlife.

Rural places sometimes become identified with the presence of wildlife species characteristic to the area, particularly if these species are valued for their rarity, beauty, or importance to humans. This identification may be particularly strong during hunting seasons. Small towns and rural areas are dominated by hunting-based totemic display, such as blaze orange and camouflage clothing in storefronts, "Welcome, Hunters" signs on many places of business, "big buck" contests, high school classes and places of employment devoid of males on opening day, and special "Hunters' Breakfasts."

Wildlife-based identities are not limited to places. Individuals can develop personal identity-based interactions with wildlife. Interactions with wildlife, especially hunting, are mechanisms to transmit culture, skills,

Wildlife—in this case the ruffed grouse—is the identifying feature of this small Wisconsin town.

beliefs, and attitudes representative of a particular group or area. Contact with wildlife extends beyond the actual participants. Other people might also be socialization agents, might participate in some aspects of the hunt, have positive beliefs about hunting, and perceive that they receive benefits from hunting. This extension of the hunting culture is especially common in rural areas.

It would be a mistake to think of rurality as stable and the relationships between rural people and wildlife as unchanging. There is widespread agreement that the traditional rural orientation is declining. Urbanization has resulted in a steady decline of people being socialized in rural areas. This phenomenon is reflected in a continuous decline in hunter participation. USFWS numbers show that hunter participation is dwindling; 11.2 percent of the population hunted in 1960, 8.4 percent in 1985 (a 25-percent decline over 25 years). The pace of this decline is accelerating; the percentage of people hunting dropped to 7.4 percent in 1991 (a 12 percent decline in just 6 years). An especially sharp drop occurred in the recruitment of new, younger hunters. The two most important reasons for the decline in hunter numbers are linked to rural change: the percentage of people socialized in rural communities and current rural residence.

Urbanization is not the only factor salient to rural change. Remaining rural areas themselves are changing through immigration and linkages (information- and transportation-based) with urban areas. It is important to have a realistic idea of what "rural" means: Even a "rural renaissance" is not likely to bring about a return to traditional rural attitudes and socialization mechanisms concerning wildlife.

—Thomas A. Heberlein and Richard C. Stedman

See also
Animal Rights/Welfare; Recreational Activities.

References
Conover, Michael R., William C. Pitt, Kimberly K. Kessler, Tami J. DuBow, Wendy A. Sanborn. "Review of Human Injuries, Illnesses, and Economic Losses Caused by Wildlife in the United States." *Wildlife Society Bulletin* 23, no. 3 (1995): 407–414.

Decker, Daniel J., and Gary R. Goff. *Valuing Wildlife: Economic and Social Perspectives.* Boulder, CO: Westview Press, 1987.

Heberlein, Thomas A. "Stalking the Predator: A Profile of the American Hunter." *Environment* 29 (September 1987): 6–12, 30–33.

Kellert, Steven R. *The Value of Life: Biological Diversity and Human Society.* Washington, DC: Island Press/Shearwater Books, 1996.

Marks, Stuart A. *Southern Hunting in Black and White.* Princeton, NJ: Princeton University Press, 1991.

Miller, John. *Deer Camp: Last Light in the Northeast Kingdom.*

Cambridge, MA: MIT Press; and Middlebury: Vermont Folklife Center, 1992.

Tober, James A. *Who Owns Wildlife?: The Political Economy of Conservation in Nineteenth-Century America.* Westport, CT: Greenwood Press, 1981.

U.S. Department of the Interior, Fish and Wildlife Service, and U.S. Department of Commerce. *1991 National Survey of Fishing, Hunting, and Wildlife-Associated Recreation.* Washington DC: U.S. Government Printing Office, 1993.

Wine Industry

All individuals and companies involved in the production, transportation, marketing, and sale of wine grapes, wine, and wine-related products to domestic and international consumers. The United States has a large, well-established wine industry, which especially since the 1960s has emerged as a world-class producer of high-quality wine. The first section of this entry is a general overview of American wine production and the types of wine produced. Next, the U.S. system of winery regulation is contrasted with that of France. This is followed by a brief discussion of the history of the American wine industry. The final two sections focus on the structure of the American wine industry and a discussion of the problems facing the industry.

Wine Production

As of 1990, the United States ranked sixth in the world in wine, producing only about a quarter of that put out by the world's largest wine producer—France. Although at least some wine from grapes is commercially produced in almost all 50 states, the industry is dominated by California, which accounts for about 90 percent of U.S. production. The U.S. wine and brandy production industries employ about 14,000 people; and many more thousands are involved in distribution and sales. An unknown and constantly fluctuating number of migrant farmworkers tend vineyards, mostly in California.

Prior to the twentieth century, wine was made in the eastern United States from the fruit of the native American *Vitis labrusca* vine (the muscadine in the South and the Niagara and Concord varieties in the Northeast). *Labrusca* grapes are now used mostly for jellies, juice, and other nonwine grape products. American wine is now predominantly made in the European style from *Vitis vinifera* (Eurasian) grape varieties. American wineries produce all of the commonly accepted wine types, including red and white table wines, sparkling wines, and fortified wines. They also produce large quantities of flavored

A Concord grape vineyard in upstate New York. In the nineteenth century such native grape varieties were the source of all U.S. wine production; a century later most American wine is produced from Eurasian varieties.

wines, such as vermouth and proprietary brands such as Boone's Farm, and wine coolers—although wine coolers increasingly use a malt-beverage base. Significant amounts of grape wine brandy are produced in California. Rootstock grafting, hybridization, and more careful site selection has enabled the expansion of *vinifera* wine production to the northeastern and southern states, where it was formerly barred by climate. *Vinifera* grape wine is also produced in Canada and Mexico.

The most common dry red table wine varieties produced in the United States include Cabernet Sauvignon, Zinfandel, Pinot Noir, and Grenache; white varieties include Chardonnay, Chenin Blanc, and Colombard. There are three basic price/quality market segments for American wine. The premium segment consists of wines priced at $12 and higher for a 750-milliliter (ml) bottle. Most of these wines are produced on a small scale by small wineries. However, several larger wineries also have premium product lines. At the other end of the spectrum are the low-priced, mass-produced wines, about $6 or less per 750 ml. Many of these wines are sold in large jugs,

although most wineries have been moving away from this bottling practice. A third, mid-priced market segment has emerged in the 1980s and 1990s. These wines are produced on a relatively large scale and are marketed to consumers who are interested in quality wines at a reasonable price.

Regulation

American wine regulation is predicated on a varietal-entrepreneurial model that focuses on taxation, sanitation standards, minimum and maximum alcohol levels, marketing and distribution ordinances, and so on. This contrasts with the French chateau-appellation model, in which wineries must not only conform to basic regulations, but must make their wine according to the stylistic dictates of their appellation (wine district). How an American winemaker chooses to adjust the character of his or her wine is of no concern to regulators. American wine is mostly labeled by grape variety, again contrasting with France, in which a given wine carries the name of the chateau that produced it. Most individual American wineries produce at least two or three different types of wine, usually some combination of red and white table wines, or table wines and sparkling wines. Wine is not a true niche product; wineries compete with one another based on their image and the popular acceptance of their product. From the perspective of the consumer, there are only marginal subjective differences between wines in the same price classification.

Bureau of Alcohol, Tobacco, and Firearms (BATF) regulations stipulate that at least 95 percent of a wine labeled with a vintage year must be made from grapes harvested that year, that at least 90 percent of the wine be of the variety named on the label, and that at least 75 percent be produced from grapes grown within the appellation on the label. The BATF also allows the marketing of semigeneric wines using "borrowed" names such as champagne, chianti, sherry, or burgundy. Nonvarietal blends with proprietary names such as Hearty Burgundy or Thunderbird also are permitted. Some premium wineries are beginning to follow the French chateaux by giving their varietal blends proprietary names; a well-known example is Opus One, a Cabernet Sauvignon–Merlot blend produced by a Robert Mondavi–Baron Philippe de Rothschild joint venture. BATF regulations also provide for a system of established American viticultural areas (AVAs) created through a petition process. As of 1986, there were 84 AVAs in the United States, 49 of them in California. In an effort to heighten the exclusivity of their product, some California winemakers recently advocated the creation of subappellations within already established AVAs.

History

Vinifera grape varieties were introduced to California by Spanish missionaries in the seventeenth century. The so-called Mission variety, which made an inferior wine, dominated viniculture in the state until the mid-nineteenth century. Prior to the Gold Rush, commercial winemaking was centered in Los Angeles. A virulent vine disease, urban development, and the economic attraction of the prospering San Francisco area all helped move the industry's center of gravity to the more climatically hospitable northern coastal area. In 1870, California became the leading wine-producing state, surpassing Missouri and Ohio. Industry growth was spectacular; from 1880 to 1910, vineyard area expanded 600 percent.

The onset of Prohibition in 1919 devastated the wine industry without completely destroying it. Home winemaking was still legal, and large quantities of grapes and grape concentrates intended for winemaking, many of which were shipped with packets of yeast, were exported east from California by rail. Although many wineries closed down, others survived by producing wine for sacramental and medicinal purposes, also still legal under Prohibition. Thus, at Repeal in 1933, at least some wine industry infrastructure still existed, and the industry gradually recovered.

Throughout its history, the American wine industry underwent many cyclical fluctuations. The most recent boom began in the late 1960s in California. In 1960 there were approximately 200 wineries in the state, a post-Prohibition low. That number nearly tripled by the mid-1980s to over 700 (about the current number). While large-scale wine production grew during this period, the most significant growth was in small wineries. Many entrepreneurially minded investors, flush with capital from the state's booming economy and attracted to the rural idyll that winemaking seemed to promise, became winemakers. They encountered consumers who, for a series of economic and cultural reasons connected with postwar affluence, expressed increased interest in lifestyle-enhancing products such as wine. The American wine industry shifted from providing a relatively undifferentiated product to immigrants, housewives, and the occasional wine connoisseur to a higher-quality product differentiated by winery image and popularity.

Industry Structure

The 1980s and 1990s saw a liberalization in U.S. winemaking regulation, which spurred the revival of the small winery sector in New York as well as the new development of small winery production in other states, most notably Oregon, Washington, and Texas. It is legal for home winemakers to make up to 200 gallons of wine per year, and many amateur winemakers are active in both rural and urban settings.

Most commercial wine in the United States is produced with grapes purchased from growers. This occurs across the winery size spectrum, although small wineries are more likely to grow their own grapes. Growers usually enter into long-term contracts with wineries, which specify the type of grapes, growing methods, and minimum quality standards. Often there are disputes between growers and wineries over quality and price, particularly with larger wineries that have significant market power.

Generally, the wine industry conforms to a standard tripartite production/distribution structure: winery to distributor to retailer. Most wineries bottle their own wine, some using the services of mobile bottling contractors, and then sell it to distributors, who place it in retail outlets. Some boutique wineries market directly to restaurants and wine shops. U.S. law prohibits direct winery ownership of retail outlets, although on-site sales, which constitute a major source of revenue for many small wineries, are allowed.

It is possible to distinguish three distinct winery size categories. About 10 percent of American wineries have storage capacities in excess of 1 million gallons. The 10 largest wineries account for about 80 percent of wine shipments. The largest American winery, E & J Gallo, produces about 25 percent of all wine consumed in the United States. Gallo operates its own glass bottle and aluminum screw cap factories and owns a trucking company that it uses both to haul grapes and to distribute finished wines. Most large wineries market their own brands, although several ship wine in bulk to other wineries, which blend it with their own wines. The majority of American wineries fall into the medium-sized category. These range from fairly large producers of premium wines to smaller producers fighting for a share of the mid-priced varietal market. Finally, there are the microwineries, which produce small quantities of premium-quality wine. Many microwineries find it difficult to make a profit because of the rise in vineyard land costs, the high cost of equipment, the vagaries of weather, and the fickleness of consumers. Some of the wineries in this category consist of winemakers who buy grapes and rent excess production capacity from other winemakers. Many others are owned by affluent professionals or business executives for whom winemaking is a hobby.

Most American wineries are privately owned, often by a single family or by a partnership. This includes wineries of all sizes, from the gigantic Gallo, which is still owned by the Gallo family, to most smaller wineries. Wine and wine-grape cooperatives are virtually nonexistent in the United States. Foreign investment, which is in excess of about $1.5 billion, comes in two forms. The first consists of multinational beverage producers such as Seagram, Nestlé, and Heublein, which have portfolios of investments in both large and small wineries. Grand Metropolitan, a British firm with significant holdings in food processing, retailing, and hotels, is the second-largest producer of wine by volume in the United States. The second most important form of foreign investment in the American wine industry comes from European producers who are seeking to expand their wine production and are stymied by the lack of expansion potential in their home regions. This is best exemplified by sparkling wine producers like Taittinger, Moët-Hennessy (France), and Codorniu (Spain), which have established high-profile operations in the Napa and Sonoma areas of California. French interests, both individual and corporate, have also moved into other parts of the United States, most notably New Mexico, Texas, Oregon, and Virginia.

Problems Facing the Wine Industry

Although overall alcohol consumption in America has declined, the shift in wine has been from quantity to quality; or in the words of wine industry analysts, Americans are drinking less but drinking better. The decline in alcohol consumption coincided with the proliferation of small, premium wineries and mid-priced varietal producers. Larger producers responded by improving the quality of their wines, or in some cases, by repackaging their jug wines in smaller bottles with more attractive labels. Despite this seemingly benign quality-consumption shift, however, the widespread revival of antialcohol sentiment has increased the pressure in what is already a brutally competitive market. Increasing urbanization and the natural limit of available land in appropriate climatological zones have led to huge increases in vineyard land values. Economic recession and banks unwilling to make loans to wineries led to numerous bankruptcies and sell-outs to larger, better capitalized interests. New winery startups in California declined every year after their peak in 1980. A recent outbreak of Phylloxera (a vine-destroying pest) in the Napa and Sonoma Valleys placed an extra burden on many smaller wineries, forcing them to replace entire vineyards, which resulted in a three- to four-year production hiatus. Creeping suburban development and pressures caused by tourism and nonwinery development have fueled the ongoing, acrimonious debate over the implementation of special agricultural protections in the Napa Valley.

—*James Curry*

See also
Addiction; Marketing; Migrant Farmworkers; Temperate Fruit Industry.

References
Adams, Leon D. *The Wines of America*. 2d ed. New York: McGraw-Hill, 1990.
Blue, Anthony D. *American Wine: A Comprehensive Guide*. Rev. ed. New York: Harper and Row, 1988.
Eysberg, Cyees D. *The Californian Wine Economy: Natural Opportunities and Socio-Cultural Constraints*. Utrecht: Netherlands Geographical Studies, 1990.
Jackisch, Philip. *Modern Winemaking*. Ithaca, NY: Cornell University Press, 1985.

Johnson, Hugh. *Vintage: The Story of Wine*. New York: Simon and Schuster, 1989.

Muscatine, Doris, Maynard A. Amerine, and Bob Thompson, eds. *The Book of California Wine*. Berkeley: University of California Press/Sotheby, 1984.

Stuller, Jay, and Glen Martin. *Through the Grapevine: The Business of Wine in America*. New York: Wynwood Press, 1989.

Teiser, Ruth, and Catherine Harroun. *Winemaking in California*. New York: McGraw-Hill, 1983.

Unwin, Tim. *Wine and the Vine: An Historical Geography of Viticulture and the Wine Trade*. London: Routledge, 1991.

Wagner, Paul M. *Grapes into Wine: The Art of Winemaking in New York*. New York: Knopf, 1982.

Women
See Rural Women.

Wool and Sheep Industry

The production, processing, and marketing of wool and other products from sheep. This entry discusses the wool industry and its place in the rural United States. Since it is not possible to understand the wool industry without considering aspects of lamb production and marketing, lamb and wool production patterns and practices will be discussed first. U.S. wool policy is then considered, followed by a discussion of the market demand for lamb and wool. The concluding section considers world markets and trade in wool.

Sheep Husbandry: Lamb and Wool Production

The sheep industry has been a mainstay of the rural economy for centuries. The sheep, domesticated around 12,000 years ago, was one of the first animals domesticated by humans. Providing both meat and fiber, it has been one of humankind's most useful domesticated animals. Judging from the wild sheep of today, it is likely that the ancestors of wild sheep had shaggy, colored coats and gave birth to single lambs. Over centuries of domestication, shepherds selected lambs to retain in the breeding stock that possessed the most desirable characteristics and thus altered considerably the genetic base of the world's sheep population. Wool production, carcass characteristics, hardiness, and the prevalence of multiple births or twinning are desirable traits for commercial sheep production in the United States. Sheep are used for meat, milk, and fiber. All sheep can produce these three products, but specialized breeds are used in commercial production of each.

Although some flocks are kept for milk production, the vast majority of sheep in the United States are used in lamb and wool production. There are about 10 commercially important sheep breeds in the United States. Each of these produce both lambs and wool. However, each of these breeds is used to generate a particular mix of lamb and wool outputs or a particular quality of lamb or wool. For example, Rambouillet or Merino are used for high-quality, fine wool production, while Colombia, Corriedale, or Hampshire are used if lamb production is the primary objective. In most sheep operations, both lambs and wool are produced for market from the same sheep flock.

There are generally two types of sheep operations in the United States: range flocks and farm flocks. Typically, range flocks are located in Texas, South Dakota, the Rocky Mountain states, and the Pacific Coast states, or the "territory states." Range flocks take most of their feed in the form of standing forage that could not be harvested economically by any other means. They usually represent a primary source of income for the ranching unit. Range flocks typically consist of wool breeds, as they are hardy and excellent foragers. Wool from these areas, called "territory wools," tends to be finer and well suited to apparel. It is not unusual for range operations to cross purebred, wool breed ewes with meat breed rams. This strategy results in high-quality wool from shearing the ewes and high quality crossbred lambs for meat production. About two-thirds (about 6 million) of U.S. sheep are managed in range flocks, but only about one-fifth of producers are range-flock operators. The territory states, though dominated by range flocks, have some farm flocks. These states contain about 75 percent of U.S. sheep.

Most other sheep are in Virginia, West Virginia, Pennsylvania, states north of the Ohio River, and on the Great Plains ("fleece states"). Sheep in these areas are typically managed in farm flocks. Farm flocks are generally small flocks (less than 40 head) kept in farming areas. They are usually a supplementary source of income to the owner. They typically graze in fenced areas, for only a part of the season, and are more intensively managed. Farm flocks account for only about one-third (about 3 million sheep) of the sheep and wool production in the United States, but are kept by the majority of U.S. sheep producers. Sheep in these areas tend to be meat breeds, and most of the wool produced is medium grade, used to make coats, sweaters, and blankets. Some farm-flock operators use specialized breeds to produce colored or otherwise unusual fleeces for spinning and weaving by craftspeople.

The sheep industry has been in decline in terms of

Black-faced sheep on a farm in Waitsfield, Vermont. About one-quarter of U.S. sheep are grazed on such farms; most operations are larger-scale range flocks in the West.

breeding flock size and lamb and wool production since the early 1960s. One explanation for this decline is that the sheep enterprise has been less profitable than other enterprises that the farmer or rancher could undertake. Among the reasons cited for this decline are the unavailability and high cost of herder labor in sheep production, large losses to predators in range-flock areas, relatively low-cost imports, high marketing costs, and increasing marketing margins. Whatever the reason, the U.S. sheep industry has declined steadily for the past 30 years, from over 33 million head in 1960 to less than 9 million head in 1995.

U.S. Wool Policy

The sheep industry has been supported by various U.S. government programs since 1938. The wool incentive program has supported wool production since 1955. It provides payments to sheep producers when the market price of wool falls below the wool incentive price, a price set under the federal farm bill. In recent years, the incentive price has been more than twice the market wool price. However, Congress passed legislation in 1993 to phase out the wool incentive program. Payments were reduced in 1994 and 1995. After 1995, no incentive payment was received. The loss of the wool incentive program was a serious blow to wool production in the United States. For many years, incentive payments had accounted for over one-fifth of producers' total receipts from the sheep enterprise. Thus, the absence of incentive payments will reduce the producers' motivation to keep the sheep enterprise and will encourage breed choice away from the wool breeds and toward the meat breeds. U.S. sheep numbers were already showing a decline by 1995, 13 percent since 1993.

Wool Consumption

Wool is a natural fiber used for thousands of years. Wool is unique among natural fibers; unlike cotton, silk, flax, hemp, and jute, it is a result of livestock production. Along with that of other natural fibers, wool's position in the marketplace has been challenged by synthetic fibers. Wool is used in a variety of textile products, including fine suits, sweaters, outerwear, carpets, blankets, and decorative textile products.

Wool is classified into two categories: apparel wool and carpet wool. Carpet wool, with a fiber diameter of greater than 30 microns, is shorter and less uniform than apparel wool. Carpet wools are used in carpets. Most apparel wool is processed by the worsted or the woolen process. The worsted process uses the longer, finer fibers. The wool is carded, combed, and drawn into a thin strand of apparel fibers spun together to form a strong, thin yarn. Under the woolen system, shorter wool is carded and drawn into long, softly twisted strands spun into a bulky yarn that lacks the strength of the worsted yarns. Tops and noils are intermediate products of the worsted and woolen processes. Tops are created by carding the longer wools and removing the shorter fibers, called noils. Twisting top fibers together forms rovings, which are spun into worsted yarns.

U.S. consumers use an average of between 1 and 1.5 pounds of wool each year in textile products. This is compared to about 27 pounds of cotton, 40 pounds of synthetic fibers, and 3 pounds of flax and silk per person. Wool currently accounts for about 1.7 percent of each U.S. consumer's annual fiber consumption, compared to 9 percent in 1939. Synthetic fibers, rather than cotton, displaced wool in U.S. consumers' textile selections. Cotton and wool do not compete for most end uses, and they are rarely blended in fabrics. A major factor in the decline in wool use has been the loss of the carpet market to synthetic fibers, mainly nylon. Although synthetic fibers displaced wool, resulting in low consumption, synthetics have been unable to duplicate adequately the desirable properties of wool such as heat and flame resistance, excellent dying properties, resistance to soiling, and moisture absorption properties. Recent developments in wool processing enhanced wool fabric's ability to hold a crease and keep its shape.

Lamb Consumption

On average, the U.S. consumer eats about 170 pounds of red meat (carcass weight) each year. Only about 1.6 pounds of that meat is lamb. The demand for lamb has both seasonal and geographic qualities. Lamb is a product often used for special occasions and holiday observance. Thus, the demand for lamb is highest during the spring and early summer. About half of the lamb consumed in the United States is consumed in the northeastern and mid-Atlantic regions. Thirty percent is consumed in New York alone. About 17 percent is consumed in California. These descriptors characterize lamb as a specialty meat used by relatively few consumers and during relatively limited times of the year. The primary competitors for lamb in the marketplace are beef, pork, and chicken. The prices and production of other meats can cause substantial shifts in lamb prices and consumption. For example, it is estimated that a 10 percent increase in the total supply of beef will cause a 3 percent decline in the retail price of lamb.

Retail prices are much higher than farm prices for lamb. The difference between retail and farm prices, the marketing margin, is based on the cost to transform a live lamb into a retail meat product. It takes about 3.3 pounds of live lamb to equal 1 pound of boneless, trimmed retail lamb product. The value added by slaughterers, processors, distributors, and retailers, among others, goes into the farm to retail marketing margin. This margin has been increasing in recent years.

World Markets for Wool

Australia is the world's leading wool producer and exporter. Australia produces over 1 billion pounds of wool each year and often exports 90 percent or more of its production. Approximately 60 percent of the wool traded in world wool markets is of Australian origin. New Zealand, Argentina, Uruguay, and South Africa are also major wool-producing and -exporting countries. These five countries account for 96 to 98 percent of the world's wool exports. Thus, most of the world's exportable surplus of wool comes from the Southern Hemisphere.

The countries making up the former USSR and China are also major wool producers, but because of large populations and intensive consumption are not exporters. Over 35 percent of the world's wool is processed and used in the former Soviet Union and China. The European Union and Japan account for about 30 percent of world wool use. Although the United States is not a large consumer or importer of wool by world standards, wool imports are important to U.S. textile consumers. Over 88 percent of the wool consumed in the United States in 1993 was imported. The United States imports three-quarters to two-thirds of the wool processed in U.S. textile mills. However, most U.S.-imported wool is already in the form of manufactured textile products.

Because of the size of its industry and a heavy reliance on world markets to sell its wool crop, Australia has taken an active stance in the international wool market. The Australian Wool Corporation (AWC) was formed in 1972 to aid in the domestic and international marketing of Australian wool. Competition from synthetic fibers was recognized as a problem, and the AWC worked to enhance the competitive qualities of Australian wool. The AWC improved the grading and presentation of raw wool. Virtually all Australian wool is tested for yield, vegetable matter content, and fiber diameter, and is sold by sample. The industry is moving toward sale by description with further testing for fiber length, fiber strength, and color. Objective measurement and sorting for consistency reduce the fiber users' costs and improve wool's competitiveness with other fibers. World wool markets are generally as free and unrestrained by government policy as any world agricultural markets.

—Glen D. Whipple and Dale J. Menkhaus

See also

Agricultural Programs; Clothing and Textiles; Livestock Industry; Livestock Production; Marketing; Pasture; Policy, Agricultural; Textile Industry; Trade, International.

References

American Sheep Industry Association. *U.S. Sheep Industry Market Situation Report: 88–89.* Denver, CO: American Sheep Industry Association, 1990.

Botkin, M. P., Ray A. Field, and C. Le Roy Johnson. *Sheep and Wool Science Production and Management.* Englewood Cliffs, NJ: Prentice-Hall, 1988.

Government Accounting Office. *Wool and Mohair Program, Need for Program Still in Question.* GAO/RCED-90-51 (March). Washington, DC: Government Accounting Office, 1990.

Purcell, W. D., J. Reeves, and W. Preston. *Economics of Past, Current and Pending Change in the U.S. Sheep Industry with an Emphasis on Supply Response.* MB 363. Blacksburg: Virginia Tech University, Department of Agricultural Economics, 1991.

Shapouri, Hosein. *Sheep Production in 11 Western States.* Staff Report No. AGES 9150. Washington, DC: U.S. Department of Agriculture, Economics Research Service, Commodity Economics Division, 1991.

Sheep Industry Development Program. *Sheep Industry Development (SID): Sheep Production Handbook.* Denver, CO: Sheep Industry Development Program, 1992.

U.S. Department of Agriculture. "Fibers Background for 1990 Farm Legislation." *Agriculture Information Bulletin* No. 951. Washington, DC: U.S. Department of Agriculture, Economic Research Service, National Agricultural Statistical Service, 1990.

Work

Activities that contribute to the material survival or livelihood of individuals and their households. The work that rural Americans do encompasses a wide variety of activities. Included are jobs or businesses in which rural people are formally employed as well as other kinds of work they do as part of their household livelihood strategies, such as work in the informal economy and self-provisioning activities. Household maintenance, child care, and other domestic activities are included in this definition of work. Such a broad conception of work is necessary not only to describe the work that rural Americans do but to understand how this work has changed in recent decades.

Recent changes in the structure of work in rural America are highlighted in this entry, with special emphasis on how those changes are related to divisions of labor between rural and urban areas and between women and men. The entry begins with a discussion of the economic restructuring that occurred in both the formal and informal sectors. The subsequent section relates this transformation to the gender division of labor in rural America. The restructuring of work in rural America is also related to other social divisions of labor, such as divisions by class, ethnicity, and age. Special consideration is given to the gender division of labor because it is the primary basis for allocating work within households.

The Restructuring of Work in Rural America

Alphonse Karr's (1849) comment, *plus ça change, plus c'est la même chose* (The more things change, the more they remain the same) applies to the restructuring of work in rural America. Work in rural America was transformed by a profound economic and social restructuring during the latter part of the twentieth century, but the hierarchical spatial division of labor between rural and urban areas remains, as does the gender division of labor within rural households. The restructuring of work in rural America began long before the economic and social restructuring that captured the nation's attention in the 1970s and 1980s. Central to the earlier restructuring in rural America was the transformation of agriculture. Agricultural work became highly mechanized, greatly reducing the number of farmers and farm laborers as tractor power fostered a move toward larger and fewer farms. As a consequence of this transformation of agriculture, less than 10 percent of rural Americans work in agriculture in the 1990s. And among the rural Americans who do continue to farm, most rely upon off-farm work as part of their household livelihood strategies.

The shift away from agricultural work in rural America has produced an industry structure that is similar to the structure of industries in urban America. In 1992, more than half of all rural workers employed in the formal economy worked in the service sector. In addition, another third worked in either the manufacturing or the

The workload on a farm often requires rising with the sun.

government sector (U.S. Department of Agriculture 1995). While the industry structure of rural America became more like that of urban America, the division in the work done in rural and urban America remained very much the same through a persistent spatial division of labor. Similar to farmers' historical role of providing cheap food for urban populations, a primary role of rural workers in nonagricultural industries today is to provide cheap labor for urban-managed industries.

The general pattern of the spatial division of labor is for work in rural America to be concentrated in routine production activities, while a disproportionate share of the professional and managerial work within an industry is located in urban areas. A consequence of this spatial division of labor is that rural economies have become more vulnerable to downturns in the national and world economies, as routine production jobs are often the first to be cut back during recessions. Moreover, rural workers are more likely to experience underemployment, and the resultant low hours and low earnings, than are urban workers (McGranahan 1983).

The restructuring of work in rural America involved more than changes in the kinds of work that rural people do in the formal economy. There also has been a restructuring in the informal and domestic spheres of work in rural America. The major change in the informal sphere is tied to the shift away from agriculture. Farm households have a long tradition of informal exchanges of labor and materials related to their farms' production. In the nonfarm household, the informal work activities relate more to household reproduction, such as the informal exchange of personal services or commodities for household consumption (which is not to deny the significance of "egg money" to many farm households).

One implication of this shift is that the informal work activities of rural nonfarm households are similar to the informal work activities of urban households. Informal work is especially important to households in the most remote rural areas, where informal work activities compensate for the local lack of services and job opportunities in the formal economy (Jensen, Cornwell, and Findeis 1995). With regard to the restructuring of work in the domestic sphere, the major change has involved the increased dependence of rural households on women, who in addition to their domestic work have increased their participation in the formal economy. This aspect of the restructuring of work in rural America is related to a persistent gender division of labor in the formal economy and within households.

Restructuring Work and the Gender Division of Labor

Despite the profound economic and social restructuring of work in rural America, much remains the same. Considerable change occurred in the kinds of work that rural Americans do, but the relation of their work to the spatial and gender divisions of labor has not changed fundamentally. As a consequence, work opportunities for rural Americans remain tied to persistent divisions of labor in the organization of work. The spatial division of labor helped preserve a division in the kinds of work that rural and urban Americans do. Likewise, the gender division of labor has helped preserve a division in the kinds of work that rural women and men do. Women hold a wide range of positions in the work structure of rural America. Yet they typically have less access to certain kinds of work and less control over the products of their labor than do men. This gender inequality in work opportunities and power is related strongly to the household division of labor. Within rural and urban households, men usually have an inordinate control over the household's disposable income and any capital or means of production the household owns. Conversely, cooking, child care, and other work in the domestic sphere is almost exclusively allotted to women.

Even within farm households, where women often do the bookkeeping and other clerical work for the farm enterprise and participate extensively in physical agricultural labor, men usually control the technology that is incorporated into agricultural production. As the cost-price squeeze pushed more and more farms to part-time farming, farm women often found themselves not only entering the formal labor market while maintaining their own farm and domestic work, but also expanding their farm production duties to fill in for their male partners who also were working off the farm. Because much of household labor is indispensable, women are unable to adjust the time they spend on household labor to their paid labor demands. It does not appear that farm men have been contributing very extensively to the domestic sphere of their households' livelihood strategies. With more women entering the paid labor force there has been an increase in household labor by men. Yet this increase has been slight, especially when compared with the increase in women's paid labor time (Shelton 1992).

A gender division of labor remains in the formal economy as well, with rural women being most likely to work in clerical, operative, and personal service jobs, whereas rural men are more likely than women to work in skilled manual jobs. Semyonov (1983) has pointed out that the increased labor force participation by women in rural areas accentuates the general pattern of occupational segregation by gender, with women being even more concentrated in low-status, low-wage jobs than in areas where relatively few women work outside the home. Men in rural areas with high levels of women's participation in the formal economy also are more likely to receive low wages for the work they do in the formal economy (Tigges and Tootle 1990). Therefore, the increased significance of women's participation in the formal economy to many rural household's livelihood strategies occurred in conjunction with a diminished earnings capacity of rural men and women. However, while rural men's and women's earnings capacities are adversely affected by women's increased labor force participation, gender earnings inequality remains. The gender gap in earnings has become even more critical for rural women in conjunction with the increased proportion of female-headed households in rural America.

The gender division of labor also is related to the allocation of informal work in rural America. Men's work in the informal sphere usually involves their physical labor, such as repair work or landscaping. Women's work is likely to be an extension of their domestic work, such as child care for other households or the selling of food commodities produced in their home.

One of the recent trends in the informalization of work has been for rural women to increasingly take on industrial homework as part of their household's livelihood strategy. Industrial homework refers to employers' contracting work out to households, with the work usually performed by women for minimal wages and with few benefits. Gringeri (1993) has argued that the acceptance of industrial homeworking as a rural economic development strategy has been facilitated by traditional beliefs about women's roles within the household and the labor market. The instability, low wages, and limited benefits of industrial homework are justified through the assumption that these jobs are secondary and supplemental to the work of men in the household.

Women involved in industrial homeworking, much like women who work outside the home, often find they are doing double the work as they remain primarily responsible for child care, household maintenance, and other forms of domestic work. This imbalance in work responsibilities within the rural household continues to be a dominant factor shaping gender divisions in both the formal and informal spheres of work in rural America.

To understand work in rural America, therefore, it is important to consider the various activities that rural Americans get involved in as they strive to meet their households' livelihood needs. It also is important to recognize that work opportunities for rural Americans remained tied to the spatial and gender divisions of labor, despite the considerable changes that have occurred in the kinds of work that rural Americans do. The more things have changed, the more they remain the same.

—*Leonard E. Bloomquist and Bridget E. Murphy*

See also
Careers in Agriculture; Division of Household Labor; Employment; Foresters; Labor Force; Miners; Rural Women; Underemployment.

References
Gringeri, Christina A. "Inscribing Gender in Rural Development: Industrial Homework in Two Midwestern Communities." *Rural Sociology* 58, no. 1 (1993): 30–52.
Jensen, Leif, Gretchen T. Cornwell, and Jill L. Findeis. "Informal Work in Nonmetropolitan Pennsylvania." *Rural Sociology* 60, no. 1 (1995): 67–107.
Karr, Alphonse. *Les Guêpes* (Janvier 1849).
McGranahan, David A. "Changes in the Social and Spatial Structure of the Rural Community." Pp. 163–178 in *Technology and Social Change in Rural Areas*. Edited by Gene F. Summers. Boulder, CO: Westview Press, 1983.
Semyonov, Moshe. "Community Characteristics, Female Employment and Occupational Segregation: Small Towns in a Rural State." *Rural Sociology* 48, no. 1 (1983): 104–119.
Shelton, Beth Anne. *Women, Work and Time: Gender Differences in Paid Work, Housework and Leisure*. New York: Greenwood Press, 1992.
Tigges, Leann M., and Deborah M. Tootle. "Labor Supply, Labor Demand, and Men's Underemployment in Rural and Urban Labor Markets." *Rural Sociology* 55, no. 3 (1990): 328–356.
U.S. Department of Agriculture. *Understanding Rural America*. Washington, DC: U.S. Department of Agriculture, Economic Research Service, 1995.

Workers' Compensation

A state-administered system that provides employees and their families with definite and sure compensation, together with a prompt and efficient remedy for injury or death suffered in the course and scope of employment.

This entry examines the duties of employers to their employees, the advantages and disadvantages of providing agricultural employees with workers' compensation benefits, the compulsory nature of workers' compensation in light of the agricultural exception, and the means of finding the best insurance carrier. The entry also explains the advantages and disadvantages of purchasing other liability insurance coverage for agricultural employees in place of workers' compensation coverage.

Employers' Duties to Employees

Employers must provide employees with a reasonably safe workplace and safe tools, and must issue rules and warnings so that work can be done in safety, plus ensure that all workers are reasonably competent. If the employer breaches any of those duties and an employee is injured, then the employer is financially responsible. It is well known that agriculture is a hazardous business. Agricultural workers operate hazardous machinery, handle unruly animals, and are exposed to dangerous chemicals, infectious diseases, and extremes of weather—and in some cases, even to dangerous gasses like ammonia, hydrogen sulfide, and methane, produced by manure pits. If the employer does not have insurance to cover an employee's bodily injures and medical expenses, both the employer and employee may face devastating financial consequences.

The Case for Workers' Compensation

Workers' compensation insurance offers both advantages and disadvantages to the employer and the employee. It is a quid pro quo system, in which each of the parties gives up something in order to be in a stable and predictable system to handle work-related injuries.

For the employer, in most situations, it provides the exclusive remedy to claims filed by an employee. For example, the worker who is entitled to compensation under a state workers' compensation act cannot sue the employer under state product liability laws or wrongful death statutes, or bring any negligence claim against the employer. This limits the employer's financial exposure to the amounts set forth in the state workers' compensation act.

However, even workers' compensation will not preclude an action by an employee who is intentionally injured by the employer. Similarly, few states have adopted the "substantially certain" doctrine. The doctrine allows an employee to sue an employer outside the workers' compensation remedy if the employee has been placed in a position where harm is substantially certain to occur, regardless of the employer's intent. For example, a group of workers repeatedly exposed to toxic fumes in a manufacturing plant were allowed to sue their employer outside the workers' compensation statutes because the employer had repeatedly failed to eliminate the toxic fumes.

Workers' compensation insurance guarantees the employee compensation and medical care even if the employee was at fault. The employer cannot raise the employee's own negligence or fault as a defense. An insured worker is entitled to compensation for any personal injury caused by an accident or disease arising out of and in the course of employment, so long as the injury is caused by, or related to, the employment.

The worker is compensated according to a schedule of benefits. For each injury, depending on whether the injury is permanent or temporary, the employee will be paid for a certain number of weeks, at a fixed percentage of the worker's average weekly wage, up to a maximum amount.

However, employees will find that they may not be fully compensated for their injuries. Workers' compensation frequently does not provide compensation for impotency, pain and suffering, psychological damage, or disfigurement. The system also does not provide compensation to family members for loss of consortium or companionship.

Is Workers' Compensation Compulsory?

In analyzing insurance needs, an agricultural employer must first determine whether state law makes workers' compensation insurance coverage compulsory. At least a dozen states require that workers' compensation coverage be provided for agricultural workers as for their nonagricultural counterparts.

In those states, if an employer fails to purchase compulsory workers' compensation, he or she loses certain common-law defenses in any lawsuit filed by an injured employee. One example is contributory negligence. This defense looks at the employee's own carelessness. If the injury is more the fault of the employee than the employer, the employee's monetary recompense is either denied, or reduced. A second example is assumption of risk. This defense applies if the employee was aware of the work dangers and chose to be exposed to the dangers. In this situation, he or she may not be entitled to compensation. But remember, both of these defenses may be lost if compulsory insurance is not obtained. Also, the employer loses the benefit of any other liability insurance he or she

might have. Liability policies commonly state that there is no coverage under the policy for injured employees when state law requires them to be covered under workers' compensation insurance.

The Agricultural Exemption

A majority of states exempt some farm laborers from state workers' compensation statutes. However, there is much variation between states. Some exclude all agricultural workers. Others exclude only the workers of farmers who employee less than a certain number of employees, have an annual payroll less than a certain amount, or whose employees work less than a specified number of hours each year.

In interpreting the state exemption for agricultural workers, some courts have found concentrated poultry or hog operations to be commercial activities outside the agricultural exemption. In those cases, workers' compensation insurance was found to be compulsory.

Similarly, if an employee regularly shifts from strictly farm work to nonfarm work, even if an agricultural exemption exists, the worker must be covered by workers' compensation insurance. An employer who has an employee constantly operating or repairing nonfarm machinery, or repairing other nonfarm equipment or buildings, may find the agricultural exemption inapplicable if the worker gets injured. Even those states that exclude agricultural workers from compensation coverage, however, usually give the employer the right to bring their agricultural workers under the state workers' compensation act.

Finding the Right Coverage

If employers choose to provide workers' compensation insurance for their employees, they must also decide what insurance is best for them. There are three basic ways to secure workers' compensation insurance under state workers' compensation acts. Many states permit what is known as self-insurance, which is simply a program whereby the employer regularly sets aside sufficient assets to cover potential liability claims. The states that do permit self-insurance have specific regulations for setting up such programs.

For many employers, self-insurance is not a viable option because of the amount of assets that must be set aside to take care of potential claims. In some states it is possible to obtain workers' compensation at competitive rates through a state fund. Information about these funds can be obtained through an insurance agent or the state's workers' compensation commission. For most employers, state law (as well as economics) requires purchase of workers' compensation coverage through a private insurance company. Employers should shop around, because insurance company rates for workers' compensation vary greatly. Employers should check for reputation, reliability, and financial stability.

There are several services that rate insurance companies. A. M. Best is probably the best known. Under its ranking system, the most reliable insurance companies receive an A+ rating. Standard & Poor, Duffy & Phelps, and Moody's Service are also helpful in selecting a reliable insurance company.

The actual cost of workers' compensation insurance will vary greatly with the type of operation, number of employees, and size of payroll. The more employees, the greater the payroll, and the more dangerous the operation, the higher the premiums. An operation's safety record is also a factor.

Other Insurance Coverage

If state law gives the option of not purchasing workers' compensation insurance and an employer considers exercising that option, or lives in one of the few states that does not provide coverage for agricultural employees, an important question should be asked. What sort of insurance will best protect the employer and his or her employees?

The employer may already have a Farmer's Comprehensive Personal Liability Policy (FCPL) or a Commercial General Liability Policy (CGL) and believe that coverage is sufficient. If so, the employer is probably flirting with economic disaster. Most FCPL policies and CGL policies do not provide protection for injured employees. Instead, they specifically exclude coverage for bodily injuries and any medical payments for those employees.

Employers who already have other insurance can modify their coverage to protect themselves and their employees. FCPL policies and CGL policies can be expanded to provide bodily injury coverage for employees and some medical compensation. This is done by means of an employer's liability and employee's medical payments endorsement to the standard liability policy. It is important, however, to understand what is and what is not covered under the endorsement.

An employer's liability and employee's medical payments endorsement does not provide coverage if the employee's injuries should have been covered by workers' compensation or are already covered by disability bene-

fits, employment compensation, or similar laws. The endorsement will not cover injuries to an illegally employed person, if the employer had knowledge of the illegal employment. For example, a 15-year-old boy was not covered for injures received while operating a defective manure spreader because state law prohibited anyone under 18 years of age from cleaning moving machinery or being employed in any hazardous job.

Similarly, the endorsements provide incomplete coverage for occupational diseases. The endorsement commonly excludes coverage of any claims or suits brought more than 36 months after the end of the policy period. However, unlike a traumatic injury, an occupational disease may not manifest itself until many years after the worker's exposure to the particular hazard.

The endorsement also excludes coverage for certain types of damages. Punitive damages are not covered under the employer's liability and employee's medical payment endorsement. These are damages assessed against a wrongdoer in addition to any compensatory damages the wrongdoer must pay. Punitive damages are assessed to deter the wrongdoer from engaging in similar reckless and willful misconduct in the future. For example, if an agricultural employer was ordered to pay $50,000 to a worker whose lungs were injured by ammonia, and then was ordered to pay an additional $100,000 in punitive damages for unlawfully failing to warn the worker of the dangers associated with being exposed to ammonia, the insurance company would pay the $50,000, but not the $100,000, even if the employer's liability policy provided coverage in excess of $150,000.

Endorsements also exclude coverage for consequential damages sought by the spouse, child, parent, or sibling of an injured farm employee. These are damages that other family members might be able to receive as a result of the injuries suffered by the family worker. A classic example would be a wife who sues for loss of consortium because her husband's injuries made him impotent.

If an agricultural employer decides to obtain an employer's liability and employee's medical payments endorsement, the cost will depend on the number of persons employed and whether they are full-time or part-time workers. For rating purposes, full-time employees are those who work 180 days or more per year. Part-time employees are divided into those who work more than 40 but fewer than 180 days per year, and those who work 40 or fewer days per year. The endorsement typically contains a schedule on the declarations page, specifying the total number of employees in each classification. The schedule also lists those employees to whom the provisions of the endorsements do not apply.

—*John D. Copeland*

See also
Agricultural Law; Employment; Fringe Benefits; Injuries; Insurance; Labor Force; Labor Unions; Work.

References
Copeland, John D. *Understanding the Farmers Comprehensive Personal Liability Policy: A Guide for Farmers' Attorneys and Insurance Agents*. Fayetteville, AR: National Center for Agricultural Law Research and Information, 1992.
———. *Recreational Access to Private Lands: Liability Problems and Solutions*. Fayetteville, AR: National Center for Agricultural Law Research and Information, 1995.
Jerry, Robert H., II. *Understanding Insurance Law*. New York: M. Bender, 1987.
Larson, Arthur. *The Law of Workmen's Compensation*. New York: M. Bender, 1952 and subsequent years (unnumbered, loose-leaf).
———. *Workmen's Compensation for Occupational Injuries and Death*. New York: Matthew Bender, 1972.
Looney, J. W., J. Wilder, S. Brownback, and J. Wadley. *Agricultural Law: A Lawyer's Guide to Representing Farm Clients*. Chicago: American Bar Association, Section of General Practice, 1990.
Nackley, Jeffrey V. *Primer on Workers' Compensation*. Washington, DC: Bureau of National Affairs, 1989.
National Conference of State Legislatures. *The State of Workers' Compensation*. Denver, CO: National Conference of State Legislatures, 1994.
National Safety Council. *Accident Facts*. (Annual.) Itasca, IL: National Safety Council, 1994.
National Underwriter Co. *Fire Casualty and Surety Bulletins*. Cincinnati, OH: National Underwriter Co., 1990 and 1994–1995.
Tramposh, Anne. *Avoiding the Cracks: A Guide to the Workers' Compensation System*. New York: Praeger, 1991.
Victor, Richard A. *Challenges for the 1990s*. Cambridge, MA: Workers Compensation Research Institute, 1990.

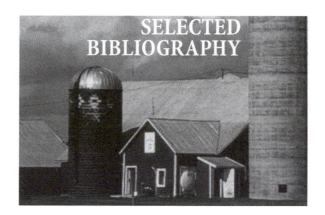

SELECTED BIBLIOGRAPHY

The following books and monographs, written since 1980, pertain to various aspects of life in rural America. These interdisciplinary references were selected by the editor and contributors and represent the variety of topics addressed in this encyclopedia. Many more references could be included in the bibliography; these are provided as a starting point for additional exploration.

Adams, Jane. *The Transformation of Rural Life: Southern Illinois, 1890–1990.* Chapel Hill: University of North Carolina Press, 1994.

Adams, M. A., and R. W. McLellan. *Use of Nonindustrial Private Land for Public Recreation: An Annotated Bibliography.* Clemson, SC: Clemson University, U.S. Department of Agriculture, Soil Conservation Service and Department of Parks, Recreation, and Tourism Management, n.d.

Agency for Health Care Policy and Research. *Delivering Essential Health Care Services in Rural Areas: An Analysis of Alternative Models.* AHCPR Pub. No. 91-0017 (May). Washington, DC: U.S. Department of Health and Human Services, Agency for Health Care Policy and Research, 1991.

Agriculture and Biosystems Engineering Department. *Conservation Tillage Systems and Management, Crop Residue Management with No-Till, Ridge Till and Mulch Till.* Midwest Plains Service, MWPS-45, 1st ed. Ames: Agriculture and Biosystems Engineering Department, Iowa State University, 1992.

Albin, R. C., and G. B. Thompson. *Cattle Feeding: A Guide to Management.* 2d ed. Amarillo, TX: Trafton Printing, 1996.

Albrecht, Don E., and Steve H. Murdock. *The Sociology of U.S. Agriculture: An Ecological Perspective.* Ames: Iowa State University Press, 1990.

Allen, James P., and Eugene J. Turner. *We the People: An Atlas of America's Ethnic Diversity.* New York: Macmillan, 1988.

Allen, John C., and Don A. Dillman. *Against All Odds: Rural Community in the Information Age.* Boulder, CO: Westview, 1994.

Allen, Patricia, ed. *Food for the Future: Conditions and Contradictions.* New York: John Wiley and Sons, 1993.

Altieri, Miguel A., ed. *Crop Protection Strategies for Subsistence Farmers.* Boulder, CO: Westview, 1993.

Altieri, Miguel A., Richard B. Norgaard, Susanna B. Hecht, John G. Farrell, and Matt Liebman. *Agroecology: The Scientific Basis of Alternative Agriculture.* Boulder, CO: Westview, 1987.

Ambler, Marjane. *Breaking the Iron Bonds: Indian Control of Energy Development.* Lawrence: University Press of Kansas, 1990.

American Farmland Trust. *Farming on the Edge: A New Report on the Importance and Vulnerability of Agriculture near American Cities.* Washington, DC: American Farmland Trust, 1993.

American Poultry Historical Society. *American Poultry History, 1974–1993.* Mt. Morris, IL: Watt, 1996.

———. *American Poultry History, 1823–1973.* Madison, WI: American Printing and Publishing, 1974.

Andreas, Carol. *Meatpackers and Beef Barons: Company Town in a Global Economy.* Niwo: University Press of Colorado, 1994.

Andrews, David. *Ministry in the Small Church.* Kansas City, MO: Sheed and Ward, 1988.

Appalachian Land Ownership Task Force. *Who Owns Appalachia?* Lexington: University of Kentucky Press, 1983.

Arendt, Randall. *Rural by Design.* Chicago: APA Planners Press, 1994.

Arno, Stephen F., and Ramona P. Hammerly. *Timberline: Mountain and Arctic Forest Frontiers.* Seattle: The Mountaineers, 1984.

Arntzen, Charles J., and Ellen M. Ritter, eds. *Encyclopedia of Agricultural Science.* 4 vols. San Diego: Academic Press, 1994.

Arthur, Eric, and Dudley Witney. *The Barn: A Vanishing Landmark in North America.* New York: Arrowood Press, 1988.

Axton, W. F. *Tobacco and Kentucky.* Lexington: University Press of Kentucky, 1975.

Ayres, Janet, F. Larry Leistritz, and Kenneth E. Stone. *Revitalizing the Retail Trade Sector in Rural Communities: Lessons from Three Midwestern States.* Ames, IA: North Central Regional Center for Rural Development, 1989.

Ayres, J. S., R. Cole, C. Hein, S. Huntington, W. Kobberdahl, W. Leonard, and D. Zetocha. *Take Charge: Economic Development in Small Communities.* Ames, IA: North Central Regional Center for Rural Development, 1990.

Baharanyi, Ntam, Robert Zabawa, and Walter Hill, eds. *New Directions in Local and Rural Development.* Tuskegee, AL: Tuskegee University, 1992.

Barkley, David L., ed. *Economic Adaptation: Alternatives for Nonmetropolitan Areas.* Boulder, CO: Westview, 1993.

Barkley, Paul W., and Gene Wunderlich. *Rural Land Transfers in the*

United States. AIB 574. Washington, DC: Economic Research Service, U.S. Department of Agriculture, 1989.

Barlett, Peggy F. *American Dreams, Rural Realities: Family Farms in Crisis.* Chapel Hill: University of North Carolina Press, 1993.

Barnard, Freddie L. *Banker's Agricultural Lending Manual.* Austin, TX: Sheshunoff Information Services, 1993.

Barnes, Robert F., Darrell A. Miller, and C. Jerry Nelson. *Forages.* Vol. 1: An *Introduction to Grassland Agriculture.* 5th ed. Ames: Iowa State University Press, 1995.

Barritt, Bruce H., and K. Bert van Dalfsen. *Intensive Orchard Management: A Practical Guide to the Planning, Establishment, and Management of High Density Apple Orchards.* Yakima, WA: Goodfruit Grower, 1992.

Barry, Peter J., Paul N. Ellinger, C. B. Baker, and John A. Hopkin. *Financial Management in Agriculture.* 5th ed. Danville, IL: Interstate, 1995.

Barry, Robert D., Luigi Angelo, Peter J. Buzzanell, and Fred Gray. *Sugar: Background for the 1990 Farm Legislation.* Staff Report No. AGES 9006. Washington, DC: U.S. Department of Agriculture, Economic Research Service, Commodity Economics Division, 1990.

Bartlett, Richard A. *Rolling Rivers: An Encyclopedia of America's Rivers.* New York: McGraw Hill, 1984.

Bath, D. L., F. N. Dickinson, H. A. Tucker, and R. D. Appleman. *Dairy Cattle: Principles, Practices, Problems, Profits.* 3d ed. Philadelphia: Lea and Febiger, 1985.

Baumgardt, Bill R., and Marshall A. Martin, eds. *Agricultural Biotechnology: Issues and Choices.* West Lafayette, IN: Purdue University Agricultural Experiment Station, 1991.

Baur, Donald, et al. *Natural Resources Law Handbook.* Rockville, MD: Government Institutes, 1991.

Beaulieu, Joyce E., and David E. Berry, eds. *Rural Health Services: A Management Perspective.* Ann Arbor, MI: Aupha Press, 1994.

Beaulieu, Lionel J., ed. *The Rural South in Crisis: Challenges for the Future.* Boulder, CO: Westview, 1988.

Beaulieu, Lionel J., and David Mulkey. *Investing in People: The Human Capital Needs of Rural America.* Boulder, CO: Westview, 1995.

Bell, Edward L. *Vestiges of Mortality and Remembrance: A Bibliography on the Historical Archaeology of Cemeteries.* Metuchen, NJ: Scarecrow, 1994.

Bender, Lloyd D., Bernal L. Green, Thomas F. Hady, John A. Kuehn, Marlys K. Nelson, Leon B. Perkinson, and Peggy J. Ross. "The Diverse Social and Economic Structure of Nonmetropolitan America," Rural Development Research Report No. 49. Washington, DC: U.S. Department of Agriculture, Economic Research Service, 1985.

Bennett, John. *Of Time and the Enterprise: North American Family Farm Management in a Context of Resource Marginality.* Minneapolis: University of Minnesota Press, 1982.

Berardi, G. M., and C. C. Geisler. *The Social Consequences and Challenges of New Agricultural Technologies.* Boulder, CO: Westview, 1984.

Berman, David. *County Governments in an Era of Change.* Westport, CT: Greenwood Press, 1993.

Berry, Brian, John B. Parr, Bart J. Epstein, Avjit Ghosh, and Robert H. T. Smith. *Market Centers and Retail Location: Theory and Applications.* Englewood Cliffs, NJ: Prentice-Hall, 1988.

Bhat, Mahadev G., Burton C. English, Anthony F. Turhollow, and Herzon O. Nyangito. *Energy in Synthetic Fertilizers and Pesticides: Revisited.* Oak Ridge, TN: Oak Ridge National Laboratory, 1994.

Billington, Ray Allen. *Westward Expansion: A History of the American Frontier.* New York: Macmillan, 1949. 5th ed., 1982.

Bird, Elizabeth Ann R., Gordon L. Bultena, and John C. Gardner, eds. *Planting the Future. Developing an Agriculture That Sustains Land and Community.* Ames: Iowa State University Press, 1995.

Blank, Steven C., Colin A. Carter, and Brian H. Schmiesing. *Futures and Options Markets: Trading in Commodities and Financials.* Englewood Cliffs, NJ: Prentice Hall, 1991.

Blatz, Charles V., ed. *Ethics and Agriculture: An Anthology on Current Issues in World Context.* Moscow: University of Idaho Press, 1991.

Blevins, Winfred. *Dictionary of the American West.* New York: Facts on File, 1993.

Boardman, John, John A. Dearing, and Ian D. L. Foster. *Soil Erosion on Agricultural Lands.* New York: John Wiley and Sons, 1990.

Boehlje, Michael D., and Vernon R. Eidman. *Farm Management.* New York: John Wiley and Sons, 1984.

Bolen, Eric G., and William L. Robinson. *Wildlife Ecology and Management.* 3d ed. Englewood Cliffs, NJ: Prentice-Hall, 1995.

Bollier, D. *The Importance of Communications and Information Systems to Rural Development in the United States. Report of an Aspen Institute Conference.* Turo, MA: Aspen Institute for Humanistic Studies, 1988.

Bonanno, Alessandro, Lawrence Busch, William Friedland, Lourdes Gouveia, and Enzo Mingione. *From Columbus to ConAgra: The Globalization of Agriculture and Food.* Lawrence: University Press of Kansas, 1994.

Boodley, J. W. *The Commercial Greenhouse.* Albany, NY: Delmar, 1981.

Botkin, M. P., R. A. Field, and C. L. Johnson. *Sheep and Wool Science Production and Management.* Englewood Cliffs, NJ: Prentice Hall, 1988.

Brady, N. C. *The Nature and Properties of Soils.* 10th ed. New York: Macmillan, 1990.

Brickell, Christopher, Elvin McDonald, and Trevor Cole, eds. *The American Horticultural Society Encyclopedia of Gardening.* New York: Dorling Kindersley, 1993.

Bridwell, R. *Hydroponic Gardening.* Santa Barbara, CA: Woodbridge Press, 1990.

Briody, Elizabeth K. *Household Labor Patterns among Mexican Americans in South Texas.* New York: AMS Press, 1986.

Brown, David, et al., eds. *Rural Economic Development in the 1980's: Preparing for the Future.* Rural Development Research Report No. 69 (September). Washington, DC: U.S. Department of Agriculture, Agriculture and Rural Economy Division, Economic Research Service, 1988.

Brown, D. L., D. R. Field, and J. J. Zuiches. *The Demography of Rural*

Life. University Park, PA: Northeast Regional Center for Rural Development, 1993.

Brown, John Gary. *Soul in the Stone: Cemetery Art from America's Heartland*. Lawrence: University Press of Kansas, 1994.

Brown, Linda Keller, and Kay Mussell, eds. *Ethnic and Regional Foodways in the United States*. Knoxville: University of Tennessee Press, 1984.

Brown, T. D. *Quality Control in Lumber Manufacture*. San Francisco: Miller Freeman Publications, 1982.

Browne, William P. *Cultivating Congress*. Lawrence: University Press of Kansas, 1995.

Browne, William P., Jerry R. Skees, Louis E. Swanson, Paul B. Thompson, and Laurian J. Unnevehr. *Sacred Cows and Hot Potatoes: Agrarian Myths in Agricultural Policy*. Boulder, CO: Westview, 1992.

Brunvand, Jan Harold. *The Study of American Folklore: An Introduction*. 3d ed. New York: W. W. Norton, 1986.

Bruyn, Severyn T., and James Meehan. *Beyond the Market and the State: New Directions in Community Development*. Philadelphia: Temple University Press, 1987.

Bryan, Frank. *Politics in the Rural States: People, Parties and Processes*. Boulder, CO: Westview, 1981.

Bull, C. Neil, ed. *Aging in Rural America*. Newbury Park, CA: Sage Publications, 1993.

Bull, C. Neil, and Share D. Bane, eds. *The Future of Aging in Rural America*. Kansas City, MO: National Resource Center for Rural Elderly, University of Missouri at Kansas City, 1992.

Burt, Brian A., and Stephen A. Eklund, eds. *Dentistry, Dental Practice and the Community*. 4th ed. Philadelphia: W. B. Saunders, 1992.

Busch, Lawrence, and William B. Lacy. *Science, Agriculture and the Politics of Research*. Boulder, CO: Westview, 1983.

Busch, Lawrence, and William B. Lacy, eds. *The Agricultural Scientific Enterprise: A System in Transition*. Boulder, CO: Westview, 1986.

Butler, Margaret A. *The Farm Entrepreneurial Population, 1988–1990*. Washington, DC: U.S. Department of Agriculture, Economic Research Service, 1993.

Buttel, Frederick H., Olaf F. Larson, and Gilbert W. Gillespie, Jr. *The Sociology of Agriculture*. Westport, CT: Greenwood Press, 1990.

Buzzanell, Peter, and Ron Lord. *Sugar and Corn Sweetener: Changing Demand and Trade in Mexico, Canada, and the United States*. Agriculture Information Bulletin Number 655 (April). Washington, DC: U.S. Department of Agriculture, Economic Research Service, 1993.

Calkins, Peter H., and Dennis D. DiPietre. *Farm Business Management: Successful Decisions in a Changing Environment*. New York: Macmillan, 1983.

Callicott, J. Baird. *In Defense of the Land Ethic: Essays on Environmental Policy*. Albany: State University of New York Press, 1989.

Carlson, Robert V. *A Case Study of the Impact of a State-level Policy Designed to Improve Rural Schools in the State of Vermont*. Occasional Paper No. 36. Charleston, WV: Appalachia Educational Laboratory, February 1994.

Carroll, Matthew S. *Community and the Northwestern Logger: Continuities and Changes in the Era of the Spotted Owl*. Boulder, CO: Westview, 1995.

Carson, Rachel. *Silent Spring*. Boston: Houghton Mifflin, 1962.

Carter, Harold O., Henry J. Vaux, Jr., and Ann F. Scheuring, eds. *Sharing Scarcity: Gainers and Losers in Water Marketing*. Davis: University of California Agricultural Issues Center, 1994.

Carter, M. R. *Conservation Tillage in Temperate Agroecosystems*. Baco Raton, FL: Lewis, CRC Press, 1994.

Carter, Timothy J., G. Howard Phillips, Joseph F. Donnermeyer, and Todd N. Wurschmidt. *Rural Crime: Integrating Research and Prevention*. Totowa, NJ: Allanheld, Osmund, 1983.

Cassidy, Frederic G. *The Dictionary of American Regional English*, Volumes I, II, and III. Cambridge, MA: Harvard University Press, 1985, 1991, 1996.

Castle, Emery N., ed. *The American Countryside: Rural People and Places*. Lawrence: University Press of Kansas, 1995.

Chan, Sucheng. *This Bittersweet Soil: The Chinese in California Agriculture, 1860–1910*. Berkeley: University of California Press, 1986.

Cheeke, Peter R. *Impacts of Livestock Production on Society, Diet/Health and the Environment*. Danville, IL: Interstate, 1993.

Chibnik, Michael. *Farm Work and Fieldwork: American Agriculture in Anthropological Perspective*. Ithaca, NY: Cornell University Press, 1987.

Childs, Alan W., and Gary B. Melton., eds. *Rural Psychology*. New York: Plenum Press, 1983.

Chicago Board of Trade. *Commodity Trading Manual*. Chicago: Chicago Board of Trade, 1989.

———. *Grains, Production, Processing and Marketing*. Chicago: Chicago Board of Trade, 1982.

Chicago Board of Trade, Education and Marketing Services Department. *Introduction to Agricultural Hedging*. Chicago: Chicago Board of Trade, 1988.

Chicago Mercantile Exchange. *A Self-Study Guide to Hedging with Livestock Futures*. Chicago: Chicago Mercantile Exchange, 1986.

Childs, Alan W., and Gary B. Melton, eds. *Rural Psychology*. New York: Plenum Press, 1983.

Christensen, James, Richard C. Maurer, and Nancy L. Strang. *Rural Data, People, and Policy: Information Systems for the 21st Century*. Boulder, CO: Westview, 1994.

Christenson, James A., and Cornelia B. Flora. *Rural Policies for the 1990s*. Boulder, CO: Westview, 1991.

Church, D. C. *Livestock Feeds and Feeding*. 3d ed. Englewood Cliffs, NJ: Prentice-Hall, 1991.

Clark, E. H. II, J. A. Haverkamp, and W. Chapman. *Eroding Soils: The Off-Farm Impacts*. Washington, DC: Conservation Foundation, 1985.

Clay, Daniel C., and Harry K. Schwarzweller. *Household Strategies. Research in Rural Sociology and Development*, Vol. 5. Greenwich, CT: JAI Press, 1991.

Claytor, Diana L., coord. *Bibliography of Fruit, Vegetable, Tree Nut, and Ornamental Publications*. U.S. Department of Agriculture handout, prepared for the 1994 Produce Marketing Association Convention and Exposition, San Antonio, TX, October 1994.

Cleland, Charles L., Will Fontanez, and Brian S. Williams. *Rurality*

Scores for U.S. Counties, 1994 (map). Agricultural Experiment Station Bulletin 689. Knoxville: University of Tennessee, 1994.

Coastal Georgia Regional Development Center. *Rural Solid Waste Management: Regional Planning User Guide.* Brunswick, GA: Coastal Georgia Regional Development Center, 1994.

Cobia, David W., ed. *Cooperatives in Agriculture.* Englewood Cliffs, NJ: Prentice-Hall, 1989.

Coburn, Andrew, Sam Cordes, Robert Crittenden, J. Patrick Hart, Keith Mueller, Wayne Myers, and Thomas Ricketts. *The Rural Perspective on National Health Reform Legislation: What Are the Critical Issues?* Prepared for House Committee on Agriculture. Columbia: Rural Policy Research Institute, University of Missouri, 1994.

Coburn, Carol K. *Life at Four Corners: Religion, Gender, and Education in a German-Lutheran Community, 1868–1945.* Lawrence: University Press of Kansas, 1992.

Cochrane, Willard W. *The Development of American Agriculture, A Historical Analysis.* 2d ed. Minneapolis: University of Minnesota Press, 1993.

Cocklin, Chris, Barry Smit, and Tom Johnston, eds. *Demands on Rural Lands: Planning for Resource Use.* Boulder, CO: Westview, 1987.

Commission on Agricultural Workers. *Report of the Commission on Agricultural Workers.* Washington, DC: U.S. Government Printing Office, 1993.

Comstock, Gary, ed. *Is There a Moral Obligation to Save the Family Farm?* Ames: Iowa State University Press, 1987.

Conger, R., D. Conger, and Glen H. Elder, Jr. *Families in Troubled Times: Adapting to Change in Rural America.* New York: Aldine de Gruyter, 1994.

Conrat, Maisie, and Richard Conrat. *The American Farm: A Photographic History.* San Francisco: California Historical Society and Boston: Houghton Mifflin, 1977.

Cook, Peggy J., and Karen L. Mizer. *The Revised ERS County Typology: An Overview.* Rural Development Research Report No. 89. Washington, DC: U.S. Department of Agriculture, Economic Research Service, 1994.

Cook, Roberta L. *North American Free Trade Agreement: Fruit and Vegetable Issues, Volume IV.* Park Ridge, IL: American Farm Bureau Research Foundation Project, 1991.

Copeland, J. D. *Recreational Access to Private Lands: Liability Problems and Solutions.* Fayetteville, AR: National Center for Agricultural Law Research and Information, 1995.

Copeland, J. D. *Understanding the Farmers Comprehensive Personal Liability Policy: A Guide for Farmers' Attorneys and Insurance Agents.* Fayetteville, AR: National Center for Agricultural Law Research and Information, 1992.

Corbin, David. *Life, Work and Rebellion in the Coal Fields: The Southern West Virginia Miners, 1880–1922.* Urbana: University of Illinois Press, 1981.

Cotterill, Ronald W. *Competitive Strategy Analysis for Agricultural Marketing Cooperatives.* Boulder, CO: Westview, 1994.

Council for Agricultural Science and Technology (CAST). *Effective Use of Water in Irrigated Agriculture.* Ames, IA: Council for Agricultural Science and Technology, 1988.

Coward, Raymond T., and Jeffrey W. Dwyer. *Health Programs and Services for Elders in Rural America: A Review of the Life Circumstances and Formal Services That Affect the Health and Well-Being of Elders.* Kansas City, MO: National Resource Center for Rural Elderly, University of Missouri, Kansas City, 1991.

Coward, Raymond T., Gary R. Lee, Jeffrey W. Dwyer, and Karen Seccombe. *Old and Alone in Rural America.* Washington, DC: American Association of Retired Persons, 1993.

Coward, Raymond T., C. Neil Bull, Gary Kukulka, and James M. Galliher, eds. *Health Services for Rural Elders.* New York: Springer, 1994.

Coward, Raymond T., and Gary R. Lee, eds. *The Elderly in Rural Society: Every Fourth Elder.* New York: Springer, 1985.

Coward, Raymond T., and William M. Smith, eds. *The Family in Rural Society.* Boulder, CO: Westview, 1981.

Cramer, Gail L., and Eric J. Wailes, eds. *Grain Marketing.* 2d ed. Boulder, CO: Westview, 1993.

Crispeels, M. J., and D. E. Sadava. *Plants, Genes, and Agriculture.* Boston: Jones and Bartlett, 1994.

Critchfield, Richard. *Trees, Why Do You Wait?* Washington, DC: Island Press, 1991.

Dacquel, Laami T., and Donald C. Dahmann. *Residents of Farms and Rural Areas: 1991.* Bureau of the Census, Current Population Reports, P20-472. Washington, DC: U.S. Government Printing Office, 1993.

Dana, S. T., and S. K. Fairfax. *Forest and Range Policy.* New York: McGraw-Hill, 1980.

Danbom, David B. *Born in the Country: A History of Rural America.* Baltimore: Johns Hopkins University Press, 1995.

Daniel, Pete. *Breaking the Land: The Transformation of Cotton, Tobacco, and Rice Cultures since 1880.* Urbana: University of Illinois Press, 1985.

Dary, David. *Cowboy Culture: A Saga of Five Centuries.* New York: Knopf, 1981. Lawrence: University Press of Kansas, 1989.

Daugherty, Arthur B. *Major Uses of Land in the United States: 1992.* AER-723. Washington, DC: U.S. Department of Agriculture, Economic Research Service, 1995.

Davidson, Osha Gray. *Broken Heartland.* New York: Free Press, 1990.

Davidson, R. H., and W. F. Lyon. *Insect Pests of Farm, Garden, and Orchard.* 8th ed. New York: Wiley, 1987.

Davis, R. C., ed. *Encyclopedia of American Forest and Conservation History.* 2 vols. New York: Macmillan, 1983.

Davis, Robert Murray. *Playing Cowboys: Low Culture and High Art in the Western.* Norman: University of Oklahoma Press, 1992.

DeBraal, J. Peter. *Foreign Ownership of U.S. Agricultural Land.* Statistical Bulletin No. 879. Washington, DC: U.S. Department of Agriculture, Economic Research Service, 1994.

DeBraal, J. Peter. *Taxes on U.S. Agricultural Real Estate, 1890–1991, and Methods of Estimation.* SB-866. Washington, DC: U.S. Department of Agriculture, Economic Research Service, 1993.

DeBuys, William. *Enchantment and Exploitation: The Life and Hard Times of a New Mexico Mountain Range.* Albuquerque: University of New Mexico Press, 1985.

Decker, Daniel J., and Gary R. Goff. *Valuing Wildlife: Economic and Social Perspectives.* Boulder, CO: Westview, 1987.

DeGrove, John M., and Deborah A. Miness. *The New Frontier for Land Policy: Planning and Growth Management in the States.* Cambridge, MA: Lincoln Institute of Land Policy, 1992.

Dethloff, Henry C. *A History of the American Rice Industry, 1685–1985.* College Station: Texas A&M University Press, 1988.

Detomasi, Don D., and John W. Gartrell, eds. *Resource Communities: A Decade of Disruption.* Boulder, CO: Westview, 1984.

DeYoung, Alan J. *The Life and Death of a Rural American High School: Farewell, Little Kanawha.* New York: Garland, 1995.

DeYoung, Alan J. *Rural Education Issues and Practices.* New York and London: Garland, 1991.

Dicks, Michael R., and Katharine C. Buckley, eds. *Alternative Opportunities in Agriculture: Expanding Output through Diversification.* Agricultural Economic Report No. 633. Washington, DC: U.S. Department of Agriculture, Economic Research Service, 1989.

Dillman, Don, and Daryl Hobbs. *Rural Society in the U.S.: Issues for the 1980s.* Boulder, CO: Westview, 1982.

Doeksen, Gerald A., et al. *A Guidebook for Rural Solid Waste Management Services.* Mississippi State, MS: Southern Rural Development Center, 1993.

Dolbeare, Cushing N. *Conditions and Trends in Rural Housing. A Home in the Country: The Housing Challenges Facing Rural America.* Fannie Mae Office of Housing Research, October 30, 1995.

Doppelt, B., M. Scurlock, C. Frissell, and J. Karr. *Entering the Watershed: A New Approach to Save America's River Ecosystems.* Covelo, CA: Pacific Rivers Council, 1993.

Dorman, Robert L. *Revolt of the Provinces: The Regionalist Movement in America, 1920–1945.* Chapel Hill: University of North Carolina Press, 1993.

Duncan, Cynthia M., ed. *Rural Poverty in America.* New York: Auburn House, 1992.

Duncan, Dayton. *Miles from Nowhere: Tales from America's Contemporary Frontier.* New York: Viking, 1993.

Durham, Weldon B. *American Theater Companies, 1888–1930.* New York: Greenwood Press, 1987.

Dyson, Lowell K. *Farmers' Organizations.* Westport, CT: Greenwood Press, 1986.

Edwards, Franklin R., and Cindy W. Ma. *Futures and Options.* New York: McGraw-Hill, 1992.

Egerstrom, Lee. *Make No Small Plans.* Rochester, MN: Lone Oak Press, 1994.

Elliott, R. L., and M. E. Jensen, eds. *Design and Operation of Farm Irrigation Systems.* 2d ed. ASAE Monograph No. 3. St. Joseph, MI: American Society of Agricultural Engineering, 1997.

Ensminger, M. E. *Animal Science.* 9th ed. Danville, IL: Interstate, 1991.

———. *Dairy Cattle Science.* 3d ed. Danville, IL: Interstate, 1993.

Ensminger, Robert F. *The Pennsylvania Barn: Its Origin, Evolution, and Distribution in North America.* Baltimore: Johns Hopkins University Press, 1992.

Erickson, Duane E., and John T. Scott, eds. *Farm Real Estate.* NCR No. 51. Urbana: University of Illinois, 1990.

Estes, E. A., ed. *Look through the 90's: The U.S. Fruit and Vegetable Industry.* Proceedings of the S-222 Regional Research Committee Workshop on the U.S. Fruit and Vegetable Industry. Overland Park, KS: Packer, Vance Publications, June 1990.

Evans, Bernard, and Greg Cusack, eds. *Theology of the Land.* Collegeville, MN: Liturgical Press, 1987.

Ewert, Alan W., Deborah J. Chavez, and Arthur W. Magill. *Culture, Conflict, and Communication in the Wildland-Urban Interface.* Boulder, CO: Westview, 1993.

Eysberg, Cyees D. *The Californian Wine Economy: Natural Opportunities and Socio-Cultural Constraints.* Utrecht, Netherlands: Netherlands Geographical Studies, 1990.

Fahl, R. J. *North American Forest and Conservation History: A Bibliography.* Santa Barbara, CA: Forest History Society, 1977. Updated annually in computerized database by Forest History Society, Durham, NC.

Fairbanks, Carol, and Sara Brooks Sundberg. *Farm Women on the Prairie Frontier: A Sourcebook for Canada and the United States.* Metuchen, NJ: Scarecrow Press, 1983.

Fairchild, Deborah M., ed. *Groundwater Quality and Agricultural Practices.* Chelsea, MI: Lewis, 1987.

Falk, William W., and Thomas A. Lyson. *High Tech, Low Tech, No Tech: Recent Occupational and Industrial Changes in the South.* Albany: State University of New York Press, 1988.

Falk, William W., and Thomas A. Lyson. *Rural Labor Markets.* Research in Rural Sociology and Development. Greenwich, CT: JAI Press, 1989.

Fanning, D. S., and M. C. B. Fanning. *Soil Morphology, Genesis, and Classification.* New York: John Wiley and Sons, 1989.

Faust, Miklos. *Physiology of Temperate Zone Fruit Trees.* New York: John Wiley and Sons, 1989.

Ferleger, Lou. *Agricultural and National Development: Views on the Nineteenth Century.* Henry A. Wallace Series. Ames: Iowa State University Press, 1990.

Fett, John. *Sources and Use of Agricultural Information: A Literature Review.* Madison: Department of Agricultural Journalism, University of Wisconsin, 1993.

Finlayson, Max, and Michael Moser. *Wetlands.* Oxford, UK: International Waterfowl and Wetlands Research Bureau, Facts on File, 1991.

Fink, Deborah. *Agrarian Women: Wives and Mothers in Rural Nebraska, 1880–1940.* Chapel Hill: University of North Carolina Press, 1992.

Fishback, Price. *Soft Coal, Hard Choices: The Economic Welfare of Bituminous Coal Miners, 1890–1930.* New York: Oxford University Press, 1992.

Fitchen, Janet M. *Endangered Spaces, Enduring Places: Change, Identity, and Survival in Rural America.* Boulder, CO: Westview, 1991.

———. *Poverty in Rural America: A Case Study.* Boulder, CO: Westview, 1981.

Fite, Gilbert C. *American Farmers: The New Minority.* Bloomington: Indiana University Press, 1981.

Fleisher, B. *Agricultural Risk Management.* Boulder, CO: Lynne Rienner, 1990.

Flint, M. L., and R. Van den Bosch. *Introduction to Integrated Pest Management.* New York: Plenum Press, 1981.

Flora, Cornelia B., and James A. Christenson, eds. *Rural Policies for the 1990s*. Boulder, CO: Westview, 1991.

Flora, Cornelia Butler, Jan L. Flora, Jacqueline D. Spears, and Louis E. Swanson, with Mark B. Lapping and Mark L. Weinberg. *Rural Communities: Legacy and Change*. Boulder, CO: Westview, 1992.

Fluck, Richard C., ed. *Energy in Farm Production*. Vol. 6, *Energy in World Agriculture*. B. A. Stout, editor-in-chief. Amsterdam: Elsevier, 1992.

Follett, R. F., and B. A. Stewart. *Soil Erosion and Crop Productivity*. Madison, WI: American Society of Agronomy, 1985.

Foth, H. D. *Fundamentals of Soil Science*. 8th ed. New York: Wiley, 1990.

Francavighia, Richard V. *Hard Places: Reading the Landscape of America's Historic Mining Districts*. Iowa City: University of Iowa Press, 1991.

Fraser, Andrew F., and Donald M. Broom. *Farm Animal Behavior and Welfare*. 3d ed. Philadelphia: Bailliere Tindall, 1990.

Fraser, James. *The American Billboard: 100 Years*. New York: Harry N. Abrams, 1991.

Free, John B. *Insect Pollination of Crops*. London, England: Academic Press, 1992.

Freier, George D. *Weather Proverbs: How 600 Proverbs, Sayings and Poems Accurately Explain Our Weather*. Tucson, AZ: Fisher Books, 1989.

Frenzen, Paul D. *The Medicare and Medicaid Programs in Rural America: A Profile of Program Beneficiaries and Health Care Providers*. Staff Paper No. AGES9604. Washington, DC: U.S. Department of Agriculture, Rural Economy Division, Economic Research Service, 1996.

Freudenberger, C. Dean. *Food for Tomorrow?* Minneapolis: Augsburg, 1984.

Friedland, William H., Amy E. Barton, and Robert J. Thomas. *Manufacturing Green Gold: Capital, Labor, and Technology in the Lettuce Industry*. New York: Cambridge University Press, 1981.

Fuguitt, Glenn V., David L. Brown, and Calvin L. Beale. *Rural and Small Town America*. New York: Russell Sage, 1989.

Fuller, Varden. *Hired Hands in California's Farm Fields*. Giannini Foundation Special Report. Davis: University of California, Davis, June 1991.

Fuller, Wayne E. *The Old Country School: The Story of Rural Education in the Middle West*. Chicago: University of Chicago Press, 1982.

———. *One-room Schools of the Middle West: An Illustrated History*. Lawrence: University Press of Kansas, 1994.

Galaty, John G., and Douglas L. Johnson, eds. *The World of Pastoralism: Herding Systems in Comparative Perspective*. New York: Guilford Press, 1990.

Galbraith, Michael W., ed. *Education in the Rural American Community: A Lifelong Process*. Melbourne, FL: Krieger, 1992.

Galeski, Boguslaw, and Eugene Wilkening. *Family Farming in Europe and America*. Boulder, CO: Westview, 1987.

Gamboa, Erasmo. *Mexican Labor and World War II: Braceros in the Pacific Northwest, 1942–1947*. Austin: University of Texas Press, 1990.

Gard, Robert, and Kolhoff, Ralph. *The Arts in the Small Community: A National Plan*. Washington DC: National Assembly of Local Arts Agencies, reprinted 1984.

Garreau, Joel. *The Nine Nations of North America*. Boston: Houghton Mifflin, 1981.

Gaventa, John. *Power and Powerlessness: Quiescence and Rebellion in an Appalachian Valley*. Urbana: University of Illinois Press, 1980.

Geisler, Charles C., and Frank J. Popper, eds. *Land Reform, American Style*. Totawa, NJ: Rowan and Allanheld, 1984.

Gendel, Steven M., A. David Kline, D. Michael Warren, and Faye Yates, eds. *Agricultural Bioethics: Implications of Agricultural Biotechnology*. Ames: Iowa State University Press, 1990.

General Accounting Office. *Pesticides: A Comparative Study of Industrialized Nations' Regulatory Systems*. Washington, DC: Program Evaluation and Methodology Division, GAO, July 1993.

———. *U.S. Agriculture: Status of the Farm Sector*, GAO/RCED–95–104FS. Washington, DC: General Accounting Office, March 1995.

George, Henry. *The Land Question*. New York: Robert Shalkenbach Foundation, 1881/1982.

Ghelfi, Linda M., ed. *Rural Conditions and Trends: Special Census Issue* 4, no. 3. Washington, DC: U.S. Department of Agriculture, Economic Research Service, 1993.

Gibbons, Diana C. *The Economic Value of Water*. Washington, DC: Resources for the Future, 1986.

Gibson, Eric. *Sell What You Sow: The Grower's Guide To Successful Produce Marketing*. Carmichael, CA: New World, 1994.

Gilbert, Jess, ed. "Minorities in Rural Society." *Rural Sociology* (Special Issue) 56 (1991): 175–298.

Gilbert, Richard, J., ed. *The Environment of Oil*. Norwell, MA: Kluwer, 1993.

Gilford, Dorothy M., Glen L. Nelson, and Linda Ingram, eds. *Rural America in Passage: Statistics for Policy*. Washington, DC: National Academy Press, 1981.

Ginsburg, Leon H. *Social Work in Rural Communities*. 2d ed. Alexandria, VA: Council on Social Work Education, 1993.

Glasmeier, Amy K. *Rural America in the Age of High Technology*. New Brunswick, NJ: Center for Urban Policy Research, Rutgers University Press, 1991.

Glasmeier, Amy K., and Michael E. Conroy. *Global Squeeze on Rural America: Opportunities, Threats, and Challenges from NAFTA, GATT, and Processes of Globalization*. A Report of the Institute for Policy Research and Evaluation, Graduate School of Public Policy and Administration. College Park: Pennsylvania State University, 1994.

Glenn, George D., and Poole, Richard L. *The Opera Houses of Iowa*. Ames: Iowa State University Press, 1993.

Goldman, Robert, and Stephen Papson. *Sign Wars: The Cluttered Landscape of Advertising*. New York: Guilford, 1996.

Goodwin, John W. *Agricultural Price Analysis and Forecasting*. New York: John Wiley and Sons, 1994.

Gopalakrishnan, Chennat. *The Economics of Energy in Agriculture*. Aldershot, UK: Avebury, 1994.

Gordon, Robert B., and Patrick M. Malone. *The Texture of Industry:*

An Archaeological View of the Industrialization of North America. New York: Oxford, 1994.

Goreham, Gary. *The Rural Church in America: A Century of Writings—A Bibliography.* New York: Garland, 1990.

Goreham, Gary A., David L. Watt, and Roy Jacobsen. *The Socioeconomics of Sustainable Agriculture: An Annotated Bibliography.* New York: Garland, 1993.

Government Accounting Office. *Wool and Mohair Program, Need for Program Still in Question.* GAO/RCED-90–51 (March). Washington, DC: Government Accounting Office, 1990.

Graf, William L., ed. *Geomorphic Systems of North America.* Boulder, CO: Geological Society of America, 1987.

Graham, Joe M., John T. Ambrose, Lorenzo L. Longstroth, eds. *The Hive and the Honey Bee.* Hamilton, IL: Dadant and Sons, 1992.

Gregory, James Noble. *American Exodus: The Dust Bowl Migration and Okie Culture in California.* New York: Oxford University Press, 1989.

Grey, Gene, and Gregory Smith. *So You Want to Be in Forestry.* Bethesda, MD: American Forestry Association and Society of American Foresters, 1989.

Griffith, David, and Ed Kissam. *Working Poor: Farmworkers in the United States.* Philadelphia: Temple University Press, 1995.

Grigg, David. *The Dynamics of Agricultural Change: The Historical Experience.* New York: St. Martin's Press, 1982.

Gringeri, Christina E. *Getting By: Women Homeworkers and Rural Economic Development.* Lawrence: University Press of Kansas, 1994.

Gulliford, Andrew. *Boomtown Blues: Colorado Oil Shale, 1885–1985.* Niwot: University Press of Colorado, 1989.

Gunn, Christopher, and Hazel Dayton Gunn. *Reclaiming Capital: Democratic Initiatives and Community Development.* Ithaca, NY: Cornell University Press, 1991.

Hadwiger, Don F. *The Politics of Agricultural Research.* Lincoln: University of Nebraska Press, 1982.

Hahn, Steven, and Jonathan Prude, eds. *The Countryside in the Age of Capitalist Transformation: Essays in the Social History of Rural America.* Chapel Hill: University of North Carolina Press, 1985.

Halcrow, H. G., E. O. Heady, and M. L. Cotner, eds. *Soil Conservation Policies, Institutions, and Incentives.* Ankeny, IA: Soil Conservation Society Press, 1982.

Hall, Carl W., Nelson E. Hay, and Walter Vergara. *Natural Gas: Its Role and Potential in Economic Development.* Boulder, CO: Westview, 1990.

Hall, J. D., J. Leloudis, R. Korstad, M. Murphy, L. Jones, and C. B. Daly. *Like a Family: The Making of a Southern Cotton Mill World.* Chapel Hill: University of North Carolina Press, 1987.

Hallam, Arne. *Size, Structure, and the Changing Face of American Agriculture.* Boulder, CO: Westview, 1993.

Hallberg, Milton C. *The U.S. Agricultural and Food System: A Postwar Historical Perspective.* Publication No. 35. University Park: Northeast Center for Rural Development, Pennsylvania State University, 1988.

Hallberg, Milton C., Robert F. G. Spitze, and Daryll E. Ray, eds. *Food, Agriculture, and Rural Policy into the Twenty-first Century: Issues and Trade-offs.* Boulder, CO: Westview, 1994.

Hammerman, Donald R., William M. Hammerman, and Elizabeth L. Hammerman. *Teaching in the Outdoors.* Danville, IL: Interstate Printing, 1985.

Hammerman, William M., ed. *Fifty Years of Resident Outdoor Education.* Martinsville, IN: American Camping Association, 1981.

Haney, Wava G., and Donald R. Field. *Agriculture and Natural Resources: Planning for Educational Priorities for the Twenty-first Century.* Boulder, CO: Westview, 1991.

Haney, Wava G., and Jane B. Knowles, eds. *Women and Farming: Changing Roles, Changing Structures.* Boulder, CO: Westview, 1988.

Hanou, John. *A Round Indiana: Round Barns in the Hoosier State.* West Lafayette, IN: Purdue University Press, 1993.

Hargett, N. L., and J. T. Berry. *Commercial Fertilizers 1990.* TVA Bulletin Y-216. Muscle Shoals, AL: Tennessee Valley Authority, National Fertilizer, and Environmental Research Center, 1990.

Harl, Neil E. *The Farm Debt Crisis of the 1980s.* Ames: Iowa State University Press, 1990.

Harper, Sarah. *The Greening of Rural Policy: Perspectives from the Developed World.* London and New York: Guilford Press, 1993.

Harsh, Stephen B., Larry J. Connor, and Gerald D. Schwab. *Managing the Farm Business.* Englewood Cliffs, NJ: Prentice-Hall, 1981.

Hart, G. L., R. A. Rosenblatt, and B. A. Amundson. *Rural Hospital Utilization: Who Stays and Who Goes?* WAMI Rural Health Research Center, working paper series, March 1989.

Hartel, Peter G., Kathryn Paxton George, and James Vorst, eds. *Agricultural Ethics: Issues for the 21st Century.* ASA Special Publication no. 57. Madison, WI: Soil Science Society of America, American Society of Agronomy, Crop Science Society of America, 1994.

Hassebrook, Chuck, and Gabriel Hegyes. *Choices for the Heartland: Alternative Directions in Biotechnology and Implications for Family Farming, Rural Communities, and the Environment.* Ames: Iowa State University, Technology and Social Change Program, and Walthill, NE: Center for Rural Affairs, 1989.

Hassinger, Edward W., John S. Holik, and J. Kenneth Benson. *The Rural Church: Learnings from Three Decades of Change.* Nashville, TN: Abingdon Press, 1988.

Hatch, Upton, and Henry Kinnucan, eds. *Aquaculture: Models and Economics.* Boulder, CO: Westview, 1993.

Havir, Linda Marie. *But Will They Use It? Social Service Utilization by Rural Elderly.* New York: Garland, 1995.

Havlin, John, Alan Schlegel, Kevin C. Dhuyvetter, James P. Shroyer, Hans Kok, and Dallas Peterson. *Enhancing Agricultural Profitability and Sustainability: Great Plains Dryland Conservation Technologies.* S-81. Manhattan: Cooperative Extension Service, Kansas State University, 1995.

Hawley, Amos H., and Sara Mills Maize, eds. *Nonmetropolitan America in Transition.* Chapel Hill: University of North Carolina Press, 1981.

Hayes, Robert G., ed. *Early Stories from the Land: Short-Story Fiction from Rural American Magazines, 1900–1925.* Ames: Iowa State University Press, 1995.

Haynes, Richard W. *An Analysis of the Timber Situation in the*

United States: 1989–2040. USDA General Technical Report RM-199. Washington, DC: U.S. Department of Agriculture, Forest Service, 1990.

Heady, Harold F., and R. Dennis Child. *Rangeland Ecology and Management*. Boulder, CO: Westview, 1995.

Hedges, Elaine, and William Hedges. *Land and Imagination: The Rural Dream in America*. Rochelle Park, NJ: Hayden Book Company, 1980.

Heffernan, William, Douglas Constance, Robert Gronski, and Mary Hendrickson. *Concentration of Agricultural Markets*. Columbia: Department of Rural Sociology, University of Missouri–Columbia, 1996.

Heimlich, Ralph, and L. Langer. *Swampbusting: Wetland Conversion and Farm Programs*. Agricultural Economics Report No. 51. Washington DC: U.S. Department of Agriculture, Natural Resource Economics Division, Economic Research Service, 1986.

Heiser, Charles B., Jr. *Seed to Civilization: The Story of Food*. San Francisco: W. H. Freeman, 1981.

Heitschmidt, Rodney K., and Jerry W. Stuth, eds. *Grazing Management: An Ecological Perspective*. Portland, OR: Timber Press, 1991.

Helge, D., guest editor. Special Topical Issue: Rural Special Education. *Journal of Exceptional Children* 50, no. 4 (1984): 293–369.

Helsel, Zane R., ed. *Energy in Plant Nutrition and Pest Control*. Vol. 2: *Energy in World Agriculture*. B. A. Stout, editor-in-chief. Amsterdam: Elsevier, 1987.

Hewitt, Marcia E. *Defining "Rural" Areas: Impact on Health Care Policy and Research*. Staff Paper, Office of Technology Assessment. Washington, DC: U.S. Government Printing Office, 1989.

Heywood, V. H., ed. *Global Biodiversity Assessment*. New York: Cambridge University Press, 1995.

Hickey, Joseph V. *Ghost Settlement on the Prairie: A Biography of Thurman, Kansas*. Lawrence: University Press of Kansas, 1995.

Hickman, John, Jeff Jacobsen, and Drew Lyon. *Best Management Practices for Wheat: A Guide to Profitable and Environmentally Sound Production*. Washington, DC: Cooperative Extension Service and National Association of Wheat Growers Foundation, 1994.

Hillel, Daniel. 1991. *Out of the Earth: Civilization and the Life of the Soil*. Berkeley: University of California Press.

Hirschfelder, Arlene, and Martha Kreipe de Montano. *The Native American Almanac: A Portrait of Native America Today*. New York: Prentice Hall General Reference, 1993.

Hoban, Thomas J., and Patricia A. Kendall. *Consumer Attitudes about Food Biotechnology*. Raleigh: North Carolina Cooperative Extension Service, 1993.

Hodgson, John. *Grazing Management Science into Practice*. New York: John Wiley and Sons, copublished with Longman Scientific and Technical, 1990.

Hoffman, G. J., T. A. Howell, and K. H. Solomon, eds. *Management of Farm Irrigation Systems*. ASAE Monograph. St. Joseph, MI: American Society of Agricultural Engineering, 1990.

Hoffman, Linwood A., Sara Schwartz, and Grace V. Chomo. *Wheat: Background for 1995 Farm Legislation*. Agricultural Economic

Report No. 712. Washington, DC: U.S. Department of Agriculture, Economic Research Service, 1995.

Holechek, Jerry L., Rex D. Pieper, and Carlton H. Herbel. *Range Management: Principles and Practices*. Englewood Cliffs, NJ: Prentice Hall, 1989.

Holland, I. I., G. L. Rolfe, and D. A. Anderson. *Forests and Forestry*. Danville, IL: Interstate, 1990.

Hopkin and Associates. *Transition in Agriculture: A Strategic Assessment of Agricultural Banking*. Washington, DC: American Bankers Association, 1986.

Hoppe, R. *The Role of the Elderly's Income in Rural Development*. Rural Development Research Report 80. Washington, DC: U.S. Department of Agriculture, Economic Research Service, 1991.

Horan, Patrick M., and Charles M. Tolbert II. *The Organization of Work in Rural and Urban Labor Markets*. Boulder, CO: Westview, 1984.

Housing Assistance Council. *Rural Homelessness: A Review of the Literature*. Washington, DC: Housing Assistance Council, 1991.

Howell, F. M., Y. Tung, and C. W. Harper. *The Social Cost of Growing-up in Rural America: A Study of Rural Development and Social Change during the Twentieth Century*. Mississippi State, MS: Social Science Research Center, Mississippi State University, October 1995.

Hoxie, Frederick E. *A Final Promise: The Campaign to Assimilate the Indian, 1880–1920*. Lincoln: University of Nebraska Press, 1984.

Hubka, Thomas C. *Big House, Little House, Back House, Barn: The Connected Farm Buildings of New England*. Hanover, NH: University Press of New England, 1984.

Hughes, Dean W., Stephen C. Gabriel, Peter J. Barry, and Michael D. Boehlje. *Financing the Agricultural Sector*. Boulder, CO: Westview, 1986.

Humstone, Mary. *Barn Again! A Guide to Rehabilitation of Older Farm Buildings*. Denver, CO: Meredith Corporation and National Trust for Historic Preservation, 1988.

Hunter, Kent R. *The Lord's Harvest and the Rural Church*. Kansas City, MO: Beacon Hill Press, 1993.

Hurt, R. Douglas. *American Agriculture: A Brief History*. Ames: Iowa State University Press, 1994.

Hurt, R. Douglas. *The Dust Bowl: An Agricultural and Social History*. Chicago: Nelson-Hall, 1981.

Ilic, Pedro. *Southeast Asian Farmers in Fresno County: Status Report 1992*. Fresno: Fresno County Office of University of California Cooperative Extension, 1992.

Inge, M. Thomas, ed. *Agrarianism in American Literature*. New York: Odyssey Press, 1969.

Isern, Thomas D. *Bull Threshers and Bindlestiffs: Harvesting and Threshing on the North American Plains*. Lawrence: University Press of Kansas, 1990.

Iwata, Masakazu. *Planted in Good Soil: A History of the Issei in United States Agriculture*. New York: P. Lang, 1992.

Jackson, Kenneth, and Camillo José Vergara. *Silent Cities: The Evolution of the American Cemetery*. New York: Princeton Architectural Press, 1989.

Jain, R. K., L. V. Urban, G. S. Stacey, and H. E. Balbach. *Environmental Assessment*. New York: McGraw-Hill, 1993.

Janick, Jules. *Horticultural Science.* 4th ed. New York: W. H. Freeman, 1986.

Jansson, AnnMari, Monicao Hammer, Carl Folke, and Robert Costanza, eds. *Investing in Natural Capital: The Ecological Economics Approach to Sustainability.* Covelo, CA: Island Press, 1994.

Jarvis, Lovel S. *The Potential Effect of Two Biotechnologies on the World Dairy Industry.* Boulder, CO: Westview, 1994.

Jasper, James M., and Dorothy Nelkin. *The Animal Rights Crusade: The Growth of a Moral Protest.* New York: Free Press, 1992.

Jellison, Katherine. *Entitled to Power: Farm Women and Technology.* Chapel Hill: University of North Carolina Press, 1993.

Jenkins, J. Craig. *The Politics of Insurgency: The Farm Worker Movement of the 1960's.* New York: Columbia University Press, 1985.

Jensen, M. E., ed. *Design and Operation of Farm Irrigation Systems.* ASAE Monograph No. 3. St. Joseph, MI: American Society of Agricultural Engineering, 1983.

Johannessen, S., and C. A. Hastorf, eds. *Corn and Culture in the Prehistoric New World.* Boulder, CO: Westview, 1994.

Johanson, Harley E., and Glenn V. Fuguitt. *The Changing Rural Village: Demographics and Rural Trends since 1950.* Cambridge, MA: Ballinger, 1984.

Johnson, Kenneth M. *The Impact of Population Change on Business Activity in Rural America.* Boulder, CO: Westview, 1985.

Johnson, Thomas, Brady J. Deaton, and Eduardo Segarra. *Local Infrastructure Investment in Rural America.* Boulder, CO: Westview, 1988.

Jones, Hamlyn G. *Plants and Microclimate: A Quantitative Approach to Environmental Plant Physiology.* 2d ed. New York: Cambridge University Press, 1992.

Journal of Soil and Water Conservation 32, no. 1 (1977): 3–65. Special issue on conservation tillage in different geographic regions of North America.

Judy, Marvin. *From Ivy Tower to Village Spire.* Dallas: Southern Methodist University Printing, 1984.

Jung, Shannon. *We Are Home: A Spirituality of the Environment.* Mahwah, NJ: Paulist Press, 1993.

Jung, Shannon, and Mary A. Agria. *Rural Congregational Studies: A Guide for Good Shepherds.* Nashville, TN: Abingdon, 1997.

Jung, Shannon, Pegge Boehm, Deborah Cronin, Gary Farley, Dean Freudenberger, Judy Heffernan, Sandy LaBlanc, Ed Queen, and Dave Ruesink. *Rural Ministry: The Shape of the Renewal to Come.* Nashville, TN: Abingdon Press, forthcoming 1997.

Kabacher, J., and V. Oliveira. *Structural and Financial Characteristics of U.S. Farms, 1992: 17th Annual Family Farm Report to Congress.* Agriculture Information Bulletin Number 72. Washington, DC: Rural Economy Division, Economic Research Service, U.S. Department of Agriculture, 1995.

Kader, Adel A., ed. *Postharvest Technology of Horticultural Crops.* Oakland: University of California, Division of Agriculture and Natural Resources, 1992.

Kadlec, John E. *Farm Management: Decisions, Operation, Control.* Englewood Cliffs, NJ: Prentice-Hall, 1985.

Kay, Ronald D., and William M. Edwards. *Farm Management.* 3d ed. New York: McGraw-Hill, 1994.

Keith, Jeanette. *Country People in the New South: Tennessee's Upper Cumberland.* Chapel Hill: University of North Carolina Press, 1995.

Keizer, Garrett. *No Place But Here: A Teacher's Vocation in a Rural Community.* New York: Viking Penguin, 1988.

Keller, Peter A., and J. Dennis Murray, eds. *Handbook of Rural Community Mental Health.* New York: Human Services Press, 1982.

Kellogg, Robert L., Margaret Stewart Maizel, and Don W. Goss. *Agricultural Chemical Use and Groundwater Quality: Where Are the Potential Problem Areas?* Washington, DC: U.S. Department of Agriculture, Soil Conservation Service, 1992.

Kelly, Eric Damian, and Gary J. Raso. *Sign Regulation for Small and Midsize Communities.* Planning Advisory Service Report No. 419. Chicago: American Planning Association, 1989.

Kenny, Martin F. *Biotechnology: The University-Industrial Complex.* New Haven, CT: Yale University Press, 1986.

Kephart, William M., and William W. Zellner. *Extraordinary Groups: An Examination of Unconventional Life-Styles.* 4th ed. New York: St. Martin's Press, 1991.

Kerr, Norwood A. *The Legacy: A Centennial History of the State Agricultural Experiment Stations 1887–1987.* Columbia: Missouri Agricultural Experiment Station, University of Missouri, 1987.

Killian, M. S., L. E. Bloomquist, S. Pendleton, and D. A. McGranahan, eds. *Symposium on Rural Labor Market Research Issues.* Staff Report AGES860721. Washington, DC: U.S. Department of Agriculture, Economic Research Service, 1986.

Kingsolver, Barbara. *Holding the Line: Women in the Great Arizona Mine Strike of 1983.* Ithaca, NY: ILR Press, 1989.

Kirschenman, Frederick. *Switching to a Sustainable System: Strategies for Converting from Conventional/Chemical to Sustainable/Organic Farm Systems.* Windsor, ND: Northern Plains Sustainable Agriculture Society, 1988; Emmaus, PA: Rodale Press, Holding Library, 1996.

Kloppenburg, Jack R., Jr. *First the Seed: The Political Economy of Plant Biotechnology, 1492–2000.* New York: Cambridge University Press, 1988.

Knobloch, Frieda. *The Culture of Wilderness: Agriculture as Colonization in the American West.* Chapel Hill: University of North Carolina Press, 1996.

Knutson, Ronald D., C. Robert Taylor, John B. Penson, and Edward G. Smith. *Economic Impacts of Reduced Chemical Use.* College Station, TX: Knutson and Associates, 1990.

Kohl, David M. *Weighing the Variables: A Guide to Ag Credit Management.* Washington, DC: American Bankers Association, 1992.

Kohls, Richard L., and Joseph N. Uhl. *Marketing of Agricultural Products.* 7th ed. New York: Macmillan, 1990.

Korsching, Peter F., Timothy O. Borich, and Julie Stewart, eds. *Multicommunity Collaboration: An Evolving Rural Revitalization Strategy.* Ames, IA: North Central Regional Center for Rural Development, July 1992.

Kraenzel, Carl. *The Social Cost of Space in Yonland.* Bozeman, MT: Big Sky Press, 1980.

Krause, Tina B., ed. *Care of the Earth: An Environmental Resource Manual for Church Leaders.* Chicago: Lutheran School of Theology at Chicago, 1994.

Kromm, David E., and Stephen E. White, eds. *Groundwater Exploitation in the High Plains.* Lawrence: University Press of Kansas, 1992.

Krout, J. A. *The Aged in Rural America.* New York: Greenwood Press, 1986.

Krout, J. A., ed. *Providing Community Based Services to the Rural Elderly.* Thousand Oaks, CA: Sage, 1994.

Lampkin, Nicolas. *Organic Farming.* Ipswich, UK: Farming Press Books, 1980.

Land, Aubrey, ed. *Bases of the Plantation Society.* Columbia: University of South Carolina Press, 1969.

Langhans, Robert W. *Greenhouse Management: A Guide to Structures, Materials Handling, Crop Programming, and Business Analysis.* 3d ed. Ithaca, NY: Halcyon Press of Ithaca, 1990.

Lapping, Mark B., Thomas L. Daniels, and John W. Keller. *Rural Planning and Development in the United States.* London and New York: Guilford Press, 1989.

LaRoe, Edward T., Gaye S. Farris, Catherine E. Puckett, Peter D. Doran, Michael J. Macs, eds. *Our Living Resources: A Report to the Nation on the Distribution, Abundance, and Health of U.S. Plants, Animals, and Ecosystems.* Washington, DC: U.S. Department of the Interior, National Biological Service, 1995.

Larson, Olaf F., Edward O. Moe, and Julie N. Zimmerman. *Sociology in Government: A Bibliography of the Work of the Division of Farm Population and Rural Life, U.S. Department of Agriculture, 1919–1953.* Boulder, CO: Westview, 1992.

Lasley, F. A. *The U.S. Poultry Industry: Changing Economics and Structure.* A.E. Report No. 502 (July). Washington, DC: U.S. Department of Agriculture, Economic Research Service, 1983.

Lasley, F. A., W. L. Henson, and H. B. Jones. *The U.S. Turkey Industry.* A.E. Report No. 525 (March). Washington, DC: U.S. Department of Agriculture, Economic Research Service, 1985.

Lasley, F. A., H. B. Jones, E. E. Easterling, and L. A. Christensen. *The U.S. Broiler Industry.* A.E. Report No. 591 (November). Washington, DC: U.S. Department of Agriculture, Economic Research Service, 1988.

Lasley, Paul, F. Larry Leistritz, Linda M. Lobao, and Katherine Meyer. *Beyond the Amber Waves of Grain: An Examination of Social and Economic Restructuring in the Heartland.* Boulder, CO: Westview, 1995.

Lee, Warren F., Michael D. Boehlje, Aaron G. Nelson, and William G. Murray. *Agricultural Finance.* 8th ed. Ames: Iowa State University Press, 1988.

Leistritz, F. Larry, and Steven H. Murdock. *The Socioeconomic Impact of Resource Development: Methods for Assessment.* Boulder, CO: Westview, 1981.

Lesser, William H. *Marketing Livestock and Meat.* Binghamton, NY: Food Products Press, 1993.

Leuthold, Raymond M., Joan C. Junkus, and Jean E. Cordier. *The Theory and Practice of Futures Markets.* Lexington, KY: Lexington Books, 1989.

Lewis, Ronald L. *Black Coal Miners in America: Race, Class and Community Conflict.* Lexington: University Press of Kentucky, 1987.

Lewis, Steven. *The Wisdom of the Spotted Owl.* Covelo, CA: Island Press, 1994.

Libbin, James D., Lowell B. Catlett, and Michael L. Jones. *Cash Flow Planning in Agriculture.* Ames: Iowa State University Press, 1994.

Lieb, Robert C. *Transportation.* 4th ed. Houston, TX: Dame Publications, 1994.

Lincoln, C. Eric, and Lawrence H. Mamiya. *The Black Church in African-American Experience.* Durham, NC: Duke University Press, 1990.

Linder, Marc. *Migrant Workers and Minimum Wages.* Boulder, CO: Westview, 1992.

Lingeman, Richard. *Small Town America: A Narrative History, 1620–the Present.* Boston: Houghton Mifflin, 1980.

Lobao, Linda M. *Locality and Inequality: Farm and Industry Structure and Socioeconomic Conditions.* Albany: State University of New York Press, 1990.

Long, Patrick, Jo Clark, and Derek Liston. *Win, Lose, or Draw? Gambling with America's Small Towns.* Washington, DC: Aspen Institute, 1994.

Longstreth, Richard. *The Buildings of Main Street: A Guide to American Commercial Architecture.* Washington, DC: Preservation Press, 1987.

Looney, J. W., J. Wilder, S. Brownback, and J. Wadley. *Agricultural Law: A Lawyer's Guide to Representing Farm Clients.* Chicago: American Bar Association, Section of General Practice, 1990.

Lovejoy, Stephen B., and Ted L. Napier, eds. *Conserving Soil: Insights from Socioeconomic Research.* Ankeny, IA: Soil Conservation Society Press, 1986.

Lovell, T. *Nutrition and Feeding of Fish.* New York: Van Nostrand Reinhold, 1989.

Lucier, Gary, coord. *Vegetables and Specialties: Situation and Outlook Report.* TVS-263 (July). Washington, DC: U.S. Department of Agriculture, Economic Research Service, 1994.

Luebke, Frederick, ed. *Ethnicity on the Great Plains.* Lincoln: University of Nebraska Press, 1980.

Luh, Bor S., ed. *Rice: Production and Utilization.* 2d ed. Vol. 2. New York: Van Nostrand Reinhold, 1991.

Luloff, A. E., and Louis E. Swanson. *American Rural Communities.* Boulder, CO: Westview, 1990.

Lyle, John Tillman. *Regenerative Design for Sustainable Development.* Wiley Series in Sustainable Design. New York: John Wiley and Sons, 1994.

Lyson, Thomas A. *Two Sides of the Sunbelt: The Growing Divergence between the Rural and Urban South.* New York: Praeger, 1989.

Lyson, Thomas A., and William W. Falk, eds. *Forgotten Places: Uneven Development in Rural America.* Lawrence: University Press of Kansas, 1993.

MaCC Group. *Waste Reduction Strategies for Rural Communities.* Washington, DC: American Plastics Council, with support from the Tennessee Valley Authority, 1994.

McCloskey, Amanda H., and John Luehrs. *State Initiatives to Improve Rural Health Care.* Washington, DC: Center for Policy

Research, National Governors' Association. Published in cooperation with Office of Rural Health Policy, Health Resources and Services Administration, Public Health Service, U.S. Department of Health and Human Services, 1990.

McCoy, John H., and M. E. Sarhan. *Livestock and Meat Marketing.* 3d ed. New York: Van Nostrand Reinhold, 1988.

MacDonald, June Fessenden. *Agricultural Biotechnology: A Public Conversation about Risk.* Ithaca, NY: National Agricultural Biotechnology Council, 1993.

———. *Agricultural Biotechnology and the Public Good.* Ithaca, NY: National Agricultural Biotechnology Council, 1994.

McDonald, Thomas D., Robert A. Wood, and Melissa A. Pflug. *Rural Criminal Justice.* Salem, WI: Sheffield, 1996.

McEowen, R., and Harl, N. *Principles of Agricultural Law.* Eugene, OR: Ag Law Press, 1996.

McFague, Sallie. *The Body of God: An Ecological Theology.* Minneapolis: Fortress Press, 1993.

McFate, Kenneth L., ed. *Electrical Energy in Agriculture.* Vol. 3, *Energy in World Agriculture.* B. A. Stout, editor-in-chief. Amsterdam: Elsevier, 1989.

McGranahan, David A., J. Hession, F. Hines, et al. *Social and Economic Characteristics of the Population in Metro and Nonmetro Counties, 1970–1980.* Rural Development Research Report No. 58. Washington, DC: U.S. Department of Agriculture, Economic Research Service, 1986.

McKibben, Bill. *Hope, Human and Wild: True Stories of Living Lightly on the Earth.* Boston: Little, Brown, 1995.

McLaughlin, Edward W., and D. J. Perosio. *Fresh Fruit and Vegetable Procurement Dynamics: The Role of the Supermarket Buyer.* Cornell Food Industry Management Program publication R.B. 94–1 (February). Ithaca, NY: Cornell University, Department of Agricultural, Resource, and Managerial Economics, 1994.

McMichael, Philip. *Food and Agrarian Orders in the World Economy.* Westport, CT: Greenwood Press, 1995.

McMurry, Sally. *Families and Farmhouses in Nineteenth Century America.* New York: Oxford University Press, 1988.

McNall, Scott G., and Sally Ann McNall. *Plains Families: Exploring Sociology through Social History.* New York: St. Martin's Press, 1983.

Majka, Linda C., and Theo J. Majka. *Farm Workers, Agribusiness and the State.* Philadelphia: Temple University Press, 1982.

Malia, James E., and Janice Morrisey. *Rural Communities and Subtitle D: Problems and Solutions.* Knoxville: Tennessee Valley Authority, 1994.

Malone, Bill. *Country Music, USA.* Rev. ed. Austin: University of Texas Press, 1985.

Manchester, Alden. *Rearranging the Economic Landscape,* AER-660. Washington, DC: U.S. Department of Agriculture, Economic Research Service, 1992.

Marcus, Alan I. *Agricultural Science and the Quest for Legitimacy: Farmers, Agricultural Colleges, and Experiment Stations, 1870–1890.* Ames: Iowa State University Press, 1985.

Maril, Robert Lee. *The Bay Shrimpers of Texas.* Lawrence: University Press of Kansas, 1995.

Marotz-Baden, Ramona, Charles B. Hennon, and Timothy H. Brubaker. *Families in Rural America: Stress, Adaptation, and Revitalization.* St. Paul, MN: National Council on Family Relations, 1988.

Marshall, Robert, ed. *Standard Methods for the Examination of Dairy Products.* 16th ed. Washington, DC: American Public Health Association, 1992.

Marti, Donald B. *Women of the Grange: Mutuality and Sisterhood in Rural America, 1866–1920.* New York: Greenwood Press, 1991.

Martin, Guy R., Traci J. Stegemann, and Karen Donovan. *Water Conservation: The Federal Role.* Washington, DC: American Water Works Association, 1994.

Martin, Lee R. *A Survey of Agricultural Economics Literature: Economics of Welfare, Rural Development and National Resources in Agriculture, 1940's to 1970's.* Vol. 3. Minneapolis: University of Minnesota Press, 1981.

Martin, Philip L., and David A. Martin. *The Endless Quest: Helping America's Farm Workers.* Boulder, CO: Westview, 1993.

Martin, Russell. *Cowboy: The Enduring Myth of the Wild West.* New York: Stewart, Tabori, and Chang, 1983.

Mason, J. *Commercial Hydroponics.* Kenthurst, NSW, Australia: Kangaroo Press, 1990.

May, Roy. *The Poor of the Land: A Christian Case for Land Reform.* Maryknoll, NY: Orbis Books, 1991.

Mayberry, B. D. *A Century of Agriculture in the 1890 Land-grant Institutions and Tuskegee University, 1890–1990.* New York: Vantage Press, 1991.

Meffe, Gary K., and C. Ronald Carroll. *Principles of Conservation Biology.* Sunderland, MA: Sinauer Associates, 1994.

Meier, Matt S., and Feliciano Ribera. *Mexican Americans/American Mexicans: From Conquistadors to Chicanos.* New York: Hill and Wang, 1993.

Meinig, Donald W. *The Shaping of America: A Geographical Perspective on 500 Years of History.* Vol. 1: *Atlantic America, 1492–1800.* New Haven, CT: Yale University Press, 1986.

Meinig, Donald W. *The Shaping of America: A Geographical Perspective on 500 Years of History.* Vol. 2: *Continental America, 1800–1867.* New Haven, CT: Yale University Press, 1993.

Meinig, Donald. W., et al., eds. *The Interpretation of Ordinary Landscapes.* New York: Oxford University Press, 1979.

Metcalf, R. L., B. M. Francis, D. C. Fischer, and R. M. Kelly. *Integrated Pest Management for the Home and Garden.* 3d ed. Urbana-Champaign: Institute for Environmental Studies, University of Illinois, 1994.

Metcalf, R. L., and W. H. Luckman. *Introduction to Insect Pest Management.* 3d ed. New York: Wiley, 1994.

Metcalf, R. L., and R. A. Metcalf. *Destructive and Useful Insects: Their Habits and Control.* 5th ed. New York: McGraw-Hill, 1993.

Meyer, Richard E., ed. *Cemeteries and Gravemarkers: Voices of American Culture.* Logan: Utah State University Press, 1992.

———, ed. *Ethnicity and the American Cemetery.* Bowling Green, OH: Bowling Green State University Press, 1993.

Michrina, Barry P. *Pennsylvania Mining Families: The Search for*

Dignity in the Coalfields. Lexington: University Press of Kentucky, 1993.

Milbrath, Lester W. *Envisioning a Sustainable Society.* Albany: State University of New York Press, 1989.

Miller, James P. *Survival and Growth of Independent Firms and Corporate Affiliates in Metro and Nonmetro America.* Washington, DC: U.S. Department of Agriculture, Economic Research Service, 1990.

Miller, John. *Deer Camp: Last Light in the Northeast Kingdom.* Cambridge, MA: MIT Press and Middlebury: Vermont Folklife Center, 1992.

Miller, S. *The Economic Benefits of Open Space.* Portland: Maine Coast Heritage, 1992.

Miller, Sandra E., Craig W. Shinn, and William R. Bentley. *Rural Resource Management: Problem Solving for the Long Term.* Ames: Iowa State University Press, 1994.

Molnar, Joseph J., and Henry Kinnucan, eds. *Biotechnology and the New Agricultural Revolution.* Boulder, CO: Westview, 1989.

Moltmann, Jurgen. *God in Creation: A New Theology of Creation and the Spirit of God.* San Francisco: Harper and Row, 1985.

Monk, David H. *Disparities in Curricular Offerings: Issues and Policy Alternatives for Small Rural Schools.* Paper prepared for the Appalachia Educational Laboratory. Ithaca, NY: Cornell University, Department of Education, February 1988.

Monk, David H., and Emil Haller. *Organizational Alternatives for Small Rural Schools.* Ithaca, NY: Cornell University, Department of Education, 1986.

Montmarquet, James A. *The Idea of Agrarianism: From Hunter-Gatherer to Agrarian Radical in Western Culture.* Moscow: University of Idaho Press, 1989.

Mooney, Patrick H. *My Own Boss? Class, Rationality and the Family Farm.* Boulder, CO: Westview, 1988.

Mooney, Patrick H., and Theo J. Majka. *Farmers' and Farm Workers' Movements: Social Protest in American Agriculture.* New York: Twayne, 1995.

Morrison, Peter A., ed. *A Taste of the Country: A Collection of Calvin Beale's Writings.* University Park: Pennsylvania State University Press and Rand Corporation, 1990.

Morse, R. A., and K. Flottum, eds. *The ABC and XYZ of Bee Culture.* 40th ed. Medina, OH: A. I. Root, 1990.

Morse, R. A., and T. Hooper, eds. *The Illustrated Encyclopedia of Beekeeping.* New York: E. P. Dutton, 1985.

Mortensen, Viggo, ed. *Region and Religion: Land, Territory and Nation from a Theological Perspective.* International Consultation, Brazil, 1993. LWF Studies No. 4. Geneva, Switzerland: Lutheran World Federation, 1994.

Muckle, M. E. *Basic Hydroponics.* Princeton, BC, Canada: Growers Press, 1982.

Murphy, Dennis. *Safety and Health for Production Agriculture.* St. Joseph, MI: American Society of Agricultural Engineers, 1992.

Murray, J. Dennis, and Peter A. Keller, eds. *Innovations in Rural Community Mental Health.* Mansfield, PA: Mansfield University Rural Services Institute, 1986.

Muse, Ivan, and Ralph B. Smith, with Bruce Barker. *The One-Teacher School in the 1980s.* Ft. Collins, CO: Eric Clearinghouse on Rural Education and Small Schools, 1987.

Nachtigal, Paul M. *Rural Education: In Search of a Better Way.* Boulder, CO: Westview, 1982.

Napier, Ted L., ed. *Implementing the Conservation Title of the Food Security Act of 1985.* Ankeny, IA: Soil Conservation Society Press, 1990.

———, ed. *Outdoor Recreation Planning, Perspectives and Research.* Dubuque, IA: Kendall/Hunt, 1981.

Napier, Ted L., Silvana M. Camboni, and Samir A. El-Swaify. *Adopting Conservation on the Farm: An International Perspective on the Socioeconomics of Soil and Water Conservation.* Ankeny, IA: Soil and Water Conservation Society Press, 1994.

Napier, Ted L., Donald F. Scott, William K. Easter, and Raymond J. Supalla, eds. *Water Resources Research: Problems and Potentials for Agriculture and Rural Communities.* Ankeny, IA: Soil and Water Conservation Society of America Press, 1983.

National Center for Health Statistics. *Common Beliefs about the Rural Elderly: What Do National Data Tell Us?* Hyattsville, MD: U.S. Department of Health and Human Services, Public Health Service, Centers for Disease Control, National Center for Health Statistics, 1993.

National Geographic Society. *Life in Rural America.* Washington, DC: National Geographic Society, Special Publication Division, 1978.

National Research Council. *Managing Global Genetic Resources: Livestock.* Washington, DC: National Academy Press, 1993.

———. *Valuing Ground Water.* Washington, DC: Water Science and Technology Board, Commission on Geosciences, Environment and Resources, forthcoming 1997.

National Research Council, Board on Agriculture. *Alternative Agriculture.* Washington, DC.: National Academy Press, 1989.

National Rural Health Association. *Study of Models to Meet Rural Health Care Needs through Mobilization of Health Professions Education and Services Resources.* Vol. 1. Washington, DC: Health Resources Services Administration, 1992.

National Telecommunications Information Infrastructure. *Survey of Rural Information Infrastructure Technologies.* Washington, DC: U.S. Department of Commerce, September 1995.

Nelson, P. V. *Greenhouse Operation and Management.* 4th ed. Englewood Cliffs, NJ: Prentice Hall, 1991.

Neth, Mary. *Preserving the Family Farm: Women, Community, and the Foundations of Agribusiness in the Midwest, 1900–1940.* Baltimore: Johns Hopkins University Press, 1995.

Nettl, Bruno. *Folk and Traditional Music of the Western Continents.* 3d ed. Englewood Cliffs, NJ: Prentice-Hall, 1989.

Neyland, Leedell. *Historically Black Land-Grant Institutions and the Development of Agriculture and Home Economics, 1890–1990.* Tallahasee: Florida A&M University Foundation, 1990.

Noble, Allen. *Barns of the Midwest.* Athens: Ohio University Press, 1995.

Noble, Allen G. *Wood, Brick, and Stone: The North American Settlement Landscape.* 2 vols. Amherst: University of Massachusetts Press, 1984.

Norris, Kathleen. *Dakota: A Spiritual Geography*. Boston: Houghton Mifflin, 1993.

O'Brien, Sharon. *American Indian Tribal Governments*. Norman: University of Oklahoma Press, 1989.

Office of Technology Assessment. *Health Care in Rural America*, OTA-H-434 (September). Washington, DC: U.S. Congress, Office of Technology Assessment, 1990.

————. *A New Technological Era for American Agriculture*. Washington, DC: U.S. Government Printing Office, 1992.

————. *Technology, Public Policy and the Changing Structure of American Agriculture*. Washington, DC: U.S. Government Printing Office, 1986.

Olkowski, N., S. Door, and H. Olkowski. *Common-sense Pest Control*. Newton, CT: Tauton, 1991.

Orloff, Tracey M., and Barbara Tymann. *Rural Health: An Evolving System of Accessible Services*. Washington, DC: National Governors' Association, 1995.

O'Rourke, A. Desmond. *The World Apple Market*. Binghamton, NY: Haworth Press, 1994.

Ortolano, Leonard. *Environmental Planning and Decision Making*. New York: John Wiley and Sons, 1984.

Osborne, Diana, and Lise Fondren, eds. *National Rural Health Policy Atlas*. Chapel Hill: University of North Carolina Health Services Research Center, 1991.

Osteen, Craig D., and Philip I. Szmedra. *Agricultural Pesticide Use Trends and Policy Issues*. Agricultural Economic Report No. 622 (September). Washington, DC: U.S. Department of Agriculture, Economic Research Service, 1989.

Ostler, Jeffrey. *Prairie Populism: The Fate of Agrarian Radicalism in Kansas, Nebraska, and Iowa, 1880–1892*. Lawrence: University Press of Kansas, 1993.

Overton, Patrick. *Grassroots and Mountain Wings: The Arts in Rural and Small Communities*. Columbia, MO: Columbia College, 1992.

————. *Rebuilding the Front Porch of America: Essays on the Art of Community Making*. Columbia, MO: Columbia College, 1996.

Paarlberg, Don. *Farm and Food Policy: Issues of the 1980s*. Lincoln: University of Nebraska Press, 1980.

Palerm, Juan Vicente. *Farm Labor Needs and Farm Workers in California, 1970–1989*. Sacramento: California Agricultural Studies, Employment Development Department, 1991.

Palmer, Tim. *Lifelines: The Case for River Conservation*. Washington, DC: Island Press, 1994.

Parker, Blaine F., ed. *Solar Energy in Agriculture*. Vol. 4: *Energy in World Agriculture*. B. A. Stout, editor-in-chief. Amsterdam: Elsevier, 1991.

Parker, Edwin B., Heather Hudson, and Don A. Dillman. *Rural America in the Information Age*. Boston: University Press of America, 1989.

Parker, Edwin B., Heather E. Hudson, Don A. Dillman, Sharon Strover, and Frederick Williams. *Electronic Byways: State Policies for Rural Development through Telecommunications*. 2d ed. Washington, DC: Aspen Institute, 1995.

Parks, Arnold G. *Black Elderly in Rural America: A Comprehensive Study*. Bristol, IN: Wyndham Hall Press, 1988.

Parlin, Bradley W., and Mark W. Lusk. *Farmer Participation and Irrigation Organization*. Boulder, CO: Westview, 1991.

Patton, Larry. *The Rural Homeless*. Washington, DC: Health Resources and Services Administration, 1987.

Peart, Robert M., and Roger C. Brook, eds. *Analysis of Agricultural Energy Systems*. Vol. 5: *Energy in World Agriculture*. B. A. Stout, editor-in-chief. Amsterdam: Elsevier, 1992.

Peat, Marwick, Mitchell, and Co. *The Economic Impact of the U.S. Horse Industry*. Washington, DC: American Horse Council, 1987.

Pedigo, L. P. *Entomology and Pest Management*. New York: Macmillan, 1989.

Pence, Richard A. *The Next Greatest Thing*. Washington, DC: National Rural Electrical Cooperative Association, 1984.

Penson, John B., Jr., and David A. Lins. *Agricultural Finance: An Introduction to Micro and Macro Concepts*. Englewood Cliffs, NJ: Prentice-Hall, 1980.

Perez, Agnes M. *Changing Structure of U.S. Dairy Farms*. Agricultural Economics Report 690, July. Washington, DC: U.S. Department of Agriculture, Economic Research Service, 1994.

Perlin, John. *A Forest Journey: The Role of Wood in the Development of Civilization*. Cambridge, MA: Harvard University Press, 1991.

Peterson, Fred W. *Homes in the Heartland: Balloon Frame Farmhouses of the Upper Midwest, 1850–1920*. Lawrence: University Press of Kansas, 1992.

Peterson, George L., Cindy Sorg Swanson, Daniel W. McCollum, and Michael H. Thomas. *Valuing Wildlife Resources in Alaska*. Boulder, CO: Westview, 1991.

Petulla, Joseph M. *American Environmental History*. 2d ed. Columbus, OH: Merrill, 1988.

Phillips, R. E., and S. H. Phillips, eds. *No-Tillage Agriculture: Principles and Practices*. New York: Van Nostrand Reinhold, 1984.

Phillips, Willard, and Barton D. Russell. *Rural Government: A Time of Change*. Washington, DC: U.S. Department of Agriculture, 1982.

Physicians Task Force on Hunger in America. *Hunger in America: The Growing Epidemic*. Middletown, CT: Wesleyan University Press, 1985.

Pigg, Kenneth E. *The Future of Rural America*. Boulder, CO: Westview, 1991.

Pimentel, David. *Handbook of Energy Utilization in Agriculture*. Boca Raton, FL: CRC Press, 1980.

————. *The Handbook on Pest Management in Agriculture*. Boca Raton, FL: CRC Press, 1991.

Pimentel, David, and H. Lehman. *The Pesticide Question*. New York: Champman and Hall, 1993.

Plater, Zygmunt J. B., Robert H. Abrams, and William Goldfarb. *Environmental Law and Policy: A Coursebook on Nature, Law, and Society*. St. Paul, MN: West Publications, 1992.

Platt, Rutherford. *This Green World*. 2d ed. New York: Dodd, Mead, 1988.

Poincelot, Raymond P. *Toward a More Sustainable Agriculture*. Westport, CT: AVI, 1986.

Ponting, Clive. *A Green History of the World: The Environment and the Collapse of Great Civilizations*. New York: St. Martin's Press, 1991.

Powell, D. S., J. L. Faulkner, D. R. Darr, Z. Zhu, and D. W. MacCleery. *Forest Resources of the United States, 1992.* General Technical Report RM-234. Washington, DC: U.S. Department of Agriculture, Forest Service, 1994.

Powers, Nicholas J., *Marketing Practices for Vegetables.* Agricultural Information Bulletin No. 702 (August). Washington, DC: U.S. Department of Agriculture, Economic Research Service, 1994.

Price, Larry W. *Mountains and Man: A Study of Process and Environment.* Berkeley: University of California Press, 1981.

Purcell, Wayne D. *Agricultural Futures and Options.* New York: Macmillan, 1991.

Purcell, W. D., J. Reeves, and W. Preston. *Economics of Past, Current and Pending Change in the U.S. Sheep Industry with an Emphasis on Supply Response.* MB 363. Blacksburg: Department of Agricultural Economics, Virginia Tech University, 1991.

Quinn, Bernard. *The Small Rural Parish.* New York: Glenmary Home Missioners, 1980.

Rasmussen, Wayne D. *Taking the University to the People: Seventy-five Years of Cooperative Extension.* Ames: Iowa State University Press, 1989.

Reeder, Richard, and Anicca A. Jansen. *Rural Governments—Poor Counties, 1962–1987.* Washington, DC: U.S. Department of Agriculture, 1995.

Regan, Tom. *The Case for Animal Rights.* Berkeley: University of California Press, 1983.

Relf, Diane, ed. *The Role of Horticulture in Human Well-Being and Social Development.* Portland, OR: Timber Press, 1992.

Resh, H. M. *Hydroponic Food Production.* 5th ed. Santa Barbara, CA: Woodbridge Press, 1995.

Resh, H. M. *Hydroponic Home Food Gardens.* Santa Barbara, CA: Woodbridge Press, 1990.

Resh, H. M. *Hydroponic Tomatoes for the Home Gardener.* Santa Barbara, CA: Woodbridge Press, 1993.

Rheingold, Howard. *The Virtual Community: Homesteading on the Electronic Frontier.* Reading, MA: Addison Wesley, 1993.

Riebsame, William E., Stanley Changnon, Jr., and Thomas Karl. *Drought and Natural Resources Management in the United States: Impacts and Implications of the 1987–1989 Drought.* Boulder, CO: Westview, 1991.

Rifkin, Jeremy. *Beyond Beef: the Rise and Fall of the Cattle Culture.* New York: Dutton, 1992.

Riney-Kehrburg, Pamela. *Rooted in Dust: Surviving Drought and Depression in Southwestern Kansas.* Lawrence: University Press of Kansas, 1994.

Rodgers, Harrell R., Jr., and Gregory Weiher. *Rural Poverty: Special Causes and Policy Reforms.* Prepared under the auspices of the Policy Studies Organization. New York: Greenwood Press, 1989.

Roe, Keith E. *Corncribs in History, Folklife and Architecture.* Ames: Iowa State University Press, 1988.

Rogers, Denise M. *Leasing Farmland in the United States.* AGES-9159. Washington, DC: U.S. Department of Agriculture, Economic Research Service, 1991.

Rogers, Denise, and Gene Wunderlich. *Acquiring Farmland in the United States.* AIB 682. Washington, DC: U.S. Department of Agriculture, Economic Research Service, 1993.

Rogers, Everett M., Rabel J. Burdge, Peter F. Korsching, and Joseph F. Donnermeyer. *Social Change in Rural Societies: An Introduction to Rural Sociology.* 3d ed. Englewood Cliffs, NJ: Prentice Hall, 1988.

Rollin, B. E. *Farm Animal Welfare: Social, Bioethical, and Research Issues.* Ames: Iowa State University Press, 1995.

Rooney, John F., Jr., Wilbur Zelinsky, Dean R. Louder, eds. *This Remarkable Continent: An Atlas of the United States and Canadian Society and Cultures.* College Station: Texas A&M University Press, 1982.

Rosenbaum, Walter. *Environmental Politics and Policy.* 2d ed. Washington DC: Congressional Quarterly, 1991.

Rosenblatt, Paul C. *Farming Is in Our Blood: Farm Families in Economic Crisis.* Ames: Iowa State University Press, 1990.

Rosenblatt, Roger A., and Ira S. Moscovice. *Rural Health Care.* New York: John Wiley and Sons, 1982.

Rosenblum, Jonathon D. *Copper Crucible: How the Arizona Miners' Strike of 1983 Recast Labor-Management Relations in America.* Ithaca, NY: ILR Press, 1995.

Rosenfeld, Rachel Ann. *Farm Women: Work, Farm, and Family in the United States.* Chapel Hill: University of North Carolina Press, 1985.

Rowles, Graham D., Joyce E. Beaulieu, and Wayne W. Myers, eds. *Long-Term Care for the Rural Elderly.* New York: Springer, 1996.

Rowley, D. Thomas, and Peter L. Sternberg. *A Comparison of Military Base Closures Metro and Nonmetro Counties, 1961–90.* Staff Report No. AGES 9307, April. Washington, DC: U.S. Department of Agriculture, Agriculture and Rural Economy Division, Economic Research Service, 1993.

Royer, J. P., and C. D. Risbrudt, eds. *Nonindustrial Private Forests: A Review of Economic and Policy Studies.* Durham, NC: School of Forestry and Environmental Studies, Duke University, 1983.

Rural Policy Research Institute. *Block Grants and Rural America* P95-4 (November), Iowa State University, University of Missouri, University of Nebraska. Columbia: University of Missouri, November 1995.

———. *Opportunities for Rural Policy Reform: Lessons Learned from Recent Farm Bills.* P95-2 (April). Iowa State University, University of Missouri, University of Nebraska. Columbia: University of Missouri, 1995.

Rural Sociological Society. *Persistent Poverty in Rural America.* Rural Sociological Society Taskforce on Persistent Rural Poverty. Boulder, CO: Westview, 1993.

Russell, Howard S. *A Long, Deep Furrow: Three Centuries of Farming in New England.* Hanover, NH: University Press of New England, 1982.

Ruttan, Vernon W., ed. *Health and Sustainable Agricultural Development: Perspectives on Growth and Constraints.* Boulder, CO: Westview, 1994.

Ryugo, Kay. *Fruit Culture: Its Science and Art.* New York: John Wiley and Sons, 1988.

Sachs, Carolyn E. *Gendered Fields: Rural Women, Agriculture, and Environment.* Boulder, CO: Westview, 1996.

Salamon, Sonya. *Prairie Patrimony: Family Farming and Commu-*

nity in the Midwest. Chapel Hill: University of North Carolina Press, 1992.

Sanders, H. C. *The Cooperative Extension Service*. Englewood Cliffs, NJ: Prentice-Hall, 1966.

Sargent, Frederic O., Paul Lusk, José A. Rivera, and María Varela. *Rural Environmental Planning for Sustainable Communities*. Washington, DC: Island Press, 1991.

Savory, Allan. *Holistic Resource Management*. Washington, DC: Island Press, 1988.

Schmandt, J. F. Williams, R. H. Wilson, and S. Strover, eds. *Telecommunications and Rural Development: A Study of Business and Public Service Applications*. New York: Praeger, 1991.

Schmidt, G. H., L. D. VanVleck, and M. F. Hutjens. *Principles of Dairy Science*. 2d ed. Englewood Cliffs, NJ: Prentice Hall, 1988.

Schmuck, Richard A., and Patricia A. Schmuck. *Small Districts, Big Problems: Making Schools Everybody's House*. Newbury Park, CA: Corwin Press, 1992.

Schnaiberg, Allan, and Kenneth Allan Gould. *Environment and Society: The Enduring Conflict*. New York: St. Martin's, 1994.

Schoenrich, Lola. *Case Studies of Seven Rural Programs Cooperatively Marketing Recyclables*. St. Paul: Minnesota Project, 1994.

Schor, Joel. *Agriculture in the Black Land-grant System to 1930*. Tallahassee: Florida A&M University, 1982.

Schultz, LeRoy G. *Barns, Stables and Outbuildings: A World Bibliography in English, 1700–1983*. Jefferson, NC: McFarland, 1986.

Schwager, Jack D. *A Complete Guide to the Futures Market*. New York: John Wiley and Sons, 1984.

Schwartzweller, H. K. *Research in Rural Sociology and Development*. Vol. 1: *Focus on Agriculture*. Greenwich, CT: JAI Press, 1984.

Scott, Shaunna L. *Two Sides to Everything: The Cultural Construction of Class Consciousness in Harlan County, Kentucky*. Albany: State University of New York Press, 1995.

Sears, David W., and J. Norman Reid. *Rural Development Strategies*. Chicago: Nelson-Hall, 1995.

Senate Committee on Environment and Public Works. *Rural Transportation Issues: Hearings before the Subcommittee on Water Resources, Transportation, and Infrastructure of the Committee on Environment and Public Works* (August 20, 1990, Boise, Idaho). 101st Congress, Second Session, 1990.

Senauer, Ben, and Jean Kinsey, eds. *Final Report by the Food and Consumer Issues Working Group, 1995 Farm Bill Project*. Washington, DC: National Center for Food and Agricultural Policy and St. Paul, MN: University of Minnesota, Hubert H. Humphrey Institute of Agricultural Policy, March 1995.

Seroka, Jim. *Rural Public Administration: Problems and Prospects*. Westport, CT: Greenwood Press, 1986.

Setia, Parveen, Nathan Childs, Eric Wailes, and Janet Livezey. *The U.S. Rice Industry*. Washington, DC: U.S. Department of Agriculture, Economic Research Service, 1994.

Shallat, Todd. *Structures in the Stream: Water, Science, and the Rise of the U.S. Army Corps of Engineers*. Austin: University of Texas Press, 1994.

Shapouri, Hosein. *Sheep Production in 11 Western States*. Staff Report No. AGES 9150. Washington, DC: U.S. Department of

Agriculture, Economic Research Service, Commodity Economics Division, 1991.

Sheldon, Ian M., and Philip C. Abbott. *Industrial Organization and Trade in the Food Industries*. Boulder, CO: Westview, 1994.

Sherman, Arloc. *Falling by the Wayside: Children in Rural America*. Washington, DC: Children's Defense Fund, 1992.

Shifflett, Crandall. *Coal Towns: Life, Work, and Culture in Company Towns of Southern Appalachia, 1880–1960*. Knoxville: University of Tennessee Press, 1991.

Shinagawa, Larry Hajime, and Michael Jang. *Atlas of American Diversity*. Newbury Park, CA: Sage Publications/Altamira Press, 1996.

Singer, Peter. *Animal Liberation*. New York: Avon Books, 1990.

Slatta, Richard W. *The Cowboy Encyclopedia*. Santa Barbara, CA: ABC-CLIO, 1994.

———. *Cowboys of the Americas*. New Haven, CT: Yale University Press, 1990.

Sloan, David Charles. *The Last Great Necessity: Cemeteries in American History*. Baltimore: Johns Hopkins University Press, 1991.

Smil, Vaclav, Paul Nachman, and Thomas V. Long II. *Energy Analysis and Agriculture*. Boulder, CO: Westview, 1983.

Smith, Duane A. *Mining America: The Industry and the Environment, 1800–1980*. Niwot: University Press of Colorado, 1993.

———. *Rocky Mountain Mining Camps: The Urban Frontier*. Niwot: University Press of Colorado, 1992.

Smith, R. K., E. J. Wailes, and G. L. Cramer. *The Market Structure of the U.S. Rice Industry*. Bulletin 921. Fayetteville: University of Arkansas, Arkansas Agricultural Experiment Station, 1990.

Snipp, C. Matthew. *American Indians: The First of This Land*. New York: Russell Sage Foundation, 1989.

Society of American Foresters. *Task Force Report on Sustaining Long-Term Forest Health and Productivity*. Bethesda, MD: Society of American Foresters, 1993.

Solid Waste Association of North America. *Rural Solid Waste Management Series*. Silver Spring, MD: Solid Waste Association of North America, 1994.

Soule, Judith D., and Jon K. Piper. *Farming in Nature's Image: An Ecological Approach to Agriculture*. Washington, DC: Island Press, 1992.

Southern Rural Development Center. *Decision Aids for Municipal Solid Waste Management in Rural Areas: An Annotated Bibliography*. Mississippi State, MS: Southern Rural Development Center, 1995.

Stam, Jerome M., Steven R. Koenig, Susan E. Bentley, and H. Frederick Gale, Jr. *Farm Financial Stress, Farm Exits, and Public Sector Assistance to the Farm Sector in the 1980's*. Agricultural Economic Report No. 645 (April). Washington, DC: U.S. Department of Agriculture, Economic Research Service, 1991.

Steiner, Frederick R. *The Living Landscape: An Ecological Approach to Landscape Planning*. New York: McGraw-Hill, 1991.

———. *Soil Conservation in the United States: Policy and Planning*. Baltimore: Johns Hopkins University Press, 1990.

Stern, Joyce D. *The Condition of Education in Rural Schools*. Washington, DC: U.S. Department of Education, Office of Educational Research and Improvement Programs for the Improvement of Practice, 1994.

Stewart, B. A., and D. R. Nielsen, eds. *Irrigation of Agricultural Crops*. Agronomics Series No. 30. Madison, WI: American Society of Agronomy, 1990.

Stewart, James B., and Joyce E. Allen-Smith, eds. *Blacks in Rural America*. New Brunswick, NJ: Transaction, 1995.

Stinson, Thomas F., Patrick J. Sullivan, Barry Ryan, and Norman A. Reid. *Public Water Supply in Rural Communities: Results from the National Rural Communities Facilities Assessment Study*. Staff Report No. AGES 89–4. Washington, DC: U.S. Department of Agriculture, 1989.

Stock, Catherine McNicol. *Main Street in Crisis: The Great Depression and the Old Middle Class on the Northern Plains*. Chapel Hill: University of North Carolina Press, 1992.

Stokes, Samuel N., A. Elizabeth Watson, Genevieve P. Keller, and J. Timothy Keller. *Saving America's Countryside*. Baltimore: Johns Hopkins University Press, 1989.

Stokowski, Patricia A. *Riches and Regrets: Betting on Gambling in Two Colorado Mountain Towns*. Niwot: University Press of Colorado, 1996.

Stone, Kenneth E. *Competing with the Retail Giants: How to Survive in the New Retail Landscape*. New York: John Wiley and Sons, 1995.

Stone, Lynn. *Old America Plantations*. Vero Beach, FL: Rourke, 1993.

Stone, Michael E. *Shelter Poverty*. Philadelphia: Temple University Press, 1993.

Stone, Ted, ed. *100 Years of Cowboy Stories*. Roundup Series. Red Deer, Alberta: Red Deer College Press, 1994.

Storer YMCA Camps. *Nature's Classroom: A Program Guide for Camps and Schools*. Martinsville, IN: American Camping Association, 1988.

Strange, Marty. *Family Farming: A New Economic Vision*. Lincoln: University of Nebraska Press, 1988.

Strover, S., and F. Williams. *Rural Revitalization and Information Technologies in the United States*. Report to the Ford Foundation. New York: Ford Foundation, 1990.

Stull, Donald, Michael Broadway, and David Griffith. *Any Way You Cut It: Meat Processing and Small-Town America*. Lawrence: University Press of Kansas, 1995.

Summers, A., J. Schriver, P. Sundet, and R. Meinert. *Social Work in Rural Areas: The Past, Charting the Future, Acclaiming a Decade of Achievement. Proceedings of the 10th National Institute of Rural Areas*. Columbia: University of Missouri at Columbia, School of Social Work, 1987.

Summers, Gene F., ed. *Technology and Social Change in Rural Areas: A Festschrift for Eugene A. Wilkening*. Boulder, CO: Westview, 1983.

Summers, Gene F., et al., eds. *Agriculture and Beyond: Rural Economic Development*. Madison: University of Wisconsin–Madison, Department of Agricultural Journalism, 1987.

Sun, Ren Jen, and John B. Weeks. *Bibliography of Regional Aquifer-System Analysis Program of the U.S. Geological Survey, 1978–91*. Water-Resources Investigations Report 91–4122. Reston, VA: U.S. Geological Survey, 1991.

Surrey, Peter. *The Small Town Church*. Nashville, TN: Abingdon Press, 1981.

Suter, Robert C. *The Appraisal of Farm Real Estate*. 3d ed. Lafayette, IN: Retus, 1992.

Swanson, Linda L., and David L. Brown, eds. Population Change and the Future of Rural America. Staff Report No. AGES 9324. Washington, DC: U.S. Department of Agriculture, Economic Research Service, Agriculture and Rural Economy Division, 1993.

Swanson, Louis, ed. *Agriculture and Community Change in the U.S.: The Congressional Research Reports*. Boulder, CO: Westview, 1988.

Sweeten, J. M. *Cattle Feedlot Waste Management Practices for Water and Air Pollution Control*. B-1671. College Station: Texas Agricultural Extension Service, Texas A&M University, 1990.

Tanzer, Michael. *The Race for Resources: Continuing Struggles over Minerals and Fuels*. New York: Monthly Review Press, 1980.

Taylor, Harold H. *Fertilizer Use and Price Statistics, 1960–93*. Statistical Bulletin No. 893 (September). Washington, DC: U.S. Department of Agriculture, Economic Research Service, 1994.

Teiser, Ruth, and Catherine Harroun. *Winemaking in California*. New York: McGraw-Hill, 1983.

Teske, Paul, Samuel Best, and Michael Mintrom. *Deregulating Freight Transportation: Delivering the Goods*. Washington, DC: AEI Press, 1995.

Thomas, M. G., and D. R. Schumann. *Income Opportunities in Special Forest Products*. Agriculture Information Bulletin No. 666. Washington, DC: U.S. Department of Agriculture, Forest Service, 1993.

Thompson, Paul, and William Stout, eds. *Beyond the Large Farm*. Boulder CO: Westview, 1991.

Thornton, Russell. *American Indian Holocaust and Survival: A Population History since 1492*. Norman: University of Oklahoma Press, 1987.

Thurston, H. David. *Sustainable Practices for Plant Disease Management in Traditional Farming Systems*. Boulder, CO: Westview, 1991.

Tichi, Cecelia. *High Lonesome: The American Culture of Country Music*. Chapel Hill: University of North Carolina Press, 1994.

Tin, Jan S. *Housing Characteristics of Rural Households: 1991*. Bureau of the Census Current Housing Reports, Series H121/93-5. Washington, DC: U.S. Government Printing Office, 1993.

Tisdale, Samuel L., Werner L. Nelson, James D. Beaton, and John L. Havlin. *Soil Fertility and Fertilizers*. 5th ed. New York: Macmillan, 1993.

Tober, James A. *Who Owns Wildlife? The Political Economy of Conservation in Nineteenth Century America*. Westport, CT: Greenwood Press, 1981.

Todd, David Keith. *Groundwater Hydrology*. New York: John Wiley, 1980.

Tomek, William G., and Kenneth L. Robinson. *Agricultural Product Prices*. 3d ed. Ithaca, NY: Cornell University Press, 1990.

Tooch, D. E. *Successful Sawmill Management*. Old Forge, NY: Northeastern Loggers Association, 1992.

Troeh, F. R., J. A. Hobbs, and R. L. Donahue. *Soil and Water Conservation.* 2d ed. Englewood Cliffs, NJ: Prentice-Hall, 1991.

Troeh, F. R., and L. M. Thompson. *Soils and Soil Fertility.* 5th ed. New York: Oxford University Press, 1993.

Tromp, Solco W. *Biometeorology: The Impact of the Weather and Climate on Humans and Their Environment (Animals and Plants).* London: Heyden, 1980.

Tullis, F. L., and W. L. Hollist. *Food, the State, and International Political Economy.* Lincoln: University of Nebraska Press, 1985.

Upton, Dell, and John Michael Vlach. *Common Places: Readings in American Rural Architecture.* Athens: University of Georgia Press, 1982.

Upton, Dell, ed. *America's Architectural Roots: Ethnic Groups That Built America.* Washington, DC: Preservation Press, 1986.

U.S. Commission on Civil Rights. *The Decline of Black Farming in America: A Report of the United States Commission on Civil Rights.* Washington, DC: United States Commission on Civil Rights, 1982.

U.S. Congress. House. *Hunger in Rural America, Hearing before the Subcommittee on Domestic Marketing, Consumer Relations, and Nutrition of the Committee on Agriculture.* 101st Cong., May 17, 1989, serial 101–15. Washington, DC: Government Printing Office, 1989.

———. Office of Technology Assessment. *Agriculture, Trade, and Environment: Achieving Complementary Policies.* Washington, DC: U.S. Government Printing Office, 1995.

———. Office of Technology Assessment. *Health Care in Rural America,* OTA-H-434 (September). Washington, DC: U.S. Government Printing Office, 1990.

———. Office of Technology Assessment. *A New Technological Era for American Agriculture,* OTA-F-474. Washington, DC: U.S. Government Printing Office, 1992.

———. Office of Technology Assessment. *Rural America at the Crossroads: Networking for the Future.* Washington DC: U.S. Government Printing Office, 1992.

———. Public Law 99–603. *Immigration Reform and Control Act of 1986.* 99th Cong., November 6, 1986.

———. Public Law 97–470. *Migrant and Seasonal Agricultural Act, 1983.* 97th Cong., January 14, 1983.

———. Senate. Committee on Agriculture, Nutrition, and Forestry. *Circle of Poison: Impact on American Consumers.* 102d Cong., 1st sess., September 20, 1991.

———. Senate. Committee on Agriculture, Nutrition, and Forestry. *Farm Structure: A Historical Perspective on Changes in the Number and Size of Farms.* 96th Cong., 2d sess. Washington, DC: Government Printing Office, 1980.

U.S. Department of Agriculture. *Agricultural Conservation Program: 1993 Fiscal Year Statistical Summary.* Washington, DC: U.S. Department of Agriculture, Agricultural Stabilization and Conservation Service, 1994.

———. *Agricultural Food Policy Review: Commodity Program Perspective.* Agricultural Economic Report No. 530 (July). Washington, DC: U.S. Department of Agriculture, Economic Research Service, 1985.

———. *Agricultural Income and Finance: Situation and Outlook Report.* USDA-ERS, AIS-52, February. Washington, DC: U.S. Department of Agriculture, Economic Research Service, 1994.

———. *Agricultural Resources and Environmental Indicators.* Agricultural Handbook No. 705. Washington, DC: U.S. Department of Agriculture, Economic Research Service, 1994.

———. *The Basic Mechanisms of U.S. Farm Policy.* Miscellaneous Publication No. 1479 (January). Rockville, MD: U.S. Department of Agriculture, Economic Research Service, National Agricultural Statistics Service, 1990.

———. *Economic Indicators of the Farm Sector: Costs of Production, 1993—Major Field Crops and Livestock and Dairy.* Report No. ECIFS 13–3. Washington, DC: U.S. Department of Agriculture, Economic Research Service, 1995.

———. *Education and Rural Economic Development: Strategies for the 1990s.* ERS Staff Report No. AGES 9153 (September). Washington, DC: U.S. Department of Agriculture, Agriculture and Rural Economy Division, Economic Research Service, 1991.

———. *Focusing on the Needs of the Rural Homeless.* Washington, DC: Rural Housing Service, 1996.

———. *Labor Market Areas for the United States.* Washington, DC: U.S. Department of Agriculture, Economic Research Division, 1987.

———. *The Physical Distribution System for Grain.* Agricultural Information Bulletin No. 457. Washington, DC: U.S. Department of Agriculture, Office of Transportation, 1990.

———. *Report and Recommendations on Organic Farming.* Washington, DC: U.S. Department of Agriculture, July 1980.

———. *The Second RCA Appraisal: Soil, Water, and Related Resources on Nonfederal Land in the United States.* USDA Misc. Publ. No. 1482. Washington, DC: U.S. Department of Agriculture, 1989.

———. *Sugar and Sweetener: Situation and Outlook Yearbook.* USDASSRV18N2 (June). Washington, DC: U.S. Department of Agriculture, Economic Research Service, 1993.

———. *A Time to Choose: Summary Report on the Structure of Agriculture.* Washington, DC: U.S. Department of Agriculture, 1981.

———. *Understanding Rural America.* Washington, DC: U.S. Department of Agriculture, Economic Research Service, 1995.

———. *Yearbook of Agriculture.* Washington, DC: Superintendent of Documents, various years.

U.S. Department of Agriculture, Agricultural Research Service. *USDA Plant Hardiness Zone Map.* A.R.S. Misc. Publ. 1475. Washington, DC: U.S. Government Printing Office, 1990.

U.S. Department of Agriculture, Forest Service. *An Analysis of the Timber Situation in the United States: 1989–2070.* General Technical Report RM-199. Ft. Collins, CO: Rocky Mountain Forest and Range Experiment Station, 1990.

U.S. Department of Agriculture, National Agriculture Library. *Periodicals Pertaining to Alternative Farming Systems.* Beltsville, MD: Alternative Farming Systems Information Center, 1993.

———. *Sustainable Agriculture in Print: Current Books.* Beltsville, MD: Alternative Farming Systems Information Center, 1993.

U.S. Department of Agriculture, Soil Conservation Service. *SEEP-*

PAGE: A System for Early Evaluation of the Pollution Potential of Agricultural Groundwater Environments. Engineering Geology Technical Note 5. Chester, PA: Northeastern National Technical Center, 1988.

U.S. Department of Health and Human Services, Office of Rural Health Policy. *Mental Health and Rural America: 1980–1993*. Washington, DC: U.S. Government Printing Office, 1993.

U.S. Department of the Interior, Fish and Wildlife Service, and U.S. Department of Commerce. *1991 National Survey of Fishing, Hunting, and Wildlife-Associated Recreation*. Washington DC: U.S. Government Printing Office, 1993.

U.S. Environmental Protection Agency. *Another Look: National Survey of Pesticides in Drinking Water Wells (Phase 2 Report)*. Report No. 570/9–91–020 (January). Washington, DC: U.S. Environmental Protection Agency, Office of Water, 1992.

———. *National Water Quality Inventory: 1988 Report to Congress*. EPA 440–4–90–003, Washington, DC: U.S. Environmental Protection Agency, April 1990.

———. *Risk Assessment, Management and Communication of Drinking Water Contamination*. Report EPA 625–4–89–024. Washington, DC: Environmental Protection Agency, Office of Water, 1990.

———. *The United States' Experience with Economic Incentives to Control Environmental Pollution*. Report 230–R–92–001. Washington, DC: U.S. Environmental Protection Agency, Office of Planning, Policy and Evaluation, July 1992.

———. *The Worker Protection Standard for Agricultural Pesticides: How to Comply*. EPA 7354-B-93-001. Washington, DC: U.S. Environmental Protection Agency, 1993.

U.S. Government Accounting Office. *Drinking Water: Stronger Efforts Essential for Small Communities to Comply with Standards*. Report No. US GAO/RCED-94–40. Washington, DC: U.S. Government Accounting Office, 1994.

U.S. Travel and Tourism Administration. *Rural Tourism Handbook: Selected Case Studies and Development Guide*. Washington, DC: U.S. Department of Commerce, U.S. Travel and Tourism Administration, 1994.

Utley, Robert M. *The Indian Frontier of the American West, 1846–1890*. Albuquerque: University of New Mexico Press, 1984.

Valente, C., and W. Valente. *Introduction to Environmental Law and Policy*. St. Paul, MN: West Publications, 1995.

Vandeman, Ann, Jorge Fernandez-Cornejo, Sharon Jans, and Biing-Hwan Lin. *Adoption of Integrated Pest Management in U.S. Agriculture*. Agriculture Information Bulletin No. 707. Washington, DC: U.S. Department of Agriculture, Economic Research Service, September 1994.

Van Kooten, Cornelis G. *Land Resource Economics and Sustainable Development*. Vancouver, Canada: UBC Press, 1993.

Vasey, Daniel E. *An Ecological History of Agriculture, 10,000 B.C.–A.D. 10,000*. Ames: Iowa State University Press, 1992.

Vavrek, Bernard. *Assessing the Information Needs of Rural Americans*. Clarion, PA: Department of Library Science, Center for the Study of Rural Librarianship, Clarion University of Pennsylvania, 1990.

———. *Assessing the Role of the Rural Public Library*. Clarion, PA: Department of Library Science, Center for the Study of Rural Librarianship, Clarion University of Pennsylvania, 1993.

Vesterby, M., R. E. Heimlich, and K. S. Krupa. *Urbanization of Rural Land in the United States*. AER-673. Washington, DC: U.S. Department of Agriculture, Economic Research Service, 1994.

Vitek, William, and Wes Jackson. *Rooted in the Land: Essays on Community and Place*. New Haven, CT: Yale University Press, 1996.

Vroomen, Harry, and Harold Taylor. *Fertilizer Trade Statistics, 1970–91*. Statistical Bulletin No. 851. Washington, DC: U.S. Department of Agriculture, Economic Research Service, January 1993.

Wagenfeld, Morton O., J. Dennis Murray, Dennis Mohatt, and Jeanne C. DeBruyn. *Mental Health in Rural America: 1980–1993*. Washington, DC: National Institute of Mental Health, 1993.

Wagner, Paul M. *Grapes into Wine: The Art of Winemaking in New York*. New York: Knopf, 1982.

Wahl, Richard W. *Markets for Federal Water: Subsidies, Property Rights, and the Bureau of Reclamation*. Washington, DC: Resources for the Future, 1989.

Wallace, H. A., and W. L. Brown. *Corn and Its Early Fathers*. Rev. ed. Ames: Iowa State University Press, 1988.

Walzer, Norman. *Rural Community Economic Development*. New York: Praeger, 1991.

Ward, Fay E. *The Cowboy at Work*. Norman: University of Oklahoma Press, 1958, 1987.

Warner, Paul D., and James A. Christenson. *The Cooperative Extension Service: A National Assessment*. Boulder, CO: Westview, 1984.

Weisheit, Ralph A., David N. Falcone, and L. Edward Wells. *Crime and Policing in Rural and Small Town America*. Prospect Heights, IL: Waveland Press, 1996.

Welsh, Roger L. *Of Trees and Dreams: The Fiction, Fact, and Folklore of Tree-Planting on the Northern Plains*. 2d printing. Lincoln: University of Nebraska Press, 1988.

Westman, Walter. *Ecology, Impact Assessment, and Environmental Planning*. New York: John Wiley and Sons, 1985.

Westwood, Melvin N. *Temperate-Zone Pomology, Physiology and Culture*. 3d ed. Portland, OR: Timber Press, 1993.

White, Robert H. *Tribal Assets: The Rebirth of Native America*. New York: Henry Holt, 1990.

Wilhite, Donald. *Drought Assessment, Management, and Planning: Theory and Case Studies*. Dordrecht, Netherlands: Kluwer, 1993.

Wilhite, Donald, and William Easterling, eds. *Planning for Drought: Toward a Reduction of Societal Vulnerability*. Boulder, CO: Westview, 1987.

Wilkinson, Alec. *Big Sugar: Seasons in the Cane Fields of Florida*. New York: Alfred A. Knopf, 1989.

Wilkinson, Charles F. *Crossing the Next Meridian: Land, Water, and the Future of the West*. Washington, DC: Island Press, 1992.

Wilkinson, Kenneth P. *The Community in Rural America*. New York: Greenwood Press, 1991.

Williams, M. *Americans and Their Forests: A Historical Geography*. Cambridge, MA: Cambridge University Press, 1989.

Wimberley, Ronald C., and Libby V. Morris. *The Southern Black Belt: A National Perspective—Dependence, Quality of Life, and Policy,* forthcoming.

Winter, C. K., J. Seiber, and C. F. Nuckton. *Chemicals in the Human Food Chain.* New York: Van Nostrand Reinhold, 1990.

Worster, Donald. *Dust Bowl: The Southern Plains in the 1930s.* New York: Oxford University Press, 1982.

Wright, John B. *Rocky Mountain Divide: Selling and Saving the West.* Austin: University of Texas Press, 1993.

Wright, R. Dean, and Susan E. Wright. *Homeless Children and Adults in Iowa: Addressing Issues and Options in Education, Services and the Community.* Des Moines: State of Iowa, Department of Education, 1993.

Wunderlich, Gene. *Land Ownership and Taxation in American Agriculture.* Boulder, CO: Westview, 1992.

———. *Owning Farmland in the United States.* AIB 637. Washington, DC: U.S. Department of Agriculture, Economic Research Service, 1991.

Wunderlich, Gene, and John Blackledge. *Taxing Farmland in the United States.* Agricultural Economics Report No. 679. Washington, DC: U.S. Department of Agriculture, 1994.

Wyckoff, William, and Larry M. Dilsaver. *The Mountainous West: Explorations in Historical Geography.* Lincoln: University of Nebraska Press, 1995.

Yarborough, Paul. *Information Technology and Rural Economic Development: Evidence from Historical and Contemporary Research.* Washington, DC: Office of Technology Assessment, U.S. Congress, 1990.

Yoder, Don. *Discovering American Folklife: Studies in Ethnic, Religious, and Regional Culture.* Ann Arbor, MI: UMI Research Press, 1990.

Young, John A., and Jan M. Newton. *Capitalism and Human Obsolescence: Corporate Control vs. Individual Survival in Rural America.* Montclair, NJ: Allanheld, Osmun, 1980.

Zabawa, Robert, Ntam Baharanyi, and Walter Hill, eds. *Challenges in Agriculture and Rural Development.* Tuskegee, AL: Tuskegee University, 1993.

Zeitlin, Steven J., Amy J. Kotkin, and Holly Cutting Baker. *A Celebration of American Family Folklore: Tales and Traditions from the Smithsonian Collection.* New York: Pantheon Books, 1982.

Zelinsky, Wilbur. *The Cultural Geography of the United States.* Englewood Cliffs, NJ: Prentice-Hall, 1992.

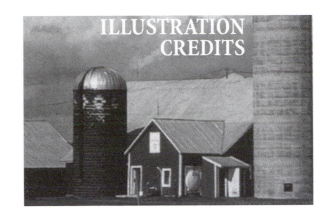

ILLUSTRATION CREDITS

ABOUT THE CONTRIBUTORS

Charles W. Abdalla is associate professor, Department of Agricultural Economics and Rural Sociology, Pennsylvania State University. His research and extension work involves economic assessments of water management technologies; groundwater values; environmental, groundwater, and farm policy; and community conflict over pollution from animal agriculture.

Don E. Albrecht is associate professor, Department of Rural Sociology, Texas A&M University. He specializes in agricultural sociology, agricultural mechanization, environmental and natural resources, and human ecology and has interests in the sociology of leisure, sports, and recreation. He is the book review editor for *Rural Sociology*. He is the author (with Steve H. Murdock) of *The Sociology of U.S. Agriculture: An Ecological Perspective* (1990).

Ralph Alcock is chair, Department of Agricultural Engineering, South Dakota State University.

Marilyn Aronoff is assistant professor, Department of Sociology, Michigan State University, and a community sociologist in the Rural and Environmental Sociology program. Her work examines the processes of change in rural Michigan communities as well as community response to economic and environmental crisis and their impacts on changing rural community identity.

Donald E. Arwood is associate professor, Department of Rural Sociology, and associate director, Census Data Center, South Dakota State University. He has conducted research on the agricultural, social, and demographic characteristics of South Dakota and the Upper Great Plains. His current research focuses on rural-urban differences in low birth weight, suicide, and crime.

Julian H. Atkinson is professor, Department of Agricultural Economics, Purdue University. He devotes time to extension work with farmers, farm managers, appraisers, lenders, and landowners. His areas of work include farm financial management, leasing, family farm business arrangements, and land prices and investment.

Dean A. Bangsund is research associate, Department of Agricultural Economics, North Dakota State University. He is currently assessing the economics of noxious weed control methods.

Peggy F. Barlett is professor, Department of Anthropology, Emory University. Her current interests are in economic development theory and the globalization of culture. She is active in rethinking ways to teach these issues in anthropology. She is the author of *American Dreams, Rural Realities: Family Farms in Crisis* (1993).

Freddie L. Barnard is associate professor, Department of Agricultural Economics, and director, Agricultural Banking School, Purdue University. He conducts the extension program in agricultural lending and serves on the Farm Finance Standards Council to promote uniformity in financial reporting and analysis in agriculture. Barnard is the author of *Banker's Agricultural Lending Manual* (1993).

C. Phillip Baumel is professor, Department of Economics, and Charles F. Curtiss Distinguished Professor in Agriculture, Iowa State University, Ames. He specializes in the economics of grain transportation and distribution systems and of genetically modified corn and soybeans.

Michael M. Bell is assistant professor, Department of Sociology, Iowa State University.

G. Andrew Bernat, Jr., is chief, Analysis Branch, Regional Economic Analysis Division, Bureau of Economic Analysis, U.S. Department of Commerce. His research includes regional input-output modeling, econometric modeling, and economic growth particularly with the role of manufacturing.

Michelle Beshear is a graduate student, Department of Agricultural Economics, Oklahoma State University.

Sampson Lee Blair is assistant professor, Department of Sociology, Arizona State University, Tempe. His research involves the division of household labor by adolescents to determine how parents assign tasks to children and by retired couples to examine the effect of retirement on division of housework. He also analyzes marital quality among American couples.

Anita D. Bledsoe is research assistant, University of Akron, and a doctoral student studying sociology and social psychology.

Leonard E. Bloomquist is associate professor, Department of Sociology, Anthropology and Social Work, Kansas State University. His research interests include rural work structures, the organization of rural communities, and the impacts of economic and social restructuring on rural localities.

Michael D. Boehlje is professor and head, Department of Agricultural Economics, Purdue University, West. He has written on farm management, megatrends impacting agriculture such as industrialization of agriculture, and farm finance issues such as rural credit markets and agricultural lending decisions. Among his publications is *Farm Management* (1984, with Vernon R. Eidman).

Rosemarie Bogal-Allbritten is professor, Department of Sociology, Anthropology, and Social Work, Murray State University. Her research interests include service delivery to victims of domestic violence and rape, the use of self-help groups (Parents Anonymous) to work with abuse parents, and campus efforts to address date rape and dating violence.

Janet L. Bokemeier is professor, Department of Sociology, Michigan State University. She specializes in studies of gender, work, family, and agriculture in rural America. Her current research involves multiple jobholding and underemployment, how changes in the dairy industry affect farm families and communities, and children, rural poverty, and school readiness.

David O. Born is professor and chair, Division of Health Ecology, University of Minnesota School of Dentistry. He directs research and training programs on rural dental health issues, focusing on health professional recruitment, retention, and placement programs. He has served on the National Health Council's Task Force on Health Manpower Distribution.

Regina Broadway is a graduate research assistant, Department of Agricultural Economics and Rural Sociology, Auburn University. She is studying the horse industry.

Ralph B. Brown is assistant professor, Department of Sociology, Anthropology, and Social Work, Mississippi State University. He studies subsistence and informal economic activities of individuals and communities in the Mississippi Delta and is studying the social impacts of large automotive manufacturing plants locating in southern rural communities.

Carolyn Junior Bryant is assistant professor of social work, Department of Sociology, Anthropology, and Social Work, Mississippi State University. She is pursuing an international research agenda studying Ghanaian women living with HIV and AIDS.

Steven T. Buccola is professor, Department of Agricultural and Resource Economics, Oregon State University. He has interests in the economics of producing and processing agricultural products in the United States and abroad. He conducts research on agricultural cooperatives and the pricing of agricultural goods and is a past editor of the *American Journal of Agricultural Economics*.

William W. Budd is professor, Program in Environmental Science and Regional Planning, Washington State University. He examines environmental regulations and policies, including the carrying capacity of the land.

Gary Burkart is director, Center for the Rural and Small Town Church, and chair, Department of Sociology, Benedictine College, Atchison, Kansas. He advises the North American Forum on the Cathecumenate regarding rural parishes, and he completed a needs assessment for the Catholic Archdiocese of Kansas City, Kansas to be used for long-range planning.

Jeffrey Burkhardt is professor, Institute of Food and Agricultural Sciences, Department of Food and Resource Economics, University of Florida. He teaches courses on agricultural and natural resource ethics. His research interests focus on the ethical implications of new technologies in agriculture, especially new biotechnology.

Lowell Bush is professor, Department of Agronomy, University of Kentucky. He conducts research on alkaloid biosynthesis in tobacco, which examines the enzymes and chemical intermediates in the biosynthetic pathways, genetic and biologic regulation of formation, and use of nicotine by the plant.

Terry F. Buss is chair and professor, Department of Public Administration and Urban Studies, University of Akron. He also works with the National Academy of Public Administration and the Advisory Council on Intergovernmental Relations to evaluate infrastructure benchmarking practices by state and local governments across the United States.

Frederick H. Buttel is professor, Department of Rural Sociology, University of Wisconsin, Madison. His research focuses on agricultural and environmental movements with particular emphasis on the influence of these movements on agricultural research and emerging technologies. He is coauthor of *The Sociology of Agriculture* (1990).

Robert V. Carlson is professor emeritus, Department of Education, University of Vermont. He continues to teach, consult, and advise doctoral students on topics related to rural education. His most recent book is *Reframing and Reform: Perspectives on Organization, Leadership, and School Change* (1995).

Dewey M. Caron is professor, Department of Entomology and Applied Ecology, University of Delaware; he teaches entomology and apiculture. He has won international recognition for his projects involving Africanized bees in Panama and Bolivia and conducts research on bee pollination and the biology of queen replacement in honey bees.

C. Ronald Carroll is a professor and associate director, Institute of Ecology, and director of the Conservation Ecology and Sustainable Development graduate training program, University of Georgia. His projects include integrated pest management in Guatemala, restoration ecology training in Ecuador, and southeastern ultisols native communities restoration. Interest areas include biodiversity protection through ecosystem management.

Peter R. Cheeke is professor, Department of Animal Sciences, Oregon State University. His studies include contemporary issues in animal agriculture and comparative animal nutrition, and he co-developed the Program for the Study of Contemporary Issues in Agriculture affiliated with the Philosophy Department's Program for Ethics, Science, and the Environment. He is the author of *Impacts of Livestock Production on Society, Diet/Health and the Environment* (1993).

Neale R. Chumbler is assistant professor, Department of Sociology, Western Michigan University. He is studying the elderly in Arkansas to determine how rural-urban and within-rural variations in health and community support service use affect older adults with dementia and their family caregivers.

Rodney L. Clouser serves as acting district extension director, Florida Cooperative Extension Service, University of Florida, Gainesville. His primary area of interest is in public policy on issues of working with local government, taxation, and land use policy.

David W. Cobia is professor, Department of Agricultural Economics, and director, Quentin N. Burdick Center for Cooperatives, North Dakota State University, Fargo. He conducts research on new, emerging value-adding contract agricultural cooperatives and edited *Cooperatives in Agriculture* (Prentice-Hall, 1989).

Jack T. Cole is professor and director of special education, Department of Special Education/Communication Disorders, New Mexico State University. He worked in rural regular and special education for 30 years, was the director of the ERIC Clearinghouse on Rural Education and Small Schools, and is executive editor of *Rural Special Education Quarterly*.

John D. Copeland is director, National Center for Agricultural Law Research and Information, University of Arkansas. He specializes in agricultural law, worker's compensation, and the impact of environmental legislation on livestock producers.

Sam Cordes is professor, Department of Agricultural Economics, and director, Center for Rural Community Revitalization and Development, University of Nebraska. He studies community economic development with emphasis on rural health care delivery. He served on the U.S. Department of Health and Human Services' National Advisory Committee on Rural Health. His publications include *Recreational Access to Private Lands: Liability Problems and Solutions* (1995) and *Understanding the Farmers Comprehensive Personal Liability Policy: A Guide for Farmers' Attorneys and Insurance Agents* (1992).

Arthur G. Cosby is professor of sociology and director, Social Science Research Center, Mississippi State University. He conducts societal monitoring, policy research, and futuring and focuses on the visualization of social and economic phenomena and the growth of legalized gaming and gambling in the United States. He led the 1995 U.S. Survey of Gaming and Gambling.

Connie Coutellier is director, Professional Development, and past president, American Camping Association. She directed camps in Ohio, California, and Michigan and is integrating camp director education courses into a development plan for camping professionals. She is author of *Management Risks and Emergencies* and the Camp Fire Boys and Girls *Outdoor Book*.

Raymond T. Coward is professor of health policy and epidemiology, affiliate professor of sociology, and director, Institute for Gerontology, University of Florida. His research focuses on the affect of race and residence on the process of aging and on health and human services delivery to older adults and their families. He is coauthor of *Health Programs and Services for Elders in Rural America: A Review of the Life Circumstances and Formal Services That Affect the Health and Well-Being of Elders* (1991) and *Old and Alone in Rural America* (1993).

Cynthia M. Cready is a sociology Ph.D. student, Texas A&M University. Her dissertation examines African American population size and the impact of desegregation on public school finances and White enrollment in the nonmetropolitan South. Other research involves the effect of mate availability on African American family structure and minority group intermarriage.

Susan J. Crockett is dean, College for Human Development, Syracuse University. She co-authored "Environmental Influences on Children's Eating," one of three plenary papers presented at the National Conference on Healthy Eating for Children: A Policy Dialogue, sponsored by the National Partnership to Improve the American Diet.

John B. Cromartie is geographer, Economic Research Service, U.S. Department of Agriculture. He studies rural migration, settlement patterns, and minority populations. His current work involves examining post-1990 rural migration and labor market changes and mapping national settlement patterns using census tracts.

James Curry teaches at the Departamento de Estudios Norteamericanos (Department of North American Studies), El Colegio de la Frontera Norte, Tijuana, B.C., Mexico. He has written on the California wine industry and the restructuring of agri-industry.

David B. Danbom is professor, Department of History, North Dakota State University, Fargo. He studies agrarian ideology in the United States, and wrote *"Born in the Country": A History of Rural America* (1995).

Jacqueline M. Davis-Gines is assistant professor, Department of Sociology, University of Memphis. She researches racial stacking in Southeastern Conference football between 1969 and 1994 and the social psychological effects of *The Wonderful World of Disney* on young children.

Lesley Deem-Dickson is a graduate student, Department of Entomology, University of Illinois at Urbana-Champaign. She is studying pest management.

Janaan Diemer is special education coordinator, supervising programs for the Seriously Emotionally Disordered Students, Psychology, and Social Work Department, Las Cruces Public Schools, Las Cruces, New Mexico. She taught regular and special education for 14 years, has been an administrator for 6 years, and is working on a doctorate in educational administration.

David M. Diggs is associate professor, Department of Geography, Central Missouri State University. He has published research on climate perceptions of Great Plains farmers and their drought adjustment strategies. He is currently conducting a comparative analysis of governmental drought adjustment programs in the U.S. Great Plains and the Russian Steppe.

Otto C. Doering III is professor, Department of Agricultural Economics, Purdue University, and a public policy specialist working on agricultural and resource issues. He coordinates environmental policy research through the School of Agriculture for the state and federal government and is co-authoring a book on the evolution of the 1996 Farm Bill.

Frank Dooley is assistant professor, Department of Agricultural Economics, North Dakota State University. He studies costs of the wheat supply chain, effects of hazardous materials regulations on fertilizer plants, flour mill inventory practices, effects of preferred buyer programs on inventories, and the interrelationship between corn milling plants and the livestock industry.

Michael Duffy is associate professor, Department of Economics, Iowa State University. He studies natural resource and environmentally related agricultural concerns such as agrichemical use on farms.

Thomas J. Durant, Jr., is professor, Department of Sociology, Louisiana State University. His research interests include criminology, gerontology (alienation of rural elderly), minorities (African American plantation church), and global development. He is president elect and program chair of the Mid-South Sociological Association.

Ron L. Durst is tax team leader and senior economist, Rural Economy Division, Economic Research Service, U.S. Department of Agriculture. He holds degrees in agricultural economics, law, and taxation. His research pertains to taxation and related topics.

Terri L. Earnest is research associate, Mississippi Crime and Justice Research Unit, Social Science Research Center, Mississippi State University. Her research interests include race relations, hate crime activity, family violence, gang and delinquency behavior, and drug trafficking.

Clyde Eastman is development sociologist, Department of Agricultural Economics and Agricultural Business, New Mexico State University. He conducts research on small-scale irrigation systems and the farms they support and on farm labor in its various dimensions.

Lowell J. Endahl serves as donated equipment manager, National Rural Electric Cooperative Association, International Foundation. He has managed power plants, developed marketing, technological, and member relations programs, and traveled extensively in Europe, Africa, South America, and Asia for the United Nations' Working Party on Rural Electrification.

Robert D. Espeseth is professor emeritus, Office of Recreation and Tourism Development and Department of Leisure Studies, University of Illinois, Champaign-Urbana. He works on the Ohio River National Heritage Corridor, East St. Louis Cultural Heritage District, and the Economic Impact of Park and Recreation Areas for the National Society for Park Resource.

Edmund A. Estes is professor, Department of Agricultural and Resource Economics, North Carolina State University. His research involves determining consumers' willingness to pay higher prices for vegetables grown without synthetic chemicals and the feasibility of using extruded sweet potatoes as a substitute feed for poultry in developing countries. He edited *Look through the 90's: The U.S. Fruit and Vegetable Industry* (1990).

D. Merrill Ewert is assistant professor, Department of Education, Cornell University, where he teaches and conducts research on adult education and community development. Together with several colleagues, he studies the link between rural literacy education and community development in New York.

Gary E. Farley is director, Office of Town and Country Missions, Southern Baptist Convention. He assists churches and clergy throughout the United States to serve their rural communities. He writes extensively on churches in their rural context, describes how they function, and examines how their vitality can be enhanced.

Frank L. Farmer is professor, Department of Agricultural Economics and Rural Sociology, University of Arkansas. His research pertains to rural communities, migration, and poverty, and recently to rural health care policy, prenatal care, and infant mortality.

Jill L. Findeis is associate professor, Department of Agricultural Economics and Rural Sociology, Pennsylvania State University. Her research projects assess the value of farmworker housing, examine off-farm employment, and assess the impacts of alternative income sources on the distribution of income among rural households.

Price V. Fishback is professor, Department of Economics, University of Arizona, Tucson. He has written reports about insurance rationing and workers' compensation for the National Bureau of Economic Research and is the author of *Soft Coal, Hard Choices: The Economic Welfare of Bituminous Coal Miners: 1890–1930* (1992).

Emmett P. Fisk is extension organizational effectiveness specialist, Department of Rural Sociology, Washington State University. He studies resolution of environmental conflicts.

Harrison L. Flint is professor, Department of Horticulture, Purdue University. He has written several books and journal articles on landscape plants.

Cornelia Butler Flora is director, North Central Regional Center for Regional Development, Iowa State University, Ames. Her writings pertain to sustainable agriculture and appropriate technology, community-based economic development, quality of life, and social capital development. She coauthored *Rural Communities: Legacy and Change* (1992) and coedited *Rural Policies for the 1990s* (1991).

Richard C. Fluck is professor, Department of Agricultural and Biological Engineering, University of Florida. His projects involve the Florida Agricultural Energy Consumption Model, educational materials on energy use in sustainable agriculture, and budgets to evaluate energy productiveness of alternative production practices for North Florida commodities. He is the editor of *Energy in Farm Production.* Vol. 6, *Energy in World Agriculture* (1992).

Charles A. Francis is professor and director, Center for Sustainable Agricultural Systems, University of Nebraska, Lincoln. He has studied intercropping systems in Columbia, Philippines, and the Midwest United States. He is currently developing and testing innovative learning environments and designing diverse, resource-efficient farming systems.

C. Dean Freudenberger is professor, Christian Social Ethics and Rural Ministry, Luther Seminary. He studies agricultural ethics, hunger, poverty, and the integration of theology and ecology. He believes the environmental crisis is symptomatic of a human spiritual crisis and works to change the industrialized-reductionistic paradigm to a regenerative-sustainable one. He is the author of *Food for Tomorrow?* (1984).

Jerry E. Fruin is associate professor of marketing and transportation and Extension Economist, Department of Agricultural and Applied Economics, University of Minnesota. He studies the costs, infrastructure requirements, and impact of transportation on the Upper Midwest economy, rural road maintenance, and the use of alfalfa for gasification in electricity generation.

Isao Fujimoto is professor emeritus, Department of Applied Behavioral Science and Department of Asian American Studies, University of California, Davis. His research focuses on Asian Pacific Americans and Japanese rural community revitalization.

Wayne E. Fuller is professor emeritus, Department of History, University of Texas at El Paso. He has written on rural history, including the Rural Free Delivery mail system. He is the author of *The Old Country School: The Story of Rural Education in the Middle West* (1982) and *One-room Schools of the Middle West* (1994).

D. Linda Garcia is adjunct professor, School of Foreign Service and Program on Communications, Culture, and Technology, Georgetown University, and School of Advanced International Studies, Johns Hopkins University. She specializes in telecommunications.

Melanie Gardner conducts research at the Rural Information Center, National Agricultural Library, Beltsville, Maryland.

Charles C. Geisler is professor, Department of Rural Sociology, Cornell University. He specializes in topics of land ownership, use, and control in the United States and in comparative land reform. His research addresses the social impacts associated with protected areas, ecosystem management, and new forms of landownership. He coedited *Land Reform, American Style* (1984).

Jack M. Geller is director, Health Systems Research, Marshield Medical Research Foundation, Wisconsin. He specializes in the sociology of health and medicine.

Kathryn Paxton George is associate professor and chair, Department of Philosophy, University of Idaho. She writes on ethics in agriculture, including *Animal, Vegetable or Woman? A Feminist Argument against Ethical Vegetarianism.* She co-edited *Readings in the Development of Moral Thought* (1992) and *Agricultural Ethics: Issues for the 21st Century* (1994).

Duane A. Gill is associate professor, Social Science Research Center and Department of Sociology, Anthropology, and Social Work, Mississippi State University. He conducts a panel study of freshwater anglers in Mississippi, the natural hazards in Mississippi and their economic impacts on agriculture, and the community impacts of the Exxon Valdez oil spill.

Theodore Godlaski is assistant professor of psychiatry, Multidisciplinary Research Center on Drug and Alcohol Abuse University of Kentucky, Lexington. He studies patients who received treatment in Kentucky drug and alcohol programs and is helping to plan additions capacity management across the state.

Stephan J. Goetz is associate professor, Department of Agricultural Economics, University of Kentucky, Lexington. He identifies determinants of economic growth in rural areas, such as human capital, labor force, and government policy and studies food manufacturing industry location and that industry's potential to preserve farms in rural areas.

Robert Goldman is professor, Department of Sociology and Anthropology, Lewis and Clark College, Portland. He is the author of *Sign Wars: The Cluttered Landscape of Advertising* (1996, with Steve Papson). He is working on a new book applying a theoretical model of advertising and sign value to Nike.

Chennat Gopalakrishnan is professor of natural resource economics, Department of Agricultural and Resource Economics, University of Hawaii, Manoa. His research pertains to current and emerging issues in natural resource economics and policy. He is the author of *The Economics of Energy in Agriculture* (1994), and *Natural Resource Economics: A Book of Readings* is scheduled to be published in 1997.

Gary A. Goreham is associate professor, Department of Sociology/Anthropology, North Dakota State University. He works in the areas of rural community development, rural cooperatives, churches, voluntary organizations, and sustainable agriculture. He is the author of *The Rural Church in America: A Century of Writings—A Bibliography* (1990) and co-author of *The Socioeconomics of Sustainable Agriculture: An Annotated Bibliography* (1993).

Phyllis Gray-Ray is associate professor, Department of Criminal Justice, North Carolina Central University, Durham. Her primary interests include criminology, race and ethnicity, and rural sociology.

Gary P. Green is professor, Department of Rural Sociology, University of Wisconsin, Madison. His teaching, research, and extension activities focus on the social, political, and economic forces affecting communities and regions and on local efforts to promote growth and development. He is involved in projects regarding community restructuring and the problems of low-wage labor.

John L. Green is research assistant, Social Science Research Center, Department of Sociology, Anthropology, and Social Work, Mississippi State University. He has written on plantations in the rural South.

Clyde S. Greenlees recently received a Ph.D. in sociology from Texas A&M University and holds an adjunct position in the Department of Social Sciences at Del Mar College. His research pertains to the employment patterns of Mexican immigrant women.

Charles L. Griffin is professor, School of Family Studies and Human Services, Kansas State University. He is a marriage and family therapist who has worked with a wide range of farm family, rural community, and rural mental health concerns involving crisis response, communication, stress management, conflict resolution and mediation, and community and organizational change.

Christina Gringeri is associate professor, Graduate School of Social Work, and director, Women's Study Program, University of Utah. She studies rural poverty and women, work, and development in the Intermountain West and is the author of *Getting By: Women Homeworkers and Rural Economic Development* (1994).

Charles F. Gritzner is distinguished professor of geography, South Dakota State University. His teaching and research expertise includes cultural, physical, historical, methodological, and regional geography. He has expertise in geographic education and works intensively with elementary and secondary geography and social studies educators.

James L. Groves works in the School of Hotel and Restaurant Management, Oklahoma State University. He has written on restaurants and their role in rural communities.

Robert W. Groves is professor of music, Division of Fine Arts, North Dakota State University. His specialties include piano literature and performance, oral histories and American music history, and the relief of tendon stress syndrome in computer keyboard use.

Susan Hamburger is manuscripts librarian, Pennsylvania State University. She has written a dissertation on the horse racing industry in Florida, a documentary of Civil War letters, and several biographical essays. She writes the science fiction and fantasy book review column for the *Library Journal.*

Neil D. Hamilton is distinguished professor and director, Agricultural Law Center, Drake University. He is writing *Feeding America's Future*, a study about the people and forces shaping America's food and agricultural system.

Wava Gillespie Haney is professor and chair, Department of Anthropology and Sociology, University of Wisconsin Centers. She studies rural women's roles in leadership and community development strategies and women migrants from metropolitan areas in rural southwestern Wisconsin. She involves undergraduate students in her work on rural women.

Rosalind P. Harris is associate professor, Department of Sociology, University of Kentucky. Her research includes work on the land-grant institutions, rural poverty, and rural health.

Upton Hatch is professor, Department of Agricultural Economics, Auburn University. He teaches and conducts research on the economics of aquaculture, natural resources, and the environment. He is developing instructional materials for aquaculture curricula and for estimates of the economic value of water. He edited (with Henry Kinnucan) *Aquaculture: Models and Economics* (1993).

Thomas A. Heberlein is professor and former chair of the Department of Rural Sociology, University of Wisconsin, Madison. He is currently studying environmental attitudes, valuation of natural resources, and recreation change in northern Wisconsin.

William D. Heffernan is professor, Department of Rural Sociology, University of Missouri, Columbia. He studies changes in the structure of agriculture and the concentration in agribusiness, or the agro/food complex, with special emphasis on the poultry sector. He is the coauthor of *Concentration of Agricultural Markets* (1996).

David A. Henderson works at the Piketon Research and Extension Center, Ohio State University. He studies expenditure patterns between rural elderly residents and rural-to-urban elderly migrants, with particular emphasis on previous occupation.

Shida Rastegari Henneberry is associate professor, Department of Agricultural Economics, Oklahoma State University. She studies food safety, food-processing issues, and the economic impacts and effectiveness of agricultural market development programs, such as government export promotion.

Lawrence J. Hill is head, Department of Communication and Theater Arts, Western Carolina University. He has received grants from the North Dakota Humanities Council and the National Endowment for the Humanities to research nineteenth century scenic design and preservation projects. He is treasurer, United States Institute for Theater Technology.

Thomas J. Hoban is associate professor, Department of Food Science, North Carolina State University. He focuses on how people accept new products and respond to change. He studies the impacts of biotechnology on agriculture and the environment as well as American and Japanese consumers' attitudes about food produced through biotechnology. He is coauthor of *Consumer Attitudes about Food Biotechnology* (1993).

Daryl Hobbs is professor, Department of Sociology, and director, Office of Social and Economic Data Analysis, University of Missouri. He teaches, gives presentations, and conducts research on the problems and opportunities that pertain to rural schools, health care, and community development.

Wang-Ling Hsu is a graduate research assistant, Department of Agricultural Economics and Rural Sociology, Pennsylvania State University. She is examining underemployment among disadvantaged groups in the United States and the impacts of technological change on rural labor use in India.

David W. Hughes is assistant professor, Department of Agricultural Economics and Agribusiness, Louisiana State University. He evaluates the contribution of agricultural production, processing, and agribusiness to the Louisiana economy, constructs hybrid regional input-output models, and studies the impact of industries on rural public services.

Craig R. Humphrey is associate professor, Department of Sociology, Pennsylvania State University. He studies consumer interest in certification programs that promote sustainable wood production as well as studies forest-based local economic development in various regions of the United States.

Mary Humstone is co-founder and director of BARN AGAIN!, National Trust for Historic Preservation. She provides technical rehabilitation assistance to barn owners. Humstone works with Smithsonian Traveling Exhibition Service's "Barn Again!" exhibition and with publication of the *Barn-Aid* series (barn rehabilitation guides). She is the author of *Barn Again! A Guide to Rehabilitation of Older Farm Buildings* (1988).

Chris Hurt is professor and extension economist, Department of Agricultural Economics, Purdue University. He teaches agricultural marketing to undergraduates and grain and livestock marketing to farmers and agribusiness managers. He conducts research on marketing problems of family farms.

Ronald J. Hustedde is associate extension professor, Department of Sociology, University of Kentucky. He specializes in public issues education and community development in rural Kentucky. His educational work focuses on teaching public conflict resolution skills to elected officials and community leaders in rural areas.

Thomas Isern is professor, Department of History, North Dakota State University, Fargo. His research interests include the history and folklore of the North American Plains and the history of agriculture. He is the author of *Bull Threshers and Bindlestiffs: Harvesting and Threshing on the North American Plains* (1990).

Harvey M. Jacobs is professor and chair, Department of Urban and Regional Planning, and professor, Institute for Environmental Studies, University of Wisconsin, Madison. His research focuses on the anti-environmental movement in America and the development of urban fringe and agricultural land retention policy in Eastern Europe and the former Soviet Union.

Leif Jensen is associate professor, Department of Agricultural Economics and Rural Sociology, and senior research associate, Population Research Institute, Pennsylvania State University. He studies poverty among the elderly, underemployment, survival strategies among low-income families, and children's labor force participation and schooling in Chile, Peru, and Mexico.

Marvin E. Jensen is a consultant on irrigation issues. He was director of the Colorado Institute for Irrigation Management, Colorado State University, and the National Program Leader of the Water Management Research, Agricultural Research Service, U.S. Department of Agriculture. He is the editor of *Design and Operation of Farm Irrigation Systems* (1983).

Edward J. Jepson, Jr., is a doctoral student, Department of Urban and Regional Planning, University of Wisconsin, Madison. His dissertation research focuses on aspects of sustainable development and growth management.

Patrick C. Jobes is professor, Department of Sociology, Montana State University. He studies crime and delinquency, demography and human ecology, and environmental and energy concerns of the western United States.

Chandice M. Johnson, Jr., director, Center for Writers, North Dakota State University, specializes in writing and the literature of the Canadian prairies and has worked with diaries and letters of Civil War infantrymen. Johnson is editor of *Prairie Perspectives,* a regional reader used in introductory English classes.

D. Demcey Johnson is assistant professor, Department of Agricultural Economics, North Dakota State University. His research interests include agricultural price analysis, agricultural trade with focus on commodities produced in the Northern Plains, and economics of grain quality.

L. Shannon Jung is director, Center for Theology and Land, University of Dubuque School of Theology and Wartburg Theological Seminary. He writes on the theology and ethics of land use, Christian responses to contemporary moral issues, rural congregational studies, and the emergence of militias as an expression of rural rage, fear, and hopelessness. His publications include *We Are Home: A Spirituality of the Environment* (1993).

Raymond A. Jussaume, Jr., is assistant professor, Department of Rural Sociology, Washington State University. He researches the globalization of agriculture and the food industry as well as international trade, particularly in Pacific Rim countries.

Adel A. Kader is professor of postharvest physiology, Department of Pomology, University of California, Davis. His research, teaching, and extension activities focus on postharvest biology and technology of horticultural crops in relation to quality maintenance and loss reduction. He served as president of the American Society for Horticultural Science in 1995–1996. He is the editor of *Postharvest Technology of Horticultural Crops* (1992).

Aileen A. Kader is a consultant on gardening and photography and a master gardener. Her interests are to better understand plant-people interactions with a focus on the healing dimensions of gardens.

Cathy Kassab is research associate, Institute for Policy Research and Evaluation, Pennsylvania State University. She researches changes in job quality, strategies used by low-income households to enhance economic well-being, and barriers to health care services use among nonmetropolitan populations such as the elderly.

Jean Kayitsinga is a Ph.D. candidate, Department of Sociology, Michigan State University. His research interests include rural families, sociology, demography, and statistical methodologies.

Eric Damian Kelly is dean, College of Architecture and Planning, Ball State University, and is a planner and lawyer. He writes on issues in planning law and planning implementation, and coauthored (with Gary J. Raso) *Sign Regulation for Small and Midsized Communities* (1989), a Planning Advisory Service Report of the American Planning Association.

Jean Kinsey is professor, Department of Applied Economics, University of Minnesota, and director, Retail Food Industry Center, where she studies the operations, competitiveness, and productivity of the food chain. Her research involves changes in the food industry, consumer lifestyles, and preferences for types of food.

James B. Kliebenstein is professor, Department of Economics, Iowa State University, and specializes in economic evaluation of livestock production systems, assessment of animal health management, and structural adjustment in the livestock industry. He focuses on environmentally sound, economically profitable, and socially acceptable livestock production systems.

Timothy J. Kloberdanz is associate professor, Department of Sociology/Anthropology, North Dakota State University. His research includes folklore of the Great Plains and Rocky Mountain regions, genetic Alzheimer's disease, and ethnic persistence in the major grassland regions of the European steppes, North American prairies, and South American pampas.

Peter F. Korsching is professor, Department of Sociology, Iowa State University. His work pertains to adoption, diffusion, and impacts of new technologies on farming populations and rural communities. His studies involve sustainable agriculture practices and technologies and the potential of new telecommunications technologies for rural community development.

Dianne T. Koza, Auburn University, developed training materials to teach computer skills to apparel students and plant employees, and is developing software for the apparel and textiles industries.

John A. Krout is professor and director of the Gerontology Institute, Ithaca College, NY. He has published articles and books on rural aging and senior centers, such as *Providing Community-based Services to the Rural Elderly* (1994). His research is on senior centers and other community-based services, the rural elderly, and knowledge and use patterns of health and social services.

Fred M. Lamb is professor and extension specialist, Department of Wood Science and Forest Products, Virginia Polytechnic Institute and State University. He is involved in teaching, research, and technology transfer. His continuing education activities are in wood science and technology, with special emphasis on industrial manufacturing and wood-processing technology.

Christopher Lant is chair, Department of Geography, Southern Illinois University, Carbondale, and editor, *Water Resources Bulletin*. He works on projects to determine the willingness of farmers to enroll cropland in the Conservation Reserve Program and the Wetlands Reserve Program as mechanisms to improve water quality in agricultural watersheds.

Paul Lasley is professor, Department of Sociology, Iowa State University. He is involved in extension and research projects pertaining to farms, agriculture, and rural life. He is coauthor of *Beyond the Amber Waves of Grain* (1995).

Chiwon W. Lee is assistant professor of horticulture, Department of Plant Sciences, North Dakota State University, where he teaches horticultural science, plant propagation, greenhouse crop production, and horticultural food crops. His current research involves greenhouse crop nutrition, tissue culture, and genetic improvement of flowers and vegetables.

Irene K. Lee is extension family and child development specialist, University of Arkansas at Pine Bluff. She implemented a statewide teenage pregnancy prevention program in Arkansas that resulted in a decrease in teenage birth rate. Her teen suicide and stress prevention program contributed to a 20 percent decline in the teen suicide rate in the state.

Irene E. Leech is state coordinator, Women's Financial Information Program, Virginia Cooperative Extension, Virginia Polytechnic Institute, Blacksburg. Her programs are offered with the American Association of Retired Persons and the High School Financial Program. She offers training and educational support for financial counseling volunteer programs.

F. Larry Leistritz is professor, Department of Agricultural Economics, North Dakota State University, Fargo, and past president of the International Association for Impact Assessment. He conducts research on impacts of resource and industrial development in the rural United States. He serves on an international committee to assess a hydroelectric project in northern Quebec. He is the coauthor of *The Socioeconomic Impact of Resource Development: Methods for Assessment* (1981).

Carl G. Leukefeld is professor of psychiatry, Multidisciplinary Research Center on Drug and Alcohol Abuse University of Kentucky, Lexington. He studies drug abuse injection and crack use in Kentucky and is examining the incidence and prevalence of alcohol and drug use, abuse, and dependency in the state.

Harriett Light is professor, Child Development and Family Science Department, North Dakota State University, and editor, *Journal of Family and Consumer Sciences*. She is past Board of Directors president, American Home Economics Association, and conducts in-service training for educators, social workers, and other youth and family service professionals.

Linda M. Lobao is associate professor, Department of Rural Sociology, Ohio State University. Her research centers on economic change and its social and economic consequences for individuals, households, and communities and on the political response of social groups to the economic changes they experience. She is the author of *Locality and Inequality: Farm and Industry Structure and Socioeconomic Conditions* (1990).

Wayne Loescher is professor and chair, Department of Horticulture, Michigan State University. He assists horticultural growers and processors. He studies how carbohydrate metabolism compounds in horticultural crops relate to crop productivity, quality, and drought, cold, and salinity stress tolerance mechanisms in plants.

Robert Luedeman is a graduate of Drake University School of Law. He is attending the University of Arkansas agricultural law program.

Wilbur R. Maki is president, LEDIS, Ltd., a local and regional economic development consulting group. He was professor, Department of Agricultural and Applied Economics, University of Minnesota. He is a consultant on trade and transportation studies for the Minnesota Department of Trade and Development and the Department of Transportation.

Allan Marsinko is associate professor, Department of Forest Resources, Clemson University. He teaches forest economics, forest valuation, and an introductory course for nonforesters and conducts research on nontimber values of forests and the economic/marketing aspects of human dimensions as they relate to forests.

Steve C. Martens is associate professor, Department of Architecture and Landscape Architecture, North Dakota State University. He teaches courses that explore vernacular and regional architecture. He is a registered architect specializing in historic preservation research, building construction, and architectural design process and is president of the R.M. Probstfield Living History Farm Foundation.

Chuck Matthei is director, Equity Trust, Inc., Voluntown, Connecticut. He pioneered the equity pledge concept, wherein property owners commit a percentage of their property's resale value to affordable housing or to community land trusts. He is currently building institutional bridges between community land trusts and community-sponsored agriculture experiments.

William J. McAuley is director of research, Oklahoma Center on Aging, Oklahoma City. He is investigating migration patterns to nursing homes in two states, and is gathering data to investigate aging and health in the rural all-Black towns of Oklahoma, of which Oklahoma has more than any other state.

Cynthia A. McCall is extension specialist and associate professor of animal science, Auburn University. She is working with the Alabama Horse Council to foster better communication and understanding among the diverse elements of the Alabama horse industry and to develop a strategic plan to foster the continued expansion of the industry.

Thomas D. McDonald is professor, Department of Sociology/Anthropology, North Dakota State University. His research interests include analysis of social and correctional services in rural jurisdictions and the educational and training needs of rural criminal justice professionals. Presently he serves on the North Dakota parole board. He is the co-author of *Rural Criminal Justice* (1996).

Walter G. McIntire is director, Center for Research and Evaluation, and professor, College of Education, University of Maine, Orono. He has been a high school science teacher, school board member, consultant, and researcher, and has three decades of experience in rural and small schools. He is past editor of the *Journal of Research in Rural Education*.

James R. McKenna is associate professor, Department of Crop and Soil Environmental Sciences, Virginia Polytechnic Institute and State University. His teaching and research are in the area of crop science with special interests in sustainable agriculture and the history of American agriculture.

John C. McKissick is extension economist, Department of Agricultural and Applied Economics, University of Georgia. He develops marketing and farm management educational programs for farmers and writes about agricultural pricing alternatives, futures markets, option markets, and cash markets. He received the American Agricultural Economics Association Distinguished Extension Program award for his work in agricultural pricing alternatives.

Carol B. Meeks is professor and head, Department of Housing and Consumer Education, University of Georgia, Athens. Her research focuses on quality and affordability of housing for rural households at risk. She examines regulatory and policy issues related to manufactured housing.

Dale J. Menkhaus is professor, Department of Agricultural Economics, University of Wyoming. He studies the sheep and beef industries, with emphasis on marketing meats and consumers perceptions of and willingness to pay for meat.

Joyce M. Merkel is a doctoral student in nutrition at Syracuse University, administrative graduate assistant, and webmaster for the College for Human Development. She studies nutrition education approaches in rural settings.

Robert L. Metcalf is professor emeritus, Department of Entomology, University of Illinois at Urbana-Champaign. He has written prolifically on pest management, including *Introduction to Pest Management*, 3d edition (with W. H. Luckman, 1994).

Richard E. Meyer is professor, Department of English, Western Oregon State College, Monmouth. He has edited three books on cemeteries, serves as chair of the Cemeteries and Gravemarkers Section, American Culture Association, and edits *Markers: Journal of the Association for Gravestone Studies*. He researches early battlefield cemeteries of World War I.

DeMond S. Miller is a graduate student, Department of Sociology, Anthropology, and Social Work, Mississippi State University. He has interests in alcohol use among minorities and also is doc-umenting the natural hazards in Mississippi and their economic impacts on agriculture.

Melody S. Mobley is a forest health specialist, Forest Management Staff, U.S. Department of Agriculture, Washington, D.C. She was the first African American woman forester employed by the Forest Service and has served in a variety of positions in her 19 years with the Forest Service.

Joseph J. Molnar is professor of agricultural economics and rural sociology, Auburn University. He is working with the Alabama Horse Council to foster better communication and understanding among the diverse elements of the Alabama horse industry and to develop a strategic plan to foster the continued expansion of the industry. He is coeditor (with Henry Kinnucan) of *Biotechnology and the New Agricultural Revolution* (1989).

Patrick H. Mooney is associate professor, Department of Sociology, University of Kentucky. He works on issues related to the conversion of agricultural cooperatives to investor-oriented firms and on a project concerning the transformation of agriculture in post-communist Poland. He is the author (with Theo J. Majka) of *Farmers' and Farm Workers' Movements: Social Protest in American Agriculture* (1995).

Libby V. Morris, Institute of Higher Education, University of Georgia, conducts research in needs assessment, program planning and review, and contemporary conditions of the southern Black Belt. She is the author of *Multiculturalism in Academe* (1996) and is president, Southern Rural Sociological Association.

Bridget E. Murphy is a graduate student, Department of Sociology, Anthropology and Social Work, Kansas State University. Her research interests include rural community organization and how the gender division of labor shapes work relations; social divisions of labor based on race and ethnicity; social movements; and environmental sociology.

Ted L. Napier is professor, Department of Agricultural Economics and Rural Sociology, Ohio State University. He has expertise in soil conservation and has written on the adoption of soil and water quality protection practices by Ohio farmers. He is the coauthor of *Adopting Conservation on the Farm: An International Perspective on the Socioeconomics of Soil and Water Conservation* (1994).

Craig J. Newschaffer is research assistant professor of medicine, Jefferson Medical College, Thomas Jefferson University, Philadelphia, and adjunct assistant professor, St. Louis University, Prevention Research Center. His research includes epidemiologic investigations of breast and prostate cancer and HIV as well as chronic disease prevention in rural populations.

Garrett J. O'Keefe is professor and chair, Department of Agricultural Journalism, University of Wisconsin, Madison. Much of his current work is on the impact of environmental information programs on rural publics.

Jeffrey T. Olson is program officer in the Ford Foundation's Rural Poverty and Resources Program, New York. Prior to joining the Ford Foundation in 1994, he was director of the Bolle Center for Ecosystem Management at the Wilderness Society. He has been a member of the Society of American Foresters since 1978.

Patrick Overton is associate professor, Department of Communication and Cultural Studies, Columbia College, Missouri. His research and writing focus on providing technical assistance, resources, curricula, and organizational and professional development opportunities for rural and small community cultural development. His most recent book is *Rebuilding the Front Porch of America: Essays on the Art of Community Making* (1996).

Deborah Larson Padamsee is research assistant, Department of Education, Cornell University. Her doctoral dissertation examines rural literacy and community development issues.

Juan-Vicente Palerm is professor of anthropology, University of California, Riverside, and director, University of California Institute for Mexico and the U.S. (UC MEXUS). His work on international agricultural labor focuses on sending and receiving communities, rural life, and agribusiness. He applies his research to public policy and community development efforts. He is the author of *Farm Labor Needs and Farm Workers in California, 1970–1989* (1991).

William M. Park is professor, Department of Agricultural Economics and Rural Sociology, and senior fellow, Waste Management Research and Education Institute, University of Tennessee. He studies several aspects of rural solid waste management, including the economics of rural collection, drop-off recycling, regional cooperation, and unit pricing.

John G. Parsons is professor and head, Department of Dairy Science, South Dakota State University. He oversees the university's 160-cow dairy farm and milk processing plant. He conducts research on the analysis of dairy projects through the Agricultural Experiment Station and in conjunction with the State Dairy Lab.

Kyaw Tha Paw U is professor, Department of Atmospheric Science, University of California, Davis. He studies biometeorological exchange between the atmosphere and plants; plant response to increased carbon dioxide concentrations; carbon dioxide, water vapor, pesticides, and heat exchange between plants and the atmosphere; and soil-plant atmosphere exchange.

Chuck W. Peek is a postdoctoral fellow, Agency for Health Care Policy and Research, Center for Rural Health and Aging and Department of Health Policy and Epidemiology, University of Florida. He investigates changes in the caregiving networks of elders over time and race and residence variation in health, household composition, and long-term care.

Robert M. Pendergrass is senior research associate in agricultural economics, Auburn University. He has written on the horse industry.

Judy E. Perkin is director, Health Sciences, Santa Fe Community College, Gainesville, Florida.

G. A. Peterson is professor, Department of Soil and Crop Sciences, Colorado State University. He is the principal investigator of the Dryland Agroecosystem Project which involves water and soil conservation and efficient use of precipitation. He studies interactions of climate, soil, and crop rotation variables and team-teaches courses in crop and soil management systems.

AnnaMary Portz is a program analyst with the Division of Community Resettlement, Federal Office of Refugee Resettlement, Department of Health and Human Services. She has 20 years' experience with refugee resettlement.

Ann E. Preston is assistant professor, Department of Communication, North Dakota State University. Her research interests include movie portrayals of Vietnam veterans, social values embedded in the Nancy Drew novels, gender role stereotyping in department store mannequins in Canada, France, and the United States, and representations of Canadian prime ministers' wives.

Mark A. Purschwitz is assistant professor, Department of Agricultural Engineering and Wisconsin Center for Agricultural Safety and Health, University of Wisconsin, Madison. He conducts projects on agricultural injury prevention education and farm accident rescue training, develops educational videos, and researches farm injury causation and prevention.

Vernon C. Quam is consultant, Forestry Department, City of Fargo, North Dakota. He served as horticulture/forestry specialist, North Dakota State University Extension Service, and editor, *Windbreak Demonstrator Newsletter*. He writes articles and circulars on tree care and provides educational presentations to adults and youths on trees, their care and management.

Wayne D. Rasmussen retired after 50 years as historian of the U.S. Department of Agriculture and is writing a history of the department. He has written numerous books about the USDA and changes in the structure of agriculture, including *Taking the University to the People: Seventy-five Years of Cooperative Extension* (1989).

William O. Rasmussen is associate professor, Department of Agricultural and Biosystems Engineering, University of Arizona. He develops stochastic techniques to predict how water spreads on ground services as a way to model pollutant dispersion in saturated soil, and he examines the use of electrokinetics to establish chemical spill barriers.

Richard Rathge is professor, Departments of Sociology/Anthropology and Agricultural Economics, and director, State Data Center. His research focuses on the consequences of continuous population decline in rural areas of the Great Plains and the implications that the new federalism holds for rural communities.

Melvin C. Ray is associate professor of sociology and research scientist, Social Science Research Center, and associate vice president for research, Mississippi State University. His research interests include criminology and delinquency, social psychology, and race, ethnic, and minority relations.

Larry A. Redmon is assistant professor and extension forage specialist, Department of Agronomy, Oklahoma State University. He studies cool-season perennial forage grasses to replace or complement of wheat pasture; he seeks ways to control broomsedge invasion of introduced-species pastures to improve profitability in forage production systems.

Don C. Reicosky is soil scientist, North Central Soil Conservation Research Laboratory, U.S. Department of Agriculture. He researches soil physics, tillage, and crop residue management.

Ann Reisner works in the Department of Human and Community Development, University of Illinois, Urbana-Champaign. She is working on the role of communications in social movements affecting agriculture, primarily environmentalism and animal rights. She teaches environmental information handling and environmental social action.

C. Matthew Rendleman works in the Department of Agribusiness Economics, Southern Illinois University, Carbondale. He has ongoing research interests in ethanol production, agricultural policy, and the economics of plant and animal diseases.

Howard M. Resh is an international consultant and full-time contractor in development projects and has worked on hydroponic projects in North America, South America, the Middle East, and the Far East. He is the author of three books on greenhouse management and hydroponics; the most recent is *Hydroponic Tomatoes for the Home Gardener* (1993).

Marc O. Ribaudo is an agricultural economist, Economic Research Service, U.S. Department of Agriculture. He conducts evaluations on the USDA's water quality programs, and is working on an economic assessment of alternative agricultural chemical management strategies.

James W. Richardson is professor, Department of Agricultural Economics, Texas A&M University. He studies agricultural program issues such as crop surpluses, target prices, and program payments and investigates the impact of agricultural legislation and reduced chemical use on farms.

Don Roach II is a graduate student, Department of Forest Resources, Clemson University. He works with Dr. Allan Marsinko on a survey of forest industry hunt lease programs in the South.

Robert A. Robertson is assistant professor and coordinator, Tourism Program, Department of Resource Economics and Development, University of New Hampshire. He conducts research on tourism and the human dimensions of recreation resource management issues.

Ardath Rodale is chair of the Rodale Institute and chief executive officer of Rodale Press, Inc. The organization promotes "healthy soil, healthy food, and healthy people."

George B. Rogers served at the University of New Hampshire and wrote extensively on production, marketing, and processing in the poultry industry.

Paul C. Rosenblatt is professor, Department of Family Social Science, University of Minnesota, St. Paul. He studies rural families and how families and marriages react to tension and stress, bereavement, and economic crisis. He is the author (with Ira S. Moscovice) of *Rural Health Care* (1982).

G. Jon Roush is a consultant to environmental organizations, government agencies, and businesses. He has served as president of the Wilderness Society, Washington, DC, and executive vice president and chairman of the board of governors of the Nature Conservancy.

David C. Ruesink is professor emeritus and extension rural sociologist, Department of Rural Sociology, Texas A&M University,

and project director, Rural Social Science Education. He assists rural communities and churches with community development programs and helps denominations and seminaries with rural ministry education programs.

Julie A. Rursch is director, Information Technology, St. Ambrose College. Her work focuses on the uses of communication technologies in rural settings.

Cathy A. Rusinko is assistant professor of management, College of Commerce and Finance, Villanova University, and has worked in the U.S. Department of Agriculture. Her research interests include technology transfer in agriculture and manufacturing.

Sandra Rutland is a former graduate research assistant, Mississippi Crime and Justice Research Unit, Social Science Research Center, Mississippi State University, and now works with the Mississippi State Probation and Parole. Her interests include conjugal visitations in state prisons, race relations, and juvenile delinquency.

Rogelio Saenz is associate professor, Department of Rural Sociology, Texas A&M University. He studies rural minority group demography and racial and ethnic relations. Current projects include analyses of Mexican American entrepreneurship and interregional migration patterns and Latino demographic and socioeconomic trends.

Sonya Salamon is professor, Department of Human and Community Development, University of Illinois, Urbana-Champaign. She studies small community transformations that result from newcomers in a postagricultural economy; sociocultural barriers to adoption of sustainable farming systems; and the sociocultural impacts of an Illinois watershed with atrazine problems.

Neill Schaller is associate director, Henry A. Wallace Institute for Alternative Agriculture, Greenbelt, MD. He holds degrees in agricultural economics and sociology and has worked in the U.S. Department of Agriculture. The Henry A. Wallace Institute is a national, nonprofit organization in dedicated to increase understanding and adoption of sustainable agriculture.

Clifford W. Scherer is associate professor, Department of Communication, Cornell University. He teaches courses in risk communication and studies how consumers and leaders perceive and react to environmental and health risks. He is currently examining how best to communicate complex food safety and environmental risk to lay audiences and policy makers.

Shaunna L. Scott is assistant professor, Department of Sociology, University of Kentucky. Her research focuses on the politics of identity construction in Central Appalachia and Northern Ireland. She is the author of *Two Sides to Everything: The Cultural Construction of Class Consciousness in Harlan County, Kentucky* (1995).

Joan P. Sebastian is assistant professor, Department of Special Education, University of Utah. She coordinates the headquarters for the American Council on Rural Special Education and directs the University of Utah's Distance Teacher Education program which provides special education preparation in rural school districts throughout Utah.

Jim Seroka is professor of political science and public administration, and director, Center for Public Leadership, University of North Florida, Jacksonville. He studies ways to enhance rural administrative capacity and directs programs to provide training, technical assistance, and organizational development skills to communities and nonprofit agencies in northeast Florida. He is the author of *Rural Public Administration: Problems and Prospects* (1986).

Robert C. Serow is professor, Department of Educational Leadership and Program Evaluation, North Carolina State University. His research is on the integration of community service programs in American colleges and universities. He is a member of the North Carolina Commission on National and Community Service.

Todd Shallat is professor, Department of History, Boise State University. He has won the Henry Adams Prize and Able Wolman Award for books on the history of the federal government and public works and is currently writing a book on the culture, technology, and art of American rivers. He is the author of *Structures in the Stream: Water, Science, and the Rise of the U.S. Army Corps of Engineers* (1994).

Lisa A. Shanley is associate professor, Department of Consumer Affairs, Auburn University. She conducts research on the development of protective clothing for hazardous environments and the impact of technology on rural apparel plants. She teaches apparel design and is developing software for the apparel and textiles industries.

William C. Sherman is associate professor, Department of Sociology/Anthropology, North Dakota State University, and a parish priest at St. Michael's Catholic Church, Grand Forks, ND. He wrote *African-Americans in North Dakota* and is studying Arab-Americans in North Dakota and Eastern European folk housing on the Northern Plains.

Larry Hajime Shinagawa teaches in the Department of Sociology, University of California, Berkeley. He is the author of *Atlas of American Diversity* (1997).

James P. Shroyer is professor of agronomy and extension crops specialist, Kansas State University. He conducts applied, on-farm research trials and demonstrations with farmer assistance. He works primarily with wheat production and cropping systems.

Carol Simmons is an Environmental Protection Agency fellow and a graduate student, Department of Entomology, Iowa State University. Her research focuses on the development of farmer or consultant-oriented sampling technique for wireworms (*Coleoptera: Elateridae*) in agricultural environments, including land exiting the Conservation Reserve Program.

Richard W. Slatta is professor, Department of History, North Carolina State University, Raleigh. He is the author of *Cowboys of the Americas* (1990) and *The Cowboy Encyclopedia* (1994) and is a staff writer for *Cowboys & Indians* magazine.

Duane A. Smith is professor of history, Fort Lewis College, Durango, CO. He is writing a fourth-grade Colorado history and researching the Colorado mining man and politician, Henry Teller. He has a comparative study of a mining camp and farming town in the 1890s in press. He is the author of *Mining America: The Industry and the Environment, 1800–1980* (1993).

C. Matthew Snipp is professor, Department of Rural Sociology, and is affiliated with the American Indian Studies program, University of Wisconsin, Madison. His research interests include stratification and mobility, demography, and race, ethnic, and minority relations. He is the author of *American Indians: The First of This Land* (1989).

Edward Sponga is a program analyst with the Division of Community Resettlement, Federal Office of Refugee Resettlement, Department of Health and Human Services. He has 40 years' experience with refugee resettlement.

Jerome M. Stam is finance team leader, Rural Economy Division, Economic Research Service, U.S. Department of Agriculture. He studies regional economics, economic development, public finance, and agricultural finance issues. He has served as secretary, National Agricultural Credit Committee since 1984. He is a coauthor of *Farm Financial Stress, Farm Exits, and Public Sector Assistance to the Farm Sector in the 1980's* (1991).

Bernard F. Stanton is professor, Department of Agricultural, Resource, and Managerial Economics, Cornell University. He studies the changing structure of agriculture and its implications for the twenty-first century and represents land-grant universities as a member of the Census of Agriculture Advisory Committee on Agricultural Statistics.

Richard C. Stedman is a Ph.D. candidate in rural sociology, University of Wisconsin, Madison. His research looks at attitudes toward hunting and changing perceptions of landscape in quickly changing rural areas.

Philip H. Steele is professor, Forest Products Laboratory, Department of Forest Products, Mississippi State University. He researches the sawmill industry and kerf width in cutting softwood and hardwood lumber.

Frederick Steiner is professor and director, School of Planning and Landscape Architecture, Arizona State University. He helps the U.S. Department of Agriculture refine agricultural land evaluation and site assessment systems, assists Arizona in riparian area protection efforts, and works with rural communities on environmental protection, land-use planning, and the growth management projects.

Joyce D. Stern works for the National Education Association and the Appalachia Regional Education Laboratory to address issues of curriculum standards and accountability. She has worked with rural education programs in the U.S. Department of Education and has served as guest editor of the National Rural Education Association's journal, *The Rural Educator*. She is the author of *The Condition of Education in Rural Schools* (1994).

Thomas F. Stinson is assistant professor, Department of Applied Economics, University of Minnesota. He prepares state revenue forecasts for Minnesota and conducts research on the relationship between state and local taxes and economic growth. He is a coauthor of *Public Water Supply in Rural Communities: Results from the National Rural Communities Facilities Assessment Study* (1989).

Patricia A. Stokowski is assistant professor, Department of

Recreation, Park and Tourism Sciences, Texas A&M University. She conducts research on the social, cultural, and institutional effects of rural community tourism development. Her publications include *Riches and Regrets: Betting on Gambling in Two Colorado Mountain Towns*, University Press of Colorado (1996).

Janis Stone is extension professor, Department of Textiles and Clothing, Iowa State University. Her work involves development of personal protective clothing for farmers and greenhouse workers to prevent pesticide exposure.

Kenneth E. Stone is professor, Department of Economics, Iowa State University. He is the author of *Competing with the Retail Giants: How to Survive in the New Retail Landscape* (1995).

Louis E. Swanson is professor and chair, Department of Sociology, Colorado State University. He was resident scholar, National Center for Food and Agricultural Policy at Resources for the Future. His research emphasizes agricultural environmental and rural development policy. He is the editor of *Agriculture and Community Change in the U.S.: The Congressional Research Reports* (1988).

Anne L. Sweaney is professor, Department of Housing and Consumer Economics, University of Georgia, Athens. Her research focuses on quality and affordability of housing for rural households at risk. She has a U.S. Department of Agriculture Challenge Grant to develop policy lessons on the World Wide Web that include rural issues.

John M. Sweeten is professor and resident director, Agricultural Research and Extension Center, Texas A&M University, Amarillo. He conducts research on cattle feedlots and on their waste management practices for water and air pollution control. He is the author of *Cattle Feedlot Waste Management Practices for Water and Air Pollution Control* (1990).

Franklyn L. Tate works for the Department of Corrections, Jackson, MS. Previously he was with the Department of Public Administration, Mississippi State University.

William G. Tomek is professor, Department of Agricultural, Resource, and Managerial Economics, Cornell University. He teaches courses on agricultural markets, agricultural prices, and econometrics. His research pertains to the relationships among cash and futures prices and issues in replicating quantitive studies in economics. He is the author (with Kenneth L. Robinson) of *Agricultural Product Prices*, 3d edition (1990).

Frederick R. Troeh is professor emeritus of agronomy, Iowa State University. He continues to conduct research and to write on soil science. He is the coauthor of several books including *Soils and Soil Fertility*, 5th edition (1993).

Ronnie B. Tucker is a doctoral student in public administration, and a graduate research assistant with the National Black Graduate Student Association at the Social Science Research Center, Mississippi State University. His primary interests include affirmative action, rural government, race relations, and public policy.

Pamela Ulrich is assistant professor, Auburn University. She researches the history of the American textile industry, teaches costume history, and curates a small collection of historic apparel and textiles.

Gary L. Vacin is professor, Department of Agricultural Leadership, Education, and Communication, University of Nebraska, Lincoln. He develops computer solutions to rural issues.

Bernard Vavrek is professor of library science and director, Center for the Study of Rural Librarianship, Clarion University of Pennsylvania, Clarion. He is regularly involved in organizing national conferences on bookmobile services and conducting opinion surveys of public library users attempting to determine the impact the library has on their lives. He is the author of *Assessing Information Needs of Rural Americans* (1990).

Marlow Vesterby is agricultural economist, Natural Resource Conservation and Management Branch, Economic Research Service, U.S. Department of Agriculture. His research involves urbanization, farmland preservation, land-use change issues, land condition, national capital expenditures, depreciation, and imports and exports of farm machinery. He is a coauthor of *Urbanization of Rural Land in the United States* (1994).

Morton O. Wagenfeld is professor of sociology and community health services, Western Michigan University. His studies pertain to rural mental health services and policy and drug and alcohol epidemiology. He is a coauthor of *Mental Health in Rural America: 1980–1993* (1993).

Eric J. Wailes is professor, Department of Agricultural Economics and Rural Sociology, University of Arkansas. His research focus is on analysis and projections of the global rice economy and China's food and agricultural economy and implications for U.S. agricultural exports.

Katey Walker is professor and extension specialist, School of Family Studies and Human Services, Kansas State University. She works in leadership development for beginning and emerging leaders interested in community action and public policy. She has served as president, Association of Leadership Educators.

Rodney B. Warnick is associate professor of recreation resources management, Department of Hotel, Restaurant and Travel Administration, University of Massachusetts at Amherst. His conducts research on recreation and tourism trends and consumer behavior and marketing issues in recreation resource management.

Bruce A. Weber is professor of agricultural and resource economics, and extension economist, Oregon State University. His research focuses on the impacts of changes in federal and state fiscal and regulatory policy on rural and urban economies and income distribution. He is a member of the National Rural Studies Committee and the Oregon Rural Development Council.

Ralph A. Weisheit is professor, Department of Criminal Justice Sciences, Illinois State University, and has written extensively on marijuana industry, use, and production in rural America. He is coauthor of *Crime and Policing in Rural and Small-town America* (1996).

Glen D. Whipple is professor and head, Department of Agricultural Economics, University of Wyoming. He studies the sheep and beef industries, with emphasis on marketing meats and consumers' perceptions of and willingness to pay for meat.

Gregory K. White is associate professor, Department of Resource Economics and Policy, University of Maine. He works on projects to estimate the economic value of various functions of wetlands in Maine communities using Geographic Information Systems and other standard techniques.

Frederick Williams is professor, Center for Research on Communication Technology and Society, University of Texas at Austin. His research examines the information highway and the relationship between telecommunications and rural development.

Ronald C. Wimberley is professor, Department of Sociology and Anthropology, North Carolina State University. He conducts research on the southern Black Belt and its policy implications, social issues of rurality, agriculture and natural resources, and environmental conditions. He is a former president, Rural Sociological Society. He is the author (with Libby V. Morris) of *The Southern Black Belt: A National Perspective—Dependence, Quality of Life, and Policy* (1997).

Robert N. Wisner is professor, Department of Agricultural Economics, Iowa State University, Ames. He conducts research on grain, corn, and soybean futures and option marketing strategies.

Francis W. Wolek is professor of management, College of Commerce and Finance, Villanova University. He served as deputy assistant secretary for science and technology, U.S. Department of Commerce. His research pertains to management of technological innovation.

Mike D. Woods is professor, Department of Agricultural Economics, Oklahoma State University. He is involved in research projects to evaluate local economic development efforts such as small business incubators and downtown revitalization efforts, and he provides technical assistance and training to local communities to aid in strategic planning efforts.

Susan K. Woodward is research associate, Center for Research and Evaluation, College of Education, University of Maine, Orono. She researches and analyzes policy materials for local educational leaders and is the manuscript editor for the *Journal for Research in Rural Education*.

D. Wynne Wright is a Ph.D. candidate, Department of Sociology,

University of Kentucky. Her dissertation involves analysis of the political economy of the burley tobacco sector.

John B. Wright is associate professor, Department of Geography, New Mexico State University. He works on land conservation issues, land trusts, and the changing cultural landscapes of the Rocky Mountain West. He is the author of *Registered Places of Montana: Big Sky Country* and *Rocky Mountain Divide: Selling and Saving the West* (1993).

R. Dean Wright is professor, Department of Sociology and Anthropology, Drake University, Des Moines, Iowa, and president, Midwest Sociological Society (1997). He works with Susan Wright on issues of rural homelessness and poverty and has collected related data semi-annually in rural Iowa since 1988. Additionally, he studies minority group issues in northern India. He is the author (with Susan E. Wright) of *Homeless Children and Adults in Iowa: Addressing Issues and Options in Education, Services, and the Community* (1993).

Susan E. Wright is professor and chair, Department of Sociology and Anthropology, Drake University, Des Moines, Iowa. She works with Dean Wright on issues of rural homelessness and poverty and has collected related data semi-annually in rural Iowa since 1988. Additionally, she studies problems related to inequality. She is the author (with R. Dean Wright) of *Homeless Children and Adults in Iowa: Addressing Issues and Options in Education, Services, and the Community* (1993).

Laura C. Yancer is president, L&T Associates, a public policy consulting firm. She also works with the National Academy of Public Administration and the Advisory Council on Intergovernmental Relations to evaluate infrastructure benchmarking practices by state and local governments across the United States.

William Zawacki is a graduate student, Department of Forest Resources, Clemson University. He works with Dr. Allan Marsinko on valuation of nonconsumptive wildlife recreation based on a travel cost model.

Ervin H. Zube is professor, Department of Renewable Natural Resources and Department of Geography and Regional Development, University of Arizona, Tucson. He has written on environmental design, quality, assessment, evaluation, and policy and changing rural landscapes.

INDEX

Page numbers in boldface denote main entries.